THE MITCHELL BEAZLEY
TRAVELLER'S GUIDES TO ART

FRANCE

Michael Jacobs & Paul Stirton

Mitchell Beazley

To Janis

Authors' acknowledgments
The authors wish to thank all the museum curators and librarians, too numerous to mention individually, who were so helpful in providing facilities and information for their research. They would particularly like to thank the following: F.X. Amprimoz of the M. Crozatier (Le Puy), Clare Banks, Duncan and Nancy Caldwell, John Clark, Francis Jacobs, Charles Parley, Bernard Pfrien, Irmgard Pozorski, Stuart Wallace.

Artists' Biographies & Glossary Ian Chilvers

On the cover
Limbourg brothers, ***Les Très Riches Heures du Duc de Berry*** *(September), c. 1416, Chantilly, Musée Condé*

Editor James Hughes
Designer Nigel O'Gorman
Picture Research Celestine Dars
Assistant Editor Catherine Jackson
Editorial Assistant Barbara Gish
Production Jean Rigby

Maps and floor plans in two-colour by
Eugene Fleury, Illustra Design Ltd.,
Colin Salmon, Technical Art Services

Edited and designed by
Mitchell Beazley International Limited
87–89 Shaftesbury Avenue
London W1V 7AD

ISBN 0 85533 520 3

Filmsetting by Vantage Photosetting Co. Ltd., Eastleigh, England.

Printed and bound by
New Inter Litho, Milan, Italy

CONTENTS

FOREWORD

Our intention in researching the *Guide* has been not only to visit the maximum number of museums and galleries with art treasures, but also to bring to light little-known works that deserve recognition, as well as unjustifiably neglected artists. In addition, we have explored the relation between artists and places, and in our discussion of works of art have often given emphasis to artists whose work has a strong regional connection. We have not sought to compile an exhaustive list of works of art, but to make a full selection concentrating on fine art, with a lesser emphasis on the decorative arts or archaeological items. In consulting innumerable catalogues and publications we have tried wherever possible to verify attributions and to look at traditional masterpieces with a fresh eye.

Few guidebooks are without error, and no guidebook can ever be completely up to date. Without any warning, opening times and telephone numbers change, collections are reorganized, and museums and galleries close for restoration. While every effort has been made to ensure that all information is accurate at the time of going to press, we will be glad to receive corrections and suggestions for improvements, which can be incorporated in the next edition.

How this book is organized

The *Guide* is sectioned into areas, each with its own introduction and map, and these sections are arranged alphabetically by town and museum (see pp. 8–9 for a map of all the areas). Each area map shows (in black) the towns and villages listed in the section, and all these entries are identified by province, region and map reference relating them to the area map at the beginning of the section.

Names of areas, towns and museums are given in their French forms so that you can easily locate them when you are on the spot; a translation is given if the English name is especially familiar.

Entries for museums, galleries and châteaux

Addresses and telephone numbers are given for each entry where available. Opening times are provided for museums and galleries. Other practical information is provided in the form of symbols (see below).

Italic type is used for entry details; **bold** type for highlighting sections, rooms or individual works of art; ***bold italic*** for titles of works of art. Single or double stars denote collections and works of art that are, in our opinion, of particular or outstanding importance. Room numbers are given in Arabic or Roman numerals, according to the usage of the museum.

Special features

An introductory feature explores the range and variety of France's art treasures. Features within each area section discuss themes of regional interest such as "Cézanne at Aix-en-Provence", or "The Impressionists on the Seine". In the center of the book, a 16-page illustrated colour section reproduces works of special interest and is accompanied by a short summary tracing the development of French art. Reference sections include artists' biographies with illustrations, and a glossary of schools, styles and terms.

Cross-references

Different typefaces are employed to cross-refer to different parts of the book; thus M. MARMOTTAN refers to another museum within the same town, **GRENOBLE** to another town within the same area, and ***CENTRAL FRANCE*** to another area.

Abbreviations

As far as possible, only standard abbreviations are used. These include Mon, Tues, etc. for days of the week; Jan, Feb, etc. for months; N, S, E, W for points of the compass; C for century; c. for *circa*; m, km, etc. for measurements, mins, hrs, yrs for times. Less common abbreviations are b. for born, a. for active and d. for died.

Key to symbols

Symbols used in text

- ☆ Important collection, not to be missed
- ☆☆ Outstanding collection, not to be missed
- ★ Important work of art
- ★★ Outstanding work of art
- Entry free
- Entry fee payable
- Parking
- Guided tours available
- Guided tours compulsory
- Catalogues, guidebooks and other publications on sale
- Refreshments available
- Building of architectural interest
- ☑ Well displayed and pleasant to visit
- Garden or courtyard open to the public
- Temporary exhibitions worth investigating
- Important single artist's collection

Symbols used on maps

- ⊕ Major art center
- O Minor art center

How entries are organized

MEUDON — Red capitals for name of town

Hauts-de-Seine, Ile-de-France — Red italic type for province, region and map reference

Map C4

Meudon, once the site of two royal palaces, the more recent of which was burnt down in 1870, still has the remains of the extensive wooded parkland. In the 19thC it was a popular picnic spot for Parisians, but the gradual sprawl of the suburbs has overtaken it. The sculptor Rodin lived here from 1895 until his death in 1917.

Musée d'Art et d'Histoire — Bold red type for name of museum, gallery or château

11, Rue des Pierres

Tel. (1) 5347519 Ext. 427 (Mairie)

Open 2–6pm — Black italic type for entry details

Closed Mon, Tues

☑ — Symbols providing other practical information

Although the town of Meudon has few attractions, the museum, housed in a restored **17thC building**, is nothing short of delightful. The paintings are not outstanding, but out of a reasonable selection of 18thC–20thC French works Diaz de la Peña's ***Harem Scene*** and an anonymous 18thC ***Girl with a Doll*** are the most interesting.

(**17thC building** — Bold type for emphasis)

(***Harem Scene*** — Bold italic type to denote titles of works)

ART TREASURES *of* FRANCE

The most extensive collections of art in all Europe are to be found in the Louvre in Paris. But this rich concentration may not be an unmixed blessing. The size alone of the Louvre is exhausting, not to mention the crowds of people, many of whom have been drawn here by the ***Mona Lisa*** (which a whim of 19thC taste transformed into the best-known painting in the world). The Jeu de Paume – the Louvre's annexe devoted mainly to Impressionist painting – is much more manageable in its scope. But you need to pick your time; it is difficult to enjoy works featuring idyllic picnics on the banks of the Seine when trying to keep your balance in the middle of a constant flow of tour groups.

The recently opened Centre Pompidou, which concentrates on contemporary work, allows easier circulation around the pictures, and here the crowds positively contribute to the enjoyable fairground atmosphere of the place. It is nonetheless a relief sometimes to turn to some of the lesser-known museums in Paris, where the unexpected often awaits you, as with the villa frescoes by the 18thC Italian painter G. B. Tiepolo in the Musée Jacquemart-André.

ART *in the* PROVINCES

The same sense of discovery characterizes a tour of the provincial museums of France. After the French Revolution many of these amassed the most important private art collections in the country and, as a result, are now among the richest in provincial Europe. The scale of some of these places is startling, but they present less of a challenge than do the major Paris museums, not only because they are rarely crowded (you may well find yourself completely alone in them), but also because they contain more unfamiliar works, which will inevitably encourage a greater freshness of response in the viewer.

Viewing conditions are not always perfect, as when an incrustation of pigeon droppings obscures the main source of light entering the overhead windows. Yet, perversely, even such defects can contribute to the peculiar pleasure of visiting French provincial museums, where the atmosphere often rivals the treasures contained within. The occasional state of decay only heightens the faded civic magnificence of so many of these buildings, with their imposing marble staircases, monumental murals, and occasional forays into the exotic, as in the Musée Calvet in Avignon, where peacocks strut in the parched forecourt.

SMALL TOWNS *and* VILLAGES

A visit to the little-known museums of the smaller towns and villages of France is rarely unrewarding. These will inevitably contain much of mediocre quality and purely local interest, but the buildings in which they are housed are invariably among the most interesting in the locality, ranging from medieval palaces to 18thC town halls.

In such a setting, the occasional masterpiece can be more easily appreciated than if it were in a well-known museum surrounded by other masterpieces. The medieval Musée de l'Hospice de Villeneuve-lès-Avignon, for instance, contains in addition to an assortment of saints' relics one of the most important French 15thC paintings, the ***Coronation of the Virgin*** by Enguerrand Quarton (Charenton).

ONE-MAN MUSEUMS *and* COLLECTIONS

A special feature of France is the large number of museums and collections devoted to a single artist. Some, such as the Musée Toulouse-Lautrec in Albi, may contain the greater part of the artist's output; others, like the Musée Greuze at Tournus, or the Musée Courbet at Ornans, may lack important paintings but possess such interesting items as the artist's childhood sketches, or family memorabilia. Perhaps most fascinating of all are the artists' houses and studios. A visit to Rodin's studio at Meudon or Monet's house and garden at Giverny may develop a sympathy for these artists greater than can be had through studying their works in a large gallery.

Related to one-man museums are the substantial collections accumulated by a single patron. The Musée Fabre at Montpellier, for instance, contains a large room devoted to the paintings collected by the banker Aristide Bruyas, best known for his patronage of Courbet. Here, among the largest collection of Courbets in the world, is the famous ***Bonjour Monsieur Courbet***, showing the artist being greeted by the well-dressed bourgeois Bruyas.

ART *and the* ENVIRONMENT

Many of France's greatest art treasures, especially the medieval sculptures, may of course still be seen in their original settings: the monumental portals of Autun, Saint-Gilles-en-Provence, Chartres and Reims are major examples. Numerous churches also have attached treasuries, containing a wide range of precious ecclesiastical objects such as diamond-studded crucifixes and enamel caskets. In the almost inaccessible Auvergne village of Conques is perhaps the richest treasury of all, with its golden reliquary of Ste Foy, one of the most venerated objects of the Middle Ages.

There is an obvious pleasure in recognizing sites which feature in well-known paintings: to those with a knowledge of van Gogh's work, a first-time visit to Arles can be like re-entering a familiar and much loved territory. The countryside around Aix-en-Provence, with its hillsides covered with a combination of pine trees, rocky outcrops and patches of bright orange sand, may greatly increase your appreciation of Cézanne's colouring and the structuring of his landscapes.

There is a connection between the development of tourism in France and the places where artists have chosen to work. The forest of Fontainebleau and, later, Brittany became the most visited parts of the country in the 19thC, thanks largely to the presence of artists' colonies. The south of France, today's main area of tourism, had largely been a resort for winter travellers before being "discovered" by artists at the end of the last century. If St-Tropez had not been chosen as an ideal place by artists, it might well not have developed into the elegant and lively place it is today.

Artists continue to favour the south of France, which contains more museums devoted to modern art than any other area of Europe. This is certainly the ideal place to study the sensual art of the Fauves, Matisse or Picasso. There is something wholly appropriate about being able to wander in beachwear around many of the museums here, and afterwards, as at the Maeght Foundation in Saint-Paul-de-Vence, to sit down with a cool drink beside a Miró-designed pool.

The *Guide* groups the regions of France into eight convenient touring areas (including Paris), each one corresponding to a separate gazetteer of places with art treasures worth visiting. (Corsica has relatively little art and is therefore bracketed with South of France into one area.) This map shows major art centers only; minor centers and other towns appear on the more detailed area maps.

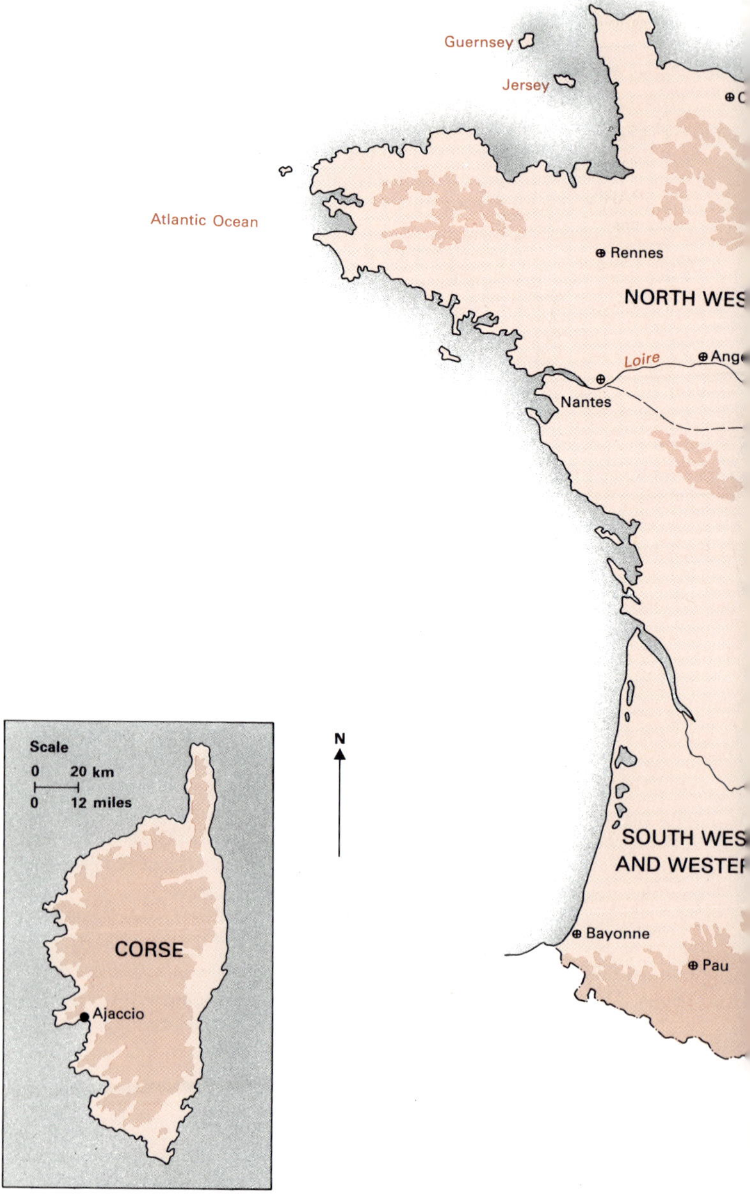

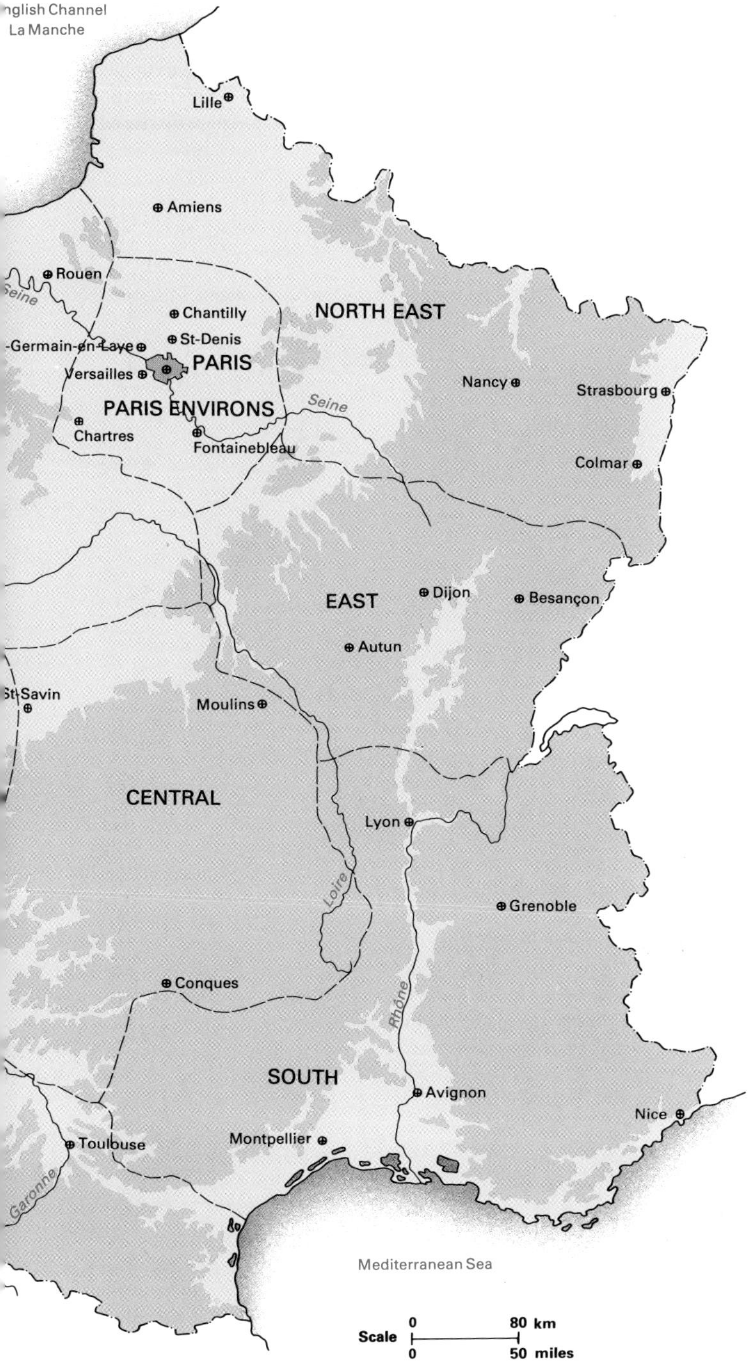
nglish Channel
La Manche
Lille
Amiens
Rouen
Seine
Chantilly
St-Denis
-Germain-en-Laye
PARIS
Versailles
PARIS ENVIRONS
Chartres
Fontainebleau
NORTH EAST
Nancy
Strasbourg
Seine
Colmar
EAST
Dijon
Besançon
Autun
St-Savin
Moulins
CENTRAL
Lyon
Loire
Grenoble
Conques
Rhône
SOUTH
Avignon
Nice
Toulouse
Montpellier
Garonne
Mediterranean Sea
Scale
0
80 km
0
50 miles

NORTH WEST FRANCE

Three regions – Normandy, the Loire Valley and Brittany – comprise this section of the *Guide*, and each one is widely different in its landscape, history and artistic tradition, making a total area of great diversity in both art and architecture.

The rolling countryside of Normandy resembles southern England more closely than it does many regions of France, and an English link was made by a member of Normandy's earliest ruling family, Duke William, who invaded England in 1066 in pursuit of his claim to the throne. The wealth and security of the medieval dukes brought about a great flowering of Romanesque and Gothic architecture in Normandy, visible today in the magnificent buildings of Caen, Bayeux, Coutances and Rouen, as well as in the collections of medieval objets d'art in many of the region's museums.

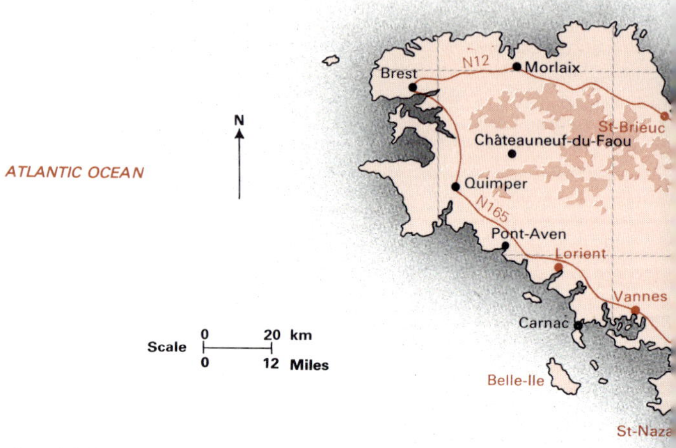

The landscape of the Normandy coast drew many artists to the seaside towns of Honfleur, Trouville and Dieppe in the 19thC when, following the example of Boudin and Isabey, they began to explore the natural effects of light and atmosphere. This area saw the development of Impressionism in the work of the young Monet, who sketched and painted extensively along the beaches and cliffs of the northern coast. More recently, Normandy was the bridgehead of the Allied invasion of Europe in 1944. Most towns in the region were damaged, many were devastated, and the subsequent reconstruction has emphasized the contrast between modern urban development and the monuments of a great medieval past.

The Loire Valley's connections with the Middle Ages can be traced in the names of its provinces – Anjou, Berry, Orléanais – which are also those of the great ducal families. But the region's greatest period came in the 15thC and 16thC when it was the focal point of the royal court and saw the introduction of the Italian Renaissance into France. French architects practised the vocabulary of classical buildings at châteaux such as Blois, Chambord and Amboise, and the owners busily acquired paintings, sculpture and furnishings in the new style. Leonardo da Vinci spent his last years at Amboise as a guest of King François I, and the network of châteaux along the river valley was for nearly two centuries the heart of the French court and state.

Brittany, by contrast, has always tried to maintain its separateness from

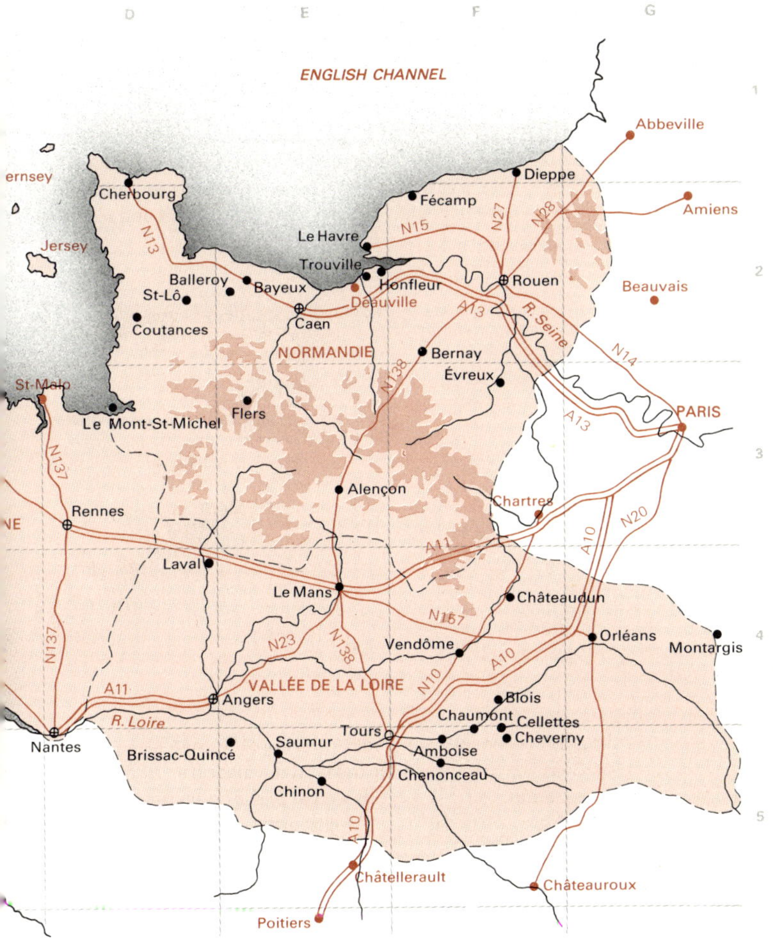

the rest of France. Its highly individual character has to a great extent been moulded by its prehistoric and Celtic past, and the menhirs (upright stones) and dolmens (stone tables) that dot the landscape are very powerful works of art, for all their crudity. Carnac, in the very south of the region, is one of the most famous prehistoric sites in Europe, and is made up of hundreds of menhirs arranged in a series of alignments. These stone monuments probably served a religious purpose, and some of them were later inscribed with crosses – an indication of the strange compromise that was reached when paganism was confronted by Christianity.

The remarkable stone calvaries, dating principally from the 15thC to the 17thC, were probably influenced by the megalithic monuments of Brittany's distant past, but it was not until the beginning of the 19thC that their expressive qualities came to be admired by Romantic artists and writers. Among the innumerable artists who came to the region in the latter years of the century were Gauguin and his followers. Their paintings – of which few have been preserved in the region – were deeply influenced by the crude simplifications of the local monuments.

ALENÇON
Orne, Normandie Map E3

The town of Alençon in lower Normandy was once the seat of a ducal court. The principal ancient building to have survived is the cathedral of Notre-Dame, which has a remarkable 16thC Flamboyant porch on the W side, covered with elaborate sculptural decoration. Unfortunately the E end was insensitively remodelled after a fire in 1744, and this has marred the overall appearance of the building. In the 17thC Alençon became the center of a lacemaking industry, giving its name to a special type known as *point d'Alençon* which is still locally manufactured.

Musée Municipal
Ancien Collège des Jésuites
Open 10am–noon, 2–6pm
Closed Mon

The new civic museum in Alençon, housed in the buildings of an old Jesuit college, brings together items that were previously held in the 15thC Maison d'Ozé and in the earlier Museum of Fine Arts in the Hôtel de Ville. The collection, consisting mainly of paintings and lace, was begun in the mid 19thC and steadily expanded as a result of a series of generous bequests. Three of these were particularly important since they helped to direct the interests of the gallery towards prints and drawings, an area in which it is now fairly strong. The drawings have come from the collections of His de la Salle and the Marquis de Chennevières, and consist for the most part of Italian 16thC–17thC and French 17thC–19thC works, including some by Giulio Romano, Watteau, Géricault and Daumier. The Godard collection provided the basis of the print department.

Many of the earliest paintings were originally church treasures from this region, confiscated during the Revolution and eventually deposited in the town. This collection has been consistently enlarged by purchases and donations until it is now strongest in examples from the Dutch, Italian and French schools between the 17thC and 19thC. There are also a few Spanish pictures, and the ***Christ carrying the Cross*** by José Ribera (1591–1652) is one of the finest works in the museum.

The Dutch paintings are predominantly from the 17thC and, apart from ***Judith and Holofernes*** by Philips Wouwermans (1619–68), reflect the four principal themes of landscape, genre, portraiture and still life found in all Dutch art of this period. The Italian works seem less interesting, and none of the paintings can rival the excellent pen drawing, frequently on public display, of an allegorical figure of ***Abundance*** by the 16thC Mannerist Girolamo di Carpi. The French paintings take up by far the largest section, and between the ***Assumption of the Virgin*** ★ by Philippe de Champaigne (1602–74) and a **still-life** by Fantin-Latour (1836–1904), both very good pictures, there are several works which greatly enhance the collection overall. Of these the ***Marriage of the Virgin*** by Jean Jouvenet (1644–1717), two **oil studies** by Géricault, a **landscape** by Courbet and two typically atmospheric **coastal scenes** by Boudin are perhaps the finest. There are also several works by local artists, such as Jean-Jacques Monanteuil, a pupil of Girodet.

The large collection of lace offers a comprehensive view of the development of *point d'Alençon* from its origins in the 17thC. It was Colbert, Louis XIV's finance minister, who first established the lacemaking industry in Alençon as part of a larger policy to encourage home production as opposed to the importation of foreign goods. At that time Venice was the center of this trade and some 30 Venetian lacemakers were settled in Alençon in 1675, after which the industry flourished under government protection. The industry still survives and the museum is able to show a good selection of the richly ornate lace which has been produced in the town over the last three centuries.

AMBOISE
Indre-et-Loire, Centre
Map F5

The little town of Amboise is dominated by the château that was the focus of the French court in the 15thC. Though it is today greatly reduced from its original size and splendour, the building remains an impressive monument.

Le Clos-Lucé (Maison Leonardo)
Tel. (47) 576288
Open Feb–Dec 9am–noon, 2–6.30pm
Closed Jan

Leonardo da Vinci came to Amboise in 1516 at the invitation of François I, and spent the last three years of his life at this modest red-brick manor house near the main château. François had long been an admirer of the Italian Renaissance, and attempted to transplant the seeds of the new learning to his court at Amboise. To this end Leonardo brought several important paintings to France, including the ***Mona Lisa*** and the ***Virgin of the Rocks***, both now in the Louvre, but the progressive paralysis of his right arm prevented him from producing any major new pictures. Le Clos-Lucé therefore possesses no original Leonardos, but an attempt has been made to reconstruct several of the sophisticated engineering and military projects described in his drawings. These reconstructions include small-scale versions of his armoured tank, swing bridge and helicopter. The upper floors have been renovated with furnishings from the 15thC and 16thC. Of the few paintings on display, the most notable is a portrait of the emperor Maximilian I, attributed to Leonardo's German counterpart, Albrecht Dürer.

ANGERS
Maine-et-Loire, Pays de la Loire
Map D4

Angers was the seat of the counts of Anjou in the Middle Ages, and still possesses a number of fine old buildings despite the upheavals of the Revolution and damage during World War II. Most impressive is the castle, one of the largest feudal fortresses in France, but the 12thC–13thC cathedral of St Maurice is equally interesting. The façade, surmounted by three towers, has some unusual Gothic sculpture, much of it badly weathered, and the building contains a series of good stained-glass windows. Angers's traditional association with tapestries, stemming from the magnificent 14thC ***Apocalypse*** series, was revived in the 1960s with ten rather undistinguished modern tapestries, ***Le Chant du Monde*** by Jean Lurcat, now hanging in the Hôtel Dieu.

Musée des Tapisseries ☆
Le Château du Roi René, Château d'Angers
Tel. (41) 874347
Open Oct–Easter 9.30am–noon, 2–5.30pm; Easter–Sept 9.30am–noon, 2–6pm;
(July, Aug)

A building of the scale and importance of the Château d'Angers can often, by its own magnificence, diminish the impact of the objects it contains. At Angers, however, the ***Apocalypse*** ★★ tapestries, which form the heart of the collection, are strong enough to stand any competition, besides being set off to good effect in a large, well-lit hall. The series, which illustrates the Apocalypse of St John, was commissioned c. 1373 by Louis I of Anjou from the Parisian workshop of Nicolas Bataille, and was celebrated from the beginning as an outstanding artistic achievement. At first it is the sheer scale of the work that impresses the most – the 70 pieces surviving from the original 90 make up a total length of about 119m (130 yards) – but this soon gives way to an appreciation of the technique, the colours, and the exuberant imagery. The relevant printed text from the Book of Revelations is set in a panel opposite each scene so that the visitor can observe how the artist, Hennequin de Bruges, transposed the visionary language of St John into these grand and vivid pictures.

Although the tapestries were from the beginning celebrated as outstanding works of art, their subsequent history strikingly illustrates how tastes change. Following the Renaissance shift away from the Gothic, they fell into a state of neglect that led to their dismemberment, sale, and ultimate use as carpets, covers and awnings. It was not until 1843, with the 19thC revival of interest in medieval art, that the bishop of Angers bought a number of pieces at a sale, and thus began the gradual restoration of the series to its present, still incomplete condition.

The tapestry museum consists of four separate buildings in the castle and, though the ***Apocalypse*** series is the principal exhibit, there are many tapestries from the 15thC to the 17thC, all of a very high quality. The **Passion cycle** from 15thC Flanders, and the single piece depicting ***Angels Bearing the Instruments of the Passion*** from the early 16thC, are perhaps the most impressive and significant. It is interesting to see how tapestry design moved away from the spare monumentality of the ***Apocalypse*** series to the richer decoration of these later works.

Musée des Beaux-Arts
10 Rue du Musée
Tel. (41) 886465
Open 10am–noon, 2–6pm
Closed Mon

Often referred to as the Logis Barrault, the original name of the 15thC former palace which it now occupies, this building was turned over to the civic museum and library as long ago as 1801, and now houses a large and impressive collection.

The galleries on the first floor, which are mainly devoted to medieval religious works drawn from the various churches in the region, contain many pieces of very good quality, but two items stand out for particular attention: an intricately carved, virtually intact ivory **tabernacle** from the 13thC or 14thC, and a near life-size funerary mask of a 13thC **abbess of Fontevrault ★**. Cast and gilded, and now exhibited on its own, this has a smooth naturalism that sets it apart from many of the miniature objects in the same room.

The paintings, displayed chronologically in a series of large galleries on the second floor, include a number of Italian, Flemish and French pictures from the 15thC and 16thC, the finest of which are undoubtedly the portraits. An anonymous 16thC **Flemish portrait**, hung in the medieval section, has the sharpness of observation characteristic of the well-known masters, and two **miniature portraits** by the Clouet circle of painters show an impressive degree of characterization.

Of the 17thC and 18thC works, Boucher's ***Reunion of the Arts*** (depicting a number of pink, fleshy children playing with paint brushes, dividers and musical instruments) is much the most lively. Boucher enjoyed treating ostensibly grand themes like this in a frivolous manner, while at the same time displaying his extravagant, fluid brushwork. In the same section, oil sketches by Tiepolo and Fragonard reveal the full abilities of high Rococo painters, the latter's ***Nymph*** being a dazzling but insubstantial mass of flesh and drapery. In contrast, Chardin's still-lifes are quiet, restrained essays in light, texture and materials. Of the three Chardins at Angers, the ***Basket of Plums*** is outstanding.

Almost all the principal figures of early 19thC French Romantic art are represented, including David, Girodet, Guérin and Géricault. The most important work in the section is Ingres' ***Paolo and Francesca*** ★ (1819), a picture with many of the characteristics of a precious Gothic work of art, painted in a deliberately primitive manner.

Perhaps because the early 19thC is so well represented, the later pictures are comparatively disappointing. A large view of ***The Seine at Paris*** by Jongkind and an unusual painting of ***St Barbara*** by Millet are really the only pictures of note, but there is a room devoted to the works of a local artist, Alexis Axilette (1860–1931) which, though hardly important, have a certain appeal.

The final section of this museum, the sculpture gallery, is housed in a separate wing beside the entrance hall and contains several important 18thC French sculptors, including Houdon, Falconet and Lemoyne. The principal figure, however, is the 18thC **David d'Angers ★** who was born in the town, and whose work fills two large galleries. David d'Angers is often thought of as a sculptor of small plaques and portrait medals, but this collection emphasizes the work he produced on a monumental and even gigantic scale: plaster casts of historical figures ten times larger than life, and a series of large heads of Goethe and Paganini. The effect, to modern spectators, is slightly surreal.

Musée Hôtel Pincé

32 Rue Lenepreu
Tel. (41) 889427
Open 10am–noon, 2–6pm
Closed Mon

The Logis Pincé is an early 16thC town house designed by Jean de l'Espine which, were it not for a poor restoration in 1886, would probably be better known. It now houses a miscellaneous collection of ancient and medieval works of art, including a few Greek vases and enamel caskets from Limoges. There are also several drawings by European artists between the 17thC and 19thC, but the character of the museum is more inclined towards oriental work and there is a large group of Japanese coloured woodblock prints from the late 18thC and early 19thC, the great period of Ukiyo-é.

BALLEROY

Calvados, Normandie Map E2

Château de Balleroy

The Château de Balleroy has an impressive situation in open parkland, with a broad drive continuing the main street of the village right up to the forecourt and principal entrance.
Tel. (31) 926061
Open Mar–Oct, 9am–noon, 2–6pm
Closed Nov–Feb, Wed

The Château de Balleroy was designed for Jean de Choisy in 1626, and has belonged ever since to his descendants, the marquises de Balleroy. As the earliest example of François Mansart's classical style it is a landmark in the history of French architecture; it is also a building to be enjoyed, as the sumptuous interior readily confirms. Among several interesting rooms the Grand Salon is notable for its paintings by Mignard (1610–95) depicting the ***Chariot of the Sun***, as well as portraits of Louis XIII and the family of Louis XIV in an illusionistic decorative cycle.

There is also a museum of ballooning in one of the outbuildings, with souvenirs of the Montgolfier brothers, pioneers of this mode of transport.

BAYEUX
Calvados, Normandie Map E2

Unlike most of the ancient towns of Normandy, Bayeux was undamaged during the Allied invasion of 1944. Today it retains the atmosphere of a quiet country town despite its popularity with tourists, most of whom come to see the famous tapestry. Bayeux, however, also possesses a large and impressive cathedral, built between the 11thC and 15thC. This has some notable sculptural decoration, particularly on the tympanums over the west and south doorways where there are 13thC reliefs of the Passion, the Last Judgment and the story of Thomas à Becket's murder at Canterbury.

Musée de la Tapisserie de la Reine Mathilde

Centre Culturelle,
Rue de Nesmond
Tel. (31) 920548
Open June–Sept 9am–7pm; Oct–Mar 9am–noon, 2–6pm; Apr–May 9am–12.30pm, 2–6.30pm

The Bayeux Tapestry ★ is one of the most famous works of art to have survived from the Middle Ages, and its imagery is familiar to virtually anyone who has ever picked up a book about medieval Europe. Despite this familiarity however it still has the power to intrigue and entertain because, first, the fabric is in very good condition for its age and, secondly, it has a strong narrative pace that carries the spectator along the full 70m (231 ft) of its length. The story, told in 58 successive scenes, is that of William of Normandy's dispute with Harold, his embarkation, and his eventual victory over an English army at Hastings in 1066. The action is lively, and for further clarification of the meaning there are inscriptions and symbols in the upper and lower borders.

In spite of its popular name the Bayeux tapestry is not, strictly speaking, a tapestry at all, but an embroidery that was almost certainly made in a Saxon workshop soon after the Conquest which it records. It was commissioned by Bishop Odo of Bayeux as a treasure to adorn the rapidly expanding cathedral, and it served in this role for centuries, being recorded in a cathedral inventory of 1476. Like all church property, the "tapestry" was under threat during the Revolution, but it survived to achieve a new significance when Napoleon, recognizing its propaganda value, brought it to Paris to stimulate support for his own projected invasion of England. Since then its fame has increased until it has become recognized not merely as a handsome medieval work of art but also as a landmark in European culture.

Musée Baron Gérard

Place de la Liberté
Tel. (31) 921421
Open June–Sept 9am–7pm; Oct–Mar 9am–noon, 2–6pm; Apr–May 9am–12.30pm, 2–6.30pm.
Closed Christmas, New Year

The Musée Baron Gérard is housed on two floors of the old palace of the bishops, and includes a fairly extensive collection of lace, furniture and ceramics as well as paintings and sculpture. From the early 19thC to the mid 20thC Bayeux had its own porcelain industry, and this ware with its "**chinoiserie**" decoration is well represented, in addition to a substantial selection of 18thC Rouen faience.

The collection of paintings is also extensive, and occupies a series of rather dull galleries on the first floor. By far the largest group are French 19thC works, many of them presented by Baron Gérard in 1894, with a predominance of realist landscapes. However, there are several interesting pictures including works by Boucher, David, Prud'hon and Caillebotte. Particularly remarkable is Baron Gros's ***Sappho Leaping From the Leucadian Rock*** (1802) which, despite its poor condition, has all the expressive lyricism of the best early Romantic art.

BERNAY
Eure, Normandie Map F2

Bernay, a small town at the confluence of two rivers SW of Rouen, grew up around a large Romanesque abbey church that was badly damaged during the French Revolution and is only now being restored. It was the home of Alexandre de Bernay, the 12thC narrative poet.

Musée Municipal de Bernay

Place de la République
Open summer 10am–noon, 3–5pm; winter 3–5pm
Closed Tues

One of the earliest municipal galleries in Normandy, Bernay's museum is housed in a modest but attractive 17thC mansion in the traditional checkerboard style, alongside the ancient abbey church. The collection of paintings, sculpture and various decorative arts is spread through a number of rooms on two floors. The furniture provides interesting examples of the Norman craft tradition of decoratively carved woodwork, but the strongest section in the museum is probably the **ceramics**. The area possessed a reasonable ceramic industry during the 16thC and 17thC, specializing in tiles, but most of these are now to be seen elsewhere, and the best pieces in Bernay's museum are from Rouen and Nevers. The series of dishes relating to the **Revolution** and the **Convention** is probably the most striking exhibit.

The paintings, by contrast, are unremarkable, though several famous names, like Constable and Bonington, are dubiously attached to canvases which, if genuine, do little for the artists' reputations.

BLOIS

Loir-et-Cher, Centre Map F4

Blois, a flourishing town in the medieval and Renaissance periods, acquired a castle as early as the 10thC. This became a royal residence in 1497, and during the next century the château at Blois was the focus of the French court, the effective capital, and the scene of many dramatic events. The town has maintained its old section of narrow streets, and contains a statue of Denis Papin, the 17thC Blois physicist and inventor of the pressure cooker.

Château de Blois

Place du Château
Tel. (54) 780662
Open Oct to mid-Mar 9am–noon, 2–5pm; mid-Mar to May 9am–noon, 2–6.30pm; June–Aug 9am–6.30pm; Sept 9am–noon, 2–6.30pm

Blois was the favourite residence of François I, under whose patronage the major **Renaissance extensions** were added to the 13thC feudal hall. The impressive **Grand Staircase**, designed by Jacques and Denis Sourdeau, projects rather awkwardly from the main part of the 16thC wing, but the ornate **octagonal tower** enclosing the staircase is generally considered one of the finest examples of French Renaissance architecture. In sharp contrast is the 17thC **Gaston d'Orléans wing**, designed by François Mansart in a severely classical style. It is nevertheless one of Mansart's masterpieces.

The present interior of Blois is largely the result of extensive restoration by a pupil of the 19thC Gothic revival architect Viollet-le-Duc. It is romantic rather than scholarly in concept, and uninspired in execution. Subsequent attempts to improve upon it have been perfunctory, and the frequently bare or characterless rooms contain dull paintings. It may be to compensate for this that the guides tend to dwell on the château's gory past in melodramatic terms.

Two small museums (not always open) have been set up in recent years, one of religious art and the other of fine arts. These contain a few interesting items, including **portraits** by the 17thC artists Corneille de Lyon and Mignard. But the overall impression left by Blois is one of contradiction. The buildings that exemplify the finest French architecture of three centuries contain nothing of a standard remotely equivalent to the exterior.

BREST

Finistère, Bretagne Map A3

Brest was almost totally destroyed by bombs during World War II, as a result of its being one of the most important of the German submarine bases. The collections of the town's former museum were also largely obliterated at this time.

Musée Municipal

Rue Émile Zola
Open 10–11.45am, 2–6.45pm
Closed Tues

The paintings of the present museum have virtually all been bought since 1958, with purchases mainly in the field of 17th–19thC art, and a particular emphasis on the Dutch, Italian and French schools. Among the most interesting works are the ***Magdalene*** by the 17thC Dutch specialist in haunting interior scenes, Godfried Schalken (whose life and strange death have been the subject of at least one work of fiction), a highly realistic still-life of fish by the 17thC Italian Giuseppe Recco, and a work full of masonic symbolism, ***Roman Elegy***, by the 18thC French painter, Charles Natoire. There is a good collection of 19thC paintings inspired by Brittany, including the ***Rose of Pen'March*** by the symbolist Lévy-Dhurmer. This is a meticulously detailed portrait of a Breton woman and child placed against a background of wild coastal scenery. The artist has intended the work to look like an icon by making the figures stare stiffly out towards the spectator and putting a halo above them. The Pont-Aven School is also represented, with works by Sérusier, Maurice Denis, Maxime Maufra, and Gauguin's former stock exchange colleague, Schuffenecker.

BRISSAC-QUINCÉ
Maine-et-Loire, Pays de la Loire
Map E5

The tiny hamlet of Brissac-Quincé is totally dwarfed by the neighbouring château.

Château de Brissac
Tel. (41) 912221
Open mid-Feb to mid-Mar 9.30–11.30am, 2.15–4.15pm, mid-Mar to June 9.30–11.30am, 2.15–5.15pm, July–Aug 9.30–11.30am, 2.15–5.45pm, Sept to mid-Nov 9.30–11.30am, 2.15–5.15pm
Closed mid-Nov to mid-Feb, Tues except July to mid-Sept

The striking appearance of this château reflects a combination of periods and styles, with an elaborate Renaissance façade linking two surviving towers of an earlier 14thC fortress. The old castle was acquired in 1502 by the ancient military family of Cossé-Brissac, who still own the château. The main section was built by Charles de Cossé, a famous public figure who begun the construction in 1606 under the direction of the architects Corbineau and d'Angluze. Because it has been in the hands of the original family for so long, the château retains a personal character despite the massive scale of many of the rooms. The **furniture, tapestries and ceramics** collected over four centuries are particularly memorable, suggesting a grand residence or stately home rather than a museum. The **large portrait gallery** is more interesting historically than aesthetically, providing as it does the background to a famous family. This is an excellent wine-growing area, and an attractive feature of the guided tour is the practice of offering visitors a glass of the local wine at the end.

CAEN
Calvados, Normandie Map E2

Caen, the capital of lower Normandy, came to prominence in the 11thC when Duke William (William the Conqueror) and his wife Matilda made it their principal residence. They began construction of the castle which overlooks the town, and founded the two abbeys, the **Abbaye aux Hommes** and the **Abbaye aux Dames**, where each of them is buried. The Abbaye aux Hommes is particularly fine, being one of the most complete and important Romanesque churches in France. It was extremely fortunate that these two buildings survived the destruction of most of Caen during the two-month battle for the city in June 1944. However, unlike many towns in Normandy that suffered serious damage, the reconstruction of Caen has been relatively successful, and the old and new elements co-exist without any major discordance.

Musée des Beaux-Arts ☆
Esplanade du Château
Tel. (31) 852863
Open summer 10am–noon, 2–6pm; winter 2–5pm
Closed Tues
(Sun and public holidays)

This museum was first established in 1809, a time when the dispersal of church treasures and aristocratic collections during the Revolution was making available large numbers of first-rate paintings, and when Napoleon's foreign campaigns were enriching French museums at the expense of the subjugated countries. This explains why a town the size of Caen should have a collection so rich in **Italian, Dutch and Flemish art**. The museum was further improved in 1872, when the collection of Bernard Mancel was donated to the town. This included the collection of Napoleon's uncle, Cardinal Fesch, which contained several very good paintings from the period between the 15thC and the 17thC, and which Mancel had purchased in Rome. Mancel was also an assiduous collector of prints, eventually amassing over 50,000 items in a collection that included **prints by Mantegna, Dürer, Rembrandt, Callot and Goya** – the greatest printmakers in the history of European art.

As a result, the museum came to possess a number of very important paintings, and it has consistently extended its range ever since. There is also a fine selection of **furniture, ceramics and decorative arts** from the 15thC to the 18thC to complement the paintings.

During World War II the original museum building, an old college of theology, was almost completely destroyed, although the collection was safely in storage. The problem of how and where the works of art should be exhibited was not fully overcome until 1970, when the authorities opened a new building in the grounds of William the

Conqueror's castle. This has a rather severe modern exterior but there is ample space, and the paintings are well displayed in a restrained and sympathetic environment.

The collection is organized chronologically, and the first room beyond the entrance hall has the 15thC or 'primitive' works. The most striking is Perugino's large ***Marriage of the Virgin*** ★★, part of the booty from Napoleon's Italian campaign and one of the finest early Renaissance paintings outside Italy. In the same room there is a magnificent ***Virgin and Child*** ★ by the Flemish painter Rogier van der Weyden. It is a pity that this superb painting is badly split down the middle of the panel, though in fact the damage need not really prevent appreciation of the artist's detailed realism. If anything, it serves to emphasize it.

In the 16thC room the most notable pieces are the Breughels and the Veroneses, but look out for the penetrating ***Portrait of a Woman*** by the Dutch painter Frans Floris (1517–70), a work that seems to anticipate Rembrandt in its depth of characterization.

The series of galleries devoted to 17thC art emphasizes by its length how extensive this section is, but includes some fine landscapes by Van Goyen and Ruisdael, as well as mythological subjects by Rubens and Poussin. Poussin's ***The Death of Adonis*** is a particularly good example of his art, with rich colour showing through the darkened surface to bring out the mournful, elegiac treatment of the subject.

The 18thC rooms have a good representative selection of Rococo paintings, including an ***Ecce Homo*** by G.B. Tiepolo and a lovely ***Pastorale*** by Boucher, but there is an overall weakening in the standard as one proceeds beyond this date. The only 19thC picture of any substance is Géricault's ***Three Jockeys.*** The collection has not been exhausted, however, and there are three further galleries in the basement where examples from the outstanding **print and drawing collection** ★ are displayed. As with the galleries on the main floor the facilities are first class.

Musée de Normandie

Logis des Gouverneurs, Esplanade du Château
Tel. (31) 860624
Open 8am–noon, 2–6pm
Closed Tues

The Museum of Normandy, just a short walk from the MUSÉE DES BEAUX-ARTS and also within the walls of the castle, is primarily a local history museum containing little of purely aesthetic interest. The displays emphasize folk crafts, antiquities and items of archaeological significance, but include several outstanding pieces, notably the brooches and metalwork from a 6thC **Merovingian treasure** discovered in the region in 1876.

CARNAC

Morbihan, Bretagne Map B4

Carnac is one of the most famous prehistoric sites in Europe, comprising a series of almost 3,000 large upright stones (or menhirs) from the New Stone Age (c.2000BC), some of which are apparently arranged in patterns of considerable astronomical accuracy. The function they originally served remains a mystery, but they were venerated by the Bretons until comparatively recent times. Many are carved with strange symbols and figures, some possibly added later; others bear crosses dating from early Christian times.

Musée Miln-Le Rouzic

Rue de St-Cornély
Open Easter to mid-July, Sept to mid-Oct 10am–noon, 2–5pm; mid-July to Aug 10am–noon, 2–6pm
Closed mid-Oct to Easter

In the middle of Carnac town is the remarkable Musée Miln-Le Rouzic, founded by the Scottish archaeologist James Miln (1819–81). Arranged chronologically, it contains almost all the finds dug up in the area, including beautiful examples of pottery and jewelry. There are also plaster casts of some of the carvings on the menhirs.

CELLETTES

Loir-et-Cher, Centre Map F5

In the great series of châteaux of the Loire valley, the modest scale of the Château de Beauregard could make it seem comparatively minor. But in fact it is one of the finest small Renaissance buildings in France, and its appearance is enhanced by its attractive location on the edge of the Forêt de Russy.

Château de Beauregard

Tel. (54) 442005
Open Oct–Mar 9.30am–noon, 2–5pm; Apr–Sept 9.30am–noon, 2–6.30pm
Closed early Jan to early Feb

The house was originally a hunting lodge for Francois I until Jean du Thier, Henri II's secretary of state, purchased it in 1545. In 1617 it was acquired by Paul Ardier, another minister of state, who added a number of rooms to the house, including the long gallery.

The interior of the château has at least two rooms which must be the envy of more famous houses. The small panelled 'cabinet des grelots' was du Thier's ***studiolo***, a type of private study where the Renaissance man could surround himself with a collection of items reflecting typically humanist concerns. This room contains several interesting illusionistic paintings. The other room is completely filled with 363 portraits of famous men and women, including François I of France, Henry VIII of England, Mary Queen of Scots, and a fair sprinkling of other European nobility. These pictures are the work of a local 17thC artist (the original court portraits which he used as models can often be recognized), and should be judged not as a collection of individual paintings but as part of an elaborate interior decoration in which the overall effect is what counts. The whole series is well set off by a floor paved with **Delft tiles**.

CHÂTEAUDUN
Eure-et-Loir, Centre Map F4

The market town of Châteaudun is attractively situated on a promontory beside the Loir. It has a fine 12thC castle with some interesting buildings, including a chapel beside the keep with several life-size statues of saints dating from the 15thC. Outside the castle walls the town also has some buildings of note, which is remarkable considering the very extensive damage it suffered not only in the Franco–Prussian War but also in World War II.

Musée Municipal de Châteaudun
3 Rue Toufaire
Tel. (37) 455536
Open mid-Mar to mid-Oct 9.30–11.30am, 2–6pm; mid-Nov to mid-Mar 10am–noon, 2–5pm
Closed mid-Oct to mid-Nov

The museum of Châteaudun combines items of local interest with four personal but unrelated bequests to the town. An immense collection of stuffed birds and animals (described by the enthusiastic guide, probably correctly, as unique), and a collection of relics from the Franco–Prussian War, are worth a look though strictly speaking outside the scope of this book. The other displays consist of collections of oriental works of art assembled by two travellers from this area. Most of the items come from India and China, and include arms, armour, ceramics, prints and dolls, all of varying size and quality. Most interesting, perhaps, are the small cult objects relating to eastern religions. These, though quite attractive in themselves, could benefit from further explanation regarding their meaning and significance.

CHÂTEAUNEUF-DU-FAOU
Finistère, Bretagne Map B3

After working with Gauguin at le Pouldu, Paul Sérusier (1863–1927) spent much of his remaining life in near total seclusion at this village in the heart of the Black Mountains. The view from his house, which still survives, inspired some of the best paintings of his later years. He also decorated the **bapistery chapel** of the local church, dedicated to the Welsh saint Teilo. These paintings, which are more interesting than beautiful, are indicative of the mystical introspection that characterized the later lives of many of Gauguin's followers.

CHAUMONT
Loir-et-Cher, Centre Map F5

The castle at Chaumont, built between 1465 and 1510, has a severe military aspect more in keeping with a feudal fortress than a Renaissance château. For this reason Marie de Medici gave it to Diane de Poitiers when CHENONCEAU was confiscated to further emphasize the latter's fall from grace. There are several emblems referring to both women on the castle buildings. Despite its reputation as an inhospitable residence, however, the château is set in a beautiful park with lovely views over the Loire.

Château de Chaumont
Tel. (54) 469802
Open Apr–Sept 9.50–11.30am, 2–5.30pm; Oct–Mar 9–11.30am, 1.35–3.35pm

The apartments at Chaumont are disappointing in comparison with the exterior, and the motley collection of furniture and anonymous 16thC paintings do little to improve matters. The Salle des Fêtes has an interesting floor of **Sicilian majolica tiles**, but the only other items of note are the **portrait**

medallions produced in the castle during the 18thC by Nini, an Italian glass engraver and potter.

CHENONCEAU
Indre-et-Loire, Centre Map F5

Château de Chenonceau
Tel. (47) 299007
Open mid-Feb to end Feb 9am–5.30pm; Mar to mid-Mar 9am–6pm; mid-Mar to mid-Sept 9am–7pm; mid-Sept to end Sept 9am–6.30pm; Oct 9am–6pm; Nov to mid-Nov 9am–5pm; mid-Nov to mid-Feb 9am–noon, 2–4.30pm

Chenonceau, considered by many to be the loveliest of all the Loire châteaux, was the gift of Henri II to his mistress Diane de Poitiers in 1547. She commissioned Philibert de l'Orme to design the graceful building that spans the river Cher, thereby creating the beautiful setting for its elegant Renaissance proportions. Diane de Poitiers also began the layout of the gardens which are now a feature of the château, but was forced to give up the residence by Henri II's widow, Catherine de Medici. It was Catherine who added an additional storey to the principal gallery on the bridge, thus giving the château its uniquely attractive look. Later the place fell into disuse until the 18thC, when the celebrated patroness of the literary arts, Mme Dupin, became proprietress. Her son was tutored at Chenonceau by Jean-Jacques Rousseau, who wrote his treatise on education, ***Emile***, at the château in 1747.

With its tearooms, waxworks, miniature railway and multilingual signs, Chenonceau is well geared to the international tourist trade, and there are usually several parties competing for space in the long gallery overlooking the river.

Out of season it is quieter, and the blazing log fires in the immense Renaissance fireplaces recall the time when Chenonceau was regularly in use as a grand residence. These fireplaces are an impressive feature of the interior, and the 16thC furniture, tapestries and painted ceilings add to a sense of the period. There are several notable paintings, including a ***Christ and the Infant St John*** by Rubens, and a life-size ***Three Graces*** by the interesting 18thC French Rococo painter Carle van Loo (1705–65). It is also a pleasure to walk in the beautiful grounds of the château bordering the river Cher, from where you can see the building to finest effect.

CHERBOURG
Manche, Normandie Map D1

Cherbourg is well known as one of the major ports of France, yet it was not until the late 19thC that it came into its own as a berth for transatlantic liners. These facilities still dominate the town, but the passing of the trade signalled the port's decline, and it now relies principally on the naval dockyards and the cross-channel ferry services.

The painter Jean-François Millet (1814–75) was born in the nearby hamlet of Gruchy, and practised as a portraitist in Cherbourg in the 1840s before moving to Barbizon near Paris.

Musée Thomas Henry
Place de la République
Open 10am–noon, 2–6pm

The original museum at Cherbourg was set up in the Hôtel de Ville to accommodate a collection of 163 pictures presented to the town by Thomas Henry in 1835. This was subsequently enriched by several other gifts, the most important of which were works by Millet and a bequest of sculptures and antiquities from the studio of the sculptor A. le Veel. The collection was dispersed for safekeeping in 1940, and it was not until 1981 that a new museum building was opened to bring together the various sections of fine and decorative arts.

The fine art section is not large but has a number of excellent works. The two earliest pictures, a ***Virgin and Child*** by the so-called Master of St Ursula, and a small predella panel of the ***Conversion of St Augustine*** ★ by the 15thC Florentine painter Fra Angelico, are the finest. But there are several other very good paintings, especially from the French, Flemish and Dutch schools of the 17thC and 18thC. A **landscape** by Paul Bril, two **still-lifes** by Chardin, and an early study by the great Neoclassical painter J.L. David are outstanding here.

There is a separate room for the **Millet collection**, including letters and photographs, as well as a number of paintings and drawings. The most interesting of these are the early works, such as the ***Portrait of Pauline Ono***, produced before the artist took up the scenes of peasant life on which his reputation is based.

CHEVERNY
Loir-et-Cher, Centre Map F5

Completed in 1634 by Hurault de

Cheverny, Cheverny is unlike most of the châteaux in the Loire valley in that it was built in a single phase, and during a period more concerned with elegant proportions than with defensive power. Its classical façade, therefore, is in marked contrast to other buildings in the region, as is the brilliance of its white tufa stone. The extensive grounds are well-known for hunting, and outbuildings contain the kennels of a pack of hounds and a trophy room with 2,000 antlers.

Château de Cheverny

Tel. (54) 799629
Open Nov–Feb 9.30am–noon, 2.15–5pm; Mar 9am–noon, 2.15–5.30pm; Apr to mid-May 9am–noon, 2.15–6.15pm; mid-May to mid-June 9am–noon, 2.15–6.30pm; mid-June to mid-Sept 9.30am–6.30pm; mid-Sept to Oct 9am–noon, 2.15–6pm
Closed major public holidays

The interior of the château reflects the sophisticated life style of the 17thC, and since it is still in the hands of the family of the original duke, the furnishings, tapestries and paintings are all appropriate to a grand residence. The finest items are the series of five Gobelin tapestries, ***The Labours of Ulysses***, from cartoons by Simon Vouet (1590–1649), and the murals in the dining room by Jean Mosnier (1600–1656) depicting scenes from the ***Travels of Don Quixote***. The overall richness of decoration, however, is the most notable aspect of the apartments, as in the elaborately carved staircase with its abundance of humorous decorative motifs – cupids, laurels and fruit – cut into the pillars and balustrade. The craftsman who executed this work is unknown apart from the enigmatic inscription 'F.L. 1634' near the base.

CHINON

Indre-et-Loire, Centre Map E5

Chinon, a small, ancient town on the banks of the river Vienne, is overlooked by the extensive remains of three castles – the strategically important plateau behind the town was repeatedly fortified from Roman times onwards. The town itself has retained much of its medieval character with an old quarter of narrow rambling streets and attractive buildings, many of which have associations with famous figures or events from the past. It was here, for instance, that Joan of Arc met the future Charles VII and persuaded him to challenge the occupying English armies, an event which set in train the removal of the English from France.

Musée des Amis du Vieux Chinon

44 Rue Voltaire
Open 10am–noon, 3–6pm
Closed Tues

The museum in Chinon has recently transferred to a newly renovated 15thC town house, and the small collection of Gallo-Roman antiquities, medieval works of art and later paintings and decorative works is well displayed in a modern but sensitive manner very much in keeping with its surroundings. Many of the finest exhibits come from the partly ruined church of St Mexme in the town, notably a Carolingian bas-relief of the **Crucifixion**, and St Mexme's 11thC **cope**. Being perishable, medieval textiles are rare, but this piece was a holy relic brought back from the Middle East during the crusades and has been well cared for, so that it is not only attractive but also a considerable treasure.

The other principal item in the museum is a full-length portrait by Delacroix of Chinon's most famous son, ***François Rabelais***. This impressive work is well hung in a large room that again has a significance above and beyond its contents; for it was here that, in 1428, Charles VII called the Estates General, the effective parliament of the country, an event that for many people marks the resurgence of French power and prestige.

COUTANCES

Manche, Normandie Map D2

This ancient hilltop town in western Normandy is dominated by a magnificent **13thC cathedral**, whose history is bound up with the noble families that supported William the Conqueror.

Musée de Coutances

2 Rue Quesnel-Morinière
Tel. (33) 451192
Open 10.30am–noon, 2–5pm
Closed Wed

Following considerable damage during the last war, the museum of Coutances is now located in the former Hôtel Poupinel, an attractive 18thC house at the entrance to the public gardens. The collection covers a wide range of interests, including ceramics, tapestries and Gallo-Roman antiquities, especially an impressive **bronze portrait bust** of the emperor Hadrian. A mixed collection of paintings includes a number of local and national figures, but the principal work is undoubtedly Rubens' ***Lions and Dogs Fighting***. Rubens painted a number of pictures of animals in combat, combining brilliant colouring and exotic subject matter in a way that made them very popular with early 19thC artists, notably Delacroix.

DIEPPE

Seine-Maritime, Normandie Map F1

Dieppe has been a busy port since the 16thC, and its extensive docks, surrounded by grey stone buildings, give the town much of its character. But Dieppe is also a popular seaside resort, for its beaches are the closest of any to Paris. In the late 19thC the town with its coastline was considered an attractive sketching place and was visited by a number of painters, including Monet, Gauguin, Whistler and Sickert. The town suffered during the last war, and the Dieppe Raid of 1942, an abortive Allied assault on German coastal defences, is commemorated in a museum of World War II relics just outside the town.

Le Musée Dieppois

Le Château, Dieppe
Tel. (35) 841976
Open 10–11.30am, 2–5.30pm
Closed Tues

The museum is housed in a formidable castle at the top of the cliffs, a medieval building which, though attractive in itself, does not display the pictures to their best advantage, and the collection is not really strong enough to overcome this handicap. In fact, considering the significance of Dieppe as a meeting place for artists in the late 19thC, the museum's content is unexpectedly disappointing.

Of the 17thC and 18thC paintings (which are hung in two panelled rooms roped off from the public and therefore not available for close examination) a minor landscape by Ruisdael is overshadowed by a larger Dutch marine picture in grisaille (grey monochrome). There is also an unusual shipwreck scene by Bonaventura Peeters (1614–52) entitled ***Tempête en le Grand Nord***, which at least provides an insight into the 17thC European conception of the Arctic. It portrays a group of bears watching a foundering ship that is flanked by a whale and a walrus – the latter clinging desperately to an ice floe.

The 19thC section is markedly stronger, with good paintings by Renoir and Pissarro – a **portrait** from the 1870s and a late **townscape** respectively – but an early portrait by Courbet appears simple to the point of crudeness. Boudin, a locally based artist who strongly influenced Monet, is represented only by a single oil sketch, and among the artists associated with the area only Sickert stands out with two prosaic renderings of the town in its aspect as a holiday resort.

Two attractive pictures by the French Romantic painter Eugène Isabey (1803–86) might be overlooked because of their small scale, but well repay closer inspection. One is a street scene, possibly in Dieppe, and the other depicts the **Disembarkation of Queen Victoria** at Tréport, just along the coast. The queen appears to be coming ashore in a large bathing machine pulled by two carthorses – a reminder of the early recreations of the beach. Dieppe became a popular resort after 1824, when the Duchesse de Berry began the vogue for sea bathing, and this aspect is emphasized by a display of early bathing costumes and deck chairs dispersed around the picture gallery.

The 20thC section consists mainly of prints by Braque, donated by the family of the Cubist sculptor Henri Laurens, and this is the only part of the museum that is not dominated by the all-pervasive theme of the sea. A large part of the building is taken up with ivory carvings made from elephant tusks that Dieppe sailors brought back from West Africa, thus giving rise to this specialized local craft. From the 17thC onwards ivory was used for a number of decoratively carved domestic items, including fans, hair clasps, hat pins, brooches and book covers. The pride of the collection is a group of highly wrought tobacco rasps.

EVREUX

Eure, Normandie Map F3

Evreux, capital of the Eure district in Normandy, has had a long history of misfortune, culminating in the devastation caused by successive German and Allied bombing raids in World War II. As a result much of the town has been rebuilt, although the Flamboyant Gothic cathedral survived relatively unscathed and still has some good carved woodwork and beautiful stained glass. The former abbey church of St-Taurin also has some interesting features, including the **Shrine of St Taurinus**, an impressive 13thC silver and enamel reliquary in the form of a miniature chapel, showing St Taurinus holding his crosier.

Musée Municipal

Rue Charles Corbeau
Tel. (32) 393435
Open 10am–noon, 2–5pm, Sun 2–6pm
Closed Mon

The museum at Evreux is housed in the 15thC bishop's palace which forms, with the cathedral, a very attractive courtyard enclosed on three sides by good late Gothic architecture, meticulously restored. The museum itself is notable for the excellent presentation of the exhibits. The main floor is devoted to prehistoric, Gallo-Roman and medieval archaeology, and includes two very good **1stC bronze statues**, a Jupiter and an Apollo, which were found locally. The two upper floors contain a collection of paintings, furniture and ceramics, all very well displayed in a series of rooms that recreate the various period styles of the 18thC and 19thC. This manner of exhibition brings out the best in the paintings because there are very few individual works of particular merit. However, a large gallery of **19thC academic pictures** is strengthened by some good paintings of **coastal scenes** by Boudin. In the company of overworked history paintings and dark Realist works Boudin's naturalism is very refreshing, and he provides an appropriate conclusion to this enjoyable museum.

FÉCAMP

Seine-Maritime, Normandie Map F2

According to the legend, a mysterious vessel landed at Fécamp in the 1stC AD, carrying a leaden box with the miraculously preserved drops of Christ's blood. As a result, the town became in medieval times a very important place of pilgrimage. The relic still survives in the 12thC church of La Trinité, a large and handsome building containing several fine sculptures, but the town, though attractive, has little otherwise to show for its medieval heritage.

Musée Municipal

21 Rue Alexandre Legros
Tel. (35) 283199
Open 10am–noon, 2–5pm
Closed Tues

Tucked discreetly off one of the main streets of Fécamp, this museum is remarkably attractive though lacking in any outstanding individual items. The building is of a scale and design that creates an intimate atmosphere – an effect increased by the warmth and humour of the staff – and the displays themselves are excellent. Thus the **maritime section** on the top floor, which contains a large number of naive marine paintings surrounded by fishermen's nets, might have appeared pretentious, but here has a refreshing simplicity.

The paintings in the main section include works by Jordaens from the 17thC and Largillière from the 18thC, and among the French 19thC pictures there is a good landscape by Diaz and two interesting works by the little-known Post-Impressionists Luce and Schuffenecker. There is also a good group of **Gothic sculptures** drawn from various churches in the area.

The finest items of the collection, however, are to be found among the **ceramics**, where there is a wide range including examples of Delft, Sèvres, Rouen and Maiolica porcelain and pottery.

FLERS

Orne, Normandie Map E3

This small industrial town in the Bocage district of Normandy has an interesting 16thC moated castle, but unfortunately most of the older buildings were destroyed during World War II. André Breton, the poet and founder of Surrealism, was born in Flers in 1896.

Musée du Bocage

Hôtel de Ville, Château de Flers
Tel. (33) 650047
Open Easter–Oct 2–6pm
Closed Nov–Easter

This small museum in the Hôtel de Ville is largely a local history collection with an archaeology section, documentation of local industries, and a few items of late medieval religious art from the churches in the region; but it does also have an interesting collection of paintings, most of which are from the 19thC. The **Barbizon school** of 19thC French landscape painters is well represented and there are paintings by many of the principal figures, including Corot, Diaz de la Pena and Daubigny. There is also a good section of local painters most of whom, like Charles Leandre in ***The Song of the Bride***, seem to have concentrated on peasant life and customs of the region.

LE HAVRE

Seine-Maritime, Normandie Map E2

Le Havre is the principal seaport of northern France and a town of considerable size, but the extensive rebuilding under Auguste Perret after its devastation in World War II has given it a rather uniform and lacklustre appearance. Most of the artists of the Normandy coast in the 19thC worked here at some stage, including

Boudin, Monet and Pissarro. The painter Raoul Dufy was born here in 1877.

Musée des Beaux-Arts (André Malraux) ☆

Boulevard J.F. Kennedy
Tel. (35) 423397
Open 10am–noon, 2–6pm
Closed Tues

The museum is housed in a box-like structure of concrete, steel and glass in the manner of Le Corbusier, with an immense and slightly intimidating concrete sculpture projecting from the façade. By contrast, the interior is relaxed and well lit, with clear open spaces in which some of the paintings are hung on suspended lattice screens.

The early pictures in the collection, although not numerous, are quite diverse, with examples of the Dutch, Spanish and Italian schools from the 16thC and 17thC. Of these the ***Portrait of a Man*** by Agnolo Bronzino (c.1550) and ***St Peter*** by a follower of the 17thC Spanish artist Ribera, are probably the finest. The early French pictures, with the exception of two good landscapes by Gaspard Poussin, are not particularly notable.

Oil sketches by Fragonard, Baudoin and Greuze demonstrate the virtuosity of brushwork that was so highly admired in 18thC France; and another fine oil sketch, by Delacroix (a study for the mural in St-Sulpice, Paris, entitled ***Heliodorus Driven from the Temple***) opens the Romantic section. The 19thC and early 20thC is the strongest period in the collection: from Géricault's ***Study of a Mastiff*** (c.1820) to a large group of Fauvist works dating from around 1905, scarcely a single French artist or movement of note is not represented. Among a considerable number of pictures illustrating the increasing naturalism and colouristic brilliance of French art, works by Courbet, Fantin-Latour, Renoir, Pissarro and Vuillard stand out. There is also a group of four paintings by Monet, two of which, ***Towers of Westminster*** ★ (1903) and ***Nymphéas*** ★ (1904), are probably the finest in the whole gallery.

Two important bequests play a significant part in forming the overall character of the museum, not least because of the amount of space devoted to them. First is an extensive collection of oils, watercolours and drawings by **Eugène Boudin** ★, numbering in all over 300 items, which were presented by the artist's brother in 1900. This bequest, combined with the pictures already purchased, is the largest single holding of the artist's work anywhere. Unfortunately, however, the amount on display does not increase one's appreciation: in fact quite the reverse. Boudin's art is impressive in its naturalism but very narrow in its range, so that a display of over 100 pictures, many of them rather slight, tends to diminish their effect. As a result, works like ***The Pardon of Sainte-Anne-la-Palud***, a Breton village festival, tend to remain in the mind longer than the more common beach and harbour scenes.

A similar observation could be made about the other bequest, consisting of over **70 works by Raoul Dufy** from the collection of the artist's wife. Dufy's technique and subject matter, usually drawn from the social life of the beach and the racecourse, did not change much after about 1920, and when a number of his paintings are gathered together they have a nagging similarity that is soon boring. However, this group is to some extent retrieved by the careful selection of the best work and a sympathetic display that complements the simplicity of the art.

HONFLEUR

Calvados, Normandie Map E2

This fishing port near Le Havre has retained many of its old timber and slate-hung buildings, including the 15thC church of Sainte-Catherine, which is built almost entirely of wood and employs early shipbuilding techniques in its construction. The picturesque appearance of the town made it popular with artists, and there was a thriving colony of landscape painters working there in the second half of the 19thC. Eugène Boudin (1824–98), the central figure of this group, was born in Honfleur, as was the early 20thC composer and friend of Picasso, Erik Satie.

Musée Boudin

Place Erik Satie, Rue de l'Homme de Bois
Tel. (31) 891647
Open Easter–Sept 10am–noon, 2–6pm; Oct–Easter 10am–noon (Sat and Sun only), 2.30–5pm

Located in the old part of Honfleur, this museum has recently been rebuilt and extended to create an attractive gallery on three floors, with very good facilities for displaying pictures. The bulk of the collection is devoted to the artists who worked either in Honfleur itself or along the adjacent coastline, but it should on no account be dismissed as provincial, including as it does **landscapes** by Isabey,

Courbet, Jongkind and Monet, as well as a reasonable 20thC section with works by Dufy, Marquet and Villon. The principal interest, however, is obviously **Eugène Boudin**, the artist after whom the gallery is named.

Boudin was the son of a river pilot working at Honfleur, and his experience of the port provides the background to much of his art. He and the Dutch painter Johan Jongkind (1819–91) were among the first to depict the fleeting effects of light and atmosphere, and their paintings of the harbours, shipping and landscape around Honfleur had a profound influence on the young Monet. The two rooms devoted to Boudin here do not give a comprehensive account of his achievement – for that you must visit the Musée des Beaux-Arts in LE HAVRE – but his interest in the everyday and the commonplace is well reflected in numerous sketches of beach scenes. Boudin turned away from historical subjects and famous beauty spots to concentrate his attention on the more significant demands of naturalism, as can be clearly seen from the pictures in this collection.

LAVAL
Mayenne, Pays de la Loire Map D4

This is a sleepy, attractive old town with fine medieval and Renaissance buildings. It is also the home town of Henri (le Douanier) Rousseau (1844–1910), the most famous of all so-called "naive" painters, who is buried in the Jardin de la Perrine just south of the Château. Rousseau was a customs official for most of his life, and only began painting when he was comparatively old. His talents were recognized at the turn of the century by avant-garde artists such as Picasso. Rousseau supposedly told Picasso that the two of them were the greatest painters of their age, "You in the Egyptian style and myself in the modern."

Musée Municipal
Place de la Tremoïlle
Open Apr–Sept 9am–noon, 2–6pm; Oct–Mar 10am–noon, 2–6pm
Closed Tues

The town's museum, which has a large collection of funerary sculptures, is housed in one of Laval's most impressive buildings, the Vieux Château, with parts dating from the 11thC to the 16thC. This also contains a small, recently arranged museum of "Naive Art" in recognition of Rousseau. Unfortunately, however, it has only one, extremely slight painting by him. The rest of the collection is devoted to contemporary "naive" artists from all over the world, whose work is not so much naive as appalling. The concept of the "naive" in art, which regrettably Rousseau did so much to promote, has led to the acceptance of the most self-consciously childlike daubs. One might reflect that one either does something well (as Rousseau did) or badly. One does not deliberately do anything "naively".

LE MANS
Sarthe, Pays de la Loire Map E4

Le Mans is associated in most people's minds with the famous 24-hour motor race which takes place there every year, but in fact the town has an impressive history, much of it linked to the Counts of Anjou and the Plantagenets in the Middle Ages. Henry II, the first Plantagenet king of England, was born in Le Mans in 1133 and later was exiled there by his son Richard I Coeur de Lion.

There is still a medieval quarter with a number of old buildings, among which the 11thC–14thC cathedral with its elaborate apse construction and early stained glass windows is the most spectacular. The 12thC sculpture on the S porch is in a native Gothic style similar to that on the cathedral at Chartres, and in the Baptistery there are two fine **Renaissance tombs**, that of Charles d'Anjou (d.1472) being the work of the Venetian sculptor Francesco Laurana. The nearby 12thC–14thC Eglise de la Couture, a former abbey church, also has some impressive features including a range of Gothic architectural sculptures, some 16thC–18thC tapestries and a white marble **Madonna** (1571) by the French Renaissance sculptor Germain Pilon.

Musée des Beaux-Arts (Musée de Tessé)
Rue de Tessé
Tel. (43) 849797
Open 10am–noon, 2–6pm
Closed Tues

The Musée des Beaux-Arts, generally known as the Musée de Tessé, occupies the impressive mansion of the early Marshall of Tessé and is surrounded by wooded gardens. The building later served as the bishop's palace before becoming the museum, and has been altered to provide temporary exhibition space, as well as allowing for the display of a good permanent collection.

One of the first items is a **12thC**

enamel plaque of Geoffrey Plantagenet, father of Henry II and founder of the Plantagenet dynasty of English kings. Le Mans was Geoffrey's principal seat, and this piece depicting him with a sword and shield in an ornamental Romanesque building came from his tomb in the cathedral.

The paintings are remarkably diverse, with examples from all the major European schools. From the Italian there is a fine early Renaissance panel of ***David's Penitence*** by the 14thC Sienese painter Pietro Lorenzetti, and, from the Dutch and English schools, good landscapes by Ruisdael in the 17thC and Constable in the 19thC.

French paintings predictably constitute the largest single section in the museum, with the 17thC and the 19thC particularly well represented. From the former there are works by Simon Vouet, Le Sueur and Georges de La Tour, as well as a very fine group of three pictures by Philippe de Champaigne: an early ***Adoration of the Magi*** from the period when his work was heavily influenced by Rubens, a ***Vanitas*** or still life, and ***The Dream of Elijah*** which was once the altarpiece of Notre Dame de la Couture in LE MANS. The 19thC works are biased towards Romanticism, with paintings by Géricault and Delacroix, but the finest picture in the whole section is an impressive ***family portrait*** ★ attributed to David and thought to represent the well-known revolutionary Michel Gérard with his children.

MONT-SAINT-MICHEL
Manche, Normandie Map D3

This is one of the most famous tourist sites in Northern France. Built on an island rock joined to the mainland by a causeway, it comprises a fortress, ramparts, a small town, and a monastery. The whole resembles a pyramid, the apex of which is the spire of the 11thC abbey church. The place owes its existence to the 9thC Bishop, St Aubert, who had a vision in which St Michael commanded him to build an oratory at the top of the rock. Afterwards it became an exceptionally popular pilgrimage center, and was probably no less crowded and bustling a place in the Middle Ages than it is now. Its attraction to today's tourists lies in the beauty both of its position and of its medieval architecture.

Musée historique
Open Mar to Sept 8am – 7pm
Closed Oct to Feb

The museum here has some 15thC–17thC alabasters and paintings on copper, but is really only worth a visit for those interested in clock mechanisms (of which there are 25,000) and in local history.

MONTARGIS
Loiret, Centre Map G4

An industrial town on the river Loing, Montargis was once the capital of the Gatinais region. Little remains of the medieval castle today, but the church of La Madeleine, built between the 12thC and 16thC, has some good features. The early Romantic painter Anne-Louis Girodet (1767–1824) was born in Montargis, and the museum houses a magnificent collection of his work.

Musée Girodet
Mairie de Montargis
Tel. (38) 852816
Open 9am – noon, 1.30 – 5.30pm
Closed Mon

Montargis is an example of the unexpected pleasures that French provincial museums can offer: the Hôtel de Ville of this otherwise undistinguished town houses a large gallery with a collection of paintings, sculpture and objets d'art far superior to those of much larger towns. In the first room a 15thC **polychrome wooden figure** of St Michael from the abbey of Ferrières is one of the finest of its type, and there are also several good paintings from the School of Fontainebleau (the group of 16thC artists who were encouraged by François I to develop an Italian Renaissance manner), including a particularly handsome ***Madonna*** by Douet.

A number of good paintings in later rooms include, from the 17thC, Zurbaran's ***St Jerome*** and a landscape by van Goyen, and, from the 18thC, a lively sketch by the Italian painter Francesco Solimena. The French 19thC section is also strong, but the core and principal attraction of the whole collection must be the large group of **paintings and drawings by Girodet** ★ presented to the town by the artist's family.

Girodet, a pupil of David, was an important painter in his own right, for he was one of the first to emphasize the imaginative qualities and poetic sensibility that became a hallmark of high Romantic art. A version of ***The Burial of Atala***, a key picture for this tendency, is here, as is ***The Deluge*** (1806). Girodet retained a certain coldness in his art, as can be seen from the rather remote portrait of Napoleon, but he was capable of charming and intimate works like ***The Boy Looking at Figures from the Bible***.

A better indication of the artist's range emerges from the large collection of Girodet's drawings, most of which are on permanent display. Some are impressive for technique alone, but others help to illustrate contemporary cultural preoccupations with, for example, landscapes and subjects from Homer. Girodet also signals the interest in fantastic and exotic subjects shown by the next generation. There are scenes from *Ossian*, a cycle of Celtic myths subsequently discredited as a forgery, and an impressive painting of ***A Turk***, much admired by Stendhal, that marks the introduction of Orientalism into French 19thC art.

MORLAIX

Finistère, Bretagne Map B2

Built up around the Dossen estuary, Morlaix was once one of the most important ports in Brittany. It is dominated by an enormous aqueduct, a masterpiece of 19thC engineering. Dwarfed beneath this is a charming old quarter, with various medieval and Renaissance buildings. The museum is on the western edge of this district and is housed in an attractive 15thC church which once formed part of a monastery. The building has undergone an extremely unusual conversion, in that it is now divided in two, with a fish market on the ground floor, and the museum above.

Musée Municipal

Place des Jacobins
Open 9am–noon, 2–6pm
Closed Tues

The tiny museum of Morlaix is much more than an amusing curiosity. It has an excellent and well laid out ethnographic section, and a surprisingly good collection of 19thC paintings, including **portraits** by Courbet and Couture, and two Trouville **beach scenes** by Boudin. A famous native of Morlaix was the 19thC art critic, Gustave Geoffroy, a friend of the Impressionists, and in particular of Monet, whom he introduced to the island of Belle-Ile off the rocky S coast of Brittany. Monet painted a famous series of pictures of the spectacular rock formations on the part of Belle-Ile known as la Côte Sauvage; subsequently the island became extremely popular with artists, attracting most notably Rodin, Matisse and Derain. The Society of the Friends of Geoffroy has made several donations to the museum, including one of Monet's **Belle-Ile paintings**, a Rodin **bust**, and a number of canvases by Maurice Denis.

NANTES

Loire-Atlantique, Bretagne Map D4

Nantes, the largest town in Brittany and a rival to Rennes as the capital of the province, became the seat of the ducal court in the 16thC, and much of the extensively remodelled castle dates from this period. The greatest phase in the town's prosperity came in the 18thC, when it was the leading port in France for a lucrative trade in sugar and slaves. The main quarter of the town has a fair mixture of buildings from the 15thC to the present day, including the imposing **cathedral of St-Pierre-et-St-Paul**. This was begun in 1434 and contains some interesting sculpture, particularly the handsomely carved **tomb of François II**. This work, made between 1500 and 1507 by Girolamo da Fiesole and Michel Colombe, is one of the earliest mature examples of French Renaissance art.

Musée des Beaux-Arts ☆

10 Rue Georges Clemenceau
Tel. (40) 745324
Open Mon–Sat 10am–noon, 1–5.45pm; Sun 11am–5pm

The fine art museum in Nantes was set up during a euphoric period of civic pride following the Revolution, and in its early years it also benefited from the government's policy of redistributing works of art confiscated from churches and private collections. Under Napoleon it gained a number of works seized during his foreign campaigns, so that by the early years of the 19thC the museum was already well stocked. The town officials themselves were active during this period, and in 1810 they purchased the collection of the Cacault brothers, one of whom had been ambassador in Rome. This impressive collection consisted of a large number of Italian paintings from the 13thC to the 18thC, and it has since been enriched by further purchases and bequests. It now has over 7,000 items, of which only a certain number can be shown at any one time.

The present museum building was opened in 1900, and it is of a scale and grandeur characteristic of national collections. The large traditional galleries provide an appropriate setting for many of the more commanding pictures, as well as giving space for the smaller-scale works. The extensive collection includes a few sculptures and a good department of prints and drawings, but the bulk of it is made up of paintings from most schools and movements between the 15thC and the 20thC. Some of the Italian paintings are even older, and there are some very good early Renaissance panels, including a ***Virgin in Majesty*** by the Florentine Master of the Bigallo (c. 1250) and a ***Madonna and Saints*** by Bernardo Daddi, pupil of Giotto (c. 1340). Both of these pictures came from the Cacault collection as did the two finest works from the 15thC: ***Scenes from the Life of St Benoît***, a predella panel of 1490 by the Lombardesque painter Bergognone, and ***Sts. Anthony and Sebastian***, one section of a larger altarpiece by Perugino which was probably painted around 1475. The latter picture is not well known, but for its age it is in remarkably good condition and even apart from the elegance of the figures it is an excellent piece of craftsmanship.

The 16thC is best represented by portraits from Tintoretto, Bronzino and, particularly, Moroni's penetrating character study of ***Lucia Vertova*** ⋆ while for the 17thC Italian school there is a good group of religious works by Neapolitan followers of Caravaggio. This section is completed by paintings that exemplify the last great phase of Italian art, with two views of ***Venetian Festivals*** by the 18thC artist Francesco Guardi which were originally part of a larger series based on drawings by Canaletto.

The Dutch and Flemish works are mainly from the 16thC and 17thC, and generally consist of landscapes and still lifes; but a large religious picture by Rubens, ***Judas Maccabaeus Praying for the Dead***, (originally painted for the cathedral at Tournai in 1635) provides a dramatic contrast.

The French pictures begin unremarkably with a few anonymous 16thC Mannerist works, but the 17thC Vouet's ***Allegory of Peace***, and the three paintings by Georges de La Tour (1593–1652), bring out forcefully the outstanding quality of this section. This is probably the strongest representation of his work to be found in any museum. The ***Virgin and Child*** and the ***Denial of St Peter*** are particularly impressive, and ***The Hurdy Gurdy Player*** ⋆ is one of the finest examples of the powerful naturalism characteristic of this artist's early work. The 18thC has fewer pictures of such quality, although a ***Harlequin*** by Claude Gilot has been linked to Watteau, but with Ingres's ***Portrait of Mme. de Senonnes*** ⋆ the 19thC opens with a work that is equally superb. Ingres is not known as a colourist, but in this picture of 1815 he elaborates the complex design with large areas of vivid plum and gold.

The 19thC and early 20thC section is probably the largest, with works by Géricault, Delacroix, Monet, Dufy and Rouault generally on display. The most considerable painting here is Courbet's ***The Corn Sifters*** ⋆, which is justifiably given pride of place. Painted in 1855, the artist's greatest period, this picture was purchased by Nantes in 1861, becoming the first of Courbet's works to enter a public collection.

Finally, there are a number of works by artists from this region, including two mythological pieces by the successful 19thC academic painters Henry Picou and J.E. Delauney. James Tissot, born in Nantes in 1836 and later associated with Degas and Whistler, is represented by four canvases depicting in a contemporary setting the biblical story of the ***Prodigal Son***. One interesting feature of this is the fact that the second in the series, ***In a Far Country***, is set in Japan, a country whose culture exerted a powerful attraction and influence on French artists and writers of the late 19thC.

Musée Dobrée

Place Jean V
Tel. (40) 893432
Open 10am–noon, 2–6pm
Closed Tues

The Musée Dobrée is the creation of a connoisseur from Nantes, Thomas Dobrée, who bequeathed his collection to the city in 1894, and employed the Gothic Revival architect Viollet-le-Duc to design a building for it. Viollet-le-Duc was responsible for restoring many famous monuments, including Mont-Saint-Michel and Carcassonne, but by the 1890s his medievalism had become even more entrenched and severe. His design for Dobrée's museum produced a formidable mansion in the Romanesque style that makes little concession to decoration or enjoyment. But the austerity of the interior, though gloomy in effect, is perhaps appropriate since many of the exhibits are medieval and ecclesiastic.

The collection contains a good number of enamels, manuscripts, church vestments, reliquaries and the like, but perhaps the most important item is an unusually complete retable of nine **15thC alabaster sculptures** from Nottingham, England. The exhibit that stays in the memory, however, is the **gold casket** containing the extracted heart of Anne of Brittany (1477–1514) –

extraction and preservation of famous people's hearts being a gory but accepted medieval practice.

The top floor of the museum has a special section devoted to the Revolutionary civil war of the 1790s, when this region, known as the Vendée, was the centre of royalist opposition to the republican government in Paris. Of these items, which mainly consist of documents, costumes and other memorabilia, the most interesting is a **Roman-style sword** designed by Jacques-Louis David (1748–1825), the leading artist of the Neoclassical movement. David was the official artist who recorded the events of the Revolution, as well as an active supporter of Robespierre, and he designed pageants, uniforms and ceremonial arms in an appropriately classical style. Many of these designs are well known and frequently referred to, but they are not often seen on display.

The Manoir de Jean V, a separate building (though part of the same complex), houses the ethnography section of Egyptian, Etruscan and Oceanic items. There is also a small collection of Greek pottery with red- and black-figure vases from the 6thC and 5thC BC.

ORLÉANS
Loiret, Centre Map G4

Joan of Arc became the "Maid of Orléans" after her famous relief of this town from an English siege on May 8 1429, a date that is still celebrated in the town. The principal street is the Rue Jeanne d'Arc, the various scenes of her exploits are commemorated, and many shops seem to claim some link with St Joan, to judge from their names. Unfortunately, not much of the town that Joan saved is still in existence, though the old quarter retains its original layout even if the buildings are modern. The main architectural feature is the cathedral, an amalgam of every style between the 13thC and the 19thC surmounted by two unusual towers appropriately known as "Wedding cake" by the local citizens. Nowadays Orléans is an important business and manufacturing town.

Musée des Beaux-Arts

Place Ste-Croix
Open Apr–Sept 10am–noon, 2–6pm; Oct–Mar 2–5pm
Closed Tuesday

Established in 1825, the Orléans museum has been able to amass a reasonable collection of paintings and sculpture which, although lacking in well-known masterpieces, is generally of high quality and fairly wide range. Until recently it was housed in the Hôtel des Crenaux, an ornate 15thC mansion that provided an attractive setting but was too small to allow a full display of the collection. This problem has now been solved with the construction of a completely new gallery which, in compensation for its bland appearance, has good modern facilities.

Among the earliest works in the collection a 15thC ***Virgin and Child with Angels*** by the Italian painter Matteo di Giovanni stands out from its neighbours, as does the bronze bust of ***Jean de Morvillier***, a bishop of Orléans, by the French 16thC sculptor Germain Pilon. The 17thC rooms contain a wider range with a correspondingly greater number of notable works. An impressive early Velasquez of ***St Thomas*** ★ has pride of place, but there are other works which can do more than simply hold their own. ***Bacchus and Ariadne*** by Louis Le Nain (1593–1648) is a rare mythological painting by an artist better known for his peasant scenes, and ***St Sebastian nursed by Irene*** from the studio of Georges de La Tour (1593–1652) has the luminosity and restraint typical of this painter.

Of the 18thC and 19thC French paintings the finest are virtually all portraits, ranging in treatment from the light decorative style of Perronneau's portrait of his wife as ***Aurora***, to Prud'hon's more dramatic ***Portrait of M. Lavalée***. The best sculptures from this period are also portraits, with good busts in terra cotta by Houdon and Pigalle, two of the finest French sculptors of the 18thC.

The pattern is broken with Gauguin's ***Fête Gloanec*** ★ (1888), and this glowing still life from the artist's Breton period stands out as the greatest of the modern works, perfectly in keeping with pictures by 20thC artists such as Soutine and Rouault.

The modern section also has a room devoted to the work of Max Jacob, who lived in this area until his arrest by the Nazis and subsequent death in 1940. Jacob is better known as a poet and close friend of the Cubist painters than as a painter in his own right, but he did produce gouaches which, according to Picasso, were "made with a bit of tobacco, a bit of saliva and very little paint". From the sale of these he eked out little more than an existence, but they provide an interesting memorial to the man whom Picasso regarded with special favour, calling him "one of the wittiest and most comical . . . in the world"

Artists of the Normandy Coast

The Normandy coast was first made popular by the English, who came here in large numbers in the early 19thC to indulge their new love for sea-bathing. This bathing fashion soon caught on in France, particularly among the aristocracy: the most famous of the seaside resorts that were built up here at this time was **DEAUVILLE**, which acquired a celebrated casino in 1825. The popularity of the coast increased considerably after 1843, when the railway from Paris reached Rouen, and again after 1863 when it was extended to Deauville. This century tourists have tended increasingly to favour sunnier coasts, and Normandy's once fashionable resorts have developed an old-fashioned, somewhat neglected character.

The arrival of the first holidaymakers to Normandy in the early 19thC coincided with a sudden interest in the area taken by artists. Appropriately this first group of artists included numerous leading English painters such as Turner, Cotman, Girtin and Bonington. Bonington, who was perhaps the English artist with the strongest enthusiasm for the coast, acted as a vital link figure between English and French art; and it is perhaps not entirely coincidental that his closest French artist friends, Isabey and Delacroix, became themselves habitués of the coast. Thereafter the area attracted most of France's major landscape artists, from Courbet up to the Fauves. **TROUVILLE** had a particular appeal for Courbet, who in 1866 brought here his American friend, Whistler: these and other artists stayed at the now destroyed Hôtel des Roches Noires. The main artist associated with adjacent Deauville was the Fauve society portraitist van Dongen, who lived here for much of his life to be near some of his richer clients. Etretat, with its spectacular cliffs, has been much painted, and features in important works by Courbet, Manet, Félix Valloton and Matisse. **DIEPPE**, once one of the most snobbish of Normandy's coastal resorts, became especially popular in the 1880s thanks to Degas, who attracted here such admirers of his as Whistler and the English painter Walter Sickert.

In 1844 the Honfleur-born landscapist Eugène Boudin, the best known of Normandy's native artists, set up a book shop and stationers in **LE HAVRE**, where he also exhibited his earliest works. These were seen that same year by

HONFLEUR

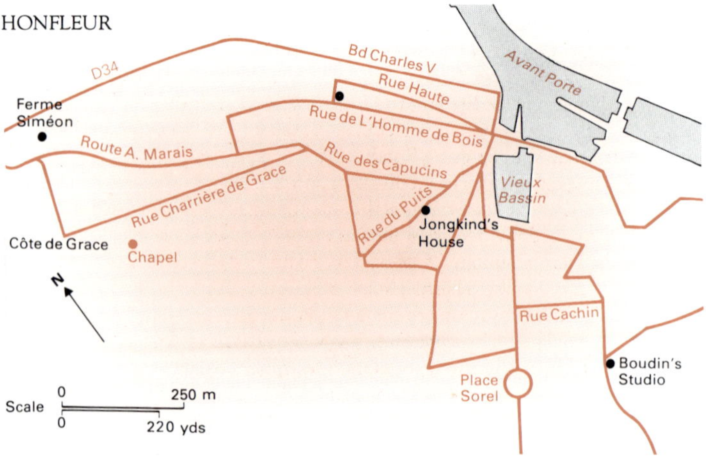

Late 19thC Etretat, Normandy, with its much painted cliffs

Isabey, who one year later met at Le Havre the Dutch-born artist Jongkind, whose atmospheric, freely painted seascapes were to have – like those of Boudin – a great influence on the Impressionists. Isabey encouraged Jongkind to go and study in Paris. Also in 1845 the five-year old Monet came with his parents from Paris to settle at Le Havre, where his father bought a grocery shop. As Monet grew up, he developed a talent for doing caricatures, and was introduced to Boudin. Boudin, who by this date had begun to acquire a considerable local reputation, subsequently took care of the young artist's education, and prepared him for art school in Paris. In 1866 Monet was in a desperate financial position, and his parents offered to look after him in their summer house just outside Le Havre at Sainte-Adresse. It was then that he painted his famous picture of his family, ***The Terrace at Sainte-Adresse***, (Metropolitan Museum, New York). Of greater consequence was the work which he executed of the port at Le Havre in 1872. The title that he gave to this, ***Impression Sunrise*** (Paris, M. Marmottan) inspired a critic to dub him and his fellow artists the Impressionists when they first showed their works together in Paris in 1874.

Virtually alone among the Normandy coastal resorts **HONFLEUR** retains a number of monuments with close artistic associations. Boudin's birthplace, for instance, survives at 27 Rue Bourdet (plaque). The studio where he worked for much of his life is at the top of a steep, charming alley which joins the Rue de l'Homme de Bois with the Rue Haute. The house which Jongkind moved to a year after meeting Boudin in le Havre in 1862 is at 23 Rue du Puits (plaque). Just outside the town on the road which leads up to the celebrated beauty spot, the Côte de Grâce, is the so-called Ferme Siméon, which was one of the most renowned artist inns in France. Isabey came here in 1825, and afterwards, Diaz, Daubigny, Corot, Troyon and Courbet. Monet brought his talented friend Bazille to Honfleur in 1864, and found lodgings in the center of the town, but always came to eat at the Ferme. Since the 1950s the once modest inn has been a luxury hotel. The Côte de Grâce, about a ten-minute walk from the hotel, is now a popular picnic spot with numerous wooden benches and telescopes. Most of the artists who worked in Honfleur painted the extensive views to be had from here of the Seine estuary, now partly ruined by the industries of Le Havre.

Artists in Brittany

In the latter years of the 19thC, the part of Brittany known as La Cornouaille – so named by 5thC Celtic settlers from Cornwall in Britain – became exceptionally popular with artists from France and other countries. By 1880 the town of Pont-Aven was the most famous and crowded artists' colony in Europe, and in the next decade a largely American offshoot had developed in the nearby fishing port of Concarneau.

Curiously, it was the Americans who did more than any other nationality to awaken an appreciation of this region of Brittany, which was "discovered" by a group of American artists, headed by Robert Wylie as early as 1866. Americans were attracted to Concarneau not least by the presence of Alexander Harrison, the most renowned American painter then working in France. At Concarneau – once referred to as Sardineopolis on account of its pungent sardine industry – all the artists stayed at what is still the Hôtel des Voyageurs in the main square of the new town, overlooking the walled medieval quarter.

The town of Pont-Aven, situated a few miles inland from Concarneau, has a conventionally pretty appeal – the Concarneau artists disparagingly referred to its "ready-made motifs as if made for female English watercolourists". Today it is almost solely known for its associations with Gauguin and his followers, who in fact did not come there till the second half of the 1880s. By that date the American expatriates were so predominant in Pont-Aven that they had initiated a series of baseball matches with the rival colony at Concarneau.

Artists were also attracted to Pont-Aven by the cheapness of its two legendary hotels: the Hôtel des Voyageurs and the Pension Gloanec. The Hôtel des Voyageurs was originally in the Place de l'Hôtel de Ville, and today is marked by a plaque to its famous proprietress Julia Guillou, known to everyone as "la mère des artistes". The Pension Gloanec stood in the square now known as the Place Gauguin, on a site currently occupied by the Maison

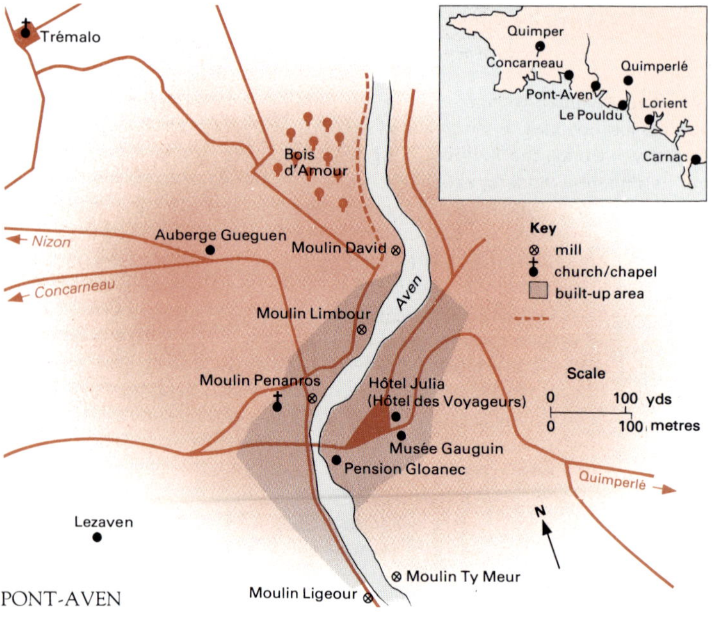

PONT-AVEN

de la Presse, where its rowdy atmosphere had earned it the reputation of being Pont-Aven's "true Bohemian home" long before Gauguin arrived in 1886. But the plaque on the building lists only the latter artist and his associates, such as Émile Bernard (1868–1941), Charles Laval (1862–94), Paul Sérusier (1865–1925) and Maurice Denis (1870–1943). Between 1886 and 1891 Gauguin was the focus for these and other artists, misleadingly known as the "Pont-Aven School" (several members of the group had hardly even visited the town). The Pont-Aven School rejected the naturalism of Impressionist painters in favour of pure unmodulated colours to express emotions and ideas, frequently using Breton peasant subjects. Gauguin's ***The Vision after the Sermon*** (1888), probably inspired by a painting by Émile Bernard, is perhaps the Pont-Aven School's most important work, with its use of colour to express emotional and symbolic significance in a non-naturalistic style.

The Bois d'Amour, haunt of the 19thC Pont-Aven painters

Pont-Aven's principal studio, a former manor house called Lezaven, still survives just outside the town. Here Gauguin painted two of his most famous Pont-Aven works, the ***Yellow Christ*** (1889) and ***La Belle Hélène*** (1889), as well as numerous landscapes of the immediate surroundings. Previously it had been used by Wylie and his American painter friends.

The most painted part of Pont-Aven was the Bois d'Amour, a wooded park to the N of the town. Today a board records the spot near the Moulin David where Sérusier, under Gauguin's supervision, painted his famous and influential ***Le Talisman*** (1888), a near-abstract work which stressed subjective perceptions rather than naturalistic representation. A beautiful uphill path through the woods leads to the Chapelle de Trémalo, where the yellowish 15thC crucifixion that inspired Gauguin's ***Yellow Christ*** can still be seen. Just 1·5km (1 mile) SW of this is the church of Nizon, famous for the primitive carved calvary group that features in his ***Green Christ*** (1889).

In the summer of 1889 Gauguin decided that there was an 'abominable crowd' in Pont-Aven, and moved to Le Pouldu, a fishing hamlet 30km (19 miles) to the SE. Here he was joined by Charles Laval, Charles Filiger, Mayer de Haan and J.F. Willumsen. The small inn where they stayed, the Auberge de Marie Poupée, is now gone, but a memorial to these artists can be found next to the Chapelle Notre-Dame-de-la-Paix.

PONT-AVEN
Finistère, Bretagne Map B3

In the late 19thC this pretty town on the wooded banks of the river Aven was the home of a thriving artists' colony (see pp. 32–3). Several of the more elderly residents here still wear the traditional Breton costume that was once such a major source of inspiration to the artists, including those of the so-called Pont-Aven School.

Musée Gauguin
Place de l'Hôtel de Ville
Open mid-June to mid-Sept 10am–12.30pm, 2–7pm
Closed mid-Sept to mid-June

It is a strange fact that not a single work of art from the town's heyday as a colony has been preserved here. The museum is only open in the summer, when it holds loan exhibitions devoted to the minor followers of Gauguin, and occasionally displays the odd work by Gauguin from private collections in Brittany. No attempt has been made to chronicle in words and photographs the extraordinary artistic history of the town. However, the Bois d'Amour, the wooded park north of the town, has placards indicating the places that inspired the Pont-Aven painters. Above the wood is the Chapelle de Trémalo, where the 15thC wooden crucifixion that inspired Gauguin's ***Yellow Christ*** (1889) can still be seen in its original setting.

QUIMPER
Finistère, Bretagne Map B3

Quimper, the ancient capital of Breton Cornouaille, has a remarkably well-preserved medieval quarter, with tall gabled houses and narrow streets offering glimpses of the fine 14thC cathedral of St-Corentin. All in all, this is one of the most beautiful towns in Brittany.

Musée des Beaux-Arts
Place Saint-Corentin
Tel. (98) 954520
Open Nov–Mar 10am–noon, Apr–Oct 9.30am–noon, 1.30–7pm
Closed Jan, Tues

The museum, housed in the 18thC former town hall, was reopened after extensive modernization in 1976, and is now very clearly arranged if a trifle bland in character. Brittany has had a limited and unsophisticated native artistic tradition, and the early collections in this museum are made up of works that have no relation to the region. The 17thC is best represented by Dutch and Flemish paintings, including two bizarre works by the Dutch Italianate painter Cornelis van Haarlem, a sketch by Rubens, and a ***Mater Dolorosa*** by Jacob Jordaens. Among 18thC masters there are competent decorative pieces by Boucher, Oudry, Fragonard and G.B. Pittoni.

With its 19thC collections the place livens up considerably. Foreign artists working in Brittany during this period are inadequately represented, but there are two very interesting works by American painters: ***The Breton Fortune Teller***, a sombre genre scene by Henry Mosler who was in Pont-Aven in the 1870s; and ***Concarneau Seascape***, a pastel by the largely unknown Charles Fromuth. Fromuth's arresting pastels attracted the attention of Rodin, who visited the Philadelphia artist at Concarneau in 1901.

Paintings of Breton scenes by French artists, many of whom were fascinated by the region's past and the people's spirit of independence, naturally receive much more extensive coverage. Among many scenes of heroic Breton exploits, Jules Girardet's powerful ***The Rebels of Fouernant*** is outstanding. Breton traditions and costumes often provided material for artists, notably Charles Cottet, who is here represented by four canvases. Of these the most impressive is ***The Burnt Church***, showing Breton peasants kneeling before the charred remains of their church – a striking evocation of the sombre, mysterious atmosphere that attracted so many Symbolist artists to Brittany. Paintings by Gauguin's followers, the artists misleadingly referred to as the Pont-Aven School, are well represented though there are no paintings by Gauguin. Of special importance is a series of highly simplified studies of Breton women by Emile Bernard; ***The Old Woman of Le Pouldu***, a haunting landscape with solitary figure by Paul Sérusier; and Maxime Maufra's enormous ***Pont-Aven Landscape***. A small sketch by Clairin is of great historical interest, as it shows the interior of Lezaven, the Pont-Aven studio where Gauguin, Mosler and numerous other artist visitors worked.

RENNES
Ille-et-Vilaine, Bretagne Map D3

Rennes, the capital of Brittany, was badly damaged in World War II. However, the absence of very early buildings is mainly due not to the bombing but to a devastating fire of 1720. The rebuilding programme that followed has produced an arrangement of streets and squares typical of 18thC town planning, and there are many attractive buildings from this period, notably the town hall with its curved façade designed by Jacques Gabriel. Earlier is the 17thC Palais de Justice, a substantial stone building that originally housed the Breton parliament and was able to withstand the fire. The interior retains many original features, including the gilded woodwork and painted ceilings by the 17thC artist Noel Coypel, a follower of Poussin.

Musée des Beaux-Arts ☆

20 Quai Emile Zola
Tel. (99) 308338
Open 10am–noon, 2–6pm
Closed Tues

Situated in an impressive former university building near the town center, and overlooking the Vilaine canal, the Rennes museum of fine arts fills a series of well appointed galleries that do justice to an excellent collection of paintings and ceramics, as well as to a smaller holding of sculpture and of antiquities.

Among the 15thC and 16thC paintings there are some notable works, such as Veronese's ***Perseus and Andromeda***, but it is with the 17thC that you can begin to recognize some of the highlights of the collection. There is a good landscape sketch by the Dutch painter Cuyp, and a vibrant picture of a ***Tiger Hunt*** by Rubens, both hung in the second room, which also contains a marvellous ***Nativity*** ★ by Georges de La Tour. Here the humble figures are completely transformed by the luminosity of the colour and tone.

The 18thC section is larger, with two excellent still lifes by Chardin. One of these, the ***Basket of Plums*** ★ is an unquestionable masterpiece, but it is also worth looking at an interesting series of four 'disasters' by the Anglo-French painter P. J. de Loutherbourg, apparently illustrating the dangers of travel in the 1780s. De Loutherbourg's lively, expressive manner of treating dramatic subjects may have been helped by his experience as a scene painter for David Garrick in the Drury Lane Theatre, London.

The 19thC section is considerably larger again, with examples of most of the principal French art movements, including very good pictures by Gros, Couture, Boudin and Sisley. Mid 19thC paintings of oriental scenes are in evidence, particularly Louis Mouchot's ***Carpet Bazaar in Cairo*** and Louis Devedeux's ***Slave Market***, both of which demonstrate the rich colour that generally accompanies these exotic subjects.

The School of Pont-Aven is well represented with works by Emile Bernard, Meyer de Haan, Georges Lacombe and Paul Ranson, all imbued with the doleful sentiments so frequently associated with Breton landscape and peasantry by artists of the later 19thC. The section includes one of Sérusier's finest paintings, ***Solitude***, but by far the most impressive painting here is a small ***Still Life*** by Gauguin, confirming his position as leader of the group and easily the most important artist among them. In fact several of the early 20thC pictures in the collection are clearly influenced by Gauguin, although paintings by Picasso and Robert Delaunay lend some breadth to this section.

The collection of prints and drawings in the museum is very good, with fine examples of the work of Leonardo, Dürer and Rembrandt. Not all can be displayed at the same time, but there is usually an interesting temporary exhibition of items selected from the main collection.

Musée de Bretagne

20 Quai Emile Zola
Tel. (99) 308387
Open 10am–noon, 2–6pm
Closed Tues

The Musée de Bretagne, though situated in the same building as the Musée des Beaux-Arts, is an altogether separate institution concerned wholly with the region of Brittany. Beginning with geology and prehistory, the museum displays the Gallo-Roman history of the province before proceeding to the better-known folk art and life style of the Breton peasants. Displays of furniture, costumes, farm implements and even a weaver's loom help the visitor to understand why Breton life held such a fascination for the French intelligentsia in the late 19thC. The museum is notable for its imaginative presentation, and there are good audio-visual displays.

ROUEN

Seine-Maritime, Normandie Map F2

Rouen today is a thriving industrial city as well as a busy port on the Seine, despite being some 129km (80 miles) from the sea. The major part of the town has been built in the last 30 years, due partly to economic expansion, and partly to the severe bomb damage suffered in World War II. It is a testament to the powers of determined restoration that the old town has maintained a strong sense of its historic past.

Rouen's significance was established in the 10thC by the dukes of Normandy, and for the remainder of the Middle Ages and the Renaissance it was the focal point of considerable activity. Richard Coeur de Lion was crowned there in 1189, as was his brother John ten years later; Joan of Arc was tried there and then burnt to death in a place near the town center in 1431; during the 16thC Wars of Religion the town was alternately ravaged by Huguenots and Catholics.

There is still a clearly identifiable old quarter to the town, containing three important Gothic churches. Of these the glorious Cathedral of **Notre-Dame**, built between 1201 and 1514, is one of the greatest Gothic buildings in existence. The cathedral carries extensive and beautiful sculptural decoration of the 13thC to the 16thC on the elaborate W front surmounted by two irregular towers, on the main W doorway, and on two subsidiary portals on the N and S. Of these the **Portail des Libraires** (Booksellers' Doorway) on the north side is probably the finest.

The interior is a masterpiece of mature Gothic architecture and design, particularly the chancel. There are also some impressive tombs, including that of **Richard Coeur de Lion**. In the Lady Chapel you can see two outstanding examples of **French Renaissance sculpture**: the tomb of the Cardinals of Amboise (1515–25) by Roulland le Roux, and the tomb of Louis de Brézé (c.1544) by Jean Goujon.

The other two churches in the area are **St-Ouen** and **St-Maclou**. The first, a former abbey church from the 14thC to 15thC, is less highly decorated, but the lack of sculpture helps to bring out its orderly proportions and simple, pure lines. St-Maclou is in a striking Flamboyant Gothic style, with good Renaissance sculpture on the central doorway.

Musée des Beaux-Arts ☆☆

26bis Rue Thiers
Tel. (35) 712840
Open 10am–noon, 2–6pm
Closed Tues, Wed mornings

Rouen's principal museum was set up in 1800, and acquired a number of paintings that had been dispossessed during the Revolution. Donations, purchases and state deposits steadily enlarged the collection until the original premises in the Abbey of St-Ouen proved too small, and in 1887 a new building was opened, where the bulk of the collection can still be seen.

The size of the museum makes it an attractive prospect for those with an interest in fine or decorative art, since it offers several hours of pleasurable diversion just to get round the numerous galleries. Nor is the museum as busy as some, so you can be assured of relative peace and quiet. But a variable standard is inevitable in so large a collection, and some sections are more appealing than others. However, there are without doubt a number of outstanding pieces, some of which are without parallel anywhere.

The decorative arts section has an excellent **collection of pottery**, reflecting the fact that Rouen was the scene of an important ceramics industry between the 16thC and the 18thC. The collection includes examples from all the major regions as well as a comprehensive survey of the finest local faience. Acquired in 1864, it is one of the **best ceramics collections in Europe**.

On entering the fine art section on the first floor, the visitor is inevitably drawn to a late 15thC painting, set in its own specially constructed alcove and obviously considered as the jewel of the whole collection. This is the ***Virgin and Saints*** ★ by the Flemish painter Gerard David. It is clearly a picture of great quality, both in conception and execution, but not everyone might agree that the shrine-like presentation is justified, especially since there are other excellent works on display. But it is the finest of the early works, overshadowing a small predella panel of the ***Adoration, Baptism and Resurrection*** by Perugino, the 15thC Italian master.

The 16thC and 17thC galleries contain a number of magnificent pictures: ***The Man with a Globe*** ★ (or ***Democritus***) by Velazquez is possibly the finest, but Caravaggio's ***The Flagellation***, Guercino's ***Visitation***, and Georges de La Tour's ***St Sebastian Tended by Irene*** are all works of great quality. There are also several very pleasant Dutch pictures: **landscapes** by Ruisdael and van Goyen, and genre pieces such as Jan Steen's ***Wafer Seller*** and Terborch's ***The Music Lesson***.

The 17thC Flemish gallery opens with a striking picture of a ***Dead Woman in Bed*** by an unknown artist, treated with a clinical detachment that would not have been out of place in the 19thC. The gallery continues with a landscape by Paul Bril (1554–1626) and Rubens's ***The Adoration of the Shepherds***, a large altarpiece originally in the church of the Cappadocians at Aachen. This is an impressive example of Rubens's mature style. A small oil sketch nearby demonstrates the artist's fresh and lively brushwork in the early stages of a picture's development.

In the early French paintings, François Clouet's ***Bath of Diana*** (c.1570), an elaborate figure composition in the Italian Renaissance manner, is prominently featured. But this is followed by two superb paintings by Nicolas Poussin, each indicating a different aspect of his art. ***Venus Arming Aeneas*** ★★ is an outstanding work in the mythological vein for which he is best known; ***The Storm*** ★ demonstrates his ability as a landscapist of great power. Although he spent most of his active life in Rome, Poussin was born in Normandy, and a number of his followers from the district are represented in the Rouen museum. Unfortunately, a comparison only emphasizes how far their work falls short of the master's.

The 18thC galleries are predominantly French. Among the many first-rate works, look for Hubert Robert's ***View of Tivoli***, Deshay's ***Monkey*** (or ***Imitation Painter***), Jean Restout's poised and self-conscious ***Portrait of Dom Louis Baudoin***, and, best of all, Fragonard's dazzling oil sketch of ***The Laundresses*** ★ – a prime example of the Rococo painter's freedom and dexterity in the handling of paint. In this group, too, there is a good ***Stormy Landscape*** by the English artist George Morland that does not appear the least out of place, which is surprising in view of the supposed gulf between the schools.

The 19thC section is also dominated by French artists, and the size of the collection offers a rare opportunity to trace the various themes and traditions that run through the period. David, in many respects the father of French 19thC art, is represented by two good portraits, ***Mme. Ducreux*** and ***M. Songeolier***. A particularly fine portrait, ***Mme. Aymon*** (or ***La Belle Zélie***) by David's famous pupil, Ingres, hangs near by. Both painters have succeeded in striking an interesting balance between the subjects' personalities or emotions and a cool description of features.

A large group of pictures by **Théodore Géricault** ★, a native of Rouen, fills Room 22 and is quite simply the most comprehensive representation of his work to be found anywhere. Géricault was an ambitious painter who died before most of his projects could be realized, but for each stage of his career he left a series of sketches and paintings documenting the obsessional nature of his work. The Rouen collection includes studies of horses, soldiers, animals, landscapes, and a series of macabre still lifes of dismembered limbs that were used in the preparatory stages for his greatest work, ***The Raft of the Medusa*** (*LOUVRE*). This group also includes a portrait study of the young Delacroix, an early associate of Géricault's whose own immense ***Justice of Trajan*** ★ hangs in a special gallery beside a later but equally large painting by the academic artist Rochegrosse, entitled ***Andromache and Astyanax***. A comparison of the two paintings emphasizes Delacroix's use of rich but controlled colour to animate a picture that is classical in both subject and design, in contrast to Rochegrosse's melodramatic and conspicuously sadistic scene from ancient Troy, littered with hideously mutilated corpses.

A number of late 19thC academic pictures indicate contemporary preoccupations in their range of subject matter, and contrast interestingly with works by artists from the Barbizon and Impressionist groups who are much better known nowadays. The Impressionists are well represented, with several good pictures by leading figures of the circle, notably Sisley's ***Inundation***. But Monet's ***Rue Montorgueil Decked out with Flags*** (1878), a dazzling display of colour and broken brushstrokes, is the outstanding picture in this department. Fittingly, there is also one of Monet's paintings of ***Rouen Cathedral***, part of the series of variations on different colour harmonies observed on the cathedral facade. But to get the full effect of the artist's conception you should really visit the Jeu de Paume in *PARIS*, where several are displayed alongside each other.

The modern section is definitely less impressive, but there are two interesting displays in a separate wing off the entrance hall. One of these consists of a large collection of works by J.-E. Blanche (1861–1942), a society portraitist who painted many of the leading writers, musicians and intellectuals of his day. Here you can see portraits of André Gide, Bergson, Cocteau, Valéry and Stravinsky, among others. In a separate room further along there is a small exhibition of works by the Duchamp family, who were natives of Rouen at the beginning of this century. Of these it was Marcel Duchamp who exerted the most powerful influence on subsequent 20thC art, but both Jacques Villon and Raymond Duchamp-Villon were prominent in the avant-garde circle of the Cubists. Marcel Duchamp is represented by an early sketch and also by the later small-scale reconstruction of all his major works known as the ***Boite en Valise***. As the name implies, this is a travelling museum in a suitcase – an ironic exhibit on which to end this tour of one of the most extensive and rambling museums in France.

Musée des Antiquités de Rouen

198 Rue Beauvoisins
Tel. (35) 985510
Open 10am – noon, 2 – 5.30pm
Closed Thurs

The museum of antiquities is housed in an old 17thC convent redolent of cloistered religion, with a tradition of sacred objects extending back to the Middle Ages. Such an atmosphere could hardly be more appropriate for a collection dominated by ecclesiastical treasures, including reliquaries, enamels, stained glass windows, illuminated manuscripts, altarpieces, icons and sculptures in wood, ivory and alabaster. There is even a faint smell of incense to emphasize the impression of ancient church ritual.

The museum also has an interesting selection of medieval and Renaissance furniture, some ceramics, and a good antique section with Greek vases and a large Roman mosaic of ***Apollo and Daphne*** from Lillebonne (the Roman town of Juliobona).

SAUMUR

Maine-et-Loire, Pays de la Loire Map E5

Famous for its wine and its cavalry school, the town of Saumur on the Loire is best known for its magnificent château. Begun in the 14thC by Louis I, Duke of Anjou, the building was depicted around 1413 by the great manuscript illuminators, the Limbourg brothers, appearing as the backdrop to the September page of the Duc de Berry's ***Très Riches Heures*** (now in the Musée Condé at ***CHANTILLY***).

Château de Saumur

Tel. (41) 513046
Open Sept – Mar 9.30 – 11.30am, 2 – 5pm; July – Aug 9am – 7pm, 8.30 – 10.30pm
Closed Tues (Nov – Mar)

Besides being one of the most attractive of the Loire châteaux, Saumur contains two museums on widely different subjects. The Musée de Cheval, a miscellaneous collection of items relating to horses, is housed on an upper floor and will no doubt appeal to riding enthusiasts. The Musée d'Arts Decoratifs, a more traditional museum, consists mainly of the Comte de Lair's collection presented to the town in 1919. It includes tapestries, ceramics, manuscripts and small sculptures from the Gothic period to the 19thC, and is particularly notable for its **range of ceramics**. The collection has little that is strictly relevant to the château or its origins, but the items are well displayed and provide an enjoyable diversion as you pass through what would otherwise be a series of bare stone rooms.

ST-LÔ

Manche, Normandie Map D2

The capital of Normandy's Manche region, St-Lô was the focal point of German resistance in 1944, during the Battle of Normandy. As a result it suffered terribly from Allied bombardment and has been almost completely rebuilt since the war, giving it the appearance of a rather anonymous new town.

Musée de l'Hôtel de Ville

Place de la Mairie
Tel. (33) 575701
Open July – Aug 10.30am – noon, 2.30 – 5pm, Sept – July 2.30 – 5pm
Closed Tues

Like the rest of the town, the original museum of St-Lô was destroyed with most of its contents during the 1944 devastation of this area, and the present rather sad display in the basement of the Hôtel de Ville represents those items that were removed for safekeeping by a concerned curator. Pre-eminent among these is the series of eight Flemish tapestries, ***The Loves of Gombaut and Macée***, depicting 16thC pastoral life in a charmingly light-hearted fashion. Tapestries with a lively anecdotal content are rare, particularly after the Gothic period, and this series is refreshingly different from the innumerable solemn productions of the tapestry workshops in the following century.

Apart from these there is little of note in the St-Lô gallery, with its unremarkable collection of 19thC paintings by Gros, Corot, Rousseau and Millet, hung in rather cramped conditions. An unusually large Boudin from the 1870s is interesting both for its size and strong colouring, since this artist tended to work with a limited palette and on a smaller scale. In this company it is surprising to find four drawings by the 18thC Venetian artist Gian-Domenico Tiepolo, even though these are not outstanding and do not greatly strengthen the collection.

TOURS
Indre-et-Loire, Centre Map F5

Capital and main touring base for the region, Tours is a fair-sized industrial town with origins dating to Roman times. Under Gregory of Tours in the 6thC it developed into an important place of learning, and in the 8thC it possessed a court school of copyists and manuscript illuminators, founded by Alcuin of York, that produced some of the finest examples of early medieval painting and calligraphy.

Tours' greatest period was in the Middle Ages, when the cult of St Martin (d. AD397), the Roman legionary who became the town's bishop and patron saint, brought a great influx of pilgrims into the city. Thereafter, from the 17thC to the beginning of the 19thC, Tours suffered a period of economic decline, and was considerably damaged by enemy action in the Franco-Prussian War of 1870 and in World War II.

Enough of the old town survives, however, to maintain something of its character. The best preserved of the principal buildings is the **Cathedral of St-Gatien**, begun in the 13thC. A number of famous figures have been associated with Tours, including the painters Jean Fouquet (15thC) and François Clouet (16thC), and the great 19thC novelist, Honoré de Balzac.

Musée des Beaux-Arts ☆
Ancien Palais Archépiscopale,
18, Place François-Sicard
Tel. (47) 056873
Open April–Sept 9am–noon, 2–6pm;
Oct–Mar 9am–noon, 2–5pm
Closed Tues (Oct–May)

The Tours museum of fine arts, founded at the time of the Revolution, is located beside the cathedral of St-Gatien in the former palace of the archbishops. This elegant 17thC–18thC building provides a fine setting for the collection, and in the interior too an attempt has been made to harmonize the exhibits with their architectural setting: several rooms are comprehensive recreations of the Regency, Louis XV and Louis XVI styles of the 18thC, complete with carpets, wall panelling, furniture and objets d'art.

The early Italian section is particularly strong, with good panels from the 15thC by the Venetian Antonio Vivarini and the Florentine father and son, Lorenzo di Bicci and Bicci di Lorenzo (the same names tend to recur in family workshops). Like most early Renaissance pictures, these are panels from altarpieces, as are the two pictures by Mantegna, the ***Agony in the Garden*** ★ and the ***Resurrection***.

These were originally panels from the San Zeno altarpiece, Mantegna's early composition painted in Padua in 1459, and were brought to France by Napoleon in 1798 as part of the spoils of the Italian campaign. The third panel, a ***Crucifixion***, is now in the Louvre (although by a coincidence there is a 19thC copy of it by Degas in the Tours museum). Significantly, none of these pictures was returned in the restitutions of 1815. The Tours ***Agony in the Garden*** closely resembles a larger version in the National Gallery, London, and is probably the finest of these two Mantegnas. Both, however, are outstanding examples of the artist's excellent draughtsmanship and crisp technique.

The later Italian pictures cannot match this impressive standard, but from the large group of 17thC works in the style of Caravaggio, the ***Triumph of Silenus*** by Mattia Preti (1613–99) is impressive. It has recently been cleaned, and now reveals a wealth of incident in a harmonious design.

Among the northern European pictures there are a few early Flemish works, including an early 16thC ***Virgin and Child*** by Quentin Massys (1464–1530), but the main group is 17thC, consisting of works by Rembrandt and Rubens, as well as by followers and contemporaries of these two leading lights. Rubens' ***Madonna and Child with Two Donors*** is a rather formal work enlivened by characteristically rich colour and brushwork. Rembrandt's small ***Flight into Egypt***, one of the artist's earliest paintings, is more dramatic, with violent contrasts between light and shade. There is also a notable recent addition to this section, the ***Portrait of a Young Woman*** by van Ravesteyn (1570–1657). This work by a less well-known contemporary of Rembrandt is by no means overshadowed by these two 17thC masters.

The extensive collection of French paintings is displayed chronologically in a series of rooms throughout the museum, and includes examples of most periods and styles between the 15thC and the 19thC. Not all the pictures are a pleasure to see – there are numerous rather dry academic works from the 17thC and 18thC – but in a collection of this size there is still plenty to catch the eye. Two paintings by Boucher in the Salon Louis XV display the exuberant handling and colour characteristic of this 18thC decorative master. In his treatment of these subjects derived from ***Silvia and Aminta***, a 16thC Italian pastorale, Boucher's light-hearted approach emphasizes the humour and eroticism of the story, and is typical of the Rococo tradition. A ***self-portrait*** by Jean-Baptiste Perronneau (1715–83) in the same room, as well as ***Portraits of M. and Mme. de Flandre de Brunville***, two rooms further on, by Alexandre Roslin (1718–93), demonstrate the intimacy and freshness of Rococo portraiture. All these works have a delicate pastel colouring that can appear superficial, but the relaxed poses and informal settings reveal a personal approach to portraiture that was quite new at the time.

The section of 19thC pictures on the top floor opens impressively with two paintings of **Oriental subjects** by Delacroix and one of his followers, Chassériau, but the rest of this section is patchy. The Cazin family of painters, who treated a number of religious and secular themes in the naturalistic style popular in the late 19thC, is well represented, perhaps not surprisingly since Jean-Charles Cazin was director of the museum between 1869 and 1872. It may be that this paucity of important artists has its advantages, allowing other artists who would not normally appear to be exhibited, but the fact remains that this section is far weaker than the earlier periods. Not till we reach Monet's small sketch of the ***Seine at Vétheuil***, from the 1880s, do we come across a clearly recognizable artistic landmark. The 20thC rooms are no better, with a **mobile** by the American artist Alexander Calder as the only work of note. The contrast is all the more striking in view of the strength and quality of the earlier rooms in the gallery.

The museum has a good collection of drawings, including the excellent study by David for his painting, ***The Oath of the Horatii***. There is also a number of Greek vases from the archaic and classical periods (6thC and 5thC) bequeathed by the archaeologist Camille Lefèvre. Some of these are of very good quality and make a worthy addition to this attractive gallery.

The following works of art in the Tours Museum of Fine Arts are of particular interest:

1 ***Agony in the Garden***, Andrea Mantegna
2 ***Resurrection***, Andrea Mantegna
3 ***Triumph of Silenus***, Mattia Preti
4 ***Virgin and Child***, Quentin Massys
5 ***Madonna and Child***, Peter Paul Rubens
6 ***Flight into Egypt***, Rembrandt van Rijn
7, 8 ***Scenes from Silvia and Amynta***, François Boucher
9 ***Self-portrait***, Jean-Baptiste Perronneau
10 ***Portrait of Mme de Flandre de Brunville***, Alexandre Roslin
11 ***Comédiens ou Bouffons arabes***, Eugène Delacroix
12 ***Maréchal-ferrant arabe***, Theodore Chassériau
13 ***Seine at Vetheuil***, Claude Monet
14 ***Mobile***, Alexander Calder

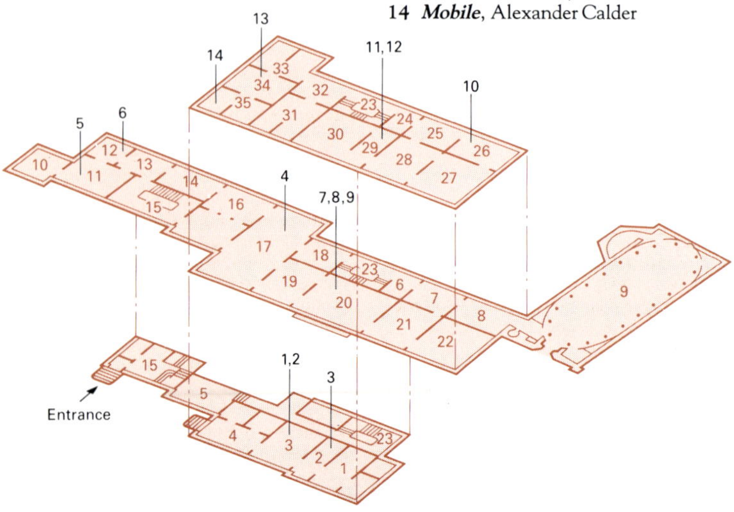

Hôtel Gouin

25 Rue du Commerce
Open mid-Mar to Sept 9am–noon, 2–7pm; Oct to mid-Mar 9am–noon, 2–5.30pm
Closed Jan, Dec

The central area of Tours has a modern appearance, having been badly damaged during World War II, and it is therefore surprising to find the ornate Renaissance mansion known as the Hôtel Gouin in the heart of this rebuilt area, apparently unaffected. In fact, however, the building has been skilfully restored for the Touraine Archaeological Society, and now houses their collections. Much is of mainly local interest, with the two vaulted rooms in the basement given over to the prehistoric and Gallo–Roman remains found in the area, but two of the other three floors have displays of **furniture, decorative arts and paintings** from the Gothic period to the 18thC. The late medieval works are perhaps the most interesting, with several sculptures from the churches of the Touraine. As a curiosity, one of the rooms on the first floor has the laboratory used by Jean-Jacques Rousseau when he lived at CHENONCEAU.

TROUVILLE

Calvados, Normandie Map E2

Trouville and its companion, Deauville, on the other side of the river Touques, were fashionable resorts throughout the second half of the 19thC, frequented as much for the gambling as for the waters. The popularity of the two seaside towns continues, but today there is an air of slightly faded elegance about them. During its great period Trouville was also popular with artists, who were attracted to the scenery of the beach and coastline. A number of important painters, including Courbet, Whistler, Boudin and Monet, worked there at significant stages in their careers.

Musée Municipal

Villa Montebello,
64 Rue General Leclerc
Tel. (31) 881626
Open Apr to mid-June (Sat, Sun) 3–7pm; mid-June to Sept (Wed–Mon) 3–7pm
Closed Oct–Mar, Tues

The museum of Trouville is situated at a prudent distance from the resort's main attractions – the casino and the beach. The collection includes a number of fairly traditional landscapes, portraits and genre paintings from the 19thC and 20thC, but there are some memorable **sketches and paintings** by Boudin, who worked in this area for most of his life. Several pictures by local artists, whose interest in natural scenery formed the basis of the School of Normandy in the mid-19thC, are also to be recommended. Of this group, Charles Mozin is perhaps the most interesting since it was his work that first drew the attention of Parisians to this region in the 1840s. Artists continued to visit Trouville in the early 20thC, and the collection contains representative works by Bonnard, Dufy and Kees van Dongen. These artists used a much richer palette for painting the local scenery than did their 19thC predecessors, but the naturalism of Boudin and Mozin seems more in tune with the atmosphere of the place.

VENDÔME

Loir-et-Cher, Centre Map F4

Vendôme has a delightfully picturesque appearance, being built over a series of small islands in the river Loir. The imposing Benedictine abbey church of the Holy Trinity, built between the 11thC and the 16thC, has impressive Romanesque and Gothic elements.

Musée Municipal

Cloître de la Trinité
Tel (54) 772613
Open 9am–noon, 2–6pm
Closed Tues and holidays

The museum of Vendôme is part of a group of buildings around the large church which once formed the abbey cloisters, and there is still a pleasant enclosed garden in front of the entrance. Inside the museum the abbey's influence seems to persist, since the collection begins with **medieval works** of a principally religious character, and some of the carved stonework is in fact taken from the fabric of the church. As you ascend through the five floors, however, the atmosphere becomes more secular, with costumes, craft items, ceramics and paintings on display. The quality or standard unfortunately deteriorates accordingly. A dull collection of paintings on the first floor, some of them attributed to Boucher, is followed by a series of rooms in a general state of neglect containing pictures that have little to recommend them. This may seem unfair considering that most of the work is local in origin, but there are also landscapes and portraits by minor academic artists which are not noticeably superior. Fortunately there is usually an interesting temporary exhibition.

Renaissance art of the Loire châteaux

The concentration of Renaissance art and architecture in the Loire Valley owes much to the Hundred Years War between France and England. After the Battle of Agincourt in 1415, most of northern France (including Paris) was under English control, displacing the French court and nobility to the Touraine. Here it led a depressed, itinerant existence, moving from one feudal stronghold to another. The formidable castle at Chinon, for example, was the site of Joan of Arc's first meeting with the Dauphin (later Charles VII) in 1429; but the gradual resurgence of French spirit from this date also corresponds with the spread of Renaissance art and manners. As a result, the French nobility asserted its renewed vigour in an ever increasing programme of building and patronage of the arts. Artists included the king's painter Jean Fouquet, himself a native of TOURS and without doubt the most sophisticated French artist of the 15thC, who supplied altarpieces and illuminated manuscripts to such figures as Etienne Chevalier and Guillaume Juvenal des Ursins, the new administrators.

With the accession of Charles VIII in 1483, the taste for Italian art increased at the French court, and was given further impetus as a result of military campaigns in Italy. These drained the royal finances but increased the collection of paintings, tapestries, furniture and jewelry, especially at AMBOISE. However, this amounted to very little when compared to the acquisitions and activities of François I (1494–1547), the greatest royal patron of the arts, a devoted admirer of Italian culture, and in many respects the personification of the Renaissance in France. François's court was one of the most outstanding in Europe, enhanced by poets, musicians and scholars who interpreted the new learning for a rising generation of Frenchmen.

Amboise, the first royal residence in France, was largely built by Charles VIII. It was already an outpost of Renaissance ideals when François came to the throne in 1515, but the new king gave it increased splendour with lavish entertainments – fêtes, tournaments and balls – which were designed to display the wealth and brilliance of the court. François also brought his considerable collection of Italian paintings and sculpture to Amboise, and eventually persuaded the ageing Leonardo da Vinci to take up residence in the nearby manor house of CLOS-LUCÉ. In fact Leonardo was unable to paint for most of his short period at Amboise, but he did bring a number of

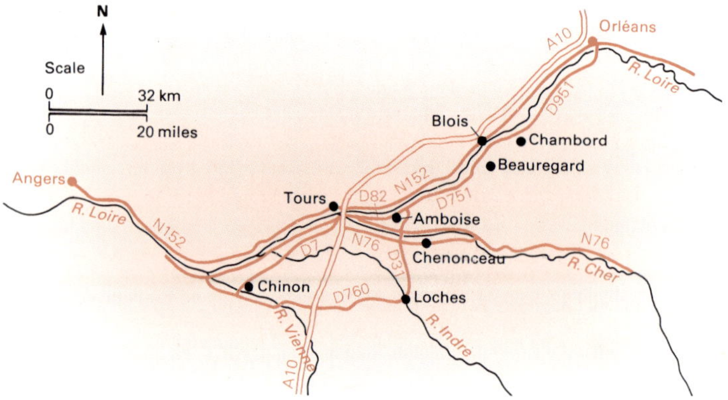

Fouquet's ***Road to Damascus****, c. 1460 from the* Heures d' Etienne Chevalier.

important works to France (now in the Louvre) which must have exerted a powerful influence on many of the native artists. An ironic counterpart to Leonardo's presence at Amboise reveals the political pragmatism behind French Renaissance ideals: at Loches, just 32 km (20 miles) away, the painter's erstwhile patron from Milan, Ludovico Sforza (Il Moro), spent the last eight years of his life decorating the walls of a dungeon with a range of curious Renaissance motifs and graffiti.

Leonardo has often been suggested as the possible designer of the elaborate spiral staircase at Blois, although there is very little stylistic evidence to support this. It is certainly the most striking feature of the building, but the heavy forms and traditional arrangement suggest the work of a French architect in the service of François I. The king embarked on the extension to Blois in the first year of his reign and succeeded in creating a Renaissance building with a clear strong character. It is on a grand scale, and from the N the exterior façade has an orderly arrangement that does nothing to lessen its towering, cliff-like appearance. Blois did not occupy the king's interest for long, however. By 1519 François had thrown all his enthusiasm and money into the building of an immense new palace at **CHAMBORD**. Employing an army of workmen and a team of French and Italian designers, it slowly rose in the heart of an extensive estate complete with deer forest and a diverted river. It was sufficiently advanced by 1539 for the king to receive the Emperor Charles V at Chambord on a state visit, but the château was still unfinished at his death in 1547. One reason for this was that François had become interested in yet another project; a palace of equally large proportions at Fontainebleau, with the result that the Loire Valley lost its cultural prominence. The Renaissance did not stop there however. The minor châteaux continued to attract ambitious patrons, and at **BEAUREGARD** and **CHENONCEAU** the most important work was done in the later 16thC.

NORTH EAST FRANCE

The area covered by the northeastern section of the *Guide* encompasses an immense diversity of art and, for that matter, an immense concentration of different cultural traditions within its tenuous boundaries, not to mention the richness of the collections themselves. The resorts and fishing ports of the Channel coast with their obvious links with Normandy; Alsace and Lorraine, the two bilingual districts on the German border; the rich industrial heritage of the Franco–Flemish area around Lille; the cathedral country of the Île de France – in every case a relatively short distance can quite easily mark the transition from one culture to another.

The section takes in roughly four regions, each with their various *Départements:* the Nord, Pas de Calais and Somme, much of which was traditionally Picardy; the Vosges area with Alsace and Lorraine in the extreme east; Champagne taking in the Ardennes and the Marne; and, closest to Paris, the eastern wing of the Ile de France.

Whether or not any one of these areas is more interesting than another, it is the contrast between them which sharpens up their respective identities.

But the northernmost section has perhaps the strongest historical associations. It is often the first sight of France which the visitor sees from a ferry, and its seaward face runs clearly into Belgium and Holland. Indeed many of the towns of this *Blooteland* have a Flemish ring to them, and the architecture of town halls such as the Stock Exchange at **LILLE** or the main square at **ARRAS** finds an echo in Bruges or Amsterdam rather than in France. Traditionally the main industry was textiles, the basis for much Flemish power in the late Middle Ages, but although this survives in Lille it has been overtaken by mining, steel and manufacturing industries which gives much of the landscape a harsh and work-soiled appearance.

The sense of being at the fringe of French society, evident in the Nord, becomes even more pronounced in Alsace and Lorraine. Linked together since the 18thC, when Lorraine was acquired by the Bourbons, these regions continually shuttled between France and Germany in successive conflicts. Towns like STRASBOURG, MULHOUSE or METZ have a distinctively Germanic style of architecture, but to many Germans the culture of the region seems equally Frankish and, as has often been pointed out, the Vosges was the birthplace of Joan of Arc, the embodiment of French nationalism.

As one moves inland towards the middle such problems of identity disappear, for the area of southern Picardy, Champagne and the Île de France is in many respects the heartland of the country. Champagne of course produces the famous sparkling white wine of that name, but the region also contains many of the great Gothic cathedrals, including the two finest, AMIENS and REIMS – the latter being the place where the kings of France were crowned. Any list of other great church buildings would have to include Laon, Soissons, Senlis and many more, but it is an indication of the wealth of medieval monuments in the region that they are too numerous to deal with even in passing.

If any single thing were to link the diverse features of the NE it would be the landscape. Flat and rolling until it gives way to the slopes of the south-eastern borders, it is interspersed by a series of navigable rivers and characteristically poplar-lined roads. This was the countryside that bore the brunt of three major wars, and particularly World War I. To this day the rivers Marne and Somme have a special significance to all Frenchmen.

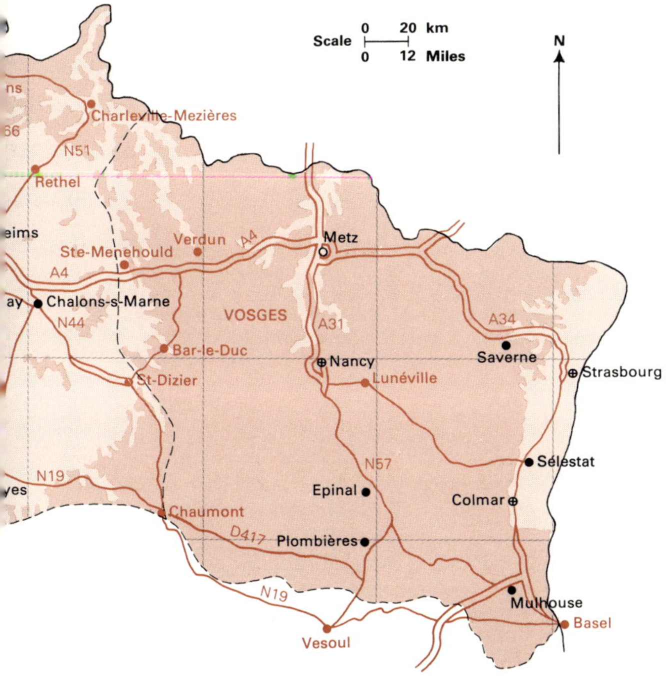

ABBEVILLE
Somme, Picardie Map A3

Abbeville lies on the main road between Paris and the channel ports. Until 1940 it was a town with many attractive medieval features but during the war, the city was virtually levelled by bombardment, and has been rebuilt in the anonymous style that has come to be associated with the urban architecture of the 1950s.

Musée Boucher de Perthes
24 Rue du Beffroi
Tel. (22) 240849
Open May–Sept 2–6pm; Oct–Apr, Sun 2–6pm
Closed May–Sept Tues; Oct–Apr Mon–Sat

The handsome 13thC belfry at the entrance of the Abbeville museum gives a misleading impression of its interior and contents. For unfortunately the galleries, opened in 1954, represent a rather dull municipal version of contemporary design, and the collection of paintings and sculpture does little to improve the situation. Several very weak pictures are attributed unconvincingly to Fragonard and Gaspard Dughet. A work by François Lemoyne (1688–1737) entitled ***Time Carrying Truth and Resisting the Attacks of Envy and Discord*** is well painted but the title gives some idea of the clumsy and, to modern eyes, silly allegorical subject. The two most interesting paintings in the museum are a 15thC triptych of the ***Virgin and Saints*** by Jacob of Amsterdam and ***The Return to the Village*** (1777) by Henri Theulon, a pupil of Greuze.

A separate room on the first floor contains a number of late medieval **ars sacra** consisting of enamels, tapestries and small sculptures in wood, ivory and alabaster. The bulk of the upper gallery, however, is devoted to palaeontology. Jacques Boucher de Perthes, after whom the gallery is named, was a renowned local archaeologist and "prehistorian", so it is only right and proper that his collection of archaeological objects, for the most part gathered during excavations in the Abbeville area, should be given due prominence.

AMIENS
Somme, Picardie Map B3

A lot has changed since Ruskin wrote *The Bible of Amiens* in the 19thC, extolling the virtues of the town. After two world wars there is very little of the medieval town left and in its place one now encounters a rather dull if not drab commercial city. However, if its general appearance is disappointing there are still some individual attractions, and chief among these is the superb 13thC Gothic **cathedral of Notre-Dame** ★. The exterior, and especially the façade, is lavishly decorated with free-standing and relief sculpture, but this could almost be taken as a mere introduction to the interior, which is of such grand and noble proportions that the effect on entering is quite breathtaking. Ruskin described the **apse** as "not only the best, but the very first thing done perfectly in its manner by Northern Christendom". The apse also has a beautiful series of elaborately carved wooden choir stalls dating from the early 16thC, and some successful Baroque accretions like the main altar. Unfortunately the Treasury was greatly depleted during the Revolution but there are still some reliquaries from the 13thC and 14thC on display.

Musée de Picardie
48 Rue de la République
Tel. (22) 913644
Open 10am–noon, 2–6pm
Closed Mon

The Musée de Picardie was set up in a slightly unorthodox manner. Having begun to gather documents and antiquities in 1839 the Société des Antiquaires de Picardie quickly felt the need for a museum to house and display their collection, but they were short of the finance required for such a project. When the ground was offered by the state therefore, they began running lotteries to raise the building costs – a venture that proved very successful. By 1856 they had amassed enough money to begin work on a large building, perfectly in keeping with the conspicuous ostentation of the Second Empire. In fact the Empire collapsed in 1870 before the new building could be formally opened, but two years later it began to serve as the city museum, a role which it fulfils to this day.

As an initial impression the building itself is a grand if not particularly attractive edifice, and the scale of the galleries and staircase, complete with **murals** by Puvis de Chavannes, make it seem more like a state institution. As for the collection, as a result of the interests of the original society a large part of the ground floor still represents the archaeology of the region. Picardy has proved to be very rich in prehistoric and Gallo–Roman sites, many of which were identified by aerial photography, and excavation has yielded a considerable amount of implements and vessels.

The painting collection on the first floor divides into the various national schools, but first there is an interesting **group of pictures** produced in Amiens during the 15thC, 16thC and 17thC. The religious society known as the *Confrerie du Puy Notre Dame d'Amiens* were in the habit of holding annual poetry competitions on the theme of the Virgin, for which an image was commissioned by each year's president, to be hung eventually in the cathedral. This practice continued until 1666 when it was felt that the cathedral was becoming cluttered, and in 1723 many of the panels were taken down and destroyed. The 16 which survive in the museum are all glorifications of the Virgin in a slightly naive manner, but the finest of them are at least engaging, and one or two are very good indeed.

Given Amiens' proximity to the Low Countries it is understandable that there should be a large collection of Flemish and Dutch pictures, mostly from the 17thC. There is, for example, a good series of landscapes by Jan van Goyen, and a ***Portrait of Professor Langelius*** in typically muted tonality by Frans Hals. Beyond this the Spanish paintings include a ***Portrait of a Man*** by El Greco and ***The Miracle of St Donatus of Arezzo*** by Murillo, but by far the strongest area of the collection is the **French pictures from the 18thC**. Most of the principal artists from this phase in French art are represented, but it is worth drawing attention to some in particular. Maurice Quentin de La Tour's ***Self-Portrait*** ★ is one of this artist's masterpieces, while Fragonard's ***Laundresses*** ★ is a display of technical virtuosity that very few painters could equal. The nine ***Hunting Scenes***, each painted by a different artist between 1736 and 1738, are essentially decorative and were hung in the apartments of Louis XV at the palace of Versailles. From the 19thC there are **works** by Géricault, Delacroix and Gauguin and a reasonable number of early 20thC pictures by Matisse, Bonnard and the lesser figures of the so-called School of Paris. But these later works suffer by comparison with the 18thC collection, which is not only more numerous but of higher quality. Many seem out of place in such large and somehow inappropriate galleries, but the museum is currently in the process of undergoing a major renovation and this will probably improve the facilities for exhibiting less traditional works. In any case, the collection itself contains a number of first-class paintings.

ARRAS

Pas-de-Calais, Nord Map B2

A major wool town and focus of banking in the Middle Ages, with an international reputation for its tapestry manufacturing, Arras was largely destroyed in World War I, when it was virtually in the front line of the fighting. Few of its medieval monuments survive, yet it has kept against all odds – and thanks to skilful restoration – two outstanding 17thC squares. Both are completely Flemish in character and lined with tall gabled houses with arcades. The **Place des Héros**, the smaller of the two, is dominated at one end by the tall and very elaborate Flemish-style town hall, built in the 15thC, but reconstructed after 1918. The vast **Grande Place**, which is almost completely cobbled and now cleared of cars (a car park has recently been constructed underneath) can be claimed without exaggeration to be one of the most beautiful squares in Europe.

The largest old buildings in Arras are the former Abbey of St-Vaast and the adjoining Cathedral of St-Vaast (once the abbey church). The abbey was founded in the 7thC, but the present buildings date from the mid 18thC. They are cold in character and almost inhuman in their proportions.

Musée des Beaux-Arts

22 Rue Paul Doumer
Tel. (21) 212643
Open Apr–Sept 10am–noon, 2–5.30pm; Oct–Mar Mon, Wed–Sat 10am–noon, 3–5pm, Sun 3–5.30pm
Closed Tues

The monastic living quarters of the former **Abbey of St-Vaast** house the town's art gallery. Its collections, although extensive, seem dwarfed by the building, and they contain few works that really engage the attention. The ground floor displays a miscellaneous range of works of art from the Middle Ages up to the 19thC. Among the medieval statuary kept here is a particularly gruesome **15thC tomb effigy** by Guille Lefrançois: the body, carved in black marble, appears in an advanced stage of decay and is covered in maggots.

Only one **15thC tapestry** considered to have been manufactured in Arras is on display. But Arras tapestries are rare: despite the fame of the town's products in the Middle Ages, there today exists only one set which can definitely be ascribed to Arras (the one that is in Tournai Cathedral).

The tapestry industry in Arras was at its height after 1384, when the town was annexed to the Duchy of Burgundy. The local tapestry factories were lavishly patronized by the Burgundian court and, through the alliance between Burgundy and England, were allowed to export their goods to England, as well as to import English wool. They began to decline in the 15thC, as they were superseded in importance by those of Tournai, now in Belgium.

The most important paintings on the ground floor of the museum are a group by the 17thC Italian artist, Giovanni Baglione, representing ***Apollo and his Muses***. These rather stiff and awkward works were highly esteemed by contemporaries of Baglione, who today is known almost exclusively as a writer (in particular for his invaluable account of late 16thC and early 17thC painters, sculptors and architects). In his time, however, he was an extremely successful painter, and in 1620 he received the commission for the paintings now at Arras from the Duke of Mantua. Four years later the duke presented the paintings to Marie de Medici, then Regent of France. She had them hung in the Palais de Luxembourg in ***PARIS*** in the very room for which, several years later, Rubens painted his celebrated ***Marie de Medici*** cycle (now in the Louvre, ***PARIS***).

The other paintings on the ground floor include a large number of landscapes by the undistinguished local artist, Constant Dutilleux, a friend and follower of Corot. The most interesting 19thC painting in this part of the museum is by Paul Mathey, and is of the painter ***Ernest Duez*** (1876). This is one of a series that Mathey painted of his artist contemporaries.

The first floor contains a good collection of 18thC Tournai and Arras pottery. There is also an enormous room full of large-scale 17thC French religious paintings, including works by Laurent de la Hyre and Jouvenet, as well as Philippe de Champaigne's ***Presentation of the Virgin at the Temple***. The same room also contains the masterpiece of Joseph Parrocel, the ***Shaming of John the Baptist*** (1694). Parrocel's vivid handling of paint and colour, and his dramatic contrasts of light and shade, distinguish this work sharply from the cold classicism found in most of the French contemporaries of Parrocel, whose painting anticipates the art of Delacroix. Parrocel was trained mainly in Venice, and seems to have learnt much from the works of Venice-based artists such as Tintoretto, Veronese, Domenico Feti, Filippo Strozzi and Jan Liss.

Most of the museum's 19thC and 20thC collections are housed on the second floor. One of the few works here worth singling out is a painting by the Neoclassical artist Cochereau, which illustrates the interior of ***David's Studio***, with artists drawing from a nude male model. Another room here contains the donation of Madame Louise Weiss, which has numerous **watercolours** by Dufy, and a marble bust of Madame Weiss' husband, incorporating in its base a chain from an Auschwitz prisoner and a fragment of metal from Hiroshima.

BERGUES
Pas-de-Calais, Nord Map B1

Once an important wool town, Bergues is now one of the most delightful places in this area of France. It has retained its **fortifications**; and many of its old buildings – such as the medieval Abbey of St-Winoc and the 17thC almshouse – have been excellently restored. With its gabled houses and encircling canal, Bergues seems like a miniature replica of the Belgian town of Bruges.

Musée Municipal
Mont de Pieter, Place St-Martin
Tel. (20) 685044
Open 10am–noon, 2–5pm
Closed Fri

The **17thC almshouse**, with its elaborate sculpted exterior, is the masterpiece of Wenceslaus Coeburger (1561–1634), who combined the activities of architect, engineer, painter and economist, and was also responsible for introducing almshouses to Flanders. The well-preserved interior of the one at Bergues, which retains all its charming brick fireplaces, houses the local museum.

The art collection comprises for the most part indifferent 16thC and 17thC Flemish and Dutch paintings and drawings (the latter only partly displayed at any one time). It has, however, one outstanding painting, which has generally been considered as an original by Georges de La Tour ever since the 1972 Paris retrospective of this artist. This, the ***Hurdy-Gurdy Player*** ★, is one of a number of versions of the subject by La Tour, the other important ones being at ***NANTES*** (Musée des Beaux-Arts), possibly Remiremont (Musée), and Brussels (Musée Royal des Beaux-Arts).

The Bergues version, which comes from the former Abbey of St-Winoc, is notable for its small dog and extremely simplified still-life of bread in the left foreground. Only one other painting in the museum is worth special mention. This is a Breton landscape, ***The Fog*** (***Dunes at Poulignac***) by the French follower of Gauguin, Maxime Mauffra; it was painted in 1886, just before Mauffra fell under Gauguin's influence.

BOULOGNE-SUR-MER
Pas-de-Calais, Nord Map H2

Most people associate Boulogne with the ferry traffic to and from the south coast of England, but fishing plays a much larger role in the town's economy, and the activities of the port are everywhere in evidence. However, several historic buildings survive in the old town, particularly the **medieval castle** enclosed by ramparts dating from the 13thC. A number of later buildings are also of interest, including the 18thC **Hôtel de Ville** and the 19thC **Basilica of Notre-Dame**, which replaced a much earlier cathedral destroyed after the Revolution. This had been a place of pilgrimage since 636, when a vision of the Virgin Mary was seen by worshippers at the same time as the arrival, at the port, of a mysterious vessel carrying a statue of the Virgin.

Musée des Beaux-Arts et d'Archéologie
34 Grande Rue
Tel. (21) 805155 (Ext 385)
Open 10am–noon, 2–6pm
Closed Mon, Tues

The museum in Boulogne was set up to house the collection of the Vicomte de Barde, given to the town in 1824. Since this consisted mainly of natural history exhibits, the authorities gradually had to collect a range of other items to broaden its spectrum, and they have subsequently acquired a number of paintings and medieval objects as well as a considerable amount of ceramics. The paintings are not particularly distinguished – those by Pieter Lastman (1583–1633) and Corot, along with a group of 18thC French drawings, are the most memorable and interesting – but the **ceramic collection** is of considerable importance. It includes examples of most of the major French ceramics manufacturers, such as Sèvres, Rouen and Nevers, as well as pieces from pre-Columbian Peru. But the finest section overall is undoubtedly the Classical and Archaic Greek work, which includes some excellent **red- and black-figure vases** from Attica. The finest piece in the whole museum is a magnificent amphora depicting the **Death of Ajax**, and attributed to the Athenian potter Exekias, 6thC BC.

CALAIS
Pas-de-Calais, Nord Map A2

Calais is only 38km (24 miles) from the English coast and is the principal ferry link between the two countries, a fact which dominates the life and appearance of the town. In one sense it is really a border town, and has suffered the fate of all such communities, being regularly attacked and besieged. The great siege of 1346–47 led to the most famous episode in the town's history, when King Edward III of England demanded six prominent burghers for execution as an alternative to the total destruction of the town and its inhabitants. The event is commemorated in the famous **sculptural group** ★ by Rodin (1895) which stands in a park beside the Hôtel de Ville.

Musée Municipal des Beaux-Arts et de la Dentelle
25 Rue Richelieu
Tel. (31) 979900
Open 10am–noon, 2–5.30pm
Closed Tues'

Among the new provincial museums in France, many of which seem to conform to a certain pattern, consisting of an open central area surrounded by an upper gallery, Calais must be one of the more successful; the building itself is pleasant, light and above all unobtrusive. This arrangement lends itself to the display of sculpture, and the main area beyond the entrance has a number of **20thC bronzes** by sculptors such as Epstein, César and Zadkine. In 1884 the civic authorities of the town commissioned Rodin to design a monument to the ***Burghers of Calais***, those six men whose lives were offered up to appease a besieging English army. This is perhaps Rodin's finest completed work, and despite the fact that the city fathers were not at all pleased with it in 1886, the various studies and maquettes in plaster and bronze now have pride of place in a gallery of 19thC French sculpture. There are other earlier sculptures on the upper floor, although this is primarily devoted to the varied but relatively weak collection of paintings. There are pictures by Salvator Rosa, Boudin, Dufy and Derain but the most interesting works are by less well-known artists. ***Calais from the Sea*** (1840) by the English marine painter E. W. Cooke is a good mixture of the traditional Dutch manner and Turner's vibrant colour; an oil sketch ***Temptation*** by the Russian artist Ilya Repin (1844–1930) is a lively piece of work. There are also some good 19thC watercolours by artists such as

R. P. Bonington, but they are not always on display. However this gallery does have an interesting programme of temporary exhibitions which goes some way towards compensating for the weaknesses in the collection overall.

CAMBRAI
Pas-de-Calais, Nord Map C3

Cambrai was a town of some importance in medieval Flanders, but virtually all traces of the Middle Ages have been swept away, leaving only the traditional layout within the old town walls. One notable feature that links Cambrai more with Belgium than with northern France is the Flemish appearance of the major ecclesiastical building, the **Grande Seminaire**, which is in a mature 17thC Baroque style. This foundation is remarkable also for its treasury of religious art from the Middle Ages up to the 19thC. The nearby church of St-Géry contains a large painting of ***The Entombment*** attributed to Rubens.

Musée Municipal
15 Rue de L'Epée
Tel. (20) 813803
Open 10am–noon, 2–5pm
Closed Tues

The Cambrai Museum, like so many others in France, was initially set up during the Revolution when it was able to acquire church treasures displaced in the upheaval, and to this day it is the **sculptures** from the old 12thC cathedral and the Hôpital St-Jacques-au-Bois which are the most interesting parts of the collection. These pieces are supplemented by a number of later sculptures, such as ***St Sebastian*** and ***The Capture of Cambrai*** by the local 17thC artist Barthélemy Marsy, and as if to maintain this trend the museum also has sculptures by Rodin and Bourdelle.

The paintings on the first floor are drawn mainly from the Dutch, Flemish and French schools, and the most interesting of these are the works attributed to Rubens, Ingres and Boudin. Look also for a painting of ***The Entombment*** by the Flemish Mannerist Hendrik de Clerck which, though perhaps not to everyone's taste, is a fine and really quite unusual piece of work. The museum also has a few more modern pictures by artists such as Le Sidaner and Utrillo, and a reasonable selection of **20thC drawings** by Matisse, Dufy and Vlaminck. Unfortunately, this latter group cannot be placed on permanent exhibition for fear of deterioration.

CASSEL
Pas-de-Calais, Nord Map B2

A medieval town in the northeastern corner of France, Cassel is situated on the top of a hill and has a distinctly Flemish look, with its low limewashed buildings and winding, cobbled streets. Not much of the old quarter is left, for it was the scene of fierce hand-to-hand fighting during World War II, but the **Grande Place** retains much of its medieval and Renaissance heritage.

Musée d'Art, d'Histoire et de Folklore
Grande Place
Tel. (28) 424013
Open Mar–Oct, Sat, Sun 2.30–7pm
Closed Nov–Feb, Mon–Fri

Like the town itself, the museum of Cassel suffered much damage in 1940, and most of its items were lost forever. Although it has been reorganized it has very little to offer in the way of works of art, but it is housed in an elegant 16thC **Renaissance building** on the main square.

LE CATEAU-CAMBRÉSIS
Pas-de-Calais, Nord Map C3

A tiny industrial town in a pleasant valley, Le Cateau-Cambrésis is famous as the place where Henry II of France and Philip II of Spain signed an important treaty in 1559. It was also here that one of France's greatest painters of this century, Henri Matisse, was born. Matisse's parents (his father was a grain merchant) in fact lived in the nearby village of Bohain. His mother, however, had parents who had a house at Le Cateau, and it was while staying with them here in 1869 that she gave birth to her son; this house (**45 Rue de la République**) can still be seen.

Musée Matisse
Rue Charles Seyeoux
Tel. (20) 841315
Open Sat, Sun, holidays, 3–5pm
Closed Mon–Fri

Matisse stayed occasionally with his grandparents at Le Cateau during his childhood, but had otherwise relatively little to do with the town. Nonetheless in 1951 Le Cateau decided to honour its connections with him by creating in the town hall a museum of contemporary art, for which they were lent minor works by the Musée National d'Art Moderne in *PARIS*. This in turn gave Matisse the idea of presenting to the town a number of his own works in different media: he gave 5 sculptures, 2 paintings, 1 tapestry, 2 hangings, 27 engravings, 35 drawings and 10 illustrated books.

The museum of contemporary art was subsequently called the Musée Matisse, and was the first one devoted to this artist, as well as the only one which Matisse would live to see (he died in 1954). The same year that it was inaugurated Matisse also donated a stained glass window entitled ***Les Abeilles*** to a nursery school in the town. This was his last work in this medium, and he created it just after the famous stained glass windows in his chapel at *VENCE* in Provence. It occupies the largest room in what is now the **Ecole Matisse** in the Rue du Général Morland. Although the work is not exceptional, and is set in a dull modern building, it gains from being in a room which is scattered with toys and books, and constantly enlivened by playing children.

In the course of the 1970s the Musée Matisse received several donations from members of the artist's family, and plans were made to transfer the museum from the town hall to an 18thC building, the Palais Fénélon, belonging to the municipality. The new Matisse museum was opened in the autumn of 1982. The rather ugly Palais Fénélon has been drastically modernized inside to form a series of pleasantly and spaciously arranged rooms from which you can look down into the beautiful town park. The ground floor of the museum is taken up by the work of the two local contemporary artists, Auguste Herbin, and his great-niece Geneviève Claisse. Herbin, who spent his youth at Le Cateau, was in turn a Cubist, Orphist and founder member of the group of pioneering French abstract artists called *Abstraction création*. The Le Cateau museum has a wide selection of his cold, linear works dating from 1903 to 1960. Claisse's works represent the dreariest extreme of decorative hard-edge abstract painting characteristic of the 1960s.

The Matisse collection is all kept on the museum's first floor. Despite the lavish care which has been taken in the presentation, they are relatively minor and unexciting works. The most interesting are those done in his youth, all of which illustrate the artist's very tentative beginnings: these works include a series of academic nude studies executed in the Bouguereau Academy in Paris, an early oil copy of Chardin's ***The Ray*** in the *LOUVRE*, and an almost monochromatic flower still-life in oils (c.1894). Among his later works are an oil ***Self-portrait*** done in Nice in 1918, a 1946 Gobelins tapestry entitled ***The Lute***, and a number of studies in different media for his chapel at *VENCE*.

CHÂLONS-SUR-MARNE
Marne, Champagne-Ardenne
Map D4

The ancient town of Châlons, 161km (100 miles) due E of Paris, is today a busy industrial and commercial center, but there are a few buildings which testify to its eminence in the Middle Ages. The Collegiate church of Notre-Dame-en-Vaux and the large Cathedral of St-Etienne were begun in the 12thC and 13thC respectively, and both have been able to preserve fine examples of their original **stained glass**. The church of St-Alpin, which lies between the two, has a fine series of **Renaissance windows** from the 16th–17thC and some late medieval sculpture. There is also the church of St-Loup, which has a small altarpiece of the ***Adoration of the Magi*** attributed to Jan van Eyck.

Musée Municipal
Place Godart
Tel. (26) 685444
Open Mon, Wed–Sat 2–6pm, Sun 2.30–6.30pm
Closed Tues

The Musée Municipal at Châlons at first appears to be on the point of dispersal, because the Gallo–Roman and medieval antiquities displayed on the large ground floor hall are laid out in a manner so haphazard as to suggest imminent departure. In fact this is the permanent collection, although it looks like an auctioneer's rooms, and alongside some unusual Indian sculptures, primitive implements and fossils there are several fine polychrome wooden figures and church fittings from the Gothic period.

The paintings on the first floor are displayed in a long gallery, and the surprising feature of the collection is the fact that among such a large number of works there should be so few of any quality. ***A Winter Landscape*** by the 17thC Dutch artist Joos de Momper is perhaps the only picture with a convincing label, and there are a number of very weak paintings dubiously attributed to Jordaens, Manet, Degas, Monet and Sisley.

Cloître de l'Eglise Notre-Dame-en-Vaux
Rue Nicolas Durand
Tel. (26) 640387

Open May–Sept 10am–noon, 2–6pm; Oct–Apr 10am–noon, 2–5pm
Closed Tues

When work began in 1960 to clear and excavate the ground to the N of the church (an area that had once been the abbey cloisters, demolished in the late 18thC), there was good reason to expect that some remains would come to light. As it turned out, a fair amount of 12thC carved and sculpted stonework from the **Gothic cloisters** had been incorporated in the foundations and walls of later buildings on the same site, and although much of it was badly damaged, many pieces retained clear, fresh stone carving in faces, hair and drapery. The cloisters must have been an excellent example of early Gothic sculptural decoration, as several of the reconstructed column figures clearly demonstrate, and one wonders at the indifference to work of this quality before the revival of interest in the 19thC. Fortunately it is now very well displayed in a new gallery on the site which goes a long way towards restoring the original conception of the sculpted arcade.

COLMAR
Haut-Rhin, Alsace Map F5

Located close to the heart of the wine country of Alsace, not far from the first foothills of the Vosges, Colmar's **old quarter** has remained remarkably intact with its narrow streets, intricately half-timbered houses and carved façades. But Colmar is not only famous for its beautiful architecture; it also possesses one of the most outstanding museums in France; located in the 13thC former Dominican convent of Unterlinden (so named because of its lime trees). This is the home of the Isenheim Altarpiece by the great painter generally known as Grünewald (his real name was probably Mathis Gothardt-Neithardt).

Only a short walk from the Unterlinden museum is the **church of the Dominicans**, where you can see another magnificent painting, previously displayed at the **church of St-Martin**. This is the ***Virgin of the Rosebush*** ★ (1472) by the Colmar artist Martin Schongauer.

Musée d'Unterlinden ☆☆
Place Unterlinden
Tel. (89) 418923
Open Apr–Oct 9am–noon, 2–6pm; Nov to Mar 9am–noon, 2–5pm
Closed Tues (Nov to Mar), Nov 1

The buildings of the former convent of the Unterlinden Dominicans, where this superb museum is housed, include a large chapel and enclose some beautiful late **13thC cloisters**. The museum was originally founded in 1849 to preserve a rather unremarkable Roman mosaic from nearby Bergheim, and also to prevent the convent itself from demolition. In 1852 it received a large collection of works of art from various religious communities in the Colmar area.

This is one of the most visited museums in the whole of France, and the crowds around the Isenheim Altarpiece in particular can be extremely dense, especially on summer weekends. Guidebooks in several languages are available, both on the museum and on the Isenheim Altarpiece.

The layout of the museum is clear and uncluttered, with the first part devoted to Rhenish primitives from the 15thC. Among the many fine paintings is a particularly striking ***Crucifixion*** by an unknown master, and the ***Altarpiece of the Collegiate church of St-Martin*** by Gaspard Isenmann of Colmar (d. 1492).

The museum's greatest works, however, are in the old chapel. Colmar's most famous artist, Martin Schongauer, is represented by the fine ***Orlier Altarpiece***, and the master probably had a hand in the nearby ***Altarpiece of the Dominicans of Colmar*** by the School of Schongauer. There are also facsimiles of Schongauer's engravings.

The various panels of Grünewald's ***Isenheim Altarpiece*** ★★ take pride of place in the chapel. These represent 9 of his 20 known paintings, the whole group being completed in 1515 for the church of the Hospital of St Anthony at Isenheim, near Colmar. Little is known about Grünewald, but in originality and expressive power his work exceeds that of all his contemporaries, including even Dürer. The Isenheim Altarpiece, with its grandiose compositions and gory details, is acknowledged as his supreme achievement.

On the other side of the cloister, beyond a wine cellar displaying wine presses and old casks, a series of rooms are devoted mainly to stone engravings and sculptures from the 12thC to the 16thC. You can also see here some fine stained glass windows from the 15thC and two early 15thC tapestries, including a particularly impressive ***Fountain of Youth***.

On the next floor you can enjoy a fine view from the gallery to the chapel below with its magnificent paintings, already mentioned, as well as varied collections of 19thC and early 20thC children's toys, paintings of Colmar and the surrounding region, various items of period furniture, displays of ceramics, arms and armour, 18thC faience and porcelain (mainly from the major producing center of Strasbourg) and rooms devoted to the Revolution and to the Empire. There is also a room with a fine painted ceiling from the 18thC, and collections devoted to the popular arts of Alsace.

The basement of the museum contains the archaeological section, including the undistinguished Roman mosaic from Bergheim which was partly responsible for the original creation of the museum. A collection of modern art is also displayed here, with works by Renoir, Monet, Rouault, Braque, Léger, Picasso and others. But although this is quite an impressive collection, these paintings appear strangely incongruous in this setting.

Musée Bartholdi

30 rue des Marchands
Tel. (89) 419060
Open 9am noon, 2–5pm
Closed Tues

This small museum is dedicated to the memory of the Colmar-born sculptor Bartholdi who, though little known outside his native country, was responsible for perhaps the most famous massive sculpture of modern times: the ***Statue of Liberty*** at the entrance to New York harbour. Located in the house where Bartholdi was born, on 2 August 1834, the museum exhibits historical items on its ground floor with pottery, sculpture, maps of old Colmar and various historical documents.

The first floor contains period furniture from Bartholdi's time, and examples of the artist's work, including paintings, watercolours and drawings from his travels in Egypt and Abyssinia. More immediately interesting, perhaps, are several maquettes or preliminary models of his ***Statue of Liberty***, and of his other well-known massive work, the ***Lion of Belfort*** (Jura).

Colmar owns numerous works by Bartholdi, scattered around Colmar, as any stroll around the town will show, and these include a statue of General Rapp and the ***Fontaine du Vigneron***, commemorating the wines of Alsace.

DOUAI

Pas-de-Calais, Nord Map B2

Despite the ravages of two world wars Douai has been able to preserve its traditional appearance. In the old quarter a warren of narrow streets open out on the quays of the river Scarpe which bisects the town. Among many buildings of note, the **14th–15thC belfry** with its carillon of 62 bells is the most famous. It was described by Victor Hugo in 1837 and painted by Corot in one of his finest pictures, now in the *LOUVRE, PARIS*. The painter Jean Bellegambe (1470–1534), who was born in Douai, maintained a thriving workshop in the town during the latter half of his life, producing altarpieces in a style derived essentially from the great Flemish masters of the 15thC.

Musée Municipal (La Chartreuse)

4 Rue des Chartreux
Tel. (27) 872663
Open 10am–noon, 2–6pm
Closed Tues

The museum at Douai was first set up during the Revolution and subsequently enriched by a large bequest of paintings from the collection of Dr Escallier in 1857. Before turning to these, however, it is well worth taking a look at the building itself. This is the old **Chartreuse**, a plain but beautiful brick building dating, in part at least, from the 16thC. It now houses the paintings and ceramics which survived the destruction of the main part of the former museum in World War II. There are few museums which can boast such an attractive setting, and the collection, itself of a high standard, is well displayed.

The first galleries present a selection of **ceramics** from a wide range of sources, including examples of all the major French factories such as Sèvres, Nevers and Rouen, some local works from St-Omer, and pieces from further afield such as India, China and Japan. Behind this, in a separate gallery which was once the refectory of the Chartreuse, are the more important Flemish works of art: a series of **altarpieces** from the 15thC and 16thC, overlooked by a **Brussels tapestry** and surrounded by various medieval ivories, enamels and alabasters. There are **panels** attributed to Jan Provost and the Master of Flémalle in this group, but even more impressive are those by Jean Bellegambe and Jan van Scorel. Bellegambe, the leading artist of his day, was active in Douai during the early 16thC and is represented by two good works, ***Virgin Protecting the Order of the Citeaux*** and the **Retable of Anchin** depicting the ***Adoration of the Trinity***. Scorel's elaborate ***Polyptych of the Marchiennes*** is quite different in style (since he had visited Italy in the 1520s) and much larger in scale. The various panels of the

Madonna and the ***Last Judgment*** have now been detached and are exhibited individually, although there is a photographic reconstruction to demonstrate the original relationship of the parts.

At the opposite end of the ground floor galleries there are two curious Flemish 16thC paintings, a grotesque ***Mocking of Christ*** by Jan van Hemessen and ***The Trials or Misfortunes of Job*** by Jan Mandyn, both of which reflect the influence of Bosch in their imagery. But before this there is a good selection of Italian Renaissance pictures. Beginning with the earliest panels, an ***Adoration*** by Starnina and ***Christ Blessing*** by Barna da Siena, this section covers a fair range with **works** by Veronese, Vasari and Ludovico Carracci as well as a bronze ***Venus*** by the great Florentine Mannerist sculptor Giambologna.

The rooms on the first floor open with 17thC Dutch and Flemish pictures, of which Ruisdael's large ***Forest Landscape***, Berckheyde's ***View of Haarlem***, and van Dyck's sober ***Portrait of a Man*** are the most interesting. Following these, Salomon de Bray's ***Rebecca and Eliezer*** is an unexpectedly attractive work. Painted on a long narrow panel, indicating perhaps that it was intended for a piece of furniture, the biblical subject is set against a lovely landscape background.

The French paintings in the two longer galleries on the first floor have as wide a range as the other schools, covering the period between the 17thC and the 20thC. However, this section is something of a paradox because pictures by the most famous artists are easily outshone by those of lesser painters. David, Courbet and Delacroix are each represented, but it is the **landscapes** of Isabey, Jongkind and Boudin that are the most attractive. Another example of this can be seen in the portraits by Lebrun and J. M. Nattier at opposite ends of this same room. Lebrun's large equestrian ***Louis XIV*** is an impressive but dry and formal public work whereas Nattier's ***Portrait of a Woman*** ★, (thought to be Madame de Dreux-Brèze) has a dazzling surface texture and sharp characterization. The French rooms also include some good late 19thC works by Pissarro, Renoir and Sisley, but here again the less well-known artists, Henry Cross and Le Sidaner are more impressive. Nevertheless, it is a bronze by Rodin, ***The Prodigal Son*** ★, that stands out as almost certainly the finest work in this section.

The museum at Douai also has space for temporary exhibitions in the chapter-house beyond the cloisters. Like the other parts of the building, this has been well adapted to its new function, and has several interesting pieces of early sculpture distributed around the corridors.

DOULLENS
Somme, Picardie Map B3

Doullens is a small quiet town with a strong 19thC atmosphere.

Musée Lombart
7 Rue du Musée
Tel. (22) 770686
Open Thur–Fri 2–5.30pm
Closed Sat–Wed

The local museum of Doullens, which was inaugurated in 1908, was the conception of a wealthy local philanthropist and chocolate manufacturer, J-F. Lombart. It comprises exclusively his own extensive but mediocre collections. The archaeological section of the museum has mainly Egyptian and Far Eastern works, and is housed in a 19thC chapel. A small but ostentatious art gallery was built next to this to display Lombart's contemporary copies of Rubens, a painting dubiously attributed to Boucher, souvenirs of the chocolate trade, and other such objects. The museum's most charming feature is its small garden, which is dominated by a pond once crowned by a Carpeaux sculpture. The latter was stolen early in 1983.

DUNKERQUE
Pas-de-Calais, Nord Map B1

Dunkerque, which derives its name from a former church (or kirk) on the dunes, has had a troubled history: throughout the 16thC and 17thC it was the center of a dispute between the Spaniards, French, English and Dutch. Then, in 1940, it became the scene of a famous military offensive against the Germans which destroyed almost the entire town. It has subsequently grown up again to become the third largest port in France.

Recent attempts have been made to instil some cultural life into this ugly and characterless town. These include the building of two art galleries.

Musée des Beaux-Arts
Place du Général de Gaulle
Tel. (20) 665100 (Ext 432)
Open 10am–noon, 2–6pm
Closed Tues

The oldest of Dunkerque's galleries, the

Musée des Beaux-Arts, is on the town's market square. It was opened in 1973 and contains municipal collections that have been built up since 1841, but it is a dull building in a dated modernistic style imitative of the work of Le Corbusier. The paintings, which are well if unimaginatively displayed on a series of movable panels, mostly occupy the building's first floor, and have all been excellently restored or cleaned. The collection is strongest in Dutch and Flemish 16thC and 17thC works, most notable among which is an enormous ***Martyrdom of St George*** by Frans Pourbus, taken from a local church; an unusual ***Temptation of St Anthony*** by the little-known Flemish artist van der Vinnen; and an anonymous late 16thC Flemish ***Portrait head*** of a young boy.

The French collection has some interesting late Baroque and Rococo works, including Sébastien Bourdon's vividly painted ***Attack of the Travellers*** and the ***Bulgarian Rider*** by François-Joseph Casanova, brother of the celebrated lover. In the 19thC collection there is one of a series of monastic cell scenes by the romantic artist François-Marius Granet, an indifferent ***View of Dunkerque*** by Corot, and a **bronze** by Antoine-Louis Barye (1796–1875) of a tiger eating a crocodile, the first work to be acquired by the municipal authorities. Much of the 20thC collection is taken up with works by Maurice Marinot. Although associated with the group of early 20thC painters known as the Fauves, Marinot was at his most successful as a craftsman in glass. The Dunkerque gallery has a large group of his brash early Fauve paintings, and a case full of his delicate glasswork.

The ground floor, undoubtedly the most popular part of the museum, is devoted mainly to models of early ships. One also finds here – unexpectedly – a large and very impressive painting of a **Port** by the 19thC French artist Isabey, and a collection of paintings of local historical events and personalities. The most striking of these works is by the Russian artist Hirschfeld, and portrays **Arrival in Dunkirk** in 1901 of Tsar Nicholas II. The town's history during World War II is illustrated by a series of photographs and documents shown in the museum's basement.

Musée d'Art Contemporain de Dunkerque

Jardins de Sculptures
Tel. (28) 652165
Open 10am – 7pm
Closed Tues

The collections for the Musée d'Art Contemporain de la Ville de Dunkerque began to be assembled in 1974; but the museum itself, situated in a specially built sculpture park, was only inaugurated in December 1982. The park comprises a series of neatly mown hills punctuated at long intervals by bits of stone and twisted metal, and other such objects. Each of these art works is linked by a tiled concave path which would be ideal for skateboarders. The bleak ensemble blends in excellently with the surrounding landscape of shipbuilding yards and pretentious modern tower blocks. In the middle of the park is a large pond out of which rises the museum – a dazzlingly white structure capped by three large glass pyramids serving no apparent purpose. Enormous glass doors open automatically as one crosses the bridge leading into the museum, and bring one into what looks like a modern, hygienic version of a classical amphitheatre. This is used for experimental ballet and performance art, and adjoins a cafe with "High Tech" furniture. Little space has been left for the museum's collections. Contemporary American artists such as the abstract expressionist Sam Francis and the pop artist Andy Warhol are represented by some of their worst works. There is a whole room devoted to recent works by the Dutch artist Karel Appel, who once said that he painted "like a barbarian in a barbaric world". He has subsequently done little painting and specializes instead in colourful wooden reliefs resembling children's toys. The greater part of the collections are of French works of the 1970s. These are mainly chic, derivative and vacuous, but carry high-flown titles.

ÉPERNAY

Marne, Champagne-Ardenne
Map C4

Épernay, on the Marne south of Reims, is in the heart of the Champagne wine growing area. It was the wealth created by this industry that gave rise to the town's expansion during the 19thC.

Musée des Beaux-Arts

13 Avenue de Champagne
Tel. (26) 514991
Open Mar–Nov Mon, Wed–Sat 9am–noon, 2–6pm, 2–5pm
Closed Mar–Nov, Tues

In a street where all the great names of Champagne wine have their offices it comes as no surprise to find that a section of the museum is devoted to wine production and even that the archaeology department should have been organized by the Comte Chandon-Moët. In fact the imposing house set back from the Rue de Champagne has three museums, "Vin du Champagne" and "Archéologie" as well as "Beaux-Arts" although the latter is very much the poor relation of the group. The Beaux-Arts collection consists of a few indifferent French paintings from the 17thC to the 19thC and a reasonable amount of faience ware from Rouen and Nevers. In general, however, the wine presses, old bottles and diorama of the wine museum are more alluring.

ÉPINAL
Vosges, Lorraine Map E5

Épinal is a pleasant if unremarkable Vosges town, through which the river Moselle runs, forming an island in the middle. A wooded hill with a park containing the fragmentary remains of a castle dominates the town, which has a number of attractive buildings from various periods. These include the church of St-Maurice and an arcaded central square. The city library has an annex with magnificent bookcases taken from the abbey of Moyenmontier, and some fine old books and **illuminated manuscripts**.

Épinal is best known as a result of its manufacture of coloured images or prints, an industry associated with the Pellerin family in the 18thC but with antecedents that go back at least to the 17thC, if not earlier. The industry, which survives to this day, began with depiction of popular religious themes (coloured prints of saints in particular) but in its heyday (the first part of the 19thC) historical and patriotic topics predominated, as well as moral messages such as "Keep out of Debt".

The Departmental Museum now includes an International Museum of Colour Prints and the visitor can also look around the most famous workshop, the Imagerie Pellerin, located on the riverbank a little N of the town center. A tour of these buildings is very rewarding and nicely complements the visit to the museum.

Musée Départemental des Vosges/Musée International de l'Imagerie
Place Lagarde
Open Oct–Mar, 10am–noon, 2–5pm; Apr–Sep, 10am–noon, 2–6pm
Closed Tues

The original purpose of the Musée Départemental, founded in 1822, was to house the **collection of the Princes of Salm**, a tiny independent principality high in the Vosges, which survived till the French Revolution. According to a catalogue drawn up in 1799, the collection consisted of 164 paintings, 143 drawings and 2,355 prints. It was dispersed during the Revolution, part going to Anhalt in Germany (where it can still be seen in the castle) and part to the Épinal prefecture, where many of the works were destroyed by fire. The surviving paintings ended up in the museum.

In 1829 a further fine collection of paintings came to the museum through the generosity of the Duc de Choiseul. These two collections form the nucleus of the paintings in the museum, though there have been numerous later donations, including the remarkable **Oulmont collection** of drawings (1917).

In 1951 the museum underwent radical transformation when the Musée International de l'Imagerie was created and housed in the same building, an undistinguished early 19thC structure at the tip of the island formed by the Moselle and a canal.

There is no comprehensive catalogue of the exhibits, but a small brochure, issued free of charge at the door, is quite adequate. The ground floor contains a collection of local Roman and Gallo-Roman works, including a substantial mosaic, a room with medieval, 16thC and 17thC sculpture, and a room dedicated to life in the Vosges. The latter is fully equipped with period furniture, marriage coffers, clothes, pottery and household objects of various kinds.

At the top of the stairs a narrow gallery on the left (containing 16thC stained glass from the abbey at Autrey) leads to a room with 17thC and 19thC paintings by Sebastiano Ricci, Nicholas Bellot (a view of Épinal as it was in 1626), Odilon Redon and others. From the middle of this room a staircase goes up to the building's attic, where you can see the museum's famous paintings, mainly from the collections of the Princes of Salm and the Duc de Choiseul.

Of these, the most outstanding works are Rembrandt's ***Virgin Mary***, painted in 1661 towards the end of his career, and ***Job Visited by his Wife*** by Georges de La Tour, a native of Lorraine. There are also two characteristically **fine paintings** by Claude Lorrain, as well as works by Sebastiano Ricci, Largillière, Primaticcio, van Goyen, Jan "Velvet" Brueghel, Annibale Carracci, Palma Vecchio, and many others.

Returning to the first floor, and

passing through galleries displaying 19thC and early 20thC paintings, faïence and porcelain from the Vosges, a collection of glasswork, and an entertaining display of decorated pipes, the visitor finally reaches the small but crowded room where you can see the excellent Oulmont collection. This consists of many **drawings** from such masters as Hubert Robert, Boucher, several Tiepolos and Guardis, Fragonard, Watteau and Bonington. Beyond this is a gallery entirely dedicated to **modern painting**, including a Léger and a Picasso.

The International Museum of Imagery occupies the final section of the building, taking up one large room, long and windowless, with a gallery going all the way round it. The prints on show are frequently changed, with new ones put on display, but the layout and organization of the exhibits remains substantially the same.

This begins with some medieval woodcuts, showing how the industry got under way, followed by exhibits organized by theme and period. There are also playing cards and other exhibits. The ground floor is primarily devoted to products from Épinal itself, the upper gallery to prints from other areas in France and from other European countries.

LA FÈRE
Aisne, Picardie Map C3

La Fère lies on the river Oise between Laon and St-Quentin, in territory that has seen much military activity. For this reason, perhaps, it contains a large army barracks, and this feature strongly influences the appearance and daily life of the town.

Musée Jeanne d'Aboville
Place de l'Esplanade
Open 1.45–5.45pm
Closed June–Sept Tues; Oct–May Wed, Sun

Housed in a rather musty building opposite the barracks, this museum consists almost exclusively of the collection of paintings donated in 1860 by the Comtesse d'Héricourt de Valincourt, born d'Aboville. The works, drawn from the French, Italian, German and Flemish schools, are numerous but generally dull and, despite the guide's claims for their importance, of dubious quality beneath the discoloured varnish. Nevertheless, as you might expect in a collection of this size, there are a few pictures that are well worth looking at, and perhaps the most interesting of these are the early German works: an anonymous 15thC ***Flagellation*** and a ***Calvary*** questionably attributed to Martin Schongauer. Among the French pictures a ***Basket of Plums*** by Pierre Dupuis (1610–82) is one of the finest works in the gallery, and a few 18thC paintings also make an impression, such as Elizabeth Vigée-Lebrun's portrait of Louis XV's daughter, ***Mademoiselle Adelaide***, and Hubert Robert's ***Caves of Posilippo at Naples***.

HAZEBROUCK
Pas-de-Calais, Nord Map B2

Hazebrouck is a small commercial town which has been largely rebuilt since World War II. It has two old buildings of note – the austere, Neoclassical **town hall** in the main square, and the former **convent of the Augustinians** in the attractive Place Georges Degrotte.

Musée Municipal
Place Georges Degrotte
Tel. (28) 416782
Open 8am–noon, 2–5pm
Closed Tues, Fri

The old Augustinian convent, dating from the 17thC, houses the tiny municipal museum of Hazebrouck. It is a dusty, unkempt place, strong in atmosphere if rather weak in its collections and the way in which its paintings are displayed. All its objects are jumbled together in a sometimes surprising fashion. Thus a small collection of charred 17thC paintings of religious subjects is placed next to a group of tailors' dummies wearing motheaten military costumes from World War II.

The two most interesting paintings in the museum both come from the French Government collections once housed in the Palais du Luxembourg in Paris. They are to be found in a gallery dominated at the far end by three gigantic puppets used in local festivities. One of these paintings is a full-length portrait (dated 1885) by the little known late 19thC painter Paul Mathey. The subject is ***Georges Clairin***, who is shown at work at an enormous allegorical composition. The other is a dark portrait of ***Monsieur Simon Hayem*** by Jules Bastien-Lepage. It is an early work by this artist, painted in 1875, three years before he became established as one of the most renowned painters of peasant life in the 19thC. Of purely historical interest is a mid-19thC portrait of ***Rose Doise*** by De Coninck, a painting which rejoices in the subtitle ***Victim of a Legal Error***. Attached to the picture is a story which tells how this woman was accused of stabbing her father to death and was subsequently acquitted. The museum's 20thC holdings consist exclusively of an unlabelled and unframed abstract canvas hung at an angle against a sack-cloth backing.

LAON
Aisne, Picardie Map C3

Laon is unusual among towns in northern France by virtue of its impressive position at the top of a rocky outcrop, and its winding streets are still enclosed by **medieval ramparts**. Surmounting this acropolis are the seven towers of the 13thC **cathedral of Notre-Dame**, a building that is not only striking in its appearance, but also of seminal importance as one of the earliest and most unified Gothic buildings in France. The façade contains some good sculpture, especially the bulls high up on the front towers, and there are original stained glass windows, but it is the unity of the building as a whole that is really striking, together with the interaction of the architectural forms. Laon was the birthplace in the 17thC of the famous genre painters, the Le Nain brothers, Antoine, Louis and Mathieu, who were all active in Paris by 1630.

Musée Archéologique Municipal
32 Rue Georges Ermant
Tel. (23) 232205
Open April–Sept 2–6pm, Oct–Mar 2–5pm
Closed Tues

Before going into the museum at Laon it is worth spending some time in the garden, where there is a small **Romanesque chapel** founded by the Knights Templars in the 12thC. Laon was one of the last outposts of the order before it was suppressed in 1407. Inside the chapel and scattered around the garden are numerous pieces of sculpture, some very fine, from the cathedral and other buildings in the area. Most impressive is the *transi* or **tomb effigy** depicting the decomposing body of Charles VI's doctor, Guillaume d'Harcigny (d. 1393).

The ground floor of the museum is largely devoted to a collection of Classical and Egyptian items gathered by P. M. de la Charlonie and bequeathed to the town on his death in 1937. Numbering in all over 17,000 items, the collection covers a wide range of interests in the ancient world. The Roman marble sculptures and the Greek painted pottery, particularly the red- and black-figure vases, are perhaps the most interesting items in this large collection.

Unfortunately the paintings on the first floor have much less to recommend them. Most of the exhibits are weak copies after well-known masters such as Jordaens and the Le Nain brothers, and even those paintings ostensibly by artists like Corot seem very unlikely attributions.

LILLE
Pas-de-Calais, Nord Map B2

At the heart of a vast urban and industrial area numbering nearly 1,250,000 people, Lille is a lively if not especially attractive place. The town grew up in the 11thC around an island formed by the river Deuse (hence its name of The Isle, Lille) and became in the 15thC one of the residences of the Burgundian court. It was here that the great Flemish painter Jan van Eyck served as *valet de chambre* to the Duke of Burgundy, Philip the Good.

The city has been much devastated by wars in the course of its history, being besieged no fewer than 11 times, including a famous episode in 1792 when the Austrians unsuccessfully attacked the city with an army of 35,000. Much of the city's unharmed older areas succumbed to bombing and shelling during World Wars I and II, but to this day Lille still retains in the vicinity of the cathedral a pleasant **old quarter** with numerous 17thC buildings in the Flemish style, and the occasional medieval monument such as the **Hospice Comtesse**. The former **Stock Exchange** stands at the edge of this, in a square named after one of Lille's most famous sons, General Charles de Gaulle. Although surrounded by especially hideous 19thC and early 20thC civic buildings, this is a masterpiece of Flemish Baroque architecture. It has a beautiful courtyard that is delightful to visit after undergoing the ordeal of the city's noise and traffic.

Musée des Beaux-Arts de Lille
Place de la République
Tel. (20) 570184
Open 9.30am–12.30pm, 2–6pm
Closed Tues

The main tourist attraction in Lille is its art gallery. This dominates one end of the enormous Place de la République, in the middle of which is the main station of the most modern underground system in Europe. The idea of a town museum dates back to 1792, when the painter Louis Watteau, nephew of Antoine, suggested to the town council that they should make publicly accessible the works seized from local religious institutions in the wake of the Revolution. In the course of the 19thC the museum was augmented by several important donations, the most important being that of the Chevalier Wicar (1834), which included one of the major **collections of drawings** in Europe. In 1881 the city authorities decided to build the Palais des Arts to rehouse the museum; this was inaugurated in 1892.

This massive and highly pretentious building lays claim to having one of the finest provincial art collections in France. It is certainly true that a number of outstanding works of art are to be found here; yet the atmosphere of the place is dark and musty, the display of the works poor and old-fashioned, and the condition of the paintings generally lamentable. The ground floor is taken up by collections of local and other porcelain, and sculpture. Among the latter are a famous marble relief by Donatello of the ***Feast of Herod*** ★ and a wax ***Head of a Woman*** which was for a long while the star piece in the museum, attributed variously to Raphael and Leonardo da Vinci. Today it is thought to be a 17thC work by the Flemish sculptor François Duquesnoy. Both pieces are from Chevalier Wicar's collection, which also consists of an enormous quantity of drawings, including one of the largest collections anywhere of drawings by Raphael. You can sometimes see part of this magnificent collection in the exhibition hall on the ground floor.

The paintings are all kept on the first floor, and, as you might expect, many of the rooms display Netherlandish paintings from the 15thC to the 17thC. Particularly striking among the earlier works are two panels by Dieric Bouts, representing ***Hell*** ★ and ***Paradise*** ★. Bouts was born in the Dutch town of Haarlem, but spent most of his working life in a Flemish town, Louvain, and came under the influence of the Flemish artist van der Weyden. The ***Hell*** panel in the Lille museum is one of the most celebrated, as well as one of the most gruesome, depictions to have come down from the 15thC. In his rendering of fantastical demons, Bouts shows, in this work, that he is almost the equal of Hieronymus Bosch. Also of interest in this section of early Netherlandish paintings are ***Bullfighting in Ancient Times*** by Maerten van Heemskerck (1498–1574) and ***The Resurrection of Lazarus*** by Wtewael (1566–1638).

Next comes a series of rooms filled with enormous altarpieces by Rubens – ***The Descent from the Cross*** from the Capuchin convent in Lille, and ***Martyrdom of St Catherine*** – and also Jordaens' early ***Temptation of the Magdalene*** and van Dyck's ***Christ on the Cross***. These rooms are peculiarly depressing, despite the celebrity of the painters on show.

The Lille gallery has a worthy collection of Dutch 17thC works, including a fine ***Entombment*** by Rembrandt's teacher Pieter Lastman, and an impressive painting (***The Ecstasy of St Francis***) by Rembrandt's brilliant companion from his early Leyden days, Jan Lievens. Rembrandt himself could have been represented by the famous ***Man with the Golden Helmet*** (now in the Glasgow Art Gallery) but in 1894 the Lille authorities failed to purchase it. There is also a good Ruisdael (***Wheat Field***), and an attractive Emanuel de Witte (***Interior of the New Church at Haarlem***), as well as two charming little monochromatic genre scenes by Pieter Codde, ***The First Pipe*** and ***Contentment with Little***.

Of the Italian pictures, special mention must be made of Veronese's ***Martyrdom of St George***, and ***Moses Saved from the Waters*** by Johann Liss (c.1597–1631), a remarkable German painter who lived most of his life in Venice, and was strongly influenced by Rubens and the Venetian 16thC masters.

Among the 18thC paintings there are two interesting British works – ***The Count of Kelly*** by David Wilkie, and an oil sketch by Thomas Lawrence of ***Sir John Cuypage***. But the most famous and impressive of the 18thC foreign schools of painting are two magnificent works by Goya. One of these, ***Time, or the Elderly Woman*** ★★ shows a grotesque old woman (considered by some to be a portrait of the Spanish queen Maria Luisa) covered in make-up and staring at herself in a mirror which has the inscription *Que Tal?* (How are you?); behind her is the winged figure of Time. The other, ***The Letter, or The Young Woman*** ★★, is a full-length genre scene of a woman in a landscape.

The museum has a very extensive collection of 18thC and 19thC French works. Among the former is a good pastel portrait of ***Madame Pelerin*** by Quentin de La Tour, and two amusing panels entitled ***Modern Virgins*** and ***Ancient Virgins*** by Jean Raoux, an artist whom Voltaire claimed was on occasion the equal of Rembrandt. There are also a number of paintings by Louis-Léopold Boilly (1761–1845). Boilly, who belongs in spirit to the 18thC, perpetuated into the 19thC a fashion for intimate genre scenes of middle-class life. He came under suspicion during the Revolution, and was only vindicated by the Revolutionary Tribunal after painting ***The Triumph of Marat***, which is the largest of his works in the Lille museum. Of greater popular appeal today is a *trompe-l'oeil* still-life which he painted on top of a real desk. Boilly's more politically-minded contemporary, Jacques-Louis David, is represented by what today seems one of his silliest works, a preciously erotic scene of ***Apelles Painting Campaspe in the Presence of Alexander***. To compensate for this disappointment there is an excellent oil sketch by Géricault, ***Horse Race in Rome***, and a large and famous painting by Delacroix, ***Medea***, now in a rather depressing condition.

Among the several works in the museum by Courbet, the best-known is ***Afternoon at Ornans***. This enormous canvas features life-sized figures seated around a table in a dark interior, and has something of the character of an overblown Dutch genre scene. It was the first and most conventional of a group of canvases, executed by Courbet in the late 1840s and early 1850s, that were intended by the artist to shock the public with their realism. The canvas at Lille was painted with a great deal of bitumen, and has now deteriorated to such an extent that it is really best seen in reproduction. Among the more attractive 19thC landscapes in the museum are Harpignies' ***Landscape near Moncel-sur-Seille*** and Théodore Rousseau's ***Seine at Villeneuve-St-Georges***. Millet is represented by a fairly typical ***Woman Teaching Village Children***, but Millet's great successor as a painter of peasant life, Jules Bastien-Lepage, has a very uncharacteristic work on display, painted while he was still an art student: ***Priam Imploring Achilles***, his only known classical subject.

A number of good full-length portraits include ***Lady with a Dog*** (1870) by Émile Carolus-Duran, and Amary Duval's nude, ***Birth of Venus*** (1862), a work often illustrated in art books to show the type of nude painting considered acceptable when Manet caused such a scandal with his ***Olympia*** (Jeu de Paume, *PARIS*).

Next there is a room of unremarkable paintings by the Impressionists and their French followers. The best of these works are probably Monet's ***Thames Scene*** and Suzanne Valladon's **half-nude of a woman**. The contemporary French works are also unimpressive, apart from Sonia Delaunay's ***Abstraction***, but few paintings would shine out in the grimy, bleak 19thC setting of this museum.

The Lille Museum of Fine Arts possesses many excellent works of art, among which the following are particularly impressive:

1 ***The Feast of Herod,*** Donatello
2 ***Hell,*** Dieric Bouts
3 ***Paradise,*** Dieric Bouts
4 ***Descent from the Cross,*** Peter Paul Rubens
5 ***The First Pipe,*** Pieter Codde
6 ***Contentment with Little,*** Pieter Codde
7 ***Medea,*** Eugène Delacroix
8 ***Afternoon at Ornans,*** Gustave Courbet
9 ***Martyrdom of St George,*** Paulo Veronese
10 ***Time, or The Elderly Woman,*** Francisco de Goya y Lucientes
11 ***The Letter, or The Young Woman,*** Francisco de Goya y Lucientes
12 ***Abstraction,*** Sonia Delaunay

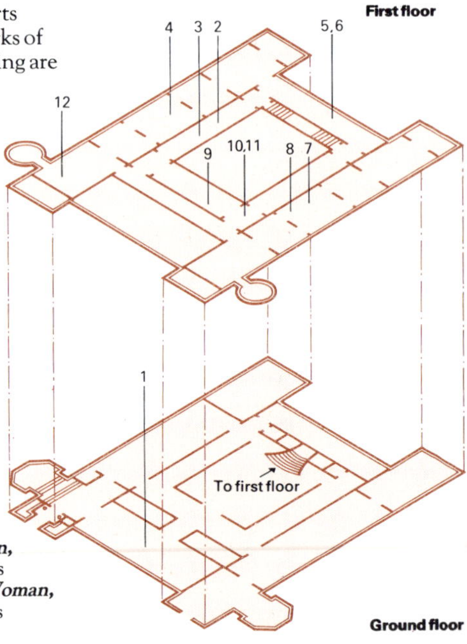

METZ
Moselle, Lorraine Map E4

Metz is in the industrialized northern part of Lorraine but unlike many of the towns in this area, which are rather grim and have been hard hit by the economic recession, Metz itself is a lively town with a distinctive character. It has always been an important place, from Roman times onwards, as is apparent from the **Roman baths** under the City Museum and from the **church of St-Pierre-aux-Nonnains**, which is believed to be the earliest Christian church in France. There is also a magnificent cathedral, a large number of turreted medieval houses, and a fascinating arcaded square, the **Place St-Louis**. Another sign of Metz's former importance is the sheer number of churches of all periods scattered through the city and the size of its **medieval quarter**, built during its heyday as a rich merchant city state.

The exterior of the **Cathedral of St-Etienne** is a fine example of Gothic architecture, more impressive in its total effect than in any particular detail. One of the two towers, dated to the 15thC, contains the famous bell called Dame Mutte that traditionally sounds on all great occasions. The interior of the cathedral is brilliantly lit by stained-glass windows of many styles and periods, from the 13thC to the 20thC. Particularly fine is Herman de Munster's 14thC **rose window** in the W end, but Marc Chagall's glass in the choir ambulatory, and Jacques Villon's work in a side chapel (both of 1960) provide interesting contrasts to the predominantly medieval effect.

There is also a Treasury attached to the Cathedral which, though much depleted as a result of the Revolution, still contains such interesting items as the so-called **Cope of Charlemagne**, a textile of 11thC Byzantine origin made of purple and gold thread. There is also a model of the famous "Graoully" dragon of Metz, mentioned by Rabelais (who lived in the city).

Metz Museums
Ancien Couvent des Petits Carmes, Rue Chèvremont
Tel. (8) 77510/8
Open Apr–Sept 10am–noon, 2–6pm; Oct–Mar 10am–noon, 2–5pm
Closed Tues
(Wed only)

Metz has a number of museums, all located in the same complex of buildings close to the cathedral, and with a common entrance. A museum has existed on this site since 1839 in the former convent of the Petits-Carmes, and during the expansion of this museum between 1935 and 1937, the remains of a **Gallo-Roman baths complex** were discovered under the building and became an integral part of the new museum. Today, a Gallo-Roman museum, a museum of Architecture, and a museum of Fine Arts are all combined on the same tour, merging into one another.

It was in 1980 that the existing museum was again extended to include a museum of Architecture, located partly in the **Grenier** (granary) **de Chèvremont**, a magnificent medieval building dating from 1457 and situated just behind the Couvent des Petits-Carmes. A number of architectural exhibits have been brought from other parts of Metz and reconstructed around the courtyard next to the Granary.

The interesting buildings, and the extensive and varied collections, make the Metz museums a pleasure to visit, and the layout is extremely modern. The rooms unfold in more or less chronological sequence and are dedicated to specific periods or themes until a certain point where the modernized part of the museum ends. Beyond this the rooms are more jumbled, but there are plans to continue the chronological layout at a later date. A complete tour takes a long time with plenty of stairs to go up and down and, since many of the rooms are windowless, it is hard to keep a sense of direction. The visit begins with the Archaeological Museum, arranged around the ruins of the **Roman baths** down in the basement. Here there are some very fine sculptures and, in particular, a cylindrical room containing the remains of the impressive **Merten Column**. In addition to Gallo-Roman remains there are also some fine Merovingian exhibits.

Going up and down some more stairs, you next come to the Architectural Museum. Here is a magnificent room containing the intricately sculptured remains of the **chancel of St-Pierre-des-Nonnains** from the early Middle Ages. The sound of Gregorian chanting in the background provided by a concealed sound system, emphasizes the archaic atmosphere of the place.

In the next few rooms, sculptures, windows, doors and other bits of the architectural legacy of medieval Metz are laid out, and you can also go into the courtyard where various buildings have been reconstructed. From here you enter the ground floor of the Grenier de Chevremont. Perhaps the most interesting rooms in the whole museum are the ones you enter when returning to the main building, and which contain **13thC pointed wooden roofs**. These are among the best preserved of their type in Europe, and besides being very rare are also extremely beautiful. Dating from 1225, they formerly were part of a mansion elsewhere in Metz, and were discovered by accident in 1896. More rooms follow with 14thC and 15thC furniture and decoration. The Fine Arts Museum comes next, and although this has some attractive paintings, it is nevertheless the least original part of the whole museum complex. There are, however, a number of agreeable **17thC paintings** of the Dutch, Flemish and French schools, and the 18thC and 19thC are also quite well represented. In the last rooms of all are exhibits related to the research work currently being carried out in French museums, with regard to such aspects as the restoration of paintings, or ways of detecting fakes. The aim here, as elsewhere, seems to be to instruct. But the layout is so good, and the exhibits so interesting, that this approach does not become tediously didactic.

MULHOUSE
Haut-Rhin, Alsace Map F6

Mulhouse, the third major town in Alsace along with **STRASBOURG** and **COLMAR**, became a place of importance long after the others, developing rapidly only in the 19thC and 20thC with the growth of its textile and then its potash industries. It is now an extensive industrial city and lacks the attractive urban landscapes of Strasbourg and Colmar. Nevertheless it is far from unpleasant and possesses a remarkable number of specialist museums, including a railway museum with steam trains made as long ago as 1844; a fire engine museum on the same site; a superb automobile museum with over 500 cars, mainly from 1920–40 and including some very rare Bugattis (whose plant was and is in Molsheim in Alsace); and the museum of printed fabrics which is described below. Three other museums to be seen in Mulhouse are of less originality but deserve to be included in any art guide of the region, namely, the Musée Historique, the Musée des Beaux-Arts and the small museum contained in the Chapelle St-Jean.

Musée de l'Impression sur Étoffes
Rue des Bonnes-Gens
Open Jan–Mar 10am–noon, 2–5pm; Apr–Dec 10am–noon, 2–6pm
Closed Tues
(mornings)

The printed fabrics and textiles industry of Mulhouse dates from the mid 18thC and was largely responsible for the rapid development of the town. As long ago as the 1830s there was a move to establish a collection of some of the finer productions from the different enterprises active in the town, and this developed into the present full-scale museum, which has now become one of the richest of its kind anywhere. In addition to the displays there is a massive reference library, and further information is available in the very detailed guidebook sold at the entrance. All in all, the museum has considerable historical as well as artistic interest, despite its specialized subject matter.

The ground floor contains machinery and equipment used in the industry, as well as large collections of textiles. Above this is a gallery with fabrics from all over the world: painted *toiles* from Persia and India, batiks from Indonesia, *tapas* from Polynesia, works using the *Ikat* technique from Cambodia, and many others, some dating back to the 18thC. Production from all over France is well represented, and in addition to work from Mulhouse itself there is a fine collection of material from the factory at Jouy, featuring many 18thC genre scenes. These include historical themes such as the American Declaration of Independence (from the Agnes Holding collection), and others depict political campaigns, jubilees, the 1848 revolution, and so on.

Musée Historique
Place de la Réunion
Open mid-June to Sept 10am–noon, 2–6pm; Oct to mid-June 10am–noon, 2–5pm
Closed Tues
(first Sun of month)

This museum is located in the restored **16thC town hall**, a very fine building situated in the most attractive square in Mulhouse. The historical museum was installed in this building in 1969.

The ground floor contains, in addition to a small collection of prehistoric and Gallo-Roman items, some fine 15thC and 16thC sculptures and the splendid 15thC **retable of Rheinfelden**. Some of the exhibits come from the original church of St-Etienne, just opposite, which was demolished and rebuilt in the 19thC.

The 16thC Hall where the Grand Council of Mulhouse used to meet is on the first floor, and is still used for sessions of the Town Council. This is a magnificent room with a beautiful ceiling and fine period stained-glass windows.

A series of rooms on the next floor offers a miscellaneous but interesting collection of items: old furniture (including a superb 18thC folding bed), costumes, documents, porcelain and glass, paintings and sculptures. Numerous portraits and miniatures of Mulhouse personalities, and a series of caricatures by Henri Zislin, a satirical Mulhouse journalist, help to flesh out the history of the town. A good collection of old toys and games includes some packs of playing cards from the French Revolution. These have "equalities" and "liberties" instead of kings and queens.

Musée des Beaux-Arts

4 Place Guillaume Tell
Closed for restoration
🏛

This museum, located in an 18thC building close to the middle of the town, is currently closed for restoration, and at the time of writing it is uncertain when it will reopen. Its collection includes a variety of 17thC and 18thC works by artists such as Teniers and Ruisdael, as well as paintings by local artists – the portraitist Henner (1829–1905) and Lehmann are represented.

Musée de la Chapelle St-Jean

Open May–Sept 10am–noon, 2–5pm
Closed Oct–Apr, Tues

This chapel of the Knights of Malta, built in 1268, stands on the site of an even older building, of which some remains have been found. Restored on several occasions, it has had a varied history including a period as a brewery. Between 1515 and 1521 it was embellished by a lively series of **wall paintings**, probably the work of Mulhouse artists under the direction of painters from the Basel school of Hans Herbster, where Holbein had worked in his youth. Today the chapel provides an attractive setting for a collection of **religious sculpture** and funeral statues. It is a pity that the museum is only open in summer.

NANCY

Meurthe-et-Moselle, Lorraine Map E5

Nancy, one of the two major cities of Lorraine, has a very different atmosphere from its great rival METZ, being both more elegant and less lively. Its elegance stems from the period of Stanislas Leczynski, the dethroned king of Poland, who was put in charge of Lorraine in the mid 18thC by his son-in-law Louis XV, on condition that Lorraine would become an integral part of France on Stanislas's death. The town had previously been the capital of the dukes of Lorraine, and the **medieval ducal palace**, reconstructed and heavily restored on several occasions, now houses the Lorraine Historical Museum. This building is surrounded by the nucleus of the old town, bounded on the north by an impressive gate (the **Porte de la Craffe**) and numerous old mansions, which give a general impression of disrepair and neglect.

Stanislas, whose fat pudgy face stares cheerfully out at the visitor from numerous portraits in the Lorraine Historical Museum, became extremely popular in the region, being responsible for the magnificent architecture of its three main squares: **Place Stanislas, Place de la Carrière** and **Place d'Alliance**. The first of these, which is embellished with superb ironwork by Jean Lamour, is one of the most elegant 18thC squares in France.

Nancy grew very rapidly in the late 19thC, mainly as a result of an influx of refugees from Alsace and the occupied part of Lorraine after the conclusion of the Franco–Prussian war in 1871. During this period the city became one of the major European centers of "Art Nouveau" in the form of the so-called École de Nancy, which played an important part in the decorative arts of the time. The legacy of this movement is preserved in a special museum, and also in some very fine houses scattered around the city (although a number have been destroyed or disfigured), particularly to the W of the station.

Musée Historique Lorrain

Palais Ducal Grande Rue
Tel. (8) 3321874
Open 10am–noon, 2–5pm; mid-June–Sep 10am–noon, 2–6pm; Oct–mid-June 10am–noon, 2–5pm
Closed Nov, Tues
🏛

This rambling museum spreads throughout the former ducal palace and its annexes, and even extends to the church and convent of the Cordeliers across the road. It is concerned with all aspects of Lorraine's past, and the collections include archaeology, ethnography, medieval sculptures, ceramics, religious items (including a Jewish room), tapestries, furniture, and countless portraits and miniatures of the dukes of Lorraine and other Lorraine notables.

There are no guidebooks or catalogues on sale within the museum to help the visitor around the many rooms, though a fair amount of information can be gleaned from a booklet on the history of the museum, dated 1976, which is on sale at the entrance. A 1948 guide can be tracked down in Nancy bookshops by persevering visitors, and much of the information is still valid, although the museum's layout has greatly changed. All in all, the museum is not suited for a quick visit. The atmosphere is musty, and a tour of all the rooms is hard work.

The pavilion across the courtyard from the entrance is devoted to archaeology, and the ground floor mainly to medieval art, particularly sculpture. Climbing a fine staircase you reach the rebuilt Galerie des Cerfs, where there are many portraits and mementoes of the dukes of Lorraine. Also on this floor are two small rooms that contain the most famous works of art in the museum. The first is dedicated mainly to the **engravings** and **etchings** of Jacques Callot (1592–1635), a native of Lorraine. The series entitled ***Miseries of War*** is particularly striking, recording as it does incidents from the Thirty Years War that decimated Lorraine. The other room contains paintings by Georges de La Tour, another artist from Lorraine, of which the ***Woman with the Flea*** ★ is particularly fine.

An adjacent and larger room contains several paintings by two other well-known painters of Lorraine origin, Jacques Bellange (active 1600–17) and Claude Deruet (1588–1660). But Claude Lorrain himself is hardly represented.

Few of the other paintings in the museum are worth singling out. The arrangement is mainly historical, with rooms devoted to particular periods and themes, and with paintings jumbled in with all the other exhibits. The visitor who is still full of energy at this stage would do best to wander at random.

It is worth keeping something in reserve, however, for a guided tour of the church of the Cordeliers across the road (it cannot be visited without a guide), for this contains a series of impressive **tombs of the dukes of Lorraine**, as well as the curious ducal chapel where the heir to the Hapsburg throne, Otto of Hapsburg, was married in 1951.

Musée des Beaux-Arts

Place Stanislas
Tel. (8) 3376501
Open 10am–noon, 2–6pm
Closed Mon (morning), Tues

The museum, located in a fine 18thC building on the W side of Place Stanislas, retains its façade but has been modernized internally and considerably extended to the rear.

The museum's layout is clear and the collection is extensive, but no catalogues or guidebooks are available, nor is there any literature on any of the painters or paintings represented in the museum, although there are a few catalogues on sale from long-forgotten exhibitions in the past. The connection with Lorraine is not stressed – well-known Lorraine artists such as Claude Lorrain, Georges de La Tour and Callot are not represented – and few of the paintings have Lorraine as their subject.

Most of the 19thC and 20thC paintings occupy one long room on the ground floor of the museum. Two highly characteristic heads by Modigliani, a number of Dufys, including a **self-portrait**, and **paintings** by Utrillo, Vlaminck, Vuillard, Manet, Signac, Bonnard and Matisse make up the best of the modern works. The upper level of this main gallery has several Lorraine scenes and some works by Lorraine painters such as Auguste Desch, Guillaume and Ventrillon. A little side room to the left has some earlier 19thC paintings, including ***The Death of Charles the Bold at the Battle of Nancy***, a large battle scene by Eugène Delacroix.

Before going up the main stairs, look for a little room on the right which has some magnificent pieces of glass and crystal from the École de Nancy and Art Deco periods. Nancy's **'cristalleries de Daum'** are famous, and it was the glass-maker Gallé (1846–1904) who founded the École de Nancy.

At the top of the stairs there is a handsome ***Transfiguration*** by Rubens, and the two rooms on the same floor displaying Flemish and Dutch paintings also include his work, in addition to landscapes by Ruisdael and paintings by Maes, van Goyen, van der Velde and David Teniers. The same floor has Italian and French paintings, with an ***Entombment*** by Tintoretto and paintings by Bassano and Vasari. Beyond this is a second room that is also devoted to Italian paintings, with works by Pietro da Cortona and Pesarese, as well as Caravaggio's superb painting of ***The Annunciation***.

Further on there are a few rooms overlooking the Place Stanislas in the 18thC part of the building. The views over the square are very fine, but the paintings are less exciting, consisting mainly of 18thC French contemporaries of Boucher, who is also represented. There are also two interesting works by Magnasco, and paintings by Stanislas Leczynski's court painter, Girardet. From these rooms an elegant 18thC staircase leads down to the exit.

Musée de l'École de Nancy ☆
38 Rue Sergent-Blandan
Tel. (8) 3401486
Open 10am–noon, 2–6pm (2–5pm Oct–Apr)
Closed Tues

This very enjoyable museum, first opened in 1964, is devoted to the work of the so-called **École de Nancy**, a group of decorative artists who worked in the Art Nouveau style in Nancy during its period of rapid growth at the turn of the century. It is a little hard to find, but lies in the 19thC part of Nancy to the W of the station near the Parc Ste-Marie. The movement was formally founded in 1901 as the "École de Nancy, Alliance Provinciale des Industries d'Art" by Émile Gallé, the glass-maker. It consisted of architects, painters, glassworkers and painters on glass, ceramic workers, furniture makers, and various other designers, decorators and industrial patrons.

The achievement of the École de Nancy should not be seen in terms of individual performance, in spite of the talent of artists such as the Daum brothers, for the school represented a certain style, flowing and full of movement, which permeated these various disciplines and helped to form an interdependent whole in which structure and decoration merged into one another. Its chief claim to fame, however, tended to be in its furniture, ceramics and glasswork, with its painting proving the least successful and distinctive.

The museum has an evocative atmosphere that conveys a good feeling of the period. It is located in a house contemporary with its collections, though less impressive in its exterior architecture than many others of the same period in Nancy. A particularly good example can be seen further down the street, at Number 30.

Before entering the house it is worth taking a brief stroll around the garden, which contains two items of interest: a small period funerary monument and, in particular, a rather strange little building that used to be an aquarium.

Inside the house, collections of items brought from many places blend together well with each other, though few of the furnishings come from the original house. Unfortunately, there is not enough space to show the entire range of exhibits, but there are plans to build a new extension in the garden.

The way that the items are labelled often makes it hard to identify which artist is responsible for which work, even with the help of the small guidebook describing the museum and its contents (a separate guidebook deals with the glass collection, which is very impressive). But this is the kind of museum that invites the visitor to stroll at random rather than to examine each object systematically. In addition to the **outstanding stained-glass collection** there is a reconstructed dining room on the ground floor that is very striking, as well as **fine watercolours by** V. Prouvé and numerous works by Sellier.

After mounting the stairs, look for a **magnificent bed** by Gallé, dating from 1904 and entitled ***Dawn and Dusk***, and the impressive bath of the Marquise de Ganay. The top floor contains some more very fine furniture, with fireplaces, desks, beds, mirrors, crystalwork, tapestries, stained-glass windows, and much else besides.

PLOMBIÈRES-LES-BAINS
Vosges, Lorraine Map E6

Plombières, below the Vosges mountains, has been a spa town since Roman times, and the salt mineral waters have been the source of the town's prosperity for about 2,000 years. The period of its greatest popularity was in the 18thC when it was patronized by King Stanislas of Lorraine, who built the Maison des Arcades and after whom several streets are named. It was at Plombières that, in 1858, a meeting took place between Napoleon III and Cavour which decided the future of Italy and the union of Savoie with France.

Musée Louis Français
30 Avenue Louis Français
Tel. (29) 660024
Open May–Sept, 2–6pm
Closed Oct–Apr, Tues

The recently renovated museum in Plombières is named after the landscape painter Louis Français, who left his house and collection to the town of his birth in 1897. Français, who was one of the first clients at Père Ganne's famous inn at Barbizon (see p. 184), was described by Baudelaire as one of the greatest French landscapists of his day. In fact his work is a pale reflection of that of his Barbizon colleagues, who are also represented in this museum. You can see typically elegant works by Français' teacher Corot, and pleasant paintings by other 19thC landscapists such as Henri Harpignies and Constant Troyon. Courbet and Adolphe Monticelli, though not active members of the Barbizon group add further distinction to a rather pleasant setting.

REIMS
Marne, Champagne–Ardenne
Map C4

In 496 Clovis, the king of the Franks, was baptized at Reims by St Rémi, a momentous event in the Christianization of Europe and in the evolution of France, and one which brought great renown to the city during the Middle Ages. It certainly lent prestige to the bishopric of Reims, and this found physical expression in the magnificent 13thC **Gothic cathedral** where the kings of France were crowned. It was here for example that Joan of Arc insisted on the elevation of the Dauphin to the title of King Charles VII, took part in his coronation and confirmed her resolve to expel the English. The other principal religious building in the city is the 11thC **Basilica of St-Rémi** in a Benedictine abbey where most of the early kings and bishops were interred. Both of these buildings have suffered to some extent from war damage, as did most of the city in 1914, but they have been restored, along with the Neoclassical area round the Place Royal which was designed and laid out in the 18thC. The rebuilding of Reims after World War I introduced some new heavy industries, but the traditional ones continue and it is still one of the principal centers of the Champagne wine trade.

Musée St-Denis
8 Rue de Chanzy
Tel. (26) 472844
Open 10am–noon, 2–6pm
Closed Tues

For a town of the size and importance of Reims the Musée St-Denis, the principal museum, is slightly disappointing. The basis of the present collection came to the town as long ago as 1752 with the donation of Ferrand de Monthélon, the first director of the school of art, and other gifts and purchases have supplemented it ever since 1800, when it was opened to the public. Large as it is, the collection scarcely fills its premises in the 18thC abbey of St-Denis, a huge building where there is an impression of excessive space, as if the enormous galleries could never be adequately filled. The scale of some of the rooms is so vast that it has the unfortunate effect of diminishing the works.

Most of the ground floor concentrates on the history of the town, with portraits of local dignitaries. There is also a large collection of ceramics which include examples from all main French pottery areas as well as a number of less well-known manufacturers, and pieces from Italy, Germany and England. A series of small plaster caricatures from the 1840s looks interesting, but the significance of the individual items is not immediately apparent.

The fine art collection is on the first floor. Two important cycles of wall-hangings precede the painting displays, and these are of considerable interest. One, a tapestry from a 16thC Flemish workshop, illustrates ten scenes from the ***Life of St-Rémy***. The other wall-hanging, depicting ***Scenes from the Old and New Testaments***, uses a curious medium of painted and dyed material.

The first painting gallery contains mainly Flemish and German works from the 15thC and 16thC that are not particularly notable, but in a separate area to the side is a group of **portrait drawings** ★ by Cranach the Elder and his son (Cranach the Younger), which are probably the most remarkable works in the whole museum. Detailed studies, taken from life, for larger court portraits, these depict a variety of German princes, and are treated with a sensitivity of featural description, particularly those by the younger Cranach, that gives them a sharpness of characterization and a sense of intimacy rare in later works. This quality is strong enough to overcome the marks and damage to some of the sheets, for apparently Antoine Ferrand de Monthélou used the drawings for teaching purposes, and several have suffered at the hands of over-zealous students. But the quality of the original character still shines through.

Apart from this early group and a few isolated examples later on, such as Jordaens' ***Satyr***, the bulk of the collection consists of a rather impressive variety of French pictures from the 17thC to the early 20thC. From the 17thC there are two works by Poussin, ***Achilles at Scyros*** and a ***Landscape with a Woman Washing Her Feet***, a storm scene by Gaspard Dughet, two pictures by the Le Nain brothers and a very good portrait of ***The Children of Habert de Montmor*** by Philippe de Champaigne. In the latter, each of the subjects has obviously been studied separately, and in working it up the artist has not made a completely satisfactory ensemble, but the individuals are beautifully described. The 18thC section is a little thinner with only two outstanding works: an ***Odalisque*** by Boucher and a chalk drawing of a park by Fragonard, but with the 19thC the collection overall moves into its richest area. Géricault, Delacroix, Courbet and Puvis de Chavannes are all represented by good pictures, and this encouraging start prepares the way for a fine **group of landscapes** by artists associated with Barbizon in the middle years of the century. Works by Daubigny, Rousseau and Millet lead up to a room containing no fewer than 25 landscapes by Corot. Unfortunately Corot's art, like that of his contemporary Boudin, tends to be fairly narrow in its range, which makes a large display such as this slightly monotonous. A large number of works by one individual can nevertheless have its own attractions. Appropriately, there is a good group of Impressionist paintings to follow this, including two landscapes by Monet, ***Belle Île*** and ***Ravines of the Creuse***, and an excellent townscape by Pissarro of the ***Avenue de l'Opéra*** in Paris.

The last room, by contrast, illustrates the tendency away from naturalism towards the expressive qualities of the Fauves. An early **work** by Matisse is rewarding, but the most important pictures are undoubtedly two **still-lifes** by Gauguin and the Nabis paintings of Vuillard, Bonnard and Maillol. At this stage, the museum comes to an abrupt halt both physically and historically, because the modern works in the collection are awaiting suitable accommodation. This is being planned but there is no projected completion date, and until then the museum will be left with this unsatisfactory conclusion.

Musée du Vieux-Reims (Le Vergeur)

36 Place du Forum
Tel. (26) 402075
Open 2–6pm
Closed Mon

A museum of old Reims is a necessary institution since most of the town had been destroyed by 1918. It occupies the **Hôtel Le Vergeur**, an attractive bourgeois house bequeathed to the town by a M. Krafft in 1935, and dating from the 13thC with a Renaissance wing built in 1523. It is decorated throughout with a number of good pieces of furniture from the 17thC and 18thC, and the garden contains fragments of sculpture and decorative carving saved from the older buildings in the area. Most of the exhibits are chosen because they are illustrative of the old town, but there are some paintings and engravings of wider interest, including a large group of Dürer's prints given to the museum in 1963 and now displayed in a room on their own. The principal work is a complete set of the ***Apocalypse*** series, Dürer's early masterpiece in woodcut, and this is supplemented by the ***Passion*** and a few individual prints such as ***The Men's Bath*** and ***Adam and Eve***.

Palais du Tau

2 Place du Cardinal Luçon
Open 10am–noon, 2–6pm

The cathedral of Notre-Dame at Reims is without doubt one of the finest and most complete expressions of Gothic art in Europe. It was begun in 1211, after a fire had destroyed the earlier church, and virtually completed by the early 15thC. Conceived and built during the greatest phase of the Gothic style, this glorious building has remained free from the alterations and additions which mar so many churches of the same period. It is this unity which gives the building overall such a majestic appearance, but you soon notice the ravages of time. Apart from the war damage the stone has weathered badly, and while this has not interfered with the clear lines of the interior or the forms of the façade and structure, many of the sculptures are so worn that their features have been obliterated. It was for this reason that the authorities in 1927 began to replace as much of the sculpture on the building as possible with casts or copies, so that the originals could be protected in the controlled environment of a museum. These pieces are now displayed in the newly renovated Bishop's Palace or Palais du Tau (so named because of its T Shape).

Something will always be lost in an exercise like this. The figures from the Kings' Gallery, for instance, were designed to be seen from a distance as part of a larger scheme. This is no longer possible but, viewed at close quarters, they have an admirable authority and monumentality that might otherwise have escaped notice. This effect is what marks out the Reims figures from other Gothic sculpture; the confident, flowing poses at Reims are more reminiscent of classical then Gothic art. The drapery on the figures, as in ***The Visitation*** ★ is treated in a rippling diaphanous manner that may very probably derive from an antique source. Of them all, the figure of ***The Synagogue*** ★ from the S transept is perhaps the most striking. An elegant balanced pose enhanced by the naturalistic drapery turns into something quite dramatic through the fact that the face is blindfolded, suggesting the stubbornness and failure of the old order.

Beyond these sculptures the museum also has a collection of tapestries and goldsmiths' work from the cathedral treasury. Curiously enough most of the reliquaries and such like are from the 19thC, as are the costumes and decoration in the throne room, but that was probably the period when the trappings of royalty were most in evidence.

ST-OMER

Pas-de-Calais, Nord Map B2

St-Omer, with its well preserved old quarter built up around a slight hill is one of the most attractive towns in northeastern France. Although it has a major **medieval cathedral** (begun around 1200 and completed by the end of the 15thC) the character of the town has been influenced essentially by its 17thC and 18thC buildings. Prominent among these is the former **Jesuit chapel** (now turned into a school) in the Rue du Lycée, which has an enormous tiered Flemish-style façade (c.1639) covered in sculptures.

Musée De l'Hôtel Sandelin

14 Rue Carnot
Tel. (21) 380094
Open 10am–noon, 2–6pm (Thurs, Fri 2–5pm)
Closed Mon, Tues

One of the town's most elegant 18thC buildings is the **Hôtel Sandelin** on the Rue Carnot. This houses the town's art gallery, which is an example of the perfect small provincial museum. Not only is its setting so beautiful but also the objects are wonderfully displayed, and it has one major work of art.

The art collections are principally on the ground floor, where a section is devoted to medieval sculpture and applied art. Then, on its own in a darkened room, you see the museum's greatest treasure, the 12thC ***Foot of the Cross of Saint-Bertin*** ★, attributed to the Meuse Valley craftsman Godenfroid de Huy, and perhaps commissioned from him by the Abbé Simon II of Saint-Denis. It is gloriously executed in a combination of gold and enamel work, with golden figurines of the Evangelists and of the four elements (water with a fish, air with a lifted hand, fire with a salamander, and earth with a spade), and enameled scenes from the Old Testament prefiguring the Crucifixion.

The paintings on the ground floor include 15th–17thC Dutch and Flemish works, most notably a ***Portrait of a Woman*** by Thomas de Keyser, ***Portrait of a Man*** by Terborch, and a genre scene by Jan Steen. The 18thC rooms of the building provide an excellent setting for a small but choice collection of 18thC and early 19thC French paintings, shown alongside furniture of this period. These include a series of fascinatingly detailed scenes of middle-class life by Louis-Leopold Boilly, notably the ***Jealous Old Man***. There is also a portrait by Greuze thought to represent ***Saint-Just***, and a coyly erotic painting by Nicolas-Bernard Lépicié, ***Fanchon Rising*** (1773), which shows a pretty, half-naked young peasant girl getting up from a bed.

On the staircase of the museum is a large painting, ***The Sirens***, by a local 19thC artist, Louis Belly, who was best known as a painter of oriental scenes. This early work is in fact almost directly copied from one of Rubens' Marie de Medici cycle now in the ***LOUVRE*** in Paris. There are works by other local artists on the first floor, including ones by the 19thC specialist in military scenes, Alphonse Deneuville. The rest of the museum is taken up by over 700 pieces of porcelain, and a most intriguing collection of clay pipes: pipe-making was an important St-Omer industry from the 17th to the 19thC.

ST-QUENTIN

Aisne, Picardie Map C3

St-Quentin in Picardy has an attractive aspect in spite of being an industrial town of some size. It is situated on a gentle hill that has the Collegiate church on its summit. This large Gothic basilica, begun in the 12thC, was only completed in 1976 when the finishing touches were added to the steeple. It is visible from a considerable distance and dominates the skyline. The town is one of the key communication points on the river Somme, and as a result was the scene of intense military activity during World War I.

Musée Antoine Lécuyer

28 Rue Antoine Lécuyer
Tel. (23) 623971
Open 10am–noon, 2–5pm
Closed Tues, Sun 10am–noon

The Musée Lécuyer owes its origin to a bequest made in 1807 by the town's most famous son, the 18thC pastellist and portrait painter, Maurice-Quentin de La Tour. La Tour, who was born and died at St-Quentin, possessed a brilliant virtuosity of style that made him very popular at all levels of society in Paris, where he was a regular exhibitor at the Salon. His ability to catch the movement of life and spontaneity of his subjects has perhaps never been surpassed, and can be seen to its best effect here in a museum containing some 80 of his **portraits**.

La Tour was notoriously radical in his views, abrupt to the point of rudeness with his aristocratic clients and a champion of the artist's rights, so it was perhaps to be expected that the fruits of his successful career should be put to good and practical use. He initiated several prizes in Picardy and Paris and made a large bequest of paintings and money to set up a museum and school of art in St-Quentin, the funds for this to be supplemented by the proceeds from a sale of his pictures. Fortunately the derisory results from the first sale persuaded the executors to hold on to the remaining works and to place them on display in the Abbaye de Fervacques. In 1877 a more suitable venue became available when the Hôtel Lécuyer was donated to the town and the pictures were transferred there, but this building was destroyed during the bombardment of 1917. A new gallery with an appropriate interior in 18thC style was opened in 1932, only to be closed in 1939. But it was eventually reopened in 1947, and has stayed so ever since.

The museum possesses a few medieval ivories, some tapestries and a number of French paintings between the 17th and 20thC, but there can be no doubt that the **collection of pastel portraits** by La Tour is the principal feature and attraction of the Musée Lécuyer. In the words of the Goncourts, who saw the collection in the mid 19thC, it is "an entire gallery hung from top to bottom, populated, encumbered even on the return walls, with the master's works, a collection of more than 80 portraits completed or merely begun, highly finished or simply sketched, a collection that composes a procession of his contemporaries of the various social levels, of the types of his epoch, showing side by side in the inescapable jostling of contemporaneity, the philosopher Rousseau and the financier La Reynier, Mlle Camargo the dancer and the Duc d'Argenson, the clown Manelli and the Prince Xavier de Saxe. . . ."

Today the setting has changed and there are now contemporary furniture and decoration, but the overall impression remains remarkable. The sheer number of works allows one to study the artist's technique and especially the way he achieved such lively, animated likenesses. The men for example, and particularly the marvellous ***Abbé Hubert***★, all show a "5 o'clock shadow" laid in with a subtle blue over the warmer pinks of the face. At times it is clear that La Tour aimed for an easy effect, occasionally using short cuts or abbreviations that can result in a certain blandness, but it is equally true that these same devices bring out the sharpness of characterization around the eyes and mouth that distinguishes his greatest works. One can only repeat the Goncourt's own summing up of the collection as "an astonishing museum of the life and humanity of a whole society".

SAVERNE

Bas-Rhin, Alsace Map F4

Saverne has an attractive location by the Rhine–Rhone canal on a previously strategic site in the valley of the Zorn near the German border. The town is an old one with period architecture, and there is a good Renaissance house (built in 1606) in the main street. The principal building, however, is the large **Château** built by Cardinal Rohan in the late 18thC as a retreat for the bishops of Strasbourg.

Musée Municipal

Château de Rohan
Place du General de Gaulle
Tel. (88) 911852
Open May–Sept, 10am–noon, 3–5pm
Closed Oct–Apr; Jul–Aug Mon; May–June, Sept Mon–Sat

The municipal museum in the S and more recent wing of the château is mostly archaeological in its emphasis, giving special prominence to the Gallo-Roman implements excavated in the Saverne area. Apart from these, there are a few medieval sculptures in wood and stone, some folk art from Alsace, and a collection of paintings by two local artists of the 19thC, Gustave Brion and Alfred Roll.

SÉLESTAT

Bas-Rhin, Alsace Map F5

Sélestat is a sleepy-looking town, which seems of little interest either from the railway or from the road linking Strasbourg to Colmar. In fact it has a number of attractive streets and fine old houses (such as the 16th century **house of Stephen Ziegler**), and two impressive churches, the Romanesque church of Ste-Foy, and the Gothic church of St-George.

Bibliothèque Humaniste

Place Gambetta
Open 8am–noon, 2–6pm
Closed Sat afternoon, Sun

Sélestat's most unusual feature may be its **Humanist Library**. The late 15thC and early 16thC were a great period in the history of Alsace. At this time Sélestat was a major intellectual center and scholars came to its "Latin School" from all over Europe. Developing rapidly from 1450 onwards under such humanist scholars as Louis Dringenberg, Jerome Guebwiller and Jean Sapidus, the school had as many as 900 or even 1000 students during the 1520s. The school's library, founded in 1452, gradually grew.

The greatest treasure of the library is the remarkable **collection of volumes** donated by Beatus Rhenarus, a close friend of Erasmus, to his native town. He spent his life collecting editions of the classics, eventually accumulating 760 volumes. Apart from the Vadrana library in Switzerland, this is the only Humanist library which has survived intact.

Mainly located in one large room on the first floor of the 19thC Halle aux Blés, the Humanist Library of Sélestat is well worth a short visit. Some of the manuscripts on display date back to the 7thC. The **Book of Miracles of Ste-Foy** is a particularly beautiful illuminated codex from the 11thC.

Besides the superb medieval manuscripts there are also exhibits devoted to the history of printing in Alsace, and to the memory of the great Sélestat humanists. A number of sculptures and retables are on display in the library as well as a striking **mortuary mask** of a woman dating probably from the 12thC, and known as the "unknown lady of Ste-Foy".

SOISSONS
Aisne, Picardie Map C4

Having been an important settlement in Frankish times, Soissons returned to prominence during the later Middle Ages with the foundation of a cathedral and two abbeys. The **Cathedral of St-Gervais-et-St-Protais**, begun in the 12thC, is one of the purest examples of early Gothic architecture, seen less in the exterior, which was never fully completed, than in the interior with its simple rhythmic order. Unfortunately these buildings suffered badly during the religious wars of the 16thC and the Revolution, although this was little compared to the destruction of 1914–18, after which the town had to be rebuilt.

Musée Municipal (Ancienne Abbaye St-Léger)
2 Rue de la Congregation
Tel. (23) 591200
Open 10am–noon, 2–5pm
Closed Tues

Occupying part of the ruined 13thC Abbey of St-Léger, and none too comfortably at that, the museum at Soissons was formed during the last century by the amalgamation of several disparate collections in the town. Among these was the collection of the Historical, Archaeological and Scientific Society, which accounts for the presence on the ground floor of cases of archaeological discoveries. Paintings and sculpture occupy the staircase and upper rooms. The ground-floor section of the museum also preserves the remains from the medieval abbey, and you can also see a number of interesting Romanesque and Gothic sculptures in wood and stone from the churches in the area.

As regards the paintings, an early 17thC ***Adoration of the Magi*** by François Francken carries authority, and the landscapes by Courbet and Boudin are impressive, but even better are two works by the 18thC Venetian artist Pellegrini, ***Alexander Finding the Body of Darius*** and ***Alexander and the Family of Darius***. These are both from the College of the Oratorians, and make a considerable impact. The same cannot be said about a large ***St Sebastian*** by Daumier (1852), which was originally in the nearby Eglise de Lesges. The qualities that Daumier brought to his normally small canvases did not always translate to a larger scale, if this painting is anything to go by.

STRASBOURG
Bas-Rhin, Alsace Map G5

Strasbourg is the largest city of Alsace and indeed of the whole of northeastern France. As its name (Strasbourg, Street-town) suggests, it has always been at the crossroads where the French and Germanic worlds meet, and has changed hands several times. Many of its inhabitants still speak Alsatian, which is essentially a German dialect. During the Middle Ages, it was an independent city state within the Holy Roman Empire, and was largely run by 20 leading corporations, or groupings of guilds, after it had shaken off the domination of its bishops and its old aristocracy.

An important source of employment during this period was Strasbourg's massive **cathedral of Notre-Dame**, one of the finest examples of Gothic architecture in Europe. This took several centuries to complete, occupying artists, craftsmen and artisans of many kinds not only in its construction and embellishment, but also in its continued maintenance. Thus the cathedral represented an important stimulus for artistic activity in the town.

As early as the 13thC an organization was set up to collate the resources and to administer the construction of the cathedral. Called the Oeuvre Notre-Dame, this institution came under the direct control of the city and continued after the completion of the cathedral to maintain and restore it. It is still in existence today, and the ancient building houses many of the cathedral's finest treasures, transferred for safekeeping during the Revolution.

Strasbourg's heyday was in the 15thC and early 16thC, when it was one of the earliest and most important centers for the new craft of printing. Many painters and, in particular, sculptors were active in Strasbourg during this period. At the end of the 17thC it was annexed to France, though allowed to keep its old administrative structure, but the Revolution swept all this away and destroyed many of Strasbourg's art treasures, including some 230 statues.

Strasbourg was damaged during the successful Prussian siege of 1870, and was bombarded in 1944. In more recent times there has been some self-inflicted damage through planners' attempts to improve traffic circulation, but the old core of Strasbourg has remained remarkably intact. It is still a very beautiful city, with its rivers, canals and superb old buildings of all periods, and, especially, its magnificent cathedral. It is perhaps not surprising that the architecture of the city still has a strong Germanic feeling, attractive in the center but less so in the rather pompous extension to the town carried out during the years of German rule after 1870.

Strasbourg's rich cultural legacy is reflected in a number of fine museums, the most remarkable of which are the Musée de l'Oeuvre Notre-Dame and the collections contained in the grand 18thC Palais de Rohan.

Musee d'Art Moderne

1 Rue du Vieux Marché aux Poissons
Tel. (88) 324607
Open Apr–Sept 10am–noon, 2–6pm; Oct–Mar Sun 10am–noon, 2–6pm; Mon, Wed–Sat 2–6pm
Closed Oct–Mar Tues

Located on the edge of the river in the former customs house of the old port of Strasbourg, this building has an exterior with parts of the original 14thC structure still intact, though it has been largely reconstructed as a result of war damage in 1944.

The interior of the museum is modern, consisting of a large and rather bleak hall, almost like an aircraft hangar, which is used as Strasbourg's main exhibition room. This unfortunately has the result that much of the permanent collection can only be seen when there is no exhibition on, which in practice means the winter months. A few austere and windowless rooms to the side of the main exhibition hall, however, contain certain items from the collection that are permanently on display.

There are several works by well-known masters such as Pissarro, Degas, Signac, Vuillard and Dufy, as well as a number of works by Klee. A **still-life** by Braque carries authority and was apparently the first Cubist painting to be displayed by any French museum. Another interesting piece is ***Le Baiser***, Gustav Klimt's celebrated painting that was originally intended for the interior of the famous Art Nouveau Maison Soclet in Brussels. There are also some impressive sculptures, including fine works by Rodin.

One room is devoted to works by Jean Arp, one of the originators of the Dada movement, and his wife Sophie Tauber-Arp. Arp was a native of Strasbourg, and the collection includes a project he carried out with his wife for the interior decoration of the Aubette, the original Strasbourg art museum that was destroyed by fire in 1870. With the collaboration of Theo van Doesburg, a leading member of *de Stijl*, the Arps redecorated the Aubette between 1926 and 1928 but their work was later mutilated by unappreciative Nazi administrators.

Up some stairs and in the attic there can be seen a collection of modern stained glass that brings the ancient stained glass tradition of Strasbourg up to the present day. The setting is attractive, with the glass gleaming brightly in the darkened room, and there is a fine Art Nouveau window by J. Gruber, some interesting pieces by Theo van Doesburg, and more works by the Arps.

Musée de l'Oeuvre Notre-Dame ☆ ☆

Place du Château
Tel. (88) 320639
Open Apr–Sept 10am–noon, 2–6pm
Closed Oct–Mar Tues

The museum's existence stems from the Revolution, when original statues from the cathedral were removed to protect them from the Terror in 1793, and stored in the building of the Oeuvre Notre-Dame, located directly opposite the cathedral. In 1931 the museum was considerably expanded to house other magnificent collections, mainly of medieval and Renaissance art from Strasbourg and Alsace.

The museum now occupies a series of interconnected buildings linked by passages and enclosing various courtyards. The buildings are very beautiful and represent different periods and styles, the earliest dating from 1347. One of the buildings was destroyed in World War II but has been unobtrusively reconstructed.

The direction of the tour round the museum is clearly indicated, and attendants are located at strategic points to assist visitors wondering where to go next. The recommended order is basically chronological, leading across courtyards and up and down stairs until any sense of direction is lost. But there is a detailed and intelligently laid out guidebook on sale at the entrance.

The museum's collections are extremely rich and varied, so much so that only a superficial account can be given here. The tour begins with some fine Romanesque columns from the former cloister of Eschau, and a room of stained glass, mainly 12thC and 13thC works from the cathedral, but including the extraordinary ***Head of Christ*** from the abbey of Wissembourg, c.1050, one of the earliest known figurative works in stained glass.

The late 16thC former meeting room of the cathedral's masons comes next, containing many beautiful sculptures from the cathedral. A further room has more cathedral sculptures, including the exquisite sequence of the ***Wise and Foolish Virgins*** ★, and the allegorical figures of the ***Church*** ★ and the ***Synagogue*** ★, dating from 1230–40. Beyond this is a room with a rare curiosity indeed, namely the original architects' designs for the cathedral, drawn on parchment and dated to the 13thC–15thC.

On the upper floors are further fine examples of the 15th and 16thC sculptures in which Strasbourg is particularly rich, including the impressive head of a ***Man with Turban*** by Nicolas Gerhaert de Leyden. There are also some magnificent paintings from the same period, including a panel of ***Sts Madeleine and Catherine*** by the Basel painter Conrad Witz, and a number of paintings by Hans Baldung Grien, a pupil of Dürer who lived in Strasbourg.

A final distinctive curiosity is the room dedicated to the **still-lifes** of Sebastian Stosskopf, a remarkable 17thC Strasbourg painter specializing in this genre. Altogether, the museum's combination of architecturally impressive rooms with superb collections of period furniture, woodcarvings, ceramics and tapestries makes this a visit that is both memorable and very worthwhile.

Musées du Château des Rohan

Place du Château
Tel. (88) 324895
Open Apr–Sept 10am–noon, 2–6pm; Oct–Mar Sun 10am–noon, 2–6pm; Mon, Wed–Sat 2–6pm
Closed Oct–Mar Tues

The magnificent **18thC building** that formerly constituted the bishop's palace now houses a number of different museums. Plans for the original château were commissioned by Cardinal Armand de Rohan-Soubise in 1704, and the construction went ahead between 1731 and 1742. Before becoming a home for several museums, in 1898, the building was a town hall, a royal palace and a university building. It was badly damaged by American bombs in 1944. In its present setting it seems just a little out of place, like a grand Parisian building that has somehow strayed in among the half-timbered structures typical of Strasbourg, but it is nevertheless very attractive. The main building contains the art museum on the first and second floors, and the archaeological museum in the basement. On the right of the courtyard is a wing containing the museum of decorative arts, on the left is the Cabinet des Estampes and the Art Library. The visit should begin with the state room on the ground floor, where there is a fine sequence of 18thC rooms on a grand scale, well restored after extensive damage in World War II. These contain the well-known painting by Largillière, ***La Belle Strasbourgeoise***, in which the subject is wearing a fantastic long hat.

Musée des Beaux-Arts

The original art museum of Strasbourg was in the Aubette on the Place Kléber, destroyed by fire in 1870. The present art gallery, on the upper floors of the Château des Rohan, was largely put together through money provided by the Germans to compensate for their destruction of the old museum. The director-general of the German Imperial Museums in Berlin himself chose many of the exhibits. Among the paintings to be seen in the large collection are **works** by Memlinc, Lucas von Leyden, Rubens and van Dyck from the Flemish and Dutch schools of the 15thC–17thC; paintings by **Botticelli, Veronese, Tintoretto,**

Titian, Guardi, Correggio and many others from 14thC–17thC Italy; works by **El Greco, Murillo and Goya** among Spanish painters; and paintings by **Fragonard, Boucher, Claude Lorrain** and others from the French 17thC–18thC.

In addition, a small room, the Salle René Loyer, interestingly illustrates early 19thC taste with its period furniture and paintings. In general, however, the rooms containing the collections are unremarkable, making it all an interesting museum rather than an outstanding one. It is gradually being restored and reorganized.

Musée Archéologique

Located in the basement of the same part of the château as that containing the art museum, this is a very musty collection, giving the visitor a feeling that time has stood still. In spite of the old-fashioned layout, however, some of the pieces on display are of considerable artistic interest. There are some fine Roman sculptures and some interesting, if battered frescoes. There are also some impressive Merovingian pieces, notably the Baldenheim helmet and the Ittenheim *phaleres*.

Musée des Arts Décoratifs

This museum contains one of the major ceramics collections in France, and it is a great pity that it is currently closed for further restoration, with no certainty about when it will reopen. The collection includes many works from the Hannong factory in Strasbourg, one of the leading manufacturers in Europe in the 18thC. These, together with pieces from the Niderviller factory, founded by Baron de Beyerlé in 1748, constitute some of the finest examples of French faience and porcelain of the period.

TOURCOING

Pas-de-Calais, Nord Map B2

Known primarily for its wool industry, Tourcoing has grown in recent years to form almost part of Lille. Few of its old buildings survive, and its main landmarks are its ostentatious 19thC civic buildings such as the Town Hall.

Musée des Beaux-Arts

2 Rue Paul Doumer
Tel. (16/20) 253812
Open Wed–Fri, Sun, 10am–noon, 2.30–5.30pm; Sat 2.30–5.30pm
Closed Aug, Mon–Tues

The art gallery faces the town hall and occupies the building where Tourcoing's greatest native son, the composer Albert Roussel (1869–1936) spent part of his youth. The extremely spacious interior of this building at first encourages a feeling of being in a major museum. However, this is far from the case. Considering the great wealth of Tourcoing in the 19thC and today, its municipal art collections are very disappointing. Moreover, the items are often confusingly arranged, in bad condition and frequently unlabelled. The collections include indifferent 17thC Dutch and Flemish paintings, and many minor French Neoclassical works, but there are interesting holdings in the field of late 19thC French painting.

One whole room is devoted to the now fashionable Salon painters of this period, with a good ***Portrait*** by Léon Bonnat, and a striking full-length ***Equestrian Portrait*** by Carolus-Duran, the teacher of the American painter John Singer Sargent. You will also see, prominently displayed on an easel, a very idealized portrait by G. Clairin of the actress ***Sarah Bernhardt***, lying on a tiger's skin and swathed in a crinoline. Post-Impressionism is represented by a beach scene by Maurice Denis, and a ***pointilliste*** rendering of the Place de la Concorde in Paris at Night by La Sidaner.

TROYES

Aube, Champagne–Ardenne
Map C5

Famous in the Middle Ages as the town which halted Attila the Hun, Troyes became the capital of Champagne and received the patronage of bishops and counts alike. Among the numerous medieval buildings still to be seen, the Gothic **church of St-Urbain** and the **Cathedral of St-Pierre-et-St-Paul** particularly emphasize the town's early significance. The cathedral was conceived in the 13thC on a grand scale and, though adapted to suit changes in taste over the next 400 years, still contains some excellent early stained glass and a Treasury with good medieval ivories, enamels and textiles. From this period in the town's history dates the work of Chrétien de Troyes, the poet and author of Arthurian romances, who wrote for the court of Marie de Campagne in the 12thC.

Musée des Beaux-Arts

21 Rue Chrestien de Troyes
Tel. (25) 434949 (Ext 382)
Open Jan–Dec 10am–noon, 2–6pm
Closed Tues

The Musée des Beaux-Arts at Troyes shares the 17thC abbey building of St-Loup with museums devoted to archaeology and natural history. The space available for paintings and sculpture is not ideal, but an attempt has been made to display the collection in an interesting way, and this has to a large extent been successful.

In the main gallery on the first floor there is a preponderance of large official paintings. The title of Philippe de Champaigne's ***Reception of the Duc de Longueville into the Order of St-Esprit by Louis XIII in 1633*** is perhaps enough to indicate the rather pompous nature of this type of work. Considering the gallery as a whole, this is one of the better pictures, but fortunately there are less formal works nearby, such as Rubens' ***Portrait of a Man Playing the Lute***, to admit a more personal and intimate character.

The other large gallery is given over mainly to 18thC art, and although there are landscapes by Ballotto and Richard Wilson the majority of the pictures are French. Watteau, Natoire, Boucher and Fragonard are all represented, and the later works are further enhanced by the presence of an excellent Empire bed. Beside it hangs David's fine portrait of Danton's first wife, ***Antoinette Gabrielle Charpentier***. The 19thC paintings at the end of this section are not particularly strong, but it is worth noting a ***Nude Study*** by Prud'hon and ***Young Girl Playing the Guitar*** by the Realist painter Théodule Ribot. Finally, in a small room off the stairway, there is space for drawings and miniatures. This is a somewhat miscellaneous collection in which the red chalk studies by Oudry are the most attractive works.

Musée d'Art Moderne (Musée Levy)

Place St-Pierre
Tel. (25) 726418
Open 11am–6pm
Closed Tues

When Pierre and Denise Levy presented a large part of their huge art collection to the state in 1976, it was decided that Troyes, the donors' home town, should provide the site of a new museum displaying these works. As a result, the former Bishop's Palace, an outstanding historic building beside the cathedral, was completely renovated to house the collection of some 2,000 works, and to provide facilities for other related activities.

The collection itself includes a series of fine **African sculptures** and some 20thC ceramics and glassware, but the most significant area is the paintings and sculptures from the late 19thC and early 20thC. Virtually every major French artist from this period is represented, and among the earlier works there are **good paintings by Courbet, Millet, Daumier and Eugène Carrière**.

As the collection develops towards the 20thC, the particular interests of the donors begin to be apparent. Picasso and Braque figure prominently, as do Soutine and Balthus, and painters from the so-called Nabis group, such as Bonnard, Vuillard and Vallotton – the last with an excellent picture of a ***Woman Sewing*** ★ (1905). But by sheer weight of numbers as well as in quality it is the Fauvist paintings which predominate. Dufy, Vlaminck, Marquet and Matisse are all in evidence, and works by André Derain outnumber all others. Derain's ***Port of Collioure*** ★ (1905) is one of the finest paintings in the gallery, coming from the artist's most innovative period, but there are also some examples of his later realist work from the 1920s and 1930s.

The collection also has a complete set of Derain's numerous bronzes, although these seem less impressive alongside sculptures by Degas, Rodin and Maillol. When Derain took up modelling, Picasso, who at the time was a close associate, also tried his hand at sculpture, and the finest piece in this section is Picasso's bronze bust of a ***Jester*** (1905).

On the second floor a prints and drawings gallery displays almost exactly the same artists as in the painting section, and in something approaching the same quantities. Particularly fine in this department are the **pen drawings by Picasso and Matisse**. In general, however, it must be said that the drawings as well as the paintings and sculpture reflect a particular taste: one which is becoming outmoded in its exclusive preoccupation with the French avant garde and the School of Paris. But although this perspective is less popular today in many major galleries, there could hardly be a more sympathetic celebration of its virtues than in the museum at Troyes. Not only are the works of a high standard, but the building with its gardens overlooking the cathedral is one of the finest new galleries in France.

VALENCIENNES
Pas-de-Calais, Nord Map C2

Situated in the middle of one of the most important coal-mining areas of France, Valenciennes is an ugly town with numerous 19thC buildings and few older monuments. Incongruously it is sometimes called the "Athens of the North" on account of the many artists who have been born here. The boulevards which encircle the town in place of the former fortifications are all named after famous natives, including the medieval chronicler Froissart, the painters Watteau, Pater and Harpignies, and the sculptor Carpeaux.

Musée des Beaux-Arts ☆

Boulevard Watteau
Tel. (20) 462109
Open 10am–noon, 2–5pm
Closed Tues

The impressive, large, late 19thC art gallery is in a dusty tree-lined square off the Boulevard Watteau. This part of the town has a deserted feel about it. In front of the museum stands a rusted bandstand, apparently now rarely used. The museum itself is pitted with shrapnel and bullet holes from World War II. Inside is one of the best art collections in this part of France. There are a number of rooms with 16thC and 17thC Flemish paintings. Particularly impressive are a ***Landscape with Rainbow*** by Rubens, two large altarpieces by the same artist (the ***Descent from the Cross*** and the ***Stoning of St Peter*** from a Valenciennes church and the local Abbey of St-Arnand respectively), and a moralizing genre piece by Jordaens (***The Young Ones Play while the Old Ones Sing***).

Two rooms are devoted to Valenciennes' 18thC artists. Of these the most important was Watteau, born here in 1684 shortly after the town had been ceded from Flanders to France. One of his contemporaries once referred to Watteau as a "Flemish painter", and certainly the Flemish tradition of painting in which Valenciennes was steeped was critical to Watteau's development as a painter: the greatest influence on his art were the paintings of Rubens. The Valenciennes museum contains two works by him – a somewhat awkward early allegorical piece painted in the town in 1703 (***True Happiness***) and a superlative portrait of another Valenciennes native, the sculptor ***Antoine Pater*** ★. Watteau's pupil and rather dreary imitator, Jean-Baptiste Pater, was also born in Valenciennes, and the museum has a number of his cold, mechanical *fêtes galantes*. The 18thC rooms also have works by two other imitators of Watteau, Louis and François Watteau, the nephew and great-nephew of the artist.

Next comes a small room of modest still-lifes by the disciple of Corot, Henri Harpignies, followed by the museum's extensive collection of a single artist's work – that of the **local sculptor** Jean-Baptiste Carpeaux. Carpeaux was born in Valenciennes in 1827, the son of a mason and a lacemaker. The house where he was born, No. 53 of the quaintly decrepit **Rue Delsaux**, still survives and is marked by a plaque. He and his family left Valenciennes for Paris in 1838, where he later became the most celebrated 19thC French sculptor before Rodin. Carpeaux achieved particular notoriety for his exceptionally vital and brazenly erotic group, ***The Dance*** (now in the **LOUVRE, PARIS**), which was placed outside the Opera House in Paris in 1869 only to be violated and covered in ink immediately by shocked members of the public. Although based primarily in Paris after 1838, Carpeaux maintained his connections with Valenciennes in later life, taking refuge here during the political troubles of 1858 and executing for the town a number of important commissions. He died from cancer in 1875, suffering also in his last years from increasing paranoia.

In addition to being a sculptor, he was also relatively prolific, if not successful, as a painter. One room in the Valenciennes Museum is devoted to this lesser-known side to his work. His paintings and watercolours have a crude, agitated quality, and were mainly intended to help the artist in his very pictorial sculptural compositions. The large room in the museum full of his sculptures has several finished bronzes and marbles, but is principally interesting for its plaster maquettes of nearly all the artist's major works, including ***The Dance***. There are various maquettes for his two main Valenciennes commissions, ***The Defense of Valenciennes*** (which used to crown the Town Hall, but was destroyed in World War II and has now been replaced by a copy) and his ***Monument to Watteau***. The actual monument, executed in stone and bronze, can still be seen in the delightfully green and quiet **Place Géry**.

German Art in Alsace

Until 1648, when it was ceded to Louis XIV, Alsace was one of a series of Rhenish states within the Holy Roman Empire that eventually went to make up modern Germany. The language in much of the area is a German dialect, and it is understandable that the culture of the region in the broadest sense has a strong Germanic flavour. But Alsace's German connection is well known; what is perhaps less familar is that the region has some of the greatest masterpieces of an art traditionally considered German, from its finest period in the 15thC and 16thC.

In the 15thC Martin Schongauer (d. 1491) set up his studio in COLMAR, still one of the best preserved medieval towns in Alsace, where he developed the mature style that first asserted the Renaissance spirit in German art. Not much is known about his life except that he probably trained in the workshop of the Flemish painter Rogier van der Weyden, and he seems to have known the celebrated altarpiece of ***The Last Judgment*** in Beaune (see p. 84). The large ***Madonna of the Rosebush*** formerly in the church of St Martin at Colmar, remains the only work definitely from his hand, but there can be no question of his considerable reputation throughout Germany during his lifetime. In 1492 the young Albrecht Dürer, having completed his apprenticeship, left Nuremberg with the express purpose of meeting the Colmar master; but on his arrival he found that Schongauer had died in the previous year. Dürer and most other artists were made aware of Schongauer's work through his engravings, a medium that he and the enigmatic Master E.S., also from this area, raised to an unprecedented level. Their prints provided the basis for Dürer's own outstanding work in this field.

Colmar, or at least the nearby Anthonite monastery at Isenheim, was also the location of that extraordinary masterpiece of 16thC German art, the great altar wings (MUSÉE D'UNTERLINDEN, Colmar) painted in 1510–15 by "Grünewald" (Mathis Gothardt–Neithardt). This work is a complex series of panels that could be displayed in various combinations to serve different functions in the religious calendar. The nightmarish ***Temptation of St Anthony*** could be contrasted with the jubilant visionary light of the ***Nativity*** or the ***Resurrection***, while the famous ***Crucifixion*** was reserved for the "plague altar" during weekdays. The scourged and mutilated body of Christ seems particularly appropriate for this last role, and Grünewald emphasizes its effect with a range of expressive gestures which intensify the pathos and emotion of the scene to a level that is almost painful.

The power and superb craftsmanship of these panels tend to obscure the fact that they were commissioned to enclose an altar, and this altar must originally have been regarded as the principal feature of the whole work. Here you can see the sculpted relief by Nikolaus Hagenower of ***St Anthony of Egypt*** enthroned between St Augustine and St Jerome, an example of the Northern tradition of limewood carving that is in many respects the supreme achievement of German art. Hagenower worked mainly in STRASBOURG, an important Imperial city in the 15thC which invested considerable wealth to attract artists, and became the principal center of the Upper Rhenish school. The scale of the cathedral that was being built at this time indicates the extent of cultural activity, and the work on this building alone was sufficient to stimulate Alsatian craftsmen and to encourage a flourishing regional tradition. In this the limewood sculptors were particularly prominent, and from the 1450s the school developed a strong identity from the work of the Dutch stone and wood carver Nikolaus Gerhaert. Under the influence of the Burgundian master Claus Sluter, Gerhaert introduced a vigorous approach involving deeper cutting that became known as the "Florid Style", and his own sandstone ***Bust of a Man*** (MUSÉE DE L'OEUVRE NOTRE-DAME, Strasbourg), often thought to be a self-portrait, is a good example. Hagenower and another Strasbourg sculptor, Veit Wagner, were both exponents of this manner, and there are examples of Wagner's work in the cathedral and the church of St-Pierre-le-Vieux.

As a final link with the German tradition, and in contrast with the French experience, Alsace felt the full weight of the Reformation. In **STRASBOURG** especially, where the reformer Karlstadt was active, the roles of images in church was hotly disputed although it never reached the stage where the artists were in fear of their lives, as happened in many towns. Nevertheless, the issue of Iconoclasm came to a head in 1530 when all paintings and sculptures were removed and many destroyed in public. Those we can see nowadays are the survivors.

***The Apostles**, c. 1510, carving from the Isenheim altarpiece, Colmar.*

EASTERN FRANCE

The regions of Burgundy and the French Jura or Franche-Comté, which form the eastern section of the *Guide*, are geographical neighbours but, in many ways, cultural opposites. Burgundy impresses the visitor at once with the evidence of its abundant and diverse heritage and the extraordinary richness of its vineyards. The Franche-Comté, by contrast, seems rather like a poor relation, lacking a clear cultural tradition and consisting for the most part of remote mountainous uplands. Yet both regions have their own glories, and admirers of the Jura include such famous authorities as Goethe and Ruskin.

Most periods of history have left their mark on the rolling landscape of Burgundy. Traces of a stylish and affluent past go back at least to the 6thC BC, as the Vix Treasure of **CHÂTILLON-SUR-SEINE** clearly shows. But more conspicuous and impressive than this rich Gallo-Roman heritage are Burgundy's cathedrals, abbeys and churches, testifying to the region's seminal role in the development of Romanesque and Gothic art and architecture. Standing at the source of a major medieval pilgrimage route, the great churches of **VÉZELAY**, **AUTUN** and, above all, **CLUNY**, laid down the design and decoration of innumerable religious buildings throughout France. Though considerably depleted by time and vandalism, these structures are among the supreme masterpieces of medieval Europe.

In the 15thC the lands controlled by the dukes of Burgundy extended to the North Sea and included parts of Germany and France and virtually all of Belgium and Holland. This society saw the emergence of an independent Northern Renaissance in the art of such masters as Jan van Eyck and Claus Sluter, and the region's museums contain many of the works created for the entourage of the great dukes, Philip the Bold and John the Fearless. Sluter's powerful naturalistic sculptures for the Chartreuse at **DIJON** still survive, and

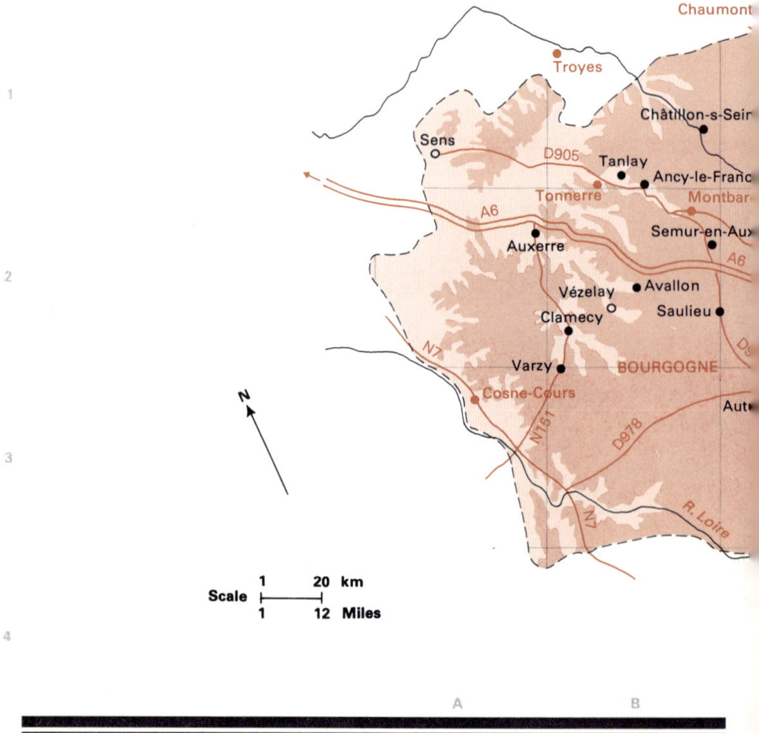

the Hôtel Dieu at **BEAUNE**, a flamboyant secular building from the 1440s, contains the magnificent original altarpiece of the ***Last Judgment*** by Rogier van der Weyden.

The vineyards of Burgundy, first exploited during the Middle Ages, now provide labels that have become household names: Chablis, Pommard, Nuits-St-Georges and above all the universally popular wines of the Beaujolais. There is more than a casual relationship between the wine trade and Burgundy's cultural inheritance. The Hôtel Dieu at Beaune, owner of some of the finest vineyards in France, traditionally holds an auction in November, and this not only sets the standard of quality and price for the year's vintage of Burgundy wine but also raises money for the hospital.

To the E of Burgundy, the Jura or Franche-Comté extends from Lorraine in the N to Switzerland, its eastern border following the crests and slopes of the Jura mountains. It is a remote area with a changeable climate and spectacular scenery, consisting of forested foothills and mountains interspersed by the great rivers, the Doubs, Saône and Rhône. Forestry, dairy farming, hunting, skiing and fishing all flourish, indicating a region that looks towards the outdoors in almost all aspects of its life. But the towns and settlements are also places of great charm. **BESANÇON**, the capital, formerly the chief place of the Gallic Sequani, is a university city of great style and culture. **DOLE**, the previous capital, has a beautiful and very well preserved old quarter. **ORNANS**, in complete contrast, huddles round the river Loue with its quaint old houses. One of these was the birthplace of the great artist Gustave Courbet, and is now the site of the Courbet museum.

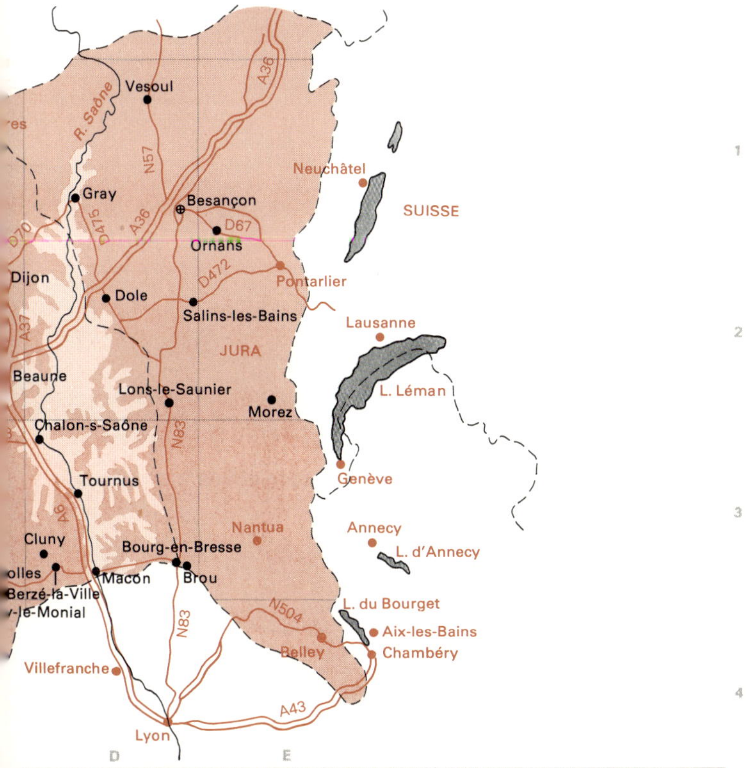

ANCY-LE-FRANC
Yonne, Bourgogne Map C2

The tiny hamlet of Ancy-le-Franc, 57km (37 miles) from Auxerre, serves as little more than a context, one might almost say a pretext, for the magnificent château of Ancy-le-Franc, one of the finest Renaissance châteaux in France.

Château d'Ancy-le-Franc
Open Apr–Oct 10am–noon, 2–6pm
Closed Nov–Mar

Begun in 1546 for Antoine de Clermont-Tonnerre, Grand Forester of France, Ancy-le-Franc was originally built to plans prepared by the celebrated Italian architect Sebastiano Serlio. It seems, however, that Antoine had definite ideas about the type of residence he wanted and the building changed considerably during its construction to suit the patron's wishes. It became more French in its exterior forms and details but, like most of his contemporaries, Antoine was an admirer of the Italian Renaissance and he commissioned Primaticcio, the leading Italian painter then working in France, to decorate the interior. In all, 18 apartments were painted with subjects drawn from classical mythology and the Bible. The finest of these are the **chapel and the two galleries**. Primaticcio himself was probably responsible for some of the work at Ancy-le-Franc, but most of it, featuring stylish figure scenes and elaborate ornamentation in the style he developed at Fontainebleau, is the work of his very able assistant, Niccolo dell'Abbate.

AUTUN
Saône-et-Loire, Bourgogne Map C3

Several interesting Roman and late medieval monuments bear witness to the former significance of Autun, a town at the edge of the Arroux valley in southern Burgundy, but in modern times its history has been unremarkable. The present century has seen some industrial expansion in the area and this has given the town a fairly lively, bustling character without detracting too much from its heritage.

Cathédrale St-Lazare ☆
Place du Terreau
Open all year

Autun's decline during the Renaissance was probably responsible for preserving the wonderful series of Romanesque sculptures that grace the **Cathédrale St-Lazare**, which would otherwise have suffered from the changes in taste and the vandalism that affected similar works from the same period. Fortunately these works were spared the normal ravages, and even the 18thC remodelling only concealed the carvings behind a screen of plaster. When this was finally removed in the late 19thC and early 20thC, lively scenes from the Old and New Testament could be seen virtually intact on the tympanum and capitals. Moreover, the two principal losses, the **Head of Christ** from the tympanum and half of a relief depicting **Adam and Eve**, have since been rediscovered, making this cycle one of the finest and most comprehensive monuments of late medieval art. There can scarcely be a better setting in which to appreciate the sinuous, fluid rhythms of Romanesque design running throughout the figure groups, or the alternately sensitive and dramatic narrative bringing a power and directness to the familiar Bible stories.

The sculpture at Autun has another remarkable feature in the fact that the craftsman broke the medieval tradition of anonymity and signed his work: "Gislebertus hoc fecit" is inscribed in the **Last Judgement** ★ on the tympanum. This is not quite unique, since several 12thC sculptural series have the signature of their creators inserted at some point in the cycle, but in Autun we can be fairly sure that virtually all the work was done by one man and probably over a single ten-year period. We have therefore one of the earliest clear indications of an artistic personality, and a range of work in the tympanum and capitals, that is both fascinating and entertaining.

Most of the sculpture is still in its proper position, but a few of the finest capitals have been replaced and the originals put on display in the **chapter house** at the top of a winding staircase to the S or right hand side of the altar. It is also just worth mentioning that a small chapel on the N side contains a large painting by the 19thC artist J. A. D. Ingres, a rather dry academic rendering of ***The Martyrdom of St-Symphorien***.

Musée Rolin
15 Rue des Bancs
Tel. (85) 520976
Open Jan to mid-Mar 10am–noon, 2–4pm (Sun 2.30–5pm); mid-Mar to Sept 9.30am–noon, 2–6.30pm; Oct to mid-Nov 10am–noon, 2–5pm (Sun 2.30–5pm); mid-Nov to Dec 10am–noon, 2–4pm (Sun 2.30–5pm)
Closed Tues, May 1, Nov 1, Nov 11

The Musée Rolin is just a few yards from the main portal of the cathedral, and one section of the museum could almost be regarded as a continuation of the visit to St-Lazare since it contains several pieces from the cathedral's sculptural decoration. The figure of ***Eve*** ★, discovered in a wall in 1866, is particularly celebrated, for it is one half of the relief that was probably Gislebertus' masterpiece (the other half is unfortunately lost). Lying in the foliage she whispers through her hand to Adam, with a glance, gesture and pose that is sensuous even to a contemporary eye and must have appeared positively salacious in the 12thC.

The rest of the museum's exhibits fall clearly into two categories: a Gallo-Roman section which contains handsome objects, like the Gallic chieftain's ceremonial helmet, that make it actually enjoyable to visit, unlike the vast majority of such collections; and a painting section occupying a series of galleries on the upper floors. Here the French 19thC academic pictures like Cibot's ***Anne Boleyn in the Tower of London*** dominate the scene in quantity, and they have been well displayed with the right amount of background information, but the finest painting in the collection is undoubtedly the 15thC ***Nativity*** ★ by the Master of Moulins. This is not only a work of the highest quality, but is also particularly appropriate in its present setting because the donor kneeling on the right of the main scene is Cardinal Rolin himself, the man whose beautifully restored family house is now the museum building.

AUXERRE

Yonne, Bourgogne Map B2

Auxerre on the river Yonne in northern Burgundy is a typical medieval town with a rambling old quarter bounded by the remains of the ancient city walls. A number of important early buildings have survived, among which the most important is the Gothic cathedral of St-Etienne, built between the 13thC and 16thC. The sculpture and stained glass depicting the ***Seven Liberal Arts*** point to the fact that the cathedral school was an important focus of learning in the late Middle Ages. The early Christian saint, Germain, was born in Auxerre in 378, and his remains were interred in a crypt beneath the abbey which bears his name.

Musée St-Germain (Cryptes de l'Abbaye)

Place de l'Abbaye St-Germain
Open 9am–noon, 2–6pm
Closed Tues and holidays

The abbey of St-Germain is a memorial to well over 1,000 years of building activity, with the earlier stages lying deep underground. At the beginning of this century archaeologists working beneath the Neoclassical and Gothic structures uncovered a number of crypts dating back as far as the 5thC; but the most exciting discovery was at the level of the 9thC Carolingian chambers. Here they found a series of frescoes depicting scenes from the ***Life of St Stephen*** which, though somewhat crude in comparison with other works of art from the period, such as manuscript illuminations, are nevertheless among the earliest paintings of their type in the whole of France.

Musée Leblanc–Duvernoy

Rue d'Egleny
Tel. (86) 524463
Open 10.30am–noon, 2–5.30pm
Closed Tues

The Musée Leblanc–Duvernoy, an 18thC house of considerable elegance, specializes in 18thC decorative arts, particularly ceramics and furniture, and has a good series of Beauvais tapestries with **Chinois** decoration.

At the time of writing, it also houses some exhibits from Auxerre's Musée d'Art et d'Histoire, which normally occupies a 16thC half-timbered house near the river on the opposite side of the town. These items include a number of pleasing **early French portraits** from the Château of ANCY-LE-FRANC, among other paintings. Auxerre's museum of art and history is in the process of complete reorganization, and is unlikely to be open to the public before the end of 1984. However, there are plans to mount some temporary exhibitions to show sections of the permanent collection, such as the extensive medieval and Gallo-Roman antiquities.

AVALLON

Yonne, Bourgogne Map C2

Avallon, with its impressive hilltop setting, was an important strategic town in the late Middle Ages, fortified with a series of towers and ramparts. Inside the walls, which still survive, the town has retained its early layout and character with a number of old buildings, the finest being the 12thC church of St-Lazare.

Musée de' l'Avallonais

Place de la Collégiale

Tel. (86) 340319
Open mid-June to Sept 10, 10am–noon, 3–7pm; school hols 2.30–6.30pm
Closed Mon, Tues, mid-Sept to mid-June (exc. school hols)

The Musée de l'Avallonais contains a miscellaneous range of exhibits, most of which have been presented to the town since the museum's creation in 1862. The medieval rooms have some good Romanesque and Gothic sculpture drawn from the churches in the area, and a few 6thC–8thC Merovingian antiquities such as decorated brooches and buckles, but the rest of the collection is patchy. One bequest by an early 20thC designer, Jean Despes, consists of silverware and furniture in a range of unattractive materials as well as ***two drawings*** by Braque and De Chirico. The paintings on the upper floors are almost uniformly dull, but at the turn of the century the civic authorities acquired a curious early painting, ***Stella Vespertina*** (1895) by Rouault in the style of his master Gustave Moreau. To supplement this, Rouault's daughter at a much later date presented a complete set of the artist's ***Miserere*** print series to the museum, and this does much to enhance the collection overall.

BEAUNE
Côte-d'Or, Bourgogne Map D3

Beaune, in the heart of what is known as the Côte-d'Or or Golden Slopes, is the chief focus of the Burgundy wine trade and has been recognized as such for centuries. There is scarcely a village or vineyard in the surrounding area whose name is not linked to one of the great wines of international repute. Beaune was also a major administrative town and it has preserved a number of fine medieval buildings, particularly the Mansion of the Dukes (Hôtel des Ducs de Bourgogne) which is now a museum of winemaking, and the Hôtel Dieu. The Collegiate church of Notre-Dame which was begun in 1120 and now displays a succession of different building styles, has an important series of tapestries of the ***Life of the Virgin*** hung in the choir. These were commissioned for the church in 1474 by Cardinal Jean Rolin and woven at Tournai to the designs of a local artist, Pierre Spicre.

Hôtel Dieu ☆
Rue de l'Hôtel Dieu
Tel. (80) 221414
Open Summer 9–11.30am, 2–6pm
Winter 9–11am, 2–5pm

The most striking features of the Hôtel Dieu are its Flamboyant design and remarkable state of preservation, but the plain stone frontage which it presents to the street gives very little indication of what to expect inside. It is only from the inner courtyard that you can appreciate the richness of the buildings and in particular the elaborately patterned tiling on the pitched roof.

Founded in 1443 by Nicolas Rolin, the chancellor of Burgundy, the Hôtel Dieu was a charity hospital set up to relieve the sufferings of the poor, and it still served this purpose as recently as 1948. At the time of its foundation several people noted that Rolin's own quest for wealth and power had probably contributed to the destitution of many of the patients, but the belief that works of public charity helped to store up good will for the afterlife was the reason behind many, if not most, of the commissions for religious art throughout Europe.

The largest building served a dual purpose as a hospital ward and as a church, enabling the patients to be present at religious services, and although the fittings are modern reconstructions, enough of the original conception has survived to evoke the atmosphere of the period. Unfortunately the other rooms are disappointing, but perhaps the guided tour through mundane offices and kitchens helps to increase the visitor's pleasurable surprise when finally confronted with the painting that is the climax of any visit: Rogier van der Weyden's ***Last Judgement*** ★★, painted for the Hôtel Dieu soon after 1443 and originally hung on the high altar of the paupers' ward.

Rogier van der Weyden was the leading Flemish painter of the 15thC after the death of Jan van Eyck in 1441, and this painting along with the ***Descent from the Cross*** in the Prado is the greatest expression of his art. The work is a polyptych or altarpiece of several panels, nine in fact, which could be opened or closed in various combinations depending on the religious festival which was to be celebrated. When fully open, as it is now exhibited, the whole scene is apparent. Beneath a Christ seated in judgement in the middle, flanked by groups of apostles and saints on the lateral panels, St Michael weighs the souls of the resurrected on a balance that tips towards evil and damnation: a tendency corroborated by the figures at the bottom, more of whom are moving in the direction of the fiery pit at the right than the gates of paradise on the opposite side. This picture is larger than most Flemish 15thC works, but the artist has succeeded in controlling the grand design around the majestic figure of St Michael while maintaining the meticulous attention to detail that is the hallmark of the early Flemish school.

The gallery also has several early tapestries which, while hardly rivaling the altarpiece, are nevertheless very attractive, notably the Flemish ***Mille Fleurs*** tapestry from the early 16thC.

Musée des Beaux-Arts

Rue Hôtel de Ville
Tel. (80) 222080
Open Apr, Oct, Nov 9am–noon, 2–5.30pm; May–Sept 10am–12.15pm, 2.15–6.30pm
Closed Dec–Mar, Tues

The Musée des Beaux-Arts in Beaune shares a 17thC convent building with the Hôtel de Ville and the main police station, but there has been very little attempt to adapt it to its new purpose. The main gallery was once the chapel, a tall bare room that is singularly unsympathetic to the display of paintings although it is now undergoing the renovations that are long overdue.

As far as the collection is concerned, there are a few pieces from different periods, including Gallo-Roman antiquities, medieval sculpture, paintings from a variety of schools and a few modern prints, but the only significant holding is the **group of paintings** and studies by the 19thC landscapist, Félix Ziem. Ziem, who was born in Beaune in 1821, worked in a late Romantic manner similar to J.M.W. Turner and, like the English artist, he produced some of his best work in Venice.

In a separate gallery on the first floor there is another collection devoted to another local celebrity, Etienne-Jules Marey (1830–1904) the pioneer of techniques for creating "moving pictures". In fact Marey was more of an experimental scientist who addressed himself to a variety of problems, but along the way he created several gadgets such as the "Zoetrope" and the "Gun Camera" which not only prepared the way for cinematography but also influenced a number of early 20thC artists such as Giacomo Balla, Umberto Boccioni and Marcel Duchamp. This collection was given to the town by the Collège de France and it includes his prints and instruments.

BERZÉ-LA-VILLE
Saône-et-Loire Map D4

This undistinguished little village SE of Cluny was once a retreat for monk pupils from the great Abbey of Cluny. The chapel lies a short distance from the main group of buildings.

Chapelle des Moines

Open Apr–Nov 9.30am–noon, 2–6pm
Closed Dec–Mar, Sun mornings, Tues afternoons

From the outside there is very little to the Priory of Berzé-la-Ville that would lead you to expect the brilliant cycle of **Romanesque frescoes** in the interior. These are not only very attractive works of art but also the only substantial group of Cluniac paintings to have come down to us, and they provide important evidence concerning the workshop manner and techniques of 12thC craftsmen. The frescoes have survived because at some stage the walls were whitewashed, and it was not until 1887 that the paintings were rediscovered by the parish priest. Beneath this protective covering the colours have survived extremely well.

The principal scene is on the vault of the chancel, depicting a ***Christ in Majesty*** presenting a scroll to St Peter. Other scenes, especially those from the lives of ***St Lawrence*** and ***St Blaise***, have a markedly Byzantine character, suggesting that there must have been a considerable traffic in art and artists between the Eastern and Western churches as late as the 12thC.

BESANÇON
Doubs, Franche-Comté Map E2

Besançon, the capital and largest town of the Franche-Comté, has a splendid location in a loop of the river Doubs, giving it a strikingly beautiful appearance when approached on the main roads. The strategic value of the site was recognized at an early stage, and successive rulers from Julius Caesar to Louis XIV have extended the fortifications. Some of these are still in evidence and the network of streets which makes up the old town is clearly circumscribed by the remains of the old ramparts. Among the buildings of Besançon the citadel with its local museums is the most impressive, but the old town also has a number of fine religious and secular buildings. These include the 16thC Palais Granvelle with its fine tapestries, and the 12thC Cathedral of Saint-Jean.

Musee des Beaux-Arts et d'Archéologie ☆

Place de la Revolution

Tel. (81) 814447
Open 9.30am–noon, 2–5.50pm
Closed Tues

The Besançon museum can claim with justice to be the oldest public gallery in France: pictures amassed by the Abbé Boisot in the 17thC, which are the nucleus of the present collection, were put on public display as early as 1694. It has of course changed considerably since then, being greatly expanded, and is now housed in the old covered wheat market overlooking a market place that is still very much alive to this day. From the outside the building does not look very promising, but the interior is pleasant if unobtrusive and the ground floor galleries, containing antiquities and decorative arts such as furniture, ceramics and glass, are well proportioned with good displays. In the upper floors mainly devoted to paintings, a curious system of ramps and half-landings has been installed, rather like a new skeleton frame in an older building, which takes some getting used to. Despite the bare concrete walls, however, it is overall a successful development because it extends the exhibition space; but not all the works, and particularly those from the earlier periods, are suited to such an environment.

The Italian Renaissance is represented by two good pictures, ***The Drunkenness of Noah*** by Giovanni Bellini and a large ***Deposition*** altarpiece by the Florentine Mannerist Agnolo Bronzino, but despite these works it is overshadowed by a superior collection of northern European art from the same period. The small ***Virgin*** is perhaps not by Rogier van der Weyden, though attributed to him, but is a fine painting nevertheless, and there are several delightful pictures by Lucas Cranach, the lascivious ***Courtesan and Old Man*** ★ being the most impressive. There are also some good portraits in this section, such as Clouet's ***François de Scepaux*** and Hans Eworth's magnificent ***Portrait of a Gentleman from the English Court***.

Following this the 17thC collection seems comparatively thin and only Zurbaran's unusual ***Flight into Egypt*** stands out conspicuously. However, the 18thC and 19thC sections are more substantial. Sharing the first floor galleries with a collection of clocks and horology, these pictures are mainly French with Boucher's decorative ***Chinois*** series taking up most of one wall, but there are a few notable exceptions. A number of late **"Black Paintings"** by Goya of cannibals and fight scenes, is gruesomely interesting. There are also several pictures by the English artists Bonington, Thomas Lawrence and Constable – rarities in French provincial museums. Otherwise the principal attraction is the room devoted to Courbet. Courbet was of course a native of this region and he is represented by some of his greatest paintings: an early ***Self Portrait***, ***The Peasants of Flagey Returning From Market***, ***The Sleep-walker*** and the large hunting scene ***Death of the Stag***. ★

Recently the town received a large number of 20thC paintings and prints from the collection of George and Adèle Besson, and these are now displayed in the new galleries on the top floor. The Bessons' taste ran primarily to the great French colourists, and their collection includes **portraits** of themselves that they commissioned from Renoir, Bonnard and Matisse. These artists, together with Marquet and Signac, represent the greatest part of the collection, although there are a number of more recent works by lesser known artists.

As well as its paintings, the Besançon museum also has an excellent **collection of French drawings** ★ with particular emphasis on the 18thC and 19thC. Virtually all the major French artists of the period are represented but it is the works by Fragonard, Hubert Robert and David that deserve highlighting for their particular quality.

Musée Historique

Palais Granvelle
96 Grande Rue
Tel. (81) 818012
Open 9.30am–noon, 2–6pm
Closed Tues

The Musée Historique in the 16thC palace of the influential Granvelle family provides a historical survey of the Franche-Comté, using paintings, prints, maps and even tapestries. These exhibits are chosen for their relevance to the area rather than for any aesthetic merit, but there are a few attractive pictures which have more than merely local significance. The portraits are the finest, particularly those of ***Nicolas Perrenot de Granvelle*** by Charles Quint and ***Simon Renard and his Wife*** by Antonio Moro, but there is also a good Dutch ***Landscape*** from the 17thC by Demarne.

Cathédrale St-Jean

Rue de la Convention
Open all year

Unlike many of the churches in France the cathedral of Saint-Jean in Besançon has a considerable number of paintings, the finest of which is the large altarpiece of the ***Madonna and Saints*** ★ by Fra Bartolommeo (on the right hand side of the choir). Painted in Rome in 1512 for Ferry Carondelet, it is one of this artist's most beautiful works, well preserved and with a sensitive handling of light and colour for so grand a picture.

In other parts of the cathedral there are pictures by the French 18thC artists Natoire, Van Loo and Troy, and a remarkable 4thC marble altar, reputedly donated by the empress Helena, mother of Constantine the Great. In the Chapter library there is an interesting collection of ecclesiastical treasures.

BROU

Ain, Bourgogne Map E4

Brou is now a suburb of the much larger conurbation of Bourg-en-Bresse, a major market town for the farming produce of southern Burgundy.

Musée de l'Ain and Eglise de Brou ☆

Boulevard de Brou
Bourg-en-Bresse
Tel. (74) 222231
Open Apr–Sept 8.30am–noon, 2–6.30pm; Oct–Mar 10am–noon, 2–4.30pm

The church at Brou was embellished in the 16thC to fulfil a vow made by Margaret of Bourbon in 1480. Her husband Count Philip of Bresse was paralysed as a result of a hunting accident, and Margaret vowed to endow a monastery at Brou if he should be restored to health. Miraculously or not, he did regain his strength, but she herself died soon after and it was not until 1504 that her daughter-in-law Margaret of Austria, whose own husband Philibert the Handsome had died aged only 24, took up the project. Given this background it is understandable that the commission should turn out to be a monument to the deceased, with the main part of the work displayed in the funerary chapel. The nave of the church itself is relatively plain with only a few pieces of sculpture to break up the main lines of the architecture, but the decorative **rood screen** gives some idea of what to expect: the **chapel** at the rear is little short of an eruption of the most elaborate Flamboyant Gothic decoration. The architecture, choir stalls, marble altarpiece, stained glass windows (and at one time even the tiled floor) all present a profusion of ornamental decoration that is breathtaking and, on closer inspection, marvellous in its technical virtuosity.

Within this setting the **three tombs** ★ of Margaret of Bourbon, Philibert the Handsome and Margaret of Austria are the principal feature. Margaret of Austria's is the finest, and it is impossible to remain unmoved by the magnificence of the baldacchino or canopy. Almost equally impressive, however, are the **two effigies** by the German sculptor Conrad Meyt, acutely observed studies of character, even in death. The purpose of the two effigies is to present both the stately and the human character of the royal personage: the figure on the catafalque has courtly robes while the lower one is in a winding sheet ready for burial. This distinction is dramatically emphasized on the tomb of Philibert, where the lower figure displays the marks of advanced decay.

Buildings of this richness are not to everyone's taste, but the chapel at Brou has come down to us virtually untouched by the ravages of time and vandalism. In the words of Erwin Panowski, it is "the most enchanting of all places dedicated to the memory of the dead".

Behind the church, the Musée de l'Ain now uses the much plainer monastery buildings to display a fairly large collection of paintings, sculpture, furniture and ceramics. The most interesting pictures are those by Canaletto, Largillière, Velvet Breughel and Defendente Ferrari. One room has a collection of portrait heads by Alphonse Baudin (1819–1902), a native of Bourg, and the local emphasis is maintained in the Salle du Coq with various representations of poultry, a major product of the area.

CHALON-SUR-SAÔNE

Saône-et-Loire, Bourgogne Map D3

Chalon-sur-Saône, one of the largest towns in Burgundy and an important industrial area, serves as a port for much of the region, for many river craft and barges can navigate the Saône for most of its length. Ever since the Middle Ages, a carnival and parade, the Foire des Sauvagines, has been held in the town in February of each year.

Musée Denon

Place de l'Hôtel de Ville
Tel. (85) 480170
Open 9.30am–noon, 2–5.30pm
Closed Tues

The impressive Neoclassical building which houses the Chalon museum is sited on an old Ursuline convent and appropriately named after Vivant

Denon, the man who organized the museum system in France under Napoleon. Inside, the large collection of mainly French and Dutch paintings is displayed in a series of fine galleries, and there is also an archaeological department in the basement and a small section of modern prints on the first floor. The most interesting pictures are the **17thC Dutch still lifes** by Bollongier and De Heem, the early portraits such as that of ***Elizabeth, Queen of Bohemia*** by Mierevelt (1622), and an excellent ***oil study of a Negro*** by Géricault – the finest of a good group of French 19thC works.

Denon himself seems to have been something of a printmaker, and several of his engravings and their copper plates are on display alongside works by his contemporaries. It must be said, however, that they are not really very good.

In the nearby Hôtel des Messageries, an 18thC town house by the river, there is a museum of photography containing early **photographic prints** and cameras commemorating the work of J.N. Niépce, a native of Chalon, who in 1826 made the world's first photograph (now in the Gernsheim Collection at the University of Texas).

CHAROLLES

Saône-et-Loire, Bourgogne Map D4

The town of Charolles in southern Burgundy is the capital of the bucolic sub-region of the Charollais, where the large white cattle of that name are bred and reared. It also possesses two small museums devoted to the work of two local artists.

Musée Jean Laronze

Rue Badinot
Tel. (85) 241397
Open Easter – Oct
Closed Nov – Easter

After a false start in a commercial career Jean Laronze took up painting in 1882 at the age of 30, and quickly achieved considerable success. He worked mainly in the Charollais, treating landscapes, seascapes and peasant scenes with a typically melancholic calm, despite his use of a rich palette. Several of these paintings, as well as prints and traditional furniture, are displayed in the 17thC courthouse.

Musée René Davoine

32 Rue René Davoine
Tel. (85) 241397
Open Easter – Oct
Closed Nov – Easter

The Musee René Davoine, in the street names after the artist, is a modest affair. Davoine (1888 – 1962) was born and died in Charolles, although he was trained in sculpture at the academy of Buenos Aires in Argentina. Most of his work is in wood, and the museum contains a range of figurative pieces with documentation of the artist's career.

CHÂTILLON-SUR-SEINE

Côte-d'Or, Bourgogne Map C2

Located on the upper reaches of the Seine, Châtillon has frequently suffered from military action in the course of its history. The town figured prominently during Napoleon's Hundred Days in 1814, when the French leader was fighting desperately against the other European powers. In 1914 General Joffre made a stand here in the opening months of the First World War. Châtillon also suffered great damage in World War II, as a result of which it has been largely rebuilt.

Musée Municipal

7 Rue de Bourg
Tel. (80) 912467
Open mid-Mar to mid-June 9am – noon, 2 – 6pm; mid-June to mid-Sept 9am – noon, 2 – 7pm; mid-Sept to mid-Mar 10am – noon, 2 – 5pm
Closed mid-Sept to mid-June Mon, Tues, Thurs, Fri

The museum at Châtillon contains a sensational treasure trove of archaeology that will also appeal to art-lovers, the so-called **Vix Treasure**. It was in 1953 that an extensive archaeological excavation took place in the area, during which the keeper of the Châtillon museum uncovered at Vix, near the foot of nearby Mont Lassois, the tomb of a woman, presumably a Gallic princess, dated to the 6thC BC. The grave goods interred with this body include numerous decorative and practical items, some in bronze and gold.

The treasure ranged from finely wrought earrings to a massive ceremonial chariot, and it now constitutes the bulk of the collection on display at the Châtillon municipal museum. The most impressive item is a large bronze vase, nearly 1.8m (6ft) in height, richly designed and skilfully executed. It has Gorgons' heads on the handles and a lively decorative frieze in relief at the neck, depicting a procession of plumed and helmeted warriors.

CLAMECY
Nièvre, Bourgogne Map C3

The old town of Clamecy is a maze of steep, winding streets and old houses clustered round the 13thC–15thC Gothic church of St-Martin, a curious building with a Flamboyant façade and tower. Strategically situated on the river Yonne, Clamecy's traditional industry used to be handling the logs that were floated downstream from the hill forests, and although this activity has died out, the channels, locks and weirs surrounding the town are a constant reminder of it. Romain Rolland, the Nobel prizewinning writer and music critic, was born in Clamecy in 1866, and is commemorated by a portrait bust in the main square.

Musée Municipal
Hôtel de Bellegarde
Avenue de la République
Tel. (86) 271799
Open 10am–noon, 2–7pm
Closed Tues

The 17thC mansion of the Duc de Bellegarde which houses the municipal museum has undergone extensive renovation in recent years, particularly in the interior, and the limited collection is now very well displayed in pleasant surroundings. This is particularly the case with the ceramics, most of which come from the Nevers potteries of the 18thC and 19thC. Of the paintings, a ***Landscape*** by the 17thC Dutch artist Jan Wijnants is probably the finest, and some small 19thC ***French Landscapes*** by Harpignies, Diaz and Troyon provide a good complement to this work.

There are also two special displays, one on the first floor devoted to *flottage*, the traditional logging activities of the town, and the other, in a separate gallery on the ground floor, consisting of ***Art Deco posters*** by Loupot from the 1920s and 1930s. The latter group was presented to the town by a friend of the artist, and it includes several experimental designs and trial printings of well-known advertisements.

CLUNY
Saône-et-Loire, Bourgogne Map D4

The first monastery at Cluny was established in 910, and soon afterwards its rapid expansion as the "mother house" of the Benedictine order required extensive rebuilding to accommodate an influx of monks and administrators. Altogether there were three successive abbey churches, of which the last, begun in 1088, was the most important. This gigantic Romanesque building had an unusual plan with five naves, a narthex and two separate transepts, but the most striking feature was undoubtedly its immense scale. At nearly 30.5m (100ft) high and 183m (600ft) long it was the largest church in Europe, and its influence on the religious life of the period as well as the architecture was immense. At one time there were more than 10,000 monks from Cluny, and 1,450 "daughter houses" in France, Germany, Italy and England. From its peak in the 13thC, however, the abbey's fortunes steadily declined and the building suffered repeated damage until the Revolution, when it was closed and almost completely destroyed. What survives, although still impressive, is merely a small part of the original abbey complex.

Musée Lapidaire du Farinière
Tel. (85) 591779
Open Apr–Sept 9–11.30am, 2–6pm, Oct–Mar 10–11.30am, 2–4pm

Musée Ochier
Palais Abbatial
Tel. (85) 590587
Open 9am–noon, 2–6.30pm (4pm winter)
Closed Dec 20 to mid-Jan

Cluny today gives an overriding impression not only of admiration at its former greatness, but also of disappointment at how little is left, and this feeling is borne out by the contents of the museums as much as by the town. Given the scale of the abbey and its importance, and even bearing in mind the destruction of several centuries, it is still surprising how much has disappeared, so that Cluny's two museums have to rely on models and reconstructions to suggest what must once have been a truly spectacular complex of buildings. Both the **Musée Farinière**, located in the surviving abbey outbuilding, and the **Musée Ochier** in the nearby bishop's palace, have some sculpted capitals and fragments on display, and the Musée Ochier has a few paintings on the first floor, but in general the collections are a bit thin. There is no sense of the scale of a building so huge that several whole streets in the present town were once the ancient passageways of pilgrims that formerly lay inside the body of the church. A room in the Musée Ochier displays scale models of the Cluny ecclesiastical buildings.

DIJON
Côte-d'Or, Bourgogne Map D2

The rise of Dijon as the adminstrative head of Burgundy dates from the 12thC when Robert I decided to move his court into the area, but it was not until the accession of the Valois dukes in the 14thC that the town became a worthy setting for the effective capital of a greatly enlarged duchy. Under Philip the Bold (1364–1404) Dijon acquired a ducal palace, a court and the attendant services, including a retinue of artists, musicians and scholars that went to make this one of the cradles of the northern Renaissance. Even after the decline of the ducal house and the absorption of Burgundy into France, the town continued to be a focal point of the region and, as the architecture reflects, a cultural center of some importance. There can be no better example of this than the two principal churches: the **Cathédrale St-Benigne**, a pure Gothic structure from the early 14thC, and, at the opposite side of the town center, the more imposing **Eglise St-Michel**, one of the finest Renaissance façades in France. Later periods and styles are likewise in evidence, and many of the houses and streets around the Palais des Ducs display the classicism of Hardouin-Mansart, the architect of Versailles. Dijon's position has been maintained into the present century mainly as a result of the railways, and its importance will presumably continue as it remains on the major routes between Paris and the south east.

Musée des Beaux-Arts ☆
1 Rue Rameau
Tel. (80) 303111
Open 10am–6pm

The Musée des Beaux-Arts of Dijon is housed in a wing of the old palace of the Dukes of Burgundy in the middle of the town. The palace was begun in the 15thC, and part of this building still survives, but there have been so many alterations and extensions in virtually every period since then that it now appears to be substantially a classical complex of the 18thC and 19thC, lacking any great architectural distinction.

The museum's entrance hall contains a scale model of the **Well of Moses**, complete with the calvary in place. The remains of this medieval masterpiece can still be seen in the nearby CHARTREUSE DE CHAMPMOL, destroyed in the 1790s, but it is appropriate that the model should be here, since the greatest works in the museum's collection were also originally in the Chartreuse before it was destroyed. These are now displayed in the Salle des Gardes, where the minstrel's gallery contains the majestic **tombs of Philip the Bold** ★ and **John the Fearless** ★; robust stone catafalques complete with reclining effigies of the dead dukes. Of the two, Philip the Bold's is the finer and it conforms to a design prepared by Jean de Marville incorporating a miniature funeral procession through Gothic cloisters underneath the figure. Marville did not live to realize the scheme, but in 1389 his pupil Claus Sluter brought a masterly genius to bear on the project and created a series of *pleurants*, or weepers, in hooded monk's habits, that express clear and individual human emotions. This monument was so much admired at the time that the eventual commission for the tomb of John the Fearless in 1443 requested little more than a copy, and Juan de la Huerta produced just that, only more elaborate in its details.

In the same room is another treasure from the Chartreuse that could almost be said to represent the same breakthrough in painting that Sluter's work achieved in sculpture. When the elaborate carved altarpiece from Champmol required further decoration in 1394, Melchior Broederlam was commissioned to paint scenes from the ***Nativity*** ★ on the outside of the shutters. Broederlam's problems were compounded by the unusual shape of the panels and the need to weave different scenes into the same space, but he produced paintings of the ***Virgin and Child*** which for virtually the first time in medieval art revealed genuine human values, pointing towards the naturalism of the succeeding generation. The maturing of this tendency can be observed in an oil painting in the adjoining room, also from Champmol, that marks the beginning of the great phase of early Flemish art. The Dijon ***Nativity*** ★, painted around 1425 by the Master of Flémalle, speaks a different pictorial language from the primitive works which surround it. Instead of the flat gold background there is a subtle transition of colour and light over an extended landscape and, what is more, an attention to detail that ushers in the age of Jan van Eyck.

The bulk of the museum's picture collection is displayed according to national schools in the first floor galleries. In the first of these are the Italian paintings from the Renaissance, among which the Venetian works such as ***St Sebastian*** by Bassano and the ***Portrait of a Woman*** by Lorenzo Lotto are the most interesting. This room is followed by a very good group of early German and Swiss paintings from the Dard collection, given to the town in 1916. Part of the attraction of these pictures is no doubt due to the fact that work of this kind is rarely seen outside the country of origin, but the **panels** by Wolgemut (who was Dürer's master), Schongauer, and especially Conrad Witz, bear comparison with most works from other schools.

Throughout the remaining galleries on the first floor it is the French and Dutch schools which predominate, with a preference for the traditional and academic artists of the 17thC and 18thC. This can be explained by the fact that Dijon had an Académie des Beaux-Arts in the 18thC which amassed a large part of the present collection and, if nothing else, it does reflect the taste of that period. There are nevertheless a number of paintings which can still be regarded as attractive as well as "important": Frans Hals' ***Portrait of a Gentleman*** and Ter Borch's ***Portrait of a Burgomeister*** are both good examples of Dutch restraint in portraiture, while the ***Virgin and St Francis*** by Rubens is in the full-blown Flemish Baroque style of the 17thC. In the rooms devoted to French art it is the 18thC pictures which are the most interesting, particularly Nattier's ***Portrait of Marie Leczinska*** (the wife of Louis XV) and Hubert Robert's ***Caprices*** and ***Ruins***. There is also a small group of works by P.P. Prud'hon – a ***Portrait of Georges Anthony*** and some sketches – who was a student in the Dijon academy between 1774 and 1780.

Local artists are in fact fairly well represented, but they do not match up to the work from the major national schools. Pompon, the animal sculptor who had considerable popularity in his native Burgundy, has a room to himself containing models and maquettes, and the painters of Dijon have a separate gallery on the second floor.

Unfortunately they are rather dull, lacking even the excesses of the fashionable Salon artists which can at least be entertaining. Blanchard's ***First Mass in America*** falls into the latter category, since it looks to be set in a botanic garden with a few Samoan extras for Indians, but the rest of the section could easily be passed over.

The modern galleries, recently refitted to accommodate the Granville Collection, are a refreshing contrast. Whoever arranged this display must have had a sense of humour because the entrance is marked by a painting entitled ***Art, Misère, Désespoir, Folie*** (J. Blin 1880). Since it depicts an artist trampling on one of his canvases with a gun in his hand and a crazed look on his face the title doesn't really require translation, but it could lead to a misunderstanding of Rodin's **Age of Bronze** in the next room, where a life size male nude is represented with his hand on his head. The collection overall is rich in 19thC French paintings and drawings. Particularly good are Manet's ***Plums*** and ***Portrait of Mary Laurent***, Monet's ***Etretat*** and Felix Vallotton's ***Woman Tying her Hair***, but there are also impressive works by Géricault, Delacroix, Victor Hugo, Millet, Boudin, Moreau and Redon. The 20thC gallery is likewise dominated by French artists, or at least artists who worked in France, and there is a very good display of paintings by Delaunay, Modigliani, Gris and Kandinsky, interspersed with the African masks which inspired some of their work. Later pictures from the School of Paris take up most of the gallery but these appear slightly anaemic in comparison with the work of Braque and Picasso, both of whom are represented by drawings.

Chartreuse de Champmol

Hôpital la Chartreuse
1 Boulevard Chanoine Kir
Tel. (80) 432323
Open 9am – 6pm

The Chartreuse de Champmol was intended as a monastery and burial place to glorify the memory of the Capetian Dukes of Burgundy, and to this end Philip the Bold commissioned an elaborate series of buildings and monuments in the 1390s from the greatest craftsmen available. One of these, Claus Sluter, a sculptor from the Low Countries, produced a large well known as the **Well of Moses** ★ and a **Portal to the Ducal Chapel** ★ with five statues which are collectively one of the most important achievements of northern monumental sculpture, majestically bridging the divide between the Gothic and the Renaissance. The Chartreuse was demolished during the Revolution, and the site is now occupied by a psychiatric hospital, but Sluter's two principal monuments survive and can still be visited.

The **Portal** has been incorporated into the hospital chapel, so the figures of Philip the Bold and his wife Margaret are still presented to the Madonna across the two doorways by their respective patron saints. Nearby, in an unusual glass structure like a 19thC greenhouse, are the remains of the **Well of Moses**. Originally there was a calvary above the hexagonal base but this has disappeared leaving the six life-size prophets as a record of the sculptor's masterpiece. Within the bulky robes that help to create their powerful sense of scale, these figures have the quality that was once described as *gravitas*: not mourning but resignation to the part they each play in the prefiguration of Christ. Traditionally Sluter was thought to have taken his models from the Dijon ghetto, and when one sees the presence and naturalism of these figures the story is easy to believe.

Musée Magnin

4 Rue des Bons Enfants
Tel. (80) 671110
Open 9am–noon, 2–6pm
Closed Tues

The Musée Magnin is a 17thC mansion with an impressive central staircase running the whole height of the building, and it has been well furnished and decorated in a mid-19thC style. As an architectural monument with a period interior it would be worthy of interest in its own right, but it has the additional attraction of a number of excellent paintings. Its original owner, Maurice Magnin, presented it to the nation in 1937, and also directed that his substantial collection of pictures should be hung there.

The lower galleries contain Italian and Flemish pictures, among which the landscapes by Paul Bril and Magnasco, and the ***Self-Portrait*** by A.R. Mengs are probably the most interesting. The suite of furnished rooms surrounding the courtyard on the first floor are devoted to French paintings. Here Poussin's ***Landscape with a Serpent*** is the earliest picture of real quality. David is represented by an oil sketch, as are his pupils and contemporaries Guérin, Girodet and Prud'hon, while Gros's ***Portrait of a Woman with a Necklace*** is the finest work in the museum. Finally there are a number of 19thC sketches and drawings, including some by Géricault and Granet. There are also some portraits by minor artists which, if they were not hung in such a sympathetic environment would probably be overlooked, but are displayed to maximum advantage in this Bourgeois setting.

Musée Archéologique

5 Rue Docteur Maret
Tel. (80) 308854
Open 9am–noon, 2–6pm
Closed Tues

The archaeology museum occupies the surviving wing of the abbey that was originally linked to the Cathédrale St-Benigne. In fact the medieval section, which is the largest in the museum, is displayed in the monks' dormitory, a big vaulted hall on the first floor. Unfortunately the scale of this gallery has the effect of making the collection seem rather sparse, but you should not overlook one piece of genuine quality: the head and torso of Christ from Claus Sluter's ***Well of Moses***. In the company of undistinguished Romanesque and Gothic carvings, Sluter's powerful naturalism comes to the fore despite the fragmentary state of the figure.

In recent years the Gallo-Roman section has been renovated and the new display in the basement goes some way towards displaying this material in a lively and interesting manner.

DOLE

Jura, Franche-Comté Map D2

Dole, on the river Doubs in the easternmost part of the Jura, has an impressive history as one of the principal administrative towns of France during the 15thC. Its significance, though diminished, continued into the 17thC and the town still shows the remains of this in a number of elegant buildings. The old quarter in particular has several attractive streets around the 16thC church of Notre-Dame. Dole was the birthplace of the great bacteriologist Louis Pasteur.

Musée Municipal

85 Rue des Arènes
Tel. (84) 722772
Open Easter–Christmas 10am–noon, 2–6pm
Closed Christmas–Easter, Tues

The museum of Dole, founded in 1822 and recently transferred to a renovated 18thC building, is now divided into two separate sections of archaeology and painting. Of the latter there are several interesting French works, including a **late 15thC panel** by the Master of St-Gilles and a picture of ***The Death of Dido*** by Simon Vouet, a court painter of Louis XIII in the first half of the 17thC.

GRAY

Haute-Saône, Franche-Comté Map D2

Gray is an agricultural town overlooking the Saône in the northern part of the Franche-Comté.

Musée Baron Martin

Château du Baron Martin
Rue Pigalle

Tel. (84) 650257
Open Apr–Sept 9am–noon, 1–6pm, Oct–Mar 9am–noon, 2–5pm
Closed Tues

Numerous signs urging a visit to Gray's civic museum appear on the roads leading to the town, and their recommendation is worth following: the 18thC mansion in the castle gardens which houses the Musée Baron Martin is indeed of interest, being crammed to overflowing with a wide range of paintings, sculpture, prints, furniture and Gallo-Roman antiquities. Formed in 1900 as a result of several bequests, the collection is displayed in a series of interconnected rooms on two floors. Many of these are decorated and furnished in 18thC and early 19thC style, which is appropriate enough since a large number of the paintings are from that period. Two rooms, for example, are devoted to a **collection of drawings and prints** by Prud'hon (1758–1823), a contemporary and rival of David who lived in Gray in the 1790s. Other periods and schools are also represented, and there are several 17thC Dutch pictures, including **landscapes** by Mompers and Hobbema, and a large number of late 19thC French Symbolist paintings such as Aman Jean's ***Blooms*** and Henri Martin's ***Apparition***. Throughout the museum there are numerous prints, and it is worth looking out for the extensive **collection of etchings** by Albert Besnard (1849–1934), an artist of local origin. These are fascinating not for their quality as works of art but as a commentary on French art and life at the turn of the century. Finally there is an archaeological section which might be overlooked because it is in the vaulted cellar of the house, but it is well displayed and lit in spite of its enclosed setting.

LONS-LE-SAUNIER

Jura, Franche-Comté Map D3

In common with several towns in the Jura, Lons-le-Saunier has long been a tourist area and a spa where visitors could sample the therapeutic effects of the salt waters. The appearance of Lons-le-Saunier is more attractive than most, however, because much of the town center was rebuilt in the 17thC and 18thC with arcades that give the shopping streets a lively and elegant appearance.

Musée Municipal

Hôtel de Ville
Place Perraud
Tel. (84) 472693
Open Mon, Wed–Fri 10am–noon, 2–6pm; Sat, Sun 2–5pm
Closed Tues

Founded in 1811, the museum at Lons-le-Saunier is one of the earliest in this region, and it has been fortunate in amassing a good collection with a strong archaeological section. The paintings and sculpture however, are not overshadowed by this, and among French, Flemish and Italian works from the 17thC and 18thC there are good pictures by Simon Vouet and Courbet, as well as an impressive ***Massacre of the Innocents*** by the 16thC Dutch painter Pieter Breughel.

MÂCON

Saône-et-Loire, Bourgogne Map D4

The ancient town of Mâcon on the Saône in southern Burgundy gives its name to the great wine-producing area of the Mâconnais, and in recognition of its distinction a national wine festival is held in the town every year in May. The writer, poet and statesman Lamartine was born in Mâcon in 1790.

Musée Lamartine

Hôtel Senecé
21 Rue Sigorgne
Open May–Sept 2–5pm
Closed Tues

The imposing and elegant Hôtel Senecé, an early 18thC house in the French Regency style, is the home of the Académie du Mâcon as well as the Musée Lamartine which celebrates the town's most famous son. The museum has preserved many of the original fittings, although it is slightly dilapidated, and contains documents and souvenirs from Lamartine's career as well as some good furniture, tapestries and a few paintings.

Musée Municipal des Ursulines

5 Rue des Ursulines
Tel. (85) 381884
Open 10am–noon
Closed Tues

The Musée des Ursulines is the kind of comprehensive civic museum that caters to a variety of interests rather than concentrating on a particular theme. All the collections are well displayed in appropriate settings, and the museum building has only recently been modernized, with considerable success. As the name implies, it was originally an Ursuline convent dating from the 17thC, and its opening in 1971 enabled the authorities to bring together disparate elements which had previously been displayed in several different locations. The paintings, sculpture, furniture and ceramics share the museum with sections devoted to ethnography, archaeology, natural history and folk customs, but this does not detract in the least from what is a fairly large collection of fine and decorative arts.

The paintings, mainly Dutch and French, occupy several large galleries on the second and third floors, and there are examples of work by Courbet, Monet and Puvis de Chavannes. There are also some good pictures by local artists that provide an interesting complement to the main national schools. Gaston Bussière, for example, was an artist whose work between the 1890s and the 1920s was fairly traditional and is therefore rarely exhibited nowadays, but it is nevertheless attractive, particularly the exotic and sensual ***Salammbo***, inspired by Flaubert's novel.

MOREZ
Jura, Franche-Comté Map E3

Morez, on the river Bienne, is in the heart of the most scenic and rugged country of the Jura. The town's principal industry has for many generations been the production of telescopes and optical instruments, and a local craftsman is credited with the invention of the pince-nez. The local museum is partly devoted to a survey of these objects, with items from different parts of the world.

Musée Jourdain
Hôtel de Ville
Tel. (84) 472693
Closed Winter

The Morez museum possesses a considerable display of telescopes, eye-glasses and optical instruments, as befits its claim to be "The Capital of Spectacle-making", but the museum has in addition a collection of landscape paintings by the so-called *petits maitres* or minor masters of the 17thC and 18thC. There is nothing of outstanding merit in this gallery, but these pictures are pleasing to look at, and make an interesting introduction to French provincial art of this period.

NEVERS
Nièvre, Bourgogne Map C4

The capital of the province of Nivernais, Nevers occupies a picturesque site at the confluence of the rivers Loire and Nièvre. The medieval town grew up on the hill overlooking the rivers, and the old quarter, with its cathedral, ducal palace and medieval churches still dominates the skyline. During the 16thC, the Gonzaga family, were largely responsible for introducing and fostering the ceramic arts for which the town has long been famous.

Musée Municipal Frédéric Blandin
16 Rue Saint-Genest
Tel. (86) 573786
Open Feb–Oct 10am–noon, 2–6pm
Closed Jan–Nov, Tues

This excellent collection has recently transferred to the old Benedictine abbey of Notre-Dame, where the exhibits can be viewed in the charming surroundings of the chapter house and nun's cells. Some of the works can be seen in an adjoining building which was once occupied by the police headquarters, and which has now been annexed and renovated by the museum.

Naturally, the strength of the permanent collection lies in its comprehensive coverage of the faience of Nevers, and the visitor walking round the museum can trace the development of the art through its various stages, from the first Italianate style, through to the Oriental influence of the middle years, and the eventual establishment of a Nivernais style. Spun glass, another speciality of Nevers, enamel work, Flemish tapestries and coins by Jacques Gallois are also on display. Perhaps surprisingly, there is also a collection of modern art which includes works by painters such as Dufy, Suzanne Valadon, Picabia and Gromaire.

Musée Archéologique du Nivernais
Porte du Croux
Rue de la Porte de Croix
Open June–Sept 2–6pm, Oct–May Sat, Sun 2–6pm
Closed Oct–May Mon–Sat, holidays

This museum occupies the square 14thC tower of the Porte du Croux, a remnant of the town's fortifications. The collection comprises **Gallo-Roman** and **medieval sculptures**, mostly of local origin, and some statues, capitals and retables from old churches in Nevers.

ORNANS
Doubs, Franche-Comté Map E2

Ornans, one of the most picturesque towns in the Franche-Comté, is built round the river Loue, where the old houses in the town center seem to huddle over the water, looking right down on it. Their reflection on the calm water is known as the *Miroir de la Loue*. The great Realist painter, Gustave Courbet, was born in the town in 1819.

Musée Gustave Courbet

Rue de la Froidière
Tel. (81) 622330
Open Apr–Oct 9.30am–noon, 2–6pm
Closed Nov–Mar (except weekends), Tues

The Musée Courbet was initially installed in 1947 by the "Friends of Gustave Courbet" in the Hôtel de Ville.
It was not until 1971 that the collection of paintings, drawings, prints and souvenirs of the artist's life was transferred to the house of his birth, overlooking the river. In all there are about 30 paintings and drawings by Courbet in the museum, including some of his landscapes of Ornans and the surrounding area, such as ***Le Miroir d'Ornans*** and ***Le Lac Noir***. There are also some works produced in Paris and in Geneva during the last phase of his career. A good example is the ***Château de Chillon*** on Lake Geneva, a scene which the artist derived from a photograph in an attempt to make his art both modern and free from the traditional associations of "High Art".

These works are expanded by a number of documents and photographs, as well as a few paintings by his contemporaries: artists such as Diaz, Bonvin, Daumier and Gautier who learned from Courbet's work and assisted in the widespread acceptance of the Realist aesthetic in mid 19thC France.

What emerges most strongly from this collection is a rounded picture of an artist who had a powerful feeling for his native region, and who transformed this feeling into an art that challenged the notions of Parisian culture.

PARAY-LE-MONIAL

Saône-et-Loire, Bourgogne Map D4

Paray-le-Monial, the economic focus of the Charollais in southern Burgundy, has two distinctive and interconnected features that link it to the religious history of the area and of the nation. The first is the church itself, a magnificent **early 12thC Romanesque building** constructed under the direction of an abbot of Cluny, and closely modelled on the destroyed abbey of Cluny. The church of Paray-le-Monial originally carried the dedication of Notre-Dame, but has been renamed Sacré-Coeur in celebration of the second important religious feature of the town, namely the fact that it is the center of devotion to the Sacred Heart of Jesus, following a series of visions received by St Marguerite-Marie Alacoque in the 1670s. The saint's remains are preserved in the Convent of the Visitation where she was a nun.

Musée Eucharistique du Hiéron

Route de Charolles
Tel. (85) 811172
Open Apr–Oct 9am–noon, 2–7pm

This museum of sacred art lies only a very short walk from the Basilica of the Sacré-Coeur, but is thematically unconnected with the great Cluniac church. It was founded in 1890 by the Baron de Sarachaga during one of the periodic fits of national devotion to a particular cult. In this case the theme of the Eucharist governed the choice of exhibits for the museum, and the subject is depicted on a number of French, Italian and Flemish paintings between the 15thC and the 18thC. The most interesting of these are the canvases by Guido Reni, Tiepolo and Charles Lebrun, but the finest item in the collection overall is a **12thC tympanum** from the priory at Anzy-le-Duc. This Romanesque relief of Christ teaching, with a series of related figures below, was detached during the Revolution to protect it from damage and found its way to the Château d'Arcy. From there it came to the collection at Paray-le-Monial.

SALINS-LES-BAINS

Jura, Franche-Comté Map E2

Salins-les-Bains was a military stronghold until the 17thC, and some of the ramparts still survive. However, as its name implies, the town first became known for its salt, and a visit to the immensely deep mine, originally worked in Roman times, is still an impressive experience. Extraction also took place from the springwaters, and the salt is still used for medicinal purposes. The great baths are no longer used for cures, however, though they continue to be a popular sight for visitors.

Musée Municipal

Place des Salines
Tel. (84) 731034
Open all year

Though principally devoted to the history of the town and its salt baths, the municipal museum of Salins-les-Bains has a few sculptures and paintings, including a 16thC **Flemish diptych** and several polychrome wooden figures from the churches in the area.

There are plans to open a new museum of religious art in the church of Notre-Dame. This will consist of the collection of paintings and sculptures put together by the Abbé Lacroix, the regional keeper of art and antiquities in the Jura who died recently, leaving an interesting assemblage of predominantly medieval works of art.

SAULIEU
Côte-d'Or, Bourgogne Map C3

Saulieu, once a popular staging post on the main road from Paris to Lyons, is now something of a backwater. Nevertheless, the medieval church of St-Andoche in the town center, begun in the 12thC, is well worth a visit. The church has suffered maltreatment over the centuries, but the carved capitals depicting scenes from the **Life of Christ** show to the full the splendid qualities of Burgundian Romanesque sculpture.

Musée Regional de Saulieu
Place de la Fontaine,
Tel. (80) 640922
Open 10am–noon, 2–7pm
Closed Tues

The small museum of Saulieu beside the church of St-Andoche has a miscellaneous series of displays, including Gallo-Roman implements, a cottage interior, a number of signed menus prepared by a celebrated local chef (Alexandre Dumain), and a cobbler-carpenter's workshop with a lathe for turning wooden clogs. These exhibits are of course of purely local interest, but there is also a collection of maquettes and studies by the animal sculptor François Pompon (1855–1933) who was born in Saulieu. Pompon designed a number of large public monuments, including one in Dijon, as well as small-scale animal pieces, his favourites apparently being tigers and polar bears.

SEMUR-EN-AUXOIS
Côte-d'Or, Bourgogne Map C2

Semur, the capital of the Auxois region, has a prominent rocky location with the impressive remains of an immense 14thC fortress above it. The four huge towers and tall ramparts give some indication of the scale of this fortification, which was traditionally regarded as impregnable.

Nearby is the 13th–14thC Gothic church of Notre-Dame which contains several good paintings and sculptures, including a late 15thC polychrome sculpture group of the **Entombment**.

Musée Municipal
Rue Jean-Jacques Collenot
Tel. (80) 970111
Open July–Aug, Wed, Fri, 10am–noon, 3–6pm
Closed Sept–June

The series of dull, stained prints arranged beside the dingy staircase of the Musée Municipal gives some indication of what to expect of this museum, with its neglected-looking interior. The building, shared with the local library (which itself has a number of illuminated manuscripts and early printed items), was originally a convent and was converted to its new purpose in the middle of the last century to display the collection of the Semur Scientific and Archaeological Society. Much of the collection therefore is devoted to local history, featuring Gallo-Roman antiquities, geological specimens, early coinage and the like. There are also several paintings and sculptures, including three ***Landscapes*** by Corot and a series of **Burgundian sculpted figures** from the 13thC to the 16thC. The 19thC sculptor Dumont, who was responsible for several famous monuments in Paris such as the statue of Napoleon on the Vendôme Column, was a native of Semur, and he is represented by a number of maquettes for his large-scale public works.

SENS
Yonne, Bourgogne Map B2

An important medieval town on the river Yonne in northern Burgundy, Sens has preserved the original layout and character of its old quarter despite its modern role as a busy market town. The historic 12thC **Cathédrale St-Etienne** is one of the earliest manifestations of mature Gothic architecture, with exquisite sculpture and stained glass. The writer and critic Emile Mâle has described the whole building as "unfolding the immensity of the world and the diversity of the works of God".

Depôt Lapidaire du Palais Synodal
Cathédrale St-Etienne
Open 10am–noon, 2–6pm (2–5pm winter)
Closed Tues

Situated beside the great cathedral

façade, the Palais Synodal has been converted into a museum to house some of the magnificent statues, bas-reliefs and fragments of sculpture that originally formed part of the main building. The bulk of the display is medieval, but there is one fine group of sculptures from the 16thC **tomb of Cardinal Duprat**. In addition, however, to this wealth of material from the cathedral, there are two curiosities: an attractively pagan Gallo-Roman mosaic, and a 16thC tapestry depicting ***Judith and Holofernes*** that belonged to Thomas Wolsey, Chancellor of England under Henry VIII.

Musée Municipal

5 Rue Rigault
Tel. (86) 650958
Open mid-May to Sept 10am–noon, 2–6pm, Sun 10am–noon, 3–6pm, Oct to mid-May 10am–noon, 2–5pm
Closed Tues

The Musée Municipal of Sens shares many of the characteristics of other French provincial museums, but emphasizes the traditional aspects to such an extent that it seems still to belong in the late 19thC. The displays, the disposition of the rooms, even the decoration, have the appearance of being unchanged since 1891, when the collection was first put together.

Sens is on the site of a large Roman town, and the medieval walls once incorporated many pieces from antique buildings and sculptures until the celebrated archaeologist Gustave Julliot recovered and assembled them at the end of the last century. These are now spread throughout the museum building, with a particularly large concentration of fragments in a huge room named after the indefatigable archaeologist himself. Here there are hundreds of fragments piled up as in some ancient stonemason's yard.

Proceeding up the stairs, the guide will lead you through rooms of shells, primitive implements, stuffed birds, beetles, Napoleonic souvenirs and other objects before unlocking the barred metal door to the Fine Art section. Here in a long gallery the pictures hang in ranks three or four high across the walls, and the sculptures are placed in a line down the middle, completing this image of a 19thC Salon exhibition. No single piece in the collection is particularly memorable, but perhaps the experience of the place is enough in itself.

Trésor de la Cathédrale St-Etienne

Ancien Archevêche de la Cathédrale de Sens
Possible opening 1985

Although the cathedral treasury is under reconstruction and an opening date is not envisaged before 1985, the treasury which is to be housed in this building, the bishop's palace adjoining the cathedral, must be mentioned for it is one of the richest in France.

The bulk of the collection, consisting of tapestries, manuscripts, reliquaries and a variety of elaborately worked pieces in gold and silver, is predictably of medieval and ecclesiastical origin. Several items, however, have an interesting history, such as the chasuble and overmantle of Thomas à Becket, the martyred archbishop of Canterbury. Others reflect the cosmopolitan nature of the medieval church in its pursuit and acquisition of treasures, including classical pieces of clearly pagan inspiration and even Islamic objects. In fact, one of the two finest pieces in the collection is a 12thC **Islamic casket**. The other is a 10thC Byzantine ivory, the so-called **Sainte Chasse**. Such pieces were hoarded to celebrate not only the glory of God but also the material power of his earthly agents.

TANLAY

Yonne, Bourgogne Map C2

The Château de Tanlay lies a few miles E of Tonerre and a few miles N of **ANCY-LE-FRANC**, with which it is often compared. Both châteaux are from the 16thC, but Tanlay lacks Ancy-le-Franc's consistency of design, being the result of various hands and styles – a fact that possibly makes it more attractive.

Château de Tanlay

Open Mar to Oct 9.15–11.30am, 2.15–5.15pm
Closed Nov to Feb, Tues

The interior of Tanlay contains some well-appointed apartments with good furniture, portraits and sculpted fireplaces from the 16thC and 17thC, but the most interesting room is in the northwestern tower. Here the Andelot brothers, who owned the château in the 16thC, gave support and protection to Huguenot conspirators. **Contemporary wall paintings** depict the developing dispute between Catholics and Protestants in allegorical form, with classical deities representing the leading figures of both parties.

TOURNUS

Saône-et-Loire, Bourgogne Map D3

Tournus was already a monastic town

when, in 875, a party of monks arrived from western France bearing the relics of St Philibert. The result was an amalgamation of two groups with their respective patron saints, Valerian and Philibert, and the erection of a majestic **early Romanesque church** in the 11thC specifically for the latter. Something of the uncertain conditions of the period is suggested by the fortifications surrounding the abbey, and the church itself has a grand austerity typical of Lombard Romanesque that is quite in keeping with these surroundings. It is, nevertheless, beautifully lit from a clerestory revealing the simplicity that was lost in later more sophisticated buildings.

Musée Greuze

Rue du Collège
Tel. (85) 511315
Open Apr–Oct 9.30am–noon, 2–6.30pm
Closed Nov–Mar, Tues, Sun mornings

Founded in 1866 as a museum and a small school of art, the Musée Greuze was intended to honour the painter Jean-Baptiste Greuze, who was born in Tournus in 1725. It is difficult nowadays to understand quite why Greuze's mawkishly sentimental works should have enjoyed such popularity during his lifetime, but critics such as Diderot apparently saw in him an antidote to the frivolous eroticism of mid 18thC Rococo art. At any rate, his moral tone found considerable support, and engravings of his work were sold throughout Europe. In some respects it is this historical significance which maintains the interest in Greuze's work, and the museum has recognized this by introducing a fair amount of comparative material. Examples of the work of artists such as Hogarth and Poussin, as well as the more closely related Boucher and David, share wall space with Greuze's ***early portraits*** and some prints and drawings.

VARZY
Nièvre, Bourgogne Map B3

Varzy in western Burgundy is an ancient town with the remains of its medieval fortifications still in evidence. The 14thC Gothic church of St-Pierre has a number of treasures, including several late medieval caskets and reliquaries.

Musée Municipal

18 Rue St-Jean
Tel. (86) 294571
Open May to mid-Sept 10am–noon, 2–6pm
Closed mid-Sept to Apr, Tues

Varzy has a good municipal gallery for a town of its size, with collections of furniture, ceramics, paintings, sculpture, antiquities and musical instruments that would do justice to a much larger place. The archaeology section includes interesting **Egyptian items** from the Taylor Collection, and several of the more memorable paintings were donated in the last century by the collector Auguste Grasset. Most of the medieval works, however, come from the churches in the area, including some **fine carvings**.

Among the paintings, which are mainly French 18thC and 19thC, look for ***The Dream of Malvina*** by Girodet, a subject from the supposed (but subsequently discredited) Celtic epic *Ossian*, and a ***landscape*** by Daubigny (1817–78) also deserves attention. Among the ceramics, there are some attractive **18thC figurines** from Nevers.

VESOUL
Haute-Saône, Franche-Comté Map D1

Situated in beautiful hilly countryside in the northern part of the Franche-Comté, Vesoul was isolated for centuries until a railway link encouraged some industrial expansion. Today it is a fairly well attended holiday resort. The Salon painter Jean-Léon Gérôme, in his time a very successful member of the art establishment and a violent opponent of the Impressionists, was born at Vesoul in 1824.

Musée Municipal Georges Garret

Ancien Couvent des Ursulines
Tel. (84) 753954
Open Thurs, Sat, 2–6pm (but telephone Hôtel de Ville for confirmation)
Closed Mon, Tues, Wed, Fri, Sat (mornings only)

The municipal museum of Vesoul was reopened in 1981 in the picturesque premises of an old Ursuline convent, bringing together items of furniture, archaeology, painting and sculpture which had previously been displayed in different buildings in the town. Even in its expanded state, however, the art collection is not very strong. It is surprising that the only local artist of renown, Jean-Léon Gérôme (1824–1904), whose highly finished and painstakingly realistic work one might expect to see, is represented only by a single minor painting. Gérôme's main concern was with oriental and archaic subjects.

VÉZELAY
Yonne, Bourgogne Map C3

Situated on a prominent hill above deep surrounding valleys, the town of Vézelay presents a spectacular image of a medieval settlement with its cluster of streets and houses ascending towards the pilgrimage church and abbey on the summit.

Basilique Ste-Madeleine ☆

The **Basilique Ste-Madeleine**, the abbey church founded in the 9thC but substantially rebuilt after a disastrous fire in 1120, is one of the greatest monuments of Romanesque culture and, together with **CLUNY**, exerted a powerful influence on the dissemination of that style throughout the rest of France.

The plan and structure of the building follow the classical principles of Romanesque design, with the simple clarity of the lines emphasized by the alternating dark and light stonework of the rounded vaulting. But it is the relationship between the forms of the architecture and the sculptural decoration that makes Vézelay such a supreme achievement. It is a pity that the façade, badly damaged during the Revolution, has been rather poorly restored, but the interior capitals and the tympanums above the inner doorway of the vast narthex are reasonably intact. **The central tympanum** ★ in particular is a masterpiece of sculpture, a work of outstanding beauty when seen in the pale light of the interior. Its subject matter is the spread of God's word on Earth, with the twelve apostles receiving the Holy Spirit in the form of rays emanating from the hands of a gigantic Christ in glory. This lofty theme contrasts with the lively narrative to be seen at **AUTUN**, Vézelay's nearest rival, but it must have seemed very appropriate to the thousands of pilgrims who flocked to the church during its heyday in the 12thC to hear the preaching of such figures as St Bernard of Clairvaux, or to begin the long pilgrimage to Santiago della Compostella in northern Spain (See p. 210).

Courbet at Ornans

In 1848, Gustave Courbet was living in Paris and poised to embark on the series of great works that would make his reputation. Shunned by the Salon, and revelling in the fact that he was outside the establishment, he moved in a circle of intellectuals, writers and critics that was the self-declared élite of the capital's avant-garde. And yet Courbet already recognized that the future for his art lay outside the limits of a rather precious Bohemianism, outside the insular debates on art and even outside the confines of Paris. Writing of Courbet's pictures in the open Salon of that year, Champfleury remarked that he would be a great painter one day, and had left "for the mountains to follow nature". The mountains that Champfleury was referring to were those of ORNANS, the area where the artist had been born and which provided him with the sources and inspiration for most of his greatest work.

Courbet came from a line of respectable landowners in the Franche Comté, and his father farmed the land around Ornans, an area with a strong identity and culture emphasized by the character of the landscape. Visiting the Doubs nowadays you cannot help but be struck by its remoteness, the ruggedness of the terrain and the dense vegetation, occasionally broken by outcrops revealing the chalk and limestone rock beneath. Courbet knew this area well. He had obviously wandered through it during his childhood and youth, and in 1848 his return there marked the opening of a new phase in his work. Many of his closest friends were also from this area, notably the anarchist P.J. Proudhon and the folklorist Max Buchon.

The first picture to demonstrate Courbet's new principles was ***After Dinner at Ornans*** (Musée des Beaux-Arts, Lille), a depiction of his father and three friends gathered round a table in a simple interior. Its importance was immediately recognized by critics, who drew attention to the fact that Courbet had dared to paint a "genre" picture life size. But this was only part of the master's intention. By displaying the everyday life of the rural bourgeoisie to the Parisian public he destroyed a series of idylls regarding country life, and firmly established his view that painting should be concerned with what was real and concrete. This reality – the countryside, the people and the habits of the Doubs region – was Courbet's birthright, and he proceeded to depict it in a series of blunt, direct and, for the period, challenging works. ***The Peasants of Flagey Returning from the Fair*** (Musée des Beaux-Arts, BESANÇON), ***The Corn Sifters*** (Musée de Nantes) and above all ***The Burial at Ornans*** (Louvre, Paris) broke the back of the academic tradition.

Courbet also began a series of pictures that might be described as roadside scenes, again observed in the Franche Comté. ***The Stonebreakers*** (disappeared, Dresden 1945), the most famous of these, was a group observed by the artists near Maisières. "I stopped to look at two men breaking stones on the road – it's very unusual to come across such a total expression of misery and destitution. The idea of a picture came to me at once."

It would be wrong however to regard Courbet's interest in these subjects as a matter of mere political expediency. He had a genuine love of his native district and he frequently painted landscapes without figures. Le Puits Noir, a spectacular site near Ornans where the river Brême is forced between steep rocks, the Grotte de Plaisir Fontaine, and the Gouffre de Conches, another beauty spot near Salins where Buchon lived, were all treated in several works which sought to communicate the essential character of the place. In this vein, the Source de la Loue was one of his most frequent and arresting subjects. This natural curiosity, where the already powerful stream gushes from a deep cave in the rock, drew from Courbet a range of responses that he recreated with variations in space, composition and colour scheme.

Landscape was also the medium through which he celebrated an immense vitality and love of physical life. The Doubs mountains, especially in winter, were the source of many pictures in which he described scenes from the hunt. Previously an upper-class preserve, this type of painting was revitalized by Courbet in such works as ***Huntsmen Training Hounds*** or ***The Kill*** (Musée des Beaux-Arts BESANÇON).

In 1870, Courbet leapt at the opportunity of real political action in the Paris Commune. He was an official of the Arts Commission, fought alongside other members of the Commune, and arranged for the destruction of the Vendôme Column as a symbol of imperialism and betrayal. For this last act he was arrested by the new Republican government and forced to pay impossible compensation. Unable to meet this, the artist went into exile in Switzerland, the area closest to his beloved Doubs. His last years were passed in disillusionment and misery, separated from the friends and environment that had fuelled his art for nearly 30 years. On his death in 1877 Courbet's body was buried in La Tour de Peilz, Switzerland. It was not until 1919, the centenary of his birth, that his remains were transferred to Ornans.

*A **Landscape near Ornans**, c. 1855, probably Valbois at Flagey.*

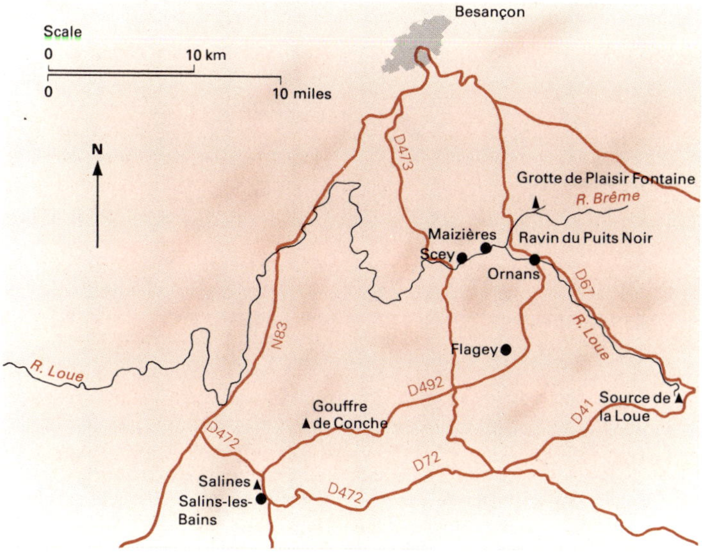

CITY OF PARIS

As an art capital, Paris had had a fitful history. Prominent in Merovingian times (AD 6th-8thC), it became one of the great cathedral cities of France in the later Middle Ages, with Notre-Dame at the heart of a cluster of excellent Gothic churches such as Ste-Chapelle and St-Germain-des Prés. But this artistic development was not sustained, for the Renaissance kings shifted the focus of power and interest to the Loire, to Fontainebleau and eventually, under Louis XIV, to Versailles. Nevertheless the 17thC, the period when Versailles was built, saw Paris emerging into something of an international reputation with the arrival of artists such as Rubens and Bernini, and from then until the 1930s the capital gradually assumed a position as the most famous and influential art center in Europe.

During the 19thC and early 20thC in particular, Paris acquired a near-mythical reputation to artists of other countries as the embodiment of everything that was modern and vital in the arts. Puccini's opera *La Bohème* merely indicated the extent to which the city has become identified with modern art in the popular imagination, with the result that artists from all countries flocked there to complete their education. A period of residence in the Latin Quarter of Montmartre was now seen as a necessary stage in the process of becoming a "true" artist. Of course behind this popular view there was a huge amount of genuine activity in Paris: this was the period when Courbet, Manet, the Impressionists, Gauguin, Matisse and Picasso all made their mark. But it is in the nature of a myth that it survives long after the original conditions have ceased to exist. Late in life, Hemingway wrote of the Paris he had experienced in the 1920s in terms that Baudelaire or Courbet might well have felt was old-fashioned in the 1850s.

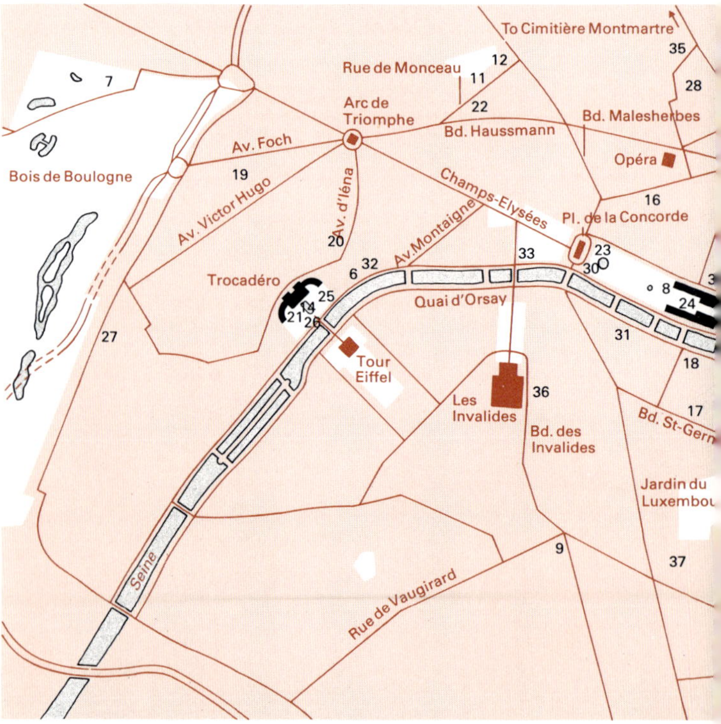

The 19thC heyday of Parisian art and society left the greatest mark on the city's appearance, for the majority of its most famous landmarks were only erected in the last century. NOTRE-DAME, the LOUVRE and several isolated pieces (such as the delightful ***Fontaine des Innocents*** reconstructed in Les Halles) are all early, of course, but the Arc de Triomphe with its sculptures by Rude, the Sacré Coeur, the Opéra, the Madeleine, and the Eiffel Tower were all completed after the time of Napoleon.

The Eiffel Tower was the focal point of an International Exhibition (1889), and these periodic exercises in chauvinism and salesmanship have had a considerable effect on Paris. The Grand Palais with its flamboyant gilded charioteers was built for the jamboree of 1900 and now houses major art exhibitions; the severe Neoclassical Palais de Chaillot, with its equally severe and Neoclassical (but very dull) figures, was erected for the exhibition of 1937. Most of the independent sculpture is fortunately superior to this, and between the façade of Notre-Dame to the Musée de Sculpture en Plein Air, with works by Brancusi and Zadkine, there is a wealth of work on view. Outdoor statuary abounds, and not merely of the commemorative type. Rodin's ***Balzac***, which might normally be shown in a museum, stands at the top of the Boulevard Raspail, while the Théatre des Champs-Elysées in the Avenue Montaigne has reliefs on the façade by Bourdelle.

Finally, if the confusion of art and life in Paris required emphasis it is clearly seen in the cemeteries. Many of the artists and craftsmen of France, as well as its writers and critics, are buried at Père Lachaise and Montmartre, and their graves (if not vandalized) are often marked by some of the finest sculpture in the city.

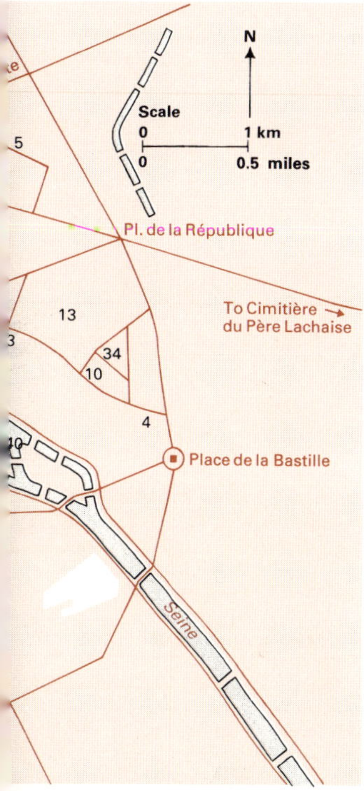

Paris museums and galleries

1 Ateliers de la Manufacture des Gobelins
2 Bibliothèque Nationale
3 Centre National d'Art et de Culture G. Pompidou
4 Maison de Victor Hugo
5 Musée de l'Affiche
6 Musée d'Art Moderne de la Ville de Paris
7 Musée National des Arts et Traditions Populaires
8 Musée des Arts Décoratifs
9 Musée Bourdelle
10 Musée Carnavalet
11 Musée Nissim de Camondo
12 Musée Cernuschi
13 Musée de la Chasse et de la Nature
14 Musée du Cinéma et Cinémathèque Française
15 Musée des Thermes et de l'Hôtel de Cluny
16 Musée Cognacq-Jay
17 Musée National Eugène Delacroix
18 Ecole Nationale Supérieure des Beaux-Arts
19 Musée d'Ennery
20 Musée National Guimet
21 Musée de l'Homme
22 Musée Jacquemart-André
23 Musée National de Jeu de Paume
24 Musée du Louvre
25 Musée de la Marine
26 Musée National des Monuments Français
27 Musée Marmottan
28 Musée Gustave Moreau
29 Musée de Notre-Dame
30 Musée de l'Orangerie
31 Musée d'Orsay
32 Musée du Palais de Tokyo
33 Musée du Petit Palais
34 Musée Picasso
35 Musée Rénan Scheffer
36 Musée National Auguste Rodin
37 Musée Zadkine
38 Sainte-Chapelle
39 Théatre-Française
40 Trésor de la Cathédrale Notre-Dame

Ateliers de la Manufacture des Gobelins

42, Avenue des Gobelins
Open Wed–Fri, 2–4pm
Closed Sat–Tues

The Gobelins Tapestry Workshops have been virtually a state or royal institution since their inception in 1601, when the official tapestry works was transferred to these buildings from Fontainebleau. Under Colbert's reorganization of the royal manufacturers in 1622, the Gobelins emerged as the central and principal factory supplying the court and the aristocracy with tapestries after famous paintings, a practice which the factory maintains to this day.

The small display of Gobelins tapestries in the former chapel includes two scenes taken from Raphael's celebrated **cycle of cartoons** in London, but the chief attraction of the factory is the tour through the workshops where traditional weaving methods are maintained, in some cases on very old hand-looms.

Bibliothèque Nationale/Musée des Médailles et Antiques

58, Rue Richelieu, 75002
Tel. (1) 2963634
Open noon–6pm (library), 1–5pm (museum)

The diverse exhibits of this museum, which benefited greatly from an extensive reorganization in 1981, have developed from the personal collections of the kings of France, accumulated since the reign of François I. They include coins from all periods and countries, exquisite **cameos and intaglios**, precious stones and jewelry, marbles and bronzes, painted antique vases, illuminated Books of the Gospels, and some pieces of 18thC furniture. The Crown gave official sanction to the collection in 1602 when Henry IV created the post of keeper of the Cabinet des Médailles. Louis XIV moved the collection to Versailles in 1684. Considerably enriched, it returned to Paris in 1741, at first residing in the town house of the Marquise de Lambert, but later transferring (in 1865) to an enormous gallery which ran the length of the Rue de Richelieu. Finally, in 1917, the collection was moved to its present location in the Bibliothèque Nationale.

As a result of a continuing series of magnificent donations, the museum has expanded under all regimes. Ironically, it was during the Revolution, when objects flowed in from the great religious institutions, that one of the museum's loveliest exhibits came into its possession: a **carved cameo**★ (from SAINTE-CHAPELLE) sent to St Louis by the Emperor of Constantinople.

Two of the leading French furniture makers of the 18thC are well represented, and you can see the interesting contrast between the more opulent pieces of the Rococo *ébéniste* (cabinet-maker) Charles Cressent, and the refined and elegant products of Jacques-Louis Cresson, who produced much of his finest work under the Neoclassicist influence of the 1780s.

Centre National d'Art et de Culture Georges Pompidou (Musée National d'Art Moderne) ☆

Plateau Beaubourg, 75191
Tel. (1) 2771233/2771112
Open Mon, Wed–Fri, noon–10pm; Sat, Sun 10am–10pm
Closed Tues
(Sun, Wed)

The Centre Pompidou, officially opened in 1977, has already taken its place as one of the most famous buildings in Paris. It is a combination of public library, modern art museum, children's workshop, cinemathèque, industrial design center and experimental music laboratory. The eight million annual visitors to the building are living evidence of the success of its aim to provide a unique and stimulating setting that "unites the different elements of modern culture and makes them accessible to everyone".

On his election to the French presidency in 1969, Georges Pompidou, a declared supporter of the arts, determined to renew Parisian cultural interest by combining two projects: a large public reference library in the middle of the city (first proposed in the 19thC), and the renovation of the National Museum of Modern Art. The Plateau Beaubourg, situated in the heart of Paris between the districts of Les Halles and Le Marais, provided the perfect site. The area was a village in the 13thC, but by the second half of the 19thC this once thriving and attractive community had degenerated into one of the worst slums in Paris. Almost total demolition between the two World Wars left the Plateau Beaubourg derelict and weed-strewn. As a result of the Pompidou project, much of the surrounding area, including the charming Gothic **church of Saint-Merri**, has been restored.

An international jury selected the final design for the museum from nearly 700 submissions, the aim being to produce a flexible and adaptable building that would both complement and extend the diversity of artistic enterprises it was to house and display. The projects included such bizarre ideas as a gigantic egg, 100m high, and an enormous open hand extended skywards, each finger to contain one department; but the jury finally chose the work of three young architects: two Italians, Renzo Piano and Gianfranco Franchi, and one Englishman, Richard Rogers. The elements of steel and glass provide the basic framework of their fashionably industrial design, which does succeed in avoiding the clutter of interior walls and staircases. The building's service systems are incorporated into part of its decorative scheme, being both visible and colour-coded: green for water-pipes, blue for air-conditioning ducts, yellow for the electrical system, and red for transportation – the main escalator has a red underbelly that you can see making its way up the Beaubourg façade. The stately progression of this glass centipede gives the visitor a very good sense of the city's dimensions as the view slowly expands before him. The Centre was intended to be a provocative building, and it aroused suitably mixed reactions when it first took shape above the streets of Paris. The Plaza of the Beaubourg is an integral part of the Centre, and has been adopted by the performing artists of Paris as their main stage. A seat by one of the vast cowled air ducts of the Centre gives you an outdoor cabaret – fire-eaters, jugglers and musicians of all varieties are but a few of the sometimes impromptu and often eccentric performers to be found here. The Place Igor Stravinsky is also worth a visit, to watch the exploits of Jean Tinguely's **Fountain**★ with its fantastic mechanical birds and beasts (including Stravinsky's Firebird), exotic colourful creatures which spout water in all directions. Underneath this area is the I.R.C.A.M. (Institut de Récherche et de Co-ordination Acoustique-Musique) which, under the directorship of Pierre Boulez, is dedicated to the development and promotion of avant-garde music.

Inside the main building, other workshops encourage both children and adults to explore new developments in art and technology. Children can experiment with their own ideas and are also allowed to examine (by touch!) the specially constructed models of the Atelier des Enfants. Adults can amuse themselves playing with the computers of the A.R.T.A. (Atelier des Récherches Techniques Avancées). The often crowded ground floor has an excellent bookshop near the main information desk and is dominated by Victor Vasarély's gigantic portrait of ***Georges Pompidou*** which hangs above the main escalator and is a popular rendezvous for Parisians.

If you have little time, you should undoubtedly avoid all other attractions and head for the third floor and the **National Museum of Modern Art**. This is the keystone to the Centre Pompidou's success in the explanation and popularization of modern visual arts. It exists as a separate entity within the Centre, but also forms the background to the numerous contemporary exhibitions that seek to explore modern art and the contemporary way of life. The collection is representative of the international scope of art (although the emphasis is obviously French and there are some gaps, notably the lack of major Italian Futurist work before 1914) and is surpassed only by the Museum of Modern Art in New York. The works are exhibited within a chronological framework, enabling the viewer to trace the upsurge of creativity evident in the artistic world between 1900 and 1914, the period when the first recognizably "modern" art was produced. All the major pioneering movements are illustrated with splendid examples, such as the beginnings of Cubism in Picasso's ***Seated Woman***★ (1909) and indications of Matisse's progression beyond the Fauvist style in ***Le Luxe***★ (1907). Works like Miró's ***Siesta*** (1925) show the preoccupation with Surrealism that was common to many of the leading artists of the interwar years, including that great showman Salvador Dali. Jackson Pollock's ***The Deep*** (1953) represents a more modern tendency. Pollock, one of the most celebrated of the American Abstract Expressionist painters, died in a car crash in 1956, and this work is probably one of the best examples of his "Action Painting" style. Also on view are paintings outside the general trends of modern art, such as Le Douanier Rousseau's ***The Snake Charmer***★ (1907), where the black temptress is set dramatically against the lush greens and sinuous forms of jungle vegetation.

The attitude of the artist to his materials is explored in one of the museum's most recent acquisitions, Balthus's cool study of ***The Artist and his Model*** (1981), while Giorgio de Chirico's prophetic ***Portrait of Guillaume Apollinaire*** provides an interesting insight into the growth of modern art. The painting shows the great poet and apostle of modernism as a profile head from a fairground shooting gallery – a bullet hole drilled neatly in his temple. The picture is dated 1914 but the bullet hole marks the spot where Apollinaire was later wounded in World War I – a wound which eventually contributed to his death after the Armistice. Other exhibits almost defy explanation, such as Joseph Beuys's ***Homogenous Infiltration for Grand Piano*** (1966). The instrument is entirely covered in brown felt – art camouflaged, insulated and protected from the ravages of the modern world.

The Centre's holdings have also been greatly enriched by the generosity of individual artists, their widows and descendants. In this respect, the **Kandinsky bequest★** is outstanding and covers all aspects of the Russian artist's development as an abstract painter. Another interesting personal collection can be found in the **studio** of the Romanian sculptor Constantin Brancusi. Brancusi spent most of his working life in Paris, leaving the contents of his *atelier* to the state on his death in 1957 on the condition that it should be preserved intact. It has now been reconstructed in a part of the new building.

Finally, one of the most successful features of the Centre Pompidou has been the series of thematic temporary exhibitions held almost annually since its foundation. Large, impressive and intriguing, if only because of their associations, these have undertaken the task of restoring the position of France to one of central importance in 20thC art; a position that was incontestable before World War II, but has sharply fallen away in international terms since then. Exhibitions such as *Paris/Moscow*, *Paris/Berlin* and even *Paris/Paris* unashamedly place the French capital back in the forefront.

Maison de Victor Hugo

Hôtel de Rohan-Guéménée
6, Place des Vosges, 75004
Tel. (1) 2721665/2721016
Open 10am – 5.40pm
Closed Mon
(Sun)

Even if you are not a devotee of Victor Hugo, the **Place des Vosges**, considered by many to be the most picturesque square in Paris, is worth a visit for itself. The subtle diversity of detail in the gables, windows and archways of its (recently restored) red brick façade gives the square a truly classical harmony. Built in 1605 under the auspices of Henri IV, it originally consisted of 36 villas or *pavillons*, each encompassing four arches, with nine *pavillons* on each side of the square. Nowadays, many of these houses have become shops, most of which sell antiques and antiquarian books, but the Place des Vosges is still one of the most luxurious residential areas in Paris. The gardens, shaded by stately chestnut trees, were once a favourite spot for aristocratic duels; today they make a charming playground for some of the city's most privileged children. Known originally as the Place Royale, the square received its current name simply because the *Département* of the Vosges was the first to pay up all its taxes to the Revolutionary government.

The Hôtel de Rohan-Guéménée is at the SW corner of the square; here Victor Hugo lived in a second-floor apartment from 1832 until 1848. The present collection of the museum, founded in 1903, has grown through various gifts and purchases, but its core is the material given to the city of Paris by Paul Meurice, one of Hugo's closest friends. The effect of the display, zealously watched by eagle-eyed attendants, is to reveal the great range of the writer's interests. The stern, bowed head of Rodin's impressive ***Bust of Hugo*** suggests a deep and powerful intellect; the wide variety of Hugo's own watercolours and drawings parallels the inspiration and imagination of his literary work. The most interesting of these compositions are the fantastic shapes achieved by experimentation with different forms of ink blots.

Hugo's interest in furniture design is well represented by two pieces in oak and a decorated mirror frame, together with a quaint writing-table. The latter is truly a record of contemporary French literature: ink-stands at each corner incorporate autographed letters from George Sand, Alexandre Dumas, Lamartine and Hugo himself. The Hugo family is depicted in a series of portraits by Louis Boulanger, along with various other memorabilia such as commemorative plates, a rack of Hugo's pipes and even one of his fine linen handkerchiefs!

Musée de l'Affiche

18, Rue de Paradis, 75010
Tel. (1) 8245004
Open noon – 6pm
Closed Tues

Elaborate painted **ceramic murals** of exceptional size decorate the entrance of the Musée de l'Affiche (Museum of Posters), a building dating from 1900 and very representative of La Belle Epoque. The murals contrast well with the contents of the museum, where the best posters illustrate the achievements of master lithographers working with a fine economy of line and colour.

One of Paris's most recently founded museums (it opened on Feb 13, 1978), the Musée de l'Affiche displays the collection of posters from the library of the Union Centrale des Arts Decoratifs, as well as keeping a close eye on contemporary poster production. The sheer quantity of works on display means that the posters have been divided up into numerous thematic and geographical categories, and there are also displays tracing the history of the poster, from early theatrical bills to present-day cabaret posters. A special place is understandably given to the **Parisian posters of the late 19thC**, when Toulouse-Lautrec's compositions, featuring the black-stockinged cancan dancers of the newly opened Moulin Rouge, first gave prominence to the poster as an art form, and when Jules Chéret's "pin-up" pictures first appeared.

Musée d'Art Moderne de la Ville de Paris ☆

11, Avenue du Président Wilson, 75016
Tel. (1) 7236127
Open Tues, Thurs–Sun 10am–5.30pm, Wed 10am–8.30pm
Closed Mon
(Sun)

The Museum of Modern Art of the City of Paris occupies a wing of the doughty building complex erected for the 1937 Exhibition between the Place de l'Alma and the Place d'Iéna. The severe lines and plain façades of these massive constructions reveal a classicizing influence in the architecture; but it is derived from the weight and bulk of Roman monumentality rather than the linear elegance and grace of Ancient Greece. A set of solid stone steps plods heavily down to the Seine Embankment; and this bare expanse – the central piazza between the two parallel wings of the building – would benefit from having its stonework cleaned and from the introduction of some official greenery, the current tufts of grass and weeds notwithstanding. A popular museum for young Parisians and art students, the gallery itself shares something of this tatty ambience, but this is due to the passage of many visitors rather than to neglect. A complete exception to this rule is the excellent bookshop, situated to the right hand of the main entrance, which has a wide range of art books and catalogues on sale.

The museum opened in 1961 and houses the municipal collection of 20thC art – a collection that is being added to continually, thanks to generous bequests and gifts, and also to the museum's judicious buying policy which keeps close contact with new developments in contemporary art. Temporary exhibitions are always worth investigating here because they cover a fair range, from conventional video displays to Max Neuhaus's ***Sound Installation*** (a totally blank white-walled room with a large notice commanding silence pinned up outside). The museum also has several rooms set aside for the presentation of the latest tendencies in contemporary art, together with recent forms of expression and new techniques.

The **permanent collection** reflects the great artistic movements of the 20thC: Fauvism (Derain, Dufy, Marquet, Vlaminck); Cubism (Picasso, Braque, Léger); Post-Cubism; Rayonism (the short-lived Russian offshoot of Cubism, practised principally by Delaunay, Ozenfant, Goncharova and its inventor Larionov); School of Paris (Chagall, Modigliani, Pascin, Soutine); Expressionism, and so on. Several major artists outside the general trends and schools of art are particularly well represented here. Over 80 **watercolours and a dozen paintings** by George Rouault give a good idea of his main themes – religious subjects, landscapes of bleak and hostile country, an occasional bouquet of flowers. The simplified forms and bright colours of Raoul Dufy's light-hearted decorative style come over clearly in the museum's holding of some 100 works by this artist. The most important of these are in the recent Reysz donation, but you should not miss the grand decorative scheme, occupying a whole room, entitled ***La Fée Electricité*** (the Spirit of Electricity). This enormous composition, executed for the Pavilion of Light at the 1937 Exhibition, is displayed in a high room at the top of the stairs leading from the first landing. It is an extraordinary piece of interior decoration, tracing the history of electricity from Archimedes to Edison and Graham Bell, and has as its central motif an enormous steel turbine!

Other artists outside general trends whose work can be seen here include Fautrier, Gromaire and Utrillo, whose sensitive and precise paintings, usually of town views, are in complete contradiction to his life as a confirmed drunkard and drug addict. Also well worth looking at are the works of contemporary sculptors, including several by Charles Despiau, and examples of Jacques Lipchitz's very personal style of openwork sculpture (***sculptures transparentes***).

One item you should make a point of seeing is Christo's model and plans of his project for wrapping up the ***Pont Neuf***. This is situated in the passageway just outside the entrance to the museum cafeteria, and is intended to reveal the beauty of simple lines of form, whether architectural or natural. Christo's notes make fascinating reading: he proposed that traffic should carry on normally while the bridge was being parcelled up, and one cannot help wishing that the city of Paris had agreed to the idea.

Musée National des Arts et Traditions Populaires

6, Avenue du Mahatma-Gandhi, 75116
Tel. (1) 7476980
Open 10am–5.15pm
Closed Tues
(Wed)

In common with several other museums in Paris, the Musée National des Arts et Traditions Populaires first came into existence as a result of one of the numerous World Fairs held in the city. In this case it was the International Exhibition of 1937, after which the basement of the Palais de Chaillot was designated a national gallery of popular or folk arts. The motivating force behind the new museum was George-Henri Rivière, its first curator, who organized the earlier folk collections of the Ethnography Museum into a coherent and separate entity. In 1966 the collections were moved to a new and very practical building at the edge of the Jardin d'Acclimatation in the **Bois de Boulogne**.

This new setting has allowed the collection to be displayed in a comprehensive and logical format, thematically arranged in categories such as agriculture, costumes, games and pastimes of pre-industrial France. There is a huge amount of material here, but in the present context the **primitive graphics and carvings** may be of the greatest interest.

Musée des Arts Décoratifs ☆ (Union Centrale des Arts Décoratifs)

Palais du Louvre, Pavillon de Marsan
107, Rue de Rivoli, 75001
Tel. (1) 2603214
Open Mon, Wed–Fri 10am–5pm, Sat, Sun 11am–6pm
Closed Tues

Despite the fact that it occupies the Pavillon de Marsan, the NW extremity of the PALAIS DU LOUVRE, the Musée des Arts Decoratifs is actually a separate and independent museum that shares the same complex of buildings with its more famous neighbour. In some respects it set out to be the Louvre's equivalent in the decorative arts, presenting in a series of grand galleries a comprehensive display of European **furniture, fabrics, ceramics, glass** and **costumes**, from medieval times up to the present day. In all, the museum covers five floors, with different periods, themes or regions on each, but unfortunately much of it will probably not be open to the public for several years until the long awaited reorganization of the building has been completed. Nevertheless the arrangement is roughly as follows.

The ground floor contains the administration and the library of the Centre Nationale d'Information et de Documentation sur les Métiers d'Art, and only on the first floor, which displays the **19thC and 20thC section**, does the collection begin in earnest. The arrangement emphasizes the prominent role of French designers, notably Hector Guimard (who designed the early Metro entrances as well as a large amount of furniture), in the dissemination of the Art Nouveau style. The second floor holds the collection of **furniture, tapestries, metalwork** and other objects from the Gothic and Renaissance periods in Europe, while the third and fourth floors are mainly devoted to French design of the 17thC and 18thC. This occupies a series of well-constructed rooms complete with paintings, furnishings and everyday items which help to recreate the lifestyle of the various periods, and the context in which different pieces were used. The paintings are by no means foils for the other exhibits, for the suites include works by Hubert Robert and Ingres as well as ceramics from all the major European factories. The upper floors also contain a collection of **Islamic and Far Eastern art**, together with works by the 20thC painter Jean Dubuffet, which looks remarkably out of place in such a setting.

Musée Bourdelle ☆

16, Rue Antoine Bourdelle, 75015
Tel. (1) 5486727
Open 10am–5pm
Closed Mon
(Sun)

This large, rambling and generally deserted museum is undoubtedly one of the great delights of Paris. Bourdelle's family donated the house and studio of the artist to the state in 1948, together with 875 of his sculptures and over 1,000 drawings and watercolours. An enormous gallery had to be built to show works for which space was lacking in the other building and the garden; today a further extension is being planned. A pleasantly eccentric daughter of the artist runs the place, which might account for some of its quirky charm.

Bourdelle was born in ***MONTAUBAN*** in 1861, and worked there initially as an assistant in his father's carpentry shop. He enrolled at the École des Beaux-Arts in Paris in 1884, and moved that same year to the studio at 16 Impasse du Maine (now the Rue Bourdelle) which he was to keep for the rest of his life. Between 1893 and 1908 he was chief assistant to Rodin, and the influence of Rodin is clearly apparent in his early work, in particular a series of bronze studies of ***Beethoven***. Later he became deeply interested in ancient Greek art, which inspired two of what are today his most popular works, a lively standing nude of a woman entitled ***Fruit*** (1906) and a tense, powerful portrayal of ***Hercules*** as an archer (1909). Unlike his contemporary Maillol, who revived the static element in classical art, Bourdelle always had a fascination with the representation of movement; indeed, one of his major official commissions – a high relief for the Champs Elysées theatre – was influenced by the choreography of Isadora Duncan.

The artist's house and studio have been little touched by time. A layer of dust hangs over everything, and personal items, such as an old pair of shoes, are haphazardly scattered around. Even the part of the house once inhabited by Bourdelle's parents has been faithfully preserved. Most of the museum's sculptures (which include versions of virtually every work which Bourdelle ever did) are kept in the adjoining gallery. This place is dominated by the cast for the gigantic equestrian monument to ***General Alvear*** , who is shown riding on a tall plinth flanked by representations of Strength, Victory, Liberty and Eloquence. This, the most important official commission Bourdelle ever received, was intended for a square in Buenos Aires. It was executed between 1912 and 1915, but was not put in place until 1925. Bourdelle was strongly criticized for showing the general in breach of military etiquette by being without a hat when riding. Bourdelle countered this by saying that the general had lost his hat in the heat of battle. A **bronze** of the horse and rider is in the front garden of the museum.

Musée Nissim de Camondo

63, Rue de Morceau, 75008
Tel. (1) 5632632
Open 10am–noon, 2–5pm
Closed Mon, Tues

As you pass through the gracious arched entrance to the courtyard of this museum, pause to read the stone tablet inset on the right-hand wall. This records the origins of the house and its collection as a memorial to Nissim de Camondo, killed in air combat during World War I. His father, Comte Moïse de Camondo, assembled the museum's entire collection of 18thC furniture and objets d'art, and also employed the architect Sergent to draw up plans for the house in the style of a Louis XVI *hôtel.* This was completed in 1914, and the Comte left the house and its contents to the MUSÉE DES ARTS DECORATIFS as a permanent memorial to his son. The trustees of the Arts Decoratifs have paid tribute to the Comte's acute aesthetic sense by leaving every item in the collection exactly where he had arranged it in a precise **re-creation of an 18thC interior**.

An outstanding range of craftmanship is on display here, with the furniture and decorative items set off against the mellow patina of original panelling. Throughout the house beautiful objects detain the visitor: exquisite chased and gilded bronze statuettes, fine porcelain, and intricate pieces of silver plate. But it is in the domain of the 18thC master *ébéniste* (cabinet-maker) that this museum reigns supreme. Among the very fine furniture to be seen here are several items made by Martin Carlin, one of the most elegant and refined furniture makers from the Louis XVI period. His work tended to be small in scale, often decorated with Sèvres plaques, as can be seen in the charming ***bureau à gradin*** ★ (a flat-topped table with a set of drawers above) in the salon. Later in the 18thC the delicacy of such pieces gave way to the taste for heavier, more sumptuous works, as seen here in the furniture of David Roentgen, a German working in Paris. The Nissim de Camondo museum possesses an imposing **mahogany cupboard** by Roentgen, its severe line offset by ornate gilt-bronze mounts. The skill and high technical ability of the Germans gave them a leading place in furniture-making, especially towards the end of the century. Among the few important French furniture-makers working in Paris during the last years of the *ancien régime,* Charles Topino is well represented in the museum. Topino specialized in small pieces and developed a very personal style of marquetry decoration.

Musée Carnavalet (Musée de l'Histoire de Paris) ☆

23, Rue de Sévigné, 75003
Tel. (1) 2722113
Open 10am–5.40pm
Closed Mon
(Sun)

One of the most entrancing museums in Paris, the Carnavalet owes much of its charm to the **Hôtel Carnavalet** itself, a beautiful house dating back to the mid 16thC. In 1578 it became the home of Françoise de Kernevenoy, whose Breton surname was corrupted to Carnavalet. The house was modernized and remodelled in the 17thC by the protagonist of classicism in French architecture, François Mansart, and the visitor's first introduction to the beauties of the house is Mansart's very handsome **façade** facing the Rue de Sévigné entrance. Later in the century, the Hôtel Carnavalet became the home of Marie de Rabutin-Chantal, Marquise de Sévigné, the celebrated hostess and letter-writer. One room of the museum is devoted to **Mme de Sévigné**, containing her elaborate gilt and lacquer desk and a delightful **oil portrait** by Claude Lefebvre. In the 18thC the Hôtel Carnavalet remained a family home, but the city authorities bought the house in 1866 and had it restored by Victor Parmentier, who added the Neo-Renaissance garden gallery. In 1880 it was opened as an annex to the Bibliothèque Historique, but soon became the more prestigious of the two institutions, benefiting from many generous gifts and donations.

The collection is primarily concerned with Paris itself, illustrating the city's changing topography as well as the principal events and varying aspects of the inhabitants' lifestyles. The well-organized displays begin with Paris in the 16thC, and a Flemish painting of c. 1650, ***The Prodigal Son in the Company of Courtesans***, shows a clear delineation of the city with the Seine curling below the towers of Notre-Dame in the background. In the section devoted to Parisian life under Louis XIII and Louis XIV, a large painting of the ***Wedding Festivities*** following Louis XIII's marriage to Anne of Austria in 1612, clearly depicts the Place Royale (now the Place des Vosges, only a few streets away from the Carnavalet) and serves as an important and precise architectural record.

Several rooms in the museum are given to suites of **decorative panelling and furniture**★ which, taken from various buildings throughout the city, help to illustrate the changing taste in wealthy Parisian households from the 17thC onwards. Luxury and elegance are not, however, the predominating factors in the museum's most important collection – **paintings** and **art objects** from the French Revolution and First Empire. Here you can see a fascinating range of exhibits, such as the anonymous portrait of ***Dr Guillotin*** (advocator of the guillotine), **Sèvres porcelain** decorated with revolutionary emblems and allegories, and a contemporary illustration of Marat's funeral. After the turbulence and bloodshed of the Revolution, however, Napoleon wanted artists who could equal the former glories of the royal court commissions. Among these First Empire painters was Gérard, whose superb portrait of ***Madame Récamier***★ is the Carnavalet's premier painting.

Musée Cernuschi (Musée d'Art Chinois de la Ville de Paris)

7, Avenue Velasquez, 75008
Tel. (1) 5635073
Open 10am–5.40pm
Closed Mon
(Sun)

A pair of recumbent lions flank the entrance to this specialist museum of Far Eastern art, but any effect of Oriental savagery is tempered by the delightful surroundings of the Cernuschi museum. The Avenue Velasquez is a street of elegant houses, embellished by wrought-iron balconies and shaded by ornamental trees, leading into the serene Parc de Monceau, a haven of pleasant walks and well-kept shrubberies for pampered Parisian lap dogs. The house containing the Cernuschi collection is a fine building, and the elegance of its façade complements the stylish displays inside.

The collection has developed from a number of bronzes brought back from the Far East in 1873 by Henri Cernuschi, a respected economist and important political figure in Paris during the second half of the 19thC. An active member of the Commune, Cernuschi travelled to the Far East to escape the turbulence of political life. It was whilst visiting Tokyo that his interest was caught by the bronzes on sale to Western visitors, and he then began systematically to buy these works. In 1896 he gave the resulting collection, together with the house he had built to display it, to the city of Paris.

Today's museum, enriched by judicious purchases over the years, concentrates on **archaic Chinese art** and, since 1953, traditional **contemporary paintings**. Apart from the archaic Chinese bronzes, the principal works on show are a variety of funerary statuettes from the Han to the T'ang dynasties (8th–3rdC BC), and Far Eastern ceramics dating from the Neolithic period to the Sung dynasty (13thC). Pride of place however must go to the bronzes, although only about 20 of these truly belong to the category of "archaic" bronzes. Other Chinese works – rather more powerful and heavy in design than the elegant delicacy of Japanese bronzes – are virtuoso pieces made for the literati of the Ancient East, and consist of items such as intricate and highly decorated brush-holders and inkstands. Although a very attractive museum to visit, the Cernuschi does tend to concentrate on a specialist interest, and you may gain a fuller idea of Oriental art from the comprehensive collections at the MUSÉE GUIMET.

Musée de la Chasse et de la Nature

Hôtel Guénégaud des Brosses, 60, Rue des Archives, 75003
Tel. (1) 2728643
Open 10am – 5.30pm
Closed Tues

This entertaining museum devotes the major part of its display to "the chase", and is therefore not for those with an aversion to blood sports. But whatever you may feel on the issue, the history of man's pursuit of animals and the development of field sports make for some very fascinating exhibits: **paintings**, **sculptures**, **tapestries**, firearms, trophies and other objets d'art relative to the subject.

The Hotel Guénégaud des Brosses was remodelled in the mid-17thC by the great François Mansart, but the building had fallen into a sadly dilapidated state by the time it was extensively restored in the 1960s, with the result that much of the original stonework has been destroyed. A fine interior staircase survives from Mansart's day, but the nearby MUSÉE CARNAVALET is a much better example of his work. The hôtel, the property of the city of Paris, owes its survival to Jacqueline and François Sommer, whose determination to found a museum for their extensive collection of hunting objects led to the restoration of this building.

Items on display date from the Late Middle Ages and include a set of **Flanders tapestries** depicting the courtly pursuit of boar and bear, and many exhibits illustrating the legend of the two saints associated with the animals of the chase, ***St Eustace and St Hubert***. Passing down the centuries, the museum traces the development of firearms – the silver and ivory inlay decoration of the 18thC guns is magnificent – and sporting accessories such as powder flasks show an equally rich decoration.

The museum also contains many fine paintings of **hunting scenes**, including several by Alexandre Desportes, the official painter of hunting for Louis XIV and Louis XV, as well as Carle Vernet's ***Hunt at Fontainebleau***, an airy, vibrant scene probably painted for Napoleon.

Musée du Cinéma et Cinémathèque Française

Palais de Chaillot (Aile de Paris, Porte Président Wilson) Place du Trocadero, 75116
Tel. (1) 5332186
Open 10am – 5pm
Closed Mon

Spreadeagled above the Trocadéro Gardens and the Seine, and commanding a fine view of the Eiffel Tower from its central piazza, the **Palais de Chaillot** (built for the World Fair of 1879) houses four museums and two theatres within its monumental walls. However, despite the ponderous majesty of the building's exterior appearance, the entrance halls to both wings of the Palais have a general air of scruffiness and clutter. Fortunately, this impression is not carried through to the rest of the building.

The Musée du Cinéma et Cinémathèque Française is tucked away in the basement of the Palais de Chaillot, and makes no great efforts to advertize its presence. By following what signs are in evidence, however, access to the museum will be found via a descent of stone steps – somewhat perilous as the stone has worn very smooth. Cinema and film enthusiasts will be well rewarded for such perseverance, for this small specialist museum has some unique items on display. The collection, founded in 1959 by Henri Langlois and moved to its present location in 1974, includes examples of very early film projectors, some rare and extremely striking **film posters and photographs** (stills and publicity shots), and a series of fascinating models and plans of various important **set designs** from avant-garde and popular films. In addition, the museum traces the origin of the cinema, not just from the heyday of the silent movie in the 1920s, but from the very first efforts at projection known to man, beginning with the oriental shadow theatre and progressing to the magic lantern – the 18thC forerunner of today's sophisticated cinematic films. Throughout the museum, small slide projectors have been set up, showing a changing succession of major moments from cinematographic history.

Musée des Thermes et de l'Hôtel de Cluny ☆☆

6, Place Paul-Painlevé, 75005
Tel. (1) 3255200
Open 9.45am – 12.30pm, 2 – 5.15pm
Closed Tues
(Wed)

In the heart of the Latin Quarter, where the boulevards of St-Germain and St-

Michel meet, you can visit two superb collections closely linked with the two buildings of the museum. Of these, the **Gallo-Roman baths** (Thermes) are among the most impressive monuments to survive from the ancient civilization that existed before the growth of the city of Paris. 19thC excavations led to a careful reconstruction of the three interconnecting rooms of the *frigidarium* (which still survives in its entirety) the *tepidarium* and the *calidarium* (both in ruins). Today, however, instead of catering to the needs of corpulent Romans, the baths display a fine collection of **Gallo-Roman antiquities** belonging to the city of Paris.

Adjoining the Thermal Baths is the **13thC house** of the abbés of Cluny, used as a lodging for the churchmen when they came on visits from the mother house of *CLUNY* in Burgundy. During the 15thC Abbé Jacques d'Amboise transformed the earlier building into the more ostentatious **Palais d'Amboise**; and it stands today as one of the first examples of a house built between a courtyard and a garden – a pattern that was to become very popular in 17thC cities. The **chapel** in the N wing reveals the art of Gothic architecture at its best, flawlessly proportioned, with exquisite decorations setting off the delicate grace of its stonework. In 1825 the house was bought by Alexandre du Sommerard, a state official whose enormous collection of works of art revealed his keen appreciation of the Middle Ages and the Renaissance at a time when work from these periods was little considered. Du Sommerard exploited the medieval setting of the House of Cluny in order to present his treasures in the best light. By 1843 the Cluny was established as a museum, to be combined with the Palais des Thermes which had recently become the home for the Paris stonework collection.

Alexandre du Sommerard's son, Edmond, inherited the task of re-classifying and re-organizing his father's collection. He also added such treasures as the famous ***Lady with the Unicorn***★★ set of tapestries from Boussac, and several unique gold pieces, including the ***golden crowns of the Visigoth kings***.

Access to the museum is from the Rue Paul-Painlevé; a wrought-iron gate leads into the charming courtyard, overhung with laburnum trees, through to the principal entrance via the former kitchens of the house – a magnificent stone fireplace remains as a reminder of medieval banquets. The 24 exhibition rooms contain, without doubt, one of the world's richest collections of medieval art from all over Europe. Superb examples of the leading trades of the Middle Ages, notably the craftsmanship of the weavers, embroiderers and workers in precious metals, are on view throughout the museum. The Cluny is justifiably proud of its **collection of tapestries**★★, among which there are two especially outstanding early pieces. The very precious and sumptuous ***Resurrection***★, woven with silk and metal thread, and intended as an altar hanging, dates from the early 14thC; and ***The Offering of the Heart***★, woven in wool, and showing a courtly gentleman paying homage to a seated lady, is one of the last manifestations of the International Gothic style of the 1400s.

The masterpiece of the collection, however, is the early 16thC ***Lady with the Unicorn***★★, whose grace and charm, together with a harmonious colour scheme, make this tapestry set one of the finest to survive from the Middle Ages. Various interpretations of the subject matter of the six hangings have been put forward, but it is now thought to represent the Five Senses – for example, ***Sight*** shows the unicorn admiring himself in a mirror held by the lady. Cluny also possesses beautiful 14thC works from England and the Rhineland (both were renowned for the quality of their embroidery) as well as fragments of Byzantine work, including a magnificent piece of blue fabric depicting a four-horse chariot, found in the Treasure of Aix-la-Chapelle.

Reliquaries, devotional objects and jewelry show the high standards attained by the medieval gold- and silver-smiths. One of the most precious objects here is ***The Golden Rose of Basle***★, an exquisite creation and the oldest known survivor of the Eastertide Vatican custom whereby the Pope presented a small golden rose tree to persons of high rank whom he wished to honour. This delicate piece, given to a bishop of Basle by Pope Clement V (1305–1314), was made by an Italian goldsmith in Avignon.

The production of enamels was another flourishing art of the Middle Ages, and the museum has a rich and varied collection of the famous **Limoges ware**. Early works carry enamelled figures on a copper background, while the later pieces show the beautiful blue background, richly decorated with polychrome rosettes, foliations and flowers, that established the fame of the Limoges craftsmen. Medieval sculptors and painters are also well represented, with numerous statues of the ***Virgin and Child*** carved in stone, marble, wood and ivory, and taken from the various churches and châteaux. The most distinguished of the sculptures here is the marble ***Presentation in the Temple*** group. But look for the altar screen of the Belgian abbey of Averbode, a masterpiece of painted and gilded wood, which depicts a rare subject, ***The Mass of St Gregory***, as well as the ***Meeting of Abraham and Melchizedek***, and well represents the specialist work of the Antwerp gilders and decorators. The Cluny also has a very rare English primitive altarpiece, c.1300, illustrating ***The Life of The Virgin***.

The climax to the rich and fascinating displays occurs in the exhibition chamber next to the chapel. Here are the most precious pieces of the Cluny, recalling the rich treasures accumulated during the Middle Ages in important churches. The principal exhibit is ***The Golden Altar of Basle***★ part of the treasure of Basle Cathedral. Many examples of these beautiful "golden tables" (designed to be placed in front of the altar) were made at the time of Charlemagne and during the 11thC. However, nearly all have been melted down and in fact only four survive in the world. The Basle altar has no enamel decoration but is made of beaten gold on a core of wood and wax. It survived the religious wars of the 16thC hidden in the vaults of the cathedral and was bought by the Cluny in the 1880s. The room also contains impressive **ivories**, dating from the 6thC, and rare religious vestments.

Musée Cognacq-Jay ☆

25, Boulevard des Capucines, 75002
Tel. (1) 7429471
Open 10am–5.40pm
Closed Mon
(Sun) ☑

A haven of calm (albeit gilded and highly ornate) in the busy shops and cafés of the *grands boulevards*, this museum reconstructs a typically wealthy bourgeois household as it would have appeared towards the end of the 18thC. Each room of the building has been arranged in the furnishing style fashionable in the reigns of Louis XV and XVI, providing an overall effect of intimate affluence. The style of the décor, with its original wood **panelling** and some exquisite **tapestries**, as well as the contents, rejects the new sobriety of 18thC Neoclassicism and avoids most of the preciousness of the earlier Rococo style.

The entire collection, together with the building, was bequeathed to the city of Paris in 1928 by Ernest Cognacq, founder of the Samaritaine chain of shops. In company with his wife, Louise Jay, this rich and astute businessman never pretended to be a connoisseur of art himself; instead he was happy to take expert advice in order to gather together paintings, furniture, porcelain and curios representative of an 18thC interior. Cognacq wisely rejected buying the grand history paintings of the period in favour of **portraits**, a more intimate 18thC genre which he regarded as more representative of 18thC art as a whole, and of particular relevance to the interior of a town house of the period.

The three rooms of the first floor contain paintings by the two French artists most associated with the gaiety and brilliant technique of the French Rococo: Jean-Honoré Fragonard and François Boucher. Four works by the latter are on display, the most attractive being a ***Portrait*** of his daughter, while ***Diana Returning from the Hunt*** serves as an example of his favourite subject matter, namely slightly risqué mythological scenes. In contrast to the frivolity of these two artists, the museum also shows works by Chardin, the finest 18thC French painter of still-life and genre, and his contemporary, Greuze. The strength of the colouring and the composition of Chardin's ***Copper Cauldron*** is especially notable, as is the tender treatment evident in Greuze's pair of **portraits** of two young boys. The second floor displays some very fine armchairs, sofas and an enormous *lit à la polonaise*. The French excelled themselves in inventing canopies for beds in the 18thC; this style has curved iron supports, forming a dome entirely swathed in curtains. These pieces represent the work of the leading *ébénistes* of the day, but you may well prefer to go straight to the museum's greatest treasures which, paradoxically, lie outside its overall concept. These consist of an exceptional and very early Rembrandt, ***Balaam's Ass***★, painted when the artist was barely 20, and ***The Feast of Cleopatra***, a detailed oil sketch by Tiepolo, the greatest Venetian decorative painter of the 18thC and a decided influence on all the French Rococo artists. Also on this floor is a collection, unusual for a French museum, of 18thC English portraits, including Reynolds' magnificent ***Earl of Northington***★.

The third floor has a fine array of pastels, the most impressive of which are **portraits** by Quentin de La Tour, and a charming ***Fêtes Galantes*** (lovers in a pastoral setting) by Watteau. In these rooms and throughout the museum you can see the exquisite **porcelain** of Meissen and Sèvres, alongside many and varied examples of the highly skilled work of 18thC gold- and silver-smiths.

Musée National Eugène Delacroix

6, Place de Furstemberg, 75006
Tel. (1) 3540487
Open 9.45am – 5.15pm
Closed Tues
(Wed)

The Musée Delacroix is tucked behind a small paved courtyard off the delightful Place de Furstemburg – a charming retreat from busy St Germain and a popular subject for the students of the École des Beaux-Arts. Delacroix's old studio and final home, where he died in 1863, gives a more intimate view of the painter's work than is provided by his famous , and enormous, canvases in THE LOUVRE. Undoubtedly the leading painter of the Romantic movement in France, Delacroix is characterized by his free handling and use of brilliant colour. A visit to North Africa in 1832 had a profound effect on this latter aspect of his work as well as providing him with a wealth of exotic subject matter. Among the numerous sketches and studies made at this period, one of the most striking in the museum is the ***Seated Turk***, where the magnificent reds and oranges of the Turk's costume contrast daringly with the dark blue-green of the background. There are also many examples of Delacroix's interest in animal painting and his delight in floral still-lifes.

Mementoes and memorabilia of the artist are also to be found here, contributing to an evocative ambience that owes much to the dedication and enthusiasm of the Delacroix Society. This association was founded in 1929 to save the building. After the first exhibition was mounted here in 1932 the house became a permanent showplace for Delacroix's works. **Paintings, drawings, pastels** and **lithographs** of Delacroix's art have been donated to the museum, the principal benefactors being Baron Vitta and Paul Jamot, so that today's visitor can enjoy the full range of the great artist's output.

École Nationale Supérieure des Beaux-Arts

14, Rue Bonaparte, 75006
11, Quai Malaquais (temporary exhibitions)
Tel. (1) 2603457 (Ext 422)
Open 1 – 7pm
Closed Tues

The origins of the École des Beaux-Arts go back to 1648, when the Academy of Painting and Sculpture was founded. The Beaux-Arts has inherited the collections of the old Academy, which focus principally on copies of important paintings of the **Italian Renaissance**, together with numerous architectural fragments and some sculptures from the Middle Ages to the Renaissance. For those interested in the "official" school of French painting, the Beaux-Arts's **collection of portraits** (both painted and sculpted) of all the leading artists and professors of the old Academy and the new École will be of particular interest. The school also houses the medals awarded under the title of the Prix de Rome – France's most prestigious artistic honour – since its foundation in 1688.

The Beaux-Arts frequently plays host to important temporary exhibitions; and on the whole these displays, together with showings of the students' work, are of more interest than the permanent collections here. The major exception is the magnificent **collection of drawings** housed in the school's library, predominantly French and dating from the 16thC to the 19thC. There is also a useful bookshop here, selling posters, catalogues and art books.

Musée National Guimet ☆

6, Place d'Iéna
Tel. (1) 7236165
Open 9.45am – 12.30pm, 1.30 – 5.15pm
Closed Tues
(Wed)

Cool and spacious, the entrance hall to the Musée Guimet provides a pleasant contrast to the dusty boulevards outside. Indeed, an airy atmosphere pervades the museum's well-lit exhibition rooms and provides an excellent setting for the rich displays of **Oriental art** housed here. The industrialist Émile Guimet, a native of Lyon and an avid collector of objets d'art from the Far East, founded the museum in 1879. Ten years later the entire contents was moved to Paris, to be given the status of National Museum in 1929. Since then, the museum has benefited greatly from the addition of several important collections, including all the works from the old Department of Asiatic Art of THE LOUVRE, a remarkable variety of **Chinese and Japanese pottery and porcelain** (Grandidier and Michel Calmann Collections) and, its latest principal donation, a range of **Chinese and Indian funerary statuettes** given by Robert Rousset in 1978.

The museum houses over 300,000 objects and documents related to the art and archaeology of Eastern Asia: India, China, Japan, Cambodia, Thailand, Pakistan, Afghanistan, Tibet, Nepal and Indonesia are all well represented. In partnership with its scientific and museological departments, the Guimet also commands a wide array of facilities, including an extensive library and a music department complete with listening booths.

Of all the fascinating objects on display, perhaps the most remarkable is the collection of **Khmer art**, including quite large items such as a beautifully carved sandstone lintel dated to the beginning of the 13thC. Just as exciting is the Guimet's extensive collection of **Chinese pottery**, from the simple earthenware jugs and bowls of its origins to the more sophisticated works of the 14thC. Examples of the Chinese potters' mastery are displayed in the first ten rooms of the second floor of the building. Over the centuries the Chinese experimented with various types of clays and glazes, eventually perfecting their technique in the production of truly exquisite vases, such as those made during the **Sung dynasty** (12thC and 13thC) where the beautifully painted decorations are covered by a fine transparent glaze. The modelling prowess of these master craftsmen stands out particularly in such works as the magnificent ***Tang Humped Oxen*** ★, models which are both realistic and also highly decorative.

Other treasures at the Guimet include a very fine selection of **Japanese prints** – the first European exhibitions of Japanese art were not held until 1854 and 1862. There is also a wide-ranging display of Indian art, from decorative terracotta wall plaques of the 1stC BC, to the wonderful **carved stone effigies** ★ of various gods and goddesses, their expressions ranging from the terrifying to the sublimely beautiful. Nor should you miss the much later but quite exquisite **miniature paintings** ★ of the 17thC, whose fine detailing complements the glowing colour.

Musée de L'Homme (Musée National d'Histoire Naturel)

Palais de Chaillot (Aile de Passy), Place du Trocadéro
Tel. (1) 5537060
Open 9.45am–5.15pm

An offshoot of the Natural History Museum, the Musée de l'Homme was founded in 1937 and takes up the major part of the Passy wing of the Palais de Chaillot. As its name implies, this museum is dedicated to the study of man, and the collections reflect the three principal "human" sciences of anthropology, palaeontology and ethnology. The museum is also a focus for teaching and research in these areas and has an extensive library. Much thought and imagination has gone into the fascinating displays on view in all the galleries here. Children seem to find it a particularly interesting and stimulating place to visit, no doubt partly because the museum provides plenty of material to satisfy a youthful delight in the macabre and the bizarre. On the first floor, devoted principally to anthropology and palaeontology, displays of relics, carvings, sacred vessels and other objects explore and reveal the spiritual, social and aesthetic differences between the varying cultures. Exhibits range from carved wood **ceremonial masks** and drinking cups from the African Congo to the beaten brass hair ornaments of a Turkish bride. Skulls abound, both ancient and modern, such as the **tattooed head** of a New Zealand Maori (one of the museum's prized exhibits) or the **skull of Descartes**, the 17thC thinker often regarded as the founder of modern philosophy.

In terms of the decorative arts the carvings of different races and cultures on display reveal great skill and beauty. The Galerie d'Afrique Noire in particular contains one of the finest existing examples of a **carved wooden drum** ★ worked in fine-grained hardwood and shaped in the form of an ox.

The second floor of the museum is concerned with ethnology, and here again craftmanship and skill is much in evidence in the wide variety of decorative, functional and symbolic items of the different races. The Galerie de Peuples Arctiques has a particularly splendid collection of **Eskimo ivory carvings**, notably a very fine broad-bladed knife whose handle is fashioned into a wonderfully simplified form of a polar bear.

Music is an extremely important element in all cultures represented here, and the large square gallery at the head of the stairs contains a comprehensive collection of musical instruments from all parts of the globe. Surrounded by displays of string, wind and rhythm instruments, the dominant central showcase contains a full range of bronze percussion instruments, including a rare **Javanese gamelan** – an orchestral ensemble with varied percussion instruments.

Musée Jacquemart-André (Institut de France) ☆

158, Boulevard Haussmann
Tel. (1) 5623994
Open 1.30–5.30pm
Closed Mon, Tues

The Musée Jacquemart-André was set up in 1913 by Madame André (*née* Jacquemart) following the terms of her husband's will which bequeathed their house and collection to the Institut de France. The collection reflects the André family's taste which, apart from several notable exceptions, tends to concentrate on **fine and decorative arts** of the Italian Renaissance and of the French 18thC. Each of the 13 rooms provides a range of items with a common link in the culture in which they were created. The Italian Renaissance rooms, for example, have works by Donatello, Mantegna, Pontormo and in particular, Uccello's ***St George Slaying the Dragon*** in a context of carved wedding chests (*cassoni*), Della Robbia **terracottas** and 15thC sculpted marble doorways. The same is true of the French 18thC rooms, where paintings by Nattier, Prud'hon and Greuze, and portrait busts of Houdon and Coysevox, are set off by contemporary furniture, Aubusson carpets and Sèvres or Meissen porcelain. In addition to these two areas there are some fine Dutch and Flemish pictures from the 17thC, including ***Hercules Strangling the Lion*** by Rubens and the ***Portrait of Amalia von Solms*** and ***Pilgrims at Emmaus*** by Rembrandt. **Portraits** by Frans Hals and van Dyck, and a **landscape** by Ruisdael command attention, but perhaps the most interesting of all is the **series of frescoes** by G.B. Tiepolo on the staircase and in three of the rooms, which originally came from the Villa Contarini in Venice. Finally, and in contrast to most of the other exhibits, there is a very good late medieval illuminated manuscript, the ***Boucicaut Hours*** by the so-called Master of the Boucicaut Hours, which once belonged to Diane de Poitiers.

Musée National du Jeu de Paume ☆☆

Place de la Concorde, 75001
Tel. (1) 2601207/2964273
Open 9.45am–5.15pm
Closed Tues
(Wed)

Although the Jeu de Paume became the principal Impressionist gallery only after the war, in 1947, it has been associated with this phase of French art for so long that it often seems as if it should have been in existence far earlier. Previously this pavilion of the Palais du Louvre had been used for temporary exhibitions and for the modern European paintings which were subsequently transferred to the Musée National d'Art Moderne (now in the CENTRE POMPIDOU), but the decision to create a new museum displaying what must be the most widely admired movement in Western art ensured its popularity from the outset. Over the next few years however, it will be subjected to another major reorganization, because the Jeu de Paume is one of the institutions that has been drawn into the orbit of the MUSÉE D'ORSAY, an immense project unifying all the art of the later 19thC. Most of the collection will be transferred to this new museum by 1986, after which the Jeu de Paume will revert to its earlier role as a venue for temporary exhibitions.

In its present form the Jeu de Paume houses the **greatest collection of Impressionist and Post-Impressionist paintings** in existence, a large number of the key pictures in the development of those movements, and a host of other paintings so well known as to be familiar even to people who profess no interest in art. How the Louvre came to possess these works in the first place is in itself an interesting story, because, in the period 1870–1900, when the Impressionists were most active, the movement did not enjoy the kind of official recognition likely to result in the purchase of their work by the state. Most of the paintings were presented to the Louvre in private donations by collectors who had supported the artists during their early and impoverished careers. After the Caillebotte bequest in 1894, which incidentally included such pictures as Manet's ***Balcony***, Renoir's ***Moulin de la Galette*** and ***The Swing***, and Monet's ***Gare St-Lazare***, there was a quickening of interest and, in the subsequent decades, major donations came in from Etienne Moreau-Nelaton, Count Isaac de Camondo, Antonin Personnaz, Paul Gachet, Dr Eduardo Mollard and Max and Rosy Kaganovitch.

The process was not without setbacks of a kind that seem fascinating, tantalizing and even infuriating to contemporary eyes. The first attempts to give Impressionist paintings to the Louvre were bedevilled by an unwritten rule over the representation of "living" artists in what was in effect a National Gallery. When this obstacle had been overcome, the curators and advisory committee, especially the chairman Léon Bonnat (a painter himself), proved stubbornly resistant to such novel pictures in a context dominated by Old Masters. Manet's ***Olympia***, one of the most famous paintings of this or any other period, was only accepted in 1890 after much dispute and a large public subscription. The Caillebotte bequest, although it did bring important works into a public collection, nevertheless contained two pictures by Renoir, eight by Monet, eleven by Pissarro and three by Cézanne that were rejected. In all, 29 paintings out of Caillebotte's total of 67, almost half, were refused – and this even as a gift. Those that were accepted, however, marked a considerable breakthrough in the struggle for official acceptance of Impressionist art, and the subsequent donations of "modern" pictures found an easier passage into the august galleries of the national art collections, a tendency which has continued to the present day. Manet's ***On the Beach***, for example, and Degas's ***Madame Jeantaud at a Mirror***, two works which seem to be part of the firmament of Impressionism, only entered the museum as recently as 1970.

When the Jeu de Paume was selected for the Louvre's Impressionist collection the building required considerable renovation. The architects wisely decided on a relatively plain interior that would not intrude on the exhibits, but nowadays this has a slightly dull and even lacklustre appearance which, were it not for the quality of the paintings, could have a depressing effect. The layout, however, is very straightforward with the galleries occupying two floors along the full length of the building, within which the collection is broken up into separate sections mainly devoted to individual artists.

For some reason Toulouse-Lautrec's oils occupy the first space beyond the entrance hall, although it is not clear why this work should be placed here. Presumably it is not a mere afterthought, because this group of paintings, which includes ***La Toilette*** ★, ***Jane Avril Dancing*** and ***Cha-U-Kao, the Female Clown***, are all first rate. Rooms I and II are devoted to Degas, and successfully encompass the various themes which preoccupied the artist at different times in his career. ***Semiramis Building a City***, an example of Degas' early attempts at history painting, is unusual and less well known than his depictions of contemporary French life as seen at the races (***In Front of the Stands***), the ballet (***The Dancing Class***), or the bars of Paris (***Absinthe*** ★). The casual and apparently unposed arrangement of ***The Bellelli Family*** was Degas' attempt to imbue this traditional type of picture with the immediacy of "modern life", a theme which he pursued in numerous studies of women engaged in everyday domestic chores, such as ***The Tub*** ★ (1886) and ***Women Ironing*** (c.1884).

Rooms III and IV, interrupted by the staircase and constantly subject to groups of people in transit, are less suitable for display purposes, and for that reason the works hung there are not necessarily Impressionist but relate to the Impressionist movement at large. There are four large portrait groups by Fantin-Latour, consisting of a fine ***Homage to Delacroix*** ★ and **portraits** of Manet, Whistler and Baudelaire, as well as the ***Studio in the Batignolles***, in which Manet is seen at work surrounded by, among others, Renoir, Monet, Bazille and the novelist Émile Zola. These paintings provide some attractive background to the history of the Impressionists as a social group, showing that they shared more than just their opposition to the Salon.

Opposite these are a few **landscapes** by Corot, Boudin and Jongkind, *plein-air* artists whose work makes an appropriate introduction to the Impressionist paintings in Room V by Monet, Pissarro and Sisley. Of this latter group Sisley's ***Snow at Louveciennes*** is probably most typical of the work produced by the movement in the 1870s. Monet's ***Women in a Garden*** (1867), the most striking picture in the room, is exceptional if only because of its large scale. Monet had attempted to produce a major work for the Salon and also to vie with Manet's ***Déjeuner sur l'Herbe*** of four years earlier. In fact Monet had already begun an even larger canvas of a similar subject, which he was forced to abandon (although a fragment of a man and two women survives in this collection).

Rooms VI and VII at the extreme E end of the building contain works by Manet and are dominated by the two famous pictures ***Déjeuner sur l'Herbe*** ★ and ***Olympia*** ★. Both of these works had something of a *succès de scandale* in the 1860s which has assured their position in the history of art, but here they are surrounded by other paintings such as the ***Fife-player***, ***Portrait of Zola*** and the Goya-inspired ***Balcony*** ★★ that are less well known but in many respects more successful as works of art. The ***Serveuse de Bocks*** ★, a waitress serving beer in a Parisian café of the 1870s, is the finer of two versions of the subject, the other being in the National Gallery in London.

Returning to the middle of the building, the next two galleries (VIII and IX) have some of Monet's most famous pictures, including ***The Poppies***, as well as **landscapes** by Pissarro, Sisley and the early works of Cézanne and Gauguin. Cézanne also occupies the first gallery at the top of the staircase, but if you want to follow the sequence of galleries you must turn right for the remaining works by Monet, Renoir and Pissarro. Room X contains Pissarro's ***Red Roofs*** and Monet's ***Gare St-Lazare***, as well as five studies of ***Rouen Cathedral*** ★★. This is the only gallery where you can fully appreciate Monet's intention in the series, which was to vary the colour harmonies between each picture of the same subject. Here you can compare several examples, making this the only setting where the effect can be clearly followed. The near-musical variation in the colour harmonies is clearly evident. The following room has other serial works by Monet such as the ***Nymphéas*** (Waterlilies) and ***The Houses of Parliament***, but in this gallery it is Renoir's pictures, notably ***The Swing*** ⋆ and ***The Moulin de la Galette*** ⋆⋆ that predominate. The end gallery (XII) has Monet's ***Bridge at Argenteuil*** ⋆, Pissarro's ***Vegetable Garden*** and Mary Cassatt's ***Woman Sewing***.

To continue with the gallery devoted to Cézanne (XIII) you must return to the middle of the building. Here there are examples of Cézanne's mature still-lifes, landscapes and figure studies, notably the ***Card Players*** ⋆ and the ***Self-Portrait*** of 1880, as well as a few of the expressive early works painted before he was introduced to Impressionism by Pissarro. ***A Modern Olympia*** of 1873 appears somewhat crude in its execution but, in contrast to Manet's cool, detached version on the ground floor, Cézanne has tried to preserve the passion associated with Delacroix's high Romanticism.

Galleries XIV and XV display works by other principal Post-Impressionists: Seurat, Gauguin and van Gogh. Of the three, van Gogh is probably the best represented with such pictures as ***Vincent's Room at Arles***, ***The Church at Auvers*** ⋆, the ***Self-Portrait*** of c.1889 and the ***Portrait of Dr Gachet***; but Seurat's curious ***Circus*** as well as Gauguin's ***La Belle Angèle*** and ***The White Horse*** are also very attractive. It may be an indication of how strong this collection is in Impressionist paintings that the Post-Impressionist section, even with works such as these, seems comparatively weak. In compensation, however, there are several minor works, such as Seurat's studies for ***La Grande Jatte*** and several of Gauguin's ceramics and wood carvings, as well as Le Douanier Rousseau's marvellous ***Snake Charmer***⋆⋆, which considerably enhance the final rooms of this outstanding museum.

Musée d'Ennery

59 Avenue Foch, 75116
Tel. (1) 5535796
Open Sun and holidays only
Apr–Oct 1–5pm, Nov–Mar 1–4pm
Closed Mon–Sat, Aug

The Musée d'Ennery contains the collection of Far Eastern art amassed by the 19thC dramatist Adolphe d'Ennery. The exhibits, mainly drawn from China, Japan and Korea, cover a wide spectrum of Oriental arts and crafts – ceramic vessels and sculpture, enamels, prints, dolls, masks and wooden reliefs. The most important section, however, is that devoted to the small **Japanese carvings** in lacquer or ivory known as *netsuke*, of which there are over 2,000. These items, which originally acted as toggles on bags and belts, were developed in the 18thC into sophisticated representations of animals and figures, and display all the virtuosity of the Japanese miniature sculptor.

The same building also accommodates a small museum of **Armenian art** devoted to the arts and crafts of that much disputed region on the Soviet–Turkish border. This collection consists of religious and folk paintings, ceramics, books and manuscripts.

Musée de la Marine

Palais de Chaillot (Aile de Passy),
Place du Trocadéro
Tel. (1) 5533170
Open 10am–6pm
Closed Tues

The oldest museum of the quartet roofed under the Palais de Chaillot, the Musée de la Marine was formally inaugurated by Royal Charter in 1827 but had already come into being in 1748, when Louis Henri Duhamel du Monceau, Inspector-General of the Marine, offered his personal collection of model vessels to the Crown. In its present form, the museum presents over one thousand years of maritime history with the aid of models, plans and records, together with a wide-ranging collection of marine objects, from figureheads to anchor winches, from ship's bells to the elegant furnishings of an 18thC sea-captain's cabin. Extremely well laid out, the displays provide a wealth of information; for example, tracing the evolution of the traditional Viking longship to its final form (as depicted on the ***Bayeux Tapestry***) as a Norman fighting ship of the 11thC. The history of naval warfare takes up a large part of the museum's display space, but the value of the oceanic trading routes is not forgotten, with the ancient design of Portuguese caravels and graceful Venetian galleys paving the way for the great merchant ships of the 17thC and 18thC. Important individual ships and battles have complete showcases to themselves, but one cannot avoid noting the intense Gallic pride which mentions the Battle of Trafalgar only as the combat in which Lord Nelson died.

PALAIS DU LOUVRE

75041, Paris

The Louvre is surely the most famous museum in the world. Even Cole Porter mentions it and the ***Mona Lisa***, its most famous exhibit, in the same song of superlatives ("You're the Tops"). It is recognized throughout the world as a byword for "culture" even by people who have never visited it, and the ***Mona Lisa*** has become the archetypal "Old Master", known as much for its inestimable value as for any aesthetic merits. The French themselves have been assiduous in promoting this view; a point recognized by Marcel Duchamp over 60 years ago when he drew a moustache on the smiling face and exhibited it with a humorously deflationary inscription.

This attitude colours the atmosphere of the Louvre, and it is almost to be expected that an institution which acts as the flagship of French culture will be formidable as well as impressive. A single visit to the Louvre may not always be an enjoyable experience. The place is not merely large, it is immense, usually very crowded, and pervaded by a somewhat overbearing sense of officialdom.

On the other hand, it is a gallery of masterpieces, pictures, sculptures and antiquities which, if one is interested in art at all, should not be missed on any account. The answer is not to attempt to see the whole museum at once, partly because this is almost physically impossible, and also because it often means restricting yourself to the most famous pieces, which in these circumstances are not always the easiest to appreciate. If only one day is available, try to identify beforehand what you would like to see and give those items priority, because otherwise you will be worn out before you have seen one quarter of the museum. Should you have more time, break the collection up into manageable sections and allow yourself to concentrate on specific areas that can be assimilated in one session. This may sound very contrived and programmatic, but the alternative is often frustrating or exhausting, and you may come away vowing never to enter another museum.

The Louvre is housed in one of the largest royal palaces in Europe. There had been a castle on the site when, in 1527, François I decided to erect a residence there in close proximity to the city. In keeping with the king's taste for the Italian Renaissance style, Pierre Lescot, an early French classicist, was commissioned to design the new building, and despite modifications under the succeeding monarch Henri II, Lescot continued to build the square château that is now the Cour Carrée at the E end. It was Henri II's widow Catherine de Medici who in 1564 began a separate palace to the W of the Louvre on a site known as the Tuileries. This she entrusted to the great 16thC architect Philibert de l'Orme. In 1595 work to link the two buildings began.

The external appearance of the Louvre owes much to Louis XIV, for he commissioned Perrault, Le Vau and Lebrun to complete the present east front between 1667 and 1670. They then went on to redesign much of the remaining exterior of the Cour Carrée.

After this, it was not until 1800 that work was resumed. Napoleon I erected the triumphal arch, the Arc du Carrousel, and then set his architects Percier and Fontaine to restore the building and design the first of the long "arms" along the banks of the Seine. His nephew Napoleon III, in emulation of the first emperor, built the bulk of the N wing, facing the Rue de Rivoli and giving the immense edifice its present symmetrical form.

The building therefore has been a royal palace for most of its existence and, even during the period of neglect in the 18thC (when it was apparently something of a mixture between a shanty town and market place) it was still the property of the royal family. There had been art classes and galleries of paintings open to the academy and artists during much of this time, but it was only after the Revolution that it became the Musée de la Republique. It has remained the principal museum of national art and antiquities ever since.

Closure of Rooms and Depts. by Rotation.

Monday and Wednesday all rooms are open "in principle"

Thursday: Oriental Antiquities – complete dept.
Objets d'Art – complete dept.
Paintings – small rooms
Sculpture – Pavillon de Flore and Wing

Friday: Egyptian Antiquities – complete dept.
Oriental Antiquities – complete dept.
Greek and Roman Antiquities – Galerie Campana
Paintings – 2nd Floor (19thC)

Saturday: Greek and Roman Antiquities – Cour du Sphinx and Galerie Campana
Oriental Antiquities – complete dept.
Objets d'Art – complete dept.
Paintings – Small rooms, Flore Wing and Zenith Gallery

Sunday: Greek and Roman Antiquities – Bronzes and Galerie Campana
Oriental Antiquities – complete dept.
Objets d'Art – complete dept.
Paintings – Small Rooms, 2nd Floor (19thC)
Sculptures – Pavillon de Flore and Wing

Musée National du Louvre ☆☆

Palais du Louvre (main entrance: Porte Denon)
Tel. (1) 2603926
Open 9.45am–5.15pm (some rooms open until 6.30pm)
Closed Tues (and see above for Closures of Rooms by Rotation)
(Sun, Wed)

Because the national art galleries of France have been centralized to a very great extent, the overall standard or quality of the works of art in the Louvre is far higher than you might expect to see in provincial galleries. **Virtually every item we mention here would carry either a single or a double star if it were being discussed elsewhere in the *Guide*. We have therefore not allocated stars to the pictures and objects referred to here.**

François I was one of the first French monarchs to acquire paintings systematically, and his policy of importing the fruits of the Italian Renaissance brought Leonardo da Vinci himself to France, together with a number of excellent paintings, including Leonardo's ***Mona Lisa*** and ***Holy Family with St Anne***, which have remained in the country ever since.

This was the nucleus of the royal collection, but François's successors added to it with considerable zeal: there is scarcely a period in French monarchical history when the king did not acquire works of one period or another, whether for personal pleasure or for the aggrandisement of his reign.

The administrators appointed by the crown were equally active in the collection of art treasures. Cardinal Richelieu possessed one of the finest art collections in Europe, including the paintings by Perugino and Mantegna from the **studiolo** of Isabella d'Este, and his successor Mazarin was an avaricious connoisseur. Both of these private collections ended up in the Louvre. Mazarin was also instrumental in acquiring a body of work which, taken together, was the most significant addition to the royal treasures. Between 1649 and 1653 Oliver Cromwell and the agents of the Commonwealth set about disposing of Charles I's paintings, the greatest collection of the 17thC, which had earlier absorbed the spectacular collection of the Gonzaga family of Mantua. Mazarin ensured that many of the greatest works from this haul, especially those of Raphael, Correggio, Titian and Caravaggio, came to France.

Throughout this time the king and his ministers did not ignore the achievements of native artists, and in addition to commissioning sculptures for the palaces they also patronized the leading French painters. In 1665 for example, Louis XIV purchased a number of works which included 13 by Poussin and 2 by Claude Lorrain, and an inventory of the royal collection at that time reports that the king owned 32 pictures by the former and 11 by the latter. By such measures and schemes the royal collection, which would eventually become public, developed and expanded into the body of work now on display in the Louvre.

Louis XVI's reign was another period of expansion in the arts and his agents greatly enlarged the royal collection. This was also a time when public interest in the arts ran so high as to prompt the idea of a public gallery – a proposal fulfilled after the Revolution and greatly encouraged by Napoleon. Throughout his campaigns Napoleon and his contemporaries considered it perfectly right and proper to strip the museums and churches of defeated countries in order to concentrate the achievements of mankind in the capital of France. During this period, therefore, the Louvre housed a collection of paintings, sculpture and antiquities the like of which had never been assembled in one place before or is ever likely to be again. In 1802 when hostilities ceased, artists and connoisseurs from all over Europe travelled to Paris to see the treasures; according to the reports of visitors like Turner and Constable the array of art treasures, particularly those picked up by Napoleon in the Italian campaign, was fabulous. Vivant Denon, the director of the Louvre, presided over this hoard with an ardency that bordered on fanaticism. Scarcely was a town overrun or a mission planned than he had prepared an itemized list of the works to be deported to France. In this way the palaces, galleries and churches of Europe were denuded of their masterpieces. In 1815 most, but by no means all, of these works were returned to their previous owners and the Louvre was forced to fall back on its own considerable resources.

One feature which had changed, however, was that the Louvre had become uneqivocally a national gallery, and although the matter of rights and possession was not cleared up until after 1870, from this time onward the museum had moved into the public domain.

Hundreds of French artists throughout the 19thC have described the Louvre as their "training ground" or "apprenticeship". Painters as disparate as Ingres, Courbet, Manet, Cézanne and Matisse drew inspiration from the work of earlier masters displayed in the great galleries as much as from their contemporaries and teachers in the formation of their art. This has also entailed a shift in the source of the gallery's acquisitions. Where it had previously had the benefit of royal purchase, in the 19thC and 20thC numerous private donations flowed in to the benefit of the collection overall. For example, an apparent oversight in the taste of Louis XV and XVI resulted in the acquisition of only one painting by Watteau (the artist's Diploma picture, deposited there on his election to the academy). The bequest of Dr La Caze in 1869 brought in eight works by this artist, as well as paintings by Ribera, Hals and Rembrandt – all under-represented in the earlier collection, dominated as it was by the royal taste for grander and more impressive art. These last two centuries therefore have seen the Louvre develop from a royal palace containing the king's treasures into an international museum of considerable range and diversity.

The Collections

The collections of the Musée du Louvre are divided into six departments: Greek and Roman Antiquities, Egyptian Antiquities, Oriental Antiquities, Paintings and Drawings, Sculpture, and Objets d'Art (Decorative Arts). Other areas are represented in separate national museums (Far Eastern art at the MUSÉE GUIMET, for example, or posters at the MUSEE DÉ L'AFFICHE). At the time of writing, a department of Islamic art is awaiting its new location at Versailles, but it must be said that this is not always open to the public. The same is true of the permanent collection, since certain sections are closed as a matter of course on specific days of the week to allow time for restoration and other work (see p. 118 for details).

This policy however, is further complicated for the visitor by the fact that the Palais du Louvre is undergoing a lengthy programme of renovation. In some rooms major building work seems likely to continue into the foreseeable future, leading to the closure or reorganization of certain galleries. This should be recognized at the outset, because the layout and disposition of many works are sure to change as the renovation continues. Nevertheless the basic structure of six departments will continue, and in the past there has been a policy of allocating each department as far as possible to a clearly identifiable area within the museum. This has not always been easy because the Louvre was built as a palace, not as a museum, and some departments have been split, because of the space available or the nature of the exhibits, between different floors or wings of the building. So if you want to explore beyond the obvious area, you need a reasonable idea of the overall layout and location of the departments and their subgroups within the building.

Paintings and Drawings

Despite an attempt by André Malraux to reorganize the arrangement of paintings so that works from different periods and countries would be juxtaposed, the traditional and time-worn pattern prevails at the Louvre: each national school is displayed separately and in a roughly chronological sequence. The French school, as one might expect, has priority and opens on the first floor, to the right beyond the ***Winged Victory of Samothrace*** on the main staircase. Beginning with the ***Parement de Narbonne***, a painted silk altar cloth from the late 14thC, the initial Salle Duchâtel also contains Jean Malouel's ***Pietà tondo*** and Henri Bellechose's ***Martyrdom of St-Denis***, all prime examples of French art in the period before the dominance of the Italian Renaissance. The earliest works in the next room, the Salon Carré or Square Salon, continue this theme with the great ***Avignon Pietà*** (c.1446) and several ***small panels*** by the Master of Moulins; but the work of Jean Fouquet, the greatest French painter of this period, clearly reveals the first signs of Italian forms. Fouquet visited Italy some time during the 1440s, and the two portraits here, ***Charles VII*** (c.1443) and ***Guillaume, Juvenal des Ursins*** (c.1460) date from before and after the Italian period that had such a powerful impact on his style. The majority of the remaining works in this large room are from the 16thC School of Fontainebleau where, under the encouragement of François I, French painters adopted the Italian manner wholeheartedly. This rather forced acceptance of a foreign style led to some fairly unusual works, notably Antoine Caron's ***The Massacre of the Triumvirate***; but with Jean and François Clouet the court had excellent portraitists, finding an enduring image with ***Diana the Huntress*** (c.1550), a combination of classical poetry and refined eroticism.

The famous Grande Galerie off the Salon is an impressive long chamber in which the masterpieces of French art from the 17thC and 18thC are arrayed in procession along the walls. This is a testament to aristocratic taste and patronage, a collection of grand public works by such Court and Salon artists as Simon Vouet, Nicolas Regnier and Claude Vignon; but right in the heart of it there is an outstanding group of pictures by Poussin. To pick out ***Echo and Narcissus, The Triumph of Flora***, ***The Inspiration of the Poet***, ***The Arcadian Shepherds*** (***Et in Arcadia Ego***), or any of the deeply felt ***Four Seasons*** is only to highlight the quality of these works, drawn from all periods of the artist's career; it is completed by the ***Self Portrait*** of 1660, originally painted for his patron and friend Paul Fréart de Chantelou. By comparison, Poussin's great contemporary Claude Lorrain seems less strongly represented with a smaller group of ***landscapes*** and ***harbour scenes***. Philippe de Champaigne and Charles Lebrun, however, both have a strong presence, the former with the ***Dead Christ*** and ***Ex-Voto***, and the latter with an exceptional group portrait ***Chancellor Séguier on Horseback with his Attendants*** (1661), an uncharacteristically vivid work that rivals the greatest portraits of the 17thC. The more naturalistic strand in French art of this period is taken up by the canvases of Georges de La Tour (***The Adoration of the Shepherds***, ***The Magdalene with a Candle*** and ***St Joseph***) and the brothers Le Nain (***The Blacksmith's Shop*** and ***The Cart***), but even in such scenes of peasant life there is still a strong classical sense of structure and restraint.

The break between the 17thC and 18thC is marked at the Tribune of the Grande Galerie by four paintings by Watteau: The ***Embarkation from Cythera***, the ***Portrait of a Gentleman***, ***Diana Bathing*** and the uncharacteristically large ***Gilles***. Nearby are two attractive works by Chardin. Then, as if to emphasize the predominance of the Rococo, the gallery continues with works by Boucher (***Vulcan's Forge***) and Fragonard (the bold and exuberant ***Women Bathing***). Most of these pictures are unsuited to the overpowering scale of their setting, but after two large paintings by Hubert Robert (***The Temple of Diana at Nîmes*** and ***The Pont du Gard***) the French collection moves into the smaller rooms of the Mollien Wing to the right where the more intimate Rococo works are taken up again. Here there are several ***Fêtes Galantes*** by Watteau and his followers; ***Still-Lifes*** by Chardin; more dazzling oil sketches and paintings by Fragonard; and the delightful ***Diana Resting after her Bath*** by Boucher. Room III of the Mollien Wing introduces a sterner note with the ***Paternal Curse*** and the companion pieces, ***Ungrateful Son*** and ***Son Punished*** by Greuze, alongside Vernet's ***Landscapes*** and Mme. Vigée-Lebrun's ***Self-Portrait with her Daughter.*** This prepares the ground for the Salle Mollien itself, in which the paintings of David and his pupils are hung.

Beginning with the ***Andromache Mourning Hector*** this momentous series of pictures by David proceeds through the great classical exhibition pieces, ***Oath of the Horatii***, ***Brutus***, and ***The Sabine Women***. But David's portraits are also very impressive, and paintings of ***M. and Mme. Seriziat***, the ***Marquise d'Orvilliers*** and ***Mme. Récamier*** reveal the supreme powers of observation in this aspect of his art. David's impact on the course of French art was enormous, and the remaining pictures in this gallery are virtually a celebration of the master's influence. Gerard's ***Portrait of Isabey*** and Guérin's ***Return of Marcus Sextus*** are obviously within David's canon, but even works such as Prud'hon's ***Divine Justice (Retribution Pursuing Crime)***, or Girodet's ***Burial of Atala*** are linked to David's cool manner. Ingres, a pupil of David, preserved the essence of his art into the second half of the 19thC, and pictures like ***Oedipus and the Sphinx***, ***The Great Odalisque*** and the portraits of ***The Rivière Family*** elaborate the rigorous principles of design first seen in the antique themes of the late 18thC.

Ingres acts as something of a bridge between the Salle Mollien and the ornate Salle Denon, where his paintings continue with the ***Portrait of M. Bertin***, ***Rogier and Angelica*** and the famous ***Bather of Valpinçon***. Then, as if to demonstrate the length of Ingres's career, the display of his work mingles with many of the Salon painters of the mid to late 19thC – Hippolyte Flandrin, Théodore Chassériau, Paul Delaroche and Thomas Couture. This room also contains a tinted plaster sculpture by Carpeaux, ***Four Parts of the World Supporting the Canopy of Heaven***, originally planned as a fountain in 1872 for the Paris Observatory.

The French school continues to a climax in the next room, the Salle Daru, where works by Gros, Géricault, Delacroix and Courbet are displayed. This room is virtually a collection of the Salon sensations of the early 19thC, beginning with Gros's ***Napoleon in the Pest House at Jaffa*** and ***Napoleon on the Battlefield at Eylau***, each one imbuing the general with the characteristics of Christ. Géricault's ***Charging Chasseur*** and ***Wounded Cuirassier*** precede the ***Raft of the Medusa***, which is in turn followed by Delacroix's ***Massacre at Chios***, ***Death of Sardanapalus*** and ***Liberty Leading the People***. In the midst of these immense compositions Delacroix's ***Women of Algiers***, the masterpiece of his later style, strikes a more quiet and thoughtful note, but the tendency to paint on a grand scale is taken up again by Courbet in his two greatest and most significant works; ***The Burial at Ornans*** of 1849 and the ***Studio of the Painter***, described by Courbet as "A real allegory – summing up seven years of my artistic life".

At this point the main galleries of French art come to a close, but the remainder of the 19thC collection, the smaller but not necessarily the less important work, begins again on the second floor of the Cour Carrée, accessible from the Egyptian room off the main staircase.

In the ten galleries along the S wing of the Cour Carrée, the development of French art throughout the 19thC is traced once again. Beginning with David and his contemporaries, the Neoclassical Room has David's striking though unfinished portrait of ***Mme. Trudaine*** and the ***View of the Luxembourg Gardens***, the artist's only landscape, painted during his imprisonment in the Luxembourg in July 1794. This room also contains Gros's romantic study of ***Napoleon on the Bridge at Arcole*** and a beautiful ***Portrait of a Black Woman*** by Mme. Benoist, one of David's leading pupils.

Gallery II, the Ingres Room, displays several of this artist's portraits, as well as ***The Turkish Bath*** of 1862, the culmination and synthesis of numerous studies on this theme throughout his career. Here you can also see works by his friends and contemporaries Marius Granet, Chassériau and Gérôme. Gallery III, which is broken up into smaller spaces for landscapes and genre paintings, includes pictures by P.M. de Valenciennes (24 studies of the ***Roman Campagna***), Boilly and Corot – the latter well represented by a large number of portraits and landscapes such as the ***View of the Coliseum***, ***The View of Tivoli*** and ***The Belfry at Douai***. Gallery IV, the Romantic Room, contains several studies by Géricault and two unusual paintings, ***The Derby at Epsom*** (the result of his sojourn to England in 1821), and the ***Madwoman***. Beside these there are some oil sketches by Delacroix as well as the ***Jewish Wedding in Morocco*** and ***Hamlet and Horatio***.

Gallery V houses the earlier part of the Moreau-Nelaton Collection (the Impressionist pictures are now in the JEU DE PAUME) which was given to the state in 1906. The donor's grandfather had bought work from contemporary painters in the middle of the 19thC, so the collection has a number of works by Géricault, Corot and Daumier as well as two beautiful paintings by Delacroix: the ***Still Life with a Lobster*** and the ***Orphan Girl in a Cemetery***. Gallery VI, known as the Picturesque-Romantic Room, has more works by Delacroix (***The Apartment of the Comte de Morny***) and Chassériau alongside paintings by relatively minor artists, Huet, Diaz de la Pena and Isabey. Room VII displays the Thomy Thierry collection, again of French 19thC art, with works by Delacroix, Corot, Barye and the Barbizon painter Théodore Rousseau (***The Oaks***). Gallery VIII, the Salle Chauchard, has yet another work by Delacroix, ***The Tiger Hunt*** of 1854, but here it is overshadowed by several peasant scenes by Millet, including the famous ***Angelus***, beloved of pious houses and Sunday schools.

Room IX defines its contents in its title, the Room of the Great Realists, and has work by Millet (***The Gleaners***), Daumier (***The Emigrants*** and ***The Laundresses***) and Courbet (***Cliffs at Etretat***). Room X, in marked contrast, has Moreau's ***Rape of Europa*** and several of Puvis de Chavannes' enigmatic easel paintings (***The Poor Fisherman*** and ***Young Girls by the Sea***). This room also displays a painting that, though not French, is quite in keeping with the period: Whistler's sombre ***Portrait of the Artist's Mother***.

Continuing into the W Wing of the Cour Carrée, the first two rooms have been set aside for the Helène and Victor Lyon Bequest comprising 65 paintings (mostly French) given to the Louvre in 1961. The first room contains mainly Impressionist works which, were they not part of a larger collection, would probably be in the JEU DE PAUME, consisting of pictures by Monet, Renoir, Sisley, Degas and Cézanne. At this stage the French collections of the Louvre are virtually complete, although isolated works do crop up in individual collections throughout the museum. The second of the two rooms containing the Lyon Bequest is more diverse, with paintings such as ***The Skaters*** and ***View of Renan*** by the 17thC Dutch landscapist Jan van Goyen, and two works by each of the 18thC Venetian artists Canaletto and Giandomenico Tiepolo.

Having followed the French School from its grand opening in the Salon and the Galerie to this relatively remote part of the museum, we can now move on to the English paintings which take up the succeeding room in the W wing of the second floor of the Cour Carrée. Unfortunately, the Louvre's collection of English pictures is so poor as to constitute a serious omission in the museum's collections overall. Many leading figures, such as Ramsay, Reynolds, Fuseli, Wright of Derby, Lawrence, Turner and Bonington, are represented, but by works well below the standard these painters were capable of achieving. Only Gainsborough and Constable are present in any strength, the former with three portraits, including ***Conversation in a Park***, which may be an early portrait of the artist and his wife, and the latter with four landscapes. The fact that these English paintings share a room with another under-represented field – German art of the Romantic period – is an indication of the weakness of this area of the collection. One painting by Caspar David Friedrich and one by Arnold Böcklin complete the Cour Carrée galleries, apart from the room containing the Princesse de Troy collection of 17thC Dutch paintings.

The Louvre has one of the finest displays of Italian art in existence, particularly in the field of the High Renaissance. It is also easier to find than other national schools because, from the moment you enter the building, there are signs pointing towards the "Mona Lisa". The urge to highlight this work above all others has led to the disruption of the normal chronological sequence, so you encounter the Italian 16thC paintings first, displayed in a large room, the Salle des Etats, between the Grande Galerie and the Salle Denon. However, this fine room is of a scale and proportion to do justice to the grandiose achievement of the High Renaissance.

On entering the room you can hardly fail to be struck by the hordes of people, sometimes hundreds, crowded in front of the ***Mona Lisa*** on the wall, and if you get close enough to catch a glimpse of the famous picture you will see that security has been the first consideration in its display. Alone among the treasures of this great museum the ***Mona Lisa*** or ***Gioconda*** sits behind bullet-proof glass in a hermetically sealed chamber, often flanked by two armed guards. Nothing is more likely to enhance its fame and popular reputation while diminishing the opportunity to see it as a work of art to be enjoyed. It is without doubt a great picture, with a surface that connoisseurs used to describe as having a "marvellous craquelure", but just a short distance away is a work of equal if not greater quality – ***The Virgin of the Rocks***, also by Leonardo da Vinci – which you can approach without all the ceremonial trappings normally associated with meeting a world-famous celebrity. In fact this room contains no fewer than six paintings attributed to Leonardo, the legacy of François I's admiration for the artist, including ***La Belle Ferronière***, the ***Virgin and Child with St Anne*** and ***St John the Baptist***.

The other paintings in the room read like a list of masterpieces: by Raphael there is ***La Belle Jardinière***, one of his finest compositions on the theme of the Holy Family, ***St Michael Overcoming the Devil***, given to François I by Lorenzo de Medici, another ***St Michael***, this time with a pendant St George, and the ***Portrait of Baldassare Castiglione***, author of *The Courtier*, a book of Renaissance manners. By Correggio there is the ***Mystic Marriage of St Catherine*** and ***Antiope Asleep***. By Andrea del Sarto ***Charity*** and ***The Holy Family***, and there are other works by the Florentine Mannerists Rosso, Pontormo and Bronzino. The same room also has an impressive display of Venetian High Renaissance art, particularly by Titian, and including the ***Concert Champêtre*** (previously attributed to Giorgione and taken to be the model for Manet's ***Déjeuner sur l'Herbe***), ***the Man with a Glove***, the ***Pardo Venus***, ***Christ Crowned with Thorns*** and the tragic ***Entombment***. To add to this group there are excellent works by the younger Venetians – Tintoretto's ***Paradise*** and ***Susanna Bathing***, Palma Vecchio's ***Adoration of the Shepherds*** and Veronese's ***Calvary***, all overlooked by the latter's vast ***Marriage at Cana***, which fills most of the N wall.

The earlier Italian pictures occupy the far or W end of the Grande Galerie, beginning with Cimabue's monumental ***Virgin with Angels*** of 1240. From here the gallery proceeds through most of the principal figures of the early Renaissance, and although the collection is patchy there are excellent panels by Simone Martini (***Christ Carrying the Cross***), Fra Angelico (***Coronation of the Virgin***), Uccello (***The Battle of San Romano***), Carpaccio (***St Stephen Preaching***), Antonello (***Portrait of a Condottiere***), and Giovanni Bellini (***The Resurrected Christ***). Two artists in this section are especially worth looking at in greater detail. Botticelli's **fresco fragments** from the Villa Lemmi, now relocated in the Percier and Fontaine Galleries (off the main staircase) are particularly good, while the paintings by Mantegna constitute the strongest group by any artist in this period. ***St Sebastian***, an example of this artist's sophisticated classicism, hangs beside a small ***Crucifixion***, the central predella panel from the ***San Zeno Altarpiece*** and the two mythological works, ***Parnassus*** and the ***Battle Between the Vices and Virtues***, which were both part of the celebrated *Studiolo* of Isabella d'Este.

Italian paintings of the 17thC and 18thC are split between two galleries. The Salle des Sept Cheminées in the first floor corner of the Cour Carrée (immediately behind the ***Winged Victory of Samothrace***) contains some of the large-scale works, the most important being Annibale Carracci's ***Hunting and Fishing***; a cycle of three paintings on the ***Legend of Hercules*** by Guido Reni; and Caravaggio's controversial but very moving ***Death of the Virgin***. The remainder are housed in the Pavillon de Flore, a long narrow gallery overlooking the Carrousel gardens. Here you can see more paintings by Carracci, Guido Reni and Caravaggio (***The Fortune Teller***); works by Gentileschi, Domenichino, Pietro da Cortona, Guercino, Rosa and Guardi; and a group of oil sketches by G.B. and G.D Tiepolo.

Beyond this group, and occupying the remainder of the Galerie Flore, is the Bestigui Collection that was given to the Louvre in 1953 on condition that it remained intact. This contains a number of disparate but very good paintings by such artists as the Master of Moulins, Fragonard, David, Ingres and Rubens, but the masterpiece of the collection is Goya's ***Portrait of the Countess del Carpio (Solana)***, conveniently placed to lead directly into the Spanish School proper in the Pavillon de Flore – the western extremity of the long S arm.

The Spanish section in the Louvre occupies five galleries in the Pavillon de Flore, but it is a mere shadow of the immense collection of Spanish paintings, assembled by Louis Philippe, which had such a marked effect on artists such as Courbet and Manet. Unfortunately, that collection was dispersed in 1853, and the present Spanish works on display have had to be gradually acquired over the last 100 yrs. Nevertheless the Louvre has examples of all the greatest Spanish artists, though the quality of the works is in some cases disappointing. Velazquez, perhaps the greatest of all Spanish painters, has three works on display, but only the ***Portrait of Mariana of Austria*** approaches this artist's best work. Much the same is true of the three pictures by El Greco, of which the ***Saintly King*** is the finest; but Ribera's ***Boy with a Club Foot***, Murillo's ***Beggar Boy*** and Zurbaran's ***Scenes from the Life of St Bonaventura***, reveal a richer vein; and Goya's ***Mariana Waldstein*** is another work of the highest quality.

Early Flemish paintings tend to be on a relatively modest scale, and are here displayed in the so-called small rooms facing the Seine (beside the Galerie Medici). This was the school which developed the use of oil paints into a technique of breathtaking refinement and there are examples of this in the work of Memlinc, Petrus Christus and Gerard David. The gallery also possesses two panels of the highest quality by Jan van Eyck and Rogier van der Weyden, the two greatest artists of 15thC Flanders. ***The Madonna of Chancellor Rolin***, originally in the cathedral at ***AUTUN*** where the sitter's family lived, is a fine example of Jan van Eyck's subtle use of light and tone to create the transition between the meticulously detailed interior and the panoramic landscape in the background. Rogier's well preserved ***Braque Triptych*** reveals this artist's more fluid linear design. The qualities embodied in these works did not survive into the following century, but there are examples of the transitional period in paintings by Jan Gossaert and Quentin Mabuse, where the signs of Italian influence are already dominant.

Sharing this suite of small *cabinets* are a number of miniature portraits by the French 16thC court painter François Clouet, together with a few early German paintings of the same period. This school is relatively thin here but again there are some notable works, the finest being Dürer's ***Self-Portrait*** of 1493, perhaps painted for his fiancée, and Holbein's portraits of ***Ann of Cleves***, Queen of England and fourth wife of Henry VIII, and ***Erasmus of Rotterdam***.

The Flemish school in the 17thC is taken up in the gallery known as the Salle van Dyck, leading on from the Grande Galerie. Here van Dyck predominates, particularly with the portraits from his English period: ***James Stuart, Duke of Lennox*** and the spectacular ***Charles I***, dismounted and in casual hunting clothes, perhaps the greatest of his royal works. But the room also contains pictures by van Dyck's contemporaries, Jordaens and his own master Rubens. In fact several aspects of Rubens's versatile output are represented here, but it is the intimate personal works, such as portraits of his second wife ***Helène Fourment***, which find most favour with contemporary taste. They are certainly in marked contrast to the grand public display of the next room, the Galerie Medici.

In 1621 Rubens was commissioned to undertake two great mural cycles, the ***Battles of Henry IV*** and the ***Life of Marie de Medici***, Regent of France, for the newly built Palais du Luxembourg. The second of these projects, comprising 21 large canvases, was completed for the Luxembourg but did not remain there, being repeatedly moved until the present gallery was fitted up to accommodate it. The paintings are undoubtedly impressive, but the liberal deployment of mythological figures, the contrived dramatic compositions, and the scale of the series make them somewhat unapproachable on anything but the most deferential level. ***The Arrival of Marie de Medici at Marseille***, complete with Neptune, tritons and naiads, is generally taken to be the greatest or at least the most characteristic of the series, but the ***Joys of Regency***, probably the only canvas painted largely by the master, is finer in its overall handling and detail.

Several other paintings by Rubens are exhibited in the *cabinets* facing the Tuileries Gardens, but this series of galleries is mainly devoted to Dutch painting of the 17thC.

The Dutch School of the 17thC is divided between two parts of the Louvre: the small rooms or *cabinets* on the N side of the Medici Gallery, and the Salle des Sept Mètres. The principal pictures are housed in the latter which opens directly off the main staircase and joins up with the Grande Galerie. Of this group, Frans Hals's ***Gypsy***, de Hooch's ***Drinker***, and **landscapes** by van Goyen and Ruisdael are all prominent, but there is no doubt that the most important works here are the 16 or so paintings attributed to Rembrandt. A few of these are probably by the artist's followers or assistants, but the group includes such masterpieces as the small ***Christ at Emmaus***, ***Bathsheba Bathing***, four ***Self-Portraits***, and a portrait of ***Hendrickje Stoffels***, his companion during the last years of his life.

Much the same period is covered in the *cabinets*, but there is greater emphasis on the so-called "Minor Masters" – painters of landscape, still-life and genre scenes, the staple of the Dutch school. This takes in such artists as Elsheimer, Hobbema, Terborch, Steen, de Hooch and Teniers, all of whom tended to work on a small scale. Vermeer, an artist who was formerly considered part of this company, but whose reputation has risen over the last century to the level of a "major master", has only one work in the collection, the small ***Lacemaker***, but the painting is a marvellous piece with all the luminosity of his greatest work.

The drawings collection, or *Cabinet des Dessins* on the second floor of the Pavillon de Flore, is not open to the general public although scholars and those with a particular interest can gain admission for the purposes of study (a letter of introduction is required). To compensate for this the department authorities organize numerous temporary exhibitions in an adjacent gallery to display aspects of the collection. Its main strength is in French drawings and pastels but, as with the paintings, there is a fairly broad range with a number of important items. These include the ***Codex Vallardi*** with drawings by Pisanello, and one of Jacopo Bellini's detailed ***Sketchbooks***, from which he and his workshop derived many of their painted compositions.

Sculpture

The sculpture department of the Louvre tends to be overshadowed by the paintings, partly because none of its items has acquired the fame of masterpieces such as the ***Mona Lisa*** or ***Bathsheba Bathing***; but one advantage of this is that the galleries are usually quiet whereas the painting rooms are distractingly overrun with visitors.

The collection is arranged chronologically in some 30 rooms along the ground floor of the long S wing. The first rooms display medieval sculpture, mostly from the Romanesque and Gothic churches of the Ile de France, as for example the fragments from St-Denis and St-Germain-des-Prés; but the later tomb sculptures, such as Room 5's monumental ***Effigy of Philippe Pot*** supported by life-size *pleurants* or "weepers", are slightly different, for these are complete in themselves and not merely parts detached from a larger scheme.

The medieval sculpture on display represents for the most part pieces that have survived from churches destroyed in the Wars of Religion, the Revolution, or one of the more recent conflicts. The heads from ***CLUNY*** provide a fine example of this category.

Sculpture played an important role in the development of the French Renaissance, and there are pieces by all the French sculptors of the 16thC, as well as some examples of the Italian models that they emulate: Della Robbia **terra cottas**, a ***Virgin and Child*** attributed to Donatello, and Cellini's ***Nymph of Fontainebleau*** (which originally decorated Diane de Poitier's château at Anet). The Palais du Louvre is of course itself a Renaissance monument, at least in the Cour Carrée, with sculptural decoration by Germain Pilon and Jean Goujon; both these sculptors are represented by independent works (Pilon's ***Three Graces*** and Goujon's ***Nymphs and Tritons*** from the Fontaine des Innocents in Paris). The same is true of Michel Colombe (***St George Slaying the Dragon***) their leading contemporary.

There is also some late medieval sculpture from outside France, such as the German ***Isenheim Virgin*** attributed to Veit Stoss, Tilman Riemenschneider's ***Virgin of the Annunciation***, and Gregor Erhart's ***Mary Magdalene***.

The 17thC galleries consist mainly of French works (Puget and Coysevox) as do those of the 18thC, when there was undoubtedly a flowering of this art in France (see Bouchardon's ***Cupid***). Successive generations of sculptors are represented, many of them by the small trial pieces which were designed to display the artist's skill – Pigalle's ***Mercury*** is perhaps the finest example of this type of work. The 18thC also saw the emergence of a fine tradition of portrait sculpture, the greatest exponent of which was Houdon. Houdon's **busts** of eminent figures such as Voltaire, Diderot and Rousseau provide the main source for our knowledge of what these people looked like.

An exception to the dominance of French work in this section occurs in the Neoclassical room, where Canova's delicately sensual ***Psyche Revived by Cupid's Kiss*** is the principal exhibit, but in the 19thC rooms the French monopoly returns in the form of the four principal Romantic sculptors: David d'Angers, Barye, Rude and his pupil Carpeaux. These artists take you almost to the end of the century, and the final room on the ground floor completes the period with one major work by Rodin, the ***Age of Bronze***.

In addition to the main sculpture galleries there are two rooms on the lower level of the Pavillon de Flore which house the most important items in the department. The first of these has works by Duquesnoy and other Baroque sculptors, while the main room contains the ***Slaves*** by Michelangelo, installed there in 1975 to commemorate the fifth centenary of the artist's birth. Executed between 1513 and 1520 for the huge tomb of Julius II in St Peter's, they arrived in France in 1550 as a gift to Henri II long after the project had been abandoned. This explains their unfinished state, a condition that preserves the power of the artist's conception. Michelangelo's theories of art are well known, especially his attitude to marble carving, where he felt himself to be freeing the figure imprisoned in the block. Michelangelo carved many unfinished creatures, but few works illustrate this concept of liberation more forcefully than these powerfully roughed out ***Slaves***.

THE LOUVRE: SELECTED WORKS AND LOCATIONS

Greek and Roman Antiquities

1	***Woman of Auxerre***	Room 6
2	***Winged Victory of Samothrace***	Main staircase
3	***Husband and Wife*** Sarcophagus	Room 14
4	***Black Figure Amphorae*** by Exekias	Galerie Campana (II)

Oriental arts

5	Stele of ***King Naram-Sin***	Room I (103)
6	Statues of ***Gudea***	Room II (104)
7	Statue of ***Ebih-il*** (The Intendant)	Room III (105)
8	***Archers of the Persian Kings***	Room VIII (110)

Egyptian Antiquities

9	Stela of ***King Djet*** (The Serpent King)	Room III (133)
10	***Head of King Didoufri***	Room VI (131)
11	***Seated Scribe***	Room XI (129)
12	Painted relief of ***Sethi I***	Room XI (125)
		Galerie Henri IV
13	Statue of ***Queen Karomama***	Room 246

Sculpture

14	Effigy of ***Philippe Pot***	Room 5
15	***Nymphs*** from Fontaine des Innocents, Jean Goujon	Room 7 (Salle Jean Goujon)
16	***Mercury***, J-B Pigalle	Green Gallery
17	***Slaves*** from tomb of Julius II, Michelangelo	Room 9, Pav. de Flore

Objets d'Art and Furniture

18	Tapestries of ***Maximilian's Hunt***	Room 6 Cour Carrée
19	Ivory ***Harbaville Triptych***	Room 4
20	Ivory ***Virgin*** from Ste-Chapelle	Room 5
21	**Cabinets** by A-C Boulle	Room 13
22	**Monkey Commode** by Charles Cressent	Room 16
23	**Jewel Cases by** Jacob-Desmalter	Room 36

Paintings

24	***Avignon Pietà***	Salon Carré
25	***Et in Arcadia Ego***, Poussin	Grande Galerie
26	***Ex-Voto***, Philippe de Champaigne	Grande Galerie
27	***Portrait of Chancellor Séguier,*** Charles Lebrun	Grande Galerie
28	***The Embarkation from Cythera***, Watteau	Grande Galerie
29	***Women Bathing***, Fragonard	Grande Galerie
30	***Diana Resting after her Bath***, Boucher	Mollien Wing
31	***Oath of the Horatii***, David	Mollien Gallery
32	***Raft of the Medusa***, Géricault	Salle Daru
33	***Death of Sardanapalus***, Delacroix	Salle Daru
34	***Burial at Ornans***, Courbet	Salle Daru
35	***Virgin of the Rocks***, Leonardo	Salle des Etats
36	***Mona Lisa***, Leonardo	Salle des Etats
37	***La Belle Jardinière***, Raphael	Salle des Etats
38	***Portrait of Baldassare Castiglione***, Raphael	Salle des Etats
39	***Crucifixion***, Mantegna	Grande Galerie
40	***The Entombment***, Titian	Salle des Etats
41	***The Marriage at Cana***, Veronese	Salle des Etats
42	***Bathsheba***, Rembrandt	Salle des Sept Mètres
43	***The Death of the Virgin***, Caravaggio	Salle des Sept Cheminées
44	***The Madonna with Chancellor Rolin***, Van Eyck	Cabinets Seine
45	***The Lacemaker***, Vermeer	Cabinets Tuileries
46	***The Cycle of Marie de Medici***, Rubens	Medici Gallery
47	***Portrait of Charles I***, Van Dyck	Salle Van Dyck

A Paintings
B Graphic Art
C Sculpture
D Greek and Roman Antiquities
E Egyptian Antiquities
F Oriental and Islamic Art
G Objets d'Art and Furniture
Closed to public

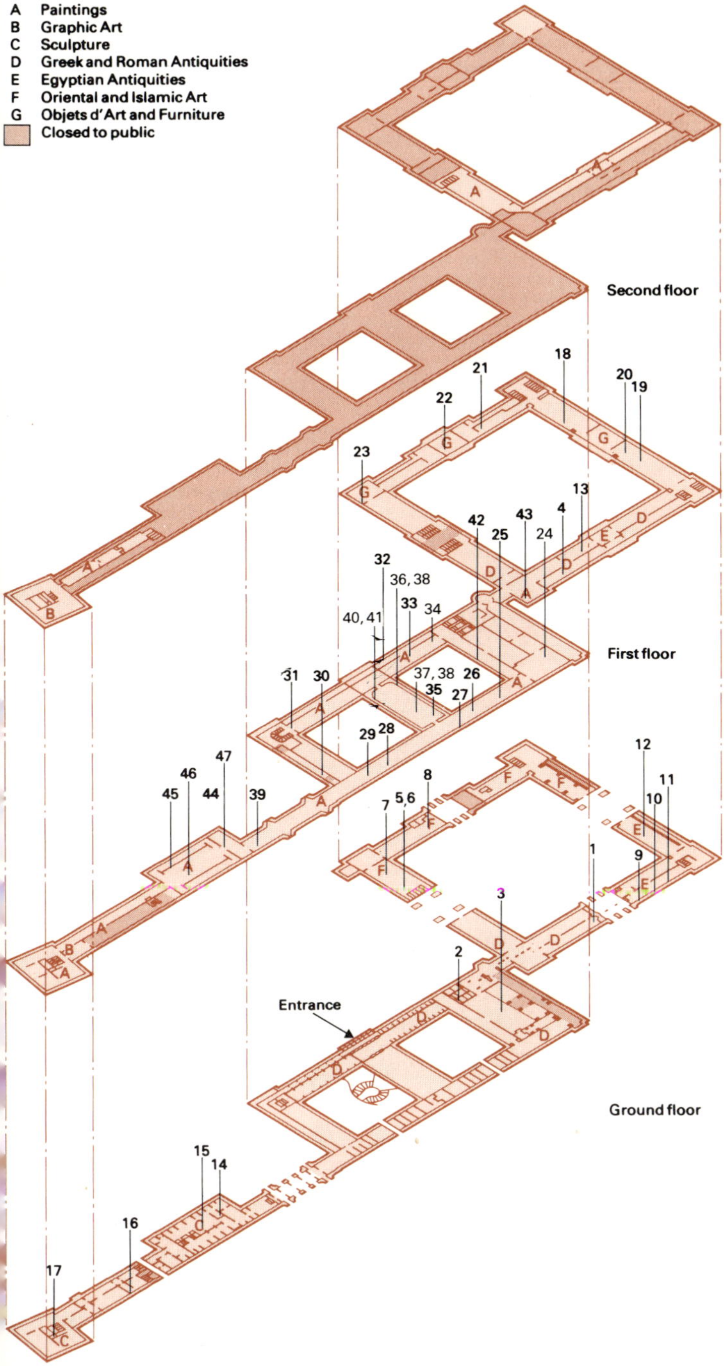

Greek and Roman Antiquities

You are plunged into the antique collections almost as soon as you enter the Louvre, since the Salle Denon, through which most visitors pass, is flanked by two rows of Roman sarcophagi. These are generally ignored in the haste to reach more famous exhibits, but include fine pieces such as the legends of ***Meleager*** and ***Achilles***. The main staircase at the end is dominated by the dramatically placed ***Nike*** or ***Winged Victory of Samothrace***, a 3rdC Hellenistic statue that acts as a focal point for the whole museum. However, the main part of the collection occupies a series of rooms on the ground floor beyond the staircase.

The most famous and popular exhibit is still the ***Venus de Milo***, and this is in some respects surprising. Changes in taste and our understanding of Greek art during the present century now conclusively reveal the figure for what it actually is – a rather over-refined Hellenistic statue of the 2ndC emulating the classical style of two or three centuries earlier. This highlights one of the major shortcomings of the collection for, apart from a few fragments from the Parthenon and Olympia, the Louvre is notably lacking in good classical sculpture. In fact, the **Salle des Cariatides** with its group of much-copied figures is closer to 19thC academic taste than to a modern gallery of ancient Greek art. Here you can see such figures as the ***Borghese Warrior***, the ***Versailles Diana***, the ***Aphrodite of Cnidus*** and the ***Diadoumenos*** (youth binding his head) of Polycleitus – or rather the copies after these lost works – but despite their influence in the past they do not command much interest nowadays as examples of the Greek achievement in sculpture. One reason for this apparent gap may be the fact that the French were less active than their British and German counterparts in excavating the important Greek sites during the 19thC and 20thC, the period when our understanding of the antique world underwent a radical revision. French interests seem to have been more concerned with the Egyptian and Mesopotamian civilizations, which helps to explain the corresponding strength of those departments.

The Salle des Cariatides itself is nevertheless very interesting. One of the oldest rooms in the Louvre, it was built for Henri II by Pierre Lescot and became an important state chamber. Mary Stuart married the future François II here, and in 1591 Henry IV had three members of the assembly hanged in it. The caryatids that support the minstrel's gallery on the end wall, and give the room its name, are by the French Renaissance sculptor Jean Goujon. Though heavy in comparison with the antique figures, they are nevertheless an interesting example of early French classicism inspired by many of the sculptures on display.

The classical sculpture may be disappointing, but there are a number of very interesting earlier works. The ***Woman of Auxerre*** (Room 6), a small figure of Cretan origin, is impressive, as is the ***Rampin Head***, though the torso and horse are casts from the originals in the Acropolis Museum in Athens. This and the beautifully columnar ***Hera of Samos***, two archaic works from the 6thC BC, indicate the sense of volume in Greek art that reached its climax in the 5thC.

Rooms 14 and 15 are devoted to the Etruscans, a people who established a flourishing society in central Italy during the first millennium BC. Their emergence was contemporary with that of the ancient Greeks, and many of their products, particularly the painted pottery, was either derived from Greek art or heavily influenced by it. Their burial customs, however, were quite different and gave rise to their most characteristic and enduring images, for the terracotta sarcophagi that were used for interments regularly featured a stylized reclining likeness of the deceased on the cover. The 6thC ***Husband and Wife***, a double portrait from Cerveteri, is one of the finest examples of this type. It must have been a popular exhibit for some time because it appears in one of Degas's most famous prints, ***Mary Cassat at the Louvre*** in the 1880s.

The Etruscans were eventually overcome by the Romans in the 4thC BC but not before they had passed on many aspects of their way of life to the conquerors. The sarcophagi in the Salle Denon are a good example of this influence but the Romans also shared the Etruscans' respect for Greece, and a large proportion of Roman art is either in emulation of Greek work or, at worst, derivative in a debased way. There is nowadays very little interest in Roman art, but from the works on display in Rooms 16 and 19 it is clear that there was great vitality in the areas unaffected by Greece. Roman portraiture, as seen in the bust of ***Livia*** and a series of emperors, demonstrates the level of realism that artists were presumably encouraged to bring to even the most aristocratic of sitters, and the **Pompeiian frescoes** in Room 19 reveal a freshness in landscape art that was not matched until the 17thC.

The Greek and Roman collection continues in the Salle des Bijoux on the first floor of the Cour Carrée (behind the ***Winged Victory***), where you can see a selection of Roman decorative arts. This includes cameos and ivories as well as a number of silver vessels from the ***Treasure of Boscoreale***, found in a well near Pompeii where they had presumably been left for safekeeping during the eruption of Vesuvius in 79AD. The 102 pieces of decorative silverware were purchased by the Baron de Rothschild, who gave them to the Louvre in 1895. In another case nearby a similar collection, the ***Treasure of Notre Dame d'Alençon***, consists of two silver repoussé masks dedicated to the goddess Athena.

The nine rooms of the Galerie Campana house the collection of painted pottery and terracotta figurines, many of which came from the Campana estate, purchased in 1863. This has been supplemented with gifts and purchases, so that the Louvre now has a very good collection of Attic pottery from the Geometric, Black, Red and White Figure styles, as well as examples of Corinthian and other provincial styles. The beauty of this work is at least in part due to the vitality of the design and draughtmanship found at all levels, but several excellent pieces have been attributed to specific artists, notably Exekias, the master of the Black Figure style, and Euphronios, whose large krater depicting the fight between ***Hercules and Antaeus*** is one of the finest Red Figure vases.

This department finishes in the Salle Henri II (Salle La Caze) with a collection of bronze sculpture and ornaments drawn from the whole period of the antique world. Though diverse in appearance, quality and origin, the display includes fine items such as a 5thC ***Head of an Athlete*** from Beneventum and a slightly later statue of ***Apollo*** which, like most surviving bronzes, was found in the sea.

Egyptian Antiquities

Egyptology could almost be described as a French creation, for the serious study of Egyptian antiquities begins with the scientific expedition which accompanied Napoleon to Egypt in 1798. It was then that parts of the present collection were first assembled under the curatorship of the great scholar Champollion, whose contribution to the art of decipherment led to the first successful interpretation of hieroglyphics – the picture-writing used on many ancient Egyptian monuments. Before his death in 1852 Champollion added greatly to the early nucleus of the department, notably in 1826 when he acquired the extensive collection of Henry Salt, the British Consul in Cairo. This policy continued throughout the 19thC and early 20thC, with the result that the Egyptian Department of the Louvre is now recognized as one of the finest in the world.

The Egyptian rooms occupy part of the ground and first floors of the Cour Carrée and are best reached from the Greek and Roman Department, although there is a direct entrance (not always open) from the Porte Champollion facing the river. The ground floor rooms contain most of the monumental statuary and the large-scale stonework, including such items as inscriptional reliefs, carved and decorated sarcophagi, columns, and a **complete Mastaba** or chapel, as well as effigies of one kind or another and various funerary items such as place settings, statuettes and model boats. Several pieces from this array are particularly striking: the 3rd millennium BC ***Stela of King Djet*** (the Serpent King) in Room III (133) the ***Head of King Didoufri*** from the Old Kingdom (Room VI/131), the ***Seated Scribe*** and the XIX Dynasty painted relief of ***Kings Sethi*** and ***Hathor*** (Room XI/125).

Among the galleries and crypts on the ground floor there is a small Coptic section displaying Alexandrian pieces from the period after the Roman conquest and the rise of Christianity. The most characteristic works from this period are also funerary, but the emphasis shifted from the cult of the dead towards commemorative portraiture in a wax encaustic medium. Some of this, particularly the ***Fayum Portrait***, combines naturalism and poetic feeling to a degree that has rarely been equalled.

The first floor rooms are devoted to small statuary, furniture and what is described as "minor arts", although it is doubtful if this distinction would have been recognized in ancient Egypt. An example of the type of item subsumed under this heading is the ***Knife of Gebel-el-Arak*** (Room 236) from c.3400BC. The ivory handle of this very early piece is carved with battle and hunting scenes which, apart from the intrinsic beauty of the craftsmanship, reveal interesting information about the implements, dress and habits of the earliest Egyptians. Among the other exhibits on the first floor is a considerable amount of jewellery, some from the tomb of ***Rameses II*** (Room 240c), funerary furniture from the tomb of ***Chancellor Nakht***, c.2510BC (Room 238b), the **golden cup** given by Pharaoh Thoutmosis to General Thoutii (Room 240c), the painted limestone head of a man, known as the ***Salt Head*** (Room 244e), and the elegant bronze statue of ***Queen Karomana*** (Room 246f).

The upper galleries are again completed by some Coptic/Alexandrian works, in this case Ptolemaic statuary, ceramics and jewellery. These emphasize clearly the curious admixture of Eastern, Hellenistic and Egyptian cultures that went to make up this last phase of the Nile civilizations.

Oriental Arts

Oriental Arts is something of a misnomer as a description of the contents of this department, which actually deals with the products of the Middle East through several millennia. (The Far Eastern antiquities are displayed in the MUSÉE GUIMET.) It does nonetheless cover a huge geographical area – Arabia, North Africa and the countries of the Eastern Mediterranean. In ancient times this region saw the emergence of the Sumerian and Babylonian civilizations of Mesopotamia, and felt the impact of the Hittites, Phoenicians and Assyrians. Later, the area fell before Alexander the Great, becoming part of the Hellenistic world and then of the eastern Roman Empire.

The collections, housed in the northern half of the Cour Carrée on the ground floor, are arranged in a roughly chronological sequence while maintaining the identity of each culture in separate galleries. Sumerian works have priority and are exhibited in the first four rooms. This was the civilization that saw the emergence of cuneiform or "wedge-shaped" writing in the 4th millennium BC, a development of epoch-making proportions which was used by most of the succeeding cultures of the Levant. Cuneiform writing is clearly seen on a number of the exhibits, but most significantly on the famous Babylonian ***Code of Hammurabi***, a black basalt slab upon which the 282 laws are inscribed. Known mainly in its simplified version, "An eye for an eye and a tooth for a tooth", it was one of the earliest codes of law and fashioned the life of Mesopotamian society. The Mesopotamians were accomplished sculptors and from this collection four items are particularly notable. The ***Stela of Eannatum*** (known as the Stela of the Vultures) and the ***Stela of King Naram-Sin*** are both early examples of high quality relief carving, while the statue of ***Ebeh-il*** (the Intendant) and ***Gudea Seated***, the latter being one in a series of 11 figures, demonstrate the powerful sculptural qualities in the free-standing works.

To the casual observer it is often the Assyrian and Achaemenid (Persian) sculpture that is most impressive, partly because of the scale of the works, most of which were to decorate palaces and temples of huge proportions. The collection here is no exception, but pieces like the large ***capital from the palace of Artaxerxes at Susa*** are also works of great beauty. Two great bulls, back to back at the top of a column and carved with immense grandeur to express the strength of the structure, supported the mammoth crossbeams of the roof. In the following room (VIII/110) are some of the glazed brick panels depicting the ***Archers of the Persian Kings***. These were known as the Immortals, and there were originally 10,000 of them in the palace of Darius at Susa. Further on the Assyrian rooms have a series of similar **reliefs** from palaces at **Dur-Sharrukin** (Khorsabad) and **Nineveh** in the 8th and 7thC BC which were probably the source for the Persian works at Susa.

Islamic Art

The collection of Islamic Art, presently displayed in the middle of the Oriental rooms, will only remain in the Louvre until new premises at ***VERSAILLES*** are ready for occupation. The area covered by this department is geographically much the same as that of Oriental Antiquities, but represents the period after the Islamic conquests of the 7thC and 8thC. The resulting art forms were an amalgam of Arabic design and the indigenous artistic traditions of the conquered countries, tempered by the requirements of the new religion. Colour, ornament and calligraphy were given precedence over figurative art, but this did not diminish the potential or the quality of the work produced in the countries of Spain, North Africa and the Middle East.

Ceramics were probably the most widespread and influential medium, giving scope to different types of decoration and formal experiment, as you can see from works as diverse as the 10thC ***Samarkand Dish with Cream Background***, the 9thC ***Persian Dish with Standard Bearer***, the 13thC ***Mameluk Chalice*** (or so-called ***Sultanabad Cup***) or 16thC ***Turkish Peacock Dish***. The same motifs are found in other media such as the metal ***Barberini Vase*** (Syria 1256) and ***St-Louis Font*** (Egypt c. 1300) or the 10thC Persian silk ***Shroud of St-Josse*** named after the abbey in northern France where it was placed after the First Crusade. Moslem metalworkers were renowned for the quality of their arms. The collection here includes an Ottoman helmet, the ***Mogul Dagger*** and the ***Sefevid Sabre***, all fine examples of the armourer's art.

Objets d'Art

The Galerie d'Apollon on the first floor of the Louvre (entered from the Rotonde d'Apollon to the left of the ***Winged Victory of Samothrace***) seems appropriate for the collection of objets d'art, since the gallery itself has something of the elaborate encrusted decoration one finds in many of the exhibits. The room was originally built in the reign of Charles IX (16thC) to link the Cour Carrée with the Grande Galerie, but it was burned down in 1661. Louis XIV began the restoration immediately under Le Vau and commissioned Lebrun to execute the decoration. Under this painter, who had already received considerable royal favour, a cycle was prepared celebrating the "Sun King" with the theme of Apollo, although the project was broken off when Louis diverted his attention and resources to Versailles. After this, several attempts to proceed with the decoration were initiated but it was only in 1850, when Delacroix painted ***Apollo Triumphing over the Serpent Python*** in the middle of the ceiling, that the scheme was completed.

As if to maintain the tenor of the decoration, most of the exhibits in this first major gallery have royal associations, not least the crowns used in the coronation of Louis XV and Napoleon I. There are also the **crown jewels** and surviving **regalia** of the treasure begun by François I (several celebrated brooches, gems, ornaments and ceremonial arms) but the most interesting works come from the **Treasure of St-Denis**, and in particular the **porphyry vase** in the form of an eagle which was commissioned by the great Abbé Suger in the 12thC.

From here the Department of Objets d'Art continues in the Colonnade Galleries (beyond the Egyptian collections in the Cour Carrée) which have been appointed with the panelling and decoration of several important 17thC rooms. The ceiling and wainscoting of Room I were originally in the Queen's Council Chamber at Châteauneuf de Vincennes (1654–58) while those in Room II formed part of the king's bedchamber on the site of the Salle des Sept Cheminées in the 17thC, when the Louvre was a royal palace. Room III has many fittings from the King's state chamber in the Palais du Louvre, planned by Lescot and Scibec de Carpi in the 16thC. These three rooms also have some fine **carpets** and **tapestries** to complete the ensemble, but the remainder of the collection is displayed in a more traditional manner.

By its very nature, a large department of decorative arts will contain a huge number of exhibits, including as it does such fields as ivories, enamels, reliquaries, ceramics and glassware, tapestries, carpets, furniture, gold and silverware, chinoiserie as well as several personal or period collections. Obviously the only way to appreciate its quality is to spend a considerable amount of time in the museum, but here we may identify works which are generally regarded as being of particular importance.

Among the ivories two Byzantine works, a 6thC ***Imperial Diptych*** and the 10thC ***Harbaville Triptych*** (Room 4), and a 13thC French ***Virgin from the Treasure of Ste-Chapelle*** (Room 5) are pre-eminent. In fact medieval church treasures or "ars sacra" constitute the majority of the early works, and another magnificent piece is the 13thC enamel ***ciborium*** (vessel to hold consecrated wafers) by the Limousin master G. Alpais (also in Room 5). The Italian Renaissance is best represented by the series of 16thC bronze statuettes, particularly those by Riccio, such as the ***Poet Arion*** in Room 6 and the curious ***Gnome Astride a Snail*** by a contemporary Florentine Mannerist. The same room also has a collection of medals, one of the most characteristic and highly admired art forms of the Renaissance, especially in the hands of such masters as Pisanello and Matteo de'Pasti. Tapestry was a craft that flourished in France to such an extent that workshops in Paris and Beauvais were considered the finest in Europe by the 17thC, and there are several examples of Gobelins and Beauvais weaving. But the most interesting tapestries in the collection are in the series known as ***Maximilian's Hunt*** commissioned by Charles V in 1535 and woven in Belgium to designs by the painter Bernard van Orley.

Of the furniture, the cabinets in Room 13 by A.-C. Boulle, Louis XIV's cabinet-maker and the first great *ébeniste*, are probably the finest, particularly the two large ebony cupboards formerly owned by William Beckford and the Duke of Hamilton in London. Equally impressive is the lighter Rococo furniture of Charles Cressent in Room 16, notably a pair of kingwood cabinets with gold fittings from the de Selle collection, and a **commode** with bronzes of children swinging a monkey. Another small piece of furniture, the ***Necessaire (dressing-case) of Marie Leczinska*** wife of Louis XV, is more interesting for its contents – objects such as the delicate silver gilt dolphins and china that the queen presumably carried with her on journeys.

The Impressionists and the Seine

Impressionist works today enjoy enormous popularity, and many visitors who daily crowd the JEU DE PAUME in Paris may be curious to see the famous places associated with these artists. Unfortunately, many of these sites are now in drab suburban or industrial areas that seem to have little in common with the colourful, cheerful places portrayed in the Impressionists' canvases. Yet a visit to the north-western environs of Paris, where most of the best-known Impressionist sites are to be found, can still be an interesting and indeed memorable experience.

Many of these sites were chosen by the Impressionists because they lay less than an hour away from Paris by public transport and were easily accessible by train. The Gare St-Lazare was the Paris station that served most of them, and it too inspired a controversial work by Monet (now in the Fogg Art Museum, Cambridge, Massachusetts).

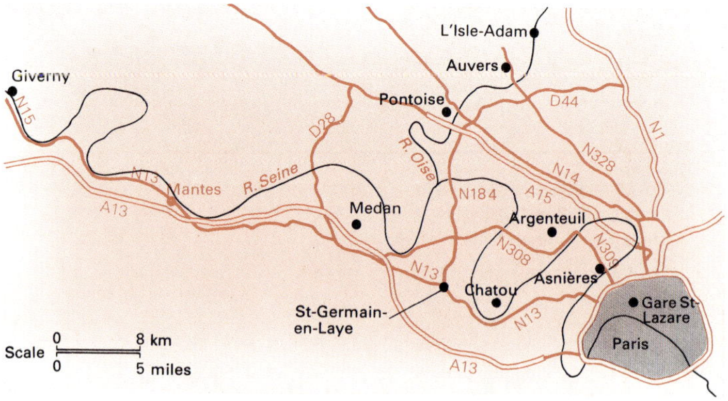

The stretch of the Seine near Chatou, where the first railway to be built in France crossed the river towards St-Germain-en-Laye, became a popular place for Parisians to spend their Sundays. One of the riverside resorts here, La Grenouillère, was regularly painted by Monet and Renoir. In the early 1870s Monet acquired a house at Argenteuil about 10km (6 miles) along the Seine to the N of Chatou, where Renoir frequently worked with him, and the two were often joined by Manet, Berthe Morisot and others. Though described in 1869 as a "pretty little town", Argenteuil was already being absorbed into the industrial sprawl of Paris when the Impressionists started to go there. But the artists prefered to show only the more attractive aspects of the place, despite their reputation for realism.

Following the Seine back to Paris you come to the island of the Grand Jatte, a 19thC park and pick-up place for prostitutes, where the Post-Impressionist artist Seurat painted his famous ***Sunday Afternoon at the Grande Jatte*** (The Art Institute, Chicago). His equally well-known ***Bathing Scene at Asnières*** (National Gallery, London) shows how heavily industrialized this part of the Seine valley had become by early 1883. Today not even the park of the Grande Jatte survives. By contrast the valley of the Oise, the Seine's tributary, remains in many parts as beautiful as when the Impressionists and others painted it. From 1866 Camille Pissarro lived nearby at Pontoise, where there is modest museum to him, and was joined in 1872 by

Seurat's ***Bathers at Asnières,*** *1883, shows industrial smoke in background.*

Cézanne. On the hilly, wooded western banks of the Oise, going N towards Auvers, you can still clearly recognize the scenes and locations chosen by Pissarro and Cézanne when they painted along this stretch of the river.

The largest house in Auvers is still the one that once belonged to the eccentric Dr Gachet, a great patron of avant-garde art at this time. Cézanne moved here to be near the doctor in 1873, and the Barbizon landscapist, Daubigny, was also then living in the village (there is a memorial bust of him on the main road leading to the parish church).

Auvers's most famous association, however is with van Gogh, who came here in May 1890 after his period in the mental asylum at St-Remy in Provence. The village has changed remarkably little, and much will be familiar to anyone with a knowledge of van Gogh's work: the church, for instance, which was a favourite motif of the artist. At the bottom of the village near the railway station there is a communal park with an idealized statue of van Gogh by Zadkine.

Further on you reach the former Café Ravoux, now the "Maison van Gogh", where a plaque records his residence at the café, and his death there. In July 1890 he shot himself in the fields behind the village and died soon afterwards in his room here. You can visit this small dark room which looks out on the Town Hall, itself the subject of many of the artist's paintings. The artist and his brother Theo are buried side by side next to the L wall of the village cemetery, just outside the village beyond the church. Immediately behind the wall stretches the enormous wheatfield that inspired the greatest works of the artist's last months. The road leading up to the cemetery has been named the Rue Émile Bernard in homage to the Symbolist painter who attended van Gogh's funeral and was later moved to paint it from memory.

Finally Giverny, not far from Auvers, though much prettified and subjected to chic renovation, should be the main pilgrimage point for anyone touring the Impressionist sites. For this is where Monet settled in 1883 and made his famous garden and lily pond. The Monet family burial plot is in the cemetery behind the apse of the church.

Musée National des Monuments Français

Palais de Chaillot (Aile de Paris), Place du Trocadéro
Tel. (1) 2723574
Open 9.45am–12.30pm, 2–5.15pm
Closed Tues
(Wed)

Perhaps the most extraordinary feature of this museum is that all the exhibits are reproductions. Founded in 1882, the collection owes much to Viollet-le-Duc, the renowned scholar of the Middle Ages, and his lifelong concern with the artistic heritage of France. All the casts and copies were moved to the Palais de Chaillot when the building was restored for the 1937 World Exhibition.

The collection is divided into two sections, sculpture and wall-paintings. The first aims to present the visitor with an all-encompassing vision of French monumental sculpture, and the vast display shows famous works from all regions and all periods. It is interesting to trace the continuing development of theme and style in French sculpture, but you may find that the density and diversity of the exhibits make it almost impossible to grasp the particular merits of individual sculptors. However, certain of the casts are outstanding, such as the elegant and restrained work of Jean-Antoine Houdon, the most celebrated French sculptor of the 18thC – notably his ***St Bruno*** (the original is in Santa Maria degli Angeli, Rome). The more dramatic style of Jean-Baptiste Carpeaux, famous for his freize of ***The Dance*** on the Paris Opéra, is well represented by an excellent cast of his pediment for the Pavillon de Flore of the Louvre (1863).

In the galleries devoted to wall-paintings, the displays show the murals as they appear in their original architectural settings. This gives a good idea of the development and increasing sophistication of wall-painting techniques, running parallel to stylistic developments in architecture and the interior decoration of the great religious houses and châteaux. Works from the Carolingian period to the Early Renaissance (9thC–14thC) have been selected from all regions of France, including magnificent examples from the ancient church of Saint-Savin.

Musée Marmottan ☆

2, Rue Louis Boilly
Tel. (1) 2240702
Open 10am–6pm
Closed Mon

The origins of the Musée Marmottan date from 1932 when Paul Marmottan bequeathed his father's house and art collection, which he himself had considerably enriched, to the Institut de France. At that stage it consisted of some good medieval works, including tapestries, furniture and 15th–16thC wooden sculpture (***The Fourteen Intercessors***); a considerable amount of French 18thC and early 19thC fine and decorative arts such as Empire furniture and **paintings** by Gérard, Guérin and Vernet; and a miscellaneous collection of early Italian and North European pictures. From this latter group, now housed on the first floor, the most interesting are Nicholaes Maes', ***Portrait of a Young Girl***, ***Crucifixions*** by Dieric Bouts and Martin Schongauer, and two wings of an **altarpiece** by Frans Pourbus depicting the donors in adoration of a missing Virgin.

This already attractive range of works was extended with the addition of several very good 19thC French pictures from the collection of Mme. Donop de Monchy. The greatest of these is the famous ***Impression-Sunrise***★ by Monet, a picture which appeared in the first Impressionist exhibition of 1874, and from which the very term "Impressionism" was derisively coined.

Perhaps because this picture was already in the collection, Claude Monet's son Michel decided in 1966 to give a large number of his father's works to the Musée Marmottan. This donation occupies a newly appointed gallery in the basement of the house, and with reasonable attention to the setting the curators have created a very good display. The surroundings are quiet and unobtrusive, allowing the pictures to shine through in their scintillating colour and light. The bulk of these works was produced by Monet during the latter half of his career in the studio and garden that he prepared at Giverny. Here he devoted most of his attention to the seemingly endless series of ***Nymphéas***★★ or Waterlilies, and from the range of these works at the Marmottan you can appreciate how the sense of space alters as the paint attempts to describe the insubstantial blossom suspended in translucent, reflective water. The sheer number of canvases devoted to this theme has the effect of drawing you into the artist's obsession; but the museum also possesses earlier Impressionist pictures by Pissarro and Renoir, although here again Monet outnumbers all others. ***Camille and her Cousin on the Beach at Trouville***, (1870) ***The Gare St-Lazare*** (1872), ***The Tuileries*** (1876) and the excellent ***Rouen Cathedral***★ in pink, blue and yellow (1894) are perhaps the finest paintings in a body of work that virtually constitutes a monument to a single artist. The fact that Monet's pen, pipe, palette and other **memorabilia** are also on display further increases this impression.

As an addendum to this outstanding collection, as recently as 1980 Daniel Wildenstein presented a large number of late medieval **illuminated manuscripts** to the museum, and these will be on display from time to time as facilities and space are available.

Musée Gustave Moreau ☆

14, Rue de la Rochefoucauld, 75007
Tel. (1) 8743850
Open 10am–12.45pm, 2–4.45pm
Closed Mon, Tues
(Wed)

In his own lifetime, Gustave Moreau (1826–98) acquired a reputation as something of an eccentric. Until the age of 30 he led a highly social life, travelling widely and taking an interest not only in art, but also in music and the theatre. In 1859, however, after a period of 2yrs spent in Italy, he retreated from public view and devoted himself to painting elaborate Biblical and mythological fantasies in a detailed, almost encrusted, manner, evolving the subject matter and technique over many years. Nonetheless, despite his hermetic tendencies, Moreau emerged from the sequestered world of his studio in the 1890s to take up a post at the École des Beaux-Arts.

Rouault, Matisse and Marquet were amongst the pupils who benefited from his tolerant and intelligent teaching. Indeed, when Moreau left his studio and its contents to the French state in his will, he designated Rouault as the collection's first curator. As a result of Moreau's bequest, this small and enchanting museum houses a truly astounding display consisting of almost his **total artistic output**; over a thousand works are here.

A visit to Moreau's house and studio is a unique and extraordinary experience. Paintings cover every available inch of wall space, and the building's dark panelling and twisted wooden staircases contribute to a feeling that you are entering a very private and precious world. The blurred outlines and sombre colouring of an early ***Self-Portrait*** show how, at the age of 24, the artist saw himself as a shadowy, insubstantial character. A later ***Self-Portrait*** drawing, done in middle age, reveals the pensive stare of a deeply contemplative nature. The intensity of colouring of ***Centaur with Dead Poet***, a picture painted at the same time as the latter self-portrait, indicates the development of Moreau's vivid and powerful imaginative vision.

The incredible detail and rich colouring so representative of Moreau's best work owes much to the influence of medieval tapestries, as can be seen in ***The Unicorns***, an exquisite ensemble of courtly grace, with the nude stretched languorously in the foreground giving the painting a disturbing, semi-erotic air. ***Jupiter and Semele*** ★ provides the most complete manifestation of the artist's vision and aims. In a long note to the museum catalogue, Moreau sums up this extraordinary painting as a hymn to divinity, or the explanation of the great mystery of Life. Another extremely interesting work is ***The Life of Humanity***, a series of nine panels mounted in a framework of richly gilded wood, which combines Moreau's biblical and mythological source material.

Not all the works on display concentrate on this subject matter: there is a magnificent oil sketch of a ***Galloping Horseman*** flying across a great plain beneath a stormy, eerily lit sky, and a host of Italian landscapes. These are among the smaller works, which range from slight sketches to detailed watercolours, and are displayed in a series of hinged frames along the side walls of the principal rooms.

Incidentally, the catalogue is worth buying as it contains fine reproductions and helpful footnotes to the works.

Musée de Notre-Dame

10, Rue du Cloître-Notre Dame
Tel. (1) 3254292
Open 2.30–6pm
Closed Mon–Fri

Devoted entirely to the history of the Cathedral of Notre-Dame, this charming little museum came into being in 1951 as a result of the combined efforts of the diocesan authority, the Cathedral chapter, and the Society of the Friends of Notre-Dame. The fascinating and comprehensive display of **manuscripts**, **plans**, **paintings**, **prints** and other objects on view owes much to the assiduous work of Pierre Joly, curator of the museum from 1951 to 1971. Notre-Dame was founded in the 7thC by the Breton king, Judicael, and you can see fragments of stonework attributed to this period; these were discovered when the ground of the *parvis* (the open space around a church) was excavated.

Paintings, drawings and prints reveal the changing appearance of the cathedral, but perhaps more interesting are the records and plans which show the various architectural alterations and additions which have taken place over the centuries. Much work was done in this respect during the 18thC: Robert de Cotte was responsible for the rebuilding of the choir in 1714, and Jacques Soufflot, the greatest of the French Neoclassical architects, later undertook the introduction of Roman regularity and monumentality to the inherent structural lightness of the cathedral's Gothic architecture. The Gothic revival of the 19thC saw Viollet-le-Duc, scholar, restorer and exponent of the Gothic style, contributing much to the preservation of Notre-Dame's earliest stonework. Other showcases concentrate on the cathedral's role in the national history of France, displaying and explaining the celebration of important state occasions such as the entry of the kings and the consecration of Napoleon. There is also an absorbing section dedicated to liturgical music.

Musée de l'Orangerie

Place de la Concorde/Quai de Tuileries, 75001
Tel. (1) 2659948
(Closed for restoration – no definite date given for re-opening)

The Orangerie, like the JEU DE PAUME on the opposite side of the Tuileries, was built in 1853 as part of a move to expand the Louvre complex at the start of the Second Empire. For the past 50yrs it has been best known as the location of Monet's greatest ***Nymphéas*** ★★ or Water-lily cycle, one of the artist's grandest projects and the masterpiece of his last years. The pictures, conceived at Giverny (see ***PARIS ENVIRONS***), are displayed in a circular format that occupies the full range of the spectator's vision and gives free rein to the liberation of light and colour – themes that are in many respects the central preoccupation of all Monet's art. The paintings were offered to the state in 1922 (though Monet continued work on them right up to his death in 1926) and were installed in a specially prepared room in the Orangerie where they have remained ever since. Unfortunately, in recent years at least, it has been difficult to see the pictures because the building has been under constant repair or renovation. While this work is in progress, and there is no definite date for completion, the ***Nymphéas*** paintings will continue to be unavailable to the public.

Musée d'Orsay

9, Quai Anatole France, 75007
Tel. (1) 5444185
(Museum in preparation. Opening 1986)

The 19thC splendour of the former Gare d'Orléans, combined with the older and rather more refined elegance of the Hôtel d'Orsay, will be the setting for this prestigious new museum. At the time of writing, extensive restoration work is in progress, under the guidance of the Italian architect Gae Aulenti (also responsible for the imminent redesigning of the Modern Art Museum at the Centre Pompidou) and is expected to be completed by 1986. The handsome façades, roofs and principal interior decoration of both buildings are to be conserved and restored as integral parts of the new museum. Adjoining buildings in the Rue de Lille and Rue de Bellechasse are also included in this ambitious scheme of refurbishment, both for their historical value and to provide better access to the museum. An enormous area some 20,000 sq. m (72,000 sq. ft) in total, has been allocated for the Musée d'Orsay's permanent collection. As befits a principal museum of the arts, this will display a broad diversity of artistic output – **paintings, sculpture, drawings, posters, photographs** – drawn entirely from works of the 19thC and 20thC. There will also be a variety of imaginative and informative displays to define the links and parallels that exist between the plastic arts, literature and music. The major paintings destined for the Musée d'Orsay are on show in the PALAIS DE TOKYO and include not only a large number of important works by Toulouse-Lautrec and Odilon Redon, but also a magnificent Neo-Impressionist collection featuring Seurat's ***Winter Circus*** and some very considerable works by the Nabis Brotherhood, in particular those of Pierre Bonnard. Eventually the contents of the famous Impressionist gallery, the JEU DE PAUME, will come to be housed in the Musée d'Orsay as well, making the Tuileries building available for temporary exhibitions.

Musée du Palais de Tokyo (Ancien Musée National d'Art Moderne)

13, Avenue du Président Wilson
Tel. (1) 7233653
Open 9.45am–5.15pm
Closed Tues
(Wed)

Still known as the old National Museum of Modern Art, the Palais de Tokyo (which occupies one wing of the solid classicizing building constructed for the 1937 International Exhibition) now houses temporary exhibitions from the adjacent MUSÉE D'ART MODERNE and the uncompleted MUSÉE D'ORSAY. These give some indication of the pictures destined for the new museum across the Seine, and it is clear that the Musée d'Orsay will have an outstanding collection. Most of the works to be seen here are **Post-**

Impressionist and, as one might expect, all the principal figures such as Seurat, Cézanne, Gauguin and van Gogh, will be well represented. Also on display will be a number of lesser but equally interesting painters from the late 19thC and early 20thC.

Musée du Petit Palais ☆

Avenue Winston Churchill, 75008
Tel. (1) 2651273
Open 10am–5.40pm
Closed Mon
(Sun)

The enormous domed entrance hall of the Petit Palais lives up to expectations aroused by the ornate splendour of the building's exterior façade. Gleaming marble pilasters soar up to the expansive curves of the ceiling, flamboyantly decorated by Albert Besnard during the first decade of the 20thC. Besnard's commission was to present the principal sources of art, and his statuesque forms and luxuriant foliage represent four main subjects: Antique Art; Nature, or the Living World; Christian Art; and the Thinker, or Human Intellect.

Designed by Charles Girault, the building itself was erected in the closing years of the 19thC as the Palais des Beaux-Arts de la Ville de Paris. Soon known affectionately as the Petit Palais, its original task was to house the retrospective of French art shown in the 1900 exhibition. It was then given to the city of Paris to house the latter's considerable art collection, which contained a large number of modern French works. In 1902, the young museum was given a further dimension through the presentation of the Dutuit Collection – a truly magnificent array of paintings and objets d'art that had been carefully and knowledgeably put together by the two young Dutuit brothers. They also presented their library of over 10,000 books to the Petit Palais. Further generous donations to the museum resulted in the rich and varied items on view today.

Indeed, the diverse chronology and geography of the objects can make a visit to the Petit Palais a confusing experience. You may leave the place with a mass of differing images: **Egyptian bronzes** juxtaposed with fine **medieval tapestries**, elegant **Greek amphorae** set against the strong colouring of Italian **16thC Maiolica ware**. However, any culture shock you may feel as a result of the rich variety of paintings and objects in the collection should not be taken as an indication of equal confusion in the museum's display techniques. On the contrary, each spacious room – the exhibition galleries curve round the central courtyard – is carefully laid out with an obvious theme connecting the items on display.

Among the beautiful, rare and exciting objects in the Petit Palais, you should not miss the work of the master potters and vase painters of Ancient Greece, represented here by several fine **amphorae** decorated in the early Black Figure technique as well as examples of the later, more naturalistic Red Figure style. Moving to Europe in the Middle Ages and Early Renaissance, the Petit Palais possesses notable religious reliquaries, ivories, carved wood friezes, **tapestries** and **enamels** – a particularly exquisite pair of the latter being attributed to **Godefroy de Huy**, the master enameller of Limoges. Precious manuscripts from these periods are also on view, including the beautifully illustrated ***History of Alexander*** ★ originally from the library of the dukes of Burgundy.

The museum's ceramics range from the decorative lead-glazed earthenware produced by the French St-Porchaire pottery to the delicate brilliance of **Sèvres porcelain**, the finest works from this factory being produced in the latter half of the 18thC. This period is well represented not only by porcelain and paintings but also by elegant furniture and wall-hangings.

The Petit Palais's collection of pictures includes several beautiful **medieval paintings** and an excellent cross-section of 17thC **Dutch art**, with fine examples of **still-lifes, landscapes** (especially by Hobbema, van Goyen and Ruisdael) and interiors. Rembrandt's ***Portrait of the Artist in Oriental Costume*** shows the painter, resplendent in tasselled waistcoat and turban, with a stern set to his jaw – possibly embarrassed by his exotic appearance.

French art of the 19thC and early 20thC, the original section of the museum and still in many respects the strongest, is represented by virtually all the leading names – David, Géricault, Delacroix, Corot, Manet, Monet, Renoir, Pissarro, Cézanne, Redon, Bonnard and others. Some of these items are exceptionally good, particularly an outstanding **group of pictures by Courbet** ★ that includes three of his greatest works: ***Self-Portrait with a Dog***, ***Portrait of Proudhon and Family*** and ***Women beside the Seine***. There are also some individual collections covering the work of, for instance, J. J. Henner, Felix Ziem, and the Danish painter H. Brokman, as well as a large number of **drawings** by Puvis de Chavannes.

Artists of Montparnasse

Montparnasse, named after the classical mountain home of the Muses, carries associations that suggest its importance to artists. Its original development as an artists' quarter arose as a result of its proximity to the École des Beaux-Arts, and by the beginning of the 20thC it had superseded Montmartre as the place of liveliest cultural activity in Paris. So it remained until World War II, after which most of its major writers and artists left the area. But whereas Montmartre today seems over-prettified and rather artificial, Montparnasse is less spoiled and more human, despite some very brash modern urban development. It probably gives a better idea of what an artists' quarter was once like.

Montparnasse's greatest beauties are hidden. Leaving the main boulevards you will come across numerous alleyways and charming courtyards crammed with ramshackle studios, many of which are not mentioned in guidebooks. A tour of these places will pleasantly complement a visit to the delightful studio-museums of BOURDELLE and ZADKINE.

Rodin's celebrated statue of Balzac stands at the busy midpoint of Montparnasse, where the boulevards of Montparnasse and Raspail intersect. Here you can see the three large cafés – La Coupole, La Rotonde and La Dôme – which were once among the main cultural meeting-places in Paris. The walls and wooden panels of La Dôme are covered with photographs of all the famous (and not so famous) artists, writers and musicians who have eaten and drunk here, including Picasso, Cocteau and Stravinsky. Further down the Boulevard Montparnasse is another café, La Closerie des Lilas, which was once patronized by Proust and Hemingway and, though today rather expensive, continues to be a haunt of artists and writers.

A minute's walk S of La Dôme along the Boulevard Raspail will bring you to the Rue Huygens, where the gateway to no. 6 leads into a small courtyard of studios once used by members of Les Six, a group of (six) composers that included Milhaud and Poulenc. Continuing down the Boulevard Raspail you will almost immediately reach the Rue Campagne Première, where every building once had its group of studios. Plaques commemorate the studios of Modigliani (no. 3), Soutine (no. 17), and the photographer Eugène Atget (no. 17 *bis*), but the restaurant of La Mère Rosalie, once one of the celebrated eating-places in the district, famous for its liveliness and its cheapness, has been replaced by a rather dull and expensive restaurant.

Further on, a right-hand turning leads into the Passage d'Enfer, a cobbled pedestrian street with tall, decrepit 19thC houses. The private art school now occupying nos. 24–27 of this street was once the studio of the leading 19thC sculptor Rude, famous for his sculptures on the Arc de Triomphe. The Passage d'Enfer takes you back to the Boulevard Raspail. Heading towards the Place Denfert-Rochereau, you will pass no. 281 Boulevard Raspail, where the eccentric Baroness Oettingen once used to organize famous salons attended by such prominent members of the Montparnasse colony as Picasso, Léger, Zadkine, Blaise Cendrars, Apollinaire, Max Jacob, Gino Severini, de Chirico and Modigliani. The Fauve van Dongen had a studio at no. 33 Rue Denfert-Rochereau, formerly the scene of some of the most riotous and orgiastic costume balls of the 1920s.

One of the largest and most attractive groups of studios in Montparnasse, the Cité Fleurie, may be found at no. 65 Boulevard Arago, off the Place Denfert-Rochereau. This decaying group of buildings is situated round a courtyard largely obscured by trees and dense vegetation, which in turn hide all sorts of sculptures, from plaster casts of classical works to abstract pieces in chrome metal. The studios were built in 1878 with materials from

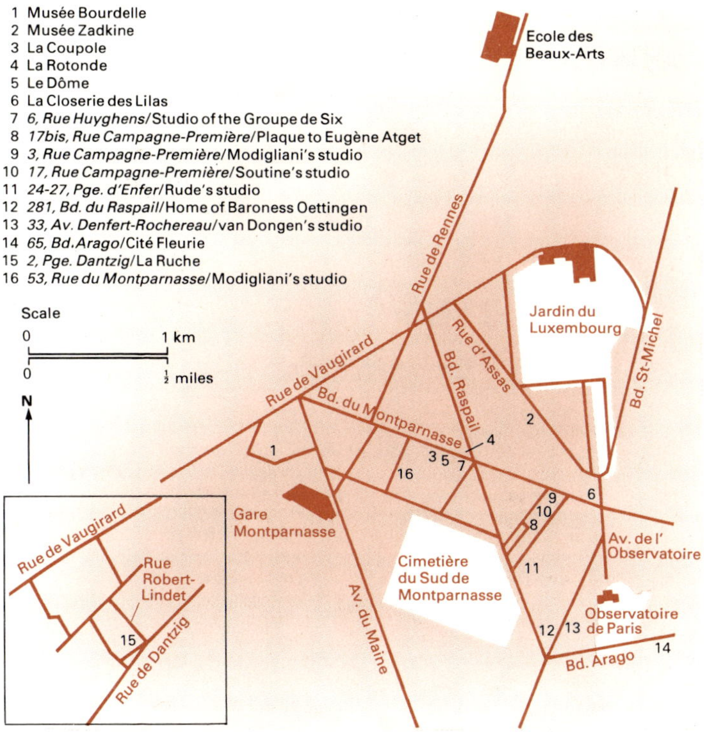

the Food Pavilion in the Great Exhibition of that year. One of them was occupied by Limet, who acted as technical adviser and photographer to such leading sculptors as Rodin, Bourdelle and Maillol. In 1896 Gauguin sent his canvases to another studio here, belonging to his friend Daniel de Monfried, when he returned to Tahiti. Closed down in 1940, the Cité Fleurie was used again by artists after World War II, and only a few years ago these managed to prevent its demolition to make room for a tower block.

The other major group of Montparnasse studios is La Ruche, at no. 2 Passage Dantzig, about 20 minutes' walk to the W of the Musée Bourdelle. An enormous rotunda with caryatids flanking its main door contains most of the studios here under its strange conical roof. Built in 1900 for a wine exhibition, it was bought in 1905 by a philanthropic sculptor, Alfred Boucher, as a place where artists could live and work for practically nothing. One of Boucher's best works, *To the Goal*, can be seen in the delightful garden surrounding the Rotunda. But living conditions at La Ruche were extremely squalid – the only toilet was simply a hole in the ground. Fernand Léger was the first major artist to work at La Ruche, and virtually all the major 20thC emigré Russian artists, such as Chagall, Lipchitz, Soutine and Zadkine, began their careers here. Soutine moved in 1920 to no. 17 Rue Campagne Première where, unloved and impoverished, he threw himself out of his studio window.

Also at La Ruche with Soutine was Modigliani, perhaps the most notorious of the Montparnasse artists. He also had a studio at no. 53 Rue de Montparnasse, where he worked alongside his model and fellow hashish enthusiast, Beatrice Hastings.

Musée Picasso

Hôtel Salé, 5, Rue de Thorigny, 75003
Tel. (1) 7233653
(Museum in preparation. Opening date to be announced)

This exciting new museum is still in preparation inside the **Hôtel Salé**, a very fine 17thC town house built in 1656 by Jean Bouiller de Bourges for the tax-collectors of the Gabelles Aubert de Fontenay. The name of the house (*salé* means salt) refers to the *gabelle* or salt tax imposed on the French people during the 17thC and 18thC. It is rather appropriate that the works destined for the new museum (at present stored in THE LOUVRE) are themselves a tax payment – they were given to the French government in lieu of death duties.

The collection is extensive and includes not only over **200 paintings** by Picasso but also some **150 sculptures**, **3,000 drawings**, prints, ceramics, pottery, manuscripts and books, all from the artist's studio. In its entirety, this considerable display will set out to show all aspects of Picasso's art, and also to reveal the artist's development in terms of attitude, subject matter and technique. Other works by Picasso or painted as tributes to him will also be on view. Moreover, a large part of Picasso's personal collection, including **works** by Cézanne, Matisse, Douanier Rousseau, Renoir, Derain and Braque, has also been given to the museum by the artist's heirs. In addition to the impressive show of paintings and other works of art, several rooms will cover the influence of Picasso's work on 20thC poets and writers, and his role in the worlds of theatre and ballet.

Musée Rénan-Scheffer

16, Rue Chaptal
Tel. (1) 8749538
Open 10am – 5.40pm
Closed Mon

This, Paris's most recent museum, was opened in June 1983 to display the collections of the Musée CARNAVALET relating to 19thC artistic and literary life in Paris. It is situated in a part of the city which in that period was so popular with artists and writers that it became known as the Nouvelle-Athènes. The early 19thC house which it occupies belonged from 1830 onwards to the portraitist and history painter Ary Scheffer, whose many distinguished dinner guests included Ingres, Delacroix, Turgenev, George Sand, Liszt, Chopin and Lamartine. Another was Ernest Rénan, who married Scheffer's niece in 1856. Their daughter Noémi later took possession of the house, and had a famous salon here frequented by members of the left-wing élite of the third Republic, including Zola, Clémenceau and Jean Jaurès.

The house, reached by a tiny alley leading off the Rue Chaptal, is charmingly situated in a tree-lined courtyard, and has an especially attractive small garden. The interior has been reconstituted in a 19thC style. The ground floor now contains a collection of material relating to the writer George Sand, a frequent visitor to the house, who lived nearby in the Square d'Orléans. This includes an excellent pastel of Sand's great-grandfather, the ***Maréchal de Saxe***, by Quentin de La Tour, a **portrait drawing** by Ingres, a **bust** by Houdon, and an **oil portrait** of Sand by Couture. There is also a fan with an entertaining caricature drawing by Auguste Charpentier, showing George Sand surrounded by her friends: Liszt is portrayed prostrate at her feet, while Delacroix stands possessively behind her. The museum has a considerable collection of material relating to Ary Scheffer which cannot yet be shown. However, an oil sketch by him of ***Louis Philippe Addressing the Chamber of Deputies*** is at present displayed on the ground floor. The first floor is devoted to temporary exhibitions of material culled from the Musée CARNAVALET.

Musée National Auguste Rodin ☆

Hôtel Biron
77, Rue de Varenne,
Tel. (1) 7050134
Open 10am – 6pm
Closed Tues
(Wed)

Of all the major French 19thC sculptors, Rodin is the only one whose popularity has survived to the present day. The Rodin Museum is one of the most visited in Paris although (like the JEU DE PAUME) by no means one of the most enjoyable. Situated in the middle of the quiet and elegant Faubourg St-Germain, it occupies a **palace** built between 1728 and 1731 by Gabriel the Elder, one of the leading French architects of this time. This building, the **Hôtel Biron**, was converted shortly after the Revolution into a convent and boarding school, a conversion that entailed the construction of ugly annexes and the stripping away of all "frivolous" interior decoration. When in 1905 the nuns were expelled from the place, plans were made to demolish it. In the meantime artists and writers were allowed to use the empty apartments; among those who did so were Matisse, Jean Cocteau, and the poet Rainer Maria

Rilke. The latter, who was married briefly to a pupil of Rodin, Clara Westhoff, was for a short while Rodin's secretary. It was his enthusiasm for the Hôtel Biron which led to Rodin himself coming to work in the building from 1909 onwards. The sculptor was then at the height of his fame, and his presence at the Hôtel Biron prevented the demolition of the place. In 1911 the building was purchased by the state and chosen as the site of a future museum to be devoted to Rodin. This was opened in 1919, two years after the sculptor's death. Its collections are those which the artist donated to the state in 1916.

The former function of the Hôtel Biron as a boarding school seems to have affected the character of the museum, which is bleak and unloveable – the opposite in fact to that of the artist's studio at Meudon (see ***PARIS ENVIRONS***). Nonetheless the collections are superlative, and the visitor can see examples of work from every stage of Rodin's career. Much of the sculptor's output was connected with his major official commissions, for which Rodin executed innumerable studies (many of these served as the basis for other sculptures). One of the rooms in the museum is devoted to works relating to the ***Burghers of Calais*** (commissioned by the city of ***CALAIS*** in 1884), and shows how Rodin would make detailed anatomical studies before representing the clothed figure. No less than three rooms are taken up by his **studies** ★ for the commission which obsessed him for much of his life from 1880 onwards – the monumental bronze doors intended for the Musée des Arts Decoratifs, the ***Gates of Hell***. These doors, which portray Dante's *Inferno*, were never put in place; moreover, the first cast of them (now in the delightful Rodin Museum in Philadelphia) was not completed until 1926, seven years after the artist's death. Many of the artist's most famous sculptures, including ***The Thinker***, ***The Old Courtesan*** (known usually as ***La Belle Héalnière***) and ***The Kiss***, developed from the studies of this work, which incorporated about two hundred figures.

Much of the appeal of Rodin's art lies in its sensuality. The artist gave new life to the sculpted nude not only through the suppleness of his technique but also by departing from the staid classical prototypes followed by most of his contemporaries. Few other sculptors have been able to invest human flesh with such a lifelike quality, a quality which gives even to the struggling figures in the ***Gates of Hell*** an intense eroticism. Rodin was as sensual in his life as he was in his art, and his incessant desire for love-making even into old age left at least one of his numerous female admirers – the English painter Gwen John – thoroughly exhausted. This side to Rodin is brought out in one room of the museum, which is devoted entirely to **portrait heads** of women, many of whom – as the brochure to the museum delicately put it – "played a part in Rodin's sentimental life". Another room recalls Rodin's friendship with many of the most celebrated political and intellectual figures of his day, and has busts of ***Clemenceau***, ***George Bernard Shaw***, and ***Gustav Mahler***. Rodin was asked to execute public memorials to a number of famous men, and yet another room in the museum contains studies for monuments to ***Victor Hugo***, ***Claude Lorrain***, ***Bastien-Lepage***, ***James McNeil Whistler***, and ***Balzac***. The latter piece was the most controversial of these, and was considered by the artist himself as the most innovatory of his works. The studies for it show the artist executing numerous naturalistic nude and drapery studies before building up to the final, drastically simplified work, which was rejected by the commissioning body, the Societé des Gens de Lettres.

In addition to works by Rodin, the museum has various **paintings** by other artists. With the exception of a recently acquired and unattractive painting by Edvard Munch showing Rodin's sculpture of ***The Thinker*** under snow, these are all from Rodin's collection. There are **minor works** by Monet, Renoir, Zuloaga and the Norwegian impressionist, Fritz Thaulow. The latter, at one time the brother-in-law of Gauguin, was a close friend of Rodin and, like him, the recipient of the Legion of Honour. Finally there are three paintings by van Gogh, including the celebrated ***Le Père Tanguy***★.

The garden has a cafeteria, a late 19thC chapel used for generally very interesting exhibitions of the work of Rodin's contemporaries, and a number of large-scale Rodin bronzes, including ***The Thinker***, ***The Gates of Hell***, ***The Burghers of Calais***, and ***Balzac***.

Musée Zadkine

100 bis, Rue d'Assas
Tel. (1) 3269190
Open Wed, Fri, Sat 10am–5.40pm
Closed Sun–Tues, Thurs

The house and studio of the Russian-born sculptor Zadkine were handed over by his widow to the state in 1980. Two years later they were opened as the Musée

Zadkine. Zadkine, who was born in 1890, came to Paris in 1910 and joined up with other Russian artists in the famous group of Montparnasse studios, La Ruche (see p. 138). At first he was very influenced by Rodin, but soon developed as a Cubist sculptor. During World War II he was in New York, but afterwards returned to Paris and settled in the house which now forms part of the museum. During his later life he turned increasingly to monumental sculpture, and evolved a more extrovert and expressive style: one of the most famous works of this period is ***The Destroyed City*** in Rotterdam.

The Musée Zadkine is a delightfully peaceful enclave in the midst of a rapidly changing part of Paris. Almost all the available space in the tiny house, studio and garden is taken up by Zadkine's sculptures from all periods in his career. To see these works in such profusion is admittedly a mixed blessing, given their strongly decorative and repetitive character. A case in the museum draws attention to Zadkine's now little-known activity as a poet; he was a close friend of a number of important poets, including Apollinaire, Aragon, Tzara, and Éluard. Also on show are the artist's working bench and materials, and a **drawing** of him by his friend and one time neighbour, Modigliani.

Sainte-Chapelle

Palais de Justice, Boulevard du Palais
Open 10–11.45am, 1.30–5.45pm
Closed Tues

The **Palais de Justice**, a fascinating complex of buildings which incorporates the Sainte-Chapelle, has a history stretching back to the early Middle Ages. This was the place where the Capetian kings administered their rule, where St Louis gave counsel and, in the 17thC, where Louis XIV made the famous statement "L'Etat, c'est Moi" in defiance of the civil authority. Most of the early buildings, including the Great Hall or Salle des Pas-Perdus, have been rebuilt since the Renaissance, and the whole area was badly damaged during the Commune (1870–71), but the Sainte-Chapelle, one of the finest early Gothic chapels in Europe, has survived reasonably intact despite several attempts to "restore" it.

Built by St Louis, and consecrated in 1248 as a shrine to house the various sacred relics that the Saint King had acquired, the tall slender structure is an excellent example of Gothic design, albeit on a small scale. The interior is split into two levels, the lower for the retainers and the upper for the services and state occasions attended by the royal family. The upper floor is remarkable for its abundance of **stained glass windows**★ which take up all the wall space between the columns. Some of these windows date from the 13thC and are among the oldest in Paris. Scenes from the Old and New Testaments are beautifully depicted in 14 lancets, while another theme relates the history of the True Cross and the background to the Saint King's relics, which include fragments of the True Cross and the Crown of Thomas. The **rose window** is slightly later, being a gift of Charles VIII in the 15thC, and illustrates the **Apocalypse** with 86 panels.

Théatre Française

Place André-Malraux

The Théatre or Comédie Française on the newly renamed Place André-Malraux is the home of the French national theatre company and, as befits its position and history, contains in its entrance hall and staircase a number of interesting portrait sculptures. Chief among those is Houdon's famous portrait of ***Voltaire***, and nearby there are busts of ***Mirabeau*** by Rodin and ***Dumas fils*** by Carpeaux as well as a statue of ***Talma***, the great actor manager of the revolutionary period, by David d'Angers. As a curiosity the theatre also displays the chair on which Molière was taken fatally ill on stage during a performance of *Le Malade imaginaire*.

Trésor de la Cathédrale Notre-Dame

Cathédrale Notre-Dame
Open 10am–5pm
Closed Sun

It is easy to miss the entrance of this tiny museum, situated half-way up the right-hand aisle of the cathedral; but the treasures it contains are well worth viewing – particularly if, as happens to so many visitors, the thronging crowds of sightseers and school parties have succeeded in lessening the impact of Notre-Dame's magnificent stonework and truly marvellous stained glass windows. The Treasure of the Cathedral has been displayed in the Sacristy since 1970 and consists of numerous objects donated to the cathedral over the centuries. The most important items are undoubtedly the beautifully wrought 15thC ***Reliquary of St Judicael***, almost certainly given by Marguerite de Foix, second wife of François II and mother of Anne of Brittany, and a **carved ivory crucifix** of exquisite detail dating from the 18thC.

DEVELOPMENT *of* ART *in* FRANCE

Any attempt to identify the individual characteristics of a nation's art involves, as Nikolaus Pevsner recognized, not only the history but also the geography of art. The development or transmission of new forms becomes less important than the nature of the work produced in a specific area. There may be objections to this whole line of thought – is there such a thing as national character? – but in the end we are still drawn to the question: Do peoples express their identity, their self-consciousness, their sense of nationality through their art as they may in their language, and if so how does one identify it? With France there are particular problems because it has retained its modern borders only since the 16thC or 17thC.

Charlemagne was perhaps the first ruler to exercise some control over the style of the art and architecture, at least in the court schools. But not until the pilgrimage routes of the Romanesque period do we find that particular unity and diversity, the free exchange and transmission of ideas within a clear overriding pattern, that can be described as French. At Vézelay, Moissac, Souillac, Conques, Poitiers or Toulouse we can observe the elaboration of similar themes controlled by the central demand of glorifying Christ in the building as a whole. The cathedral became the highest expression of medieval culture, and it was the French who first used sculpture on these buildings as part of a scheme celebrating the life and teachings of the patron saint.

The Gothic style of building, first developed in France at Senlis and St-Denis, introduced a range of new motifs in sculpture. These are best seen in the West Portal at Chartres, and this wonderful building also affords a rare opportunity of seeing the original stained glass – an important feature of the new church decoration. Narrative cycles, Christian symbols and dedicatory images could now be depicted in vivid colours brought to life by light itself.

Not all medieval art was attached to the building. Cathedrals, monasteries and even humble churches had furnishings and treasures of *ars sacra*: items in various precious materials wrought to a high level of sophistication by the craft workshops throughout the country. Enamels developed in the Meuse valley and Limoges were carried to all parts of Europe, while the ivory carvings, gold and silverware of the Ile de France adorned houses and private chapels from Britain to Constantinople.

Manuscript illumination is another art form which had thrived in France since the early Middle Ages, and achieved a peak of assurance and sophistication during the Gothic period. The ***Très Riches Heures***, the finest of a series of manuscripts commissioned from the Limbourg brothers by the Duc de Berry, celebrates the life of the court and the landscape as seen in each month of the year. This balance between nature and an exquisite courtly refinement is the hallmark of the International Gothic style.

In the confusion which followed the collapse of the court after Agincourt, the duchy of Burgundy expanded to fill the space available, occupying lands in the east from Holland to Savoy, and shifting the center of patronage from Paris and the Loire to Dijon. The Flemish sculptor Claus Sluter executed four great works in Dijon, including a tomb for ***Philip the Bold***, in which the solidity and naturalism of the figures were uppermost. Slightly later, the technique developed by van Eyck of painting with oil glazes, in which subtle effects of light and texture could be depicted with astonishing accuracy, spread throughout France; its appeal is apparent in the work of Rogier van der Weyden and of the Master of Moulins.

However, the same period saw the emergence of two distinctly independent styles. Enguerrand Quarton (Charonton), the principal figure of the so-called School of Avignon, developed a mature style that, in his finest work, the ***Coronation of the Virgin***, has an authority of design that is quite unique. Jean Fouquet, court painter to Charles VIII, visited Italy in the 1440s and was able to see the most recent developments in Renaissance art. On his return to France he made his reputation in a series of altarpieces and manuscripts, the finest being the ***Heures d'Etienne Chevalier***, combining the spatial concerns and design of the Italian Renaissance with the Northern observation of everyday life. Then, during the 16thC, what had previously been a source for innovation became an orthodoxy. François I brought Leonardo da Vinci and a string of other Italian artists to France in an attempt to transplant the seeds of the new learning. He was completely successful, and France became the first country to embrace the Renaissance.

FRENCH ART *in the* 17THC

With the gradual strengthening of the French nation during the first half of the 17thC, French art also came of age, a moment symbolized by the foundation in 1648 of the Royal Academy of Arts in Paris. No longer had France to woo the leading Italian artists to come and work here; now she could boast of a great artistic tradition of her own. However, there was still a long way to go before Italy was to be replaced as Europe's major art center, and French art continued to be governed by Italian canons. It was essential for all French artists to spend a period of their youth in Italy, and the two most widely known 17thC French painters, Claude Lorrain and Nicolas Poussin, spent almost their entire working lives in Rome. Claude specialized in idealized views of the Roman Campagna, populated by tiny figures from classical history or mythology; his influence was not really felt till much later.

Poussin, by contrast, had an immediate impact on his French contemporaries, though his art is sometimes not easy to like or to understand, reflecting as it does an extraordinary learning both in archaeology and in philosophy. Few artists before or since have painted religious and mythological works of such intellectual complexity. His imitators borrowed the measured, austere formal elements in his art but little of its intense subtlety. When the French Royal Academy attempted to establish rigid rules as to how an artist should paint, it was the art of Poussin that was chosen for all painters to emulate, and this characteristically French desire to rationalize the art of painting led to the creation of much dull and lifeless official art. But major official artists of this period, such as Vouet, Lebrun, Philippe de Champaigne, Le Sueur, Laurent de la Hire, de Largillière and Hyacinthe Rigaud still managed to display very idiosyncratic qualities in their art.

The greatest individualists in French 17thC art were those who worked in the French provinces, where the influence of the French Academy scarcely penetrated. The dark, dramatic and intensely naturalistic art of the contemporary Italian painter Caravaggio met with a great success here, whereas in Paris it made little headway. The most famous of the so-called French "Caravaggisti" was Georges de La Tour, who worked most of his life in and around the Lorraine capital of Nancy. After his death he seems to have been almost totally forgotten until this century. Other French provincial artists of La Tour's generation, such as Guy François from Le Puy and Nicolas Tournier from Toulouse, still await the recognition they deserve.

Towards the end of the century, the French Academy was split into two factions, the "Poussinistes" and the "Rubénistes". Rubens had only just then

1

1 *Godefroy de Huy (?),* ***Cross of St-Bertin*** *(foot), 12thC, St-Omer, M. de l'Hotel Sandelin*

2 *Gislebertus,* ***Eve****, 12thC, Autun, M. Rolin*

3 *Anon., Bayeux Tapestry (det.)* ***Normans attack English****, 11thC, Bayeux, M. de la Tapisserie*

2

3

1

1 *Anon.*, **The Synagogue**, *13thC, Reims, Oeuvre de la Cathédrale Notre-Dame*

2 *Anon.*, **Apocalypse** *Tapestry (det.), c.1373, Angers, M. des Tapisseries*

3 *Enguerrand Quarton (Charonton)*, **The Coronation of the Virgin**, *1454, Villeneuve-lès-Avignon, M. de l'Hospice*

4 *Rogier van der Weyden*, **Last Judgment** *Altarpiece, c.1450, Beaune, Hotel Dieu*

5 *Melchior Broederlam*, **Crucifixion** *Altarpiece (det.), 1394, Dijon, M. B-A.*

2

3

4

5

1

2

1 *Master of Moulins,* ***Nativity****, (det.) c. 1480 Autun, M. Rolin*

2 *Limbourg brothers,* ***Les Très Riches Heures du Duc de Berry*** *("June"), c. 1416, Chantilly, M. Condé*

3 *Master of Canapost,* ***Trinity Altarpiece****, 1489, Perpignan, M. Rigaud*

4 *Claus Sluter, Tomb of Philippe le Hardi, 1404, Dijon, M. B-A.*

5 *Grünewald (Mathis Gothardt-Neithardt), Isenheim Altarpiece,* ***Nativity*** *Panel, c. 1505–16, Colmar, M. Unterlinden*

3

4

5

1

1 *Peter Paul Rubens,* **Marie de Médicis Lands at Marseille** *(Palais du Luxembourg), 1622–25, Paris, Louvre*

2 *Nicolas Tournier,* **Descent from the Cross***, c. 1633, Toulouse, M. des Augustins*

3 *Nicolas Poussin,* **Venus Arming Aeneas***, 1639, Rouen, M. B-A.*

4 *Georges de La Tour,* **The Denial of St Peter***, 1650, Nantes, M. B-A.*

5 *Claude Gellée called Claude Lorraine,* **Seaport at Sunset***, 1639, Paris, Louvre*

2

3

4

5

1

1 H. Rigaud, **Cardinal de Bouillon**, c. 1700, Perpignan, M. Rigaud

2 M.-Q. de La Tour, **L'Abbé Hubert**, c. 1742, St-Quentin, M. A. Lécuyer

3 Jean-Antoine Watteau, **Antoine Pater**, c. 1716, Valenciennes, M. B-A.

3

4 *Jean-Baptiste Chardin,* **Basket of Plums**, *c. 1760, Rennes, M. B-A.*

5 *Jean-Marc Nattier,* **Mme. de Dreux-Brèze**, *c. 1755, Douai, M. Chartreuse*

6 *Jean-Honoré Fragonard,* **Figure de Fantaisie**, *c. 1775, Paris, Louvre*

4

5

6

1

1 *Eugène Delacroix,* **Justice of Trajan,** *1813, Rouen, M. B-A.*

2 *Jacques-Louis David,* **Death of Barra,** *1794, Avignon, M. Calvet*

3 *Jean-Auguste-Dominique Ingres,* **Portrait of Granet,** *1811, Aix-en-Provence, M. Granet*

2

3

4

4 *Théodore Géricault,* **Mad Woman**, *1822, Lyon, M. B-A.*

5 *Francisco de Goya,* **The Montgolfier Balloon**, *1793, Agen, M. Municipal*

5

1

1 *Edgar Degas,* **The New Orleans Cotton Exchange**, *1873, Pau, M. B-A.*

2 *Gustave Courbet,* **The Corn Sifters**, *1854, Nantes, M. B-A.*

3 *Edouard Manet,* **The Balcony**, *c. 1868, Paris, M. Jeu de Paume*

4 *Frédéric Bazille,* **Jeune Fille**, *c. 1866, Montpellier, M. Fabre*

2

3

4

5 *Gustave Moreau,* ***Jupiter and Semele,*** *1876, Paris, M. Gustave Moreau*

5

1

2

3

1 *Paul Gauguin,* **La Fête Gloanec**, *1888, Orléans, M. B-A.*

2 *Claude Monet,* **Rue Montorgueil**, *1875, Rouen, M. B-A.*

3 *André Derain,* **Port of Collioure**, *1905, Troyes, M. d'Art Moderne*

4 *Auguste Rodin,* **Statue of Balzac**, *1897, Place Bréa-Vavin, Paris*

5 *Paul Signac,* **Port of St-Tropez**, *1899, St-Tropez, M. de l'Annonciade*

4

5

1 *Henri Matisse,* ***Still Life with Aubergines****, 1906, Grenoble, M. de la Peinture et Sculpture*

2 *Fernand Léger,* ***Mosaic façade*** *of Léger museum, 1960, Biot, M. Léger*

3 *Jean Tinguely and Nikki de St-Phalle, Fontaine Beaubourg, 1980, Paris, Place Stravinsky*

1

2

3

begun to have a wide following in France. The large series of canvases which he had executed for Marie de Medici in the Luxembourg Palace had aroused relatively little enthusiasm in France, no doubt partly as a result of the unpopularity of the patron. Now these works came to be closely studied by French artists, and were to remain among the most copied works in France until well into the 19thC. One of the artists obsessed by them was Jean-Antoine Watteau (1684–1721), who in his early days in Paris (he had been brought up in the once Flemish town of Valenciennes) was lucky enough to know someone who had the keys to the room where they were kept.

The interest taken in Rubens by Watteau and other painters of his generation is indicative of a less austere period in French art. A number of the most successful painters and sculptors of this time, including Boucher and Clodion, took not even a token interest in elevated subject matter, and often created what amounted to sophisticated pornography. By the middle of the 18thC a number of critics, most notably Diderot, had hypocritcally begun to attack the lack of morality in contemporary art. Diderot championed the painter Jean-Baptiste Greuze, who though he made most of his money through painting coyly erotic pictures of thinly draped young girls, also painted occasional scenes of everyday life with a moralistic and sentimental message attached to them. The last and most technically daring of the so-called French Rococo painters was Jean-Baptiste Fragonard. Fragonard lived to see his vividly painted and highly sensual works go out of fashion; unfortunately for him he survived the Revolution by many years, by which time he was a completely forgotten man.

ART *and the* FRENCH REVOLUTION

The Revolution marked a turning-point in French art and the beginning of the most complex and exciting period in its history. With the suppression of the church and the aristocracy, art came to reach a much wider public, especially as the confiscation of almost all the major private art collections in the country had led to France having the best series of municipal museums in Europe. The wealth of art treasures to be seen in this country increased with the advent of Napoleon, who pursued a policy of cultural imperialism alongside his territorial ambitions. Under him the Louvre in Paris became truly the major art gallery in the world.

The artist most closely associated with the Revolutionary and Napoleonic periods in France was Jacques-Louis David, who took an active part in political life and imbued his scenes from classical history with a revolutionary significance. He is generally labelled a Neoclassical painter, although the degree of emotion to be found in such works of his as the ***Death of Barra*** (Avignon) is a quality usually associated with the subsequent generation of artists. What set David apart from this later generation was the intense optimism of his work. The exile of Napoleon to St Helena in 1815 created a further mood of disillusionment among French artists and writers which the writer de Musset characterized as the "Mal du Siècle". Two of the leading painters of this so-called Romantic period were Géricault and Delacroix. The former was noted at the time for his unflinching realism, perhaps best exemplified in his series of portraits of the insane (***Mad Woman***, Lyon). The art of Delacroix was perhaps more inherently "romantic" in that it expressed the artist's desire to escape from reality and take refuge in the exotic. Delacroix, a brilliant colourist, was frequently contrasted with his great contemporary rival, Ingres, a diehard follower of the principles of Poussin and David. Long before their deaths, however, the art of both these painters had come to seem very old-fashioned.

By the mid 19thC open air landscape painting and the portrayal of everyday life had become the main artistic fashions of France's artistic avant-garde. These artists included Gustave Courbet and a large group of painters who worked in and around the forest of Fontainebleau near Paris (including Corot, Théodore Rousseau, Diaz de la Peña, Daubigny and Millet), the so-called Barbizon school. The art of these painters can be seen as part of a growing dissatisfaction with conventional academic training, and in the wake of the great political crises besetting France in the 1840s, the 'realist' art of those painters also came to be regarded as politically suspect. Count de Nieuwerkerke, head of all official patronage of art during the Second Empire, wrote of the work of the Barbizon artists: "This is the painting of democrats, of those who do not change their linen. . . . This art displeases and disgusts me.'

PARIS: ART CAPITAL *of the* WORLD

After the 1850s Paris replaced Rome as the artistic Mecca of the Western world, and remained as such until World War II. The artists who flocked to Paris from all over Europe and America found a much more enlightened attitude towards art than they had experienced in their own countries: in the words of the American painter, Howard Russell Butler, art here was "a living thing!". Not least of the attractions of Paris for the artist was the art school life here, which encapsulated the increasingly fashionable concept of Bohemia. The artistic year in Paris culminated in the government sponsored spring exhibitions known as the Salons. To have a work successfully exhibited at these meant that one was fully established as an artist.

Too much emphasis is now placed in the history of late 19thC art on the group of painters called the Impressionists (most notably Manet, Monet, Renoir, Bazille, Sisley and Pissarro), who maintained their independence from the mainstream of Parisian art by exhibiting outside the Salons. Today their achievement is considered in terms of their spontaneous compositions and vivid handling of paint and colouring. In the 19thC, however, they were thought revolutionary for being extreme realists, and for portraying unhesitatingly the most mundane aspects of everyday life. An artist who had a far greater importance than the Impressionists in the 1880s and 1890s was Bastien-Lepage, who painted grey outdoor scenes of peasant life. His art had an immense appeal at a time when rapid industrialization had begun to lead artists and writers to find solace in the unspoilt life of the countryside.

The development of French art from the late 19thC up to World War II was strongly effected by the "discovery" of the colourful sensual environment of the South of France. Almost all the leading artists in France during this period worked or lived here at some stage in their careers, including Van Gogh, Cézanne, Picasso, Derain, Matisse and Chagall. Since the War both Paris and the South of France have maintained their popularity with artists; but the once serious art produced in these places has been replaced mainly by the chic and vacuous. French art as a whole has in fact recently entered a sad decline. Nonetheless, France can indeed claim to organize some of the most ambitious exhibitions of old and modern art to be seen anywhere in the world. The interest shown in the fine arts by recent French governments has been exemplary. President Pompidou, for instance, built in Paris what is certainly the liveliest of Europe's modern art galleries, the Beaubourg. To visit this fun fair of a place, to mingle with the street musicians and other performers who always gather here, is to realize that art in France, for all its faults, is still as Butler found it in the 19thC, a "living thing".

PARIS ENVIRONS

The countryside around Paris defies a simple description, but in area it covers the ancient Ile de France, a part of the Paris basin that corresponds approximately to the six *Départements* surrounding the capital. Though not an island, the Ile de France suggests by its name the importance, geographical and historical, of a region that holds within it the quintessence of French culture. This is the heartland of the country, the first base of royal power (with the Orléanais) where Clovis carved out the kingdom of the Franks in the 5thC AD, a country with the Latin name of Francia.

The Ile de France has not only been the scene of many momentous events in French history; it has also witnessed the growth and development of the Gothic style of building in church architecture, a style that reached an unsurpassed level of achievement in the region. The style first took hold in the pointed arches and rib vaulting of the BASILICA OF ST-DENIS; it reached its superb maturity at CHARTRES, perhaps the greatest of all Gothic cathedrals, which Rodin compared favourably with the Acropolis at Athens; and it aspired to its most ambitious form at BEAUVAIS which, though only the transepts and choir were built, remains the tallest cathedral in France.

St-Denis, today a somewhat unsightly northern suburb of Paris, contains the ancient Basilica that was once the burial place for the kings and queens of France for almost a millennium. From the reign of Louis IX (St Louis), who erected the first royal tombs in the choir, to that of Louis XVIII, almost every French king was buried in the great Basilica of St-Denis. The royal tombs, though now empty, have survived relatively unscathed and in their original locations, despite a decree of the Convention in 1793 that they should be destroyed. The coffins were exhumed and the bodies cast out, but the tombs themselves had already been removed for safekeeping by the antiquary Alexandre Lenoir, to be returned to the Basilica during the reign of Louis XVIII. Seen together, they represent the finest collection of funerary sculpture in France.

The Ile de France also includes major royal palaces at FONTAINEBLEAU, COMPIÈGNE and VERSAILLES. Fontainebleau with its surrounding forests was particularly associated with the hunt. In the 16thC François I established a magnificent court there, attracting leading Italian artists such as Rosso, Primaticcio and Niccolò dell'Abbate, who introduced the principles of Italian Renaissance art to their French disciples. Artists associated with the French court at Fontainebleau during the 16thC became known as the Fontainebleau School. Heroic mythology formed the subject of many of the works painted at Fontainebleau, and François's mistress, Diane de Poitiers, was frequently depicted as Diana, the classical goddess of the hunt, thus bringing together the earlier hunting tradition of Fontainebleau with its period of glory as the center of the French Renaissance.

In view of the Ile de France's popularity with successive rulers, principal members of the court found it expedient to build their residences in the same area; at CHANTILLY, VAUX-LE-VICOMTE and MAISONS-LAFITTE you can enjoy some of the finest French architecture of the 17thC, accompanied by the spectacular garden designs of Le Nôtre, which can also be seen all over the region. At Chantilly there is also the superb Musée Condé with its exquisite medieval illuminated manuscripts by the Limbourg brothers and Jean Fouquet.

The expansion of Paris is steadily making encroachments on the countryside of the Ile de France, but it is surprising how much parkland and wooded areas have survived around the capital. The forests at Ermenonville, St-Germain, L'Isle-Adam and Fontainebleau are still reasonably intact, and

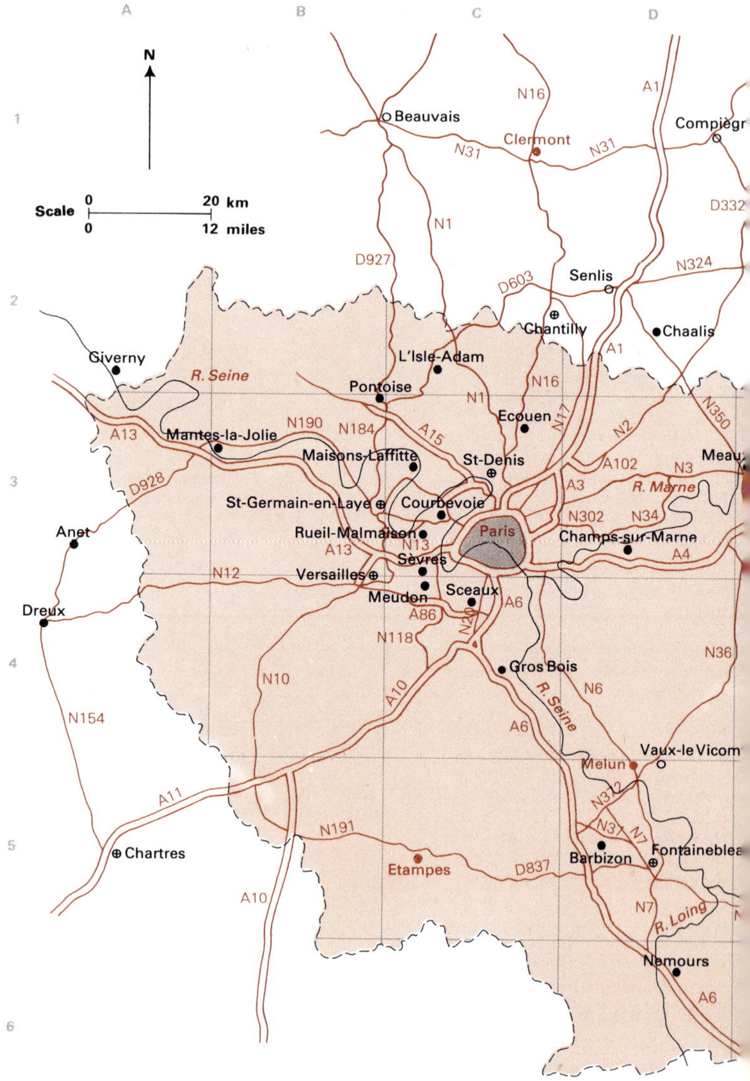

have attracted numerous landscape artists from the 19thC onwards: Corot and Millet at Barbizon, Pissarro at Pontoise, van Gogh at Auvers (where he killed himself), Sisley at Moret-sur-Loing, and Monet at Giverny.

Monet's garden at **GIVERNY** has become a popular tourist point, but many of the artists' motifs in the Seine area (see p. 132) and in the Fontainebleau Forest (see p. 184) are relatively unvisited, and still look much the same today as when they were painted. A tour of these areas can be a pleasurable and rewarding experience. Finally, there is an excellent and recently opened museum at **ST-GERMAIN-EN-LAYE**, the Musée du Prieuré. Here the Symbolist painter Maurice Denis lived from 1914 till his death in 1943, and the museum, set in a beautiful garden, contains a number of superb works by Denis and his contemporaries, very imaginatively desplayed.

ANET
Eure-et-Loire, Centre Map A3

A small town on the Eure 80km (50 miles) W of Paris which, apart from the **château of Diane de Poitiers**, also contains her funeral chapel.

Château d'Anet
Tel. (37) 419007
Open Oct–Mar Mon, Wed–Sat 2.30–6.30pm, Sun 10–11.30am, 2.30–6.30pm; Nov–Feb Sun 10–11.30am, 2–5pm
Closed Tues, Nov–Feb Mon–Sat

When Diane de Poitiers was forced out of Chenonceau on the death of Henri II in 1559, she took up residence briefly at Chaumont before moving to the château at Anet which she had already begun building to the designs of Philibert de l'Orme. On completion Anet was regarded by many as the finest château in France, and it confirmed de l'Orme's reputation as the leading and most imaginative architect in the Renaissance style. Unfortunately, it was badly damaged during the Revolution, like many other royal and ecclesiastical buildings, and only three small sections survive from the original complex. Nevertheless they are sufficient to give you a flavour of the whole château.

The **gateway**, with its confident organization of massive blocks, and its relief of ***Diana*** (a copy of Cellini's work) above the central doorway, is often singled out for particular attention, but the small **chapel** nearby is equally, if not even more attractive. Behind the simple rectilinear façade, which is partly the result of a 19thC restoration, the interior repeats and echoes the pure circular plan with arcs and spirals in the coffered dome and on the marble floor.

The **West Wing** is all that survives of the main building, and since the last century this part has been gradually refurbished with items either from the original château or in keeping with its heyday in the 16thC. The main exhibits are a series of **tapestries** from the Fontainebleau workshops, which were commissioned by Diane de Poitiers (although not for Anet itself) and several pieces of furniture such as the large four-poster bed known as the ***Lit de Diane***.

BARBIZON
Seine-et-Marne, Ile-de-France Map D5

The village of Barbizon has long since ceased to be an artist's colony (see p. 184), and today expensive weekend homes and cafés have replaced the peasant cottages and studios of the 19thC, but the landscape of the Forêt de Fontainebleau continues to offer echoes of the scenes painted by Millet, Rousseau, Diaz and Corot. The main street also retains the general outlines of its earlier appearance.

Musée Municipal de Barbizon
Grande Rue
Tel. (6) 0662238
Open 10am–noon, 2–6pm
Closed Tues

The small municipal museum of Barbizon, in the house once occupied by the landscape painter Théodore Rousseau, is primarily concerned with documenting the development and daily life of the **Barbizon School** in the 19thC. To this end there is a display of contemporary photographs, prints and memorabilia of the landscape and peasant painters who gave the "school" its reputation and character, as well as some material on Antoine-Louis Barye, the animal sculptor who lived in the village for part of his life. The paintings in the collection are without exception by minor artists, and it is a disappointment to find that there are no canvases by Millet, Corot, Daubigny or Diaz, and only a few drawings by Rousseau to give any indication of the major work produced in the village.

Maison et Atelier de J.F. Millet
27 Grande Rue
Open 9.30am–5.30pm
Closed Tues

Occupying the small house (subsequently reconstructed by the artist's American daughter-in-law) where Millet lived for nearly 30 years until his death in 1879, this museum attempts to give some indication of the artist's life and art without any examples of his paintings. In their absence, the museum offers some prints and drawings as well as several personal items such as his palette and cane. But above all it is the house itself which gives the strongest impression of the simplicity and poverty which Millet sought and maintained long after his work had achieved reasonable success.

BEAUVAIS
Oise, Picardie Map B1

One of the principal objectives of Gothic masons was for ever increasing height, and they intended the **cathedral** at Beauvais to be the tallest of them all. At 48m (155 feet) they may have overreached themselves, for insufficient buttressing led to the collapse of the roof vaults in 1284. A later building doubled the buttresses, but the tower and spire fell through the crossing in 1573. A building that would have been one of the largest in Christendom, had it been completed, consists of no more than the transept and choir in its present state. Nevertheless, even in this fragmentary condition it is still immense, and displays some of the finest 13thC Gothic stonework in the country.

Galerie Nationale de la Tapisserie

Rue Saint-Pierre
Tel. (4) 4482993
Open Apr–Sept 9.30–noon, 2–6.30pm; Oct–Mar 10am–noon, 2.30–5pm
Closed Mon

The opening in 1976 of the Galerie Nationale de la Tapisserie was the fulfilment of a proposal, made 12 years earlier by André Malraux, that Beauvais should have some tangible monument to record the town's important role in the history of tapestry weaving. In the absence of a real industry, the new gallery is particularly appropriate.

Set up in 1664 the Beauvais factory enjoyed its heyday in the 18thC, when artists such as Oudry, Boucher and Natoire produced a series of playful **bucolic designs** which were woven into rich screens, covers and hangings. Many of these designs were worked up in the 19thC, and the factory was still in production in 1939 when it was amalgamated with the Gobelins in Paris.

The collection has several examples of the finest Beauvais weaving, such as the series of ***Fables of La Fontaine*** after Oudry, but the museum places greater emphasis on frequent temporary exhibitions which fill most of the gallery space. There is also a demonstration workshop in which traditional and modern weaving techniques can be observed at close quarters.

Musée Départemental de L'Oise

Ancien Palais Épiscopal
1, Rue du Musée
Tel. (4) 4451360
Open Mar–Oct 9.30–noon, 2–6pm; Nov–Feb 10am–noon, 2–6pm
Closed Tues

The Musée Départemental, reopened as recently as 1981 after an extensive renovation, is housed in the old Bishop's Palace beside the cathedral. The building itself is very attractive, parts of it dating from the 14thC, and in fitting it out for new displays the designers have taken care to highlight the original **Gothic vaulting** and decorative stonework in some of the rooms. This in turn provides a good setting for the collection of late **medieval wood and stone sculpture**, such as ***St Barbara*** by Jean Le Pot, most of which has been gathered from the town and outlying districts.

The painting collection on the first floor has a number of Italian and French works from the period between the 16thC and the 19thC, and within this range there are two areas of particular interest. Antoine Caron, the court painter to Catherine de Medici and one of the principal French Mannerists, was born in Beauvais and there are a few of his elaborate pictures in the museum, the most important being ***The Resurrection of Christ***. Near by, and immediately noticeable by its scale, is the unfinished ***Enrolment of the Volunteers of 1792*** by the 19thC Salon artist Thomas Couture.

The second floor is devoted to the **decorative arts of the Belle Epoque** (described here as the "Années Folles") and principally to the collection of the potter Auguste Delaherche. This consists mostly of pottery, furniture and tapestries, although there are a few paintings from the early 20thC. The most interesting pictures consist of a series of seven panels entitled ***L'Age d'Or*** by Maurice Denis which fall clearly within the original description, being a light decorative ensemble displayed on the walls and ceiling of the staircase.

The third floor of the museum contains the local history and archaeology section, including some examples of the **lead-glazed ceramics** referred to by Rabelais, which were produced in the Beauvais area during the 15thC and 16thC.

CHAALIS

Oise, Picardie Map D2

The Cistercian abbey at Chaalis was founded in 1136 and soon established itself as a thriving religious community. It was particularly popular during the Renaissance, when it was visited by many artists including Tasso, and a number of frescoes were executed in the abbot's lodge in an Italianate style similar to that of Primaticcio. More recently the buildings have fared rather badly. Suppressed in 1785, the abbey was sold during the Revolution, and in the 19thC was partially restored as a country residence.

Musée Jacquemart-André

Abbaye de Chaalis
Tel. (4) 4540001
Open mid-Mar to Oct 1.30–6pm
Closed Tues, Thurs, Fri, Nov to mid-Mar

The domain of Chaalis was presented to the Institut de France in 1912 as part of the same bequest which gave rise to the excellent Musée Jacquemart-André in *PARIS*. The two properties owned by Mme. André (née Jacquemart) were filled with her private collection, but whereas the house in the Bd Haussmann in Paris is largely devoted to the finest Renaissance and 18thC work, the abbey at Chaalis has a miscellaneous selection of items gathered in the course of the donor's travels. As a result, this museum does not approach the standard or quality of its counterpart in Paris, but its setting and variety do give it a distinct identity.

The museum occupies a building known as the château, and contains paintings, sculpture, furniture and ceramics as well as a number of Egyptian and Greco-Roman antiquities. The most important items are undoubtedly the two panels by Giotto of ***St John the Evangelist***★ and ***St Lawrence***★ from an altarpiece which was originally in the church of Santa Croce in Florence. These have recently been cleaned and are now displayed in a setting which includes several pieces of **16thC Italian furniture** and **faience**. Other notable holdings are the **Louis XIV furniture** on the ground floor and the series of 18thC French portrait sculpture, including a **bust of J-J. Rousseau** by Houdon. The philosopher is further represented by some autographed writings and souvenirs.

CHAMPS-SUR-MARNE

Seine-et-Marne, Ile-de-France
Map D3

Champs-sur-Marne, some 21km (13 miles) E of Paris, is close enough to the capital to show traces of gradual suburban expansion. The village is of little interest, but immediately beyond it on the main road are the gates of the château. Designed by Bullet de Chamblain in 1703 for the successful businessman Georges Poisson, the simplicity and elegance of Champs set a standard for many French country houses of the 18thC. Poisson was imprisoned during the Regency, and the house was subsequently occupied by the Princesse de Conti and then by Madame de Pompadour. During the Revolution Champs was badly damaged, but in the 1890s the owner began restoration.

Château de Champs

Tel. (6) 0052543
Open 10am–noon, 1.30–6pm
Closed Tues, Wed

Despite the importance of the exterior at Champs, and particularly the **garden façade**, it is the interior that is of the greatest interest. Bullet de Chamblain paid considerable attention to the plan of the house, with the result that you are always conscious of the overall arrangement of the rooms and of the transition when moving from one part to another. However, the appeal of the interior depends largely on the 18thC decorative schemes, many of which have survived remarkably well. The **Salon Chinois**, for example, has a wealth of Rococo painted decoration by Huet covering walls and doors, and the **Grand Salon** has a beautiful illusionistic ceiling substituting a delicate sky in the pastel colours of the period for the traditional horde of nymphs and goddesses.

Of the oil paintings, as distinct from the "***dessus de porte***" panels by Boucher, Oudry and Desportes, the finest are a portrait of ***Madame de Pompadour as La Belle Jardinière*** by Drouais and a series of four 18thC **French landscapes**. Besides these there is some good 18thC furniture and ceramics, including **Meissen lamps**, and tapestries such as the **Beauvais "Chinois" tapestry** in the library.

CHANTILLY

Oise, Picardie Map C2

Chantilly is known for its lace and its racecourse, but above all for its château standing in a lake surrounded by extensive parkland. The château is in fact two buildings, each reflecting a different phase in its history. The older or **Petit Château** was designed by Bullant for Anne de Montmorency around 1560 and survives largely in its original form: an attractive building with some unusual features recalling Bullant's other major work at ECOUEN for the same patron.

The original **main château** was built for the Great Condé, general and principal courtier of Louis XIV, who inherited the property in the 17thC. Though designed by Mansart and with gardens by Le Nôtre, it was not regarded as the finest work of these master craftsmen, but it was nevertheless an appropriate expression of the Condé's wealth and power as well as the scene of his famous banquets. At one lavish entertainment for the whole court (according to Mme. de Sévigné's report) the chef committed suicide because the fish he had ordered did not arrive in time. The main château was destroyed during the Revolution, but in 1875–81 the Duc d'Aumale had it rebuilt on the plan of the original building.

Musée Condé ☆

Château de Chantilly
Tel. (4) 4570362
Open Apr–Sept 10.30am–6pm; Oct–Mar 10.30am–5pm

The items on display in the Musée Condé, outstanding as many of them are, can give only a partial account of the collection. This could be said of many museums but in this case it is especially true because the manuscripts which were the Duc d'Aumale's particular passion cannot be permanently exhibited. For this reason the museum's most famous treasure, the ***Très Riches Heures*** ★★ painted for the Duc de Berry by the Limbourg brothers c. 1416, is rarely seen. The ***Heures d'Etienne Chevalier*** ★★, however, less well-known but equally important, are on display in the Santuario (Room 15).

Painted by Jean Fouquet, c. 1460, for Charles VIII's treasurer, these 40 illuminations are the artist's masterpiece and perhaps the greatest example of French Renaissance art. Fouquet understood, more than any other northern painter, the principles of Italian art, but he linked this to the naturalism of his native tradition so that these scenes from the Bible and Golden Legend are couched in the terms of 15thC life and experience. In one, St James kneels while his executioner, in a single movement, receives the sword and measures his distance with an outstretched arm. In the ***Adoration of the Magi*** it is Charles VIII, accompanied by his royal guard, who presents the Christ child with frankincense and myrrh.

The same room also contains two small paintings by Raphael (***The Three Graces*** and ***The Orléans Madonna***) and a 15thC **cassone panel** attributed to Filippino Lippi which provide an excellent introduction to the extensive collection of paintings. As one might expect, this brilliant standard is not always maintained throughout the collection, and there are several lapses, but the museum undoubtedly possesses a number of excellent works which are distributed throughout the galleries of the main château. Raphael is further represented by the ***Madonna di Loreto*** ★, and of the other early Italian works Piero di Cosimo's profile ***Portrait of Simonetta Vespucci*** ★ and Sassetta's ***Mystic Marriage of St Francis*** ★ are the finest. By comparison the Dutch and Flemish schools are weaker, and apart from a small diptych of ***The Crucifixion*** by Memling in the Tribune and two good **sea pieces** by Ruisdael and van de Velde (Salle Isabelle) there is little in that area.

The French paintings, however, are plentiful and there are many of particular note. The earliest is probably Enguerrand Quarton's ***Madonna of the Misericord*** (Cabinet du Giotto) leading on to the series of 16thC–17thC portraits including an excellent group of **drawings** ★ by Jean and François Clouet. French paintings from the 17thC to 19thC also dominate the large **Galerie de Peinture** in which there are several works by Poussin, such as ***The Massacre of the Innocents*** and ***The Childhood of Bacchus***. Later works, like Fromentin's ***Hunters with Falcons***, indicate a definite taste for Oriental subjects on the part of the duke, but there is also a good ***Concert Champêtre*** by Corot in his most bucolic manner and a Romantic subject, ***The Two Foscari***, by Delacroix. In another part of the museum (the Tribune) there are four good paintings by Ingres – ***Venus Anadyomene, Antiochus and Stratonice***, a **Portrait of Mme. Devaucay** and a ***Self-Portrait*** ★ – and the **Salle Isabelle** brings together works by Géricault, Delacroix and Ingres, the three principal figures of French Romantic art.

Still inside the main château there are some ceramics and tapestries as well as a famous collection of gems and miniatures in the **Cabinet des Gemmes**, but the **Petit Château**, entered from the main vestibule, accommodates most of the decorative arts. Here, in a series of seven large rooms furnished and decorated in 17thC and 18thC styles, there are **dessus de portes** by Oudry, **Chinoiserie** decorations by J-B. Huet, **porcelain** from Sèvres and Rouen, **tapestries** from the Gobelins, and **furniture** by Riesener and J-B. Sené. This building also contains the extensive library of the Duc d'Aumale and a chapel with some stained glass and a **16thC altar** by Bullant and Goujon, brought here from ECOUEN.

CHARTRES ☆☆

Eure-et-Loire, Centre Map A5

Notre-Dame de Chartres is widely regarded as the greatest of all Gothic cathedrals, the building which introduced the classic phase of French Gothic culture; but even this reputation does not prepare the visitor for its spectacular setting, perched on an outcrop of rock.

From the E the apse rises over a deep cleft displaying the encircled series of flying buttresses, while the W aspect presents the façade supporting the asymetrical old and new towers. The most important period of construction followed the fire of 1194. The new design, based on the principles of Abbé Suger's church at ST-DENIS, deployed the tall rib vaults and pointed arches that are the hallmark of Gothic architecture.

The most striking feature of Chartres, however, is not the architecture, marvellous though it is, but the decoration in the form of **sculpture** and **stained glass**. The triple **Portal Royale** (W end) contains an elaborate sculptural cycle on the theme of prophecy and redemption. Along the supports are the elongated column figures of ***Old Testament Prophets*** ★★ who foretold the coming of Christ, and the tympanum in the central doorway concludes the cycle with ***Christ in Majesty*** ★★ flanked by the symbols of the four evangelists. These sculptures are quite simply the finest masterpieces of Gothic art, but the lateral portals, particularly the **Portal de la Vièrge** ★ to the north from 1197, provide a fascinating comparison.

Much the same could be said about the **stained glass** ★★, but in this case its significance is even greater: the 173 windows which open up the structure and refract the light into a myriad colours are the most complete series of medieval stained glass to have come down to us.

Musée des Beaux-Arts

Cloître Notre-Dame
Tel. (37) 364139
Open Apr–Sept 10am–noon, 2–6pm; Oct–Mar 10am–noon, 2–5pm
Closed Tues

It is perhaps inevitable that a museum beside the cathedral will be overshadowed by the architecture, sculpture and stained glass of Notre-Dame, but the Musée des Beaux-Arts does not offer much competition. Housed in the old Episcopal Palace, there is a generally faded air to the interior which has extended to many of the exhibits, with the result that only a few items stand out from the miscellaneous collection of polychrome wooden sculptures, medieval church treasures and paintings from the 16thC–20thC.

Zurbaran's ***St Lucy*** is the finest work on display, but there are some good 18thC French pictures, including Van Loo's ***Adoration of the Shepherds***, Chardin's ***Monkey Painter*** and a **landscape** sketch by Fragonard. There are also several good medieval enamels, such as the 13thC ***Processional Cross*** from Châteauneuf-en-Thymerais. The most recent addition to the collection consists of paintings by Vlaminck, donated by the artist's son-in-law in 1978.

COMPIÈGNE
Oise, Picardie Map D1

The town of Compiègne has several interesting buildings, such as the early 16thC town hall described by Robert Louis Stevenson as "a monument of Gothic insecurity", but it is the **royal palace** and grounds which command the greatest attention. Louis XIV, the first king to be attracted to the area, said, "At Versailles I live like a king, like a prince at Fontainebleau, and at Compiègne like a peasant." It was his two successors, however, who built the present palace, later extended by Napoleon I.

Two unrelated incidents in Compiègne's rich history stand out. Joan of Arc was captured here in 1430 by Burgundians and then handed over to the English for trial, and, much later, a railway carriage in the forest behind the town was the scene of the armistice at the end of World War I.

Musée National du Château de Compiègne

Place du Général de Gaulle
Tel. (4) 4400202
Open summer 10am–noon, 1.30–6pm; winter 9.30–11.45am, 1.30–4.45pm
Closed Tues

The château at Compiègne was begun in 1751 under the direction of the architect A.-J. Gabriel, replacing an earlier structure, and this building now houses three separate museums: the Great Apartments, the Museum of the Second Empire, and a Museum of Transport (which need not concern us here).

In the **Great Apartments** it is the bedrooms of Napoleon I and Marie-Louise, both so richly decorated that they are almost overripe, that are most memorable. One could be forgiven for thinking that the emperor had an eye on the future history of his palace as a tourist center when he chose the decoration, because his own bed is not unlike an altar, elaborately carved and gilded, draped with a tentlike covering of pink and gold satin, and topped with ostrich feathers. His wife's bed, of the same design, uses the tasteful combination of white and gold. But in Compiègne one can only welcome this excess because the rest of the palace is bare almost to the point of austerity, showing no signs of any individual character or period of occupation. Some rooms do have suites of furnishing in Louis XV, Directory or Empire style, and there are several tapestries and decorative murals, but very little could be described as memorable.

The **Museum of the Second Empire** is quite different. Under Napoleon III Compiègne came back into prominence because the emperor preferred this palace, where he held the elaborate house parties known as the "Series de Compiègne". These were rather unorthodox affairs, often mixing guests from different social and professional backgrounds, and it is this domestic character which is recalled in the everyday furniture of the rooms. One notable indication of the taste for flashy ostentation, however, is the copy of Winterhalter's portrait of ***Napoleon III and the Empress Eugénie***.

Musée Vivenel

Hôtel des Songeons, 2, Rue d'Austerlitz
Tel. (4) 4402600 (Ext 323)
Open Mar–Oct 9am–noon, 2–6pm; Nov–Feb 9am–noon, 2–5pm
Closed Tues

The Musée Vivenel was set up in 1842 with the collection of paintings and furniture left to the town by the architect Antoine Vivenel, but it was not until 1953 that it was installed in the Hôtel des Songeons, an early 19thC Empire house beside the river Oise. The collection itself is now fairly diverse, with a number of **medieval sacred art** objects, some 18thC and 19thC French furniture and ceramics, and a reasonable selection of drawings and paintings from France and other European schools. The earliest paintings are perhaps the most interesting, in particular an anonymous 17thC French ***Crucifixion*** and a retable of five panels depicting ***Scenes from the Life of Christ*** by the 15thC German painter Michael Wolgemut. The museum also possesses two **drawings** by Albrecht Dürer, who was Wolgemut's assistant in Nuremberg during the 1480s.

The ground floor of the building contains a large **archaeology display** in which the classical pieces are given prominence. Alongside marble and bronze sculptures there is an impressive collection of **Greek painted pottery**.

COURBEVOIE

Hauts-de-Seine, Ile-de-France Map C3

Courbevoie, on the edge of Paris, was until quite recently a pleasant suburb which had attracted its fair share of artists and writers. In the 1960s, however, it was drawn into, or at least overshadowed by, the immense high-rise development known as La Défense.

Musée Roybet-Fould

178 Boulevard Saint-Denis
Tel. (1) 3333073
Open Thur, Sat, Sun 2–6pm

The building which houses the collection in the Musée Roybet-Fould is itself something of a curiosity. It began life as the Norwegian and Swedish Pavilion at the International Exhibition of 1878, and was then dismantled and re-erected on its present site on the Fould estate in Courbevoie. It was not until 1927 that the painter Consuelo Fould decided to use the building as a museum to display his collection of paintings, furniture and items of local history. There are several examples of Fould's own work in the museum as well as that of F. Roybet, the late 19thC genre painter, but the most important aspect of the collection is the **sculpture, paintings, prints and drawings** by Jean-Baptiste Carpeaux, who died in Courbevoie in 1875.

DREUX

Eure-et-Loire, Centre Map A4

The repeated sieges of Dreux, especially during the Wars of Religion, resulted in the destruction of many buildings, but the 13thC **Church of St-Pierre** and an impressive **16thC Flamboyant/ Renaissance belfry**, have survived reasonably intact. In fact the latter has several good features, particularly the staircase and the interior wood panelling, although it tends to be overshadowed (undeservedly) by the **Chapelle Royale St-Louis**, a mausoleum built by Louis-Philippe in the early 19thC.

Chapelle Royale St-Louis

2, Square d'Aumale
Tel. (37) 460706
Open Easter to mid-Oct 9am–noon, 2–7pm; mid-Oct to Easter 9am–noon, 2–sunset
Closed Sun 10–11am

The Chapelle Royale at Dreux, a mausoleum to the House of Orléans and in particular to Louis-Philippe, King of France from 1830 until he was deposed by the Revolution of 1848, would perhaps better be described as a "Chapel of Rest" because it recalls many of the features of a modern funeral parlour. It is also proof that the French could produce monuments to bad taste with the same blend of historicism and piety so beloved of the Victorians.

The architecture is a combination of High Renaissance and Gothic revival, giving the interior the look of a miniature St Peter's, but the main focus is on the fittings. The windows, for example – one taken from a **cartoon** by Ingres – are not stained glass but painted with strong, even gaudy, colours using a special technique developed at Sèvres. Descending to the crypt you are confronted by a procession of marble tombs surmounted by **sculpted effigies**.

These are of variable quality, both in technique and conception. The most striking, The **tomb of the Duke and Duchess of Orléans**, shows the lady stretching a marble hand through a carved window to touch the Duke's cold reclining figure. The others merely lay claim to military or political greatness through the display of arms and inscriptions. The whole building is in fact an entertaining monument to inflated pretensions, apparent not least in the **tomb of Louis-Philippe** himself.

Musée Municipal

Place du Musée
Tel. (37) 501861
Open Sat, Wed 2–5pm; Sun 10am–noon, 2–5pm
Closed Mon, Tues, Thurs, Fri

The municipal museum at Dreux, occupying two floors of a deconsecrated chapel, is well laid out, which partly compensates for the routine character of the collection. It is mainly of local interest, containing furniture, militaria and historical documents from the area, as well as a good display of **Romanesque capitals** and **stained glass** from the 13thC collegiate church of St-Etienne de Dreux. These fragments are all that survive of the building destroyed during the Revolution. In keeping with the rest of the exhibits, the paintings are predominantly local works from the 19thC and 20thC, but there are also pictures by Le Sidaner and Vlaminck.

ECOUEN

Val d'Oise, Ile de France Map C3

Ecouen, at the edge of a forest to the N of Paris, has been associated with the Montmorency family since the 10thC. The village itself has little to recommend it but it is overlooked by the impressive 16thC château built by François I's military commander, the Constable Anne de Montmorency.

Musée National de la Renaissance

Château d'Ecouen
Tel. (3) 9900404
Open 9.45am–12.30pm, 2–5.15pm
Closed Tues

The idea of a National Museum of the Renaissance in France is an excellent one. The character and diversity of this phase of French culture are not widely known, and would offer an interesting display of the various works of 16thC artists and craftsmen. There is a prodigious amount of material in the form of paintings, sculpture, hangings, ceramics, metalwork, medals and prints, mostly on reserve in the national collections, and this would amply stock such a museum. At the same time, the choice of the Château d'Ecouen as its home would seem to be perfect, since it is a fine 16thC building which had an important position in the history of the Renaissance in France. Designed largely by Jean Bullant, the exterior was perhaps best known for the sculptures that it incorporated, namely the **two slaves** by Michelangelo intended for the tomb of Pope Julius II, but given to François I in 1546 by Roberto Strozzi. (These sculptures are now in the ***LOUVRE***).

In view of all this, it is all the more disappointing to conclude that the Musée National de la Renaissance is an opportunity missed. In spite of the advantages already mentioned and the possibility of creating a museum that would be virtually unique, as well as extremely enjoyable, for the specialist and casual observer alike, there is a blandness to the displays and an almost barren effect in many of the majestic rooms, as if the museum were either unfinished or under-stocked. Certain rooms, such as the **bedchambers of the King and the Constable**, do have some interesting frescoes, and there is a curious series of large paintings of the ***Life of Scipio*** on leather, but you can't help wishing for other exhibits which could bring the images and their setting, indeed the whole period, to life.

The **chapel** in the SE pavilion is the most attractive room, combining Renaissance and Gothic elements in an elaborate decorative scheme that includes the remains of a carved **altar** by Jean Goujon. In the other apartments however, you must look for individual items of interest, such as the two **chimney-pieces** in the Gallery of Psyche, formerly in the Cluny Museum although originally created for a house in Chalons-sur-Marne. A relief sculpture on one, depicting ***Diana and Actaeon***, is perhaps the finest work on display.

FONTAINEBLEAU
Seine-et-Marne, Ile-de-France
Map D5

The sporting opportunities of the Forêt de Fontainebleau made this area popular with the kings of France long before a palace was built there, and as early as the 12thC it was known as a royal hunting lodge. From this humble base it gradually expanded to include a hospital and monastery as well as a royal residence, but it was François I who gave it prominence as the principal seat of his court. In 1528, following his return from captivity in Spain, he began making general improvements to the château under the master mason Gilles Le Breton, and these became increasingly ambitious as his interest quickened. The **Porte Dorée** (1528–40) was the first of these works and one of the finest examples of early Renaissance architecture in France. François went on to build the **Galerie** and **Cour du Cheval Blanc** as well as to lay down plans for later extensions.

At the same time, the political turmoil in Italy enabled François to secure the services of some outstanding artists from Rome and Florence. Rosso, Primaticcio and Niccolò dell' Abbate were brought to the palace where they communicated the principles of Italian Renaissance art to a team of assistants. Paintings, sculptures and a series of architectural and decorative designs flowed from this circle, and with the aid of a printing press their work was quickly disseminated to workshops throughout the country. They also acquired a number of antique statues for the palace.

The masterpiece of this phase is still to be seen at the palace itself. In the 1530s the Italians decorated the **interior of the Galerie François I★**, combining different materials and techniques in an elaborate hybrid style that is very attractive and has come to be associated with the School of Fontainebleau.

Musée National du Château de Fontainebleau
Tel. (6) 4222740 & 4223439
Open 9.30am–12.30pm, 2–5pm
Closed Tues
(*in some parts*)

Despite its Renaissance motifs and apparently controlled façade, Fontainebleau is a haphazard building created by several hands, and has no unifying plan to its development. On closer inspection most of the wings are inconsistent or asymmetrical, but this is clearly part of their appeal. Unlike many later palaces it is on a human scale, and the steep-pitched roof, broken irregularly by dormers and taller pavilions, has a domestic character that most people intuitively recognize. The gardens likewise, although they stretch for some distance to the E, are diverse and attractive without the overpowering orchestration of nature that you find at VERSAILLES.

The buildings apart, Fontainebleau is probably best known for the 16thC decorations undertaken for François I by Rosso, Primaticcio and a team of Italian and French craftsmen. The finest surviving example of this is in the impressive **Galerie François I** on the first floor where Rosso and Primaticcio introduced the combination of painting, wood panelling and high stucco relief that became the hallmark of the School of Fontainebleau. The same principle was applied with equal success by Primaticcio to the Bedchamber of the Duchesse d'Etampes (now the **Escalier du Roi**) although in this case placing greater emphasis on the sculptural quality of the lifesize female nudes flanking the central scene. Unfortunately the paintings in both cycles have suffered some deterioration, but Rosso's **mythological scenes** glorifying the monarch in the Galerie have been restored to something approaching their original condition.

Beyond the Galerie is the series of **royal apartments** overlooking the Cour Ovale. The Salon François I has a decorative chimneypiece by Primaticcio with a medallion depicting ***Venus and Adonis***, but in general these rooms, some of which were decorated in the 19thC, are disappointing, although there are a few interesting pieces in the miscellaneous collection of paintings, furniture and tapestries. In contrast, the **apartments of Marie-Antoinette** overlooking the Jardin de Diane are more attractive, preserving the **18thC furniture and decoration** chosen by the Queen. Her bedroom, often known as the Chambre des Six Maries, a reference to the succession of women who have occupied it, is an excellent Louis XVI interior with a ceiling painting of ***Aurora*** by Berthélémy.

Returning to the main entrance and running alongside the Galerie are the **apartments of Napoleon I**. Furnished in mainly Empire Style with examples of the work of Jacob-Desmalter, these rooms are rather dull, in spite of the lavish gilding here and there. There are plans for a Napoleonic museum at Fontainebleau, and a number of items and souvenirs, such as one of the innumerable hats worn by the Emperor, are already on display.

This section also has the finest modern painting in the palace: a version of David's equestrian portrait of ***Napoleon Crossing the Great St Bernard Pass***. Never one for understatement, Napoleon can be seen to have inscribed his name on the rock beside those of Charlemagne and Hannibal who, it seems, had also passed this way.

On the ground floor, although they are not always open, are the **Petits Appartements** of Napoleon and Joséphine, again furnished in the Empire Style and there is a small collection of Oriental art in the **Chinese Museum** off the Cour de La Fontaine.

GIVERNY
Vernon, Eure, Normandie Map A2

Giverny, a small village at the confluence of the Seine and the Epte 80km (50 miles) from Paris, was already known to landscape painters when Monet took up residence there in 1883. It also became the center for a large colony of American artists some five years later. The village, Monet's own garden and the surrounding area became the subject matter of virtually all the artist's paintings until his death in 1926. He is buried beside the small Romanesque church.

Musée Claude Monet
Rue Claude Monet
Open Apr–Oct: House 10am–noon, 2–6pm; Gardens 10am–6pm Closed Nov–Mar, Mon

Judging from the large crowds and the number of tourist buses in the area at weekends, it would appear that Giverny has become something of a pilgrimage center for devotees of the lush pastoralism of Monet's late work. When the artist moved here in 1883 he began cultivating the rich garden and making the waterlily pond that became the preoccupation of his art, culminating in the ***Nymphéas*** or Waterlilies series of the early years of this century. Initially Monet designed the garden himself, but such were the demands of maintaining it that at one stage he employed a small army of gardeners. This garden has now been restored to something approaching its appearance of 60 or 70 years ago, complete with the water courses and the much-painted Japanese bridge. Monet's house and studio have also been renovated (to the extent that the interior has a strangely unused feeling, as if nobody had ever lived there) but there are no paintings by the artist on display. In view of this a visit to the Musée Marmottan in ***PARIS*** is strongly recommended to appreciate the full effect of Monet's years at Giverny.

GROS BOIS
Val-de-Marne, Ile-de-France Map D4

The plaster, brick and stone façade of Gros Bois indicates that it is a 16thC–17thC château in the traditional style of the Ile-de-France, but the details, the interior and most of the furnishings are from the period of the Empire. This was the home of Maréchal Berthier, Napoleon's chief of staff, and was frequently visited by the Emperor.

Le Château de Gros Bois
Boissy-Saint-Leger
Open Sat, Sun 2–5.30pm, Thur from May to Aug

The interior at Gros Bois has successfully retained the character of an impressive residence of the Empire period. **Furniture** by Jacob and Thomire, **sculpture** by Canova, and **paintings** by Vernet and Gros all contribute to the range and quality of its contents, while the large **Galerie des Batailles** reflects the military achievements of Maréchal Berthier. In 1910, however, some traces of the earlier 17thC decoration were uncovered in the dining room (Chambre d'Honneur), including painted beams and a **large fresco** of a marriage ceremony by Abraham Bosse.

L'ISLE-ADAM
Val d'Oise, Ile-de-France Map C2

L'Isle-Adam, on the river Oise with its parks, banks and avenues, seems perfectly equipped for the leisurely outdoor life so often depicted by the Impressionist painters in this area. Auvers, nearby, was particularly popular and both Daubigny and van Gogh died there (see p. 133). L'Isle-Adam also has a **15thC–16thC church** combining Gothic and Renaissance elements in the façade and containing a number of good furnishings such as the choir stalls and misericords.

Musée Louis Senlecq
46, Grande Rue
Tel. (3) 4691250
Open May–Oct, Sat–Mon 2–5pm
Closed Nov–Apr, Tues–Fri

The Musée Senlecq, situated in the 17thC college of the Josephites beside the church, is primarily a museum of local history; but there are also some **paintings and drawings** by artists who were associated with the town. These include the marine painter Jules Dupré, who died in L'Isle-Adam in 1889, and the landscapist Théodore Rousseau. There is also a ***Snowy Landscape*** by the Fauvist Maurice de Vlaminck.

MAISONS-LAFITTE
Yvelines, Ile-de-France Map C3

The Château de Maisons was designed by Mansart in 1642 for Louis XIII's finance minister, René de Longueil. The scale of the house and its stables, rivalling those at CHANTILLY, were an expression of de Longueil's immense wealth; but they have suffered considerably since then. In the 1840s the banker Jacques Lafitte, who had purchased the house in 1818, sold off the gardens as building plots and demolished the stables for the stone.

Château de Maisons
Maisons-Lafitte
Tel. (3) 9620149
Open 9am–noon, 2–5pm
Closed Tues, Sun mornings

Despite its formal appearance, mainly due to the destruction of its surrounding gardens, the **Château de Maisons** is probably the finest surviving building by François Mansart, the greatest French architect of the 17thC, and therefore fully deserves closer inspection. The façade with its complex centerpiece and extended wings is a masterpiece of proportion, control and sensitive disposition of the classical orders. The same can be said of the interior. Before seeing any of the contents you are confronted by Mansart's majestic **staircase** leading, as you ascend, to the playful **decoration** of carved acanthus and putti representing the Arts and Sciences. The rest of the interior decoration at Maisons is more restrained, but the main apartments on the first floor, the **Salle des Fêtes**, the **Salon d'Hercule** and the **King's Bedroom**, are richly appointed and have some good 17thC and 18thC furniture.

MANTES-LA-JOLIE
Yvelines, Ile de France Map B3

If Mantes ever was the attractive town which its name suggests, rebuilding since World War II has changed it into a dull commercial center that is almost completely lacking in character. In the midst of the uniformly modern redevelopment, however, is the beautiful 12thC–13thC Gothic **church of Notre-Dame**, which has some good sculpture and stained glass. It was built at the same time as Notre-Dame de Paris and probably shared some of the craftsmen, and the similarity of the two buildings has often been commented upon.

Musée Maximilien Luce
Hôtel de Ville, Avenue Gambetta
Tel. (3) 4774900
Open 2–5.30pm
Closed Tues

Until the renovations to the Musée Duhamel are completed, the only gallery in Mantes is the Musée Luce, containing 130 **paintings, drawings and prints** by the Post-Impressionist painter and donated to the town in 1971 by Frédéric Luce, the artist's son. Unfortunately the collection is rather one-sided, consisting almost exclusively of late work (**landscapes, working scenes** and **views of Paris**) in a dull and awkward style quite unlike the scintillating Pointillist pictures that the artist produced in the late 19thC. The Portrait of ***Felix Fenéon***, an early supporter of the Neo-Impressionists, is the only work recalling the heyday of Seurat, Luce and their circle.

MEAUX
Seine-et-Marne, Ile-de-France Map E3

Meaux is a historic town which over the centuries has endured more than its fair share of the misfortunes arising from military and religious conflicts. Partly for this reason, the only section of the town which has retained any character is the area around the large Gothic **cathedral of St-Etienne**, begun in 1180 but now badly weathered. Jacques-Benigne Bossuet, "last of the fathers of the church" and a famous theologian and preacher, was Bishop of Meaux 1681 until his death in 1704.

Musée Bossuet
Cité Episcopale,
5, Place Charles de Gaulle
Tel. (6) 4348445
Open 10.30am–noon, 2–6pm
Closed Tues

The Musée Bossuet is housed appropriately in the **Episcopal Palace**, an early building dating from the 15thC with gardens laid out by Le Nôtre in the 1640s. Much of the collection is devoted to souvenirs of Bossuet's life and times, but there are sections of **Gallo-Roman** and **medieval antiquities** and some fine and **decorative arts** of the 18thC and 19thC. The paintings include **works** by Rigaud, Lancret, Daubigny and Millet and there are **sculptures** by Bouchardon. Among the items of furniture, there is a **commode** by Charles Cressent from around 1720 which is particularly interesting.

MEUDON
Hauts-de-Seine, Ile-de-France
Map C4

Meudon, once the site of two royal palaces, the more recent of which was burnt down in 1870, still has the remains of the extensive wooded parkland. In the 19thC it was a popular picnic spot for Parisians, but the gradual sprawl of the suburbs has overtaken it. The sculptor Rodin lived here from 1895 until his death in 1917.

Musée d'Art et d'Histoire
11, Rue des Pierres
Tel. (1) 5347519 Ext. 427 (Mairie)
Open 2–6pm
Closed Mon, Tues

Although the town of Meudon has few attractions, the museum, housed in a restored **17thC building**, is nothing short of delightful. The paintings are not outstanding, but out of a reasonable selection of 18thC–20thC French works Diaz de la Peña's ***Harem Scene*** and an anonymous 18thC ***Girl with a Doll*** are the most interesting. The sculptures are stronger overall, and in this section the museum possesses works by Courbet, (***Helvetia***) Bourdelle (***Great Warrior***) and Hans Arp (***Ptolemly II***), some of which are exhibited in the beautiful gardens to the rear of the house.

Musée Rodin
Villa des Brillants, 19, Avenue Auguste Rodin
Tel. (1) 5341309
Open Apr–Oct, Sun, Mon, 1.30–6pm
Closed Nov–Mar, Tues–Sat, Apr–Oct

The Villa des Brillants, where Rodin lived during the later part of his life, is now an annexe to the Musée Rodin in ***PARIS***. It has recently been absorbed by a sprawl of suburban houses but it had lost its original character long before this. Rodin's villa survives, although it stands beside a larger building erected in 1932 on the site of the sculptor's studio, and this serves as a gallery for casts and maquettes of his most famous works. ***The Burghers of Calais, Balzac*** and the ***Gates of Hell*** are all represented and, as a particularly touching gesture, a cast of ***The Thinker*** sits overlooking the graves of Rodin and his wife.

NEMOURS
Seine-et-Marne, Ile-de-France
Map D6

Nemours, situated on a beautiful section of the Loing near Fontainebleau, was an important bridgehead in the Middle Ages.

Musée de Nemours
Château de Nemours
Tel. (6) 4282742
Open Sat–Mon 10am–noon, 2–5.30pm; Wed–Fri 2–5.30pm
Closed Tues

(*If the museum is closed during the normal hours there is a caretaker in the last house to the left of the courtyard.*)
At the time of writing, the contents of the museum at Nemours are in storage while the rooms of the castle are being renovated for display purposes, and only the prehistory section is on exhibition. As it stands, however, the **12thC castle** building is impressive in itself and the collection of **paintings, drawings, ceramics** and **tapestries** will eventually be displayed to good advantage.

PONTOISE
Val d'Oise, Ile-de-France Map B3

As a crossing point and bridgehead Pontoise had considerable historical importance. Several medieval and Renaissance buildings have survived; the **church of St-Maclou** dating from the 12thC–16thC is the most important. More recently the town was popular among the Impressionist painters, and Pissarro lived there from 1866–82, during which time he encouraged the latent talent of both Cézanne and Gauguin as well as pursuing his own work in the surrounding area.

Musée Pissarro
17, Rue du Château
Tel. (3) 9650675
Open Wed–Sun 2–6pm
Closed Mon, Tues

Considering the significance of Pontoise in Pissarro's work, it is slightly disappointing to find that this new museum has only one early painting, ***Péniches sur la Marne*** (1864), by the Impressionist master. There are a few of the artist's prints and some works by lesser-known contemporaries but, as if to compensate for this relative shortage, the museum does have a policy of mounting good temporary exhibitions of other Impressionist and Neo-Impressionist painters associated with Pissarro.

Musée Tavet-Delacour

4, Rue Lemercier
Tel. (3) 0319300 (Mairie)
Open 10am–noon, 2–6pm
Closed Tues

The arrangement of the Musée Tavet-Delacour says something about the disparate interests of the collection, because the items on display are largely drawn from different bequests, each of which is exhibited separately on the three floors of the building. There is a sense of visiting several small museums, but this is an attractive feature especially since they are all accommodated in the fine **15thC Renaissance house** that Camille Tavet presented to the town in 1890.

The ground floor clearly contains a **personal collection** in the library of Charles Oulmont which has all the characteristics of a bibliophile's private apartments. Apart from the leather bound volumes there are a few paintings of writers at work and two sketches by Carrière for his well known ***Portrait of Verlaine***. The first floor, devoted to **20thC art**, is taken up by the bequests of Otto Freundlich and his associate Jeanne Kosnick-Kloss. A German by birth Freundlich spent a large part of his career in Paris in the company of the Cubists and Constructivists. He was therefore able to acquire **works** by Arp, Picasso, Marcoussis and Sonia Delaunay. This collection also has some examples of his own work, such as the painting ***La Roseraie II*** (1942), in which colourful geometric shapes are built up into an elaborate abstract pattern.

The second floor galleries usually display temporary exhibitions in which other aspects of the collection, such as the medieval antiquities or Italian and French drawings, are given particular prominence.

RUEIL-MALMAISON

Hauts-de-Seine, Ile-de-France
Map C3

Malmaison at the western edge of Paris takes its unsalubrious name from the fact that it was a leper colony in the Middle Ages, the original house being built on the site by Christophe Perrot in the 17thC.

Musée National du Château de Malmaison

Avenue du Château
Tel. (1) 7492007
Open 10am–12.30pm, 1.30–5.30pm (5.00pm in winter)
Closed Tues

The Château of Rueil-Malmaison was the private home of Napoleon and Josephine, where they entertained lavishly to further his career, so it comes as something of a surprise to see how modest the house is. When Napoleon purchased it in 1798 he engaged the two architects Percier and Fontaine to remodel the house along lines that became known as the Empire Style. This involved designing a series of adaptable but interconnected rooms on two floors along the length of the narrow building. The two architects then supervised the design of furnishings, carpets, hangings and porcelain, making Malmaison the model for much contemporary taste. After they divorced, Josephine lived at Malmaison until her death in 1814, when most of the contents were sold.

With a house of such importance in the history of French decorative arts, quite apart from its historic associations, the task of recent years has been one of steady and painstaking restoration in an attempt to recreate its original state. In several rooms, notably **Napoleon's Study** (which suggests the interior of a military tent) and the **private apartments** on the first floor, this has already been completely successful, but some work remains to be done.

Josephine was herself a considerable art collector, with over 300 paintings in her private collection, and a few of these are on display alongside pictures by Napoleon's official artists: David, Gros, Gerard, Girodet and Prud'hon. The finest of these works are Girodet's ***Ossian Receiving Napoleon's Generals at Valhalla*** in the drawing room, a version of David's ***Napoleon Crossing the Great St Bernard Pass***, and Gros's ***Napoleon awarding Swords of Honour after Marengo***.

ST-DENIS

Seine-St-Denis, Ile-de-France
Map C3

Despite the fact that St-Denis has become an unattractive modern suburb of Paris, the Basilica alone is enough to make the trip worthwhile. Ever since its foundation as early as the 5thC, there has been a succession of abbey churches on the site where the decapitated martyr St

Denis eventually fell, having carried his head all the way from Montmartre. The most important of these was the **12thC Basilica** which, under the supervision of Abbé Suger, became one of the earliest structures to deploy the pointed arch and rib vaulting that became the hallmark of Gothic architecture. Large sections of this ancient building have survived in the present church, notably the apse, façade and narthex. However, the combination of this and later work, including a fair amount of 19thC restoration, gives it an unspectacular appearance that belies its historic importance.

Under Suger the abbey at St-Denis forged close links with the French crown, and from medieval times until the 19thC almost all the kings of France were buried there. Their tombs, reflecting the taste and aspirations of different periods, have survived reasonably intact.

Basilica of Saint-Denis ☆

Open Apr–Sept 10am–noon, 1.30–6pm; Oct–Mar 1–4pm
Closed Sun morning

The compulsory tour of the interior of St-Denis can be both frustrating and irritating, but it is the only way that you will get close enough to inspect the royal tombs ranged around the aisles of the basilica. These represent a comprehensive collection of the greatest **French funerary sculpture**★, and are fortunately still to be seen in their original location. During the Revolution St-Denis was an obvious target for anti-monarchist feeling, and on more than one occasion the tombs and their contents were pillaged. But they were saved from destruction by Alexandre Lenoir, who recognized their historical importance and transferred them to the Musée des Beaux-Arts. Under Napoleon they were restored, partly because he wanted eventually to rest in the same place.

Most of the earlier tombs date from the reign of Louis IX (St Louis) in the 13thC, and consist of the traditional catafalque or sarcophagus displaying a reclining effigy of the dead man or woman. In the Renaissance, however, such projects were more elaborately treated, and in the tomb of ***François I*** by Bontemps and Philibert de l'Orme, and of ***Henri II*** by Bontemps and Primaticcio, complex architectural structures support and enclose a number of beautifully carved figures. The ***François I*** tomb is also, as you might expect from de l'Orme, a small masterpiece in the variation of classical architectural motifs.

Musée d'Art et d'Histoire de la Ville de St-Denis

22 bis, Rue Gabriel Péri
Tel. (1) 2430510
Open Mon, Wed–Sat 10.30am–6pm, Sun 2–6.30pm
Closed Tues, Sun morning

Declared **European Museum of the Year** in 1983, this is essentially a local museum with a fairly ordinary collection for a town of this size. It has, however, been dramatically transformed at the hands of a gifted designer. The focus for this transformation is the **17thC Carmelite convent**, acquired by the town in 1972, which has been extensively remodelled in an attempt to balance the three interests of the collection: the town itself, the Carmelites, and the fine arts. The ground floor, for example, has among other local antiquities a complete reconstruction of a traditional **apothecary's shop** (which you enter through a plate glass cubicle); and the **nuns' cells** on the first floor present a series of tableaux juxtaposing the Spartan surroundings of convent life with various **church treasures**.

In complete contrast the second floor offers a large collection of **souvenirs from the Paris Commune** of 1870–71. Photographs, models, guns and uniforms, as well as some more unusual items, make up the display, and numerous contemporary cartoons and prints, including two **lithographs** by Manet, recall the effect of this momentous event on the lives of many artists.

As for the fine art collection, there are **medieval sculptures**, some **paintings of St-Denis**, and a bequest of **oils** and **water-colours** by Albert André (1869–1954) in a style close to that of the **Nabis** brotherhood. Beyond this there are a few works from the **School of Paris**, but the most interesting item is a **vase** decorated by Picasso which the artist gave to Paul and Dominique Eluard as a wedding present in 1951.

ST-GERMAIN-EN-LAYE
Yvelines, Ile-de-France Map B3

The first château at St-Germain was begun in 1124 by Louis VI on a site backed by a forest, overlooking the Seine and commanding a marvellous view across the plain to Paris. With these attractions St-Germain remained popular with the ruling family; successive buildings were erected by Charles V and François I, the latter superimposing Renaissance forms on an essentially medieval plan. In 1557 Henri II commissioned a new château from

Philibert de l'Orme, the **Château Neuf**, to stand beside the older residence. It was here in 1638 that Louis XIV was born, and he in turn continued to use St-Germain as one of the principal seats of the court until VERSAILLES, only 14km (9 miles) away, was completed in 1682. Very little now survives of the Château Neuf, but the formal gardens and **Grande Terrasse** laid out by Le Nôtre are an indication of the extravagance of the 17thC court.

In addition to the châteaux, St-Germain itself has a number of interesting features. Numerous writers, musicians and artists have been associated with the town, Dumas, Debussy and Maurice Denis being the most famous, and there are several attractive buildings from the 17thC and 18thC.

Musée des Antiquités Nationales

Château de St-Germain-en-Laye
Tel. (3) 4515365
Open 9.45am–noon, 1.30–5.15pm
Closed Tues

The old **château** at St-Germain has a formidable appearance from the outside with its dry moat and impressive ramparts, although the courtyard seems more domestic with its superficially Renaissance design. The interior was presumably in the same grand style, but when the Museum of Antiquities was installed there in 1962 a comprehensive programme of renovation transformed the various state rooms and chambers into tasteful modern exhibition galleries. You now walk through a series of rooms in which **archaeological antiquities** from the Palaeolithic to the Merovingian period are displayed in chronological order.

The earliest rooms are largely taken up with implements, pottery shards and the remains of burial sites complete with skeletons, but as you proceed through the château there is an increasing number of attractive and well-worked items to enjoy. The jewellery and armour of the Bronze and Iron Age are interesting enough, but this aspect of the collection comes into its own with the Gallo-Roman and Merovingian works on the second floor, particularly in the patterned **clasps, brooches** and **fibulae** of the 3rd and 4thC AD. Among the Roman works there are a number of stone figures and funerary stelae in the crude style characteristic of most Roman provincial work, but the **mosaic floor** from Saint-Romain-en-Gal and the **bronze statuettes** show considerable qualities of craftsmanship.

Musée du Prieuré ☆

2, Rue Maurice Denis
Tel. (3) 9737787
Open 10.30am–5.30pm
Closed Mon, Tues

At the foot of a hill on the outskirts of the town is the recently opened Musée du Prieuré, which is devoted principally to Maurice Denis and his fellow Nabis and other Symbolist contemporaries. The building itself dates from the late 17thC and was originally a hospital. After 1803 it served first as a warehouse, then as a studio for artists, and, from 1870 to 1902, as a Jesuit Priory. Maurice Denis, who was born in St-Germain-en-Laye in 1870, always loved working in the town, and after his marriage in 1893 lived in a house overlooking the Priory. He acquired the Priory itself in 1914, and kept it until his death in 1943.

Denis was a founder member of the group of artists known as the Nabis (the Hebrew word for prophets), who reacted against the naturalistic art of their contemporaries and attempted to portray the spiritual world in the flat, pure colours favoured by their mentor Gauguin. After 1900 the meetings of the group became less frequent, and its members began to follow more closely their individual artistic paths. Nonetheless, after 1914 many of them, including Denis, Paul Ranson, Roussel and Émile Bernard, would get together at the Priory to discuss art and religion, and to enjoy the atmosphere of profound calm which still pervades this place.

The museum, which is surrounded by an enchanting wooded garden with **sculptures** by Bourdelle, has items in all the many media in which Denis worked, ranging from stained glass to ceramics, mosaics and textiles. Among the oils is the serene and dazzlingly white ***The Catholic Mystery***★ (1889), painted shortly after the Nabis had been founded; the joyous and very decorative ***Ladder in the Greenery***★ (1892), which is delightfully and appropriately hung on the ceiling; two works using St-Germain-en-Laye as a setting (***The Pilgrims of Emmaus*** of 1895 and ***Dessert in the Garden***★ of 1896–97), and a late **Self-Portrait** (1921) showing the Priory in the background. There is in addition a large chapel attached to the building, covered in **murals** and other works by Denis.

Denis' contemporaries are also represented by works in a great variety of media: **posters** by Jules Chéret, **illuminated books** by Émile Bernard, **lithographs** by Carrière, **pottery** by Filiger, a **wooden bust** by Lacombe, **sculptures** by Maillol, a beautiful **stained**

glass window by Besnard, **graphic work** by Ranson, Rops and Roussel, a superlative Pointillist portrait of ***Alice Sethe*** by Theo Rysselberghe, various **oils** by Sérusier (including the excellent ***Louise or the Breton Servant***★), and **theatre designs** by Vuillard. A list of the many fine works in this museum could continue endlessly, yet ultimately it is their setting and the way in which they are displayed that leave the most memorable impression. Each room in this simple and beautifully modernized building has a very different character from the next, and each work of art seems to have been positioned with enormous thought. This is less of a museum than a place for quiet contemplation.

SCEAUX
Hauts-de-Seine, Ile-de-France
Map C4

A small town on the outskirts of Paris, Sceaux was the site of a grand house built by Perrault for Colbert, Louis XIV's finance minister. In the early 18thC the Duchesse du Maine's famous court there was patronized by such figures as Voltaire and Fontenelles, but the house was virtually demolished during the Revolution, to be replaced later by a modest building in the style of Louis XIII.

Musée de l'Ile-de-France
Château de Sceaux
Tel. (1) 6610671
Open Mon, Fri 2–6pm; Wed, Thurs 10am–noon, 2–6pm; Sat, Sun 10am–noon, 2–7pm
Closed Tues

The museum in the present Château de Sceaux is devoted to the Ile-de-France, the region surrounding Paris, and it has an impressive range of exhibits, including **costumes, furniture, ceramics, prints,** maps and implements. But the museum concentrates principally on the great houses of the region, many of which have disappeared. Each room on the ground floor is devoted to one or other of the mansions, such as St-Cloud, Meudon and Montmorency, with models, plans, photographs and furnishings arranged in an attempt to evoke the appearance and lifestyle of the 17thC and 18thC, the heyday of the French aristocracy.

Unfortunately the items on display, with a few honourable exceptions, are not of particular interest in themselves. Nowhere is this more obvious than in the paintings. Great painters depicted many of these châteaux and many more contained large decorative schemes and impressive art collections, but there is little trace of them here. Apart from a few rather weak **portraits** by Nattier and Van Loo, **landscapes** by Hubert Robert and Bonington, a room of **sketches** by Dunoyer de Segonzac, and an attractive 18thC **floral decoration** from Pantin, the pictures are unremarkable. Of the furnishings, the inlaid **wooden floor** from Château Pouget (c.1890) is probably the most striking feature, if only because you are required to wear special sheepskin slippers to walk across it.

The house itself is equally unimpressive, but **the park** is really spectacular. Laid out by Le Nôtre in typically 17thC fashion with large formal watercourses, avenues and vistas, it is reminiscent of the park at VERSAILLES (also by Le Nôtre) but smaller and in many respects more enjoyable.

SENLIS
Oise, Picardie Map D2

Senlis is one of the most ancient and historic towns in France, the seat of many early medieval kings, and the place where in 987 Hugues Capet, the ancestor of all later monarchs, was elected to the crown. It has also narrowly escaped the destruction of several wars, with the result that the old town, within two **concentric ramparts**, is virtually intact. In the heart of this, and bounded by the **Gallo-Roman wall**, are the remains of the ancient castle from which there is a good view of the beautiful Gothic **cathedral of Notre-Dame**. Begun in 1155 in a pure early style, it was partially rebuilt in a more Flamboyant manner following a fire in 1504. Nevertheless the two styles coexist happily, and the later work did not interfere with the excellent **13thC sculpture** on the W portal. The other early churches have a less successful history: one has been turned into a market, another into a garage, and a third is now a cinema.

Musée des Beaux-Arts
Place du Parvis Notre-Dame
Tel. (4) 4530080 Ext. 219
Open 10am–noon, 2–6pm
Closed Tues, Wed morning

The Musée des Beaux-Arts at Senlis has been largely turned over to an information center for the adjacent cathedral, with an audio-visual display taking up much of the gallery space. This is appropriate enough, because the **cathedral sculpture**, especially that on the main portal, just a few yards from the museum, is of the highest quality. There are also a few interesting paintings in the museum, including an unusually delicate ***Flight into Egypt*** by Philippe de Champaigne, better known for his impressive public portraits, and an early painting of a ***Weaver*** (1888) by Paul Sérusier before he fell under the influence of Gauguin.

The successful academic painter Thomas Couture, who taught many younger artists of the later 19thC including Manet, was born in Senlis. The museum possesses several **oil sketches** by this artist, but unfortunately no examples of the full-blown Salon paintings for which he was best known.

Musée d'Art et d'Archéologie

Place Notre-Dame
Tel. (4) 4530080 Ext. 247
Open Apr–Sept 10am–noon, 2–6pm; Oct–Mar 10am–noon, 2–5pm
Closed Tues, Wed morning

A cathedral building in the center of the old town houses this collection, following the closure of the Musée Haubergier. Unfortunately, lack of space prevents much of it from being displayed, and you are unlikely to see such items as the early 13thC ***Head of a Prophet*** or the medieval **enamels, reliefs** and **manuscripts**, unless they are included in one of the temporary exhibitions.

Musée de la Vénerie

Château Royal
Tel. (4) 4530080 Ext. 315
Open Apr–Sept 10am–noon, 2–6pm; Oct–Mar 10am–noon, 2–5pm
Closed Tues, Wed morning

The Musée de la Vénerie is, as its name suggests, concerned with hunting in all its aspects. Housed in one of the buildings surviving from the old castle of Senlis, it is surrounded by **gardens** which in themselves make the visit worthwhile. The museum has several paintings which reflect the aristocratic taste for having such pursuits as hunting depicted by artists of considerable ability. This genre reached its peak during the 18thC in the work of Desportes and Oudry, both of whom are represented here; the former by a ***Deerhunt*** depicting the kill, and the latter by the ***Chien à la Jatte***, a lively piece of animal portraiture.

SÈVRES
Hauts-de-Seine, Ile-de-France
Map C3

Sèvres, on the outskirts of Paris, is best known for the famous **porcelain factory** which was transferred there from Vincennes in 1756 at the behest of Madame de Pompadour. Three years later it was taken over by the king and since then it has continued as a national institution, producing fine china and porcelain for a sophisticated luxury market. In the 18thC and early 19thC Sèvres designs were at the forefront of European fashion, but since then the factory has mainly concentrated on producing copies of its own early table and decorative ware.

Musée National de Céramique

Tel. (1) 5349905
Open 9.30am–noon, 1.30–5.15pm
Closed Tues

Burdened with so formal a title as the National Ceramic Museum, the authorities at Sèvres have been concerned to present an appropriately dignified impression. The building possesses an imposing (though not especially inviting) façade in the midst of the motorway complex around the Pont de Sèvres. The interior, similarly, displays the collection in a series of large galleries on two floors with very little regard for the intimate scale of most of the pieces, or for that matter with modern techniques of lighting and display. Only in the early sections on the ground floor, where **Oriental** and **Early European pottery** are exhibited in a new setting, is there any concession to the obvious need for background information.

The main part of the collection on the first floor is predictably dominated by pieces from the Sèvres factory, including three outstanding and important **18thC services**: those of Madame du Barry (1771), Louis de Rohan (1772), and Catherine the Great of Russia (1779). There are also a few examples of the **biscuit figurines** which were modelled by such eminent 18thC sculptors as Houdon, Pigalle and Falconet. Falconet was appointed by the factory to take charge of modelling in 1757.

The collection is not restricted to Sèvres products and, apart from the other French factories at Rouen, Nevers, Marseille and St-Cloud, there are pieces from Holland, Germany, Italy, Switzerland and Spain – indeed from most of the countries of Europe and the Arab world which maintained a ceramic industry. The range is so impressive that it would be difficult to isolate one area for particular attention, but an unusual item that does remain in the memory is the large porcelain ***Animal*** produced in the Meissen factory in Germany (1732–5) but intended for a French "Palais Japonais".

VAUX-LE-VICOMTE
Seine-et-Marne, Ile-de-France Map D5

Vaux-le-Vicomte is a monument to the ambition of one man, Nicolas Fouquet, Louis XIV's finance minister; but its success in promoting his image at court also led directly to his downfall. Begun in 1657 under Le Vau, it was erected at great speed in order to achieve its purpose as quickly as possible. While masons worked on the building, gardeners planted trees, workmen dug new watercourses, and a tapestry workshop was set up in the nearby village of Maincy to produce the hangings.

The culmination of this frenetic activity was an immense fête in August 1661, to which the whole court at Fontainebleau was invited. Reports of this occasion agree that it eclipsed all previous fêtes in its scale and lavish expenditure, and culminated in a brilliant firework display at 2am. But Fouquet had overstepped the mark by outshining the Sun King, and the monarch's displeasure enabled Colbert to arrange his rival's downfall. Nineteen days later Fouquet was arrested for embezzlement; he narrowly escaped execution but spent the rest of his life in prison. One result of this whole affair was that Colbert took over the team of artists and craftsmen assembled at Vaux and put them to work on VERSAILLES where they glorified their new patron, the king.

Le Château de Vaux-le-Vicomte

Tel. (3) 4389709
Open Mar–Nov 10am–6pm
Closed 1–2pm Wed, Oct–Feb

The hasty construction of Vaux-le-Vicomte may have led to a number of weaknesses that could be described as flaws in the design. The central portico, for example, is insufficient for the scale of the building, and its connection with the façade is uncertain. Nevertheless, the vast complex of buildings, gardens and fountains is splendid and at first sight breathtaking. This was largely due to the skill of Le Nôtre who laid out the estate, although Le Vau was in overall control.

Le Vau also supervised the sumptuous decoration of the interior, bringing together the painter Lebrun, and the sculptor Girardon to develop a complex integrated scheme. Ironically, this combination of richly gilded stucco work enclosing mythological paintings, as in the **Chambre du Roi**, became known as the Louis XIV Style.

After 1661 Vaux-le-Vicomte suffered mixed fortunes, but in 1875 it was purchased by Alfred Sommier, who restored the house and gardens. He also acquired most of the **17thC furniture, tapestries and paintings**, which help to recreate its period of greatness.

VERSAILLES
Yvelines, Ile-de-France Map B3

A visit to the palace of Versailles today is an impressive experience, but the purpose behind this vast monument to 17thC magnificence owes more to political than to artistic developments. Its rise was planned by Colbert and Louis XIV as an instrument of Absolutism and a means of controlling the power of the nobility who threatened the authority of the crown. A centralized court required the attendance of all who wished preferment, and the king maintained a close surveillance on his richest and most powerful subjects, carefully manipulating their ambition and weakness to his own ends. If this policy was to succeed, the palace had to be of a scale and opulence that would eclipse all other residences, and in 1661 the arrest of Fouquet provided the means and the opportunity. He had already gathered the finest artists and craftsmen at VAUX-LE-VICOMTE, and they were soon devoting their skills to the new palace at Versailles.

Le Vau became the chief architect responsible for the developments around Louis XIII's original building, and this role was taken over by J.H. Mansart in 1676 to even greater effect. The latter completed the elegant **garden façade** with its two extensive wings, making a total length of 550m (600 yards). The equally splendid interior was under the control of Lebrun, and with the **King's Apartments**, seven rooms decorated between 1671 and 1681 on the theme of Apollo the Sun god, the Louis XIV Style reached its peak. The **gardens** had an equally important role to play in this scheme, and Le Nôtre proceeded to organize over 250 acres (100 hectares) of parkland into parterres, vistas and waterways to make the landscape into a suitable context for the main château. There were originally 1,400 fountains, and Lebrun commissioned over 100 statues for the gardens as well as a series of mythological groups, such as Girardon's ***Apollo and the Nymphs***, for the grottoes and buildings of the park.

At the center of court activity, the kind led a life of public display to a court that numbered somewhere in the region of 1,000; the attendants probably amounted to a further 5,000. All the king's activities throughout the carefully regulated day were seen by a crowd, whether he was rising, playing, eating or retiring. We are even told that Louis XV lay for several days with smallpox while the court watched him die from a safe distance. In addition to all this, the palace also become the principal patron of all the arts in 17thC France; quantities of musicians, writers, artists and craftsmen either worked at Versailles or provided the interest and entertainment that diverted the assembled aristocracy.

The palace of Versailles and its outbuildings includes several museums. Two of these (the Musée des Voitures and the Salle du Jeu de Paume) are at the time of writing closed for reorganization, while the main château is undergoing a long overdue renovation that is likely to affect the interior for some years to come. You should bear in mind, therefore, that certain rooms or exhibits may prove to be inaccessible depending on the state of the building work.

Musée National du Château de Versailles

Tel. (3) 9505832
Open 9.45am–3.30pm
Closed Mon

The Château de Versailles may well be, as the publicity claims "the greatest palace in the world" but this does not necessarily mean that it is the most attractive. From the entrance court at the Place des Armes it has a confused and overblown appearance that often makes a first impression disappointing. Tour arrangements for visitors are not always helpful. If you want to see all the apartments open to the public you must enter and pay twice to follow two circuitous routes through the building, and these give very little indication of the overall layout. Nevertheless, whatever this vast complex loses in intimacy it more than regains in sheer scale and impressiveness, and on proceeding through the building the **garden façade** comes as a marvellously unified spectacle overlooking the immense vista of Le Nôtre's *Tapis Vert* (green carpet) and Grand Canal.

The palace was in constant development and expansion for almost 300 years, and it bears the marks of different periods and successive rulers; but above all it has retained the character of its principal creator, Louis XIV. Like the buildings as a whole, the Louis XIV Style in most of the **state rooms** is impressive rather than attractive, and the designers of the **Salon de l'Abondance** or the **Salon de Vénus** tended to aim for grand effects in the heavy disposition of the parts. Colours are often strong (golds, maroons, deep blues) and the materials themselves, such as marble and porphyry, are luxurious. The way they are organized is solid and sculptural, with grand pilasters, recesses and gilded mouldings.

The painted decoration also tends towards the high Baroque, but with a French academic flavour rather than the exuberance of the Italians. Charles Lebrun was in overall charge of the decoration in the state rooms, and he prepared schemes celebrating the reign of the Sun King, invoking the powers of nature as personified by the classical gods. Another theme was that of Louis XIV in the role of conqueror and peacemaker, depicted by Lebrun in the **Salons de la Guerre** and **La Paix**, flanking the great **Galerie des Glaces** (Hall of Mirrors). This last room and the **King's Bedchamber** are the greatest examples of the Louis XIV style; thereafter the decoration becomes lighter and the rooms smaller as the **18thC Rococo** was introduced in the **Petits Appartements** such as the **Cabinet de la Pendule**.

The dispersal of the palace's original contents during and after the Revolution has left many rooms almost bare, and although there are plans to replace as many items as possible, pieces like the **Bureau du Roi** by Oeben and Riesener (1769) are virtually on their own. There is a fair amount of good sculpture, such as Coysevox's relief of ***Louis XIV on Horseback*** and Bernini's flamboyant **bust of the king** in the Salon de Diane, but the easel pictures are in general disappointing. Apart from the fairly routine portraits of the royal family, of which there are numerous examples, a few **works** by Rigaud, Philippe de Champaigne, Corneille de Lyon, Nattier and Rubens are worthy of note. Many of the later pictures came to the palace when Louis-Philippe attempted to turn it into a museum "to the Glory of France", and this partly explains why most of the works are of military subjects. The **Salle du Sacre**, for example, displays three immense Napoleonic paintings by David and Gros; ***The Presentation of the Eagles*** and ***Coronation of Napoleon*** by the former and ***Murat at Aboukir*** by the latter. The military theme continues in the Galerie des Batailles, and among the 33 dull canvases Delacroix's ***Battle of Tailleborg*** and Gros's ***Austerlitz*** stand out. Gros's finest work, however, ***Napoleon on the Bridge at Arcole***, is hung in the Historical Collection on the second floor.

Grand Trianon

Musée National du Château de Versailles
Tel. (3) 9505832
Open 9.45am–5pm
Closed Mon

The Grand Trianon, built for Louis XIV in 1687 by Mansart and Robert de Cotte, was intended as a retreat from the formal court life of the main château. With this in mind the architects designed a modest single-storey building in pink, rose and white marble with an attractive open portico linking the two wings. The original contents were scattered during the Revolution, but Napoleon I took to living there and most of the present furniture, including pieces by Marcion and Jacob-Desmalter, dates from the Empire period.

The interior of the Grand Trianon recently underwent an extensive renovation that even involved the weaving of new carpets and fabrics to the old designs. Unfortunately these have now been covered with plastic sheets for protection, thus rendering the whole scheme pointless. In addition to the decorations, the Grand Trianon displays a few paintings, including a series of **22 views of the gardens** at Versailles by Jean Cotelle and J.B. Martin.

Petit Trianon

Musée National du Château de Versailles
Tel. (3) 9505832
Open 2–5pm
Closed Mon

The Petit Trianon is the only major building at Versailles that breaks away from the pervasive influence of Louis XIV. It was commissioned from Ange-Jacques Gabriel by Louis XV as part of a series of projects in the northern sector of the park, including the "New Menagerie" (model farm) and botanical garden. The king's hobbies are less in evidence now, but Gabriel's elegant palace remains, the sober façade being one of the earliest and finest examples of French Neoclassicism.

The interior, which is equally controlled, reflects the taste of Marie Antoinette, who preferred this residence to the other châteaux. The rooms contain good **furniture** and **boiseries** (panelling) in the style of Louis XVI, and a number of decorative paintings.

In contrast to the restrained style of the house, the surrounding park, on which Marie Antoinette lavished great expense, became something of a royal playground where she and the king could indulge in some apparently absurd 18thC fantasies. Gabriel's delightful **Pavillon Français** (1751) provided a start for the series of garden buildings near the Petit Trianon, but the most famous is probably the **Hameau**, a rustic village where Marie-Antoinette could play at being a peasant.

Musée Lambinet

54 Boulevard de la Reine
Tel. (3) 9503032
Open 2–6pm
Closed Mon, Wed, Fri

A visit to the Musée Lambinet after the château offers a refreshing contrast to the scale, opulence and crowds of the palace. Here you can see a pleasant 18thC town house that has preserved most of its original **boiseries** without the interference of restoration.

Besides documents and prints recording the history of Versailles, a number of good paintings and sculptures stand out. Panini's ***Roman Ruins***, Guérin's ***Woman Adorning an Antique Bust***, Pigalle's terracotta ***Diana***, Houdon's ***Bust of the Comtesse de Sabran*** and works by Isabey, Bonington Corot and Carrière are probably the finest. However, it is their settings including, as they do, various prints, books, items of furniture and ceramics, that are most attractive. The first floor rooms are particularly well arranged.

There are some **medieval church treasures** but the main emphasis is appropriately towards the 18thC. One room is devoted to **souvenirs of Charlotte Corday** who was born in Versailles but achieved fame or notoriety for assassinating the Revolutionary leader Marat by stabbing him in his bath.

Artists of the Fontainebleau Forest

Artists first came to the Fontainebleau forest 64km (40 miles) SE of Paris in the early 16thC, when François I built one of the great Renaissance palaces there. The symbol of this court came to be Diana, the virgin goddess of the hunt, in homage to Diane de Poitiers, mistress of the king. Much of the work produced at FONTAINEBLEAU refers to her, and the surrounding forest was seen in terms of the Arcadian groves where the goddess and her maidens roamed.

Fontainebleau declined in importance after the 16thC, but from the early 19thC onwards the area rapidly developed into one of the most popular sites in Europe for artists and tourists. Now the forest was regarded, not as a setting for classical mythology, but as a primeval wilderness where Druids might suddenly appear. Artists originally came to Chailly on the W edge of the forest, but after c.1825 the hamlet of BARBIZON replaced it in popularity, becoming the "Bethlehem of modern painting" in the words of Millet's follower Jules Breton.

Barbizon attracted some of the most influential landscape artists of the 19thC, including Corot, Daubigny, Theodore Rousseau and Diaz de la Pena, as well as the greatest painter of rural subject matter, Jean-Francois Millet. This group of artists, the nucleus of the so-called "Barbizon School", generally met at an inn run by Père Ganne on the village's main street. The inn has not been in business since 1870, but a recent attempt has been made to reconstruct the interior, and the extensive decorations painted by the artist visitors and habitués of Pére Ganne have been replaced.

Continuing along the main street in the direction of the forest you will come to Rousseau's studio (now a museum) and Millet's so-called studio (now

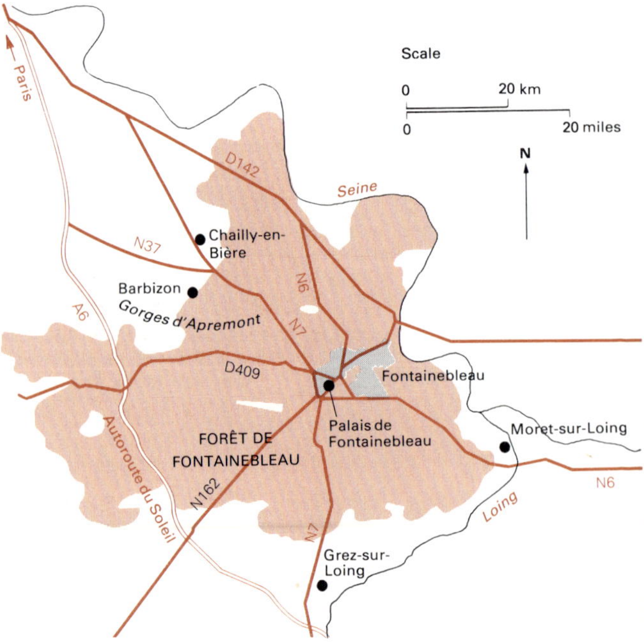

Fontainebleau artists of the late 19thC at Barbizon. In striped socks is R.A.M. Stevenson, artist cousin of Robert Louis Stevenson

also a museum) which is in fact a late 19thC replacement built by Millet's American daughter-in-law. The tombs of both artists, marked by a boulder with bronze medallion, are side by side in the church cemetery of Chailly.

Barbizon also attracted leading artists from outside France, and these came to dominate the village in the 1870s. The liveliest meeting-place was the Hôtel Siron, now the luxurious Hôtel Bas-Bréau, where a plaque records the visit of Robert Louis Stevenson – the acknowledged leader, together with his painter and artist cousin, of what they termed Barbizon's "Anglo-Saxon community". The most popular part of the forest for artists was the Bas-Bréau, which lay just beyond the Hôtel Siron. This area of massive oak trees, one of which provides the subject of a painting by Monet (now at the Metropolitan Museum of Art, New York) is backed by the intriguing rock formations known as the Chaos et Gorges d'Apremont.

Barbizon's rapidly growing popularity led to the establishment of other artist communities in the neighbourhood. Particularly popular with French artists was Moret-sur-Loing on the S edge of the forest, where the Impressionist Sisley spent the last 20 years of his life (a plaque marks his house on the Rue Château). The American and British community at Barbizon, likewise, transferred its allegiance to the nearby village of Grez-sur-Loing after its "discovery" in 1876 by a party of "Anglo-Saxons" led by the Stevensons. Grez had a river where artists could swim and go canoeing, and it attracted a number of famous American and British artists.

In the early 1880s the village of Grez received an influx of Scandinavian artists such as Christian Krogh (Munch's teacher) and Carl Larsson, as well as the Swedish dramatist August Strindberg. Grez remains today by far the most attractive of the former artist villages of the Fontainebleau area with its grey stone buildings, riverside gardens and, above all, its medieval bridge.

Present-day Barbizon, however, bears virtually no resemblance to the former quaint primitive hamlet. The agricultural plain to the W of the village, which Millet so loved to paint, is now crossed by the Autoroute du Soleil; and the site of Millet's most famous work, the ***Angelus*** (Louvre, Paris) is marked by a service station halfway along the Barbizon-Chantilly road. But the forest itself still retains much of its former appeal.

SW & W FRANCE

The landscape of the far western side of France, if you go down from the Loire estuary to the foothills of the Pyrenees, is either flat or, at the most gently undulating. The bleak expanses of the Poitevins marshes are succeeded by apparently endless vineyards around Bordeaux, which in turn give way to that vast, strange, and exceptionally monotonous area of reclaimed and forested wasteland known as the Landes. Most of this western district, which once formed part of Aquitaine, entered into English possession for some 300 years after the marriage of Eleanor of Aquitaine to the future Henry II of England in 1152. The conflict between the English and French that broke out as a result of this ownership came to be known as the Hundred Years War, and led to the destruction of many of the medieval monuments in the region.

Further devastation resulted in the 16thC, when the region's many Protestant strongholds made it a battleground of the Wars of Religion. To this day, much of Aquitaine has a sad, slightly sinister character which is well evoked in the novels of François Mauriac. Tourism has only just begun to develop here in any significant way, as more and more people come to spend their holidays along its flat, sandy coastline. Even so, a good proportion of those visiting the region are simply passing quickly through on their way to the Pyrenees or to Spain.

Yet this part of France has much to offer. There are admittedly very few important museums here (even the Bordeaux ones are something of a disappointment) but you can find many other compensations. La Rochelle – despite being the site of a major siege in the 17thC – is the best-preserved sea port in France; Saintes and the other towns and villages along the largely wooded bands of the Charente are rich in medieval monuments; and BORDEAUX is one of the finest examples in Europe of 18thC town planning.

On reaching Gascony you begin to feel strongly that the confines of France are nearing their end. Historically the region is linked to the Basque country in Spain, and many of its place-names and traditions are Basque in origin. The dramatic landscape of the Pyrenees (which has been much less spoilt than that of the Alps) may attract your attention more than the architecture or artistic treasures, but you should not overlook the fact that the region also has two of France's finest painting collections – at BAYONNE and at the beautifully situated and once thriving mountain resort of PAU.

To the E lies Languedoc, artistically the richest region in this section. TOULOUSE, its capital, is so far from Paris that in the past it was able to maintain a culture very much of its own, and has remained to this day the center of studies of the Languedoc language. Toulouse's Romanesque treasures are famous, but its 17thC-18thC painting school, which is one of the most individual of any French provincial city, deserves to be far better known. The towns surrounding Toulouse all have much to offer the tourist. ALBI, perhaps the most fascinating of these, is dominated by a 14thC cathedral built in the shape of a fortress to symbolize the invincibility of the catholic church. The cathedral was built after the suppression of the Cathar heresy which had been so powerful in the whole of Languedoc.

The handsome building that adjoins the cathedral of Albi, the Palais de la Berbie, now houses one of the most popular museums in France to be devoted to the work of a single artist, Henri de Toulouse-Lautrec. Toulouse-Lautrec came from an aristocratic local family – his birthplace in the town can still be visited – and this background has contributed to the legend of an artist who, whatever the shortcomings of his work, has exerted a powerful influence on the imaginations of succeeding generations. Other major single-artist collections are to be found in the nearby towns of MONTAUBAN and Castres. Ingres was born at Montauban in 1780, and the museum contains numerous paintings bequeathed by the artist as well as personal belongings. At CASTRES there is an extensive collection of works by Goya, where the somewhat dilapidated condition of the building reflects the mood of the superb but frequently morbid works on display.

Roussillon, the SW region of France, was a Spanish possession for much of the Middle Ages, and the greatest of its architectural monuments date from this period. You should not miss the 15thC Loge de Mer in PERPIGNAN, which is in a Catalan gothic style, or the almost contemporary ***Retable of the Trinity*** by the Master of Canapost in the Perpignan Musée Rigaud. By and large, however, this region has produced few interesting artists apart from two important exceptions: the late 17thC portraitist, Hyacinthe Rigaud, and the early 20thC painter and sculptor Aristide Maillol. Maillol worked here at a time when this still very beautiful region was "discovered" by the artistic avant garde from Paris, and the coastal town of Collioure saw a gathering of Maillol's Fauve colleagues, including Matisse, Derain and Marquet. Meanwhile, the nearby inland town of Céret attracted Picasso, Braque and other artists, with the result that Céret became known as the "Mecca of Cubism".

AGEN
Lot-et-Garonne, Périgord Map B4

A market town in the midst of a very fertile region, Agen has a great reputation among gourmets for its prunes. A number of distinguished men settled here in the Renaissance, including the potter and glass-maker Bernard Palissy and the writer, monk and diplomat Bandello, who came here after being banished from Milan; it is said that a number of Shakespeare's plays, including *Romeo and Juliet* and *Much Ado About Nothing* were based on his short stories.

Musée d'Agen ☆
Place Dr Pierre Esquirol
Tel. (56) 663527 (ext 397)
Open 10am–noon, 2–4pm
Closed Tues

Agen today has few old buildings. A group of four of the most beautiful of these, dating from the 16thC and 17thC, houses the rambling but exceptionally well displayed local museum. All the rooms have been recently renovated, but in a very tasteful and restrained way, with paintings, furniture and other objects of the same period all exhibited together in appropriate settings.

Classical and medieval statuary occupy the basement and ground floor. The most celebrated treasure here is a Hellenistic ***Torso of a Woman*** that was dug up by a local farmer in 1876. This stands on a mosaic pavement and has been dramatically spotlighted. Upstairs the layout of the museum begins with the Renaissance collections, which include two outstanding portrait heads, ***Fair-haired Man*** and ***Dark-haired Man***, both dated 1550, by Corneille de Lyon. However, the greatest paintings in the museum date mainly from the 18thC with excellent works by G.D. Tiepolo (***Dying Page***), Oudry (***Still Life with Cherries***), Drouais (***Comtesse de Barry***), Subleyras (***Distribution of Bread***), and François de Troy (***Judgment of Paris***). Best of all, there are five oil paintings by Goya. These were given to Agen – together with a collection of Spanish damasks, pottery and paintings by lesser Spanish contemporaries of Goya such as Lucas y Padilla – by a native of the city, the count of Chaudardy, the French ambassador to Madrid. The works by Goya include a sketch for an equestrian portrait of Ferdinand VII (1808) in the Academy of San Fernando, Madrid, a ***Self-portrait*** of 1783, and ***The Mass of St-Relevailles***. The latter belongs to the last period of Goya's life, and is one of several versions of the subject. It is a characteristically satirical comment on Catholic fanaticism, and records a custom, once common in southern Europe, of a young mother assisting at a mass in thanksgiving for the safe delivery of her child. But perhaps the most interesting of the Agen Goyas are ***Caprices*** ★ and ***The Montgolfier Balloon*** ★. The former is a fantasy featuring a cow and an elephant flying over a terrified crowd of people. The latter also concerns flying but was inspired by an actual event: the launching by the Montgolfier brothers of a balloon in the park of the Buen Retiro, Madrid in 1793, ten years after they had made their first attempt to do so in France. In spite of this basis in reality, Goya's rendering of the subject has the same fantastical quality of ***Caprices*** and seems also to comment on the irrational side to humanity.

Prominent among the gallery's 19thC holdings is a famous painting by Corot, ***Pond at Ville d'Avray*** ★, which is beautifully and appropriately positioned above a Neoclassical fireplace. Ville d'Avray was the village where Corot's father had bought a house in 1817. There is a large group of works by Boudin's Honfleur contemporary, Louis Lebourg, and – a complete surprise – a room largely filled with the works of one of Romania's two greatest 19thC painters, **Nicolae Grigorescu**. These were all collected by a local doctor. Grigorescu – like most of Romania's painters – spent a critical period of his life in France. In the 1860s he was for a short while at Barbizon, and was greatly influenced by the Barbizon artists. Later he returned to Romania, where he became actively involved in his country's fight for independence, and devoted himself mainly to the portrayal of the Romanian peasantry. The most striking of his paintings at Agen is a small oil portrait head of a ***Romanian Peasant Girl***, a work that combines bravura brushstroke and sensibility to delicate colour harmonies typical of this master at his best.

Only with the gallery's 20thC collection – kept on the second floor – does a serious decline in quality set in. In addition to countless Impressionist-style landscapes, there is an unremarkable still-life in oils by the Surrealist Picabia. There is also a group of works in different media, including stained glass, by the facile yet highly regarded sub-Cubist Roger Bissières, who worked in a Cubist idiom after meeting Braque in 1922, but whose later work was strongly influenced by Klee.

ALBI
Tarn, Causses Map C4

The most beautiful of the various red-brick towns in this part of France, Albi is sometimes known as "Albi la Rouge". The best view of the place can be had from across the old bridge over the river Tarn: the town's two main architectural monuments – the **cathedral** and the adjoining **archbishop's palace** – can be seen from here looming massively above the river, acquiring at sunset an unforgettably vivid hue of red.

Like most of the towns in south-western France, Albi was in the Middle Ages a Cathar city. The Cathars were a religious sect who believed that the material world was created by the devil and that the only way to salvation was to deny the world and concentrate on spiritual life. They are sometimes referred to as the Albigensians, and their creed the Albigensian heresy. But these are in fact relatively modern academic terms, the origin of which is not clear. Following a vicious crusade led by Simon de Montfort on the instigation of Pope Innocent III, the sect was suppressed by 1244. In 1276 Bernard de Castanet was appointed Bishop of Albi and revived the Inquisition in an attempt to suppress all lingering traces of heresy.

It was also during his reign that the main body of the cathedral was built (the impressive tower was added in the 15thC, and the Flamboyant S porch in the 16thC). It is a most imposing crenellated structure, whose fortress-like shape was intended to symbolize the unassailability of the Catholic church. The interior was largely embellished in the 15thC and 16thC and forms a contrast to the austere exterior. Most of the wall surface is covered by frescoes – mainly of a purely decorative nature – by a group of Italian artists. The enormous ***Last Judgment*** on the W wall however, is by an unknown 15thC French artist. Supposedly the largest painting in France, its impact was rather marred in the 17thC by the insensitive placing of an organ in front of it. Other impressive features of the interior are the elaborately carved stone **rood screen** and **choir enclosure**, both of which date from the 15thC.

Musée Toulouse-Lautrec ☆

Palais de la Berbie
Tel. (63) 541409
Open 10am–noon, 2–5pm
Closed Tues

Albi's other main attraction to tourists is its museum devoted to Toulouse-Lautrec, who was born in the town of an aristocratic family in 1864. His birthplace survives, and is still in the family's possession. A few minutes' walk from the cathedral, and in the middle of the town's picturesque old quarter, it can be visited during the summer months. Inside you can see a number of interesting family photos, a small collection of works done by the artist at an early age, and the room where he had the first of the accidents (he fell off a chair) which were to stunt the growth of his legs. It is often said that, had it not been for his deformity, he might never have become a professional artist, and would instead have led the life of a well-to-do aristocrat, combining the pastimes of drawing and horse-riding in equal proportions.

The museum dedicated to his paintings is housed in the former archbishop's palace, the **Palais de Berbie**, which was built at the same time as the cathedral and in the same fortress style. It is one of the most visited of France's provincial museums. Although Toulouse-Lautrec was really no more than an outstanding illustrator, he continues to exert an enormous popular appeal. There is a fascination both with the facts of his life – the story of the deformed man who forsook his comfortable home surroundings in favour of a life in the brothels and night clubs in Paris – and with the *fin-de-siècle* decadence which formed the main subject of Toulouse-Lautrec's art.

Like his contemporary Gustave Moreau, Lautrec was sufficiently well off not to have to rely on selling his work. As a result, the main body of it has remained intact. The Albi museum contains 600 works by him, mainly donated by the artist's mother, and also by his close friend, Maurice Joyant, to whom Lautrec's father ceded parental control over the will on his son's death in 1901.

To see virtually the complete life's output of Toulouse-Lautrec in a single place is not an unmixed blessing. Moreover, the works have begun to suffer from constant exposure to the light, a fact which seems not to concern the museum authorities. The mind occasionally begins to wander, and the superb views to be had from the building down to the exceptionally beautiful palace garden and the river Tarn may well succeed in claiming the visitor's attention.

Loving to paint and draw horses when he was an adolescent (many of these highly accomplished works are in the museum), Toulouse-Lautrec was encouraged by his first teacher in Paris to specialize in the portrayal of animals. He then fell strongly under the influence of Degas, and devoted the rest of his life to the reproduction of seedy interiors. Although Lautrec began by using oil on canvas, his favourite medium became oil on cardboard, which allowed him to work much more rapidly. He developed essentially into a graphic artist, and even the paintings that he did in later life were mainly intended as studies for lithographs.

One of the most famous of Toulouse-Lautrec's works in the museum is his large painting, ***At the Salon of the Rue des Moulins*** (1894) which shows a group of prostitutes listlessly lying around the waiting room of a brothel; a large pastel for this work hangs opposite. The museum contains all Lautrec's posters (together with the original drawings for many of them), which represent perhaps the best-known side to the artist's work. Lautrec was one of the first artists fully to exploit the possibilities of this medium, although in fact his output as a poster artist was by no means prolific (he produced only 32 posters in 10 years). In the same room as the posters is the artist's ingenious walking stick, which opens up to reveal a glass and a tiny flask of brandy.

The Albi museum is by no means totally taken up by Lautrec's works. A series of dingy rooms on the first floor preceding the Lautrec rooms contain 17thC and 18thC French and Italian works, including a good ***View of Venice*** by Guardi. The second floor has an extensive but admittedly unremarkable collection of works by such well-known artists as Bonnard, Vuillard, Matisse, Marquet, Dufy, Utrillo, Vlaminck, Rodin, Bourdelle and Maillol. Of particular interest here is a half-length ***Portrait*** by the symbolist artist Émile Bernard of his sister Madeleine in the Bois d'Amour in ***PONT-AVEN***. It was painted in 1888, at a time when Bernard was working closely with Gauguin. Madeleine acted almost as a muse of their circle, and was the center of an amorous rivalry between Gauguin and his minor follower Charles Laval.

ANGOULÊME
Charente, C. de l'Atlantique Map B2

Angoulême, a town much loved by Balzac (who described it at length in his novel *Illusions Perdues*), is most impressively sited on top of an enormous rock above the river Charente. It was already an important town in Roman times, and in the 15thC gave birth to one of the major figures of the French Renaissance, Marguerite of Angoulême, sister of François I. The city still retains its **medieval ramparts**, from which excellent views can be had of the surrounding countryside.

The 12thC cathedral, at the edge of the old city, has an interesting sculpted façade with an especially striking ***Last Judgment***. However the building has been heavily restored, most notably by the locally born 19thC architect Paul Abadie, who was also responsible for the construction of the Sacré Coeur in Paris, as well as restoration of Perigueux Cathedral. Unfortunately, the interiors of both the Angoulême and the Perigueux cathedrals are more characteristic of monumental railway stations than of religious buildings.

Musée Municipal
1 Rue Friedland
Tel. (45) 950769
Open 10am–noon, 2–6pm
Closed Tues

The municipal museum is housed in the bishop's palace next to the cathedral. This too is a heavily restored building, dating from the 12thC but considerably altered in the 15thC. Its collections are in the process of being rearranged by a young and imaginative staff. Prominent among the museum's medieval holdings are a group of **12thC sculpted capitals** from the Abbey of Beaulieu. Its Old Master paintings are for the most part uninteresting. There is an enormous Neoclassical painting, ***The Grief of Priam*** by the obscure Garnier, competent works by Rosa Bonheur, Théodore Rousseau and minor associates of the Barbizon School. A tiny room is devoted to Symbolist painting, and has been built up around a recent donation of one slight Puvis de Chavannes drawing; the other works here include some by a local heavy-handed pupil of Puvis, Claude Darras. Another room is largely taken up by the **peasant genre scenes** of a late 19thC local painter, Léonard Jarraud who, though unknown outside the region, deserves greater recognition. Born in the village of La Couronne near Angoulême, he enjoyed great success as an art student in Paris, but returned almost immediately to his native village, living the life of an irritable recluse and eventually dying there.

The great strength of the Angoulême museum is its collection of **African art**, the third most important in France. It was largely amassed by a local doctor who lives in the nearby town of La Rochefoucauld. Most of the museum's recent acquisitions have been in the field of African art, and black artists, musicians, poets and actors have been encouraged to exhibit or perform here.

Another speciality of the museum – for which it is unrivalled in France – is its collection of **original illustrations for comic strips**. This emerged out of the annual convention held in Angoulême of artists working in this field. The works are exhibited in a room – designed by the staff of the local art school – which is bound to shock purists. Its walls, floors and ceiling are largely covered in mirrors and chrome, with screens jutting out at unexpected angles. The overall result is like a futuristic – and rather dangerous – discothèque. Children will love it, but adults with a serious interest in the art of Schultz, Hergé and other such illustrators might find it disconcerting to have to look at some of their works while crawling on the ground or else being constantly on the lookout for overhead projections. Reassuringly, the glass is unbreakable, so that children can quite happily walk over original Tin-Tin and Asterix illustrations.

AUCH
Gers, Pyrénées Map B4

Auch was once the capital of Gascony. Its old quarter of tall, characteristically Gascon houses with long wooden balconies rises up steeply from the river Gers and is dominated by the 16thC **Cathédrale Ste-Marie**. The town's greatest art treasures are to be found in this building. These are the early 16thC **stained glass windows** in the ambulatory, and **sculptures** of the same date by Arnauld de Mollesse. In the ambulatory the latter carved in stone one of the most impressive **Lamentation groups** in France, a masterpiece of Renaissance naturalism. The same artist was also responsible for the superlative **choir stalls** in the cathedral, on which task he was engaged for much of his life. The profusion of naturalistic and decorative detail on these is quite remarkable. The guides who show you round this part of the building take particular pleasure in drawing attention to the numerous erotic scenes carved on the underside of the choir stools.

Musée des Jacobins
4 Place Louis Blanc
Tel. (62) 057479
Open May – Oct 10am – noon, 2 – 6pm; Nov – Apr 10am – noon, 2 – 4pm
Closed Mon

An exceptionally steep walk down from the cathedral leads to the dirty, badly displayed local museum, which is taken up mainly by mediocre examples of South American art, including early Columbian pots and morbid paintings and sculptures by naive colonial artists. One room features paintings, prints, puppets and books relating to Auch's greatest son, the 17thC soldier D'Artagnan, who was later immortalized by Dumas in his novel *The Three Musketeers*.

BAGNÈRES DE BIGORRE
Hauts-Pyrénées, Pyrénées Map B5

Although pleasantly situated near some of the highest mountains in the Pyrenees, Bagnères is an undistinguished health resort with few old buildings.

Musée Salies
Place des Thermes
Tel. (62) 950503
Open July – Sept 9am – noon, 2 – 6pm; Nov – June 2 – 6pm
Closed Oct, Tues

The Musée Salies is installed in a grubby Egyptian-style building dating from the early years of this century, and adjoins the town's equally decrepit casino and thermal baths. It has some indifferent 17thC and 18thC works of the Flemish, Italian and French schools, but is strongest in 19thC French paintings, most of which are by now little-known Salon painters. There is an especially large collection of chocolatebox-style pastel landscapes and still lifes by Blanche Odin, a woman painter of local origin.

BAYONNE
Pyrénées-Atlantique, Pyrénées Map A4

Bayonne, the capital of Gascony, is a thriving port which, like Bordeaux, belonged to the English for 300 years. It has an old quarter surrounding the Cathédrale Ste-Marie, which is built in a N Gothic style. But otherwise it is not an especially attractive city.

Musée Léon Bonnat ☆☆
5 Rue Jacques Lafitte
Tel. (59) 590852
Open mid-June to mid-Sept 10am – noon, 4 – 8pm; mid-Sept to mid-June 1 – 7pm
Closed Tues, public holidays (Mon, Wed – Fri mornings reserved for scholars)

Bayonne's greatest attraction for tourists lies undoubtedly in the Musée Bonnat, which ranks with the Musée des Augustins in **TOULOUSE** as the greatest art gallery in southwestern France. It is housed in a late 19thC building which has recently been excellently modernized. The paintings are exceptionally well displayed, and many of the rooms provide useful information sheets. It is a relatively small museum, but the standard of the collections is consistently high.

A large proportion of thc paintings on the first floor of the museum are early works by Léon Bonnat, who enjoyed exceptional fame in the 19thC, not only as a painter, but also as a teacher and collector. He was born in Bayonne in 1833 and studied at first in the Academy of San Fernando in Madrid; later he went to Paris, and then spent a critical period in Italy. As a painter, he was especially renowned as a portraitist. His pupils included many of the greatest names of late 19thC and early 20thC art, including Toulouse-Lautrec, Munch and Braque. His extraordinary collection of Old Master paintings and works by his contemporaries forms the nucleus of the museum named after him in Bayonne. His studio and many of his personal belongings have been preserved in the nearby Musée Basque, an old-fashioned but charming museum devoted to the Basque people.

Signs encourage the visitor to go round the gallery in a largely chronological sequence, beginning on the top floor. Among the earlier collections are some interesting Spanish primitives, including the 15thC ***Adoration of the Magi*** by the Master of the Chevalier de Montesa. The first major room in the museum is devoted to a collection of outstanding **oil sketches** ★ by Rubens. Some of these were sketches for a group of tapestries featuring the ***Triumph of the Eucharist*** which are now in the Convent of the Descalzas Reales in Madrid. They were commissioned from Rubens by Isabella Eugenia, Governess of the Netherlands, and were executed between 1625 and 1628. Another group of sketches (1627–31) was for a cycle of paintings – never completed – honouring the life of Henry IV, and intended as a sequel to the Marie de Medici cycle now in the Louvre, ***PARIS***. The remaining sketches – perhaps the liveliest of them all – were for a series of 100 paintings of scenes from Ovid's *Metamorphoses*, commissioned by Philip IV of Spain for his hunting lodge near Madrid, the Torre de la Parada. The actual paintings were mainly executed by Rubens' pupils, and certainly lack the vitality of the sketches. Few artists before Rubens' time, with the major exception of Titian, had been able to render the mythological world with such extraordinary passion and conviction. Rubens' oil sketches at Bayonne are exhibited in a truly dramatic manner by being spotlighted in an otherwise darkened room.

The rest of the 17thC and early 18thC collections are by no means negligible. There are good works by van Dyck (***Martyrdom of St George***), G.B. Tiepolo (a ceiling sketch), Ribera (***Woman Pulling her Hair***) and above all Vouet (***Roman Charity*** ★).

However, it is for its late 18thC and early 19thC paintings that the museum is especially famous. These begin with a small room of works by English artists and Goya. Here one finds modest works by Constable (***Hampstead Heath***) and Reynolds (an oil sketch for his dramatically posed ***Portrait of Colonel Tarleton*** in the National Gallery, London). The high point of the English collection is a half-length portrait of the painter ***Johann Heinrich Fuseli*** ★ by Sir Thomas Lawrence. It is a macabre, sinister work, in character with the art of Fuseli himself: the sitter is shown against a darkened background, his left hand nervously touching an arm rest in the form of a grimacing lion. The Goya paintings include a ***Self-portrait*** of 1798 and an oil sketch for his large, tormented canvas of the ***Last Communion of San José de Calasanz*** (1819) in the church of San Antonio de la Florida, Madrid. The most impressive of the Goyas here is a full-length portrait of the ***Duke of Osuna, Don Francisco de Borja*** ★. Goya was on close terms with the highly cultured Osuna family, who were among his greatest patrons. The bloated duke is portrayed in casual pose, with an emaciated servant looking up at him in awe.

Leading off this room is a gallery of French Neoclassical paintings that not only has some excellent portraits (including ***Napoleon***) by Anne-Louis Girodet, but also one of the best collections of Ingres paintings in any provincial French gallery. Among these is a famous half-length portrait of a ***Female Bather*** ★ (painted in Rome a few years before his famous ***Valpinçon Bather*** of 1808); a jewel-like ***Portrait of Mme Devaucay***, mistress of the French ambassador to Rome; a small painting of the medieval lovers ***Paolo and Francesca***; and a study for the figure of Victory in the ***Apotheosis of Homer*** in the Louvre, ***PARIS***. This exquisite study, if compared with the absurd and lifeless work for which it was intended, illustrates how much more subtle Ingres generally was when working on a small scale than when trying to execute enormous compositions.

The paintings by Bonnat on the first floor of the Bonnat museum consist mainly of innumerable oil copies, done in his youth, of famous paintings by artists such as Velasquez, Titian, Giorgione, Leonardo da Vinci, Veronese and Ribera, and are largely interesting for the light they throw on mid 19thC taste and on the sort of works which artists of the time were encouraged to study. The best of his paintings in this part of the museum are his small and tender portraits of members of his family, and there is also a remarkably assured ***Self-portrait*** done when the artist was 17. The first floor also contains an excellent group of paintings by Géricault (most notably ***Four Jockeys*** and ***Head of a White Horse***) as well as works by Meissonier, Corot, Daubigny and Harpignies.

Another room on this floor is dominated by a large allegorical painting by Puvis de Chavannes, ***Gentle Country***, which was intended to hang in the staircase well of Bonnat's Paris house, and was given to him by Puvis in exchange for a portrait which Bonnat did of him: the two artists had an enormous respect for each other's art. Hanging next to ***Gentle Country*** are two excellent portraits by another great admirer of Bonnat – Degas. These are of ***Bonnat*** himself and of Bonnat's step-brother, ***Enrique Melida***, himself a painter, albeit a rather mediocre one.

The ground floor houses a collection of Oriental, Egyptian and classical antiquities, as well as an excellent group of **full-length portraits** by Bonnat (including one of the animal sculptor Barye) dating from his maturity. They indicate the need for a reassessment of his now unfashionable art.

BÉZIERS

Hérault, Causses Map D4

The old town of Béziers is built on a hill which slopes down steeply to the river Orb. The 15thC Cathedral of St-Nazaire (which replaces an earlier building destroyed in 1209 by Simon de Montfort) has a large terrace with superb views.

Musée des Beaux-Arts

Place de la Révolution
Tel. (67) 283878
Open Tues – Sat 9am – noon, 2 – 6pm; Sun 2 – 6pm
Closed Sun morning, Mon

The Musée des Beaux-Arts is in a late 18thC house in a small street tucked away just behind the cathedral. Its collections are extremely varied, both in scope and quality, but are put together in rather haphazard fashion. An excellent collection of Greek Attic pots on the first floor shares a small room with a group of early Netherlandish paintings, including a good ***Portrait of a Woman*** (1562) by Michel Coxie. The other room on this floor is even more congested, displaying mainly 17thC, 18thC and early 19thC French, Flemish and Italian works. In the jumbled collection the visitor may well miss a large portrait by Domenichino of ***Pope Gregory XV and his Nephew Ludovico Ludovisi*** (c.1621 – 23) and a ***Landscape*** by the Romantic artist Philip de Loutherbourg.

The staircase well has a number of large and rather striking Salon pictures, including ones by Cabanel (***Orestes***) and Glaize (a strange symbolic work inspired by a poem by Alfred de Musset). The ground floor has a collection of 20thC paintings, most notably a ***Self-portrait*** by De Chirico (1926) and a ***Seated Nude*** by Suzanne Valadon. The art lover with a close knowledge of French museums will also experience here a sense of ***déjà-vu*** on coming across yet another collection of glasswork and paintings by the Fauve artist, Maurice Marinot.

More interesting is a case full of the studio contents of Béziers' greatest native artist, the 19thC sculptor, Injalbert. Injalbert, the son of a Béziers mason, moved to Paris in 1864, where he worked at first as an apprentice furniture-maker, and later studied at the École des Beaux-Arts. A conventional and prolific artist, Injalbert enjoyed an enormous success in his time, receiving important commissions not only in France, but also in New York, Rio de Janeiro and Mexico. In addition to a special display of maquettes and small bronzes, the museum has numerous other sculptures by Injalbert scattered around the building. A bronze ***Triton*** by him surmounts a fountain in a nearby park, the Plateau des Poètes.

BORDEAUX

Gironde, C. de l'Atlantique Map A3

Bordeaux, capital and principal town of the large region of Aquitaine, has been an important place since Roman times. Even then it was a trading port and it has maintained this role to the present day, ensuring its position under successive rulers. This activity financed the town's greatest period in the 18thC, when the elegant buildings and squares were erected, but the **Cathédrale St-André**, a mixed Romanesque and Gothic structure, testifies to a heritage stretching back to the Middle Ages and earlier. In recent years Bordeaux has seen a fair amount of modernization and the introduction of new industries. The wine trade, however, is still in the forefront and the city lends its name to the largest appellation in France.

Musée d'Aquitaine

Cours d'Albret
Tel. (56) 909160 (ext 1378)
Open 2–6pm
Closed Tues, Sun, holidays

A museum of local antiquities was first suggested in 1594 when three Roman statues were discovered near Bordeaux, but it was not until 1781 that the Académie des Belles-Lettres, Sciences et Arts de Bordeaux set up an institution to accommodate their collections. Even then it was hardly complete, since many of the pieces were kept elsewhere, and a true antiquarian museum did not exist until 1960 when the present building was opened. The intervening period had also seen the collection grow from its original limited range into a comprehensive survey of the successive civilizations of the region, from prehistory right up to the 17thC.

The collection is displayed chronologically, beginning with items found in the numerous Paleolithic and Neolithic sites in the Bordelais and Perigord. This mostly consists of the traditional remains of early human activity, grave goods, potsherds, etc., but there are a few important stone carvings such as the palaeolithic ***Venus of Laussel***, made about 20,000 years ago.

The Gallo-Roman section is considerable, with a number of interesting inscribed pedestals, relief fragments and steles (particularly those of ***Amabilis*** and of ***Fortunatus***, both 2ndC AD) but the finest exhibit is undoubtedly a 2ndC bronze statue of ***Hercules*** found in a drain beneath a house in the town.

Of the medieval works, which are again mostly sculptural fragments, the Tomb of the ***Wife of Seneschal Roger de Leyburn*** (d.1265) is the most remarkable, including as it does an effigy of the nude figure. The Renaissance and later periods are best represented by a series of detached architectural elements, notably some carved doorways from the 16thC and 17thC.

Musée des Beaux-Arts

Cours d'Albret
Tel. (56) 909160 (ext 1312)
Open 10am–noon, 2–6pm
Closed Tues, holidays

The Musée des Beaux-Arts was set up in 1801 with 14 paintings retrieved from the riots in Paris and Versailles of the previous decade. At that stage it included works by, or at least attributed to, Titian, Perugino, Veronese, Rubens and van Dyck, and this was supplemented by the acquisition in 1829 of the Marquis de Lacaze's collection consisting of over 300 paintings, most of which were 17thC Dutch works. Throughout the 19thC interest steadily grew and in 1851 a Société des Amis was set up which greatly assisted in the development of the collection, particularly in the field of contemporary French works. Two setbacks in this gradual expansion occurred with the disastrous fires of 1860 and 1870, which destroyed the early gallery in the Hôtel de Ville as well as numerous paintings – although the bulk of the collection was saved, including many of the original group. The gallery was then rebuilt in the style of most civic museums in the 19thC, and as a result it now really requires renovation to display the collection in a reasonable manner.

The pictures are presently arranged according to national schools, with Perugino's ***Virgin and Sts Jerome and Augustine*** being the most interesting from the Italian section. Of the Flemish paintings, the 17thC is the strongest with a ***Crucifixion*** by Jordaens and two works by Rubens: ***The Martyrdom of St George***, the central panel of a triptych commissioned for the College of St-Gromaire (Lierre) in 1615, and a bizarre work depicting the ***Martyrdom of St Just*** in which the saint is holding his decapitated head whilst conversing with two associates.

As a result of the Lacaze collection, the Dutch paintings are the most numerous and also of the highest quality. Beginning with a small roundel of ***Envy*** by Breughel there are examples of most types of Dutch art, including landscapes, genre scenes and still lifes by leading figures. But two works are particularly notable: Terbrugghen's ***Lute Player***, a fine work in the tradition of Caravaggio, and Jan van Goyen's ***Oak Struck by Lightning*** ★ (1638), one of three paintings by this artist in the museum, and a landscape of the first order.

Apart from a few 18thC portraits the finest French pictures are drawn from the 19thC. Chief among these are the works by Delacroix, ***Greece Expiring on the Ruins of Missolonghi*** ★ (1826) and the immense though partially destroyed ***Lion Hunt*** of 1854. Landscapes by Corot,

Diaz de la Pena and Boudin help to fill out the latter part of the century, and there are also three artists well represented who have particular associations with the city. Redon, Marquet and André Lhote were all born in Bordeaux and the museum has attempted to display the range of their achievements. Of the group Odilon Redon is probably the greatest artist and, although it is not obvious in his work, he maintained a deep attachment to his native area throughout his career. The museum possesses a number of his late pastels, including ***The Chariot of Apollo***.

Musée des Arts Décoratifs

Hôtel de Lalande
39 Rue Bouffard
Tel: (56) 909160
Open 10am–noon, 2–6pm
Closed Tues,
(Wed, Sun)

The Musée des Arts Décoratifs is in many respects the most attractive museum in Bordeaux, being housed in the Hôtel de Lalande (built 1779) which provides an appropriate setting for most of the exhibits. The bulk of the collection, or at least the finest works, come from the 18thC and indeed several rooms have inherited the fittings and panelling from other contemporary houses in the city. These include some decorative paintings such as the putti representing ***The Seasons*** in the ***Salon de Campagne*** and a number of portraits such as the bust of ***Montesquieu*** by J-B. Lemoyne, but the principal exhibits fall within the traditional range of the decorative arts.

Several items are related to the Grand Theatre, one of the most impressive buildings in Bordeaux, which was the original location of some of the Regency furniture on display. Beyond this there are some good enamels (notably a 12thC ***Crucifix*** from the Abbaye de la Sauve), silverware, ivories (a 17thC German jug depicting ***The Triumph of Silenus***) and a collection of pocket watches with painted covers rather like miniatures or cameos and known as *Oeufs de Nuremberg*.

The strongest section in the museum, however, is the ceramics, which are from most of the principal French and German factories. Some emphasis is placed on the early faience from Bordeaux with the inscription "Cartus Burdig" (Cartusia Burdigalensis, Charterhouse of Bordeaux), and bearing the arms of the noble families who supported the monastery in the 17thC. But you may well find the collection of figurative *rustique* jugs equally interesting. Similar in some respects to the English Toby Jugs, these pieces from Lille, known as *Pots-Jacqueline*, have greater variety and elegance than their often crude English counterparts.

CARCASSONNE

Aude, Pyrénées Map C4

The **medieval section** of Carcassonne (known as the *Cité*) stands on top of a hill completely separate from the rest of the town. Entirely surrounded by fortifications with excellent views over the Pyrenees, it is one of the most popular tourist sites in the whole of France. The medieval fortifications are the best preserved in existence (although admittedly they were heavily restored in the 19thC by Viollet-le-Duc) and strongly reflect 19thC attitudes towards medieval architecture (the spires crowning each of the towers, for instance, are complete whims of Viollet-le-Duc's). The *Cité* is best seen from below; but once inside you may feel as if you are in a papier-maché reproduction of a medieval city rather than the real thing. There is, however, a fine **Gothic cathedral**, with good 13thC–14thC stained glass windows, and remarkable statues of the same date decorating the choir.

Musée des Beaux-Arts

1 Rue de Verdun
Tel. (68) 478090 (ext 323)
Open 9am–noon, 2–6pm
Closed Sun

Truly peverse tourists may choose to avoid the *Cité* altogether and make their way straight to the modern town situated on the opposite side of the river Aude. Their main point of call here will be the Musée des Beaux-Arts, housed in a spacious but dull 19thC building with a small collection of pictures, some of which are interesting. A large group of works by Gamelin, the celebrated 18thC specialist in battle scenes, (who was born in the town) occupies much of the space, but pride of place in the gallery's 18thC collections – which also include good works by Rigaud and Subleyras – is given to a ***Still-Life*** by Chardin. The rest of the gallery is mainly taken up by 19thC French works, including a large canvas by Benjamin Constant (***Les Chérifas***), featuring naked slave girls, which is remarkable for its erotic content. More interesting from an artistic point of view is an excellent landscape by Léon-Germain Pelouse entitled ***Grandchamp at Low Tide***. Pelouse, who was a prominent figure in the artist colonies of

Pont-Aven and Cernay-la-Ville (in the Forest of Fontainebleau) was one of the most influential and successful landscapists of the late 19thC; today he has largely been forgotten, even by historians, and few of his works are on public display. The landscape at Carcassonne is painted with extreme technical virtuosity in different shades of brown, black and grey.

A Carcassonne follower of Seurat, Archille Lauge, is represented by several works, most notably a Pointilliste portrait of ***Mme Astre*** (1894); but the further Lauge departed from Seurat's example, the more trite his works became. A poor late Marquet, several works by his colleague Marinot, and a composition by Hans Bellmer are the only 20thC works in the museum worth mentioning.

CASTRES
Tarn, Causses Map C4

A prosperous wool town since the Middle Ages, Castres is a quiet place with a group of old houses picturesquely crowded along the banks of the river Agout. Otherwise it is undistinguished in its appearance.

Its major surviving architectural monuments – the cathedral and the former bishopric – both date from the 17thC. The latter building has a beautiful **formal garden** with extremely elaborate topiary, designed by the celebrated landscape gardener of Versailles, André Le Nôtre. It now houses the town hall and, on its top floor, the tiny Musée Jaurès (a collection of items relating to the leading socialist politician, Jean Jaurès, who was born in Castres in 1859), and the Musée Goya.

Musée Goya
Hôtel de Ville
Tel. (63) 596263
Open 10am–noon, 2–5pm
Closed Tues

A local museum was founded in Castres in 1840 after the town had acquired a number of minor canvases together with a collection of zoological and mineralogical items. Then in 1892 the son of the obscure local painter Marcel Briguiboul donated to the town his father's extensive collection of works by Goya. From that time onwards the museum has concentrated almost exclusively on collecting Spanish works of art from medieval times up to the present day. The building is in a decrepit condition (although partial restoration work has begun), the atmosphere is dark and musty, and the paintings are poorly displayed. Yet somehow all this is rather appropriate to the generally morbid works on display, many of which moreover probably once hung in equally dingy Spanish interiors.

The early rooms are mainly taken up by Spanish paintings from the 14thC up to the 18thC, interspersed with some Hispano-Moorish pottery, Flemish tapestries, and various ecclesiastical objects of different periods and schools. Most of the leading Spanish painters, including Borrassa, Ribera, Coello, Valdes Leal, and Lucas y Padilla, are represented in the museum by oil paintings, but some attributions are peculiar (a contemporary copy of a ***Portrait of Philip IV*** by Velasquez is misleadingly labelled as Velasquez), and none of these works are especially worth singling out.

What makes this museum are its Goyas, which comprise three oil paintings and examples of almost all the artist's prints. The oils are prominently, even pretentiously, displayed above two platforms and against velvet curtains. Two of them are half-length portraits – of ***Don Francisco del Mazo*** (painted in Marid in about 1820), and the artist himself wearing glasses and a green coat, generally thought to have been painted when he was in his early 40s. The main Goya canvas is ***The Junta of the Philippines*** ★, the largest painting that he ever executed, although it is now probably the least well known. The picture is so dark, the figures so small in relation to the surrounding space, and the boringly symmetrical composition so stiff and ungainly, that reproductions of the work fail to do it justice. Seen at close quarters it is a work full of fascinating details that haunt the memory. The subject is a meeting of the Spanish *Corte.* King Ferdinand VII and his ministers sit motionless like puppets at a table; the others present at the meeting are gathered in front of them, yawning, dozing, chatting and generally taking little interest in what is happening. The artist has portrayed himself on the left of the picture, an isolated figure sadly staring towards the spectator.

It seems now almost inconceivable that this bitingly satirical and technically odd work, though officially commissioned, should actually have been accepted by the king, and yet it used to hang in the Spanish Royal Palace. Like his two celebrated canvases of war, the ***2nd of May*** and the ***3rd of May*** (both now in the Prado, Madrid), it was painted in 1814, the year that the contemptible Ferdinand VII returned to the throne after a period of captivity. The next six years were some of the bleakest and most repressive in Spanish history.

Goya's prints are mainly kept in a room of their own. Most of them were executed in the then new technique of aquatint – a method of toning etchings. His main series of prints were the ***Caprichos***, the ***Disasters of War***, the ***Tauromachia***, the ***Disparates*** and the ***Bulls of Bordeaux***. The ***Caprichos***, which appeared in 1799, comment on the follies of mankind, and were done shortly after the artist had suffered a serious illness which had left him deaf. The ***Disasters of War*** were inspired by gruesome events in the Spanish War of Independence (1808–1814). The ***Disparates*** date from after 1819, and are contemporary with his so-called "Black Paintings"; they reflect the artist's mood of increased pessimism brought on by another serious attack of illness, and the consequences of Ferdinand VII's horrific rule. The ***Bulls of Bordeaux*** were carried out when in exile in Bordeaux, and show him the master of what was then another novel form of printing – lithography. The impressions of the prints in the Castres museum are of varying quality, and in addition seem to be deteriorating from constant exposure.

A series of small rooms leading off the entrance hall of the museum is devoted to late 19thC and early 20thC Spanish works, including some mediocre drawings by Picasso.

CÉRET

Pyrénées-Or., Pyrénées Map D5

A small, pretty old town clinging to the foothills of the Pyrenees, Céret attracted a large number of artists in the second decade of this century. A Catalan sculptor known as Manolo (his real name was Manuel Hugué), born in Barcelona in 1872, was the first, arriving in Céret in 1909 and staying in the town until 1928. Manolo encouraged a number of artist friends to come and join him here, and between 1910 and 1914 Céret became the haunt of a group of artists and writers associated with the artistic movement known as Cubism. Most notable among these were Picasso, Braque, Juan Gris and Max Jacob. Cubism was then at an early stage of its development, and the works painted by these artists in the town – for instance, Braque's ***Window at Céret*** – played an important part in the history of the movement. Céret came to be known as the "Mecca of Cubism", although it also had strong associations with Fauvism: the Fauves, Matisse, Derain, Marquet and Maillol – who based themselves in the nearby fishing port of Collioure – all paid regular visits to Céret before World War I.

Musée d'Art Moderne

4 Rue Joseph Parayre
Tel. (68) 872776
Open July–Sept 10am–noon, 3–7pm, Oct–June 10am–noon, 2–5pm
Closed Tues (in winter only)
(Wed)

The Museum of Modern Art at Céret was opened in 1953, largely due to the efforts of the painter Pierre Brune, who came to Céret in 1916 and lived here until his death in 1956. Brune asked all the artists who had been associated with the place – however slightly, as was the case with Chagall, Cocteau and Dali – to donate works to the museum. Most of them responded, but in almost all cases with some of their slightest works. The museum is therefore frankly a disappointment – the works range from mediocre to very bad, and are haphazardly displayed against dirty white walls. There are no oil paintings by any of the well-known Céret artists. (Braque promised to give one, but then forgot about it). Instead these artists donated drawings, lithographs and the odd gouache or watercolour. Most of these are displayed in the foyer of the museum, and are sometimes difficult to distinguish from the posters and other reproductions on sale here. By far the most generous donation to the museum was made by Picasso, to whom a whole room is dedicated. He gave lithographs and drawings (mainly dating from the early 1950s) and a **large collection of ceramics**, which constitute perhaps the main reason for visiting the museum. The less said about Pierre Brune's sub-Fauvist landscapes the better.

COGNAC

Charente, C. de l'Atlantique Map B2

A quiet little town on the banks of the Charente, Cognac is of course internationally known for the brandy which bears its name, the production of which dates from the 17thC.

Musée de Cognac

48 Boulevard Denfert-Rochereau
Tel. (45) 320225
Open June–Sept 10am–noon, 2–6pm Oct–May 2.30–5.30pm
Closed Tues (mornings from Oct–May)

The local museum is housed in an 18thC palace and adjoins a beautiful park. Its most popular section is naturally devoted to the history of the local cognac industry. This takes up the entire basement of the museum, and in addition to explaining – through a series of diagrams and scale models – how the drink is produced, has a fine collection of **Art-Nouveau posters** advertising the product.

A collection of local pottery fills up most of the ground floor, and the paintings are largely to be found on the first floor. The latter were mainly from the collection of a 19thC cognac merchant, Émile Pélisson, who acquired them in the course of his many business trips abroad, in particular to Britain, Belgium and Germany. His thriving trade with Britain helps partly to explain the proportionally high representation of British works in the gallery. These include an anonymous 16thC portrait head of ***Robert Dudley, Earl of Leicester***, a copy of a Titian painting by Bonington (whose name has been misspelt on the label), and landscapes by John-Lewis Brown and Alfred Smith, two obscure pupils of Delacroix who worked in Bordeaux.

However, the two greatest paintings bought by Pélisson were by late 16thC Flemish artists, Jan Massys (***Lot and his Daughters***) and Frans Floris (***Adam and Eve***). Among the other paintings are ***Ship with Flags*** by the Fauve painter Marquet, and yet another collection of paintings by Marquet's colleague, Maurice Marinot.

Perhaps the most attractive section of this charming old-fashioned museum is devoted to Art-Nouveau craft objects and late 19thC and early 20thC Salon pictures. Among these is a small and renowned genre scene by Antoine Bail, ***A Member of the Brass Band***, and a superlative example of academic kitsch, Dagnan Bouveret's life-sized ***Margaret at the Sabbath***. This was an enormous success in the Paris Salon of 1910–1911, and portrays the scene in Goethe's *Faust* when Margaret goes mad. The sexually provocative model for this, who is shown half naked, was a well-known actress of the time, Susanne Dolvé.

CORDES
Tarn, Causses Map C4

Dramatically situated on top of a very steep hill, Cordes is a fortified village which was built in the early 13thC by the Counts of Toulouse. Its quaint cobbled streets are now lined with souvenir shops, many of which are located in handsome Gothic buildings of the 13thC–14thC.

Musée Yves Brayer
Place de la Mairie
Tel. (63) 560040
Open 10am–noon, 2–6pm
Closed Sat, Sun morning

The medieval Hôtel de Ville has a room containing paintings and other works by the exceptionally popular contemporary French painter, Yves Brayer, who came to the village in 1945, later married a local girl, and still has a house here. Brayer is an unadventurous topographical artist whose works shun the realities of modern life.

MIRANDE
Gers, Pyrénées Map B4

Mirande is a small, lively town with little of architectural interest apart from a heavily restored 15thC church with a picturesque crenellated tower.

Musée des Beaux-Arts
Rue de l'Évêché
Tel. (62) 665287
Open 10am–noon, 2–5pm
Closed Tues

The local museum is currently housed in the barn-like interior of a decaying 19thC building overlooking the municipal park. Its collections – comprising some local pottery as well as third-rate 17thC and 18thC Italian and Flemish paintings – is currently awaiting transference to a new specially built museum. For this purpose many of the paintings, including the ***Head of a Faun*** bearing an especially dubious attribution to Rubens, have been recently cleaned.

MONTAUBAN
Tarn-et-Garonne, Périgord Map C4

Situated on a hill overlooking the river Tarn, Montauban (the Roman Mons Albanus) developed out of a *bastide* or fortified settlement founded in 1144 by the Count of Toulouse in an attempt to encourage the productivity of the area. Later it became a bastion of Protestantism, and bravely withstood a siege by Louis XIII but eventually capitulated to the king after the fall of that other main Protestant center, LA ROCHELLE. It is today a lively market town with an old quarter built of red brick and an enchanting square, the **Place Nationale**, surrounded by 17thC arcades. Among its main architectural monuments are the 14thC **Church of St-Jacques**, which briefly became a cathedral after the town was reclaimed by the Catholics. In the mid 18thC, the present enormous and rather ugly cathedral of Notre-Dame was built. The latter's main object of interest is a large 19thC painting commemorating Louis XIII's fight against the Protestants. Entitled ***The Vow of Louis XIII*** it is the work of Montauban's greatest son, the painter Jean-Auguste-Dominique Ingres.

Musée Ingres ☆

19 Rue de la Mairie
Tel. (63) 631804 (ext 20)
Open 10am–noon, 2–5pm
Closed Tues

The museum named after Ingres is housed in an impressive red-brick building, constructed in 1664 and used in the 17thC and 18thC as a bishop's palace. Its site was once that of a 14thC castle, some of the rooms of which now form the basement of the museum. This is where the museum's historical, lapidary and archaeological collections are kept: included in these is a group of particularly unpleasant torture instruments. The ground floor is taken up mainly by the work of two other Montauban artists, the 19thC sculptor Antoine Bourdelle – to whom a whole museum is devoted in ***PARIS*** – and the 20thC landscapist, Desnoyer, a facile and conventional painter whose works have nonetheless found their way into a surprisingly large number of French provincial museums.

Works by Ingres and his contemporaries fill the first floor of the museum. They were bequeathed to the museum by the painter himself, together with numerous other objects and paintings belonging to him. The rooms here have been sumptuously modernized, and the tired visitor can sink almost to the floor in blue corduroy-covered armchairs of ultra-modern design.

Ingres was born in Montauban in 1780, and received here an elementary training in painting and music from his father, who was a painter, sculptor and architect. After proceeding with his studies in nearby Toulouse, he entered David's studio in Paris. Ingres lived until the age of 87 and was one of the most successful painters of his day, although his adherence throughout his life to a rigidly classical style of painting led to him being considered as a bastion of conservative French taste. His art is frequently contrasted with that of Delacroix, which seems on the surface more emotional and impetuous, although is in fact governed by a greater intellectual discipline. It was the poet Baudelaire who was one of the first to recognize that the coldly classical art of Ingres was in fact the product of a deeply passionate and romantic temperament.

The Ingres museum is not the best place fully to appreciate Ingres' qualities as a painter. For instance, there is no portrait here equal in stature to his ***Portrait of Granet*** in the Musée Granet at ***AIX-EN-PROVENCE***, or a group of small works of such high quality as those in the Musée Bonnat in **BAYONNE**. One of the main works here is the Raphael-inspired ***Christ among the Artists***, a dull, lifeless composition painted when the artist was 82. Of far greater interest is the enormous ***Dream of Ossian*** ★, which was intended for Napoleon's bedroom. The dream is portrayed entirely in monochrome, with figures and forms blending strangely together. Unfortunately this haunting work (which admittedly has the odd silliness, like the caricature dog at Ossian's feet) is hung against a deep blue background which renders slightly insipid the predominant pale blues in the painting.

The great strength of the museum is its **collection of over 4,000 drawings by Ingres** ★★. A tiny selection of these is shown in rotation in a room on the first floor; but the museum authorities willingly allow interested visitors to look through the countless boxes of drawings kept in the museum's offices on the ground floor (it is advisable, however, to write for permission beforehand). To study these drawings is one of the most exciting experiences to be had in a provincial French museum. Ingres was undoubtedly one of the greatest draughtsmen of all time. One is struck by the sheer variety of his drawings, which range from jewel-like portrait drawings, to landscapes executed in a series of minuscule dots and dashes, to hasty compositional studies sometimes covered in colour notations, to copies after old masters (his last drawing was a copy after a Giotto ***Lamentation***), and to broadly handled and voluptuous nude studies. His drawings enable one to observe the enormous effort which went into the apparently effortless perfection of his paintings: frequently a line was drawn over and over again until the artist was satisfied with the result, and at other times even tracing paper was superimposed over a drawing to allow the artist to try out other solutions to a particular problem.

The paintings in the museum by Ingres' contemporaries such as David, Delacroix, Géricault and Granet, and by his pupils, Flandrin, Gerome, and Chassériau, are mainly unremarkable. There is, however, a charming and minutely handled oil painting by an obscure pupil of Ingres showing ***Ingres in his Rome Studio*** together with his rather homely and amply proportioned wife. Near this are cases with numerous personal belongings of Ingres, including his palette, waistcoat, and violin.

The second floor of the museum forms a great contrast to the rest of the building, being dark and unmodernized. It is crammed with flaking third-rate French, Flemish and Italian paintings from the 14thC to the 18thC. By way of compensation the rooms here have attractive painted coffered ceilings, and magnificent views down to the Tarn.

NARBONNE
Aude, Causses Map D5

Though it was the first town outside Italy to be colonized by the Romans, and the birthplace of two Roman emperors, Narbonne has preserved virtually nothing of its Roman past. In earlier times an important port, it is now an industrial town with few interesting old buildings. Two of the most important of these are the unfinished **Cathédrale St-Just** and the adjoining **archbishop's palace**. Work began on the cathedral in 1272, but was suspended in 1354 with only the choir completed. Later attempts were made to construct a transept and a nave, but only the foundations for these were laid. The massive choir is in itself bigger than most cathedrals, and in its height is only surpassed in France by those of Beauvais and Amiens. One of its chapels contains a copy by the 18thC artist Carle Van Loo of a painting which was once Narbonne's most celebrated art treasure. This, the ***Resurrection of Lazarus*** by Michelangelo's follower Sebastiano del Piombo, was acquired by the English 19thC banker, Angerstein, whose collection formed the basis of the National Gallery in London.

The cathedral's treasury contains some fine 17thC Aubusson and Gobelins tapestries, but the greatest work of art in the cathedral – and indeed in the whole of Narbonne – is to be found not in the treasury but in the former chapter house underneath. This is a large canvas, ***The Guardian Angel*** ★ by the remarkable 17thC Toulouse painter, Nicolas Tournier. As with all his few surviving works (the others are mainly in the Musée des Augustins, TOULOUSE), it combines naturalism typical of Caravaggio with mannered elegance. In this case the two protagonists – and the small dog in between them – seem on the point of levitation.

Musée d'Art et d'Histoire
Tel. (68) 323160 (ext 372)
Open mid-May to mid-Sept 10–11.50am, 2–6pm; mid-Sept to mid-May 10–11.50am, 2–5.15pm
Closed Mon (winter only)
(Wed)

The local art gallery, housed in the adjacent Archbishop's Palace, has nothing which matches the cathedral's Tournier. But the building itself – which also contains a lapidary and archaeological museum – is an interesting and enjoyable place to wander in, being a large, rambling structure built between the 12thC and 19thC.

The art gallery is on the top floor, in a series of rather dirty and neglected rooms with mainly 17thC and 18thC furnishings. Roman mosaics cover the floors of two rooms, which have fine *trompe-l'oeil* and painted coffered ceilings. The paintings are largely of the 17thC and 18thC French and Italian schools, and include a large number of very doubtful attributions to artists such as Guercino and Carlo Dolci. Two of the best works are a ***Portrait*** and ***Self-portrait*** by the Perpignan artist Hyacinthe Rigaud.

There is a small room of 19thC works, which contains a watercolour by Bonington (the ***Port of Dieppe***), and two drawings by David (both of ***Napoleon on Horseback***). Also worth looking at is a good landscape by the minor Barbizon School painter, Alexandre Défaux (***Summer at Montigny-sur-Loing***) and, for good measure, a strikingly silly painting by Abel Boye, ***Evening***, which shows a nude woman from the back staring towards the rising moon.

NIORT
Deux Sèvres, C. de l'Atlantique Map B1

Niort is a small commercial town, once known for its tanning of imported pelts from Canada, and now the headquarters of various leading French insurance companies. Its principal architectural monument is its imposing medieval **Donjon** on the banks of the river Sèvre, supposedly built by Henry II of England and his son Richard Coeur de Lion.

Musée du Pilori
Ancien Hôtel de Ville
Tel. (49) 792597
Open 9am–noon, 2–5pm (2–6pm winter)
Closed Tues

Another interesting if less prominent monument is the 16thC former town hall, which is hidden away in the oldest part of the town. This houses the Musée du Pilori, a ramshackle collection of furniture, stone carvings and assorted bric-à-brac. Its principal treasure is a statue in white marble of ***Cardinal Richelieu*** by the 17thC Italian sculptor Francesco Mochi.

Musée des Beaux-Arts

3 Rue du Musée
Tel. (49) 249784
Open 9am–noon, 2–5pm (2–6pm summer)
Closed Tues

Nearby is the town's art gallery, which occupies an 18thC oratory. The dark and dingy interior of this building displays few works of art of note. There are some 18thC Dutch *boiseries* (wooden panels) once belonging to the oratory, a ***Landscape*** by Corot, an enormous canvas of the ***Massacre of the Innocents*** by the local 19thC painter, Louis Leloir, and an excellent ***Portrait of a Woman*** in the guise of the goddess Diana by Jean Nattier.

PAU

Pyrénées-Atl. Pyrénées Map B4

Although Pau was an important town in the Middle Ages and Renaissance – King Henry IV of France was born in the castle here in 1553 – its character has been largely established by its 19thC popularity as a thermal resort for the very rich. The English were the first to see its potential and used to come here in large numbers: in 1863 the town's population of 21,000 comprised 3,000 Englishmen. Today the place has the faded elegance typical of 19thC resorts. The **Boulevard des Pyrenées**, built on the initiative of Napoleon I, is the inland equivalent of Nice's Promenade des Anglais, and commands breathtaking views of the whole range of the snow-capped Pyrenees from the Pic du Midi de Bigorre to the Pic d'Anie.

Musée des Beaux-Arts ☆

Rue Mathieu Lalanne
Tel. (56) 273302
Open 10am–noon, 2–6pm
Closed Tues

Thanks mainly to the wealth of the visitors to the town in the 19thC, Pau boasts one of the best collections of painting in southern France. The Museum of Fine Arts was inaugurated in 1864, and housed at first in the former Palais de Justice. The present building – a hideous, Neoclassical structure – dates from the 1920s.

In the very cheap and generally informative catalogue to the gallery brought out in 1978, a former mayor of the town writes of the need to transform museums into "living places". With this in mind a special educational department was set up in the museum designed to promote the enjoyment of art among the young. Unfortunately, lack of funds seems to have seriously undermined the museum's aspirations. The place is typical of those soulless institutions designed to put people off art for life: the paintings are shoddily displayed in dingy rooms, one of which serves as the "educational department" – a room full of children's doodles that are completely out of character with their austere 19thC surroundings. Most of the paintings are indicated simply by faded typewritten labels crudely stuck to the walls. In other museums one might well be suspicious if such an attribution proclaims a Rubens or a Ribera; in Pau, these makeshift labels all mean exactly what they say.

The paintings are mainly displayed according to schools. The **Spanish School** is particularly rich, with good examples of the work of the 16thC Italianate painter, Juan de Juanes, El Greco, Ribera, and the late 19thC Paris-trained Realist, Ignacio Zuloaga. The best Italian paintings in the museum are of the 17thC and 18thC. There is a striking ***Self-portrait*** by the Bergamo painter Vittore Ghislandi (portraiture was a particular speciality of Bergamo); a ***Study of a Philosopher*** by Luca Giordano, a grotesque ***Drunkenness of Noah*** attributed to the Neapolitan painter Gaspare Traversi, a ***Head of St Peter*** by Guido Reni, and a ***Preaching of St John the Baptist*** by Carlo Maratta which was given in 1701 to a great admirer of Maratta's work, Louis XIV. Mention should also be made of a genre scene, ***At the Station***, by the 19thC Genoese painter Giuseppe Ricci, a friend of Toulouse-Lautrec who accompanied the latter on a trip to London.

The Netherlandish school is not well represented at Pau, but there are three important works by Rubens – a large monochrome oil sketch for the monumental ***Last Judgment*** in Munich (1615), and two other oil sketches for a series of tapestries based on the ***Life of Achilles***, commissioned either by Philip IV of Spain or Charles I of England. Two British paintings complete the gallery's holdings of foreign artists – a ***Portrait of an Adolescent*** by George Romney, and a ***Self-portrait*** by David Wilkie (1840).

Apart from some Watteau drawings

and an oil painting by Nattier of ***Mme Henrietta as a Vestal Virgin***, the greatest treasures of the French collection are of the 19thC. Here you can see not only major works by well-known artists of this period, but also a host of fascinating paintings by artists whose popularity has not survived into this century. One such work is an 1830 ***Portrait of Mme Bail*** by a pupil of Baron Gros, Edme Jean Pigal. Mme Bail was a close friend of Chateaubriand, and she is shown in this portrait in a charmingly intimate pose, leaning backwards on her chair, her arms crossed, and a half-opened book by Chateaubriand on her knee. Also interesting is ***The Patio***, a large late 19thC canvas (recently saved from oblivion in the reserve collection) by Achille Zo. This depiction of languorous and elegantly dressed figures lost in contemplation in an Oriental setting is a stylishly painted work with echoes of the art of John Singer Sargent, and captures the *fin de siècle* taste for the exotic.

In a gesture more indicative of the French reputation for gallantry than of any latent feminism on the part of the museum's authorities, a whole room entitled *La Salle des Femmes* displays 19thC portrayals of women. The most striking among these is a ***Portrait of an Unknown Woman*** by Bonnat.

In 1875 a local aristocrat, Émile Noulibos, left a large sum of money to the Pau museum to be spent on buying contemporary French painting, and stipulated that genuinely modern works should be bought rather than mere academic art. With his money, the museum bought most of its greatest 19thC works, including excellent paintings by Daubigny (***Seascape***, 1877), Fantin Latour (***Dances***, 1891), Henner (***Head of a Young Woman***) and the little-known woman painter Louise Abbéma, a student of Carolus-Duran. Abbéma's ***Dinner in the Conservatory*** (1877) is a masterpiece: strongly influenced in its colouring by the art of Manet, it is an outdoor group portrait featuring, among others, the artists' parents and a family friend, the actress Sarah Bernhardt. The most famous acquisition made by Pau museum with the Noulibos bequest is Degas' ***Cotton Exchange in New Orleans*** ★, undoubtedly the museum's single most outstanding work. Degas visited New Orleans in 1873 to stay with his mother's family, who worked in the cotton trade. Shortly after arriving here, he wrote to his painter friend James Tissot that he was engaged on a painting featuring approximately 15 people gathered around a table on which was placed a pile of cotton. He incorporated into this picture various members of his family, including his uncle, Michel Busson (standing next to a table and examining cotton in his hands) and brother Achille (leaning against a wall on the far left of the picture). Quite apart from its purely pictorial qualities – its subtle variations of greens, whites and blacks, and the fineness of its details – the painting is one of the most lifelike and sympathetic representations of work in the 19thC. However, it was poorly received by critics at the time; the Realist writer Zola, for instance, described the draughtsmanship as pitiable and the overall work as reminiscent of an engraving in an illustrated magazine. The Pau museum was fortunately enlightened enough to buy it as early as 1878, and thus became the only public gallery to buy a work by the artist during his lifetime.

The recent acquisitions of French art made by the museum have fallen far short of the standards set by its purchasing body in the last century. A particular taste has been shown for sensational Surrealism and Photo-realism. It must be said, however, that at least some of these works do have a sense of humour, albeit of a rather adolescent kind. Visitors who have wandered around France armed with their Michelin Green and Red Guides might appreciate Alfred Courmes' ***Pneumatic Greeting***, a modern-day version of the Annunciation that shows the Michelin-Tyre man hailing with the words "Ave Maria" a sexily dressed girl in black suspenders.

PERPIGNAN

Pyrénées-Or. Pyrénées Map D5

Perpignan, the capital of the former province of Roussillon, is a lively city with a strong Spanish atmosphere. The most interesting period in its history was between the 11thC and 15thC when it belonged successively to the Spanish kingdoms of Aragon, Majorca and Catalonia. The medieval part of the town is reminiscent of the Barrio Gotico in Barcelona, and is similarly animated. At its heart is the former stock exchange, the **Loge de Mer**, an elegant arcaded building in a Catalan Gothic style.

Musée Rigaud ☆

16 Rue de l'Ange
Tel. (68) 616630
Open Mon–Sat 9.30am–noon, 2–6pm; Sun 10.30am–noon, 2–6pm
Closed Tues

The Musée Rigaud once occupied part of

the rather decrepit local art school building. It has recently been magnificently rehoused in a modernized late 17thC palace. Its collections are small, but of extremely high quality. The ground floor shows an alternating selection of the museum's extensive collection of Old Master drawings, which is particularly rich in 17thC and 18thC Italian and French works. The paintings, which have all been well restored to coincide with the move to the new building, are mainly on the first floor. One room has a group of 15thC Catalan works, most notable among which is the ***Retable of the Trinity*** ★ (1489) attributed to the Master of Canapost. Portraying the Trinity surrounded by Old Testament prophets, it is a work full of complex inconographical details. In the predella panel underneath is an extremely accurate portrayal of the ***Loge de Mer*** (Sea Lodge), which has been placed in an imaginary seaside setting (thought unconvincingly by some to represent the nearby port of Collioure).

Two other rooms are devoted to the artist after whom the museum is named – Hyacinthe Rigaud. Born in Perpignan in 1659, Rigaud was trained in Montpellier. Later he moved to Paris, where he became almost exclusively a court portraitist after 1681, when he painted a portrait of the king's brother. His portraiture combines the Baroque gusto of van Dyck with the classical restraint of Philippe de Champaigne. He also had a close interest in the intimate naturalism of Rembrandt, which he was able to show in some of his unofficial works, such as his portraits of himself and his family.

The Perpignan museum has an excellent example of the artist's grand official manner – his portrait of ***Cardinal Bouillon*** ★, shown in an expansive red garment with putti at his feet and crimson draperies blowing behind. There are also three outstanding ***Self-portraits*** ★ by Rigaud, showing him painting a portrait of Monsieur de Castagney, wearing a red turban and dressed in black velvet. The artist's obsessive interest in portraying himself may partly reflect his love of Rembrandt.

Another room in the museum is of late 18thC and early 19thC French paintings, including a sickly sweet portrait ***Head of a Girl*** by Greuze, a powerful ***Male Nude*** study by Géricault, and a celebrated full-length portrait by Ingres of the ***Duke of Orléans***. Finally, there is a small room taken up mainly by works of Roussillon's most famous artist of this century, Aristide Maillol, who was born at the nearby town of Banyuls-Sur-Mer.

Maillol worked initially as a painter (he was associated with the Fauves), but became largely known as a sculptor with a particular interest in the classical female nude. Although based mainly in Paris, he maintained his connections with Roussillon throughout his life, working frequently at Collioure and at a secluded house and garden 4km (2.5 miles) SW of Banyuls. Known as the **Métairie Maillol**, this place still survives, and contains the artist's grave, surmounted by a statue by him.

Numerous towns in the vicinity – including Céret and Banyuls – commissioned war memorials from Maillol. The Perpignan museum has one good oil by him of a ***Woman with a Bonnet*** silhouetted against a light brown background, as well as a large bronze of a crouching naked woman (***Monument to Debussy***), and a case of maquettes. Two other bronzes of female nudes by Maillol can be seen elsewhere in Perpignan – in the courtyard of the Hôtel de Ville and in the Place de La Loge: both these works are within the immediate vicinity of the Loge de Mer.

PÉZENAS
Hérault, Causses Map D4

In the middle of a dreary agricultural plain, Pézenas – the birthplace of Molière – seems at first a pleasant but dull town with little to offer the visitor. However, one only has to step back a few yards from the town's main square, the Place du 14-Juillet, to find oneself in a remarkably well preserved old quarter, full of elegant palaces dating from the 15thC to the 18thC. The cobbled **Place Gambetta**, at the heart of this tiny quarter, seems almost like a stage set.

Musée Vulliod-St-Germain
Rue A.P. Alliès
Tel. (67) 981415
Open 10am–noon, 2–5pm
Closed Mon (Oct–June), Tues

The Musée Vulliod-St-Germain is in an 18thC palace just off this square. It is a charming, old-fashioned museum, with reconstructions of local domestic interiors, fine 18thC rooms, and pleasant furniture and pottery. Unfortunately, its fine art collections are less remarkable, comprising minor 18thC French works and a group of 19thC local paintings. One room is naturally devoted to Molière. This contains the museum's most impressive work of art – a maquette by the Béziers sculptor Injalbert for his statue to ***Molière***, now in the small park adjoining the Place du 14-Juillet.

POITIERS

Vienne, C. de L'Atlantique Map B1

One of the oldest and most important university towns in France, Poitiers is now a rather ugly place whose medieval quarter has been ruined by unimaginative modern development. Nonetheless it still retains a number of remarkable Romanesque monuments. Principal among these is the 11th–12thC **Eglise Notre-Dame-de-la-Grande**, which has an exceptionally elaborate sculpted façade, with a tympanum of the ***Last Judgment***, scenes from the Old and New Testament, and highly intricate plant and animal motifs.

Musée Ste-Croix

3 Bis Rue Jean-Jaurès
Tel. (49) 410753
Open 10–11.30am, 2–5.30pm
Closed Tues

The Musée Ste-Croix has been built up around the ruins of the former Abbey of Ste-Croix. It is an adventurous, sprawling building on which much money has been spent. For all this, however, its collections are confusingly displayed, and the constant changes in floor level are likely to leave the visitor disorientated. The ground floor and basement contain the archaeological and sculptural section of the museum (which has disappointingly few examples of Romanesque sculpture). Also here are a number of rooms illustrating local industries and arts and crafts. Upstairs, the paintings comprise unremarkable examples of 17thC and 18thC French, Dutch and Flemish art, as well as French 19thC works. Among the latter are small **oil sketches** by Vuillard, Monticelli, Boudin and Sisley. More striking is a large cartoon by Moreau entitled ***The Siren and the Poet***.

ROCHEFORT

Charente-Mar., C. de l'Atlantique Map A2

Rochefort was chosen by the 17thC minister Colbert as an ideal base to defend the Atlantic coastline against English invasions. Between 1666 and 1668 he had a military port built here, with a large arsenal and shipyard rivalling Toulon in power. Today Rochefort is a quiet, slightly sinister town of empty arcaded streets and closed shutters. It has maintained its formal 17thC layout, although there are few surviving old buildings of note.

Musée Municipal des Beaux-Arts

63 Avenue Charles de Gaulle
Tel. (46) 992070
Open 1.30–5.30pm (mornings by permission)
Closed Sun, Mon

The Museum of Fine Arts is installed in the 18thC Hôtel Hèbre de Saint Clement. Its main room contains a number of 16th–18thC French, Flemish and Italian paintings, most notable among which is an oil sketch by Rubens (***Lycaon Changed into a Wolf by Jupiter***). Also here is a large collection of 19thC and early 20thC French works, including a small oil by Géricault, and a striking ***Portrait of Lola Montes*** by Rouget. Another room shows a selection of the museum's extensive **collection of drawings**, which includes a number of 16thC Italian and late 18thC and early 19thC French works. The rest of the museum is taken up by exhibits relating to the maritime history of Rochefort, and by a good ethnographic collection, which is particularly rich in **Polynesian masks**.

Maison de Pierre Loti

141 Rue Pierre Loti
Open 10am–noon, 2–5pm
Closed Apr–Sept Sun, Mon (mornings); Oct–Mar, Sun, Mon–Tues (mornings)

The visitor to Rochefort should not fail to miss the house which belonged to Rochefort's greatest son, the 19th-century writer Pierre Loti. Loti, who was born in this house in 1850 and spent most of his childhood here, bought the place in 1880, and later added a neighbouring house to it. He was an eccentric in his dress and behaviour, and an incessant traveller, and these journeys inspired the exotic novels that once enjoyed an enormous vogue. The quintessential *fin-de-siècle* dreamer, he was the friend of a number of symbolist painters, including Lévy-Dhurman, who painted a portrait of him in Turkish dress (now in the Musée Bonnat at BAYONNE). His Rochefort house is on the outside small and completely unprepossessing; inside you are immediately transported into the world of his novels. Although he took care to preserve the rooms in which he lived as a child, Loti totally transformed the rest of the house and the adjoining building by pulling down walls and ceilings, and thereby creating the impression of a spacious palace. On the ground floor is a huge Renaissance-style dining room, with **Gobelins tapestries** and **Spanish Renaissance furniture**. Connected to this is a studio which belonged to his sister, a painter; it is full of traditional

Breton furniture (Loti had an enormous influence in opening up the appreciation of Brittany in the 19thC). Greater treats are in store for the visitor upstairs. Here are a series of Turkish and Arabian rooms, partly constructed by specially imported Syrian workers, and containing parts of old mosques, Turkish tombs, and innumerable other Oriental bits and pieces ruthlessly acquired by Loti in the course of his travels. You should also note here a small painting by Loti himself: in the style of a Persian miniature, it features a beautiful ***Turkish Girl*** whom Loti fell in love with (she died shortly afterwards) and who inspired his first, and one of his most successful novels, *Aziyadé*, published in 1879. When using the Oriental rooms in his house, Loti always dressed up in Turkish costume; but for most of his life he remained a respectable naval officer whose career took him to Middle and Far Eastern places that provided the settings for his novels.

LA ROCHELLE
Charente-Mar., C. de l'Atlantique
Map A2

In the 16thC and 17thC La Rochelle was one of the most important ports in France, benefiting greatly from trade with the New World. During this same period, the town was also an important bastion of Protestantism, which led to its being subjected in 1627–28 to a notorious siege conducted by Cardinal Richelieu; most of the town's population died during the course of this. Since then the town has had a relatively quiet history, and was largely untouched during World War II. The best preserved port in France, it is an extraordinarily beautiful place. Not only is there the picturesque **fortified harbour** that has attracted innumerable artists, including Joseph Vernet, Corot and Signac, but there are also many quiet arcaded back streets full of elegant **17thC and 18thC palaces**.

Musée des Beaux-Arts
Rue Gargoulleau
Open 10am–noon, 2–5pm
Closed Sun morning

The 18thC Hôtel Legoux houses the Musée des Beaux-Arts. Unfortunately, this building has been closed for restoration work for some time, and is unlikely to reopen in the near future. The interior is noted for its original 18thC *boiseries* (wood panels) and for the fine bronze railings on its main staircase. Pride of the pre-19thC collections is a coldly classical work (***Adoration of the Shepherds***) by Poussin's contemporary, Le Sueur. Among its 19thC paintings are ***Mary Stuart Protecting Riccio against the Assassins*** by Chassériau, two oil sketches by Delacroix, and a number of works by two celebrated natives of the town, Adolphe Bouguereau (1825–1905) and Eugène Fromentin (1820–76). The former was a highly successful if rather unadventurous Salon painter best known for his bloodless nudes; the museum has principally religious works by him. The latter was especially renowned for his freely painted scenes of North African life reminiscent of those of Delacroix. ***Arab Horsemen*** in the museum is a good example of these. He was also celebrated for his writing, particularly the morbid novel of contemporary Parisian life, *Dominique*, and for an influential if rather over-subtle book about Dutch 17thC painters, *The Masters of Past Time*. His magnificent house and studio on the Rue Carnot on the outskirts of the town still survive, although they cannot be visited. Of the 20thC works in the museum, there is one late **oil** by Maurice Denis, and a group of **watercolours** by Marquet and Signac.

SAINTES
Charente-Mar., C. de l'Atlantique
Map A2

Saintes was an important town in Roman times, as well as a major stopping-off point in the Middle Ages on the pilgrims' road to Santiago de Compostela (see pp. 210–11). The principal traces of its Roman past are its **amphitheatre** and the **Arch of Germanicus**, next to which is a well-displayed museum of Roman finds. Among the town's many medieval buildings is the 12thC **Eglise Ste-Marie**, which has an excellent sculpted façade.

Musée des Beaux-Arts
Hôtel Présidial, 28 Rue Victor Hùgo, Ancien Echevinage, Rue Alsace-Lorraine
Tel. (45) 930394
Open Apr–Aug 10am–noon, 2–6pm; Sept–Mar 2–5pm
Closed Tues

The river Charente divides the town into two distinctive areas. The quietest and best preserved is that on the left bank – the **Quartier St-Eutrope**. In the middle of the pedestrian district here is the Musée des Beaux-Arts, which is housed in two separate buildings, each of architectural interest. The earlier collections are kept in a small and elegant

17thC palace known as the **Présidial** which has been tastefully and sumptuously modernized. Among the paintings here is a ***Sacrifice of Abraham*** by Domenichino, ***Pygmalion and Galatea*** by the little-known French artist, Riquarde de Nantes, attributions to Salvator Rosa and Jan "Velvet" Brueghel, and several other well-restored though unexciting 16thC, 17thC and 18thC pictures of different schools. The 19thC paintings are all in the former **bishop's palace**, a few minutes walk from the Présidial. This is an 18thC building flanked by a 15th–16thC tower. The paintings here are as well presented as those in the Présidial, and in an equally well restored interior. The great majority of them are by local artists, in particular the 19thC landscapist L.-A. Auguin. However there is also a ***Snow Landscape*** by Jongkind, a collection of works by the minor but ubiquitous Marinot, and two ***Breton Scenes*** by F. de Gout-Gérard, a conventional and little-known 19thC painter whose main claim to fame was to have been in the Pension Gloanec in Pont-Aven at the same time as Gauguin.

TOULOUSE

Haute-Garonne, Pyrénées   Map C4

Once the capital of the former province of Languedoc, Toulouse is now the fourth largest town in France. Although it was joined to the French crown in 1271, the town has enjoyed for much of its history a remarkable autonomy from the rest of France. To a large extent this has been due to its great distance from Paris. Until the Revolution Toulouse had a most unusual form of government. This was an oligarchy comprising 4–12 members known as the *Capitouls*, who were invariably chosen from among the town's rich mercantile classes. Election to this rank meant also being elevated into the nobility, which led to a large number of *Capitouls* embellishing their houses with crenellated towers (unfortunately many of these have now disappeared).

Toulouse can boast of having the oldest literary academy in Europe, founded in 1323 by a group of seven young troubadours who were anxious to maintain the language of the province (the *langue d'oc*). Originally known as the *Compagnie du Gai-Savoir*, and later as the *Académie des Jeux Floraux*, the institution continues to flourish today, making the town the main focus of Languedoc studies.

A rapidly expanding town with endless modern suburbs, Toulouse has nonetheless managed to preserve a very extensive old quarter based on the exceptionally lively **Place du Capitole**. As with other towns in this area of France, this quarter is built entirely in red brick, thus explaining why Toulouse is sometimes referred to as *la ville rose*. The oldest of its main surviving monuments is the **Basilica of St-Sernin**, work on which was begun around 1080. Although regarded as one of the finest of France's Romanesque buildings, it was heavily restored in the 19thC by Viollet-le-Duc; moreover its western façade was only completed as late as 1929. Its greatest works of art are seven late 11thC marble bas-reliefs in the ambulatory, representing ***Christ in Majesty*** surrounded by angels and apostles, and early 12thC carvings of ***Scenes from the Old and New Testaments*** on the tympanum of the Porte Miégeville.

A possibly more striking, and certainly more endearing, building than the Basilica is the nearby church of the former **Monastery of the Jacobins**, which was built in the course of the 13thC and 14thC. A fortress church like the cathedral of Albi, this extremely tall aisleless building has a most elegant interior with beautiful stained glass in its two 14thC rose windows. Of the town's secular monuments, special mention should be made of the **Hôtel Assézat**, which was built between 1555 and 1557 by Toulouse's leading Renaissance architect and sculptor, Nicolas Bachelier, and was the first major example in the town of the classical style of architecture. Originally the palace of a leading *Capitoul*, it has been for over two centuries the seat of the *Académie des Jeux Floraux*.

Musée des Augustins ☆☆

21 Rue de Metz
Tel. (61) 235507
Open 10am–noon, 2–6pm; 2–10pm Wed
Closed Tues, Sun mornings

The Musée des Augustins occupies the former monastery of the Augustinians, which was built mainly in the 14thC. From about 1500 onwards the monastery went into a long decline, and was pillaged on various occasions. Very shortly after the Revolution, it was decided to turn it into a museum. Despite its earlier troubled history, the monastery had up to that time managed to preserve virtually intact its old buildings. However, in the course of making the place suitable for use as a museum, these were badly damaged and their character insensitively altered. First the interior of the church was blocked up by a pretentious Neoclassical structure known as the

Temple of the Arts. Then the refectory was pulled down in favour of an enormous warehouse-like building designed by Viollet-le-Duc, but not constructed until long after his death.

Until the 1970s the museum was a dusty, forlorn place which was mainly visited for its medieval sculptures. Then in the course of the 1970s (during which period much of it was closed off to the public), it underwent further extensive conversion work. Now that all this has just been completed, the museum can claim to be one of the most exciting and imaginative in France, if not in Europe. Apart from its medieval sculptures, its great strength lies in its collection of 17thC and 18thC Toulouse painting. Unfortunately this is an area of art which is at present unlikely to attract large crowds of tourists: it is scarcely known outside Toulouse, let alone outside France. Yet it deserves far greater recognition: Toulouse has had a very original artistic history, which, unusually for France, developed largely independently from that of Paris; furthermore, the town produced someone who must surely be considered as one of the greatest European artists of the 17thC, Nicolas Tournier.

The main concern of the reconversion work of the 1970s was to expose all the remaining medieval walls, while at the same time making modern additions only when absolutely necessary. The sensitively restored medieval rooms adjoining the large cloister house the museum's 14thC, 15thC and 16thC sculptures, including a large group of works (once in the church of the Dalbade) by Nicolas Bachelier, architect of the Hôtel Assézat. The most famous of the works displayed here is a 15thC Virgin and Child known as the ***Nostre Dame de Grasse*★**. This masterpiece of late medieval Toulouse art is by an unknown hand: the Virgin is portrayed as an extremely elegant woman in intricately carved robes who turns away uninterestedly from her child. The monastery church, now stripped of its Neoclassical lining and revealed as an airy, spacious structure, is devoted exclusively to religious painting of the 15th–18thC. The paintings are mostly shown on the walls of the side chapels, and the aisleless nave has largely been left as an enormous empty space. The idea of showing paintings as they would be seen in a functioning church is a simple but brilliant one, and the overall effect is most moving and impressive. One's only qualm is that, in the attempt to make the building look as little as possible like part of an ordinary museum, the lighting of the works is perhaps not always as good as it could be.

The paintings here are of the Spanish, Flemish, Dutch, Italian and French Schools. The main Spanish work is Murillo's ***St Diego de Alcala de Henares in Ecstasy in Front of the Cross*** (1645–46), one of a series of 11 canvases commissioned for the small cloister of the convent of the Franciscans in Seville. It is an early work by the artist, painted before he achieved the effortless and at times facile virtuosity of his maturity. The Flemish School includes van Dyck's ***Miracle of the Mule***, and an especially dramatic Rubens, ***Christ Between the Two Thieves***, which was once the main altarpiece in the Capuchin Church in Antwerp, and is now hung as if it performed a similar function in the deconsecrated museum church. Apart from a panel of a polyptych by Perugino (***St John the Baptist and St Augustine*** c. 1495–1500), the most important Italian paintings are all of the 17thC. Principal among these are ***St Ignatius of Loyola and St Francis Xavier*** by Giovan Battista Gaulli (the decorator of the celebrated illusionistic ceiling frescoes in the church of the Gesù in Rome); ***The Mystical Marriage of St Catherine*** (c.1650) by the bizarre Lombard painter, Francesco de Cairo; and two altarpieces by the Emilian artist, Guercino, ***The Martyrdom of Sts John and Paul*** and ***Saints in Glory***. These last two works date respectively from an early and late phase in the artist's development: in between he is known to have fallen deeply under the influence of the classical theorists of his time, which helps to explain why his art changed from a highly pictorial manner, involving dramatically abrupt compositions and a powerful, irrational use of light, to a blander and more controlled way of painting.

The largest of the French School paintings are Vouet's ***Discovery of the True Cross*** (showing a dead man coming to life after contact with the cross on which he had been lying) and ***The Brazen Serpent*** (portraying a miracle of Moses); both these works used to hang in the chapel of the Black Penitents in Toulouse, and were the two most important commissions given to a Parisian painter in the town in the 17thC. These are powerful works which also undoubtedly gain by being exhibited in isolation in the nave of the church. There are other religious works by important Paris-based artists of the 17thC, most notably ***The Martyrdom of St Andrew*** by Sébastien Bourdon, ***The Marriage of the Virgin*** by Jacques Stella, and ***Descent from the Cross*** by Jean Jouvenet.

Yet the outstanding French paintings shown in the church are all of the **Toulouse 17thC school**★. Very little is known about the artists in question, and an enormous amount of scholarly research has yet to be done on them. It is difficult to characterize their work as a whole other than to emphasize how Caravaggesque and strongly anti-classsical it is in comparison to the art of their contemporaries in Paris. But each of the major Toulouse painters has a style very different from that of the others, though sharing the characteristic of being highly eccentric. The greatest of these artists was undoubtedly Nicolas Tournier, who was in Rome 1619–27, and had settled in Toulouse by 1632 after having spent a short period in Carcassonne. Almost all his complete surviving work is preserved in the Musée des Augustins. Tournier's three paintings in the church here – ***Virgin and Child***, ***Descent from the Cross***★, and ***Entombment***★ – reveal an unusual interpretation of Caravaggio's style: crude, naturalistic detail has been avoided, faces beautified, and figures given an almost balletic grace.

The three main Toulouse contemporaries of Tournier were Jean Chalette, Ambroise Frédeau and Antoine Rivalz. Chalette worked in Italy at the very beginning of the 17thC, then went to Aix-en-Provence, and was referred to as "master painter" in Toulouse in 1612. Along with Tournier he was the Toulouse painter most strongly influenced by Caravaggio. In the museum church is his ***Virgin and Child Blessing Prisoners***★, which was probably painted for a prison chapel: the artist contrasts the grotesquely realistic faces of the prisoners with a radiant vision of the Virgin and Child.

Absolutely nothing is known about the artistic background of Ambroise Frédeau. His surviving paintings suggest a greater interest in the art of 17thC Bolognese artists such as the Carracci than in that of Caravaggio. To such influences Frédeau adds a bizarre style all of his own, particularly noticeable in the very mannered ***Resurrected Christ Appearing to His Mother*** and in the disturbingly grotesque ***William of Toulouse Tormented by Demons***, which shows the face and eyes of the unfortunate protagonist being lacerated by claws. Antoine Rivalz, who was in Paris in 1685–87 and then spent 12 years in Rome, was the most conventional and prolific of the Toulouse painters. Most of his work in the Musée des Augustins, however, is not in the church, but in the main body of the museum.

In front of the W door of the church is a small cloister, the upper floor of which houses the museum's remaining foreign paintings. There is an amusing work by the Dutch Italianate painter Cornelisz van Haarlem (***Corruption of Men before the Flood***) and a van Dyck mythological scene (***Achilles Recognized by Ulysses at the Court of Lycomedes***). Otherwise the foreign holdings are strongest in 17thC and 18thC Italian works, including several fine pieces by Guido Reni, G.M. Crespi, Strozzi, Solimena, Guardi and Canaletto.

The greater part of the museum's collections are kept in the large building designed by Viollet-le-Duc to replace the refectory. For all the modernization that was undertaken in the building in the 1970s, the fantastical 19thC character of the place has been very well preserved. The interior, with its bare red-brick walls, enormous staircase well, and intentionally gloomy lighting, almost resembles a film set by Cecil B. de Mille.

On the ground floor are the museum's most famous treasures – a large group of very intricate and delicate **Romanesque capitals** from the cloisters of the churches of St-Sernin and Ste-Étienne. These are displayed on plinths made of rusted steel bars imitating classical lamp holders. Upstairs are two major rooms. One, now split into two levels, has on its lower level a large collection of 17thC French works, including a large ***Group Portrait*** by Philippe de Champaigne, a mythological scene by Mignard, and innumerable paintings by Toulouse artists. Many of the latter works were commissions from the town's *Capitouls*, for every new group of *Capitouls* had portraits of themselves done. The most impressive exhibited here is Jean Chalette's ***Christ on the Cross and the Capitouls of 1622–23***. The *Capitouls* also commissioned artists to decorate the town hall (or Capitole) with allegorical works flattering their wisdom and justice, and also scenes from Toulouse's history. There is a large group of such paintings in the museum by Antoine Rivalz, executed in a heroic, Italianate manner. A completely different side to Rivalz's art is revealed in a very realistic full-length genre piece entitled ***The Apothecary's Son***.

The most outstanding of the Toulouse paintings on show here – and in many ways the most interesting work in the whole museum – is Nicolas Tournier's ***Battle of the Roches Rouges (Victory of Constantine over Maxentius***★). This, his last known work, was originally hung, together with his ***Entombment*** and the museum's two large Vouet canvases, in the Toulouse Chapel of the Black Penitents. Once again the artist shows himself to have been greatly influenced by Caravaggio, yet he also seems to have derived inspiration from earlier Italian artists. The influence on him of Raphael's follower, Giulio Romano, has been suggested. The painting, however, has much more in common with the art of two 15thC Italian painters who were then completely out of fashion – Paolo Uccello and Piero della Francesca. In its selfconscious rendering of perspectival foreshortening, it calls to mind the former's various versions of the ***Rout of San Romano***; in its stylized simplifications it has something of the latter's ***Battle of Constantine*** in the church of San Francesco, Arezzo. Such similarities are probably fortuitous; but they point to the extreme originality of Tournier's art.

The upper level of the room is devoted to 18thC and early 19thC French paintings, and include good works by Jean François de Troy (a native of Toulouse who worked mainly in Paris), Pierre Henri de Valenciennes, Vigée le Brun, Baron Gros and the Baron Gérard. There is also a famous portrait by Ingres (***Sebastian Dermants★,***1805), which once belonged to Hitler. The late 19thC is represented principally by a **group of pastels** by Toulouse-Lautrec.

The other 19thC paintings in the museum are all hung in the main Viollet-le-Duc building. With characteristic imagination, the museum authorities have decided to abandon all conventional modern notions about the display of art, and have decided to emulate 19thC example and cover with paintings all the available wall space in this massive room. In doing this they have not only found an excellent solution to the problem of exhibiting all the museum's unfashionable Salon pictures, which would normally have languished in the reserve collections, but have also created the type of setting in which most of the works would originally have been seen. There is a large, famous painting by Delacroix (***Mulet-Abd-Ar-Rahman, Sultan of Morocco Surrounded by his Guards and Principal Officers***, 1845), an ***Ornans Landscape*** by Courbet, and a large ***Landscape*** by Corot. However it is pointless to single out individual works: it is the overall impression that counts, in this case one of sensuous Oriental scenes, obscure historical dramas, absurd allegories, and, above all naked bodies, all piled up on top of each other in glorious abandon.

Toulouse has other fine museums, although they are inevitably an anticlimax after the Musée des Augustins. The **Musée St-Raymond**, housed in a Viollet-le-Duc building opposite the Basilica of St-Sernin, has an excellent collection of **Romanesque carvings** from local churches, and reputedly the finest collection of **Roman Imperial busts** outside Italy. The **Musée Paul Dupuy**, also in the old part of the town, is devoted to applied arts from the Middle Ages to the present day. Both places are currently closed and in the process of modernization. In a quiet residential part of the town is the **Musée George Labit**, which is housed in a marvelous 19thC Moorish palace. The interior has been well modernized and contains a small but choice collection of **Egyptian and Oriental art**.

The Pilgrims' Way to Santiago de Compostela

The rise of pilgrimage places, one of the most striking features of medieval life, had its origins in the spread of Christianity. From an early stage certain virtues had been attached to the physical presence of holy men, and their relics were believed to retain something of the qualities of the saint in life. Remains were eagerly sought after, and a thriving trade developed in items which, though dubious, could make the reputation of a church or town. The most important pilgrimage center in Europe was undoubtedly the shrine of St James at Santiago de Compostela in Spain.

The cult of St James began in the early Middle Ages (c.9thC) and was based on the belief that the saint had preached in Spain before returning to Palestine, where he was martyred in AD44. The evidence for this is fairly thin, but the promoters of the cult were able to fill out the story by adding an essential last chapter, according to which the saint's body was miraculously returned to Spain in a boat without sails. The discovery of the burial site at Compostela and reports of miracles performed there made the shrine increasingly popular, until, in the 11thC, a new basilica had to be built to house and display the relics. By this time the Church encouraged pilgrimage, often as a penance, and the monks of Cluny felt it necessary to produce the *Liber Sancti Jacobi* (the Book of St James) otherwise known as the *Guide for the Pilgrims of Santiago.*

The information in this guide was indispensable to prospective pilgrims because it traced clear and reliable routes across hundreds of miles of unfamiliar territory. Unforeseen obstacles such as foul water, toll points, long distances between shelters, or the presence of robbers, could easily bring the medieval traveller to grief, so it is understandable that the routes should have become fixed and well trodden. The book identified four routes, each beginning in a different part of France: the Via Tolosana from Arles in Provence, the Auvergne route from Le Puy, a third route beginning at Autun or Vézelay in Burgundy, and a fourth linking Tours and Bordeaux (this could be extended to take in Chartres and Paris further N) All four came together at Roncevaux on the Spanish border, where they split again into two ways.

Pilgrims would gather at the four principal starting points, many having already travelled from much further afield, there to form groups for comfort and safety along the road. Churches and sanctuaries on the way provided regular staging posts for food and shelter, and also served a more profound purpose; for the pilgrimage was an act of faith, a spiritual exercise in which the journey itself included regular devotions to maintain religious fervour. Accordingly, the route was marked by the shrines of famous saints and martyrs, many of which were housed in buildings of unprecedented grandeur and beauty. The pilgrimage routes were lines of communication that masons and sculptors followed as well as pilgrims and churchmen, giving Romanesque France a unity that still allowed a variety of local styles.

The Via Tolosana began at the sacred sites in **ARLES** (the marble column of St Genest and the seven churches of the Alyschamps) and led on to **ST-GILLES**, where one of the greatest Provençal churches contained the miraculous remains of the saint in a magnificent golden sarcophagus. Past Montpellier the road took in the famous Abbey of St-Guilhem-du-Desert, founded by Charlemagne's lieutenant (part of the cloisters are now in the Metropolitan Museum in New York). The last main halt before crossing into Spain was the basilica over the tomb of St Sernin in **TOULOUSE**, a splendid

***Christ and the Evangelists**, Romanesque sculpture at St-Sernin church, Toulouse.*

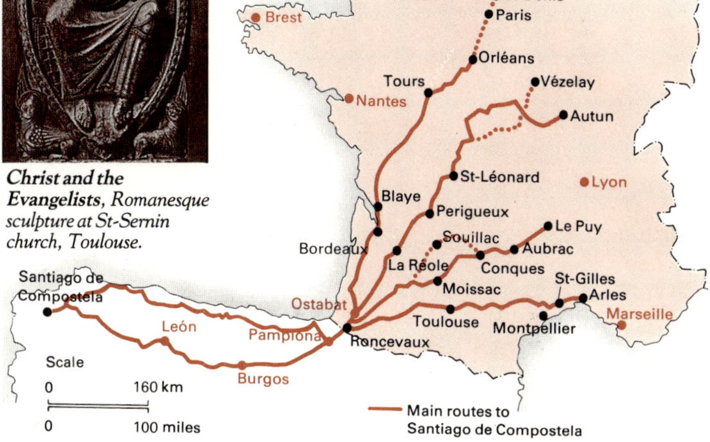

Romanesque building with some unusual relief sculpture of Christ and the Evangelists in the ambulatory.

The Auvergne route was thought to be the most hazardous, and there are stories that the great bell of the monastery at Aubrac was rung to guide pilgrims who might have lost their way at night. Nevertheless, this section does have some of the finest sights for travellers. Beginning at Notre-Dame in Le Puy, a building with unusual Islamic connections, the road proceeded to the celebrated Basilica of Ste Foy at **CONQUES**. One of the best preserved Romanesque buildings in existence, Conques was noted for its spring of pure water blessed by the power of Ste Foy. Its famous treasury included the gold figure of the saint, encrusted with precious stones and cameos, which is still in the cathedral collection. From here a spur in the road took in Rocamadour and Souillac before descending to the abbey church of St Pierre in Moissac.

The third route has the most spectacular beginning, with the two masterpieces of Burgundian Romanesque art; the cathedrals of Vézelay and Autun. Along this route the pilgrims would stop at St-Léonard (whose church was festooned with the chains of prisoners he had delivered from captivity), the church of St Front in Périgueux with its circular tomb, and the more modest churches of St Pierre at La Réole and St-Sever.

The fourth route linking up with Chartres, Paris and St-Denis began properly at Orléans, where the pilgrims could see the sacred chalice of St Euverte in the cathedral. At Tours the cathedral of St Martin had the most celebrated pilgrimage shrine in France, and the route continued through Poitou and Saintonge to pass other places of worship: St Hilaire in Poitiers, where the head of John the Baptist was venerated. St Eutrope, where the sick were cured, St Romain in Blaye, containing the grave of Charlemagne's paladin Roland, and St Seurin in **BORDEAUX**, with the ivory horn of the hero on display. The border pass near Roncevaux was marked by a huge cross erected, according to the legend, by Charlemagne.

CENTRAL FRANCE

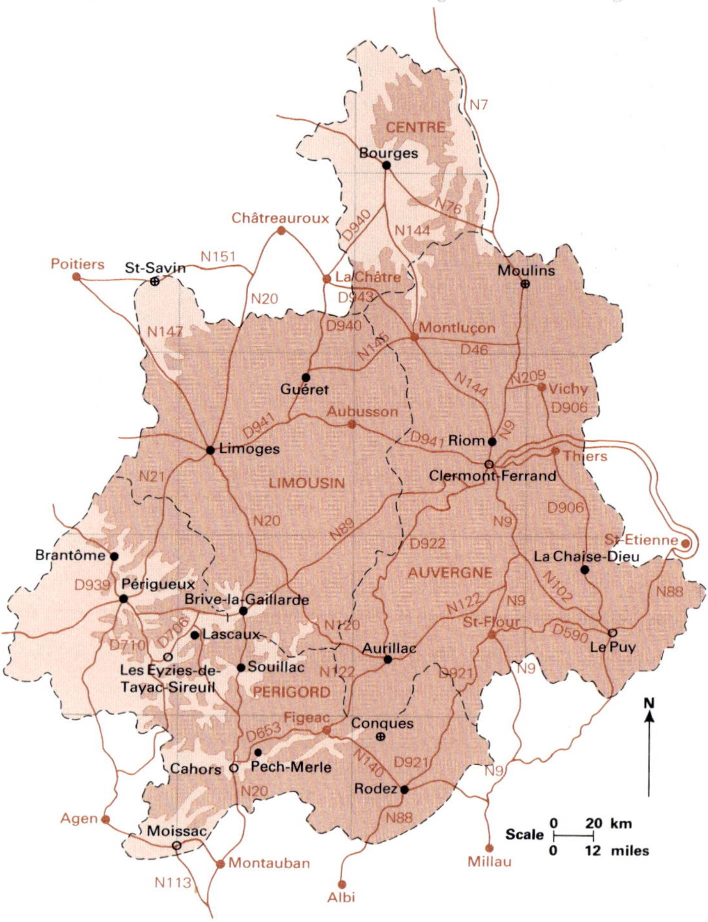

Culturally and historically, the most important regions in this section of the *Guide* lie to the north, in the area covered by the former duchies of Berry and Bourbon. In the late 14thC and 15thC respectively these places developed as thriving cultural centers, thanks to the patronage of the courts at **BOURGES** and **MOULINS**, which attracted some of France's major artists of the time. Jean de France, duc de Berry (1340–1416) commissioned a number of magnificent illuminated manuscripts, especially the Limbourg brothers' celebrated *Très Riches Heures du duc de Berry*. At Moulins Cathedral the wonderful *Virgin and Child* triptych (c.1498) by the so-called Master of Moulins carries portraits of his chief patrons, Peter II, duc de Bourbon, and his wife Anne de Beaujeu.

Going south, the landscape changes significantly. The plain of Bourges and the gently undulating countryside near Moulins give way to the high granite plateaux of the Limousin, the impressively mountainous countryside of the Dordogne, and the strange volcanic formations of the Massif Central. This is an enormous area but it has played a relatively minor role in French art and history: and much of it, for all its generally spectacular beauty, has been relatively little visited until quite recent times. The Dordogne has of course acquired of late enormous popularity, particularly among the British who buy up all its available *gîtes* or rural houses. The Massif Central is less well known, and many of the tourists who come here might well be pleasantly surprised not only by the haunting qualities of the landscape but also by the beauty of the towns. Few towns in Europe are so unusual in appearance as **LE PUY**, which is dominated by two enormous pinnacles of lava rock. The fascination of the north Auvergne towns of **RIOM** and **CLERMONT** is perhaps more unexpected: the former still remains the elegant place it became after the Duke of Berry was made also Duke of Auvergne; and the latter, for all its industrial associations, has an extraordinarily well preserved medieval center.

The artistic treasures discussed in this whole section are more scattered than those in any other area of France. Moreover not a single town here, not even Bourges or Moulins, can boast of having any truly important art gallery. There are none the less compensations for the artistically-minded traveller. The Dordogne is the most important place in the world for those interested in prehistoric art (see p. 224); and a visit to one of the region's numerous caves and rock shelters with prehistoric paintings and engravings can be a more exciting experience than seeing the objects of a purely archaeological interest that generally make up the prehistoric section of a museum.

The cave paintings of the area come from a time so long distant as to be almost unimaginable. But although the face of Europe was utterly different then, with Britain part of a continent that lay under ice and snow for much of the year, the lifestyles of the people who made the prehistoric art of the Dordogne may not have been vastly different from those of presentday hunter-gathering communities. The paintings were executed in deep caves which were not usually inhabited or put to everyday use, and it has been suggested that both the caves and the paintings were used for ritual purposes, possibly connected with sympathetic magic. However that may be, you cannot but be impressed by the skill of many of these artists of 20,000 years ago, working by the light of torches or animal-fat lamps, and drawing the strong and vivid figures by memory and without the aid of models.

Remarkable though these cave paintings are, the most impressive artistic feature of central France is the quality of the works of art belonging to its churches. Among these works are the ***Triptych of the Master of Moulins*** at Moulins, the 16th century tapestries at **LA CHAISE DIEU**, and the reliquary of Sainte-Foy at **CONQUES**, not to mention the countless **LIMOGES** enamelled objects and other fine examples of the medieval craftsman's art to be found in the many church treasuries throughout the area. In the case of the treasury at Conques – the greatest of these – the splendour of the objects is enhanced by the beauty of Conques itself, a high, remote village which has scarcely changed in appearance since the time when pilgrims passed through here on their way to Santiago de Compostela.

AURILLAC
Cantal, Auvergne Map C4

Aurillac is a largely modern and unattractive town, though it contains a pretty – but tiny – old quarter.

Musée Hippolyte de Parieu
Place de la Paix
Tel. (71) 484256
Open 10am–noon, 2–6pm
Closed Tues, Sun morning

The Musée Hippolyte de Parieu is housed on the third floor of a former barracks. The exterior of this building is singularly ugly, but fortunately the interior has been recently modernized, if not in an especially interesting way. Apart from some 17thC Italian works, the paintings are all of the French 18thC–20thC. Best among these is a small **oil sketch** by the landscapist de Valenciennes, a **portrait head** by Couture of the little known local painter M. Eloy Chapal, and a pallid portrait by Cabanel of a ***Mme. de C.*** (painted in Rome in 1858). Several **drawings** are on show, including slight works by Ingres, Delacroix, Corot and Redon. However, the painting which perhaps most catches the eye in the museum is an enormous, gruesome and clumsily composed painting by one Daniel Casey of ***St Hippolytus*** being pulled apart by horses.

BOURGES
Cher, Centre Map C1

Bourges's history dates back to before Roman times, for it was once the capital of a Celtic tribe known as the Bituriges. In the 14thC Duke Jean de Berry made it the capital of his dukedom and encouraged much artistic activity here, commissioning works from artists such as the Limbourg brothers and the sculptor André Beauneveu. Today it has become the commercial and industrial capital of the region, but retains a quiet, melancholy charm which has been beautifully described in certain passages of Fournier's novel, *Le Grand Meaulnes*.

Bourges is completely dominated by its **cathedral**, which can be seen from all over the town's surrounding plain. It was built mainly in the 13thC, and is one of the largest Gothic cathedrals in France, as well as one of the most beautiful. Its most striking feature is its interior, which has four side aisles instead of transepts, with narrow piers which soar high into a space flooded with light and colour emanating from a series of superb 13thC **stained-glass windows** in the chancel.

Palais Jacques Cœur
Rue Jacques Cœur
Tel. (48) 240687
Open Easter–Oct 9–11.15am, 2–5.15pm; Nov–Easter 10–11.15am, 2–4.15pm
Closed Tues

Bourges was the home town of the celebrated 15thC merchant, Jacques Cœur, Master of the Mint to Charles VII. His palace in Bourges was built for him between 1443 and 1453; but he was never to see it completed, being disgraced in 1451 and sent into permanent exile. It is an outstanding example of late Gothic secular architecture with an interior which though heavily restored is sumptuously decorated with fittings from this period. Eventually the paintings now kept in the reserve of the MUSÉE DU BERRY (see below) – which include works by Knupfer, Vouet, Tournier, Mignard and Lemoyne – will be moved here.

Musée du Berry
4, Rue des Arènes
Tel. (48) 704192
Open 10am–noon, 2–6pm
Closed Tues
(*Wed*)

The Musée du Berry occupies an elegant 16thC house built for a rich Florentine merchant called Durando Salvi. Its scanty and rather clumsily displayed collections are mainly of archaeological and ethnographic interest, although there are five fine **statues** of prophets executed between 1392–1401 by André Beauneveu and Jean de Cambrai for the now destroyed Sainte-Chapelle.

BRANTÔME
Dordogne, Aquitaine Map A4

Brantôme is a pretty and much visited small town hemmed in by an attractive wooded valley. Its principal monument is its **Benedictine abbey** on the willow-lined banks of the river Drôme. This was founded in the 8thC, but was substantially altered in the 11thC and 18thC. The most interesting survival from the 11thC building is the tall belfry which was built apart from the church upon a steep rock.

Musée Fernand Desmoulin
Square Pierre François Chabaneau
Tel. (53) 057021
Open Easter–Oct 10am–noon, 2–6pm
Closed Nov–Easter

In the part of the abbey building housing the town hall is to be found the Musée

Fernand Desmoulin. The museum came into existence in 1937 when the collections of the little known engraver Desmoulin were left to the town by his widow. As well as being an engraver, Desmoulin produced some amateurish and now flaking paintings while under the influence of a medium. These, a selection of Desmoulin's clumsy engravings, the odd piece of furniture, and some minor prehistoric remains constitute this dusty and justifiably neglected museum.

BRIVE-LA-GAILLARDE
Corrèze, Limousin Map B4

Brive-la-Gaillarde is a bustling, cheerful market town with a number of handsome old houses, notably the 16thC **Hôtel de Labenche** and the **Tour des Echevins**. Attractive tree-lined boulevards mark the outline of the former fortifications. The title *gaillarde* (sturdy) recognizes the qualities of the citizenry during many sieges.

Musée Ernest Rupin
15, Rue du Docteur Massenat
Tel. (55) 242137
Open Apr–Sept 10am–noon, 2–6pm; Oct–Mar 10am–noon, 2–5pm
Closed Sun

The Musée Ernest Rupin occupies one of the town's most attractive buildings, the 16thC–17thC former town residence of the priors of the Abbaye de Bonnesaigne. Its recently rearranged interior contains mainly archaeological collections, which are particularly rich in prehistoric finds. In addition there are fragments of medieval and Renaissance sculptures, a few crude religious paintings of this period, and ethnographic, numismatic and local history collections.

CAHORS
Lot, Midi-Pyrénées Map B5

Contained within a loop of the river Lot, Cahors is a quiet, beautiful place whose many surviving old monuments reflect its importance in the Middle Ages as a major university and commercial town. The most unusual of these medieval monuments is the 14thC **Pont Valentré**, a remarkable fortified bridge with three imposing towers. The town's other main monument, the **Cathédrale St-Etienne**, dates mainly from the 12thC and has a **tympanum** over the N door where you can see attractive 12thC carvings depicting the Ascension.

Musée Municipal
Rue Emile-Zola
Tel. (65) 351080
Open Apr–June 2–6pm; July–Sept 10am–noon, 2–6pm
Closed Oct–Mar, Sun

The municipal museum is housed in the former 18thC Archbishop's Palace and has varied though unremarkable collections, which include **prehistoric and Roman remains**, a few medieval and Renaissance **sculptures**, and a **painting** by Vlaminck.

LA CHAISE-DIEU
Haute-Loire, Auvergne Map D4

The village of La Chaise-Dieu, which is situated on a high, undulating plateau extensively covered with pine forests, is dwarfed by what was once one of France's greatest abbeys.

Eglise Abbatiale de St-Robert
Open Apr–May, Oct 10am–noon, 2–7pm; June–Sept 9am–noon, 2–7pm; Nov–Mar see caretaker

The Eglise abbatiale de St-Robert was founded in the 11thC, and suppressed in the Revolution. Its fortress-like church was erected in the 14thC on the command of a former monk of the abbey who became Pope Clement VI. Inside, in the choir, are some remarkable 16thC Brussels and Arras **tapestries**. These represent some of the scenes from the Old and New Testament that were included in the well-known medieval anthology, the *Bible of the Poor*: these works combine late Gothic fantasy with striking and often witty naturalistic detail. Also in the choir is a long and famous mural of the ***Dance of Death***: although much of the colour has now gone, this macabre depiction of skeletons taking away people from all walks of life retains great power.

CLERMONT-FERRAND
Puy-de-Dôme, Auvergne Map C3

Clermont-Ferrand comprises two rival towns which were amalgamated in the 17thC. Today it is the center of the vast Michelin tyre industry, and there is much unattractive development. Yet it is also a very lively place, which, moreover, can boast some of the most picturesque old quarters to be seen in any large French town. The part of the town which was originally Montferrand is crammed with elegant **15thC–17thC palaces**. More attractive still is the old district of

Clermont, which is built around the cone of one of the region's several former volcanoes (the most famous is the nearby **Puy de Dôme**). Here are steep narrow streets lined with beautiful medieval buildings, including the town's two most famous monuments, the **Basilique de Notre-Dame-du-Port** and the **Cathédrale Notre-Dame-de-l'Assomption.** The former is an outstanding Romanesque church with interesting but sadly damaged sculptures flanking the main door, and well-preserved carvings on the capitals of the choir. The cathedral, the bulk of which was built in the 13thC, replaces a Romanesque one: beautiful 12thC **stained-glass windows** from the former cathedral are to be seen in the ambulatory together with other fine windows ranging in date from the 13thC–15thC. Near the cathedral is a profusely ornamented early 16thC fountain – the **Fontaine d'Amboise** – built on a high terrace with superb views.

Musée du Ranquet

Petite Rue St-Pierre
Tel. (73) 373863
Open May–Sept 10am–noon, 2–6pm; Oct–Apr 10am–noon, 2–5pm
Closed Mon

The Musée du Ranquet (sometimes known as the Musée d'Histoire et d'Art Local) is in an attractive 16thC house right in the middle of Clermont's old quarter. Inside is a small but slightly congested display of largely unremarkable sculptures, decorative works and objects of historical interest. The best exhibits are the 11thC and 12thC **statuettes** of the ***Black Virgin*** on the ground floor. Upstairs there is pottery and furniture, and objects relating to the town's greatest son, the mathematician and moralist, Blaise Pascal.

Musée Bargoin

45, Rue de Ballainvilliers
Tel. (73) 913731
Open May–Sept 10am–noon, 2–6pm; Oct–Apr 10am–noon, 2–5pm
Closed Mon, Sun morning

The Musée Bargoin is just outside the old quarter. The building which now houses it was constructed between 1899–1903 thanks to the generosity of the local chemist, J.-B. Bargoin. The ground floor is mainly taken up by archaeological collections. However, the entrance hall is dominated by a large and impressive plaster **maquette** by Bartholdi showing Vercingétorix, leader of the Gauls, riding over a dead Roman soldier. It was either at Clermont or on the nearby Plateau de Gergovie that Vercingétorix defeated Caesar and thus temporarily brought the Roman advance on Gaul to a halt. The maquette by Bartholdi was intended for a 30m (33yd) high statue to be placed on the plateau itself.

Vercingétorix's victory is also the subject of an enormous canvas on the first floor by Chassériau which had a great success in the Universal Exhibition in Paris of 1855. This canvas is flanked by another of similar proportions by E. Devéria, representing ***Christopher Columbus being received by Ferdinand and Isabella*** (exhibited at the salon of 1861). Among other paintings on this floor are 12 interesting, anonymous early 17th C paintings once in the Château of Effiat (they show scenes from Ariosto's *Orlando Furioso*), a fine portrait of ***Vincent Voiture*** by Philippe de Champaigne, and an impressive ***View of Mont Dore*** by the late 19thC landscapist L.-G. Pelouse; however, these and other paintings in this part of the museum are frequently obstructed by crude temporary display boards featuring exhibits of local interest. The main part of the fine arts collection is on the second floor. The works are largely by relatively minor 19thC French artists, and include a large ***Quarry Scene at Fontainebleau*** by Caruelle d'Aligny, and a 19thC Salon painting by de la Foulhouse of the writer ***Musset being inspired by the Muses***. In addition there is an extensive if not especially good collection of **graphic work** by contemporary French artists such as de Segonzac, Léger, Matisse, Marquet, Lhôte, Braque and Picasso.

CONQUES

Aveyron, Midi-Pyrénées Map C5

The tiny village of Conques came into being as a result of an abbey that was founded here in the 4thC. This institution rose to fame in the 9thC when, according to legend, one of its monks stole the remains of Ste-Foy (Saint Faith), which were then guarded jealously at Agen, the scene of the young saint's martyrdom in c.303. In fact the relics were probably brought over to Conques for safekeeping at a time when much of southwestern France was suffering from Norman invasions. Following a spate of miracles reportedly caused by these relics, Conques became one of the major pilgrimage stops on the road to Santiago de Compostela (see p. 210), attracting various kings, princes and other nobles, who brought immense wealth to the abbey. Conques today is without doubt the most exciting medieval site in all central France. It has virtually everything: a spectacular position on the slopes of a steep hill above a gorge, an intact **medieval village** (admittedly somewhat over-restored in the 1970s), an outstanding **Romanesque church**, and one of the most celebrated **treasuries** in Europe. Fortunately its remoteness and the perilous, winding roads that lead to it have prevented the place from being overrun by tourists, putting it out of the reach of all but the most determined.

Eglise Ste-Foy

🏛

The tall 11thC–12thC church is all that remains of the abbey, which was devastated during the 16thC Wars of Religion. In the 19thC even the church itself, which was then suffering from over 300yrs of neglect, was almost pulled down. Only the intervention of the writer Prosper Merimée, who was in charge of inspecting historical monuments in south and central France, succeeded in saving it.

The building has been excellently restored, and is virtually as it was when first built. On the W portal you will see a superb 12thC tympanum of the ***Last Judgment*** ★ with many curious and amusing details. Look in particular for the **Hell scenes**, where, for instance, a devil points to an inscription on a parchment accusing a man and a woman underneath of fornication. Further carvings appear on many of the **capitals** inside the church. In the choir, where Ste Foy's relics were originally exposed, are some very fine **metal gates**, supposedly forged from the chains of prisoners whom the saint had released from the Moors. The relics themselves are now kept in the treasury which occupies part of the nearby presbytery.

Trésor de Conques ☆☆

Eglise Ste-Foy
Tel. (65) 698512
Open Easter–Oct 9am–noon, 2–6pm; Nov–Easter 10am–noon, 2–6pm

The famous treasury is housed in a small darkened room exhibiting a variety of reliquaries and other examples of *ars sacra* from the 9thC–16thC. The earliest and one of the finest of these objects is the early 9thC **Reliquary of Pepin**, which was given to the Abbey of Conques by Pepin II, the son of Louis the Pious (king of Aquitaine 817–838). It is made of wood covered with gold leaf and set with precious stones and translucent enamels. But the main reason for visiting the Treasury is to see the **Reliquary of Ste Foy★★**, which is spotlighted in a niche at the end of the room. This portrays the saint enthroned in majesty, and is made of wood covered with plaques of gold and gilded silver adorned with cloisonné enamels, precious stones and other pieces of jewelry. Although essentially designed in the early 10thC, it is in fact a composite work with bits and pieces from different periods: the head, possibly dating from the 4thC, may be that of a Celtic god or goddess; the crown, earrings, throne and ceratin band of filigree are of the late 10thC; the Gothic waistband is of the 14thC; and the forearms and hands are of the 16thC. Successive generations of pilgrims made their own contribution by attaching the various other ornamentations, which include antique cameos and intaglios of Egyptian, Greek, Roman and Byzantine origin.

LES EYZIES-DE-TAYAC-SIREUIL

Dordogne, Aquitaine Map A4

The village of Les Eyzies, attractively situated in a wooded river valley hemmed in by imposing stratified cliffs, is generally known as the **'capital of prehistory'**. For it was here, and in the surrounding district, that, in the mid 19thC, the first systematic attempts were made to study prehistoric man. There are countless caves and rock shelters in the vicinity, many of which have **prehistoric paintings, drawings** and **engravings** (see p. 224): among the more impressive are the Abri du Cap-Blanc, the Grotte des Combarelles, the Grotte de Font-de Gaume, the Grotte de la Mouthe, and the Abri du Poisson.

Musée National de Préhistoire

Château de Beynac
Tel. (53) 069703
Open Mar–Nov 9.30am–noon, 2–6pm; Dec–Feb 9.30am–noon, 2–5pm

The Musée National de Préhistoire is situated at the top of the village in the remains of a 13thC castle built under an overhanging cliff. This is perhaps the finest museum of prehistory in Europe, and its collections are accompanied by very helpful information panels, charts, diagrams and maps. To obtain some idea of prehistoric chronology, the visitor is strongly recommended to follow the itinerary marked out by arrows. The collections include numerous bones, flints, tools and other such items of purely archaeological interest. Much more fascinating – and also special to the region – are the many stones with **engravings** and **bas-reliefs** of animals, and the crude **statuettes** of human figures (mainly fertility goddesses).

GUÉRET
Creuse, Limousin Map B3

Guéret is a largely modern town with few surviving old monuments. One of these is the 18thC Hôtel des Moneyroux which is in the middle of a delightful flower garden. The building now houses the municipal museum.

Musée Municipal
Avenue de la Sénatorerie
Tel. (55) 520720
Open mid-June to mid-Sept 9.45am–12.15pm, 2–6.30pm; mid-Sept to mid-June 10am–noon, 2–5pm
Closed Tues

The ground floor of this pleasantly arranged museum contains 500 **dolls** dressed in local and national costumes, and **arms and armour**. The walls of the staircase leading to the first floor are lined with 17thC **Aubusson tapestries**. Upstairs are the museum's greatest treasures, a group of 12thC–15thC **Limoges enamels**, including an outstanding **processional cross** and some fine **pyxes**, or vessels where the sacramental host or bread is kept. In addition the museum has painted **enamels** from the 15thC onwards, an extensive collection of **ceramics** from different parts of France and even from Renaissance Italy, a gallery of local 15thC–18thC sculptures and a small painting collection. Although many of the paintings are indifferent 17thC and 18thC Flemish and Dutch works, there are some fine **French paintings** from the 17thC onwards by such artists as Le Sueur, Fantin-Latour, Odilon Redon and Pascin. The **graphic work** in the museum is mainly of the French 19thC and 20thC schools. There is a **drawing** by Ingres, pastels by Chéret, **watercolours** by Delacroix and Jongkind and no less than 100 drawings by an artist whom most regular visitors to French provincial museums would surely prefer to forget, Maurice Marinot.

LASCAUX
Dordogne, Aquitaine Map B4

The Lascaux caves, the most famous **prehistoric caves** in France and containing celebrated pictures of animals, were discovered by a group of local boys in 1940. They were opened to the public in 1948, but had to be closed in 1963 after the breath of countless tourists had begun to destroy the transparent mineral deposit which had preserved the paintings so well for 25,000yrs. At present an exact replica of the caves is being undertaken; but for the moment the visitor will have to make do with the film about the caves shown in the summer months at the entrance.

LIMOGES
Haute-Vienne, Limousin Map B3

Limoges is a characterless industrial town internationally famous for its **porcelain and enamel works**. The first porcelain factory was established here in 1736; a later factory was acquired by Louis XVI in 1784 with the intention that it should produce plain white ware for decoration at Sèvres. Limoges porcelain came eventually to resemble a simpler version of the Sèvres type. Today half the porcelain made in France originates in Limoges, which has a reputation for its lower-priced table wares. The Limoges enamel industry has a much larger and artistically important history, which began in the mid 12thC, when the town's enamel workshops were founded and soon came to rival those of the Meuse valley. Enamelling is the application of a vitreous substance to a metal surface. There are three main types. The *champlevé* technique is the pouring of enamel into grooves engraved into the silver, bronze or copper object to be decorated. In *cloisonné* works a network of metal bands placed on the surface of the object take the place of these grooves. The third technique – the painting of coloured enamel on to the surface – was invented in Limoges in the late 15thC since when it has been the most popular enamelling technique throughout Europe, and the one practised almost exclusively in Limoges today.

Limoges has few old architectural monuments of interest, apart from the 12thC–16thC **Cathédrale St-Etienne** which dominates a hill in the oldest surviving part of the town. Inside, in the chancel, is the mid 16thC **tomb of Jean de Langeac**, which has 14 lively and delicately carved scenes of the life of John the Baptist. Two other tombs commemorating church dignitaries are also interesting. Adjoining the cathedral is the 18thC **Archbishop's Palace**, which has an elegant terraced garden with good views down to the river Vienne. The building itself houses the town's municipal museum.

Musée Municipal

Place de la Cathédrale
Tel. (55) 337010 Ext. 575
Open June–Sept 10–11.45am, 2–6pm; Oct–May 10–11.45am, 2–5pm
Closed Tues (except July–Sept)

The Musée Municipal is a rather forlorn place, and with good reason. In January 1981, its most outstanding exhibits, a group of medieval Limoges enamels, were all stolen. Although recent guides to Limoges are tactfully silent on this point, it is only fair to warn prospective visitors that the general feeling is that these works will never be recovered. One wonders for how long the museum authorities will continue to show photographs of the lost objects in the cases reserved for them. Some medieval enamels remain, but these are all slight and third-rate works. However there is still an extensive collection of 15thC–20thC **enamels**, most of which are decorated by the painted technique. These include a number of pieces by Limoges' leading Renaissance enameller, Leonard Limosin, and others of the 17thC and 18thC by members of the Laudin family.

The rest of the museum contains a strange mixture of mainly mediocre objects ranging from a large collection of Egyptian mummies to badly displayed Gallo-Roman pots and 18thC and 19thC French paintings, mostly of local interest. The only paintings worth noting are a **portrait** by Jean Nattier, a large, unfinished **Fontainebleau landscape** by Théodore Rousseau, and two works by the greatest painter to have been born in Limoges, Pierre-Auguste Renoir. Renoir's family left Limoges when the artist was only four, but his Limoges background led him to begin his career as a painter of porcelain. The two works by this very variable artist do not do him justice: one is an early and very dark portrait (influenced by Manet) of ***Mme le Coeur*** (1866); the other, the better of the two, is a pleasant but unexciting portrait of the actress ***Colonna Romano***.

Musée National Adrien-Dubouché

Place Winston-Churchill
Tel. (88) 774558
Open 10am–noon, 1.30–5pm
Closed Tues

Limoges' other main museum, the Musée Adrien Dubouché, occupies an enormous and pompous late 19thC building in a now largely modern part of the town. Dubouché was a major collector and patron of the applied arts and founded the museum named after him, together with a school of applied arts, in 1867. The museum is devoted almost entirely to **porcelain**, and is the largest museum of its kind in France after the museum at Sèvres. All its objects are well displayed with helpful information panels; but the place lacks the warmth necessary to fire the hearts of those who feel that ceramics are best appreciated when eaten off or at least shown in more homely and domestic settings than this. The museum's coverage of styles and periods in porcelain is almost encyclopaedic, with virtually every major school of porcelain in France and elsewhere represented.

MOISSAC

Tarn-et-Garonne, Midi-Pyrénées
Map A5

The former Benedictine Abbey at Moissac was in the early Middle Ages one of the most important in southwestern France, being attached in the 11thC to the former Abbey of Cluny (see ***EASTERN FRANCE***). Today only the **Romanesque abbey church** (much altered in the 15thC) and its cloister survive; and even these only narrowly escaped being pulled down in the 19thC to make way for the Bordeaux–Sète railway. The S doorway of the church is covered in outstanding **carvings★** executed between 1100–30. The tympanum, which represents the ***Vision of the Apocalypse***, has a heavy, static quality, and is in fact very different from the contemporary tympana of Vézelay and Autun, which are more fluently and expressively carved. The ***24 Old Men of the Apocalypse*** are represented on the lintel, which is supported by three piers, the central one of which is made out of a single block of stone and contains the figures of two old men and three entwined lions. The two side piers – which have figures of ***Isaiah*** and ***St Peter***, the patron saint of the abbey – are scalloped as in Hispano–Moorish buildings: such an influence can be explained by the fact that Moissac was on one of the most frequented routes to Santiago de Compostela (see p. 210). Further **carvings★** dating from the end of the 11thC are to be seen on the capitals of the enchanting cloister, which is dominated by a gigantic cedar tree.

MOULINS

Allier, Auvergne Map C2

Moulins was, in the Middle Ages and early Renaissance, the capital of the independent Duchy of Bourbon, which, in the 15thC, under the reigns of Charles I, John II, and Peter II and his wife Anne of France, came to attract numerous musicians and artists. Among these were the Flemish composer Ockeghem and one of France's finest painters of this period, the so-called Master of Moulins. Now a bustling market town, Moulins has a small old quarter closely hugging the **cathedral**. The nave and W façade of this building are 19thC: the choir, however, which formed part of an old collegiate church, was built between 1474–1507, and has some excellent late 15thC **stained-glass windows**, including one (in the NE corner) showing ***Peter II and Anne of France worshipping St Catherine of Alexandria***. A passage leading off from the choir takes you to the **treasury** (*open 9am–noon, 2–6pm; closed Tues*), which contains the celebrated ***Triptych of the Master of Moulins*** ★★ (c.1498) together with two later triptychs, some 16thC painted enamels, and 18thC and 19thC liturgical ornaments. The room is darkened, and you have to wait while each of these latter works is spotlit in turn and discussed in a tape-recorded commentary. Just as patience is beginning to wear thin, the light is directed to the triptych itself, which is shown initially with its shutters closed; on the back of these is a monochromatic representation of the ***Annunciation***. When the shutters are finally opened, the spectator almost reels back under the shock of the triptych's vivid colours, in particular the crimsons of the draperies. The main panel shows the ***Enthroned Virgin and Child*** surrounded by angels; on the two side panels the kneeling figures of ***Peter II and Anne of France*** in the company of their patron saints are represented with marvellous naturalism. The Master of Moulins, who was clearly strongly influenced by Flemish painters such as Hugo van der Goes, has been variously identified as Jean Pérreal (the court painter to the Bourbons), Jean Prévost (a Lyonnais painter who collaborated with Pérreal), and, most recently, a Flemish painter, Jean Hay. Among other works generally attributed to the artist is ***The Nativity with Cardinal Jean Rolin*** in the Rolin Museum at Autun (see ***EASTERN FRANCE***).

Musée du Moulins

Place du Colonel Laussedat
Tel. (70) 442298
Closed for restoration

The main surviving part of the ducal castle is the austere ***donjon*** which faces the cathedral's W façade. On the other side of a small square to these two buildings is the **Pavillon d'Anne de Beaujeu** which was built by Peter II and Anne I of France as an additional wing to the pavilion. Of the original architecture only the handsome entrance porch and gallery of the main façade survive; the rest is 19thC. The pavilion now houses the local museum, which has been closed for several years and is likely to remain so for some time. Its archaeological and applied arts collections include an important group of Gallo-Roman **terra cotta figurines**, Limoges **enamels**, Moulins and other French pottery, **tapestries** and local alabasters. Among the **paintings** are some German works of the 15thC and 16thC most notably **retables** attributed to Michael Pacher and the Master of Wittenheim, and panels by Lucas Cranach. There are also 17thC and 18thC Flemish and Dutch works, and works by 19thC French Salon painters such as Gérôme, Meissonier and Cabanel.

PECH-MERLE

Lot, Midi-Pyrénées Map B5

The caves at Pech-Merle, which were rediscovered in 1922 by two 14yr old boys, contain some **prehistoric paintings**, including horses, as well as hand imprints.

Grotte du Pech-Merle

Caves open Easter–Sept 9am–noon, 2.30–6pm; Oct Mon–Sat 10am–11am, 3–4.30pm

The guided tour around these caves seems interminable; and it is certainly a relief to emerge again into the fresh air and enjoy the wonderful and extensive views of the surrounding wooded and mountainous countryside. There is a modern museum near the entrance to the caves which has good and informatively displayed collections of **prehistoric finds** from the area. The price of admission includes seeing a rather uninformative film about prehistoric art.

PÉRIGUEUX

Dordogne, Aquitaine Map A4

Périgueux, the capital of the Dordogne, was in Roman times one of the finest cities in Aquitaine. Its subsequent history was a very troubled one. Destroyed by Alemans in the 3rdC AD, it was later plundered by the Visigoths, Franks and Normans. In the Middle Ages it was one of the first towns in this part of France to answer the call of the French King

Charles V to take up arms against the English. Shortly afterwards the townsfolk entered into protracted warfare with their overlord, Count Archambaud V, who openly betrayed the king. In the 17thC the town was besieged and much damaged by the rebels known as the Frondeurs. Today the place is a rather sprawling market and industrial town which has managed to retain some sad traces of its former **Roman arena**, and a substantial old quarter, a good part of which is taken up by the enormous **Cathédrale St-Front**. This domed Byzantine-style building with a ground plan in the form of a Greek cross, was completed c.1173; it subsequently lost much of its original character after repeated restoration, culminating in the 19thC when a thorough reconstruction was undertaken by the insensitive architect Abadie. The exterior with its five white domes and four-storeyed belfry still remains intriguing; but the cavernous interior is especially bleak and uninviting.

Musée du Périgord

22 Cours Tourny
Tel. (53) 531642
Open 10am–noon, 2–5pm
Closed Tues

The Musée du Périgord, a few minutes walk from the cathedral, occupies a former Augustinian monastery which was converted into a museum in the late 19thC. Its principal treasures are its extensive **archaeological and ethnographic collections**, most notably an important group of prehistoric finds and some fine Gallo-Roman **mosaics**. The most striking painting in the small fine arts section of the museum is the crude but powerful **diptych** from Rabastens (dated 1286) by an anonymous local artist. Among the later paintings are a ***St John the Baptist and St Paul*** by Luis Morales, still-lifes and flower-pieces by the 17thC Dutch artist Jan Davidsz. de Heem and a **religious canvas** by Luca Giordano. The French holdings are mainly of the 18thC and 19thC and include a **still-life** by Oudry, and **landscapes** by Isabey and Décamps. Standing out among the handful of 20thC works are a **Honfleur scene** by Othon Friesz and a vivid oil sketch by van Dongen of a celebrated Périgueux society hostess, ***Mademoiselle Berrand***.

LE PUY

Haute-Loire, Auvergne Map D4

A market town known since the 17thC for its lace industries, Le Puy has a most extraordinary appearance. It lies on what was once the bed of an enormous lake, and is dominated by two tall and almost vertical pinnacles of lava rock thrust up by volcanic upheavals which also emptied the lake. The fascinating **old quarter** rises up on a rather more gentle volcanic mound crowned by a large Byzantine-inspired 12thC **cathedral**. In the sacristy of this is a **treasury** containing among other religious objects of later date the famous **Carolingian Theodolph Bible**, written on purple and white vellum. A path behind the cathedral leads up to one of the pinnacles, on top of which is a bronze statue of the ***Virgin Mary*** (which can be climbed) built in 1860 from cannons captured in the seige of Sebastopol. The other pinnacle lies beyond this and is capped by a small, delightful 11thC church, reached by 268 steps carved into the rock.

Musée Crozatier ☆

Jardin Vinay
Tel. (71) 093890
Open May–Sept 10am–noon, 2–6pm; Oct–Apr 10am–noon, 2–4pm
Closed Feb, Tues, Sun morning (Oct–Apr)

The Musée Crozatier is in a 19thC building in a large park to the S of the old quarter. The ground floor has collections of archaeology and local history, as well as a group of 19thC sculptures, including some rather dull Neoclassical ones by the locally-born Pierre Jullien (1731–1804). The first floor is devoted mainly to pottery and local crafts. The large room contains a display of **lace** based on a donation to the town made by the director of a local lace factory. It was the first of its kind in France, and remains the museum's greatest attraction to tourists. The far less visited **painting collection** on the second floor should nonetheless not be avoided. Among all the various mediocre 16thC–19thC works are paintings by two fascinating but little known local artists, Guy François and Charles Maurin. François was born in Le Puy c.1579, and was in Rome from about 1608–13, where he fell heavily under the influence of the leading Italian Baroque painters; the rest of his life was spent mainly in Le Puy, apart from a (probable) stay in Toulouse c.1623–26. He has been little studied, and there has been much confusion between his works, those of his son Jean and of another completely unrelated Guy François. Among the works generally ascribed to him in the Crozatier museum is the heavily restored but superb work, ***The Rosary*** (1619), which shows the virgin giving the rosary to St Dominic. In the foreground, the dog with a candle in his mouth symbolizes the Dominican order and signifies fidelity and faith. The work has a striking naturalism, though more akin to that of Annibale Carracci than to that of Caravaggio. His ***Apparition of the Virgin to St Félix de Cantalice*** has in contrast affinities with work by Toulouse artists such as Tournier, having some of the dark and dramatic characteristics of the art of Caravaggio, while at the same time retaining an ethereal elegance.

Charles Maurin was born in Le Puy in 1856, and went to study in Paris in 1870 at the Ecole des Beaux-Arts and the Académie Julien. Here he enjoyed the friendship and criticism of Vallotton and Toulouse-Lautrec, who probably influenced him in his development of a very linear and illustrative style. His best works are his bizarre symbolical fantasies, most notably two parts of a triptych now in the museum of St-Etienne. Shortly after breaking his friendship with Vallotton and Toulouse-Lautrec, he gave up painting altogether and turned to graphic work. He returned c. 1904 to Le Puy, and there started up a small art school where he eccentrically made his students copy his own works. During his years in Paris he achieved only moderate success, and died in complete obscurity in Grasse in 1914. There are three works by him in Le Puy, a naturalistic **study of a woman removing a flea from her breast**, a rather kitsch fantasy entitled ***Prelude to Lohengrin***, and a haunting ***Maternity*** ★ which has something of the power of the Ste-Etienne works (see St-Etienne ***SOUTH FRANCE***): it portrays various images of maternity surrounding a woman who is unable to have children.

RIOM

Puy-de-Dôme, Auvergne Map C3

Riom became capital of the Auvergne in the 13thC. Its importance increased after 1360 when the Duke of Berry was made Duke of Auvergne as well, and had a palace built here. In the 17thC the rapidly growing rival town of Clermont-Ferrand superseded Riom as the administrative center of the region. While Clermont-Ferrand continued to grow into the large town which it now is, Riom remained almost in a time warp. Today it is a small, quiet and remarkably well-preserved town, full of beautiful 14thC–17thC houses. Although the Ducal Palace has been replaced by the present 19thC Palais de Justice, the 14thC **Sainte-Chapelle** belonging to the duke has remained; inside are some excellent **stained-glass windows**. Riom, now often referred to as a 'Ville des Arts', has various other treasures, most notably, in **Notre-Dame-du-Marthuret**, ***The Virgin with a Bird***, a graceful and very naturalistic carving of the Virgin and child with a fluttering bird.

Musée Mandet

Rue de l'Hôtel de Ville
Tel. (73) 381853
Open summer 10am–noon, 2–5.30pm; winter 10am–noon, 2–4.30pm
Closed Mon (winter), Tues

Opposite the Sainte-Chapelle is the Musée Francisque Mandet which is housed in two adjoining buildings, both of which have just been superlatively renovated. The larger of the two – the 17thC Hôtel Chabrol-Volvic, contains the museum's paintings. These have all been well restored and are beautifully displayed in spacious elegant rooms; sadly, however, they are of little interest. The works attributed to such major artists as Frans Hals are in fact bad contemporary copies. Only minor Dutch and Flemish 17thC artists of the likes of Backer, Ykens and Brekelenkam are represented. The French holdings are marginally better, with adequate works by Raoux, Vien and Colin. The one painting which stays in the memory is a large Munch-like picture (1882) of a **family at the bed of a dead child**: it is by a Norwegian painter, Hans Olaf Heyerdahl, who was a pupil of Bonnat's in Paris between 1878–82. The other half of the museum, reached by crossing a small garden, is in the 17thC–18thC Hôtel Desaix. Here one finds a good **applied arts collection** recently donated to the town by a local barrister, Edouard Richard. This collection is very varied, and ranges from **classical marbles** and bronzes to medieval and **Renaissance enamels** and 17thC and 18thC gold and silverwork. A good proportion of the objects were locally made.

RODEZ

Aveyron, Midi-Pyrénées Map C5

If you are driving from Central France down to the South, Rodez marks a significant turning-point: the verdant mountains of the Dordogne give way to the arid plateaux of the Causses. Rodez itself stands in between these two regions on a steep hill dominated by an enormous 13thC–16thC **cathedral** which can be seen from miles around. The austere and largely unornamented lower half of the building's W façade resembles a fortress and did indeed form part of the town's now vanished ramparts. By contrast the top half of this façade, like that of the beautiful belfry, is in a profusely decorated style with late Gothic and early Renaissance detailing. Among the treasures inside the building is an elaborate 17thC wooden **organ loft**, and – in the third chapel to the right of the nave – a **Renaissance altar** with an outstanding 16thC **stone retable** of the Holy Sepulchre. The **old quarter** around the cathedral is very attractive with some fine 14thC–16thC houses.

Musée Fenaille

Rue St-Just
Open July–Aug 10am–noon, 2.30–6pm
Closed Sept–June, Mon, Sun

The Musée Fenaille is in the 14thC–16thC Hôtel Jouery, which is formed of two adjoining houses, and has a beautiful Renaissance courtyard. The collections comprise mainly prehistoric and Gallo-Roman finds, but there are some local 15thC–16thC sculptures.

Musée Denys-Puech

Place du Musée
Tel. (65) 680700 (Mairie)
Open July–Oct 9–11am, 2–5pm
Closed Sun

The Musée Denys-Puech, which is just outside the town's old quarter, was built in 1908 largely to house the sculpture of Denys-Puech. This artist was born in the nearby town of Gavenac in 1854, had a successful career in the Paris Salons, and was for a while the director of the French Academy at the Villa Medici in Rome. He was a relatively unadventurous artist who worked principally in an Art Nouveau manner: apart from his pieces in the museum, there are various other monuments by him in the town, most notably a **war memorial**. The museum has other works besides his, ranging from optimistically attributed Italian, Flemish and Dutch works from the 16thC to 18thC to a collection of slight **works** by important modern artists such as Braque, Lhôte, Picabia and Vlaminck. There are also sculptures by Denys-Puech's contemporaries including Despiau – and some appalling paintings by local 19thC and 20thC artists.

ST-SAVIN
Vienne, Poitou-Charentes Map A2

The unspoilt village of St-Savin is dominated by its former **abbey church**★ which rises from the peaceful, wooded banks of the river Gartrempe. This building, which is best seen from the village's picturesque **medieval bridge**, is all that remains of a large abbey which was destroyed during the Hundred Years War and the 16thC Wars of Religion. The 11thC–12thC church has – apart from the addition of its spire in the 14thC – remained miraculously almost as it was when first built. It is one of the finest Romanesque churches in France, with among the best and most extensive **fresco cycles**★ from this period to be seen anywhere in Europe. Frescoed scenes of the Apocalypse decorate the narthex. The greatest frescoes, however, are on the ceiling of the nave. These are all of Old Testament subjects including ***The Creation***, ***The Flood*** and ***The Crossing of the Red Sea*** – and are painted with extraordinary vitality. The nave is superb, comprising tall unfluted columns, painted to stimulate different types of marble, supporting a barrel vault. The overall impression is one of great light and serene colour.

SOUILLAC
Lot, Midi-Pyrénées Map B4

A characterless market town and tourist center, Souillac was the site of a Benedictine Abbey which was plundered during the Hundred Years War and Wars of Religion. Of the Abbey only the church remains, which now takes the place of the destroyed parish church dedicated to St-Martin. The domed building is in the style of the Romanesque-Byzantine cathedrals of PÉRIGUEUX, ANGOULÊME and CAHORS. The façade was rebuilt in the 17thC, but its 12thC **door and surrounding sculptures** were kept and placed facing the inside of this bleak church. Above are sculpted scenes from the life of the monk Theophilus, Deacon of Adna and Cilicia. Much more impressive are the two animated bas-reliefs of the prophets ***Isaiah***★ and ***Joseph*** which flank the main door.

Prehistoric Art of the Dordogne

The retreat of the Ice Age during the so-called Upper Palaeolithic period, some 40,000 years ago, left a large sheltered region stretching from the river Charente in central France to the Cantabrian mountains in northern Spain. The greatest examples of prehistoric art in the world are to be found here, and in particular in the Dordogne. About 50 of the 1,200 caves in the Dordogne seem to have been inhabited, and 25 contain examples of prehistoric art.

The richest concentration of prehistoric finds is in the valley of the Vézère, the main village of which, Les Eyzies-de-Tayac, is often referred to as the capital of prehistory. It was from here, in 1863, that two distinguished antiquarians, the Frenchman E. Lartet and the Englishman H. Christy, began to make a systematic exploration of the area's caves and rock shelters. However, the first cave in the Vézère valley to reveal traces of art on its walls was La Mouthe just outside Les Eyzies, which came to light in 1895 when a family was enlarging its wine cellar. This is a narrow, slippery cave which is not lit by electric light, and it is difficult for the layman to decipher its various line drawings of animals. The nearby caves of Font de Gaume and Les Combarelles were both first explored in the early years of this century. The former contains the finest cave paintings in the Dordogne apart from those at Lascaux, but, unlike the latter, they can be seen by tourists, which has resulted in recent deterioration of the colours. Les Combarelles has engravings of a wide variety of animals – including a giraffe and a lion.

The three main Dordogne caves outside the Vézère valley are at Rouffignac, Pech-Merle and Moissac. The cave at Rouffignac was known in the 18thC, but not the significance of the various marks on one of the walls here, which are regarded as some of the earliest examples of cave art in the

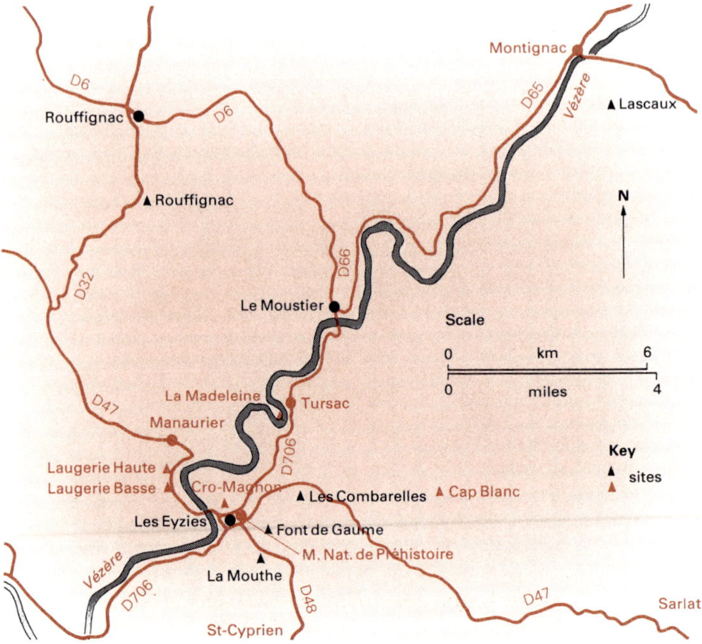

Stone carving of deer and fish, Les Eyzies, c. 15,000 BC

region. Another part of the cave was not discovered until 1956, and has some good, later paintings of animals. Pech-Merle was discovered in 1922 by some boys whose curiosity had been excited by lectures on prehistoric art given by a local priest, the Abbé Lemozzi. The cave at Lascaux, which was found eighteen years later, was also first explored by boys, in this case by ones who had heard from an old woman that the cave led to a nearby medieval castle. The freshness of the colours of the paintings here (the result of special atmospherical and geological conditions) made many sceptics feel that the paintings were a hoax, particularly in the early 1950s after a strange incident involving the surrealist writer André Breton. Breton, while visiting Pech-Merle, decided on impulse to touch one of the paintings, and was duly reprimanded; he had nonetheless made important discovery that some of the paint had come off on his finger. It was much later scientifically proved that the paint had remained fresh over the centuries because of the dampness of the cave's air.

Attempts have been made to date prehistoric art, in some cases on the dubious basis of stylistic analysis. It is generally assumed that the earliest examples of prehistoric art are the hand prints such as are to be found at Pech-Merle and Font-de-Gaume. These were made by blowing pigment from a hollow tube against an outspread hand: this spray-gun-cum-stencilling technique is still used by the Australian aborigines.

Almost all the major cave paintings and engravings are to be found in cave sites that would have been too deep for habitation. That they were executed so far down in the earth suggests some religious significance. The most likely explanation is that as prehistoric man lived largely from hunting, it was considered that the portrayal of animals (which constitutes by far the most common subject of cave art) served as some form of sympathetic magic whereby an animal would be killed simply by representing it. The hand prints that surround the animal at Pech-Merle might be intended to further the idea of human possession.

Only very occasionally are humans represented in cave art. One scene at Lascaux shows a man apparently falling under a bison. A number of carved female figures have also been found in the area, the most famous of which is the so-called Venus of Laussel (now in the Archaeological Museum at ***BORDEAUX***). The sexual attributes of this and other such works are greatly exaggerated which suggests that the figures are probably fertility symbols.

SOUTH OF FRANCE

This section of the *Guide*, which includes the most visited areas of France outside Paris, is dominated in its north-eastern part by the Alps. In the 19thC the peaks, lakes, waterfalls and extensive forests of this region had an obvious appeal to the artists of the Romantic generation, including the English painter, Turner, and later developed into one of the most thriving tourist resorts in Europe, remaining to this day exceptionally popular despite countless electricity pylons, ski lifts, wooden chalets and ugly residential blocks. The independent duchies of Savoie and Dauphiné once occupied the region, with the former extending from Lyon to Nice and across to Turin (now in Italy), and only becoming part of France after 1860. French Savoie, however, has little of artistic interest apart from a small museum at **CHAMBÉRY** filled with mainly Italian works, and another at **AIX-LES-BAINS** devoted to the Impressionists. The Dauphiné, which was amalgamated with France in the 14thC, is for the most part equally barren artistically; but its former capital, Grenoble, is a lively university and commercial town with an art gallery that, in addition to owning some outstanding 17thC paintings, was the first French regional museum to take a serious interest in contemporary art.

At the N end of the Rhone valley is **LYON**, which was once capital of Roman Gaul and is now France's second largest city. This, despite its industries, remains a surprisingly beautiful place with outstanding museums. At **ORANGE**, the environment becomes distinctly Mediterranean, and the impressive amphitheatre is only one of the many Roman monuments that make this area France's richest in terms of the classical past. "The Province", as the Romans called it, later became known as Provence and was ruled from the 12thC by counts based at the aristocratic and elegant city of **AIX-EN-PROVENCE**. The counts built many of the fine medieval castles of the region, and also commissioned such important works of art as Nicolas Froment's ***Virgin of the Burning Bush*** (Aix cathedral). But perhaps the greatest contribution to the region's artistic heritage came from the papacy, which resided in Avignon in the 14thC, and brought over some of the greatest Italian artists, writers and musicians.

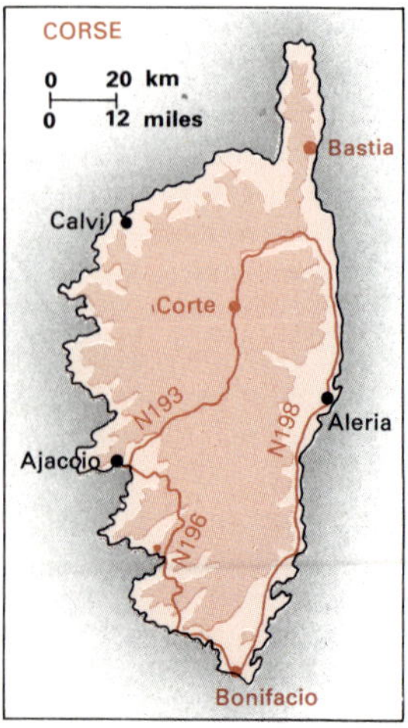

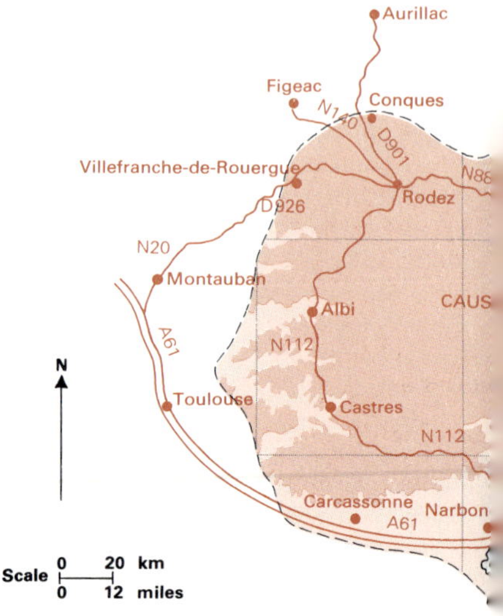

In 1482 Provence was annexed to France and gradually came to offer fewer opportunities for its artists, many of whom, such as Fragonard and Granet, moved to Paris or Rome. One of the few outstanding Provence artists of the 17thC or 18thC to undertake many commissions in his native region was the sculptor, engineer and architect Pierre Puget, whose atlantes figures made for the **TOULON** town hall are undoubtedly Provence's most outstanding Baroque works.

The beauty of the Provençal landscape has only quite recently become widely appreciated. One of the first important 19thC artists to wish to paint in the region was van Gogh, who moved to Arles from Paris in 1886, and hoped to establish what he called a "school of the Midi" similar to contemporary artists' colonies in Brittany. Nothing came of this, but not long afterwards artists started coming to the south in ever-increasing numbers, establishing themselves in towns and villages along the Cote d'Azur – an area which developed concurrently as a major tourist center. Signac and the Fauves went to St Tropez, Renoir to Cagnes, Matisse to Nice, Picasso to Antibes, Chagall to Vence, Leger to Biot, and so on. Museums devoted to these artists and their contemporaries exist throughout the Cote d'Azur.

Cézanne and Aix-en-Provence

Aix-en-Provence does not possess a single important painting by Cézanne, but a visit to the town and its surroundings is essential for anyone wishing to achieve a closer understanding of Cézanne's work. Born in Aix in 1839 (a plaque marks his birthplace at 28, Rue de l'Opéra) Cézanne spent the greater part of his life here, and found constant inspiration in the surrounding countryside. His father, who made his fortune in the hat trade and as a moneylender, was one of the town's wealthier citizens; his retail hat shop was at no. 55 in the Cours Mirabeau. The main family home was an elegant early 19thC house just outside the town in a wooded estate known as the Jas de Bouffan. This house survives (but cannot be visited), whereas the estate itself has been invaded by such unattractive landmarks as a motorway, a garish housing estate and the VASARÉLY MUSEUM.

Cézanne's house at Aix: a modern photograph.

Cézanne lived at the Jas de Bouffan whenever he came to Aix. During these periods his mistress and later wife Hortense Fiquet and their son Paul were forced to live elsewhere in the town, as the two of them were hated by the artist's sister and mother. On the death of his father in 1886, Cézanne acquired a large inheritance which enabled him to continue painting despite receiving very little recognition as an artist for most of his life. His mother died in 1897, and two years later the Jas de Bouffan was sold. Cézanne subsequently moved to an appartment at 23, Rue Boulegon in Aix (plaque), and in 1901 constructed a studio on the northern outskirts of the town (see ATELIER CÉZANNE, Aix-en-Provence). He maintained these two places until his death in 1906. A reclusive, socially awkward man, Cézanne was always regarded with deep suspicion by the inhabitants of Aix, who tended to create difficulties whenever the artist tried to rent property locally.

Cézanne, who once said that he tried to "see in nature the cylinder, the sphere and the cone," is often regarded as the precursor of abstract painting. Yet a comparison between the motifs of his which survive and his paintings of them shows the remarkable degree of fidelity with which he copied nature. Many of his earliest Aix landscapes (he never painted the town itself) were carried out in and around the Jas de Bouffan; one of these, ***The Railway***

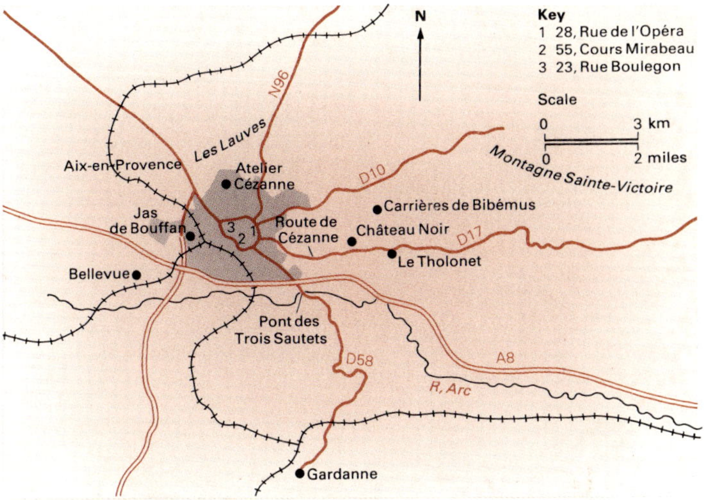

Cutting (Neue Staates-Galerie, Munich, c. 1870) – which shows the Marseille railway line at the point where it crosses the estate – features for the first time what was to be the most celebrated motif of his art, the Montagne Sainte-Victoire. The view of Montagne Sainte-Victoire from Bellevue (where a farm and dovecote that he frequently painted still survive) is interrupted by a railway viaduct, and this enhanced the classical quality of the many paintings of the mountain that he executed from this spot. To the W of the viaduct is the Pont des Trois Sautets, a bridge crossing the river Arc, which at this point is shaded by trees; Cézanne would often work here in times of hot weather.

In his early life Cézanne loved to paint near the village of Gardanne, 14 km (8.5 miles) to the S of Aix, and at L'Estaque, then a coastal village near Marseille. In the last ten years of his life, when he produced perhaps the greatest canvases of his career, he painted little around the Jas de Bouffan or Gardanne, preferring viewpoints along the road (now often referred to as the Route de Cézanne) which leads to Le Tholonet. Half way along this is a building misleadingly named the Château Noir, which is in fact a farmhouse built of yellow stone, with Gothic windows. Cézanne was obsessed by this place, and tried to buy it before eventually settling at the Rue Boulegon. Although thwarted in his attempts to purchase the Château Noir, he was allowed to rent one of the rooms in the W wing as a studio. He never painted the building from close by, but from a distance, where it can be seen to rise from above the surrounding forest of parasol pines. Within this forest are many other motifs favoured by the artist in his old age, including the millstone and other elements that were to have formed part of an oil mill.

To the N of the road that leads to Le Tholonet are the quarries of Bibémus, in whose pools Cézanne used to go swimming as a child with his close friend, Zola; it is difficult now to recognise the parts of the quarries which Cézanne often painted in later life, for they have been briefly reopened and re-worked in recent years. Just to the N of the studio which Cézanne had built in 1901 is the ridge of Les Lauves, which once commanded the most majestic views of the Montagne Sainte-Victoire. It was from here that Cézanne painted the culminating landscapes of his old age.

AIX-EN-PROVENCE
Bouches-du-Rhône, Provence
Map D4

Aix, the first Roman settlement in Gaul, was founded by the Romans in 123BC. After having been a major Roman city for many years, it went into a long decline which lasted until the 12thC, when the counts of Provence made it their capital. The greatest period in its history was the 15thC when it acquired its university and was ruled by the enlightened "Good King René", who in addition to being Count of Provence was titular King of Naples and Duke of Anjou. He was a brilliant mathematician and linguist, and a considerable patron of the arts. On the death of René's heir in 1482, Provence was annexed to France, but until 1790 remained relatively autonomous. Aix was kept on as its capital and became, from 1501, the seat of its supreme court of justice, the Parlement. The presence of wealthy and ennobled magistrates in the town led to the building of many fine **palaces** in the 17thC and 18thC. It is these buildings above all that give to the place today its dignified, aristocratic character and make it one of the most beautiful towns in the S of France.

The most important of Aix's older monuments is the **Cathédrale St-Sauveur**, which has a delightful **5thC baptistery**; the rest of the building dates mainly from the 15thC and early 16thC. The wooden **doors of the W façade** have exceptionally intricate carvings comprising Gothic and classical decorative details set round representations of the four prophets and the pagan sibyls. They were carved 1508–1510 by the Toulon artist Jean Guramand. Inside the building are four fine early 16thC **Brussels tapestries** originally from Canterbury Cathedral in England. However, the main treasure here is the ***Triptych of the Burning Bush*** ★★ painted c.1476 for King René by his court artist Nicolas Froment. The king is represented on the left-hand panel together with St Mary Magdalene, St Anthony and St Maurice; his wife Jeanne de Laval is on the opposite panel in the company of St John the Baptist, St Catherine and St Nicholas. The central panel shows the Burning Bush with the Virgin and child in its flames appearing to Moses: in the Middle Ages the Bush (which burned but was not consumed) came to symbolize the virginity of the Virgin Mary. One of the most striking features of this Flemish-inspired work is its minutely observed landscape background.

The 17thC to 18thC Archbishopric adjoining the cathedral has an important **collection of tapestries**, most notable among which is an early 18thC Beauvais group based on designs by Natoire, but carried out under the supervision of Oudry: they illustrate scenes from *Don Quixote.*

Musée Granet ☆
Place St-Jean-de-Malte
Tel. (42) 381470
Open 10am–noon, 2–6pm
Closed Tues

The Musée Granet lies just to the S of the town's main thoroughfare, the lively, tree-lined **Cours Mirabeau.** It is housed in the 17thC Priory of Malta, which is at the heart of one of the quietest and least visited parts of the town. The museum was founded in 1771 and has been in the present building since 1838. The place has changed little since then, even to the extent of there being no electric light in the main first floor galleries.

The second floor of the museum – the more modernized part of the building – contains most of the foreign school collections. The Italian School is strongest in 17thC and 18thC works, most notably a *modello* by Guercino for his ***Exhumation of St Petronilla*** in the Vatican Collections. Of the Flemish School, there is a 15thC ***Virgin in Glory*** attributed to Campin, and good **portraits** by Rubens of an unknown man and woman. The Dutch paintings include a ***Portrait of an Old Man*** by Carel Fabritius and ***Lot and his Daughters*** by Gabriel Metsu. But the supreme painting of this school represented here is a small but superlative ***Self-Portrait*** ★ by Rembrandt (c.1665).

The French paintings are all on the first floor, together with a scattering of foreign school works. A small gallery, with three paintings by Monticelli and a host of indifferent 18thC and 19thC landscapes, leads to the museum's main gallery. This enormous, dark and seedy room (which now closes 1hr before the rest of the museum) has a skylight so thick with dirt that even on the sunniest days the visitor is led to believe that a storm is brewing outside. Unlabelled paintings are hung 19thC-fashion on top of each other. It takes some time to realize that in the middle of the room there are diagrams identifying these works, kept in showcases. A large notice proclaims that the paintings are shown as they appeared in Cézanne's time. But this seems little justification for such a shoddy display.

Apart from a good mythological **scene**

by Jordaens and an **oil sketch** by Rubens, the main gallery's most important works are all of the French school. Among the earliest of these works are an amusing **Fontainebleau School painting** of young lovers observed by a jealous old man, and a portrait of about the same date of a semi-nude ***Diane de Poitiers*** in the guise of Peace. The French 17thC is represented principally by a study by Philippe de Champaigne for one of the figures in his celebrated group portrait in the *LOUVRE*, ***The Echevins of the City of Paris***. The early 18thC collections are stronger, with fine **portraits** by Hyacinthe Rigaud, de Largillière and Jean Van Loo. The last was a native of the town, and the beautiful 18thC house which he owned here – the **Pavillon de Vendôme** – is open to the public.

The greatest strength of the museum is its collection of late 18thC and early 19thC French paintings, many of which were originally in the collection of the painter François Granet. Granet, who was born in Aix in 1775, was a leading figure in the French art world of the early 19thC, and for a while was keeper of the Royal Museums; he divided his life between Paris, Provence and Italy. As a painter he is best known today for his dark and atmospheric scenes of monastic life. The Aix museum has none of these, but has instead an unfinished oil of the ***Death of Poussin*** (1834), and two **landscapes** of the Roman Campagna.

It was during his first stay in Rome that Granet met Ingres, who painted a portrait of him in 1807. ***Portrait of Granet*** ★★ which shows the artist against a severely painted background featuring the Villa Medici in Rome, is one of Ingres' greatest portraits, and arguably the most outstanding painting in the museum. Another well-known but much less subtle painting by Ingres, ***Jupiter and Thetis*** ★, dominates the end wall of the main gallery. Painted in Rome in 1811, it shows the sea nymph Thetis pleading with Jupiter on behalf of her son Achilles, who was then having a quarrel with the Greek leader Agamemnon. Thetis kneels at the god's feet, and attempts to tickle his chin, while Jupiter's wife Juno looks anxiously on, knowing only too well her husband's susceptibility to women. It is a slightly silly work with one detail which must surely have been intended as comic: the toe of Thetis delicately touches that of Jupiter. Other paintings in the gallery by Granet's French contemporaries include a dramatic **oil study** by David for the figure of Horace in his ***Serment des Horaces*** (1775) in the *LOUVRE PARIS*, a ***Portrait of a Young Boy*** (1786) by the same artist, two **oil sketches** by Géricault (including one of a standing male nude) and **portraits** by the Baron Gérard and the Baron Gros.

Another room on the first floor has minor works by the town's best known native artist Paul Cézanne (see p. 228). These include **two drawings** done while at art school in Aix (which in his time was on the ground floor of the Musée Granet), three **landscape watercolours** and a **lithographic self-portrait.**

Atelier Cézanne

9, Avenue Paul Cézanne
Tel. (42) 210653
Open June–Sept 10am–noon, 2.30–6pm; Oct–May 10am–noon, 2–5pm
Closed Tues

Cézanne's studio, which the artist had built between 1900 and 1902 and where he worked until his death in 1906, is on the northern outskirts of the town. Opened to the public in 1954, its interior has been reconstructed as it was at the time of Cézanne's death. There are reproductions of some of the artist's works, personal mementoes of his (such as his hat, cloak and clay pipe), and some of the objects that he included in his still-lifes. Alongside the actual skulls, bottles, wine glasses and other objects that Cézanne painted, the museum's curator has thought fit to place real apples and vegetables of more recent date, all of which are now in an advanced state of decay. In fact the place as a whole has a musty atmosphere, and lacks warmth.

Fondation Vasarély

Avenue Marcel Pagnol
Tel. (42) 200109
Open 9.30am–12.30pm, 2–5.30pm
Closed Tues, Nov

In an open site commanding excellent views of Mont Sainte-Victoire, is the Fondation Vasarély. The Op-artist, Vasarély, must be the only living artist in the world to have three museums devoted to him: one is in his native town of Pécs in Hungary, and the other two are both in Provence. The one at Pécs may be the best – it is certainly the smallest. Of the two in France, that at GORDES is the more enjoyable to visit, because it occupies a beautiful and well-situated 16thC castle. The Foundation at Aix not only displays his work, but is actually built to his designs. The artist paid for it himself, but the town generously provided him with the land.

Inaugurated in 1976, it was intended to serve some didactic function, the nature of which remains obscure. The artist professes to believe that his rigidly geometrical abstract works – which are at best merely chic and bland, and at worst literally painful to the eyes – help to explain man's relationship with the universe, and moreover represent some form of urban folk art. The Foundation at Aix is a monument to pretention on a scale unprecedented even in France. The ground floor of the building – which already has begun to develop ominous damp stains – comprises tall hexagonal-shaped rooms covered with enormous works by Vasarély in different media. Upstairs are a large group of cases designed by the artist to show nearly 800 of his drawings and projects. By pressing a button the works inside the case slowly begin to rotate. Visitors sit apparently mesmerized in front of them, too bored perhaps even to move. The Foundation has a large shop selling Op-prints and other works by the artist. Those who really want to posess a Vasarély would save a great deal of money by keeping the plastic bag given out at one of France's COOP stores. This has on it one of the artist's best known designs – that of the letters COOP.

AIX-LES-BAINS
Savoie, Rhône-Alpes   Map E1

Attractively situated on the lower slopes of Mont Renard, and overlooking Lake Bourget, Aix-les-Bains has been a famous thermal resort since the late 18thC, becoming particularly popular in the 19thC with wealthy English and Americans.

Musée du Docteur Faure
Villa des Chimères, Boulevard des Côtes
Open mid-Apr to mid-Oct 10am–noon, 2–6pm; mid-Oct to mid-Apr 10am–noon, 2–5pm
Closed Tues (mid-Apr to mid-Oct), Wed (mid-Oct to mid-Apr)

The Musée du Docteur Faure is in the high part of this rather haughty, old-fashioned town. Housed in a late 19thC villa, it mainly comprises the collection bequeathed to the town in 1942 by Jean Faure, a Parisian doctor who spent much of his time here. In the villa's entrance hall, which resembles that of a melancholy hotel out of season, you will see an ungainly notice board marked "The Impressionists", which crudely attempts to analyse these artists' achievements and philosophy. The board is at least indicative of the area of art in which Faure concentrated his activities as a collector. Opposite it, an example of the type of subject he particularly favoured is provided by a **watercolour** of two nude women by Foujita. The museum has an unusually large collection of nudes, including ones by Aman-Jean, Charles Cottet, le Fauconnet, Degas and Rodin (to whom a whole room is dedicated). Other works in the museum include two pastels of ***Dancers*** by Degas, a dark and dramatic early oil by Cézanne (***Lake at Bonnières***), an ***Interior*** by Vuillard and ***Landscapes*** by Boudin, Pissarro, Sisley and Marquet. All these works are of fairly high quality, even if none stands out. A pleasant feature of the museum is the wonderful view of the lake and surrounding mountains.

AJACCIO
Corse-du-Sud, Corse   Map Corsica

Ajaccio, the capital of Corsica, is a small town at the foot of mountains surrounding a most beautiful bay. It has the sleepy character of some distant colonial outpost, and seems almost an implausible place for Napoleon to have been born. Everywhere, however, the visitor is reminded of this fact: half the hotels and restaurants here are apparently named after him, and his thickset, unsmiling features seem to stare out at you wherever you go. Naturally, all the town's major monuments, (including the great man's birthplace) are connected with him.

The **Musée Napoléon** is housed on the top floor of the 19thC **City Hall.** It tells the visitor nothing of Napoleon's life, and consists simply of one large Empire-style room filled with portraits, varying in quality, of **members of Napoleon's family** by artists such as Gérard, Girodet and Winterhalter, and another smaller room containing a case of dreary Napoleonic medals.

Musée Fesch
Palais Fesch
50, Rue Cardinal Fesch
Closed for restoration

The Musée Fesch occupies one wing of an enormous **palace** built by Napoleon III that towers over the port, and is likely to be the first building you will notice if you arrive at the town by sea. The palace's other wing contains a round chapel with remains of members of Napoleon's family, including his mother, Letizia Ramolino, and her brother, Cardinal Fesch.

The museum is potentially one of the finest in the South of France, but it has been closed for many years, and – to judge by the lugubrious speed at which renovation work is being undertaken – is likely to remain so until the end of this century. Moreover, those old enough to have visited the museum when it was open would only have seen a small fraction of the collections, which have not been exhibited in their entirety for well over a hundred years.

The nucleus of the museum comprises the collections of Napoleon's uncle, Cardinal Fesch, who began to accumulate art in an obsessive way after 1796. In Paris that year he had the opportunity to purchase from the leading Belgian and Flemish galleries numerous works that were being sold to help pay for the damage resulting from the wars of the Republic and the Empire. Thereafter Fesch's ambitions as an art collector almost came to parallel his nephew's designs on Europe: he once wrote that he intended to have a gallery which would illustrate every aspect of the development of painting from the early Renaissance onwards. By 1814 he had amassed 1,600 paintings. Napoleon's downfall the following year led to the dispersal of all these and to the departure of Fesch himself, who fled to Rome where he was to remain for the rest of his life. There he began to start collecting again, and soon acquired a notable group of mainly Italian works from the 12thC to the 18thC. Owing partly to the complexities of his eccentric will, by no means all of these ended up in Ajaccio.

The museum reputedly has works by such major Italian artists as Daddi, Botticelli, Lorenzo di Credi, Cosimo Tura, Bellini, Titian and Domenichino. There are also French, Spanish, Flemish and Dutch works of the 17thC to 19thC including an important Poussin (***Midas at the Source of the Pactolus***).

ALÉRIA
Haute-Corse, Corse Map Corsica

The capital of Corsica in antiquity, Aléria is now little more than a dusty, sinister village in the only flat and ugly part of the island. The remains of the ancient city are scarcely visible.

Musée Archéologique Jérome Carcopino
Fort de Matra
Tel. (95) 570092
Open 10am–noon, 2–5pm
Closed Tues

The Musée Jérôme Carcopino is in a **16thC castle** of the type that one might expect to find in some especially barren and remote part of Spain. The unkempt museum contains local archaeological finds, including two outstanding and very unusual 5thC BC ceramic **drinking cups** ★ in the shape of a dog's and a horse's head.

ALÈS
Gard, Languedoc-Roussillon Map C4

Noted for its silks and manufacture of industrial chemicals, Alès has little to offer the tourist. The cathedral, which dates mainly from the 18thC, has an ***Assumption of the Virgin*** by the 17thC artist Mignard.

Musée du Colombier
Château du Colombier
Tel. (66) 863040
Open 9.30am–noon, 2–5pm
Closed Tues
(*Wed*)

The museum is in a nondescript 18thC house in the middle of a somewhat characterless municipal park. The interior of this building has been unimaginatively revamped in the late 1960s. On the ground floor are collections of archaeology, geology, palaeontology and local history. The paintings are on the first floor and include a relatively large collection of 17thC and 18thC French, Flemish and Italian paintings, many of unknown authorship or of dubious attribution. Two obvious imitations of Jan "Velvet" Brueghel are the pride of the collection. The best represented artist is the local 19thC painter Adrien Perrot, the titles of many of whose works (for instance, ***Does he Love Me?***) are suggestive of their quality.

ANTIBES
Alpes-Maritimes, Côte d'Azur
Map F4

A Greek trading port, then an important Roman settlement, Antibes became from the 14thC onwards a fortress town on the border between France and Savoy. The **seafront fortifications** still survive, from which fine views can be had of the coast, Nice and the Alps. Just behind them is the 13thC–16thC **castle of the Grimaldis**, and still further back a large and delightful old town.

Musée Picasso ☆
Château Grimaldi
Tel. (93) 336767
Open 10am–noon, 3–7pm
Closed Tues

The castle was turned into a museum in 1925 to house a small collection of Greek and Roman antiquities (these have now been transferred to the Musée d'Art et d'Archéologie housed in the nearby St-André bastion). In 1946 Picasso, who had just returned to his beloved Mediterranean after a period in Paris, was offered the museum by its curator as a temporary studio. He worked here from between July and Dec 1946. Three years later, in memory of his happy and productive stay in Antibes, he donated to the castle a large collection of **paintings** and **drawings**, all of which had been executed during that period. Picasso also bequeathed to the museum some of his **tapestries**, **lithographs** and **sculptures**, as well as nearly 200 ceramics made during his years in nearby VALLAURIS.

Thanks to these donations the museum has now become one of the most popular in the South of France, and during the summer months an odour of sweat and suntan lotion hangs over the place. This is nonetheless an enjoyable museum to wander round, being excellently modernized and well arranged. The main sculpture by Picasso is the amusing ***Woman with Baby Carriage***, in which the figures and pram are made up of old pots and metallic objects. The paintings by him are almost all of classical subjects, most notably a monumental oil of **two male youths** with a reed pipe, and the exuberant ***Joie de Vivre***, for which there are numerous preparatory studies.

The top floor is devoted to exhibitions of contemporary artists, some of whom – including Germaine Richier, Miró and the Provençal sculptor César – later donated examples of their work to the museum. A pleasant chapel contains the remains of the museum's former archaeological collection and a 16thC religious work by Antoine Aundi. Finally, there is a most enchanting and luxuriant garden with **sculptures** by Miró and Richier, exotic plants and trees, and a terrace overlooking the sea.

ARLES
Bouches-du-Rhone, Provence
Map C4

Arles developed as an important Roman town in the time of Julius Caesar, when it became for a while the capital of "The Province" (Provence) in place of Marseille, disgraced for having followed the Roman General Pompey. Later it was a focus of early Christianity, and it was here – in the former cathedral of St-Trophîme – that St Augustine was consecrated first bishop of Canterbury. During the Dark Ages, Arles suffered greatly from Barbarian invasions. Thereafter it played a minor role in Provence in comparison with Avignon and Aix-en-Provence, although in more recent times it came to be known as the capital of Provençal folk tradition.

Arles is also famous for having been for a while the home of Vincent van Gogh. Van Gogh came here from Paris in February 1888 and stayed until April 1889 when he was interred in the nearby mental asylum at St-Rémy (now named the Hôpital Psychiatrique Vincent van Gogh). Gauguin came to stay with him in Arles in October 1888, but left after van Gogh threatened him with a knife and then cut off his own ear. The house which they shared, the Maison Jaune in the Place Lamartine, was destroyed by bombing in 1944; but a number of the sites which van Gogh painted in the town can still be seen, including the **Café du Soir** (now a furniture shop) on the E side of the Place du Faubourg, and the quaint cemetery known as **Les Alyscamps.** The famous drawbridge just to the S of Arles, the **Pont de Langlois**, which features in many of the artist's works, was pulled down in 1926, but an exact replica was placed in honour of van Gogh at **Pont-du-Bouc** just a short way from the original bridge.

Arles is a bustling town that has suffered from bomb damage in World War II and from recent development, but it is nonetheless crammed with monuments from different periods. Everywhere you look you come across important relics of the town's past, most notably the **Arena**, the **Theatre**, the **Bath of Constantine**, and the **Cryptoporticus**. The most famous of the town's post-Roman monuments is the former **Cathédrale St-Trophîme** (now demoted to a church). The basic structure is Carolingian, but the building was much altered in the 11thC and 15thC. It has an outstanding sculpture group of the ***Last Judgment***★ on the tympanum of the W portal. Other sculptures of the same date – representing scenes from the Old Testament and even from Provençal legends – are to be found on the capitals of the church's delightful **cloister** (entered through the porch next to the Palais de l'Archevêché).

Musée Lapidaire d'Art Païen
Place de la République
Tel. (90) 963768
Open 9am–noon, 2–5.30pm

The Musée d'Art Païen is housed, like the nearby MUSÉE D'ART CHRÉTIEN, in a deconsecrated 17thC church. It has a magnificent collection of local Greek and Roman finds. Among these are three excellent mosaics (***Zodiac and the Four Seasons***, ***The Conquest of the Golden Fleece***, and ***Orpheus Charming the Animals***), the famous ***Venus of Arles*** ★ (a 1stC copy of a Greek original of the 4thC) and a large number of sarcophagi, most notably that of ***Phaedra and Hippolytus*** ★ (2ndC–3rdC) which shows in intricately carved and dramatic scenes the chase and death of Hippolytus.

Musée Lapidaire d'Art Chrétien Fernand Benoit

Rue Balze
Tel. (90) 963768
Open 9am–noon, 2–5.30pm

The Musée d'Art Chrétien has reputedly the finest **collection of early Christian sarcophagi** after the Lateran Museum in Rome. It is interesting to note how the Roman sarcophagi such as those in the Musée d'Art Païen were closely – and sometimes very crudely – adapted by the early Christians to portray Biblical scenes. Steps lead down from the museum to the vast and sinister **Cryptoporticus**, which was built by the Romans underneath their forum, and was later used for storing wheat.

Musée Réattu

Rue du Grand-Prieuré
Tel. (90) 963768
Open 9am–noon, 2–5.30pm

The local art gallery is the Musée Réattu, which is housed in the 14thC–16thC former Priory of the Knights of Malta. After the Revolution this building was acquired by the local Neoclassical painter Jacques Réattu. After the death of his daughter in 1868 his art collections were left to the town; they later formed the basis of the present museum. This is a pleasant place to walk around, with its well-modernized interior and beautiful views down to the Rhône. However, the collections are disappointing. The main works of note among the earlier paintings are a ***Self-Portrait*** by Vouet, and an amusing group portrait by the local 18thC painter Antoine Raspal showing – in a slightly naive style – the ***Artist's Family*** with the artist at his easel and his homely wife holding a ball of wool. The museum has almost all of Réattu's surviving work. Unfortunately, his paintings are dull and conventional. The most interesting is the large ***Death of Alcibiades*** which throws much light on the technical procedures of artists at this time in that it has been left unfinished, with the underdrawing taking up half of the canvas. Another local artist extensively represented in the museum is the equally mediocre 19thC landscapist, Henri Rousseau (not to be confused with the "Douanier"). There is also a large collection of **works by modern artists** who have lived or stayed in Arles. The most famous was Picasso, who in May 1970 donated to the museum 57 **drawings** executed between Dec 31 1970 and Feb 4 1971. These slight works are displayed in an unjustifiably prominent way on steel plinths. In its modern acquisitions the museum has concentrated above all on **photography**, and has an impressive collection of works by such photographers as Man Ray, Ed Weston and Cecil Beaton. These are displayed in temporary exhibitions.

AVIGNON

Vaucluse, Provence Map D4

Avignon, a substantial Gallo-Roman settlement, was an important trading point on the Rhône throughout the medieval period and later, but the key to its cultural eminence is the fact that it was the seat of the popes for much of the 14thC. Threatened by the political ambitions of the powerful Italian families, Pope Clement V abandoned Rome for the relative tranquillity of Avignon in 1309, taking with him the College of Cardinals, the Bishops Legate and the huge administrative body known as the Curia. Almost immediately the city became an international meeting-place for pilgrims, diplomats, ecclesiastics and courtiers who maintained a level of sophistication befitting the temporal and spiritual representative of Christ on Earth. The clearest indication that the popes intended to uphold their earlier position and lifestyle can be seen in the scale of the **Papal Palace**, and in their use of the finest Italian humanists and artists to enhance the new court. Petrarch, for example, spent most of his early life in Avignon, taking minor orders here in 1326; but it was Simone Martini, the greatest Sienese painter of the generation after Duccio, who served the popes most effectively. With his assistant Giovanetti, Simone supplied designs and decorative paintings for the palace, the cathedral and other buildings, developing a refined elegant manner that became known as International Gothic because it was quickly communicated to virtually all the courts of N Europe.

The strength of Avignon's new cultural identity enabled it to survive the return of the Papacy to Rome. The remaining Bishops Legate supported the emergence of a second or later Avignon school in the mid 15thC which produced some of the greatest paintings in the history of French art. The tragic ***Pietà*** ***(LOUVRE, PARIS)*** is the most famous example of this phase, bringing together elements from the Italian Renaissance, the Northern Gothic tradition and perhaps even Catalan art, allied to a unique Provençal hardiness (seen in the description of the donor). Alongside this in importance and quality is the ***Coronation of the Virgin*** in **VILLENEUVE-LÈS-AVIGNON** by Enguerrand Quarton (Charonton) one of the few masters whose name and personality have come down to us through documents. The uniqueness of this art, its reliance on traditional conventions as well as a direct and penetrating realism, had a clarity and strength that few "provincial" schools could match. But the steady polarization of power in the later 15thC, and the cultural values attached to it, led to the breakdown of painting in Avignon in favour of Fontainebleau and the royal court (see ***PARIS ENVIRONS***).

Palais des Papes

Place du Palais
Tel. (90) 860332
Open 9–11.30am, 2–6pm

The Papal Palace in Avignon overshadows all other buildings in the city, presenting a formidable aspect to the main square with its immense buttressed walls surmounted by towers and turrets. In fact it is two buildings, the old palace (**Palais Vieux**) and the new (**Palais Neuf**) disposed on adjoining sides of an interior courtyard. The Palais Vieux, built for Benedict XII in 1335 by Pierre Poisson, is the more austere and martial of the two, contrasting with Jean de Loubière's elegant designs for Clément VI in the Palais Neuf of ten years later. Both buildings however are the expression of the power and wealth of the Papacy at this time, and were once crammed with paintings, sculptures, tapestries, silverware, ivories and the like; the *ars sacra* of the late medieval church and court.

Most of this has been dispersed and, of the original contents, only the **frescoes** remain. Those by Matteo Giovanetti in the Chapels of St Jean and St Martial and the series of ***Old Testament Figures*** in the huge Grand Audience Hall are the most important, but there are other works, notably the ***Hunting Scenes*** in the Chambre du Cerf, once Clément VII's bedroom, which are, if anything, more attractive. The **frescoes** in the Banqueting Hall by Simone Martini, Giovanetti's master and the principal painter of the Papal court, were originally in the cathedral of Notre-Dame-des-Domes but were removed to the palace for safekeeping. In the process of detaching them from the cathedral walls the *sinopie* (underdrawings) were revealed, and these are now exhibited alongside the finished works demonstrating the techniques of the medieval craftsmen; you can also see, in the case of the ***Annunciation***, the process of experiment and change by which the final design was realized.

Besides these the Papal Palace also has some works from later periods, such as the **Gobelin Tapestries** in the Salle du Consistoire, the reception room by the main entrance. In recent years there has been an attempt to preserve and display some of the relics unearthed in the palace by setting up a museum in the **Salle de Jésus**. For the most part this consists of glass and pottery fragments, some tiles and a number of documents relating to the Papal seat, but there is also a collection of local antiquities which were deposited in the palace when the Museum of Old Avignon was closed in 1966.

Musée du Petit Palais

Place du Petit Palais
Tel. (90) 864458
Open 9am–noon, 2–6pm
Closed Tues

The museum housed in the Petit Palais is the most popular tourist site in Avignon after the Papal Palace, which it adjoins. The building was constructed originally in the early 14thC as the home of Cardinal Bérenger Frédol, the Grand Penitentiary of Pope Clement V. Later periods saw substantial transformations, particularly towards the end of the 15thC. In the 1970s it was converted into a museum to house the holdings of Avignon School paintings from the MUSÉE CALVET (see below), some medieval sculptures in the town's former Lapidary Museum, and a large group of Italian paintings from the 13thC to early 16thC acquired in Rome in the 19thC by the Marquis G.P. Campana. Campana's collection, which originally included over 1,000 early Italian works, was confiscated in 1861 by the Papacy when Campana had been accused of misappropriating funds belonging to the Monte de Pietà. The collection was sold to Napoleon III, who wished it to be kept together, and serve to illustrate the history of early Italian art. However, his wishes were not respected: ***THE LOUVRE*** retained the best pieces, while the others were sent off to museums all over the south of France. Many of them lay forgotten there until the creation of the present museum, the main intention of which was to bring together all of Campana's works outside the Louvre.

Although the exhibiting conditions of the museum are exemplary, the collections themselves are not as exciting as one would perhaps have expected. The main work among the Avignon School pictures is Enguerrand Quarton's (Charonton's) very sculptural ***Virgin and Child between two Saints and two Donors***, a painting which rather pales in comparison with the same artist's ***Coronation of the Virgin*** at VILLENEUVE-LÈS-AVIGNON. Of the medieval sculptures, the most striking is the morbidly expressive ***Memento Mori*** from the late 14thC tomb of Cardinal de Lagrange. By far the greater part of the museum is taken up by Campana's collection. Apart from a ***Virgin and Child*** by Botticelli, its most remarkable feature is simply its size. The minor paintings that mainly fill it have little value other than the didactic one that Napoleon III originally envisaged.

Musée Calvet ☆

Rue Joseph-Vernet
Tel. (90) 863384
Open 9am–noon, 2–6pm
Closed Tues

The Musée Calvet, which is situated in the middle of a quiet, slightly dilapidated part of the town off the main tourist circuit, could hardly be more different in character from the Musée du Petit Palais. Since 1833 it has been housed in a mid 18thC palace – the **Hôtel de Villeneuve-Martignan** – which is now greatly in need of restoration. The paintings are badly hung, and in certain cases not even hung at all: at present the museum's greatest treasure – David's ***Barra***★ – sits on the floor propped up against a wall. Yet none of this really matters, nor does the fact that most of the works on show range from the indifferent to the downright awful. The place remains one of the most enchanting of France's provincial museums. The present-day visitor is not alone in sensing the museum's old-fashioned charm. Its special qualities were recognized in the 19thC by the novelist Stendhal, who arrived at the museum in a state of morbid depression, and left completely recovered. He loved the faded elegance of the large 18thC rooms. But above all he loved the museum's parched exotic garden inhabited by peacocks. He felt here a deep serenity akin to that in Italian churches. A plaque today in the garden records his infatuation with the place.

To list the museum's pictures after having described such a glorious setting seems almost an irrelevance. Nonetheless there are fine works to be seen among the host of bad and mediocre ones. The collections are partly disposed around the two wings which flank the garden. In the right wing is a room displaying old work, as well as another one containing the museum's earliest paintings. These are of the 15thC–17thC Italian, French and Spanish schools, and include a **biblical scene** by Vasari, a ***St Bruno in the Desert*** and a ***Pietà*** by N. Mignard, a good and unusual ***St Peter Saved from the Water*** by Ribera, and a grotesque genre scene, ***The Street Vendor***, by Francesco Herrera the Elder. The most interesting works in the L wing are a series of tall, horizontal **seascapes** by Claude-Joseph Vernet incorporated into *boiseries* (panelling). Vernet was an 18thC Avignon-born artist greatly influenced by Claude; he worked for much of his life in Italy, where he befriended the English painter Richard Wilson. Of considerable appeal to children is a *trompe-l'oeil* panel representing, and actually in the shape of, a canvas on an easel with a palette and reproductions of famous paintings stuck on to it.

The high point of the Musée Calvet collections are the 19thC and 20thC paintings, all of which are housed in the main body of the building. The subject of David's ***Barra***★ is the drummer boy who in the Revolution was killed for having refused to shout "*Vive le Roi*" instead of "*Vive la République*". David himself gave a long, impassioned speech in 1794 at a programme for the elevation of Barra and Viala, another youthful hero, to the Pantheon. In the sketchy monochromatic painting of Barra at Avignon, which gives the impression of being unfinished, the boy is represented as a beautiful naked, androgynous youth against a bare background: it is a curious and not altogether satisfactory work, with the boy appearing more in the throes of orgasm than in his death agony. The other well-known painting in the museum is the rather silly ***Mazeppa*** by Joseph Vernet's son, Horace: it shows a naked man tied to the back of a rearing horse and being chased by ravenous wolves. Other 19thC works include an **Italian landscape** by Corot, an extremely dirty **still life** by Manet incorporating a hat and a guitar, and a ***Sleeping Nymph*** by Chassériau, which can perhaps claim to be the first serious portrait of a female nude which shows hair under the armpits. The 20thC collection has an unlabelled

Renoir of a child with a skipping rope, some works by Utrillo and Dufy, and three of the most outstanding paintings by the Expressionist Soutine to be seen outside Paris – ***The Village Idiot***, ***The Old Man***, and ***The Downfall***. The small rooms on the museum's first floor contain an especially dingy display of prehistoric finds.

BAGNOLS-SUR-CÈZE
Gard, Languedoc-Roussillon Map C3

Once a walled medieval town, Bagnols today has few vestiges of its past, and acts mainly as a dormitory for workers from the nearby atomic energy station at Marcoule. The arcaded square where the town's museum is situated has nonetheless a quiet charm.

Musée Bagnols-sur-Cèze
Mairie, Place Mallet
Tel. (66) 896002
Open 10am–noon, 2–5.30pm
Closed Tues
(symbols) (*Wed*) (symbols)

The museum is promoted as a museum of contemporary art but, situated as it is on the top floor of the dingy town hall the approach to it is not promising. Once inside the museum, however, you find yourself in pleasantly if not imaginatively modernized rooms containing a surprisingly good collection of exclusively late 19thC and early 20thC works of art. They were mainly amassed by a one-time curator of the museum, the painter Albert André, and his friend Georges Besson, a distinguished writer on art. The **collection of drawings and watercolours** is particularly impressive, with works by Puvis de Chavannes, Monet (a caricature done in his youth), Jongkind, Renoir, Maillol, Marquet, Signac and Gromaire. The oil paintings include a slight interior by Matisse (the ***Open Window***, 1919), a late Renoir entitled ***Young Woman in the Country*** (1910), a good Marquet (***14 July at Le Havre***, 1906) and a striking **Portrait** of Georges Besson's wife, Adèle, by van Dongen. Among the other items in the museum are a case of small **sculptures** by the Catalan friend of Picasso, Gargallo, a **wooden mask** by Gauguin, a case of medallion portraits of artists, and an attractive collection of **Moustiers pottery**. The last room in the museum, the only one not to have been modernized, is filled with the strangely assorted curiosities – such as a stuffed crocodile and an Egyptian mummy of a child – that you frequently find in a certain type of local museum. However this room also has one quite considerable artistic curiosity – a clumsy but very faithful oil copy by the young Matisse of Raphael's ***Portrait of Castiglione*** in the *LOUVRE*.

BIOT
Alpes-Maritimes, Côte d'Azur
Map F4

Set back slightly from the hectic coastal roads between Cannes and Nice, Biot is a quiet little village noted for its ceramic industry. It has a partly Romanesque church with two late 15thC retables; but its main attraction is the museum devoted to the Cubist painter Fernand Léger.

Musée National Fernand Léger ☆
Tel. (93) 334220
Open Apr–Sept 10am–noon, 2–6pm; Oct–Mar 10am–noon, 2–5pm
Closed Tues
(symbols) (*summer only*) (symbols)

Léger had in fact relatively little connection with Biot. Born in Argentan in Normandy, he lived for much of his life in Paris and died near there at Gif-sur-Yvette. However, 15 days before his death in Aug 1955 he acquired a large property at Biot – "Le Mas Saint André" – with the intention of constructing in its grounds large-scale polychrome ceramics. After his death, his widow Nadia decided to construct a museum at Biot to display **347 works** left to her in his will. This was inaugurated in 1957 and given over seven years later to the French state; it was supposedly the first specially built museum in honour of a single artist. Its architect, André Svetchine, had to incorporate into his design two enormous works by Léger – a **polychrome ceramic** ★ originally intended to decorate the Olympic stadium at Hanover, and a **stained-glass** window; these were placed on the two main façades of the building.

Léger's paintings are all kept in the light and cheerful gallery on the museum's first floor. There are examples of work from every phase in the artist's career. The earliest works – most notably a ***Portrait*** of his uncle of 1905 and a view of his ***Mother's Garden*** of 1906 – show the artist working in a straightforward representational style. From about 1911–13 he produced some of his most abstract works, including ***La Femme en Bleu*** of 1912, for which there is a fine **oil study** here. The type of Cubism which he evolved during this period has sometimes been referred to as Tubism on account of the artist's love of tubular forms.

From about 1914 onwards he moved further and further away from abstraction, and at the same time became ever more bold in his handling of forms and colour. Simple man-made objects and the lives of ordinary working people came increasingly to interest him. His socialist ideals led him also to believe in the need for an art with a universal appeal. The works of the latter half of his career mainly feature life-sized and very simplified representations of people against heavily stylized backgrounds in primary colours. In his last years he experimented with different media, most notably polychrome ceramics, which proved particularly suitable for his bold colourful statements. The larger ceramics in the Biot museum are all in the very pleasant museum garden. Others are on the ground floor together with a changing selection of drawings, watercolours and tapestries.

BORMES-LES-MIMOSAS
Var, Côte d'Azur Map E5

Bormes is an attractive medieval village on top of a hill shrouded in mimosa and eucalyptus.

Musée Jean-Charles Cazin
Hôtel de Ville
Tel. (94) 711508
In process of transference

The small local gallery used to be housed in the town hall, but is now closed while awaiting transference to a pretty 18thC palace, the **Maison Taibé**. Its holdings mainly comprise works by the highly successful Salon painter Cazin, who died in the nearby town of Le Lavandou; but there are also two **terracottas** by Rodin and works by the *pointilliste* painters Maximilien Luce, Henry Cross and van Rysselberghe.

BOURGOIN-JALLIEU
Isère, Rhône-Alpes Map D1

A small industrial town specializing in textiles, Bourgoin-Jallieu is a dull, sleepy place with little of architectural interest.

Musée Victor-Charreton
15, Rue Victor Hugo
Tel. (74) 930054
Open Mon, Wed 2.30–5.30pm, Sat 11am–noon, 2.30–5pm
Closed Tues, Thurs, Fri, Sun

The part of the town where the Musée Victor-Charreton is situated has a somewhat battered appearance. The building itself is in fact a **16thC chapel** and is one of the town's few surviving old monuments. The old-fashioned converted interior contains a pleasant hotchpotch of objects ranging from Gallo-Roman remains to local textiles. The space devoted to painting is almost entirely taken up by the third-rate local artist, Victor-Charreton (born in Bourgoin in 1864), the founder of the museum.

CAGNES-SUR-MER
Alpes-Maritimes, Côte d'Azur
Map F4

Haut-de-Cagnes, the picturesque and now very chic old part of Cagnes-Sur-Mer, rises steeply above the noisy, vulgar new town. It is crowned by a **castle** originally built in 1309, when the Lord of Monaco, Ragnier Grimaldi, became also Lord of Cagnes.

Château-Musée
Château, Haut-de-Cagnes
Tel. (93) 208557
Open Apr–May 10am–noon, 2–6pm; Jun–Jul 10am–noon, 2–7pm; Oct–Mar 10am–noon, 2–5pm
Closed Tues, mid Oct–mid Nov

The castle, which was thoroughly renovated by the Grimaldis in the early 17thC, was acquired by the town council in 1937: it has been a museum since 1946. The ground floor of the building has collections of ethnography and local history and industries. On the first floor is an enormous dining room with a **ceiling completely frescoed** in the early 17thC by the Genoese artists J.B. Carlone and G. Benso: the former painted the central scene of the ***Fall of Phaethon***, while the latter was responsible for the dramatic *trompe-l'oeil* perspectives surrounding this work.

The first floor also contains a boudoir which once belonged to a Grimaldi marchioness. It is now filled with 40 **portraits** donated to the museum by a famous artist's model, Susy Solidor. They are all of her and are by such well known painters as van Dongen, Foujita, Dufy, Marie Laurencin, Otto Friesz and Picabia.

Musée Renoir
Les Collettes, Rue des Collettes, Cagnes-Ville
Tel. (93) 206107
Open June–Oct 2.30–6pm, Nov–May 2–5pm
Closed Tues, mid-Oct to mid-Nov

On the slopes of the hill opposite the castle is Les Collettes, a property which

Renoir acquired in 1902 with the intention of building a house and saving a group of ancient olive trees then threatened with destruction. This house, where the artist lived for the last 12 yrs of his life, is now a museum to him. It includes two not very good late canvases by him on loan from the ***LOUVRE***, nine of his **sculptures** (which were executed in collaboration with the Catalan artist, R. Guido), and **portraits** of him by Maillol and Albert André.

The place is also filled with much of the original furniture and many personal mementoes. The artist's studio has been faithfully reconstructed: the wheelchair next to the easel is a reminder that the artist was severely ill in his last years with rheumatoid arthritis. This illness in fact forced him to paint with his brushes strapped to his hand, which might help partly to explain the disappointing quality of much of his later work. One of the most charming features of the museum is its **wooded garden**, which appears so frequently in the artist's paintings. It now has a statue by him of ***Venus***, as well as a regular crowd of elderly artists vainly trying to capture the scene on canvas.

CALVI
Haute-Corse, Corse Map Corsica

Calvi's most impressive feature is its well-preserved **15thC citadel**, which rises dramatically above the very popular holiday resort below and commands outstanding views of the surrounding coast and high mountains.

Among the whitewashed buildings that line the citadel's steep and winding streets is the tiny **15thC Oratory** of the Confraternity of St Anthony, which has a collection of ecclesiastical bric-a-brac, including a fine **ivory cross** attributed optimistically to the famous Venetian sculptor Jacopo Sansovino.

CANNES
Alpes-Maritimes, Côte d'Azur Map F4

The ugliest and most modern of the main resorts on the Côte d'Azur, Cannes was little more than a fishing village before 1834 when an Englishman, Lord Brougham, was forced to stop here on his way to the north Italian Riviera. He was so enchanted by the place that he had a villa built to which he returned regularly until the end of his life. Soon after his "discovery", the place became an exceedingly fashionable resort, and has remained as such until the present day. The most famous part of the town is the seaside promenade, the Boulevard de la Croisette, which features in a romantic light in Scott Fitzgerald's *Tender is the Night*, but which is now a noisy and crowded street lined with characterless modern apartment blocks (most of the town's 19thC and early 20thC buildings have been pulled down). To the W of this is the older part of the town known as Le Suquet. This is on a hillock dominating the main port and crowned by the **17thC church** of Notre-Dame d'Espérance.

Musée de la Castre
Tel. (61) 689192 Ext. 432
Open Apr–June, 10am–noon, 2–6pm; July–Sept 10am–noon, 3–7pm; Oct–Mar 10am–noon, 2–5pm
Closed Mon, Nov to mid-Dec

The citadel houses the small and pleasant Musée de la Castre, which contains mainly **Oriental, African and South American items**, collected in part by the eccentric Baron Lycklama who died in Cannes in 1900 after a lifetime of exotic travelling. The baron also had a collection of paintings, only a handful of which are on show here. These include a **portrait** of the baron in Oriental dress, and paintings by the 19thC specialist in **Oriental scenes**, Lévy Henry-Léopold. The museum in fact possesses a number of pictures by 19thC Salon painters, donated by the Baron Lycklama and other wealthy visitors to Cannes in the last century, most notably the Baron de Rothschild. This collection has up until now been kept locked away in the reserves; but soon a new museum will be opened to display it.

CARPENTRAS
Vaucluse, Provence Map D4

Carpentras is an attractive old market town with a number of interesting old monuments, including an 18thC town hall, which has collections of **Gobelins tapestries** and **Moustiers pottery**, and a **chapel** with paintings by Mignard and Parrocel. Of particular interest is the 17thC **Palais de Justice**, which has preserved much of its original interior, including a ceiling painted by Mignard.

Musée Duplessis
234, Boulevard Albain Durand
Tel. (90) 630492
Open 10am–noon, 2–6pm
Closed Wed

The Musée Duplessis is in a fine **18thC**

palace on one of the wide boulevards which have replaced the town's medieval fortifications. The ground floor of this building houses the **Musée Contadin**, an old-fashioned museum with an overwhelming smell of floor polish. The collections consist of miscellaneous items of purely local interest, such as a large collection of bells. The staircase leading up to the Musée Duplessis, which is on the first floor, has French 19thC works, including a ***Portrait*** of the model Gilbert by Ary Scheffer and ***Farniente***, a titillating but also impressively painted portrait by Adda Cabane of a recumbent woman with a breast exposed.

The Musée Duplessis is a large ugly place badly in need of restoration. It has nonetheless some interesting paintings, in particular a huge ***Fish Market Scene*** by Frans Snyders, four works by Horace Vernet, and thirteen portraits, including an excellent **Self-Portrait** ★ by the painter after whom the museum is named, J.S. Duplessis. Duplessis was born in Carpentras in 1725 and studied in Rome for four years before settling in Paris in 1752; his best known work is a portrait of ***Gluck Composing*** (Kunsthistoriches Museum, Vienna).

CHAMBÉRY
Savoie, Rhône-Alpes Map D1

Chambéry was until the 16thC the capital of Savoie, an independent state which at one time stretched from Lyon to Turin. Savoie remained independent until 1860, when it was divided between France, Italy and Switzerland. Few monuments survive from Chambéry's medieval past, save for the former **castle** of the Dukes of Savoie. This imposing 14thC–15thC building was substantially altered and added to in the 18thC; it is now the town's Préfecture.

Musée des Beaux-Arts
Place du Palais de Justice
Tel. (79) 334448
Open 10am–noon, 2–6pm
Closed Tues

The museum has been housed since 1889 on the top floor of a tall and narrow early 19thC building which once served as a grain market. It has an impressive **collection of Italian paintings** from the 13thC to 18thC. These include a ***Profile of a Young Man*** ★ generally attributed to Paolo Uccello, and a ***Crucifixion*** by Bronzino's pupil Santi di Tito, which was painted around 1595 for a monastery at Scopeto, near Florence. 17thC Italian painting is particularly well represented, with a fine ***Portrait of a Young Man*** by the Florentine artist Francesco Furini, a ***Virgin and Child*** by Guercino, two genre scenes by Monsú Bernardo (a pupil of Rembrandt who worked in Italy from 1651) and two large, violent and exceptionally powerful canvases by the Calabrian painter, Mattia Preti – ***Judith Presenting the Head of Holofernes*** ★ and ***Dido on the Pyre*** ★.

The museum's French holdings are less good, although there is a large collection of 19thC sculptures (including a **bust** by David d'Angers), an 1808 pastel of ***Mont Blanc*** by Vigée-Lebrun (who in her journal described the actual scene as a "wild one which thrills but does not charm"), and a fascinating full-length ***Portrait*** by the Salon painter Gervex of a woman decoratively posed against a red background with Japanese motifs.

DIGNE
Alpes-de-Haute Provence, Côte d'Azur Map E4

Digne is a quiet thermal resort with a pleasant tree-lined central avenue.

Musée Municipal
64 Boulevard Gassendi
Tel. (92) 314529
Open 10am–noon, 2–6pm
Closed Mon
(*Sun*)

The local museum is housed in a former 18thC hospital which was unimaginatively renovated in 1970. The interior resembles that of a dreary municipal library. Much of it is taken up by natural history collections. The paintings are all on the first floor. Apart from two slight works by the ubiquitous Ziem, they are all by local 19thC and early 20thC artists.

DRAGUIGNAN
Var, Côte d'Azur Map E4

Draguignan is a pleasant, relatively unspoilt town with an elegant 19thC district designed by Baron Haussmann, and a medieval quarter clustered around the 17thC **Tour de l'Horloge**.

Musèe Municipal
9 Rue de la République
Tel. (94) 680044 Ext. 550
Open Mon 2–6pm, Tues–Sat 9–11.45am, 2–6pm
Closed Mon morning, Sun

The museum is in the medieval quarter of the town. It has collections of antiquity, local history, furniture, and fine and applied arts, all jumbled together in a not especially attractive setting. Nonetheless there are pleasant surprises – a large collection of 19thC **Sèvres porcelain**, a **bust** by Houdin of Joseph Alphonse Omer, a ***Death of Cleopatra*** by François de Troy, an excellent view of the ***Interior of St Peter's*** by the 18thC Italian painter Panini, and some Rodin **watercolours**.

GAP
Hautes-Alpes Map E3

The most important commercial town in the Dauphiné Alps after Grenoble, Gap is an unexciting place which has little to offer the tourist apart from its situation and its museum.

Musée Départemental
4, Avenue Maréchal Foch
Tel. (92) 510158
Open July – Sept 10am – noon, 3 – 7pm; Oct – Nov, Mar – June 2 – 5pm
Closed Tues and Fri Mar – June; Dec – Feb

The museum occupies a large early 20thC building in the municipal park. The first floor has bad 16thC and 17thC Italian paintings, an oil by Monticelli (***Cock Fight***), and numerous works by local 17thC – 19thC artists. Downstairs are many cases of stuffed birds and other natural history exhibits, and a large collection of prehistoric remains, classical and medieval sculptures, and objects relating to the history of the area. But in addition to all this there is a magnificent monument to the ***High Constable Lesdiguières*** ★ (1626), which constitutes perhaps the main reason for visiting the museum. When this celebrated military commander died in Valence in 1626, his entrails remained in the town, while his heart was taken to a chapel in Grenoble cathedral, and what remained of his body to his castle chapel at Diguières, for which this monument was executed. The artist was the little known Jacob Richier. The monument, which is in black and white marble, shows the recumbent constable in a most intricately detailed coat of armour. Underneath are bas-reliefs illustrating two of his military exploits – the Battle of Pontcharra and the Siege of Grenoble.

GORDES
Vaucluse, Provence Map D4

One of the most beautiful villages in the exceptionally attractive Vaucluse region, Gordes is dramatically situated round a château on top of a steep hill.

Château et Musée Vasarély
Château
Tel. (90) 720289
Open 10am – noon, 2 – 6pm
Closed Tues

Narrow medieval streets lead up to this Renaissance castle on the hill's summit. The views of the surrounding countryside from the upper window of this building are quite breathtaking, and the main room here has one of the most outstanding **Renaissance fireplaces** in this part of France. Unfortunately the visitor to the castle has also to contend with yet another museum to the Hungarian-born Op-artist Vasarély (see Fondation Vasarély, **AIX-EN-PROVENCE**). In addition to various tapestries, paintings and kinetic works by him, there are innumerable showcases which show a literally rotating selection of his drawings.

GRASSE
Alpes-Maritimes, Côte d'Azur Map F4

Grasse, an attractive hill town, was a prosperous miniature republic from 1138 – 1227 on the medieval Italian model. Since the 17thC it has been unrivalled as a place for perfume manufacture.

The town is also the birthplace of one of France's leading 18thC painters, Jean-Honoré Fragonard, who was born at **23 Rue Tracastel** (now marked by a plaque) on April 5, 1732. From the time of the Goncourt brothers, writers on Fragonard have always emphasized how the lush environment of Provence was influential in the development of highly sensual and colourful art. In fact Fragonard spent virtually all his life in Paris, where his father, a glove-maker, moved in 1738 after having speculated and lost his entire fortune in a disastrous enterprise. Fragonard returned to Grasse in 1790 to escape from the Terror, staying with his cousin Evariste Maubert in what is now the **Villa Fragonard**.

Villa Musée Fragonard
23 Boulevard Fragonard
Tel. (93) 360271
Open June – Sept. 10am – noon, 2 – 6pm; Oct – May 10am – noon, 2 – 5pm
Closed Mon, Nov

This small, attractive 17thC villa, in a most verdant and exotic garden, has been turned into a museum. On the ground floor are copies of Fragonard's celebrated series of paintings, ***The Pursuit of Love***. These large panels were commissioned in 1770 by Madame du Barry for a building by the radical Neoclassical architect Ledoux at Louveciennes near Paris. They were turned down by her, probably because they seemed too frivolous and rococo at a time when a more austere style of painting and decoration was beginning to be favoured. Fragonard brought them with him to Grasse in 1790 to decorate the dining room of his cousin's house. In the late 17thC they were sold by heirs of the family, and eventually ended up in the Frick Collection in New York: the copies now in Grasse faithfully reflect how the originals once hung. The staircase of the villa has pleasant *trompe l'oeil* decorations attributed to Fragonard's son, Alexandre-Evariste. Minor works by the latter and his own son, Théophile, take up most of the exhibiting space on the first floor. There is just one painting by Fragonard himself – a youthful ***Self-Portrait*** in Renaissance costume.

Musée d'Art et d'Histoire de Provence

2, Impasse Mirabeau
Tel. (93) 360161
Open Apr–Oct 10am–noon, 2–6pm; Nov–Mar 2–5pm
Closed Mon

A short distance from the Villa Musée Fragonard is the Musée d'Art et d'Histoire de Provence, which is next to one of the town's most visited perfumeries, the Maison Fragonard. The museum has a pleasant old–fashioned interior, with furniture, paintings, porcelain and other objects all brought elegantly together. There are two religious paintings by the Flemish-born Jean Duret, who died in Aix-en-Provence in 1668. The modern works include a pastel by Berthe Morisot (***La Cuillette des Oranges à Cimiez***) and an oil of the ***Chapel of Saint-Cassies*** at Cannes (1922) by Maurice Denis, who also carved the frame.

GRENOBLE

Isère, Alpes Map D2

At the confluence of the rivers Isère and Drac, and bordered on two sides by dramatic cliffs and snow-capped mountains, Grenoble has a most beautiful position which is best appreciated from the **Fort de la Bastille**, a rocky promontory which rises steeply to the N of the town. Originally a small Roman settlement, Grenoble developed as an important town in the early Middle Ages, when it was ruled by the counts of Albon. In the 12thC the English-born wife of Count Guigues III gave her son the surname of Dolphin. The Gallicized version of this – Dauphin – subsequently became the title of the rulers of the region which came to be known as Dauphiné. In 1349 Dauphiné was handed over to France, and the title of Dauphin given to the eldest son of the French king.

Little survives of medieval Grenoble, which suffered much damage through the repeated flooding of the river Drac. The character of the town today reflects the prosperity which it has enjoyed since the 19thC, when it led the way in the taming of mountain streams for hydro-electric power. Apart from being a major industrial town, Grenoble is also a most lively cultural center. It has a thriving university (founded in 1339 by the last of the Dauphin counts, Hubert II) and an artistically enlightened municipal council. Visitors arriving at the town by train are immediately greeted at the station by an enormous Calder **mobile**. Other large examples of modern sculpture are scattered throughout the town, in particular in the **Parc Paul Mistral** (works by Descontin, de Wyss, Apostu, Guadagnucci and Roussil). Grenoble's reputation as a center for modern art is consolidated by the collections of the Musée des Beaux-Arts, which is one of the finest and most forward-looking in France.

Musée de Peinture et de Sculpture ☆

Place de Verdun
Tel. (76) 540982
Open 1–7pm
Closed Tues

The museum was founded in 1800 and initially comprised an outstanding series of **religious works** seized from local abbeys after the Revolution, as well as 47 well-chosen canvases acquired by the museum's founder, L-J Jay in Paris. Later the museum benefited from a number of generous donations, including one of **Spanish paintings** from the collection of General de Baylie. Then in 1923 Agutte-Sembat, the mistress of a local deputy, left to the museum a large collection of **contemporary works**. From that time onwards the Musée des Beaux-Arts has devoted most of its funds to acquiring modern art, and indeed was the first major museum outside Paris to do so.

The present museum building, constructed in 1870, has a pompous, dirty classical exterior that suggests a dingy old-fashioned interior similar to that of the Musée des Beaux-Arts at Lille. But you are in for a shock: much of the original interior has indeed been preserved and not even restored, yet everywhere there are the most surprising modern additions. To see the museum's collections in a roughly chronological way, you should avoid the temptation of walking down the garishly coloured corrugated iron tunnel at the entrance hall. Instead, go up the stairs behind the ticket desk, leading to a series of rooms with "high-tech" benches and concrete walls. The brutal simplicity of the rooms makes a perfect setting for what is one of the best **Egyptian collections** in France. Particularly fine is a superlative group of painted **tomb sarcophagi** ⋆ of the 21st Dynasty, and a **series of mummies** dramatically displayed in a darkened room. Another room here shows in rotation avant-garde works by living French artists. Such a juxtaposition of the old and new typifies the spirit of the whole museum.

Downstairs the Old Master paintings are displayed in three large rooms along the building's main axis. To one side of them (reached from the entrance hall by the tunnel) are rooms containing a further changing selection of works by young artists; to the other side are rooms housing modern works on permanent display. The decoration of the three central rooms has been left largely untouched, although works by young artists are often imaginatively placed on the floors – the effect is to give a vital character to even the most decrepit parts of the building. Other French museums should learn from this example.

The Old Master paintings include four excellent ***Still-Lifes*** ⋆ by the little known 16thC Flemish artist Osias Beert, and good works by Perugino (***St Sebastian and St Apollinaris***), Tintoretto (***Ex-voto of Mateo Soranzo***), Veronese (***Christ Appearing to the Magagdalene*** ⋆) and Bartholomeus Spranger (***Allegory of Painting, Sculpture and Architecture***). The great strength of the museum, apart from its modern holdings, is its outstanding 17thC collection, perhaps the best in France after that of the *LOUVRE*. Many of the leading European artists of this period are represented by excellent examples of their work, including ***St Gregory Invoking the Holy Spirit*** ⋆ by Rubens, ***Adoration of the Shepherds*** by Jordaens, ***St Bartholomew*** by Ribera, ***Adam and Eve*** ⋆ by Domenichino, and ***St Francis of Assisi***, a dark and early work by Annibale Carracci which was strongly influenced by Tintoretto. Best of all, however, are four large **canvases** ⋆ by Zurburan (***The Annunciation, The Nativity, The Adoration of the Shepherds*** and ***The Circumcision***). These are undoubtedly the finest works by this artist outside Spain. Zurburan, as always, impresses through the clarity of his forms and colours; one is also struck by such beautifully simple still-life details as the pitcher of water and basket of eggs in the lower left-hand corner of the ***Adoration.***

The museum has paintings by all the major French 17thC artists with the exception of Poussin and the Le Nain brothers. Among the more famous of these works is George de La Tour's ***St Jerome*** of about 1631–35 (a version of this, featuring a cardinal's hat, is in the Nationalmuseum, Stockholm), two altarpieces by Vouet (***Rest on the Flight into Egypt*** and ***Christ Healing a Possessed Man***), and a ***Landscape*** by Claude which used to hang in the 17thC Hôtel Lesdiguières in Grenoble. Particularly striking are the museum's works by Philippe de Champaigne, most notably a ***Portrait of Jean du Verger de Hauranne***, a group portrait recording the admission of the **Duke of Anjou** into the Order of the Holy Spirit, a haunting ***St John the Baptist*** ⋆ which shows the saint staring intensely towards the spectator, and an almost monochromatic portrayal of the dead ***Christ on the Cross*** ⋆ against a bizarre, sinister landscape incorporating a pyramid, a classical temple and a medieval castle. The 18thC holdings are less notable, but there are nonetheless estimable works by Guardi, Magnasco, Restout and Jouvenet, and a large and highly detailed **Still-Life** of fruit, flowers and animals by Desportes.

The relative lack of Neoclassical and 19thC works is made up for by an extensive collection of modern paintings and sculptures. These are mainly arranged according to artistic movements, and include works by virtually all the well-known artists this century. Perhaps the single outstanding masterpiece among these is Matisse's ***Still-Life with Aubergines*** ⋆, a large painting with colours subtly blending with the purple of three aubergines. The Agutte-Sembat bequest is all kept together in three small upstairs rooms. It is strongest in works by the Fauves, including further paintings by Matisse, and excellent works by Signac (***St Tropez***, 1905), van Dongen (***Amusement***, 1914) and Marquet (***Pont St-Michel***). Unfortunately one of the terms of the bequest was that the museum should have on permanent display a large group of singularly mediocre Impressionist-style paintings by Agutte-

Sembat herself. In other provincial museums these works would scarcely be noticed; but in the Grenoble museum they strike a particularly discordant note because they are in such illustrious company.

HYERES
Var, Côte d'Azur Map E5

Hyères, once a Greek trading post, was an important town in the Middle Ages when it became a base of the Knights Templars. After its castle was destroyed during the 16thC Wars of Religion, the town went into a decline, but in the 19thC it became an extremely popular resort, frequented by such notables as Queen Victoria, Tolstoy and R.L. Stevenson.

Musée Municipal
Place Lefèvre
Open Mon, Wed–Fri 10am–noon, 3–6pm; Sat, Sun 3–6pm
Closed Tues

The municipal museum is today housed on the third floor of a dreary local administrative building. Eventually its collections – the most important of which is devoted to natural history – will be moved to no less than three specially built museums. The painting collection, which is at present only partially and inadequately displayed, is not of any special note. There are minor works by the Midi artists Vernet and Ziem, and a pleasing ***Head of a Young Girl*** attributed to the 18thC Italian artist, Pietro Rotari. Best of all is ***Tragedy***, a small work, hung on an easel, by the 19thC Salon painter Cabanel.

ISLE-SUR-LA-SORGUE
Vaucluse, Provence Map D4

Known as the "Venice of the Comptat" because of the way that it is encircled and divided by various branches of the river Sorgue, L'Isle-sur-la-Sorgue is a pretty old town which has an exceptionally lively market on Saturdays. The poet René Char was born here in 1907, and still has a house in the town.

Musée Bibliothèque René Char
20, Rue du Docteur Tallet
Tel. (90) 381741
Open 10am–noon, 2–6pm

The Musée Bibliothèque René Char was opened in September 1982 in a specially converted 18thC house. Char has always had a deep interest in the visual arts, collaborating with artists in illustrated editions of his books, and being on intimate terms with a number of distinguished artists, including Giacometti, Braque, De Stael, Picasso and Viera da Silva. The museum shows a changing selection of works from his collection. The display is exceptionally spacious and pleasant, but the works themselves are what some might call delicate and sensitive and others merely slight and rather dull.

LYON
Rhône, Rhône-Alpes Map C1

Occupying a strategic position at the junction of two major rivers, the Saône and Rhône, Lyon was the capital of Roman Gaul, later becoming an important focus of early Christianity and the scene of numerous martyrdoms. After a long and uncertain period, in which the government of the place changed hands repeatedly, it gradually began to establish itself as France's second major city. By the early 16thC it had an international reputation as a mercantile and banking city, and its proximity to Italy made it an important point for the diffusion of Italian Renaissance culture. At this time, too, its celebrated silk industries began to be built up. In the 19thC many other industries were developed here, and today the city is a textile and car manufacturing center of international importance.

Although its size and industries tend to deter tourists, Lyon has perhaps more to offer than any other French city outside Paris. It is an exciting and surprisingly beautiful place. The main **Roman remains**, most notably a theater, are on top of the hill that slopes steeply down to the Saône. On the lower slopes of this hill is the exceptionally picturesque **medieval and Renaissance quarter**. This is intersected by narrow streets lined with tall, somewhat grimy but very attractive **old palaces**, including one **(8, Rue Juiverie)** with an ornate gallery designed by France's leading Renaissance architect, Philibert de l'Orme. Several of the passageways in this area tunnel their way underneath the houses, and are known as *Traboules*. Longer and more curious *traboules* dating mainly from the 19thC are to be found on the hill between the Saône and the Rhône. To the S of these, at the very heart of Lyon, you come to the most spacious and elegant part of the city.

The Place Bellecoeur, which is surrounded by fine Neoclassical houses, is one of the largest squares in France, and possesses an **early 19thC equestrian statue** of Louis XIV replacing a 17thC one by Desjardins which was pulled down in the Revolution. The **bronzes** decorating its base (representing the Rhône and the Saône) are original, however, and are by the Coustou brothers. An altogether more impressive monument is the **fountain** on the N side of Lyon's other main square, the Place des Terreaux. This is the work of Bartholdi, the 19thC Alsatian sculptor responsible for the Statue of Liberty (see Musée Bartholdi, ***STRASBOURG***), and consists of four rearing horses symbolizing rivers leading to an ocean.

Musée des Arts Decoratifs ☆

30, Rue de la Charité
Tel. (7) 8371505
Open 10am–noon, 2–5pm
Closed Mon

The early 18thC building to the S of Place Bellecoeur (the **Hôtel Lacroix-Laval**) was designed by Soufflot, one of France's leading architects of this period, and houses the Musée des Arts Decoratifs. This has extensive applied art collections displayed in rooms with a predominantly 18thC character. The rooms on the ground floor have mainly works of the **French Rococo**. The first floor is devoted more to **French Neoclassicism**, while the second floor has a wonderful case of **12thC enamels** ★, as well as a large and outstandingly good **collection of Italian Renaissance majolica**, including works from Gubbio, Faenza and Urbino.

Musée des Beaux-Arts ☆☆

20 Place des Terreaux
Tel. (7) 280766
Open 10.45am–6pm
Closed Tues

On the southern side of the Place des Terreaux is the enormous **Palais St-Pierre**, which was built between 1659 and 1687 as a Benedictine nunnery for noble ladies. Since 1801 it has housed the Musée des Beaux-Arts, which is one of the largest in France. Like the art gallery at ***LILLE*** it is a dark and somewhat decrepit place which displays most of its collections in an old-fashioned manner. Its rooms, however, although more numerous than those in the Lille museum, are less inhuman in their proportions. Moreover, its seediness gives the place a certain charm, and much of the original 17thC decoration survives, most notably in the former **chapter house** on the ground floor, adorned with flamboyant Baroque paintings and sculptures by the local artist Thomas Blanchet.

The large cloister which you cross to reach the museum's main entrance contains sculptures of different periods, including three bronzes by Rodin (***St John the Baptist, The Shadow***, and the ***Age of Bronze***), and a bust of ***Carpeaux*** by Bourdelle. Most of the ground floor of the museum is taken up by sculptures from the Middle Ages up to the 19thC. Among the earliest works are an animated **12thC Burgundian figure** in the style of those at ***VÉZELAY***, and a wooden sculpture group of ***The Annunciation*** by an artist in the circle of Nino Pisano. However, the most impressive of the museum's sculptures are of the 18thC and 19thC and are all housed in the former **church of St-Pierre**, which is the only part of the museum to have been extensively renovated in recent times.

The rather austere church, whose walls have now been painted white, provides an excellent setting for the **sculptures**. These are of high quality and are by such well-known masters as Falconet, Coysevox, Canova, Barye, Carpeaux, Daumier (a case full of **caricature bronzes**), Injalbert, Rodin, Maillol and Medardo Rosso (a characteristically suggestive marble entitled ***Veiled Woman*** ★). There is even one very recent work, a bizarre and very impressive marble full of fascinating details, ***The Agony of the Mother*** ★ by Ipoustéguy. The horizontal, slab-like format of this piece is inspired by medieval and Renaissance tomb effigies, and complements brilliantly the setting of the church. The largest group of works here is by the Neoclassical Lyonnais sculptor, Joseph Chinard. Chinard was born in Lyon in 1756, and worked here for most of his life; he did, however, spend long periods in Paris in the 1790s and first decade of the 19thC, and was a regular exhibitor at the Paris Salons. He was one of the most successful sculptors of his generation. Today his ambitious large-scale works seem cold, stiff, and lacking the imagination of his Neoclassical contemporaries such as Canova.

A more attractive side to Chinard's art is his very sensitive portrait busts. The most famous of these is of **Juliette Récamier** ★, of which the museum has two versions, one in terracotta and a later one in marble. Madame Récamier was the notoriously beautiful and flirtatious young wife of a leading Parisian banker; she was portrayed by many artists, most notoriously by David ***(LOUVRE, PARIS)***. Chinard became friends with the Récamier family in Paris in 1795–96, but did not execute his bust of her until the beginning of the following decade.

The museum's first floor is partly taken up by good and extensive **Oriental collections**. Most of the floor, however, is devoted to Lyonnais painting from the 15thC to 20thC. Room after room is filled mainly with dreary paintings by extremely minor artists. Yet visitors to this, the least popular part of the museum, should persevere. Some extraordinary works are in store for them.

In the 16thC, when the French court stayed for long periods in Lyon, the city attracted artists from different parts of Europe. The most famous was the portraitist Corneille de Lyon, who in fact came from the Dutch town of The Hague. Unfortunately the museum has only two studio works by him: a ***Portrait of François I***, and another of ***Charles d'Orléans***. The leading 17thC Lyonnais painter was Jacques Stella, whose father, François, was a Flemish painter who settled in the city in the late 16thC. Stella began his career as an engraver in Florence, and later moved to Rome, where he became one of Poussin's closest friends. Most of his paintings palely reflect the art of Poussin, and there are three in the museum: ***Adoration of the Magi, Virgin and Child with St John the Baptist*** and ***Christ and the Doctors***.

The greatest period of Lyonnais art was the 19thC. Among the city's early 19thC painters, the best known were the landscapist Caruelle d'Aligny – a follower of Corot and reputedly the first artist to work extensively in Barbizon – and Hippolyte Flandrin, a highly successful Salon painter much influenced by Ingres. The museum has a large and rather drily painted ***Fontainebleau Landscape*** by d'Aligny, and works by Flandrin, including two good ***Self-Portraits*** and an impressive ***Dante in Hell***.

Unlike Flandrin and d'Aligny, their Lyonnais contemporaries Victor Orsel and Louis Janmot are completely unknown outside the city. They represent a strong mystical streak in Lyonnais painting that developed at a time of rapidly growing industrialization. The museum not only has a large allegorical picture, ***Good and Bad*** by Orsel, and a haunting portrait of a woman covered in flowers, ***Flowers of the Fields*** (***Fleurs des Champs***), by Janmot. There is also a superb series of 18 canvases and 16 drawings by Janmot entitled ***The Poem of the Soul*** ★★. These works, which are exhibited together in a darkened room, will be a revelation to most visitors to the museum; they are never mentioned in any general histories of 19thC French art, and indeed seem to contradict conventional notions of how this art developed. Relatively little is known about the artist. Janmot apparently had the idea for these works in 1835 during a period of quarantine before reaching Rome; and he was occupied with the project until 1881, when he published a book about it in which, for the first time, the pictures were placed alongside explanatory texts. These strange, visionary works nonetheless have very precise, if complicated, meanings. A small booklet on sale in the museum's vestibule explains them clearly and is strongly recommended. In their rendering of the spiritual world with minutely observed naturalistic detail, they have much more in common with the art of the German Romantics than with that of Janmot's French contemporaries.

In the late 19thC Lyon produced a number of well known Symbolists, including Séon, who is represented here by an arresting icon-like portrait of his fellow Symbolist ***Joseph Péladan*** dressed like a monk. The greatest Lyonnais artist of this generation, however, was Puvis de Chavannes, who painted three of his most famous murals, ***Visions of Antiquity, The Sacred Wood***, and ***Christian Inspiration***, on the stairwell between the first and second floors of the museum. Unfortunately these are badly lit and in poor condition. The museum also has two other works by him, a large canvas entitled ***Autumn*** (1864), and a portrait of striking and moving simplicity of ***The Artist's Wife*** ★ (1884).

The bulk of the museum's painting collection is on the second floor. This is consistently the most impressive part of the museum in terms of the items on diaplay, but it is also the part that appears to be the worst cared for, with creaking floorboards, thick layers of dust covering the paintings under glass, and – surely to the detriment of the numerous treasures here – no proper ventilation. The earliest paintings are of the 15thC Flemish school, and include a ***Genealogy of the Virgin*** by Gerhard David, and a fine ***Virgin and Child*** by Quentin Massys. The 16thC holdings are particularly strong in Venetian works, most notably a ***Danae*** and a large ***Ex-Voto*** by Tintoretto, a ***Moses Saved from the Water*** ★ and ***Bathsheba at her Bath*** ★ by Veronese, and two rare historical scenes by Francesco Bassano, ***The Capture of Naples*** and ***Charles VIII Crowned King of Italy***. Among the 17thC Italian paintings are a fine ***Caesar and Cleopatra*** by Pietro da Cortona and a starkly expressive ***St Francis of Assisi*** by Zurburán, which shows the saint standing with arms crossed against a bare, dark background. The most important of the Dutch school paintings is an early and unusual Rembrandt of ***The Stoning of St Stephen***: the overall composition and the proportions of the figures here are bizarre and confused, but there are powerful naturalistic details. A rather more lightweight picture is ***Le Coucher à l'Italienne*** by Jacob Van Loo, a lesser known member of the Flemish family of artists who mainly settled in France. This life-sized portrait of a nude woman on the point of going to bed is little more than a very well painted pin-up. Other Flemish School paintings include two religious works by Rubens (***Adoration of the Shepherds*** and ***Saints Preserving the World from the Wrath of God***) and a mythological scene by Jordaens (***Mercury and Argus***).

Although Poussin and Claude are not represented in the museum, there are good works by most of their French contemporaries. Simon Vouet stands out particularly well in this company with a fine ***St Paul Giving Alms***, a superlative ***Crucifixion*** ★ painted in a luminous and sinister combination of cold pastel colours, and a very naturalistic and erotic representation of the ***Legend of Cupid and Pysche*** ★. Jouvenet – who represented the more Baroque tendencies in French art of the late 17thC – has two works here, a ***St Bruno at Prayer*** and a large ***Christ Expelling the Merchants from the Temple***.

The 18thC holdings of both foreign and French art are less impressive, but do not miss two good English School works – ***Portrait of a Young Woman*** by Sir Thomas Lawrence, and ***Portrait of Sophia Cumberland*** by Romney – a vividly painted landscape by Magnasco, a **portrait of a sculptor** by G.D. Tiepolo, and a well-known moralizing genre painting by Greuze, ***The Charitable Lady*** ★ featuring a woman persuading a reluctant child to see his dying father.

The quality of the museum's collections improves markedly with the 19thC French paintings, among which is a strikingly naturalistic genre painting generally attributed to David, ***Woman selling Vegetables (La Maraîchère)***. An equally vivid if rather more disturbing example of naturalistic portraiture is Géricault's ***Mad Woman*** ★. This is perhaps the most impressive of a series of portraits (others are in the Musée des Beaux-Arts at ***ROUEN***) done for a doctor friend of the artist to illustrate the effects of mental illness on physiognomy.

Two of the other main works in the museum by French Romantic artists are Delacroix's superlative oil sketch of a nude, ***Woman with a Parrot*** ★ and ***Baron Corinne at Cap Misène*** (which represents a scene from a once very popular novel by Madame du Staël), originally in the collection of Madame Récamier. Mid 19thC French works include Courbet's ***The Happy Lovers*** (one of whom is the artist himself, portrayed as an implausibly glamorous figure), a study by Corot of a naked model reading (***The Studio***), and a **portrait** of a naval officer by Millet. There is an extensive if not especially exciting **collection of works** by all the leading Impressionists with the exception of Pissarro. The other side to French art of this period is represented by a detailed ***Study of a Photographic Studio*** ★ by Dagnan du Bouverie, one of the most successful of the naturalistic Salon painters. Perhaps the most interesting of the museum's late 19thC works is Fantin-Latour's **La Lecture** ★ which is a portrait of two women, one reading, and the other staring pensively in front of her. The artist specialized particularly in double and group portraits, often brilliantly suggesting psychological relationships.

The museum's 20thC holdings include works by famous artists such as Matisse, Picasso and Dufy and Rouault, but are by and large poor in quality. The display is dominated by an enormous and dreary triptych by the academic Cubist Gleizes. Special mention, however, should be made of a powerful naturalistic work by the Futurist artist Severini, a ***Portrait of the Artist and Family*** ★.

Musée Gallo – Romaine

17, Rue Clébery
Tel. (7) 8259468
Open 9.30am – noon, 2 – 6pm
Closed Mon, Tues

The Musée de la Civilization Gallo-Romaine has a most spectacular setting. The building which houses it was inaugurated in 1975 and adjoins the **Roman theatre**. The concrete interior that spirals its way down into a hill resembles both an imaginary prison scene by Piranesi and an underground car park. Among the objects spotlit in the darkness are a 4thC Roman sarcophagus of **Dionysus**, a bronze **Neptune**, and an excellent **mosaic of a Roman circus** ★.

Musée Guimet

28 Boulevard des Belges
Tel. (7) 8932244
Open 2 – 6pm
Closed mornings, Mon, Tues

The Musée Guimet was founded in 1879

by the ethnographer Émile Guimet on his return from the Far East. Its collections of Oriental art were all transferred to Paris in 1888 (see ***PARIS***, Musée Guimet); but other such collections subsequently accumulated in Lyon, and the museum was reopened in 1912. The dull 19thC interior of the museum displays ancient Assyrian, Egyptian and Greek works, and examples of Coptic and Islamic art. Its chief treasures, however, are its **Asiatic collections**, including Khmer and Cham sculpture, Chinese pottery from the Han to the Ch'ing dynasties, and Japanese prints, paintings and ceramics. The museum is one of the only French provincial museums to have a cafeteria: unfortunately the food served here does not add to Lyon's reputation as a gastronomic center.

Musée Histoire des Tissus

34, Rue de la Charité
Tel. (7) 8371505
Open 10am–noon, 2–5.30pm
Closed Mon

The Musée Histoire des Tissus adjoins the MUSÉE DES ARTS DECORATIFS and has been completely modernized inside. It contains the largest collection of textiles in the world, ranging in date from the 4thC AD to the present day, and including ecclesiastical garments, Turkish rugs, and material designed by Sonia Delaunay (1925). But this is strictly a museum for the specialist, and it is unlikely that those previously uninterested in textiles will be converted to them by the adequate but dull way in which they are displayed here.

MARSEILLE

Bouches-du-Rhône, Côte d'Azur
Map D5

Marseille, the first major Greek settlement in Gaul, was founded by Greeks from Asia Minor in about 600BC and developed rapidly into a prosperous trading post. Later it allied itself to Rome; but in the 1stC BC the citizens ill-advisedly backed Pompey's claim to Roman leadership against those of Caesar, who reduced it to subjection. The city then went into a decline which was not arrested until the time of the Crusades, when it competed with Genoa to supply food and arms to the Crusader forces. Since then it has been France's most important port. In 1720 50,000 people of Marseille died in a plague brought to the city by sailors from Syria who avoided quarantine. The city was extensively damaged by bombing during World War II, and in addition the Germans, under the pretext of hygiene, had most of the picturesque old streets around the port destroyed in 1943.

Marseille, despite the beauty of its coastal position, is an ugly city. All that is left of the old port is a single line of houses, most of which are now seedy restaurants selling the fish soup known as *Bouillabaisse* at exorbitant prices. Behind the port runs the Canebière, in the 19thC one of the most famous and fashionable streets in Europe. Today this is still an exceptionally lively street, but it is also a dirty and slightly sinister one. Much of the rest of central Marseille has a similarly decrepit 19thC character. For a city of such size, Marseille has remarkably few interesting old buildings. The oldest is the famous **12thC cathedral**, which adjoins the hideous 19thC one.

The most famous of the innumerable modern buildings that have been built since World War II is Le Corbusier's ***Unité d'Habitation***, a pioneering block of flats conceived as a self-contained urban unit, and making free use of the Modulor (Le Corbusier's famous system of proportions). It has already begun to show its age, and now has that sad, unloved look characteristic of many of the city's older buildings.

Musée d'Archéologie

Château Borély, Avenue du Prada,
Tel. (91) 732160
Open 9.30am–12.15pm, 1–5pm
Closed Tues, Wed morning

Outside the central part of the town, in a pleasant park just off the coastal road leading to the Calanques, is an attractive 18thC palace, Le Château Borély. This contains on its ground and first floors an archaeological museum with a particularly good collection of **Egyptian works**. One of these – an enormous granite **statue of a prince** – was acquired as early as 1570 by Christophe de Vento, and was then the oldest antique to have been brought over to France. Since 1968 the second floor of the building has housed a remarkable **donation of drawings**, which includes over 200 works of the 18thC French school, as well as drawings by Breughel, Cuyp, Correggio, G.D. Tiepolo and Goya.

Musée des Beaux Arts ☆

Palais Longchamp, Boulevard Longchamp
Tel. (91) 622117
Open 10am–noon, 2–6pm
Closed Tues, Wed morning

The Musée des Beaux-Arts is housed in a wing of a grandiose 19thC palace, the

Palais Longchamp. Its interior was completely renovated in the late 1970s. On the first floor is an extensive collection of 16thC–18thC Italian paintings, and 17thC Flemish and Dutch ones: among these are Annibale Carracci's ***The Village Marriage***, which belonged to Louis XIV, a genre study (***The Adulteress***) by the 18thC Venetian painter, G.D. Tiepolo, and a group of works by Rubens, most notably the ***Adoration of the Shepherds*** ★ (once in the church of Saint-Jean in Malines).

Yet, as so often happens in art galleries in major towns, it is the work by local artists which particularly attracts the attention. On the first floor you can see two enormous canvases of astonishing power, representing in the most grotesque detail the ***Plague of Marseille*** of 1720, painted by the little-known Michel Serre. But the high point of this part of the museum are two rooms devoted to one of Marseille's greatest sons, Pierre Puget, who was born in the city in 1620 and died here in 1694. Although Puget is now best known as a sculptor, he was also a painter, architect and engineer. One room has casts of his most famous works, including the **four saints** decorating the niches in the crossing piers of Santa Maria di Carignano, Genoa (c.1661–65), and the celebrated **Milo of Crotona** (now in the ***LOUVRE***) which, on its unveiling in Versailles in 1682, supposedly elicited from the queen the rather silly remark, "Oh the poor man, how he suffers."

The museum gives full emphasis to the Baroque dynamism of these works by spotlighting them in a darkened room. An adjoining room has a collection of **original works** ★ by Puget, including a terracotta of a faun and an excellent marble medallion of Louis XIV. Puget's activity as a painter is represented by a number of small and rather indifferent religious and mythological canvases. More interesting are the artist's architectural and engineering drawings, in particular his projects for the embellishment of his native city which he executed just after his return from Italy (where he spent a critical period of his youth). These grandiose and deeply imaginative projects were turned down by the timid, conventionally-minded municipal authorities.

On the walls of the staircase leading from the first to the second floor are two murals by Puvis de Chavannes representing **Marseille as a Greek Colony** and **Marseille as the Gateway to the East** (executed the very year the Suez Canal was opened). The second floor houses French paintings from the late 18thC to early 20thC, including an early work by David, ***St Roch and the Plague Victims*** (1792), **landscapes** by Corot and Daubigny, a fine portrait by Courbet of ***M. Grangier*** and a group of oils by Raoul Dufy. A whole room is devoted to another famous native of Marseille, **Honoré Daumier**, who was born here in 1808, but lived most of his adult life in Paris. Daumier acquired particular fame as a lithographer specializing in cruel satirical depictions of contemporary French society: a series of vicious political lithographs attacking Louis Philippe and his ministers led to the artist being imprisoned for six months. The museum displays documentary photographs relating to Daumier and his times, and a large collection of his lithographs; unfortunately it possesses no important examples of his work as a sculptor or painter. An older contemporary of Daumier was the painter Adolphe Monticelli, born in Marseille in 1824. The museum has 16 of his brightly coloured paint-laden canvases that greatly influenced van Gogh.

Musée Cantini

19, Rue Erignan
Tel. (91) 547775
Open 10am–noon, 2–6.30pm
Closed Tues, Wed morning

The Musée Cantini occupies an attractive **17thC palace** which has been superlatively modernized and now contains **collections of porcelain** and of modern art – perhaps rather strangely. The collections of the former are on the ground floor and comprise nearly 600 **Provençal works**, most notably from the town of Moustiers 96km (60 miles) to the N of Marseille. The most celebrated of the Moustiers ware on display here is a large **18thC plaque** by Oléry featuring monkeys.

The collection of modern art, which is housed on the museum's first and second floors, was mainly acquired after 1968. The space for showing works here is relatively limited and is often taken up by ambitious loan exhibitions. Among the permanent collection are works by Delvaux, Léger, Hartung, Soulages, Balthus, Bacon, Masson, Vasarély and Segal. Also represented is the best-known Marseille artist of recent times, the sculptor César, who attended the local art school in the 1930s and shortly afterwards moved to Paris, where he still lives. His witty and irreverent work, which appears in many French galleries (particularly in the S) frequently makes use of unorthodox materials. From 1960 he began to compress cars, then jewels, motorcycles, and even paper. The most striking work by him in the Musée Cantini is ***Homage to Louis Renault*** ★ an enormous pillar made out of compressed car bumpers.

Musée Grobet-Labadié

140, Boulevard Longchamp
Tel. (91) 622182
Open 10am–noon, 2–6pm
Closed Tues, Wed morning

Just opposite the Palais Longchamp is a late 19thC building housing the Musée Grobet-Labadié. This was once the residence of the local violinist and painter, Louis Grobet, whose widow (*née* Labadié) bequeathed it and its collections of furniture, ironwork, porcelain, musical mementoes, sculpture and painting to the city in 1919. Although nothing in the museum is especially memorable, the place itself has considerable charm. Each of its tiny, elegant rooms is crammed with the most varied and surprising assortment of items, ranging from the signatures of Beethoven and Paganini to an old microscope. Amidst all this are minor works by Greuze, Corot, Daubigny and Monticelli.

MENTON
Alpes-Maritimes, Côte d'Azur
Map F4

Menton, like Cannes, was an obscure fishing port before becoming a major resort in the mid 19thC. Among the first to come here were an Anglican clergyman and an English doctor, who wrote a book recommending the town's climate (which is supposedly the warmest of the Côte d'Azur towns). Soon afterwards the town was overrun by the English, who established their own newspaper, club and church. Menton today is perhaps the most pleasant and leisurely of the well-known French Mediterranean resorts: it has many opulent 19thC buildings, long, elegant, tree-lined avenues, and an attractive old quarter with 17thC streets.

Musée Jean Cocteau

Quai Napoleon III
Tel. (93) 577230
Open mid-June to mid-Sept 10am–noon, 3–6pm, mid-Sept to mid-June 10am–noon, 2–5.30pm
Closed Mon, Tues

In 1957 the poet, novelist, film-maker and artist, Jean Cocteau, was asked by the mayor of Menton to decorate a room in the town hall reserved for civil marriages (see SALLE DES MARIAGES). Cocteau later expressed a desire to have a museum to himself in a small 17thC bastion which has formed part of the town's sea fortifications. Cocteau executed various **pebble mosaics** for this, and also designed special cases for the display of some of his ceramics. The museum was inaugurated in 1968, five years after Cocteau's death, and contains numerous graphic pieces by him, most notably an abysmal series of pastels called the ***Inamorati***.

It is unlikely that Cocteau would have achieved any reputation at all as an artist had he not been so talented in other fields; his strongly linear works seem merely to reflect all that was sentimental and slapdash in the art of his friend Picasso. The Cocteau museum has the character of a fashionable bistro, and the quality of its works is no better than one would expect from such establishments. Its only interesting items are a drawing of ***Cocteau*** by Picasso, and a large painting of him by another friend, MacAvoy.

Musée des Beaux-Arts

Palais Carnolès 3 Avenue de la Madonne
Tel. (93) 354971
Open mid-June to mid-Sept 10am–noon, 2–5.30pm; mid-Sept to mid-June 10am–noon, 3–6pm

The municipal art gallery is situated in a public park in the middle of a quiet and rather suburban district of Menton. It occupies the **Palais Carnolès**, which was built in the early 18thC for the Grimaldi Prince Anthony I. Later it was transformed into a casino before becoming a luxurious furnished villa let out to such illustrious visitors as Elizabeth Louisa of Bavaria, and the Prince and Princess of Metternich. It was acquired in 1896 by a rich American, Dr Edward P. Aldiss, who lived here until his death in 1947. Aldiss considerably enlarged the building and lavishly redecorated it. In 1969 it was decided to turn the place into a museum to house a large number of paintings (the Wakefield Mori collection) given to Menton by an English resident of the town. This was inaugurated in 1977.

An exceptionally ornate series of rooms houses the Old Master paintings on the first floor – a setting that overshadows the pictures, which are mainly small and uninteresting. Largely consisting of 13thC–16thC Italian and French paintings, most of these are school works (and some might well even be fakes) but there is also a fine **religious work** by the 17thC artist Philippe de Champaigne, and an unusual ***Sacrifice of***

Iphigenia (1761) by the American-born painter Benjamin West.

On the ground floor is a **portrait** of a standing man (1922) by Suzanne Valadon, and a **collection of watercolours** by Gromaire, Lhôte and Delvaux. In addition there is an **oil** by Graham Sutherland, given to the museum by the artist himself, who was an honorary citizen of the town.

Salle des Mariages

Rue de la République
Tel. (93) 578787
Open 8.30am–12.30pm, 1.30–5pm
Closed Sat, Sun

A ticket to the Cocteau museum enables one also to visit the marriage room in the town hall, which is in the middle of the old part of the town. Although Cocteau's decorations here are of only marginally higher quality than his works in the museum, it is a considerably more sympathetic place. Cocteau intended the room to look like the interior of a Greek temple, and as well as executing large drawings on the walls and ceiling, designed Classical-style brass lamp holders, red velvet chairs, and engraved mirrors. The place would make an excellent setting for a high-class confectioners.

MONACO

Principauté de Monaco
Côte d'Azur Map F4

The Principality of Monaco is a tiny sovereign state whose citizens pay no taxes and are exempt from military service. It is ruled by the oldest reigning family in the world, the Grimaldis, who acquired it in the 11thC or 12thC. It is a very crowded place with a population of 30,000 squeezed into an area of about 20sq km (8 sq miles), and with an estimated million visitors a year. Much of it resembles an American city with innumerable tall apartment blocks surrounded by flyovers.

The principality's most attractive part is the town of Monaco itself, which stands on the summit of a rock with a huge car-park complex built into it. The fact that the most usual approach to Monaco is by lift from this car park gives some indication of how artificial the town is. Although there are many old buildings here, most have been heavily restored in recent times. The square in front of the royal palace, and the palace itself, look like part of a bad film set. Tourists gather here in their thousands, adding to the confusion.

Palais du Prince

Place du Palais
Tel. (93) 301831
Open July–Sept 9.30am–1pm, 2–6.30pm
Closed Oct–June

Despite its plaster-of-Paris appearance, the palace – which can only be visited in the summer months – was originally built in the early 13thC, and then transformed in the 15thC and 16thC. The most interesting feature of the interior is the courtyard. The walls of this, and the ceilings of the surrounding *loggie*, are covered with **16thC–17thC Italian frescoes**, some of which are attributed to the Genoese painter Luca Cambiaso.

Other frescoes of about the same date decorate the ceilings of the otherwise uninteresting palace apartments. Before the Revolution the Grimaldis had a remarkable art collection, but little of this remains except for 17thC and 18thC portraits of members of the Grimaldi family, including one of James I by Largillière. You can see two fine portraits of later date in the Throne Room, depicting ***Albert I*** by Léon Bonnat, and ***Louis II*** by the immensely successful Hungarian-born high society portraitist of the first years of this century, Philip de László. This same room has also the worst painting in the palace – an outdoor **group portrait** of the present royal family dressed in casual clothes and broad smiles on all their faces. This tasteless piece of kitsch by Ralph Wolfe Cowan acquires a certain pathos with the knowledge that it was painted only months before Princess Grace's fatal road accident.

MONTPELLIER

Hérault, Languedoc–Roussillon
Map C4

Montpellier came into existence in the 8thC AD, was ruled in the 13thC by the kings of Aragon, and then by the kings of Majorca. Later it became a stronghold of Protestantism until 1622, when it was taken by Louis XIII. Its university – one of the most famous in France with a world-renowned Medical Faculty – was founded in the 13thC. Montpellier today is a lively and elegant town whose most interesting surviving monuments date mainly from the 17thC and 18thC. The most prominent among these is the **Château d'Eau**, a Neoclassical hexagonal pavilion that was the terminal for an impressive two-tiered acqueduct. The pavilion is situated at the end of a late 17thC terrace – **Le Promenade du Peyrou** – which commands wonderful views of the town and its surroundings.

Musée Atger

2 Rue de l'Ecole de Médecine
Tel. (67) 661777
Open 10am–noon, 1.30–7.30pm
Closed Sat, Sun

The Musée Atger is situated in the corner of the earliest botanical garden in France, the Jardin des Plantes, which was founded in 1593 by He nri IV. The museum is housed in a room in Montpellier's celebrated Medical Faculty, which since 1795 has occupied the buildings of a 14thC Collégiale. There are a few minor 17thC and 18thC French paintings, but the museum really only exists to show in rotation a selection of nearly **300 drawings** left to the Medical Faculty by Xavier Atger (1758–1833). The collection includes good drawings by Italian masters such a Parmigiannino, Annibale Carracci and G.B. Tiepolo; but the greater part is taken up by French 17thC and 18thC artists, such as Bourdon, Vouet, Puget, Natoire and Fragonard.

Musée Fabre ☆

13, Rue Montpellieret
Tel. (67) 660634
Open 9am–noon, 2–5.30pm
Closed Mon

The Musée Fabre is situated on the edge of the old part of the town, a district full of beautiful **17thC and 18thC palaces** with enchanting courtyards. The museum itself is in a palace built between the 15thC and 18thC, with parts added in the early 19thC when it received the town's art collections. Formed initially in 1798, these collections were enlarged in 1826 by an important bequest of works belonging to the local painter, J-F Fabre, a pupil of David and Vien who in 1787 won the *Prix de Rome*. Finding himself still in Rome at the time of the Revolution (for which he had no sympathy) Fabre decided to stay on in Italy, and did not return to Montpellier until 1826. His collection of paintings, which was amassed almost entirely in Italy, comprised mainly 16thC and 17thC Italian works, and paintings and drawings by his contemporaries.

The museum received other important donations in the course of the 19thC, most notably that of Alfred Bruyas, the wealthy son of a Montpellier banker who decided to become a patron of the arts after a trip to Italy in 1846. In Rome he met up with another native of Montpellier, Alexandre Cabanel, who was later to become one of the most celebrated Salon painters of the mid 19thC. Through his friendship with Cabanel, Bruyas came to be a friend and patron of numerous well-known artists, including Courbet, Delacroix, Tassaert and Glaize. Thanks to Bruyas, who was also the director of the Musée Fabre from 1868–76, the museum boasts one of the finest collections of 19thC French art outside Paris. In 1888 van Gogh and Gaugin paid a visit to the museum and were very excited by it. By that time, however, the place was very conservatively run: few new works were being acquired, and the collections were being poorly looked after. Thus it remained, becoming ever more dusty and dirty, until only very recently. But at the time of writing, drastic conversion work is being undertaken.

In the new vestibule of the museum you can see a fine group of 16thC and 17thC Flemish and Dutch works, which include works by Teniers, Metsu and van Ostade, and a magnificent genre scene, ***The Traveller's Rest*** ★ by Steen. Unfortunately, the museum's Italian and Spanish 16thC–17thC works cannot at present be seen. Two of the best are a ***Mystical Marriage of St Catherine of Alexandra*** ★ by Veronese, and a ***St Agatha*** ★ by Zurburán, which shows the saint calmly holding her amputated breasts on a plate. The French 18thC collection includes works by Vien, Robert, Vincent, and Avel (a powerful ***Portrait of Madame Crozat***), and is at present hung partly in the new vestibule and partly on the stairs leading down to what is now the permanent home of the museum's 19thC French paintings.

The paintings which belonged formerly to Bruyas used to hang together in a separate room. In their present setting – which though much plusher and better lit than the old one, is cramped and lacking in character – they have been split up and only partially displayed. This is a shame as Bruyas' collection demands to be seen as a single entity. What was particularly striking about the earlier arrangement was the number of times Bruyas himself appeared in his paintings. A hypochondriac who was also genuinely ill throughout his life, (Delacroix described him as a "complex of nerves, bronchitis and fever"), Bruyas was deeply introspective and obsessed by the effects of emotion on his physiognomy. All the artists with whom he came into contact were virtually obliged to paint him, sometimes in the strangest guises: Verdier, for instance, portrayed him as ***Christ Crowned with Thorns*** (1852).

This painting, together with many other such curiosities, has been demoted to the museum's reserve. Instead, only the most famous of the paintings featuring Bruyas are on show, including a portrait of ***Bruyas with a Handkerchief*** by Delacroix which made a great impact on Gauguin and van Gogh on their 1888 visit, a portrait by Courbet of 1853, and another showing (1854) Bruyas as an invalid. Bruyas was Courbet's most important patron, which is why the museum has the best collection of his work after the *LOUVRE*. Bruyas' obsession with being represented, combined with Courbet's own self-love, resulted in one of the artist's most celebrated works, ***The Meeting*** or ***"Good day Monsieur Courbet"*** ★★. This was painted in 1854 and commemorates Courbet's arrival in May of that year to be the guest of Bruyas at Montpellier. The artist is shown as a wanderer with his belongings on his back, greeting with a supercilious air the bourgeois, well-dressed Bruyas, whose servant, overwhelmed by the whole occasion, modestly looks down to the ground. This painting, which could be interpreted as genius gaining the respect of wealth, lent itself to satirical treatment by the press. Many critics noted that Courbet has painted himself as excessively handsome, and one of them observed that he was the only person in the picture worthy enough to cast a shadow on the ground.

Other paintings by Courbet in Montpellier include two excellent self-portraits – ***Self-Portrait with Pipe*** (1849) and ***Self-Portrait with Striped Collar*** (1854) – a portrait of Baudelaire, later incorporated in the ***Studio*** in the *LOUVRE*, and a view of the seaside at Palavas (1850) showing the artist taking off his hat as he first sets eyes on the Mediterranean. In a letter to a friend at this time the artist wrote, "The sea's voice is tremendous, but not loud enough to drown the voice of Fame, crying my name to the entire world." The largest picture by Courbet in the museum, ***The Bathers*** ★ of 1853, is the first in which Courbet showed his mastery in painting the female nude. But the affected pose of the two protagonists is absurd, and was rightly made fun of at the time.

The museum has many other French 19thC paintings of note, such as an early version of Delacroix's ***Femmes d'Alger*** ★ (in many ways a more likeable work than the larger, definitive painting of the same subject in the *LOUVRE*), a study of amputated feet and hands by Géricault, intended for the ***Raft of the Medusa*** in the *LOUVRE*, and an especially delicate Corot landscape, ***Memories of Ville d'Avray***. Perhaps most interesting of all are a series of works by the Montpellier-born artist, Bazille, a friend and close associate of the Impressionists who died young in the Franco-Prussian War before his talents came to be fully recognized. Bruyas took no interest in him as an artist, and it is unlikely that any of his few known works would have ended up in Montpellier had it not been for a bequest to the museum made by his family.

An excellent still life, ***Herons and Jays*** (1867), now hangs next to a painting of exactly the same subject by Sisley, and shows that at this early stage in these artists' careers, Bazille was the greater of the two in terms of crisp handling of paint and colour, and clarity of composition. More impressive still is his ***La Toilette*** ★, a scintillatingly coloured interior featuring a nude white woman and a black servant; this was exhibited at the Salon of 1870. But Bazille's particular interest was in the rendering of figures out-of-doors. His painting of a ***Peasant Girl*** ★★ against a background of the village of Castelnau (now a suburb of Montpellier) is his greatest work in Montpellier. The painting has a clarity and luminosity characteristic of Bazille at his best; and the intense stare of the girl in the foreground leaves a haunting impression on the viewer.

In recent years the museum has acquired a number of works by modern French artists, but has still a long way to go before establishing any significant representation in this field.

The Hôtel de Cabrières-Sabatiet d'Espeyran, also in Rue Montpellieret, is an annexe of the Musée Fabre devoted mainly to decorative arts of the French 18thC and 19thC. It occupies a Second Empire palace which, on the first floor, has kept its **original decoration**. The second floor has been furnished in an 18thC style, and has beautiful furniture from this period, as well as a few **paintings and sculptures** by artists such as Gauffier and Pajou.

NICE

Alpes-Maritimes, Côte d'Azur
Map F4

Nice was originally a small trading post founded in 350BC by the Greeks of Marseille. The town was almost completely obliterated after Barbarian and Saracen invasions, and only began to grow again from the 10thC onwards under the counts of Provence. From 1388 to 1860 it was under Savoy rule, and was thus attached to Italy. Supposedly that well-known Italian dish, the *pizza*, was invented here. The school of painting that flourished here in the 15thC and early 16thC, led by the Brea family, was a provincial reflection of Tuscany's. In the 18thC the town began to be a popular resort with the English (who were responsible for ordering the construction of the celebrated coastal road now known as the Promenade des Anglais). In 1864 the building of a railway to Nice led to a rapid increase in the number of visitors to the place. The town today is still a chic and thriving resort. It is also the fifth largest town in France, with a recently opened university and numerous light industries.

The **old town** of Nice is a small district tucked away between the port and the Esplanade Général-de-Gaulle. Its narrow streets and tall dirty houses, festooned with washing lines, contrasts completely with the rest of the central city, which is interesected by straight and spacious avenues lined with 19thC hotels and apartment blocks.

Musée des Beaux-Arts Jules Chéret ☆

33 Avenue des Baumettes
Tel. (93) 885318
Open 10am–noon, 2–6pm
Closed Mon, first two weeks in Nov

The Musée des Beaux-Arts Jules Chéret is in a small municipal park on the opposite side of the town to the port. The surrounding area is quiet, dignified and rather neglected despite being only a few minutes' walk from the perpetually noisy Promenade des Anglais. The art gallery is the best and most varied in Nice, yet it is also by far the least visited. Founded in 1860 when Nice was handed back to France, it was transferred in 1927 to the present site, a palace constructed c.1880 by the Russian Prince Kotschoubey and later owned by an American millionaire, James Thompson. The building – which is in the style of a late 16thC Genoese palace – is dark and dirty inside, but at the same time magnificently evocative of *fin-de siècle* Nice. Entering this museum is like stumbling upon a world which has been little touched by time, as you wander from room to room, every now and then coming across the most unusual and striking of works among the rather badly and confusingly arranged collections.

The museum's 17thC and 18thC paintings are all on the ground floor. Principal among these is an outstanding ***David and Goliath*** ★ (c.1615) which was possibly painted by the Lombard, Tanzio da Varallo, an artist known for his tense and disturbing interpretation of Caravaggio's realism. Also very impressive is a dramatic ***Portrait of the Chancellor Rigaud*** (1736) by Jean-Baptiste Van Loo, elder brother of Carle Van Loo, who was born in Nice in 1684. The ground floor also contains the largest **collection of works** by the 19thC sculptor Jean-Baptiste Carpeaux to be found outside the Petit Palais Museum in ***PARIS*** and the Musée des Beaux Arts in ***VALENCIENNES***. It was given to the museum by the sculptor's daughter, Madame Clément Carpeaux.

On the museum's first floor – which is entirely devoted to 19thC and early 20thC works – are a number of other single artist collections, all of which were likewise donated by friends and relatives of the artists. The widow of the Turner-inspired artist, Félix Ziem, left a number of her husband's colourful, freely painted landscapes, including the first painting which he exhibited at the Paris Salon, a ***View of the Grand Canal in Venice*** (1849).

Another donation came from the mother of the Russian painter, Marie Bashkirtsev, a successful portraitist who achieved posthumous fame with the publication of her remarkable journals. These are now enjoying a renewed vogue, as they make short, isolated references to the difficulties of being a woman artist. Bashkirtsev died young, as did her constant companion of later years, the celebrated painter of rural life, Jules Bastien-Lepage. The Bashkirtsev collection includes a ***Self-Portrait***, an excellent portrait of the artist by a Norwegian painter Anna Nordgrene, and two **portraits** by Lepage of his father and mother.

The museum contains almost the entire life's work of one of the museum's founders, Jules Chéret, who died in Nice in 1931. Chéret, originally a printmaker, is today best known for the Art Nouveau posters that he designed in the 1880s and 1890s – lively and boldly coloured works that had a great influence on Toulouse-Lautrec. Much of the space devoted to Chéret in the museum is taken up by large oil studies for these and later posters. As he grew older Chéret began to work more and more in the style of a latter-day Fragonard, executing flippant studies that combine the world of mythology with that of the Belle Epoque. Though instantly forgettable, these are nonetheless entertaining works with a strong nostalgic appeal.

A more obscure artist than Chéret is Gustave Adolphe Mussa, to whom two whole rooms are dedicated. Mussa, a Symbolist artist who lived most of his life in Nice, was essentially a watercolourist who specialized in the bizarre, erotic and frankly tasteless, such as a picture of ***Mary Magdalene*** exposing enormous breasts, or another of a naked woman on a crucifix. One of the most impressive of his works in the museum is ***The Glutted Siren*** showing a siren with blood dripping from her lips. In the background you can see well-known Nice buildings submerged in the sea and surmounted by pigs with dragon scales.

Tastelessness on a large scale characterizes some of the innumerable works by van Dongen that fill up another room on the first floor. Van Dongen was in early life associated with the Fauves, but became one of the most successful society portraitists of the 1920s and 1930s. Many of these portraits are on show here, including one of the Belgian ***King Leopold III***; but much more unusual – as well as silly – are a group of enormous imaginative compositions. Most notable among these is a triptych entitled the ***Tango of the Archangel*** ⭑ which features a girl, naked save for black fishnet stockings, dancing with a dinner-jacketed man with wings: all the decadence of high society between the wars seems captured in this work.

Van Dongen's Fauve colleague, Dufy, is represented by an enormous **collection of watercolours and oils** donated by his widow. Usually Dufy comes across as a pleasant but facile painter of cheerful small-scale landscapes, but the museum shows examples of a more robust side to his art, particularly a large oil of a ***Nude Emerging from a Shell*** ⭑. Dufy, like Matisse, was obsessed by music, often referring to it in his work, and another impressive painting in the museum shows a **nude on a patio** with a page of music in the foreground.

The museum has a reasonable collection of Impressionist works, including examples by Sisley, Monet, and above all Renoir. His ***Les Grandes Baigneuses*** ⭑ here is a second version of the famous painting in the Philadelphia Museum of Art. There is also a large oil (***Quai National at Puteaux***, 1878) by an Italian associate of the Impressionists, Luigi Loir, who specialized in drab, smoke-filled scenes of Paris and its surroundings.

Musée National Message Biblique Marc Chagall

Avenue du Docteur Ménard
Tel. (93) 817575
Open July–Sept 10am–7pm, Oct–June 10am–12.30pm, 2–5.30pm
Closed Tues

In the 1960s Marc Chagall, who still lives at ST-PAUL-DE-VENCE, painted 17 canvases of Biblical inspiration which he intended to present to the chapel of the Calvary in Vence. After deciding that the space would not do these works justice, he contemplated the construction of his own building to house them, and confided his plans to his friend André Malraux, then Minister of Culture. Malraux said that the government would pay for the building on condition that the artist donated the works to the state. This he agreed to do, and the museum was inaugurated in 1971. In addition to the canvases Chagall donated five sculptures, one tapestry and over 300 graphic works (most of which were preparatory studies for the paintings). He also executed three **stained glass windows** and one enormous **mosaic** of the prophet Elias specially for the building.

There is no doubt that the museum is a most delightful place, light, spacious and possessing a garden with a pool and an excellent cafeteria. But whether Chagall deserves this treatment is another matter. His enormous popularity as an artist – testified by the large crowds that daily throng the museum – can perhaps be attributed to his use of cheerful colours and sentimental sense of fantasy. There is of course nothing wrong in an artist producing what are little more than pleasing decorations. But what one does object to in the museum is the seriousness with which this art is taken, indeed the underlying pretentiousness of the whole conception. The emphasis of the museum is on the supposedly profound religious nature of Chagall's work, and, to reinforce this point, the museum library is equally divided between books on art and books on religion. Moreover, the temporary exhibitions put on here are often of a religious or mystical nature, such as displays of Tibetan prayer rolls.

Musée Matisse

164 Avenue des Arènes de Cimiez
Tel. (93) 815957
Open May–Sept 10am–noon, 2.30–6.30pm; Oct–Apr 10am–noon, 2–5pm
Closed Sun morning, Mon in Nov

Situated in the exclusive, residential district of Cimiez, and rising above the extensive Roman remains is a 17thC villa, **La Villa des Arènes** covered on the outside with 19thC *trompe-l'oeil* frescoes. On the ground floor you can look round a pleasant archaeological museum containing finds from the adjacent site. The first floor of this charmingly old-fashioned place is the Musée Matisse, and it makes a much better setting for Matisse's work than does the lavishly modernized museum to him at his birthplace, Le Cateau (see *NE FRANCE*).

Matisse was closely associated with Cimiez after 1938, working for a while in the Hôtel Régina (which is a few minutes' walk from the museum) and dying in a nearby house. Shortly after her husband's death, Mme. Matisse donated to Nice a large collection of **oil paintings, watercolours and graphic work** by him, as well as four **sculptures**. It was also she who decided on the Villa des Arènes as the most suitable place for the museum. Later the museum's collections were augmented by a donation from the artist's son, Jean, of versions of almost all the artist's **sculptures**. Although there is no single outstanding oil painting by Matisse in the museum, there are examples of his work in this medium from most stages in his career.

One of his first known paintings is his ***Still Life with Books*** (1890), which illustrates the artist's dark and rather clumsy beginnings. In 1896 he belatedly discoverd the art of the Impressionists, and soon afterwards radically changed his direction as an artist. By 1898, the date of ***La Cour du Moulin à Ajaccio***, the artist had already become interested in the representation of the sensual colours of the Mediterranean. Works from his so-called Fauvist period include the boldly Pointilliste ***Women with Umbrella*** (1905) and a **portrait of his wife** (1908). His period in Nice in the 1920s – when he reverted briefly to a more finely detailed and traditional style of painting – is represented by ***Storm at Nice***, and ***L'Odalisque au Coffret Rouge*** (1926–27). ***Window at Tahiti*** records a visit by Matisse in 1930. In the 1940s Matisse lived in VENCE, and painted ***Still Life with Pomegranates*** (1947) and the ***Rococo Armchair***. The actual armchair is also on display in the museum: perhaps its presence here is intended to remind the visitor of Matisse's famous comment that art should be "devoid of any subject matter . . . [and] as relaxing as a comfortable armchair." Between 1949–51 he was largely occupied with the decoration of the Chapel of the Rosary in VENCE, for which he executed innumerable studies. Over 50 of these are on display here, including a large number of gouache paper cutouts, his preferred medium in his last years.

The graphic work in the museum ranges from detailed academic nude studies executed in his youth to simple, joyful illustrations done in his 70s for a book on jazz. The artist's sculptures on show include the Rodin-inspired male torso, ***The Slave*** (1900) the artist's first important work in this medium; an elegant serpentine figure of a **nude woman** (1909); and three **portrait heads** of Henriette (1925, 1927–29). There are also the second and third versions of a group of large bronze reliefs of a female nude seen from the back: this group was executed over a period of years, with each figure becoming progressively more abstract.

NÎMES

Gard, Languedoc-Roussillon Map C4

In Roman times Nîmes was an important town on the road between Italy and Spain. In the 16thC it received a university and art school from François I. Today it is a large and very lively town, with extensive modern development and thriving industries, one of which is the manufacture of clothing: a type of material referred to as "de Nîmes" gave birth to the word "denim". The elegant and very well preserved old quarter of the town has a beautiful **18thC garden**, the *Jardin de la Fontaine*, as well as a famous group of Roman monuments, among which are an **amphitheatre** (smaller than the one at Arles but in better condition) and a small Roman temple, the **Maison Carrée**. The latter was probably built c.20BC by the architect of the famous nearby aqueduct, the **Pont du Gard**, and is the most important intact building of its kind in existence. It owes its excellent condition to having been used for many centuries as a town hall. Shortly after the Revolution it was restored and turned into a museum, housing both a small **group of Roman sculptures** and the municipal art collections. The former have remained in the building up to the present day, while the latter were transferred in 1907 to a specially built and rather ugly building on the edge of the town's central area.

Musée des Beaux-Arts

Rue Cité Foulc
Tel. (66) 673821
Open Apr–Sept 9am–noon, 2–6pm; Nov–Mar 9am–noon, 2–5pm
Closed Sun morning, Tues

The ground floor of the Musée des Beaux-Arts comprises a small exhibiting room and an enormous hall whose floor is half covered by an important Roman mosaic portraying in its central panel the **Marriage of Admetus**. The walls of this room are lined with large 17thC and 18thC French and Italian paintings, including works by Guido Reni, Luca Giordano, Natoire and Parrocel. On the first floor you can see 16thC Italian works, including a ***Flagellation*** by

Garofalo and ***Susannah and the Elders*** by Jacopo Bassano. There is also a large and important collection of 16thC–18thC Dutch and Flemish works. The French collections are mainly taken up with works by local painters, notably a grotesque and dramatic ***Locusta Trying out her Poisons*** by Sigalon. There is also a celebrated painting portraying ***Cromwell's Death*** by the 19thC specialist in scenes of English history. Delaroche. The museum's holdings of contemporary art are poor, and include slight works by Foujita, Yves Brayer, Rodin, and Bourdelle, as well as that almost ubiquitous feature of minor French museums – a collection of glass, paintings and drawings by the third-rate Fauve Maurice Marinot.

ORANGE
Vaucluse, Provence Map C4

An important city in Roman times, Orange became in the Middle Ages a tiny principality which was inherited in 1530 by William, Count of Nassau. William, who led the Dutch revolt against Spanish rule, came to be known as William of Orange, and was the ancestor both of William III of England and the present Dutch royal family. Together with Nîmes, Orange has the finest group of **Roman monuments** in France. Its **triumphal arch**, covered with sculptures, is the third largest in existence, and its **theatre** the best preserved in Europe.

Musée de la Ville
Place du Théâtre Antique
Tel. (90) 518006 Ext. 303
Open 8.30am–noon, 2–6.30pm

The municipal museum is across the road from the theatre. Its well-modernized interior contains on the ground floor an unremarkable **lapidary collection**, and on the first a group of miscellaneous items relating to the history of Orange, in particular during the period under William of Nassau. Strangely, the art gallery on the second floor is taken up almost entirely by **drawings** by the English artist Frank Brangwyn, and by canvases and lithographs by his English admirer and apologist William de Belleroche, a pupil of Carolus-Duran.

Brangwyn was born in the Belgian town of Bruges (where there is a museum to him), but went to England in 1877 to become apprenticed to the painter, writer and craftsman, William Morris. His work is bold and decorative, and strongly influenced by Rubens. The major commission of his life was to decorate the English Houses of Parliament with a series of murals on the theme of the British Empire (1924–30). However, they were eventually rejected by the commissioning body, being considered only suitable as colourful nightclub decorations (they are now in the Guildhall in Swansea, Wales). Brangwyn, an eccentric like his friend Belleroche, had no particular connection with Provence, and the reason why some of his and Belleroche's works have ended up in Orange remains obscure.

ST-ETIENNE
Alpes-du-Haute-Provence Map C4

A vast, ugly industrial town with no old buildings of note, St-Etienne has none the less a very active cultural life. There is an important Maison de Culture, a well-known theatre company (La Comédie de St-Etienne) and a Palais des Arts which has one of the best collections of contemporary art of any French provincial museum.

Musée d'Art et d'Industrie
Palais des Arts
8, Place Louis Comte
Tel. (77) 330485
Open 10am–noon, 2–5pm
Closed Tues, Wed morning

The Palais des Arts, a large handsome 19thC building displaying contemporary sculptures, stands in an attractive hillside park. The interior has been beautifully modernized, and its collections are excellently displayed. The ground and first floors contain objects and documents relating to mining, as well as a large and celebrated **collection of guns**.

The paintings are all on the second floor. There are some 17thC French, Italian and Dutch works, most notably two religious paintings by Charles Lebrun and Luca Giordano, a ***St Paul and St Barnabas at Lystra*** (1650) by the Dutch Italianate painter Nicolas Berchem, and an unusual genre scene, ***The Digger*** (1608) by Claes van der Back. However, the museum is principally worth visiting for its works of art dating from the late 19thC onwards. Among these is an impressive group of Symbolist paintings by artists such a A. Séon, Lévy-Dhurmer, Constantin Meunier and the extraordinary Charles Maurin (see Musée Crozatier, *LE PUY*). Here you can see two of Maurin's greatest works, ***L'Aurore du Rêve***★ and ***L'Aurore du Travail***★. Both were painted in 1892, and formed part of a triptych shown in 1892 in the exhibiting society of the Symbolists, the

Salon de la Rose Croix. The first was inspired by Baudelaire's *Fleurs du Mal* and shows a man on a park bench surrounded by female nudes; the second and more powerful of the two features expressively distorted nudes against a sinister industrial background.

Later works in the museum include pieces by Maurice Denis, Rodin, Matisse, Vuillard, Alberto Mangelli, Picabia, Léger, Villon, Max Ernst, Zadkine, Calder and Laurens. You should not miss a colourful **oil** by the Expressionist painter Franz Kupka, a sensitive Cubist-inspired still-life by Gino Severini (***Nature Morte au Journal Lacerba***, 1913), and an excellent **assemblage** by Schwitters of c.1939–44. Unlike most French provincial museums, that at St-Etienne has built up a high quality collection of works from the 1950s up to the present day. Contemporary French art is represented by such works as ***Blue Monochrome*** (1957) by Yves Klein, ***Compression of Motorcycles*** by César, a gigantic **untitled work** by Jean-Pierre Reynaud made out of white tiles (1976), and highly entertaining assemblages by Daniel Sperri (***Throw out the Baby with the Bath***, 1967) and Arnan (***Rubbish from the Studio*** and ***Accumulation of Loud Speakers*** 1964). A remarkable feature of the contemporary holdings is the high proportion of works by **leading American artists** ★ such as Jim Dine, Frank Stella, Wesselman, Warhol, Louise Nevelson, Robert Morris, Donald Judd, Sol LeWitt and Don Eddy.

ST-GILLES
Gard, Languedoc-Roussillon Map C4

St-Gilles lies on the road linking Montpellier and Arles, and is frequently bypassed in favour of the more famous Provençal cities; but you will find the medieval town behind the main street has a fair amount to offer. The most important building is the 12thC **Eglise St-Gilles-du-Gard** ★ which, like the town, takes its name from the St Egidius (Gilles) who founded a religious community here. This is one of the finest Romanesque buildings in Provence, particularly notable for the relief sculpture across its **triple-arched façade**.

Musée Archéologique
Maison Romane
Tel. (66) 873084 (town hall)
Open 9am–noon, 3–6pm
Closed Sun

The Musée Archeologique in St-Gilles occupies a 12thC town house not far from the famous church of the same period. The house itself is of considerable interest, for it is one of the few domestic buildings from the Romanesque period to have survived. The collection consists mainly of **classical and medieval antiquities**, such as capitals and tympani, drawn from the religious institutions of the area.

ST-JEAN-CAP-FERRAT
Alpes-Maritimes Map F4

This is a beautiful wooded peninsula almost entirely covered with luxurious private gardens and villas. For the ordinary tourist they seem to offer a glimpse of a world known previously only from romantic old films. The famous villas here include the **Villa des Cèdres**, which belonged to Léopold II of Belgium, and the **Villa Mauresque**, where Somerset Maugham spent his last years.

Villa Ephrussi de Rothschild
Boulevard Denis-Séméria
Tel. (93) 013309
Open July–Aug 9am–noon (gardens only) 3–7pm; Sept–June 9am–noon (gardens only) 2–6pm
Closed Mon, Nov

The only villa on the peninsula open to the public is the extraordinary **Villa Ephrussi de Rothschild**, built in the late 19thC by the Baroness Rothschild to house her own art collections and those belonging to her father and her exceptionally rich banker husband. In 1933 it was handed over to the Académie des Beaux-Arts on condition that it maintained its character as a private residence.

The interior is sumptuous and exceedingly eclectic, with each room in a style corresponding to the works displayed there. Among a large group of Renaissance works of art (the bulk of which were bought from Italian palaces fallen on hard times) is a fine late 15thC **Enghien tapestry** representing fantastical hunting scenes, and a painting of a ***Condottiere*** attributed to the Venetian artist Carpaccio.

The greatest works in the collection, however, are of the French and Italian Rococo, which was the particular interest of the baroness. There are **ceiling paintings** by the Venetian decorator Gian Domenico Tiepolo, oil paintings by Boucher (most notably a mawkishly sentimental but finely painted ***Mother and Child***), and a superlative collection of **Sèvres and Meissen pottery**, including an amusing set of Meissen figures of monkeys playing musical instruments. One room is devoted to the Impressionists and has two late **landscapes** by Renoir, a ***View of Moret-sur-Loing*** by Sisley, and a painting by Monet of ***Giverny at Dawn*** (1897) which was greatly admired by Marcel Proust. The gardens of the villa are as dreamlike as the building itself. One wanders as if in a trance from gardens in Spanish, Japanese and Florentine styles, distracted every now and then by views of the spectacular coastline leading towards Monaco.

ST PAUL-DE-VENCE
Alpes-Maritimes Map F4

A fortified hilltop village largely rebuilt in the 16thC, St-Paul-de-Vence attracted numerous artists after 1918. Today it is difficult to raise much enthusiasm for its obvious picturesque qualities, as the whole place is overrun with tourists, antique shops, and expensive hotels. One of these hotels – *La Colombe d'Or* – has an outstanding private art collection. Its founder, Paul Roux, followed the tradition dating back to the days of Père Ganne at Barbizon of allowing his many artist visitors to repay the hospitality which they received here by leaving works of art. These artists included Picasso, Matisse, Dufy, Léger Utrillo, Rouault and César. At one time tourists were freely allowed to see this collection; now they are at least obliged to have a meal in the hotel restaurant.

Fondation Maeght ☆
Tel. (93) 328163
Open May–Sept 10am–12.30pm, 3–7pm; Oct–Apr 10am–12.30pm, 2.30–6pm

In the midst of a landscape dotted with exotic trees and shrubs, and plush modern buildings, there stands one of the best museums of modern art in France. This, the Fondation Maeght, was built in the early 1960s by the gallery-owners and art-book publishers, Marguerite and Aimé Maeght. Their intention was to increase the knowledge and appreciation of modern art. In addition to a gallery, the Foundation has a library, a bookshop, and ceramic and print studios, and a number of concerts, ballets and other such events are put on here. The architect at the Fondation Maeght was the renowned Catalan, José Luis Sert, many of whose buildings reflect his original activity as a town planner. The Foundation is no exception, being conceived as an asymetrical cluster of buildings in perfect harmony with the environment. He favoured simple materials such as stones from a nearby hill, and hand-made bricks fired – as was the tradition in this area – in a wood oven.

As so often in his work, Sert designed the Foundation in collaboration with artists. Thus his friend and compatriot Miró executed numerous **ceramics**, **mosaics**, **fountains** and **sculptures** for the museum's terraces, Braque decorated a **pool** and provided **stained glass windows** for a chapel, and so on.

The museum's collection comprises works by many of the leading French or French-based artists of this century, including Braque, Bonnard, Calder, Chagall, Soulages, Tàpies, Léger, Matisse, Zadkine and Richier. It is much less strong on British, German and American art, although there is a very impressive **group of paintings** by Kandinsky. The display of the works is constantly changing, and every summer most of the gallery space is taken up by major exhibitions. On permanent show, however, is a group of **bronze figures** by Giacometti beautifully placed on the museum's patio, and the paintings by Kandinsky and Chagall.

ST-TROPEZ
Var, Côte d'Azur Map E5

Destroyed by Saracens in the Middle Ages, the seaside town of St-Tropez became a tiny self-governing republic in 1470, thanks to an offer made by a Genoese nobleman to repopulate the place on condition that it was exempt from taxes. It remained a republic until the 17thC, and later slipped into obscurity. Then in 1892 Paul Signac, the follower of Seurat and later associate of the Fauves, came to the town and was excited by its artistic potential. He was to stay here for much of his remaining life, acquiring a house called La Hune which still survives on what is now the Avenue Paul Signac.

Many other artists came to St-Tropez in his wake, most notably Bonnard and the artists associated with Fauvism – Marquet, van Dongen, Dufy, Matisse and Dérain. The port of St-Tropez, with its white, pink and yellow houses reflected against a deep blue sea, was a great inspiration to these artists, all of whom were seeking in their works for effects of ever more vivid colour.

St-Tropez continued to attract a growing number of artists and writers up to World War II. In 1944 it was largely destroyed by the Germans and, although later faithfully rebuilt, ceased temporarily to be popular. It suddenly became fashionable again after 1957 when the film director Roger Vadim brought here the then little-known actress, Brigitte Bardot, to make *And God Created Woman*. After this, the town became a playground for the rich, famous and beautiful, as well as for thousands of less glamorous holiday-makers. Today St-Tropez, for all its vulgarity and artificiality, remains one of the prettiest resorts on the French coast. Moreover it has a small but outstanding art gallery.

Musée de l'Annonciade ☆

Place Georges-Grammont
Tel. (94) 970401
Open June–Sept 10am–noon, 3–7pm; Oct–May 10am–noon, 2–6pm
Closed Tues, Nov

The Musée de l'Annonciade is situated right by the port in a deconsecrated 16thC chapel which was beautifully converted into a museum in 1955. Originally intended to display the works of modern art left to the town by Georges Grammont, the museum's collection was later augmented by a number of canvases – notably by Signac – formerly in the possession of the painter Person.

Most of the permanent collection is on the first floor, while the ground floor is often taken up by temporary exhibitions. The interior is light and spacious, and from the first floor there are beautiful views of the port and the coast leading towards Nice. Almost every painting on show is of high quality, which makes the place virtually unique among small French provincial museums.

The artists represented in the collection are for the most part those who have been closely associated with the town. There are two superlative **Views of St-Tropez** ★ by Signac in a *Pointilliste* style, a vigorous nude by Matisse entitled ***The Gypsy*** ★ (1906), another painting of the same title by van Dongen, an oil by Maillol of a **woman at her toilet**, two **views of London** by Dérain, and **St-Tropez scenes** by Marquet and Dufy. There is one view of St-Tropez by Bonnard, who, however, is best represented by an excellent **standing nude by a mirror** ★. Vuillard, a contemporary of Bonnard who also specialized in intimate interior scenes, has two small but intricately detailed and exceptionally subtle interiors, ***Le Souper d'Annette*** ★ and ***Interior with Two Chairs*** ★ (1901). In addition there are good works by the Symbolist painters Maurice Denis and Roussel, and the follower of Seurat, van Rysselberghe.

TOULON

Var, Côte d'Azur Map E5

In a deep natural harbour and protected by steep hills, Toulon is one of the most beautifully situated ports on the Mediterranean. Since the time of Louis XIV it has been France's leading naval base, and in World War II suffered severe damage from bombing. The only surviving part of the town is in the immediate vicinity of the harbour, around the rather unprepossessing Cathedral of Ste-Marie-Majeure: this is a district of tall dirty houses and menacing alleyways. The rest of the town is brashly modern, but at the same time very exciting and lacking the chic artificiality characteristic of so many other nearby coastal towns.

The town's most outstanding art treasure are two **atlantes** ★★ (1656) by Pierre Puget, which once flanked the main door of the town hall. *Atlantes* are columns in the form of male figures (they are sometimes wrongly referred to as caryatids, who are in fact their female equivalent). The town hall was destroyed during World War II, but fortunately Puget's sculptures had previously been removed for their safekeeping. They now mark the main entrance of a naval museum on the harbour's quay, occupying the same site as the old town hall. The Toulon door was the first important commission of Puget, who previously had practised both as a decorator of warships and a painter. He makes the two figures writhe under their burden as if in considerable mental and physical agony. The formal inspiration for them might be Michelangelo's *Slaves* (*LOUVRE*), but it is also possible that the artist was affected by the sight of the countless manacled convicts and political prisoners who daily shuffled through the streets of Toulon on their way to the royal galleys.

Musées Municipaux de Toulon: Musée d'Art and Music d'Histoire Naturelle

20 Boulevard Maréchal Leclerc
Tel. (94) 931554
Open 10am–noon, 2–6pm

The Musée d'Art et d'Archéologie is in the modern part of the town and shares an imposing late 19thC building with a natural history museum and municipal library. A few years ago it was an old-fashioned, uncared-for place, but since the appointment of Marie-Claude Béaud as curator in 1978, it has changed almost beyond recognition. The interior has been excellently modernized, and the museum mainly concentrates on the acquisition and display of contemporary art. However, only a small fraction of the museum's collections are shown at any one time. The spacious first-floor galleries are taken up by regularly changing exhibitions of the work of mainly young French artists. The ground floor rooms put on longer-lasting exhibitions on particular themes such as portraiture, landscape painting, and religious art. The latter exhibitions are intended to show as wide a variety as possible of the museum's collections in an imaginative and not necessarily chronological way. They include Indian, Chinese and Japanese works, two **mythological scenes** by the 17thC Italian painter Annibale Carracci, a **bust of St John the Baptist** attributed to Puget, works by the locally-born 18thC painters Joseph and Louis-Michel Van Loo, an impressive **battle scene** by de Loutherbourg, a plaster cast of a man's head by Rodin, a view of the **Spanish Steps in Rome** by Maurice Denis, and works by contemporary artists such as Francis Bacon, Christo, Sol LeWitt, Richard Long and Gilbert and George. Although it is a matter of luck what one will find on show, a visit to the museum is certainly worthwhile if simply to experience a lively and very sympathetic ambience.

VALLAURIS
Alpes-Maritimes, Côte d'Azur
Map F4

A lively little town set back from the main coastal roads, Vallauris has for centuries been noted for its ceramic industry. This industry was given a new lease of life just after World War II when Picasso settled here for six years and executed numerous ceramics (see p. 266). The great majority of these are now in the Picasso Museum in **ANTIBES**.

Musée Municipal de Vallauris
Place de la Libération
Tel. (93) 641605
Open 10am–noon, 2–6pm
Closed Tues

A 16thC castle on the town's attractive main square houses this recently opened museum, devoted largely to ceramics from Etruscan times to the present day. Many of the modern works are prize-winning ceramics from the biennial ceramics exhibition which has been held in the town since 1966. The museum also has a small collection of contemporary paintings, most notably by Alberto Magnelli, an extremely original Italian artist associated with Cubism, Futurism and Metaphysical Painting.

The chapel of the castle contains the town's most impressive works of art – two large murals by Picasso representing ***War*** ★★ and ***Peace*** ★★. These were painted on plyboard panels in the artist's studio, and then attached by screws to the chapel's windowless walls (which curve inwards to form a barrel vault). The makeshift quality of the decoration and the dark simplicity of its setting help to increase its power. The message of the virtues of Peace over the evils of War is expressed partly in the harmonious, colourful composition of the ***Peace*** mural as opposed to the sombre violent composition of the ***War*** mural opposite.

At the end of the town square opposite the chapel is a well-known but rather absurd **bronze** by Picasso of a sad-faced naked man inexplicably holding a struggling sheep.

VENCE
Alpes-Maritimes, Côte d'Azur
Map F4

Vence, now a sprawling and very crowded inland resort, is attractively situated on the slopes of a hill and has a pleasant old town bursting with antique and pottery shops. It was once very popular with artists and writers, including D.H. Lawrence, who died here.

Chapelle du Rosaire
Route de St-Jeannet

The town's main attraction is the **Chapelle du Rosaire** ★★, designed and decorated by Matisse between 1949–51 when he was in his late 70s and early 80s. It was intended as a gift to the nuns of the adjacent Dominican convent, who had looked after him during an illness. Set in a quiet suburban part of the town, the place is characterized by its extreme simplicity. It is a box-like structure which on the outside is completely bare save for an elegant wrought-iron cross on the roof. The dazzlingly white walls of the interior are decorated with black line drawings representing the **Stations of the Cross** and **Dominican monks**. The main colour note is provided by some beautiful stained glass windows. Every detail of the building down to the candles on the altar table and the vestments worn by the officiating priests was designed by Matisse. The chapel is undoubtedly one of the most moving religious buildings of recent times. It is a pity that the atmosphere of peace and serenity which it emanates is often diminished by the inevitably large number of daily visitors.

VIENNE
Isère, Rhône-Alpes Map D2

Squeezed into a bend of the Rhône valley, Vienne almost gives the impression of having been pushed aside by the motorway, main roads and railway line that closely follow the course of the river. The town has nevertheless miraculously retained a quiet and dignified character. It has numerous important old monuments, ranging from a very well preserved **Roman temple** to a 12thC–15thC cathedral with a most beautiful 15thC **sculpted façade**.

Musée des Beaux-Arts et Archéologie
Place de Miramont
Tel. (74) 855042
Open Apr to mid-Oct 9am–noon, 2–6.30pm, mid-Oct to Mar 10am–noon, 2–5pm (Sun 10am–noon, 2–6pm)
Closed Mon (Nov–Mar), Tues

Housed in a dull 19thC building in the town's main square, this has a fine collection of **pottery**, but its items of archaeology and painting are less impressive. The paintings comprise mainly French and Flemish 17thC works, and works by 19thC local artists. There are also some striking but silly Salon pictures, most notably ***The Fall of Man*** by A. Nemoz, which shows Adam and Eve as if they were disgruntled nudists on a rainy day.

VILLENEUVE-LÈS-AVIGNON
Gard, Languedoc-Roussillon Map C4

On the other side of the Rhône from AVIGNON, Villeneuve-lès-Avignon developed in the 14thC as an exclusive residential district for members of the papal court. It is a quiet place with some beautiful medieval monuments, including the 13thC **Tower of Philippe le Bel**, the enormous hilltop **Chartreuse du Val de Bénediction** (founded by Pope Innocent VI in 1356, and the largest charterhouse in France), and the 14thC **church of Notre-Dame**, which has in its sacristy a fine 13thC polychrome ivory statuette of the ***Virgin and Child***.

Musée Municipal
Rue de l'Hôpital
Tel. (90) 254540
Open Apr–Sept 10am–noon, 3–7.30pm; Oct–Mar 10am–noon, 2–5pm
Closed Tues, Feb

The Musée Municipal, which is housed on the first floor of a 17thC palace, is a dark and musty place filled with saints' relics, decaying ecclesiastical bric a brac and somewhat grim religious paintings such as a ***Crucifixion*** by Philippe de Champaigne in a bad state of preservation. But a visit here is worth it simply to see the outstanding ***Coronation of the Virgin*** ★★ (1453) by the Laon artist Enguerrand Quarton. Though born in Laon, Quarton (also called Charonton) was active in the S of France at Aix, Arles and Avignon. The Villeneuve-lès-Avignon painting, like many other works in the museum, came from the nearby charterhouse. The artist was specifically contracted to portray in the background the church of St Peter's in Rome and the Castel Sant' Angelo; but Quarton also decided to include elements of local scenery, such as Mont Sainte-Victoire, and the cliffs of L'Estaque. Quarton is also considered the painter of the celebrated ***Avignon Pietà*** in the ***LOUVRE***, which originated from the charterhouse, and is represented in the museum by a good copy.

Matisse in the South

For Matisse, who had been brought up in a grey, industrial area of northern France, the colourful and sensual environment of the Mediterranean seems to have had a remarkable liberating effect. It was undoubtedly an important factor in turning him into one of the great colourists of this century. During his early years as a painter, when he was based mainly in Paris, Matisse worked in a relatively dark and conventional style. He began to develop a greater interest in colour in 1896, after seeing a group of Impressionist works in the collection of an Australian painter in Brittany. Two years later he painted vividly coloured landscapes in Corsica, in striking contrast to those he had executed a few years previously in northern France. But his real discovery both of colour and of the Mediterranean did not begin until the early years of this century. In 1904 he was invited by Seurat's friend and follower, Paul Signac, to stay in his villa ("La Hune") at **ST-TROPEZ**. This visit inspired, ***Luxe, Calme et Volupté*** which shows female nudes bathed in brilliant sunshine beside the Saint-Tropez seashore. The following year Matisse, together with his friend and colleague Derain, went to Collioure in Roussillon and devised the first major work of his career, ***The Joy of Life***. This is a sensual Arcadian scene set in a clearing in a wood near Collioure with a view towards the sea.

Matisse began to spend an increasing amount of time near the Mediterranean after 1916, when he decided to pass the winter in **NICE**. During this and subsequent winters in the town he stayed in one of the grand 19thC hotels that line the Promenade des Anglais. Matisse was a keen viola

player and was forced to practise his instrument in a remote bathroom of the hotel so as not to disturb the other guests. In 1921 he acquired a balconied top-floor apartment in the old part of Nice, and this he retained until 1938. It was on the Place Charles Félix and had previously belonged to the American writer, Frank Harris. It was in this apartment that Matisse painted most of his celebrated ***Odalisques***, half-naked women in Oriental guise placed against a sensual, exotic background. In 1938 the artist moved into an apartment in the Hôtel Régina in the exclusive residential suburb of Cimiez. The hotel was an extremely pretentious late 19thC building that had been constructed in the hope that Queen Victoria would become a regular guest, but by Matisse's day it had long ceased to be fashionable. His room looked out on to a balcony with Rococo ironwork which often featured in the artist's work.

In 1940 Matisse fell seriously ill and was looked after by Dominican nuns in Lyon. Shortly after his recovery a year later, he moved to a small villa called "La Rêve" on the outskirts of **VENCE**. It happened quite by chance that a Dominican rest home for invalid girls was situated across the road, and one of the nuns (Sister Jacques) who had taken such good care of the artist in Lyon, now worked there. Out of gratitude for all that the Dominican order had done for him, Matisse offered to design and decorate for them a chapel at the **VENCE** rest house. In 1948 Matisse returned to the Hôtel Régina, and remained there until his death in 1954. During his last years he did much work lying in bed; using a stick with a piece of charcoal attached to it, he still managed to execute portrait drawings on the walls and ceiling of his bedroom.

Matisse at Nice, 1939, photographed by Georges Brassai.

***The Tree of Life**, stained-glass window at the Chapelle de la Rosaire.*

Picasso in the South

Unlike Matisse, Picasso was far more affected by encounters with people – particularly with women – than by the places where he lived. The topographical elements in his art are minimal, and it is hard to see any obvious differences between the works he painted in Paris and those done in the South of France, except that the latter were mainly executed during the last stage of his career. Nonetheless, the legend of Picasso lives on in the South of France more than anywhere else in Europe.

Avignon, which he visited on various occasions before World War I, was one of the first places in the South to be associated with him. However, the celebrated ***Demoiselles d'Avignon*** (1907, Metropolitan Museum of Art, New York) was in fact probably named after a street of brothels in Barcelona. According to another source, the connection with the Provençal town might have derived from a ribald suggestion that the poet Max Jacob's grandmother, who came from Avignon, had posed for one of the figures. Picasso's first major involvement with the South of France developed over the three summers he spent at the Roussillon village of Céret, 1911–13. He went there on the advice of his Catalan sculptor friend Manolo and stayed with Braque and Max Jacob in the Maison Delcros, a large early 19thC house just behind the village which soon came to be known as the "Maison des Cubistes".

Picasso made periodic visits to Provence – especially to the Riviera – in the years between the two world wars. In 1956 the poet Paul Éluard encouraged him to stay at the Hôtel Vaste Horizon at Mougins, a fortified hill village behind Cannes. By chance Dora Maar – a beautiful Yugoslav girl whom he had recently met in Paris – was holidaying at St-Tropez. She and Picasso met up in Provence and, becoming lovers, explored the region together. On one trip they discovered the village of **VALLAURIS** and found that it had a pottery industry dating back to ancient times.

It was after World War II that Provence came to play a major role in Picasso's life. In 1945 he decided to move to **ANTIBES**, and was offered the use of the Château Grimaldi (now the MUSÉE PICASSO) as a studio. He also paid a visit to the Vaucluse village of Ménerbes, where he bought for Dora Maar a beautiful and large house that formed part of the town's medieval fortifications; she still lives there. At this time Picasso had other amorous intentions; he had recently met a painter and model, Françoise Gilot, whom he was shortly to marry. She came to live with him in Antibes, and then in 1947 settled with him at Vallauris, where they bought the Villa La Galloise.

At Vallauris Picasso helped to revive the local pottery industry, and himself carried out many works in this medium. In 1950 he offered to present a bronze statue to the town, an offer that at first caused alarm among the townspeople. They knew that they would have to accept it in gratitude for all that Picasso had done for the place, and yet were worried that it would be too avant-garde for their taste. When told, however, that it was simply a naturalistic representation of a man with a sheep, the local blacksmith was heard to say, "What a pity if it looks just like any other statue." Picasso's stay in Vallauris ended in 1954 on a sad note, with Françoise walking out on him, saying that she did not want to spend the rest of her life with a historical monument. Later Françoise was to write a frank account, *Life with Picasso* (1964), which was to lead to a permanent break between Picasso and the two children he had by her, Claude and Paloma. Picasso failed to take up an offer, made by the Roussillon town of Collioure, to come and live in that town, and instead bought an early 19thC villa, "La Californie" on the northern outskirts of Cannes in 1955. He was joined there by the new love of his life, Jacqueline Roque, who was to remain with him until his death. Visitors to

"La Californie" were struck by the way Picasso had stripped the tasteless interior of the house of its furniture and carpets, and had replaced these with a chaotic jumble of works of art. In 1958, seeking to avoid the growing number of visitors and tourists who were anxious to meet him in Cannes, Picasso sold "La Californie" and acquired a 14thC château in the remote village of Vauvenargues near Mont Sainte-Victoire. This grand, princely building was an appropriate final home for a man who had come to be regarded as the giant of 20thC art. To its enormous echoing rooms, adorned with baroque fireplaces, Picasso added some of his own decorations, including, in one of the bathrooms, a mural of a piping Pan that was intended to serenade Jacqueline in her bath. Picasso died in 1973, and his grave in the garden of the château has a bronze by him, ***Women with a Vase***.

Picasso at work in his Vallauris studio, 1953

BIOGRAPHIES

This selective list of artists mentioned in the *Guide* consists mainly of French artists, but includes others whose work has been influential in France, or who have themselves been deeply influenced by French art.

Abbate, Niccolò dell' c.1512–71
Italian painter, active in France from 1552. He is most important for his landscapes with mythological figures.
Aman-Jean, Edmond 1860–1936
French painter, etcher and lithographer.
Angelico, Fra (Guido di Pietro) d.1455
Florentine painter, one of the most famous artists of the early Renaissance.
Arp, Jean or **Hans** 1887–1966
French artist, active in several fields but principally famous as one of the greatest of abstract sculptors.

Baglione, Giovanni c.1573–1644
Italian painter and writer, remembered chiefly for his *Lives of the Painters, Sculptors and Architects* (1642).
Baldung Grien, Hans 1484/5–1545
One of the outstanding German painters and engravers of the 16thC.
Balthus (Count Balthasar Klossowski de Rola) b.1908
French painter of Polish background.
Bartolommeo, Fra (Baccio della Porta) 1472/75–1517
Florentine painter, a Dominican monk. He was one of the leading artists of the High Renaissance.
Barye, Antoine-Louis 1796–1875
French sculptor (and much less importantly painter) of animal subjects.
Bastien-Lepage, Jules 1848–84
French painter, mainly of portraits and scenes of rural life.
Bazille, Frédéric 1841–70
French Impressionist painter, particularly noted for his paintings of figures out of doors. He gave much-needed financial support to Monet and Renoir and his death in the Franco-Prussian War cut short a promising career.
Bellange, Jacques a.1600–17
French Mannerist painter, engraver and decorator, active in the Duchy of Lorraine for the court at Nancy.
Bellegambe, Jean c.1470/80–c.1535
Netherlandish painter, active in Douai.
Bellini, Giovanni c.1430–1516
The greatest Venetian painter of his day. His brother **Gentile** (c.1429/30?–1507) and his father **Jacopo** (c.1400–70/71) were also painters.
Bellmer, Hans b.1902
Polish-French painter, graphic artist and sculptor.
Bernard, Emile 1868–1941
French painter and writer on art. He knew Toulouse-Lautrec and van Gogh.
Bernini, Gianlorenzo 1598–1680
Italian sculptor, architect and painter, the dominant figure in Italian Baroque art.
Besnard, Albert 1849–1934
French painter. A successful establishment figure.
Blanche, Jacques-Emile 1861–1942
French painter, primarily of fashionable portraits, also a graphic artist and writer on art.
Boilly, Louis-Léopold 1761–1845
French genre and portrait painter and lithographer.
Bonington, Richard Parkes 1802–28
English painter, primarily a landscapist, working mainly in France.
Bonnard, Pierre 1867–1947
French painter and graphic artist. He was one of the founders of the Nabis, but after 1900 he reverted to a more naturalistic style, rooted in Impressionism.
Bonnat, Joseph-Florentin-Léon 1833–1922
French painter. He made a fortune with his society portraits, painted with photographic verisimilitude.
Bontemps, Pierre c.1505/10–68
French sculptor, best known for his work on royal monuments at St-Denis.
Bosse, Abraham 1607–76
French engraver, writer on art and occasional painter.
Bouchardon, Edmé 1698–1762
One of the finest French sculptors of the 18thC. He spent a decade in Rome and his style was decisively influenced by antique sculpture.
Boucher, François 1703–70
French painter of mythology, gallantry, landscape and portraits, one of the greatest of Rococo artists. He was immensely prolific, and represents, with his pupil Fragonard, the taste of his age more than any other French artist.
Boudin, Eugène 1824–98
French painter of seascapes and beach scenes. His spontaneous brushwork concentrating on the essential, influenced the Impressionists, with whom he exhibited at their first group exhibition in 1874.
Bouguereau, Adolphe William 1825–1905
French painter, immensely popular in his day and one of the most influential upholders of the conservative values of academic art.
Bourdelle, Antoine 1861–1929
Leading French sculptor, Rodin's chief assistant from 1893–1908.

Bouts, Dirk or Dieric d. 1475
One of the greatest early Netherlandish painters.

Brancusi, Constantin 1876–1957
Romanian-French sculptor, based in Paris from 1904. He worked briefly with Rodin, but from 1907 onwards, inspired by the primitivist carvings of painter-sculptors such as Gauguin, he began to reject modelling techniques and naturalism.

Braque, Georges 1882–1963
French painter, with Picasso the originator of Cubism. Whereas Picasso soon moved on from Cubism, Braque continued to develop its ideas throughout his long career.

Broederlam, Melchior d. 1409
Netherlandish painter, active principally at Dijon, where he was court painter to Philip the Bold, Duke of Burgundy.

Bronzino, Agnolo 1503–72
Florentine Mannerist painter. He is best known for his elegant and highly polished court portraits.

Bruegel (Brueghel), **Pieter** c. 1525–69
The greatest Netherlandish painter of the 16thC. His sons **Pieter Brueghel the Younger** (1564–1638) and **Jan "Velvet" Brueghel** (1568–1625) were also painters.

Buffet, Bernard b. 1928
French painter. He had made a considerable reputation by the age of 20, and his distinctive style has hardly changed since.

Cabanel, Alexandre 1823–89
French painter, one of the most successful and influential academic artists of his day.

Caillebotte, Gustave 1848–94
French painter and collector, best known as one of the chief patrons of the Impressionists, whose exhibitions he helped to organize.

Callot, Jacques 1592/3–1635
French engraver and draughtsman, one of the greatest of graphic artists.

Campin, Robert a. 1406–44
Netherlandish painter, with Jan van Eyck the founding father of the early Netherlandish school. It is practically certain that he was the author of a number of paintings grouped under the name of the "Master of Flémalle".

Canaletto (Giovanni Antonio Canal) 1697–1768
Venetian painter. The most famous viewpainter of the 18thC.

Canova, Antonio 1757–1822
Italian sculptor, one of the most celebrated artists of the Neoclassical movement.

Caravaggio, Michelangelo Merisi da 1571–1610
The greatest Italian painter of the 17thC. His revolutionary style – characterized by bold, strongly lit, realistically painted figures emerging dramatically from dark shadow – was immensely influential in Italy, Spain and northern Europe.

Caron, Antoine c. 1520–c. 1600
French painter, decorator and festival designer.

Carpeaux, Jean-Baptiste 1827–75
The leading French sculptor of his day. His emotional expressiveness broke with the Neoclassical tradition.

Carracci, Annibale 1560–1609
Bolognese painter, one of the founders of Baroque history painting and the father of ideal landscape. With his brother **Agostino** (1557–1602) and cousin **Ludovico** (1559–1619), he played a leading role in the revival of Italian painting from the prevailing rather sterile Mannerism.

Carrière, Eugène 1849–1906
French painter of portraits and domestic scenes.

Cellini, Benvenuto 1500–71
Florentine sculptor and goldsmith, active in France as well as Italy.

César (César Baldaccini) b. 1921
French sculptor of considerable versatility and inventive power.

Cézanne, Paul 1839–1906
French painter, one of the greatest artists of the 19thC and a key figure in the development of 20thC art. His declared aim was to make Impressionism into "something solid and durable, like the art of the museums" and his rigorous analysis of structure made him an inspiration to the pioneers of abstract art.

Cézanne: *Self-portrait, 1883–5, Paris, Niarchos coll.*

Chagall, Marc b. 1887
French Russian painter who has also worked prolifically as a designer of book illustrations, stage sets and stained glass windows.

Chalette, Jean 1581–1645
French painter, active in Toulouse. Influenced by Caravaggio, he was one of the most important of the 17thC Toulouse painters.
Champaigne, Philippe de 1602–74
The greatest French portraitist of the 17thC, also a distinguished painter of religious works. A Fleming by birth (he moved to Paris in 1621), he gradually modified his Rubensian early style to suit more sober French taste.
Chardin, Jean-Baptiste-Siméon 1699–1779
French painter of still life and genre, one of the outstanding artists of the 18thC. Chardin's seriousness and sense of truth are far removed from the frivolities of the then dominant Rococo style, and few artists have approached his directness of vision or his sureness and delicacy of touch in handling oil paint. Late in life, failing eyesight caused him to give up oils and he produced some penetrating pastel portraits.

Chardin: *Self-portrait pastel, c.1771, Paris, Louvre, Cabinet des Dessins*

Charonton see QUARTON
Chassériau, Théodore 1819–56
French painter. He trained with Ingres, but deeply admired Delacroix, and combined Romantic and classical ideals in his work; his drawing is clear, but his colour is vivid and his choice of subjects often exotic. Chassériau visited North Africa in 1840 and 1846 and some of his best and most popular works are of African subjects.
Chéret, Jules 1836–1931
French printmaker, best known for his posters, which, deriving inspiration from Japanese prints, use bold colours and elongated proportions. They were a significant influence on Art Nouveau designers and on such painters as Seurat and Toulouse-Lautrec.

Chirico, Giorgio de 1888–1978
Italian painter. He was a forerunner of Surrealism, and his works are characterized by an enigmatic, dreamlike quality.
Claude Gellée called **Claude Lorraine** 1600–82
French painter, active in Rome for almost all his career. He was the most famous exponent of ideal landscape and was enormously influential. His works, which show very great sensitivity to effects of light, are much more gentle and elegiac than those of his friendly rival Poussin. He drew his subjects mainly from the Bible and classical myth.
Clodion (Claude Michel) 1738–1814
French Rococo sculptor. He made a few large statues, but is best known for his small-scale terracotta and marble groups.
Clouet, Jean d.1540/1
French portrait painter. Although he had a great contemporary reputation, there is little secure knowledge about his career and only a handful of paintings are generally accepted as his. They are sensitively characterized, with an air of reflective calmness. Clouet was succeeded as court painter in 1541 by his son **François** (c.1510?–1572). His style is more Italianate than his father's and he probably visited Italy early in his career.
Cocteau, Jean 1889–1963
French writer, film maker, painter and draughtsman, a leading figure in French avantgarde artistic circles from the 1920s. His versatility as an artist is outstanding, but his paintings and drawings rank among his lesser achievements.
Colombe, Michel c.1430 after 1512
French sculptor. Very little documented work by him survives, but that which does shows him to have been one of the most accomplished French artists of his period.
Constable, John 1776–1837
English landscape painter. His work was exhibited (with Bonington's) at the 1824 Paris Salon and was received enthusiastically by French artists, notably Delacroix.
Corneille de Lyon a.1533–74
Naturalized French portrait painter, born at The Hague and active mainly in Lyon. He worked for the French royal family and had a great contemporary reputation. His works are generally small, with bust or half-length figures portrayed in dark costumes against plain backgrounds.
Cornelis van Haarlem 1562–1638
Dutch biblical and portrait painter, one of Holland's leading Mannerist artists. His later work was more sober and influenced another Haarlem artist, Frans Hals.

Corot, Jean-Baptiste-Camille
1796–1875
French landscape and figure painter. He is one of the most important artists in the history of landscape painting, as his unaffected, clearly lit scenes broke away from stereotypes and were a major influence on the next generation. Some of Corot's more popular paintings, however, were of a more artificial, Romantic type.

Corot: *Self-portrait, c.1835, Florence, Uffizi (Alinari)*

Cottet, Charles 1863–1924
French painter and etcher. His most characteristic and important works were scenes of Brittany.
Courbet, Gustave 1819–77
French painter, the foremost exponent of Realism, who exerted an immense influence on 19thC art by his emphatic rejection of idealization. A socialist and a revolutionary, Courbet, in addition to his controversial genre paintings, treated a wide variety of non-political subjects – landscapes, sensuous nudes, still-lifes. His technique was innovatory, often featuring bold impasto applied with a palette knife.
Coustou family
Family of French sculptors from Lyon, the most important of whom were the brothers **Nicolas** (1568–1733) and **Guillaume** (1677–1746). They trained with their uncle Coysevox, and like him worked mainly for court circles.
Couture, Thomas 1815–79
French history and portrait painter. He was a highly successful academic painter and an important teacher. His most important pupil was Manet.

Coypel family
Family of French history and decorative painters, active in the 17thC and 18thC. **Noel** (1628–1707) was a follower of Poussin and worked under Lebrun at Versailles. His son **Antoine** (1661–1722) carried out some important decorative schemes, the most important of which to survive is the ceiling of the royal chapel at Versailles. Antoine's half-brother **Noel-Nicolas** (1690–1734) produced less ambitious but more charming works. **Charles-Antoine** (1694–1752), Antoine's son, painted in a rather dull Rococo style, but he enjoyed a career of exemplary academic success.
Coysevox, Antoine 1640–1720
French sculptor, whose work shows a fuller understanding of the Baroque than that of any of his French contemporaries. He did much monumental work, but was at his best as a portrait sculptor.

Daddi, Bernardo d.1349
The leading Florentine painter of the generation after Giotto.
Dagnan-Bouveret, Pascal-Adolphe-Jean
1852–1929
French painter. He began as a painter of mythological works, but then turned to peasant scenes influenced by Bastien-Lepage.
Dali, Salvador b.1904
Spanish painter, one of the best-known contemporary artists, famous for his eccentric life-style and provocative self-advertisement as well as for the quality of his work. His best paintings are among the most characteristic products of Surrealism.
Daubigny, Charles-François 1817–78
French landscape painter and graphic artist, a member of the Barbizon school. He had a studio-boat in which he travelled the rivers of France, and water was one of his principal themes. His devotion to the fleeting aspects of nature had a great impact on the Impressionists.
Daumier, Honoré 1808–79
French painter, sculptor and lithographer, considered the father of modern caricature. His brilliant lithographic cartoons (one of which – satirizing King Louis-Philippe – led to his imprisonment) are at the heart of his achievement, but he was also a remarkable painter and sculptor, with a highly original technique in both media.
David, Gerard c.1460–1523
One of the leading Netherlandish painters of his generation.
David, Jacques-Louis 1748–1825
French painter, the leading artist of the Neoclassical movement. His severe and remarkably taut compositions extolled

selfless civic virtues in episodes taken from ancient history. He took an active part in the Revolution, and during the Terror was virtual dictator of the arts. Later he became Napoleon's official painter, and after his defeat at Waterloo sought refuge in Brussels. His portraits are the best works of his later career. Gérard, Gros and Ingres were among his pupils.

David, Pierre-Jean 1788–1856
French sculptor, known as David d'Angers after his place of birth. His style was deeply influenced by classical art, but was also marked by a vigorous strain of naturalism. He left an important collection to his native city.

Degas, Hilaire Germain Edgar 1834–1917
French painter and sculptor, widely admired in his lifetime and now one of the most popular of 19thC artists. Although he is a central figure in Impressionism, he differed from his colleagues in the stress he laid on drawing and in the fact that he did not paint out of doors. His main subject was contemporary Parisian life, and he made certain themes – such as the racecourse or the ballet – his own.

Degas: *Self-portrait, c.1855, Paris, Louvre*

Delacroix, Eugène 1798–1863
French painter, one of the greatest artists of the Romantic movement. In his early career he aroused controversy because of his violent and exotic subjects, brilliant colouring and energetic brushwork but later his style was sufficiently accepted for him to receive many prestigious official commissions. He was immensely prolific.

Delaroche, Paul 1797–1856
French history painter who reconciled avant-garde and conservative tendencies by combining Romantic themes with academic drawing and painstaking realism.

Delvaux, Paul b.1897
Belgian Surrealist painter. His work often features the female nude in strange, dreamlike architectural settings.

Denis, Maurice 1870–1943
French painter, a founder of the Nabis and a central figure of the Symbolist movement. As well as painting, he designed book illustrations, stained glass and theatre sets. His work shows a desire to express his ardent Catholicism, echoing the pious simplicity of artists such as Fra Angelico and rejecting realism in favour of the decorative possibilities of pure line and colour.

Denon, Dominique Vivant 1474–1825
French engraver, draughtsman, archaeologist, writer and diplomat. In 1804 Napoleon appointed him director of national museums, and he played an important role in the development of the Louvre's collections.

Derain, André 1880–1954
French painter. In his early career he was at the center of avantgarde developments (he was one of the creators of Fauvism and was one of the first artists to appreciate the expressive stylization of primitive art) but from the 1920s his work became increasingly dry and academic.

Deshays, Jean Baptiste 1721–65
French history painter, the son-in-law of Boucher.

Desportes, Alexandre-François 1661–1743
French painter of still-life and hunting scenes, the main rival of Oudry. His lavish works are in the 17thC tradition, but the remarkably fresh landscape studies he made for the backgrounds of his paintings prefigure the work of the 19thC.

Detroy see TROY

Diaz de la Peña, Narcisse Virgile 1807–76
French painter of the Barbizon school.

Domenichino (Domenico Zampieri) 1581–1641
Bolognese painter, Annibale Carracci's favourite pupil. As well as being one of the leading fresco decorators of his time, he was one of the pioneers of ideal landscape painting.

Dongen, Kees van (Cornelius Theodorus Marie) 1877–1908
Dutch painter, working in Paris from 1897. His early work was Impressionist, but around 1905 he turned to a bolder, broader, more colourful style influenced by Fauvism.

Drouais, François-Hubert 1727–75
French portrait painter, the son-in-law of Nattier, whom he replaced as the most fashionable court painter of his day. He popularized the genre of aristocratic children in rustic disguise.

Duchamp, Marcel 1887–1968
French artist and theorist, brother of Raymond Duchamp-Villon and half-brother of Jacques Villon. He produced some Cubist-inspired paintings early in his career, but soon abandoned traditional oil painting for avantgarde works, such as his ready-mades, in which the concept behind them was more important than their appearance. His ideas, repudiating the traditional ideas of fine art, had great influence on Dada and Surrealism.

Duchamp-Villon, Raymond 1876–1918
French sculptor, much admired in Parisian avantgarde circles before World War I. His work shows a powerful fusion of mechanical and organic forms.

Dufy, Raoul 1877–1953
French painter, also a designer of mural schemes, tapestries and textiles. His work is highly distinctive: in both oil and watercolour he painted race-meetings, fashionable resorts, flowers and landscapes, using bright luminous colours and linear draughtsmanship to create charming and decorative effects.

Dughet, Gaspard (also called Gaspard Poussin) 1616–75
French landscape painter, draughtsman and etcher, all of whose career was spent in Rome. His style combined those of Poussin (his brother-in-law) and Claude.

Dunoyer de Segonzac, André 1884–1974
French painter, etcher and illustrator. After an early Cubist-influenced phase, he painted traditional subjects such as landscapes, nudes and still-lifes in sombre earth colours. Later he turned to translucent watercolour.

Duquesnoy, François 1594–1643
Flemish sculptor active in Rome. His style was classical and restrained, showing the influence of his friend Poussin. Louis XIII invited him to Paris to become court sculptor, but he died on the way.

Dürer, Albrecht 1471–1528
German painter, printmaker and writer on art, the greatest artist of the northern Renaissance. His prints were enormously influential throughout Europe, and he was the first artist of such stature to express himself primarily through engraving.

Dyck, Sir Anthony van 1599–1641
The most important Flemish painter of the 17thC apart from Rubens, primarily a portraitist. His aristocratic style – distinguished by the effortless elegance and refinement with which he invested his sitters and his incomparable skill in depicting rich materials – was the model for society portraitists until the early 20thC.

Epstein, Sir Jacob 1880–1959
American-born British sculptor.

Eyck, Jan van d. 1441
The most renowned Netherlandish painter of the 15thC. He was at one time credited with the invention of oil-painting, and although this is not true, he did bring the technique to an unprecedented degree of accomplishment, showing extraordinary skill in the use of translucent glazes to achieve a marvellous luminosity of colour.

Fabritius, Carel 1622–54
Dutch painter, Rembrandt's finest pupil and probably the master of Vermeer. He died tragically young in the explosion of the Delft ammunition depot of 1654, and his surviving output is small.

Falconet, Etienne-Maurice 1716–91
One of the leading French sculptors of the 18thC, also a prolific writer on art. His most characteristic works are small marble statues, often gently erotic in style, which were frequently reproduced in porcelain (from 1757–66 he worked at the Sèvres factory). He also, however, worked convincingly on large scale compositions.

Fantin-Latour, Henri 1836–1904
French painter and lithographer. He is best known as one of the finest of all flower painters, but he was intellectually involved with some of the leading avantgarde artists of the day and produced some interesting portraits of them.

Fantin-Latour: *Self-portrait, 1883, Florence, Uffizi (Alinari)*

Flandrin, Hippolyte 1809–64
French painter. He worked in an academic style specializing in religious works, notably decorative schemes in several churches in Paris.

Foujita, Tsugouharu 1886–1968
Japanese-born French painter and graphic artist, active in Paris from 1913. He was part of the circle of Chagall, Modigliani and Soutine, produced a wide variety of paintings and illustrated numerous books.

Fouquet, Jean or **Jehan** c. 1420–81
The leading French painter of the 15thC and the first well-defined personality in French art. He produced both miniatures and panel paintings, and his work in both media is clearly drawn, sober and poised, with a convincing solidity of form and sense of space that shows his knowledge of Italian art (he was in Italy in the 1440s).

Fragonard, Jean-Honoré 1732–1806
French painter of mythology, gallantry and landscape. His gift for witty characterization, delicate colour and vivacious brushwork were ideally suited to the light-hearted and erotic subjects in which he excelled. The demand for his frothy, titillating, quintessentially Rococo paintings ceased with the Revolution and he died virtually forgotten.

François, Guy c. 1578–1650
French Caravaggesque painter. He spent the early part of his career in Rome, and on his return to his native Le Puy (1613) he supplied a large number of altarpieces for local churches (mostly still *in situ*). Strikingly naturalistic, his work has certain affinities with Toulouse artists such as Tournier and Challette.

Friesz, Othon 1879–1949
French painter. In his early career he worked and exhibited alongside some of the most progressive artists of the day, but his later work was conservative.

Froment, Nicolas a. 1450–90
French painter from Languedoc, working mainly in Avignon. His work reveals the influence of Rogier van der Weyden in the sculptural quality of the modelling.

Fromentin, Eugène 1820–76
French painter, novelist and art critic. In his time his Orientalist paintings were much admired, but he is now remembered chiefly for his book *Masters of Past Time* (1876), a penetrating critique of earlier Netherlandish painting and its influence on French artists.

Gauguin, Paul 1848–1903
French painter, sculptor and printmaker, one of the founding figures of modern art. His rejection of the naturalism of the Impressionists in favour of subject matter provided by the imagination and depicted by expressionist means was his most influential contribution to the development of Western art. He also pioneered appreciation of the simple and primitive, a taste that led him to Martinique, Tahiti and finally to the Marquesas Islands, where he died.

Gauguin: *Self-portrait, Sao Paulo (Brazil), Museo d'Arte (Alinari)*

Géricault, Théodore 1791–1824
French painter and graphic artist, one of the founders of Romanticism. His highly-charged subject matter and his powerful and spontaneous brushwork became hallmarks of the Romantic style. Delacroix was the greatest of the many successors who felt his influence after his tragically early death.

Gérôme, Jean-Léon 1824–1904
French painter, particularly of Oriental subjects. Anti-innovatory, especially anti-Impressionist, he painted in a highly finished, painstakingly realistic style and was a pillar of the art establishment. From 1878 he turned mainly to sculpture.

Giacometti, Alberto 1901–66
Swiss sculptor and painter. He studied sculpture under Bourdelle in Paris from 1922 to 1925, and in 1930 joined the Surrealist group. Public recognition finally came in 1948 with an exhibition in New York. The catalogue to this exhibition carried an important foreword by his friend Sartre.

Giordano, Luca 1634–1705
The most important Neapolitan painter of the later 17thC, known as "Luca fa presto" (Luke go quickly) for the speed at which he produced his enormous output in oil and fresco. His light, airy style anticipates the Rococo.

Giotto di Bondone c. 1267–1337
Florentine painter and architect, one of the most celebrated figures in the history of art. He is considered the founder of the main tradition of Western painting because of the way he broke away from

the flat Byzantine tradition and introduced the concern with an illusionistic pictorial space. Later artists developed his innovations, but few approached his grandeur and human sympathy.

Girardon, François 1628–1715
With Coysevox, the leading French sculptor of Louis XIV's reign. His style was more classical and severe than Coysevox's, and he represented the ideal of the Académie Royale de Peinture et de Sculpture more completely than any other sculptor of the time.

Girodet de Roucy, Anne-Louis 1767–1827
French painter. His work is transitionary between Neoclassicism and Romanticism, being classical in its firm drawing and references to the Antique, Romantic in its atmospheric lighting and expressive elongation of figures. In 1812 he gave up painting and devoted himself to writing tedious poems on aesthetics.

Gislebertus a. 1st half of 12thC
French Romanesque sculptor, active in Burgundy. He was a great artist, but his name has survived solely because he signed the tympanum of the ***Last Judgment*** at Autun Cathedral. His style had a strong influence in Burgundy, particularly at Vézelay, where he probably worked himself.

Giulio Romano 1499?–1546
Italian painter and architect, the chief pupil and assistant of Raphael and one of the most important Mannerist artists. His paintings, which extend the Mannerist tendencies of Raphael's late work and combine them with a muscularity derived from Michelangelo, were widely influential.

Gleizes, Albert 1881–1953
French painter. His early works are Cubist and he was co-author of the first book on Cubism (1912). After a religious experience in 1917, he became preoccupied with the expression of spiritual meaning in art.

Godefroy de Huy (Godefroy de Claire) a. mid 12thC
Metalworker from Huy, now in Belgium. There are several early documentary references to his great artistry, but almost nothing is known of his career and the attributions to him are highly speculative.

Gogh, Vincent van 1853–90
Dutch painter, one of the greatest and most influential artists of the 19thC. He began to paint in 1880 and his early works are sombre in mood and colour. In 1886 he moved to Paris, where his work changed dramatically, becoming vibrant in colour and concerned with aesthetic rather than social problems, although

Gogh, Vincent van: *Self-portrait, 1889, London, Courtauld Institute Galleries*

still broadly humanist. The astonishing emotional intensity of his work, his complete integrity as an artist, and his battles with poverty and mental instability, culminating in his suicide, have made him one of the great cultural heroes of modern times.

Goujon, Jean c. 1510–68
The leading French sculptor of the mid-16thC. He worked mainly in Paris, but the beginning and the end of his career are obscure. His style shows influence from the school of Fontainebleau.

Goya y Lucientes, Francisco de 1746–1828
Spanish painter and printmaker, the most powerful and original European artist of his period. His work developed from charming Rococo scenes to devastating indictments of human cruelty and corruption, and because of his bitter opposition to tyranny he left Spain in 1824 and settled in Bordeaux.

Goyen, Jan van 1596–1656
Dutch landscape painter. He was a pioneering figure in the development of Dutch realistic landscape, his paintings – often virtually monochromatic – being marked by a sense of airy freshness and poetic tranquillity. His output was huge and he was highly influential.

Granet, François-Marius 1775–1849
French painter of interior scenes and landscapes. Appointed Curator at the Louvre in 1826 and at Versailles in 1830, he devoted only part of his time to painting. During the 1848 Revolution, he returned to his native Aix-en-Provence and founded the Musée Granet there.

Greco, El (Domenikos Theotokopoulos) 1541–1614
Painter, sculptor and architect, born in Crete and trained in Italy, but considered one of the greatest artists of the Spanish school (he had settled in Spain by 1577).

His highly individual style reflects the atmosphere of intense religious zeal in his adopted country.

Greuze, Jean-Baptiste 1725–1805
French painter. His anecdotal genre scenes made him the most popular painter in mid 18thC France, but when their popularity faded with the growth of Neoclassicism he turned increasingly to sentimental pictures of young girls.

Greuze: *Self-portrait, c.1760, Paris, Louvre*

Gris, Juan (José González) 1887–1927
Spanish painter, working in Paris from 1906. He made an individual contribution to Cubism and had a highly varied output.

Gros, Baron Antoine-Jean 1771–1835
French painter, a major figure in the development of Romanticism. He travelled with Napoleon as official war painter and recorded his campaigns in epic canvases. After the fall of Napoleon, he turned mainly to portraiture. His pupils, among them Géricault, Delacroix, Barye and Bonington, were strongly influenced by his dramatic subject matter and bold technique. He committed suicide.

Grünewald (Mathis Gothardt-Neithardt) c.1470/80–1528
German painter. He was one of the greatest and most individual artists of his time, but he remained so little known for centuries after his death that his real name was not discovered until the 1920s – "Grünewald" is a mistake of a 17thC historian. The small body of his work that survives is exclusively on religious themes.

Guardi, Francesco 1712–93
The best-known member of a family of Venetian artists. He painted various subjects, but is remembered almost exclusively for his views of Venice.

Guercino, Il (Giovanni Francesco Barbieri) 1591–1666
One of the most individual of Italian Baroque painters. His early works are characterized by grand forms, dramatic lighting, rich colour and distinctive soft modelling.

Guérin, Baron Pierre-Narcisse 1774–1833
French Neoclassical painter. He painted epic scenes from Roman history and French classical drama, combining gracefulness with disciplined form. As the teacher of Géricault, Delacroix, Delaroche and Scheffer, he was an important transitional figure in the Romantic movement.

Hals, Frans 1581/85–1666
The first great painter of the 17th Dutch school and one of the greatest of all portraitists. His ability to capture a sense of fleeting movement and spontaneous expression is the key to the tremendous vivacity of his portraits. The appreciation of his genius came only in the 19thC, when the freedom of his brushwork was an inspiration to the Impressionists.

Harpignies, Henri 1819–1916
French landscape painter, a follower of the Barbizon school, noted for his soft lyrical treatment of trees. From the 1870s onwards he achieved fame and success.

Haussmann, Baron Georges-Eugène 1809–91
French civil servant and town planner. From 1853 he was in charge of Napoleon III's grandiose rebuilding and modernization of Paris. He planned the great straight boulevards leading to such focal points as the Arc de Triomphe and the Opéra and thus has had a greater effect on the appearance of Paris than anyone before or since.

Heem, Jan Davidsz. de 1606–83/4
The best-known and most brilliant member of a large family of Dutch still-life painters.

Henner, Jean-Jacques 1829–1905
French painter. He was immensely successful in his day, but his reputation has declined sharply since his death. His most characteristic works are idealized female heads and sensuous nudes.

Houdon, Jean-Antoine 1741–1828
The greatest French sculptor of his period, celebrated chiefly for his portraits. He portrayed many of the leading men of his times with astonishing vivacity and psychological perception, displaying a brilliant gift for capturing quirks of gesture and expression. His fame was such that in 1785 he was called to America to make a statue of George Washington.

Ingres, Jean-Auguste-Dominique 1780–1867
French history and portrait painter, one of the leading, but also most personal, exponents of Neoclassicism. His severely classical teaching, championing line before colour, was deeply influential on his many pupils, but his own paintings are often at variance with his ideals, being notable for their mannered gracefulness. Chassériau was the only one of Ingres's pupils to attain lasting distinction, but Degas, Picasso and Matisse were all influenced by his supreme draughtsmanship.
Ipoustéguy, Jean Robert b. 1920
French artist. He has worked in various media, notably stained glass and painting, but since 1954 has concentrated on sculpture.
Isabey, Jean-Baptiste 1767–1855
French painter, the most celebrated miniaturist of his day. He was patronized by Napoleon and, after a short exile in England following the fall of the Empire, by subsequent French monarchs.

Jacob, Max 1876–1944
French writer and painter, a friend of Modigliani and Picasso. He is best known as a poet, but he produced some attractive gouaches of Parisian life.
Jongkind, Johan Barthold 1819–91
Dutch painter and etcher who spent much of his life in France and was an important precursor of Impressionism. He exhibited with the Barbizon school painters, but his work shows more spontaneity, and Boudin and the young Monet were particularly impressed with the freshness of his sketches.
Jordaens, Jacob (Jacques) 1593–1678
Flemish painter, etcher and tapestry designer, the leading figure-painter in Flanders after the death of Rubens.
Jouvenet, Jean 1644–1717
French history painter, a pupil of Lebrun.

Lancret, Nicolas 1690–1743
French painter of genre and *fêtes galantes*, with Pater the chief of Watteau's imitators. His *fêtes galantes*, which were very popular in his time, are ravishing in colour, but he never approached Watteau's psychological penetration.
Largillière, Nicolas de 1656–1746
French painter, with Rigaud the most successful portraitist of the last years of Louis XIV's reign. He trained in Antwerp and London.
Lastman, Pieter 1583–1633
Dutch painter of biblical, historical and mythological scenes, remembered principally as Rembrandt's teacher.

La Tour, Georges de 1593–1652
French painter, working in Lorraine. Although he had a considerable reputation in his lifetime, he was virtually forgotten for almost three centuries after his death, and has only recently been acclaimed as perhaps the greatest of Caravaggesque artists. His mature works – majestic and severe religious paintings, often lit by a single candle – are characterized by monumental simplification of forms and exquisite handling of light.
La Tour, Maurice-Quentin de 1704–88
The most successful French pastellist of the 18thC. His eccentric personality and brilliant virtuosity made him in demand at all levels of society. He presented his sitters in a vivacious – often rather theatrical – manner.

La Tour, Maurice-Quentin de:
Self-portrait, c. 1770, Paris, Louvre

Lawrence, Sir Thomas 1769–1830
The most fashionable English portraitist of his period. His fluid, glossy technique was admired by Delacroix.
Lebrun, Charles 1619–90
French painter, the most important artist of Louis XIV's reign and the chief formulator of French academic doctrine. He was Director of the Gobelins factory, which produced everything needed for the furnishing of royal palaces, and much of his energy went into the decoration of Versailles.
Léger, Fernand 1881–1955
French painter who created one of the most distinctive styles of any 20thC artist. Inspired by Cézanne and early Cubism, he had a life-long preoccupation with formal simplification and monumental structure, which he used to celebrate modern urban and technological culture.
Lemoyne, François 1688–1737
French painter of history and mythology, an important figure in the transition from Baroque to Rococo. Boucher and Natoire were his pupils. He committed suicide.

Le Nain brothers
Three French painters, **Antoine** (c.1588–1648) **Louis** (c.1593–1648) and **Mathieu** (1607–77), born in Laon, but all active in Paris by 1630. The demarkation of the oeuvres of the three brothers is one of the most controversial problems in the history of art, for all their signed paintings bear only the surname, and none is dated later than 1648, when all three were alive. Those attributed to Louis are the most important – sober genre scenes of peasants, painted with great dignity.

Le Nôtre, André 1613–1700
French designer of formal gardens, the greatest and most famous practitioner of his art. His father and grandfather were royal gardeners, and he studied painting (with Vouet) and architecture as well as all aspects of gardening. From the 1650s he designed, altered or enlarged gardens for many of the finest châteaux in France.

Leonardo da Vinci 1452–1519
Florentine artist, scientist and writer, one of the greatest of Renaissance painters and perhaps the most versatile genius who has ever lived. His immense prestige and fame helped to raise the status of the visual arts, and the idea of the artist as a creative thinker rather than an artisan stems chiefly from him. In 1516, at the invitation of François I, he settled in France, dying at Cloux. No works certainly from Leonardo's brief French period are known, but he brought several of his pictures with him, which explains why the Louvre, via the French royal collection, has the world's largest collection of his paintings.

Le Sueur, Eustache 1616–55
French history painter. Poussin was his chief inspiration, but Le Sueur's work is less heroic and more tender and reflective than his model.

Limbourg brothers
Netherlandish illuminators, **Herman, Jean** and **Pol** de Limbourg, all of whom were dead by 1416, probably victims of an epidemic. They worked for Philip the Bold of Burgundy and, after his death in 1404, for his brother Jean de Berry, achieving a privileged position at court. Their miniatures, exquisite and beautifully observed reflections of contemporary life, are among the greatest expressions of International Gothic.

Lorenzetti brothers
Sienese painters, **Ambrogio** (d.1348?) and **Pietro** (d.1348?), among the leading Italian artists of their generation. Both probably died in the Black Death of 1348.

Lotto, Lorenzo c.1480–1556/7
Venetian painter. He was something of a stylistic maverick and his work is uneven, but at his best he was an artist of great distinction.

Lurçat, Jean 1892–1966
French artist. He worked in various fields, including painting and lithography, but is best known as one of the most important figures in the 20thC revival of interest in tapestry design.

Magnasco, Alessandro 1667–1749
Italian painter of religious works and fantastic eerie landscapes.

Maillol, Aristide 1861–1944
French sculptor, devoted almost entirely to the female nude. His figures are usually calm and monumental, with a sense of classical dignity, and he received many commissions for public monuments.

Manet, Edouard 1832–83
French painter and graphic artist, one of the most important artists of the 19thC and often regarded as the father of modern painting. Although his paintings incorporate many motifs from the Old Masters, their directness of approach (in, for example, showing contemporary women nude and unidealized) and their freshness of technique, made them often appear shocking to the public. He never exhibited with the Impressionists, but they looked upon him as an inspiration.

Manolo (Manuel Martinez Hugué) 1872–1945
Spanish sculptor, active for much of his career in France.

Mantegna, Andrea c.1430–1506
Italian painter and engraver, one of the most renowned artists of the early Renaissance. His paintings reveal his devotion to classical antiquity, but although his style is precise it is never dry – indeed he was one of the wittiest of great painters.

Maratta or **Maratti, Carlo** 1625–1713
The leading painter in Rome in the second half of the 17thC. He is best known for his calm and dignified religious work.

Marinot, Maurice 1882–1962
French artist, working in various fields but best known as a glass designer. His output as a painter is remarkable more for its quantity than its quality.

Marquet, Albert 1875–1947
French painter. He collaborated closely with Matisse at the beginning of his career, but did not go on to develop the more radical possibilities of Fauvism.

Massys (Matsys, Metsys), **Quentin** 1464/5–1530
One of the leading Flemish painters of his period. He painted religious works and portraits, and in the latter field popularized a new type – the scholar in his study.

Master of Canapost a. 15thC
Obscure Spanish painter, named after an altarpiece in the church of San Esteban de Canapost in the province of Gerona in NE Spain. Gerona borders on France and the Master of Canapost's style is similar to that of southern French painters such as Quarton (Charonton).
Master of Flémalle see CAMPIN
Master of Moulins a. late 15thC
One of the finest French painters of the 15thC, named after the exquisite triptych of the ***Virgin and Child*** in Moulins Cathedral. Several other works are convincingly attributed to the same hand. Their style suggests that the artist trained in Flanders.
Matisse, Henri 1869–1954
French painter, one of the greatest and most influential artists of the 20thC. He was one of the creators of Fauvism, and subsequently he sought to eliminate illusionistic description of volume and space from his work, emphasizing instead the flatness of the picture surface and the abstract purity of line, decorative pattern and colour. Although crippled by arthritis, he worked until his death, and was a forceful sculptor and illustrator as well as a painter.

Matisse: *Self-portrait, 1907, Copenhagen, Statens Museum for Kunst*

Maurin, Charles 1856–1914
Born at Le Puy, he went to Paris in 1870 where he worked with Toulouse-Lautrec and Vallotton. In 1904 he returned to Le Puy where he started an art school. He died in obscurity in 1914.
Metsu, Gabriel 1629–67
Dutch genre painter. He is best known for his refined and delicately painted bourgeois interiors.
Michelangelo Buonarroti 1475–1564
Florentine, sculptor, painter, draughtsman, architect and poet, one of the supreme giants of world art. His contemporaries called him "divine", and his influence on European art has been incalculable.
Mignard, Pierre 1612–95
One of the most successful French painters of his day. His history paintings are in a cold classicizing style much influenced by Poussin, and his portraits (in which the sitters are often fitted out with allegorical trappings) are now considered his best works. His brother **Nicolas** (1606–68) was also a popular painter of portraits and religious subjects.
Millet, Jean-François 1814–75
French painter and graphic artist. He was of peasant stock and is best known for his depictions of rural life, in which he moved from a prettified Arcadian style to a more robust, realistic approach. His more pious scenes were once among the most famous images in art and were endlessly reproduced. In the 1860s, through the influence of his friend Théodore Rousseau, he turned increasingly to pure landscape.
Miró, Joan 1893–1983
Spanish painter, one of the most original and versatile of 20thC artists. In 1917 he moved from his native Catalonia to Paris, and in 1924 signed the Surrealist manifesto. His most characteristic works show brightly coloured organic forms against a large plain background.
Modigliani, Amedeo 1884–1920
Italian painter and sculptor, living in Paris from 1906 and often considered French by adoption. In painting, he concentrated almost exclusively on portraits and female nudes (often highly erotic), showing an archaic simplification and distortion of form, a superb sense of linear design, and a sensitive, if limited, use of colour. In sculpture, he produced a series of figures and heads of primitive power, reflecting his friendship with Brancusi. His amorous, dissolute life and early death have contributed to his fame.
Monet, Claude Oscar 1840–1926
French painter, one of the leading figures of Impressionism. Monet painted the picture after which the movement is named (***Impression: Sunrise***, Paris, Musée Marmottan), and he is often considered the Impressionist *par excellence* because his commitment to its ideas was total throughout his career and he developed them most single-mindedly. His intense concern with the changing effects of light is shown most clearly in the various series of painting he did of the same subject seen at different times of day.
Monticelli, Adolphe 1824–86
French painter of landscape, portraits and still-lifes.

Mor, Anthonis 1519–75
Netherlandish painter, active at numerous European courts as the leading international portraitist of his day (he is also known by the Spanish and English versions of his name – Antonio Moro and Sir Anthony More).

Moreau, Gustave 1826–98
French painter, one of the leading Symbolists. His allegorical, mythological and fabulous scenes, painted in rich, jewel-like colours, are haunted by an ambiguous image of a powerful, seductive, evil woman, and are some of the finest evocations of the *femme fatale*. He was an important teacher, Matisse and Rouault being among his pupils.

Morisot, Berthe 1841–95
French Impressionist painter. She was the first women to join the group and was influential in persuading Manet (her brother-in-law) to take up *plein-air* painting.

Morland, George 1763–1804
British painter of rustic scenes.

Moroni, Giovanni Battista c.1525–78
Italian painter, best known for his sober, thoughtful portraits.

Murillo, Bartolomé Esteban 1618–82
Spanish painter. He is best known for two types of painting: sentimental genre scenes of peasant children; and devotional paintings (particularly of the Immaculate Conception) appealing to popular piety.

Natoire, Charles-Joseph 1700–77
French history painter and decorator. His prettily coloured Rococo style was best suited to light-hearted scenes and his attempts at serious subjects are less successful. From 1751 he was Director of the French Academy in Rome.

Nattier, Jean-Marc 1685–1766
Fashionable French portrait painter at the court of Louis XV. His best works are his female portraits; they rarely convey much sense of character, but they have a pleasing sense of intimacy.

Oudry, Jean-Baptiste 1686–1753
French painter. He produced a few portraits (Largillière was his teacher) and histories, but is best known as a painter of hunting scenes and hunting still-lifes.

Parrocel, Charles 1688–1752
French painter of battles. He spent a year in the cavalry and his knowledge and love of horses comes out in his numerous paintings of Louis XV's campaigns. His father **Joseph** (1648–1704) was also a noted battle painter.

Pascin, Jules (Julius Pincas) 1885–1930
Bulgarian-born French painter who later became a naturalized American. Taking his inspiration from Degas and Toulouse-Lautrec, but lacking their sharpness of observation, he concentrated on female figure studies in which delicacy of line and colour compensate for a certain repetitiveness. He committed suicide.

Pater, Jean-Baptiste 1695–1736
French painter of *fêtes galantes*, the pupil of Watteau and with Lancret his principal imitator. Pater's work is so close to Watteau as to be pastiche, but his characterization is much less penetrating and his works often have a note of suggestiveness quite foreign to the master. His father **Antoine** (1670–1747) was a sculptor.

Peeters, Bonaventura the Elder 1614–52
The most important member of a family of Flemish painters.

Perronneau, Jean-Baptiste 1715?–83
French portraitist and engraver, a pupil of Natoire. He worked in oils but is best known for his vigorous pastel portraits. He eschewed the technical virtuosity of Maurice-Quentin de la Tour, whose popularity in Paris led Perronneau to seek work in Italy, Holland and Russia.

Perronneau: *Self-portrait, c.1745, Tours, Musée des Beaux-Arts*

Perugino, Pietro (Pietro Vannucci) c.1445–1523
Italian painter, named after his native Perugia. His style has a distinctive sweetness and grace, qualities he passed on to the young Raphael, whom he probably taught.

Picabia, Francis 1879–1953
French painter. At first successful as a late Impressionist, he changed course around 1911 and played an important role in disseminating avantgarde ideas among proto-Dada circles.

Picasso, Pablo 1881–1973
Spanish painter, sculptor, graphic artist and stage designer, the most renowned artist of the 20thC, whose protean development encompassed the majority of its progressive movements. His prodigious capacity for work and his fluency of invention have perhaps exceeded those of any other artist, and his range extends from delightful humour to tragic political statements. He first visited Paris in 1900 and settled there in 1904. From 1947 till his death he lived in the South of France.

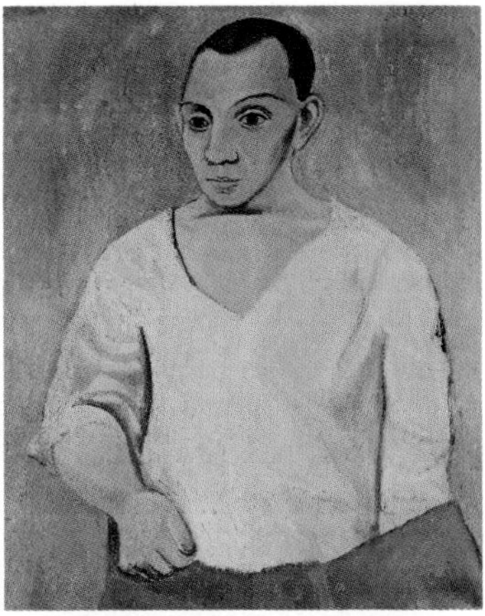

Picasso: *Self-portrait, 1906, Philadelphia Museum, Gallatin coll.*

Piero di Cosimo 1462–1521
Florentine painter, one of the most charmingly idiosyncratic painters of his time.
Pigalle, Jean-Baptiste 1714–85
The leading French sculptor of his period. He was extremely versatile, creating with equal skill charming genre pieces and monumental tombs. Added to his versatility were a formal inventiveness and technical accomplishment that place him among the greatest sculptors of the 18thC.
Pilon, Germain 1527–90
The greatest French sculptor of the 16thC. His early style was based on the decorative manner of Primaticcio and the Fontainebleau school. Subsequently his work became more naturalistic but his figures always tended to be expressively elongated.
Pissarro, Camille 1830–1903
French painter, one of the leading Impressionists. Although as an artist he is not so greatly esteemed as some of his associates, he was central to the movement, and was the only artist to exhibit at all eight Impressionist exhibitions. He was a kindly father figure, much respected by the other Impressionists, among whom he had an important role as a peacemaker. His son **Lucien** (1863–1944) was a painter and book illustrator. He settled in England in 1890 and played a significant role in transmitting French avantgarde ideas to English artists.
Pompon, François 1855–1933
French sculptor. He worked for a long time as Rodin's assistant and success came to him late in life with his animal sculptures, in which he was the foremost specialist of his day.
Poussin, Nicolas 1593/4–1665
French painter, active in Rome for almost all his career. He was the chief formulator of the French classical tradition in painting, his works being based on a profound study of ancient literature and art. His paintings were generally fairly modest in size and produced for a highly cultivated circle of private clients. Lebrun's academic doctrines, which shaped French art for generations, were based on Poussin's work, and the great masters of Neoclassicism looked to his example.
Preti, Mattia (Il Calabrese) 1613–99
Italian painter, widely travelled and prolific.
Primaticcio, Francesco 1504/5–70
Italian painter and architect, active mainly in France, particularly at Fontainebleau, where he collaborated with Rosso on the decoration of the great royal residence there.
Prud'hon, Pierre-Paul 1758–1823
French painter, a leading figure in the transition from Neoclassicism to Romanticism. He received numerous official commissions, and was a favourite painter of the wives of Napoleon I, the Empresses Josephine and Marie-Louise.
Puget, Pierre 1620–94
The most powerful and individual French sculptor of the 17thC, active mainly in his native Marseille and in Toulon. He made several visits to Italy and the emotional intensity of his work is based on the Italian Baroque and on Michelangelo. His style was too personal to win success at court and his headstrong temperament also hindered his career – his final years were embittered.
Puvis de Chavannes, Pierre 1824–98
French painter, immensely popular in his day and highly influential on younger artists, particularly the Symbolists. His work is distinguished by its static, timeless, soulful qualities, and he used colour non-naturalistically to convey the message of the painting. He carried out many large decorative commissions, but worked in oil rather than fresco.

Quarton (Charonton), **Enguerrand** c.1410–66
French painter, born in Laon and active at Aix, Arles and Avignon. He is one of the few medieval French artists whose career is well documented, but only two works certainly by him survive (at Chantilly and Villeneuve-lès-Avignon). They are majestically conceived, sharply drawn and imaginatively rich, retaining something of the decorative beauty of manuscript illumination, even though they are impressive in scale.

Ranson, Paul 1864–1909
French painter, a founder member of the Nabis.

Raphael (Raffaello Sanzio) 1483–1520
Italian painter and architect, in whose works are found the most complete embodiment of the ideals of the High Renaissance. For three centuries after his death he was almost universally regarded as the greatest of all painters – the artist who had expressed the loftiest ideals of Christianity with the grace and grandeur of the Antique. Poussin and Ingres are two of the painters most clearly indebted to him.

Redon, Odilon 1840–1916
French painter and lithographer, one of the leading Symbolists. Many of his works are in charcoal and lithography – fantastic images often inspired by the poetry of Edgar Alan Poe – and he embarked on his highly coloured paintings and pastels only about 1892.

Redon: *Self-portrait, 1867, Paris, Ari Redon coll.*

Rembrandt Harmensz. van Rijn 1606–69
Dutch painter, etcher and draughtsman, one of the supreme geniuses in the history of art. He was extraordinarily versatile, but his greatness comes out most forcibly in his portraits and religious works, which show his unsurpassed ability to express the depth and complexity of human feelings. Academic critics long objected to what they considered his vulgarity but his work was sought after and influential in 18thC France, and in 1851 Delacroix was perceptive enough to prophesy that one day Rembrandt would be considered a greater artist than Raphael.

Reni, Guido 1575–1642
Italian painter. His pure, classical style brought him immense fame, and in the 18thC he was considered by many critics second only to Raphael.

Renoir, Pierre Auguste 1841–1919
French Impressionist painter. His sensuous appreciation of colour and light, his ample, glowing nudes, the charm and poetry of his works, have made him one of the best-loved artists of the 19thC. Beautiful women, children and people enjoying themselves remained his favourite subjects even in old age, when – in a wheelchair and partially paralysed – he realized his earthy female nudes in sculpture "dictated" to his assistants.

Restout, Jean 1692–1768
French painter, the nephew of Jouvenet, best known for his religious works, which stand out from those of his contemporaries because of their gravity and intensity.

Reynolds, Sir Joshua 1723–93
British painter (primarily of portraits) and writer on art. The first President of the Royal Academy (founded in London in 1768), he was the central figure in British art in the second half of the 18thC, and his intellectual standing and social success did much to raise the status of the artist in Britain.

Ribera, Jusepe (José) **de** (called Lo Spagnoletto) 1591–1652
Spanish painter, etcher and draughtsman, all of whose career was spent in Italy, especially Naples, where he settled in 1616.

Richier, Germaine 1904–59
French sculptress, a pupil of Rodin and Bourdelle. Her most characteristic works have a distinctive macabre imagery, responding to the horror and destruction man inflicts upon himself and the world – her figures are often half-human, half-insect, decomposing, torn and withered.

Rigaud, Hyacinthe 1659–1743
With Largillière, the most successful French portrait painter of the last years of Louis XIV's reign. His grand style is derived from the Flemish Baroque, but has a greater air of restraint.

Rivalz, Antoine 1667–1735
The best-known member of a family of French history painters, active in

Toulouse in the 17thC and 18thC. He returned from Rome in 1700, influenced by Maratta, and from 1726 ran an academy that was the center of a Toulouse school quite independent of Parisian influence and inspired by the Roman rather than the Flemish Baroque.

Robert, Hubert 1733–1808
French landscape painter. He was in Italy from 1754–65 and he is best known for romantic, often rather melancholic landscapes and ruin-pieces inspired by the Roman Campagna.

Rodin, Auguste 1840–1917
French sculptor. In the history of sculpture he occupies a place even more important than that of his great contemporaries Cézanne, Gauguin and van Gogh in painting, for single-handedly he brought sculpture back to the mainstream of art after it had occupied a secondary position for half a century. The expressive power of his figures, often marked by formal simplification and exaggeration and a rough "unfinished" quality in the modelling, made sculpture once more a vehicle for personal feeling.

Romney, George 1734–1802
British painter, principally a portraitist.

Roslin, Alexander 1718–93
Swedish portraitist in oils and pastel, active mainly in France. He arrived in Paris in 1752, and his skill in painting complexions and fine clothes rapidly made him one of the most sought-after and prolific painters in the city.

Rosso Fiorentino 1495–1540
Italian Mannerist painter who spent the last decades of his life in France, where he worked with Primaticcio at Fontainebleau. The many engravings made of his work were an important factor in the spread of the Mannerist style in France.

Rouault, Georges 1871–1958
French painter and designer of tapestries, prints, book illustrations and stained glass windows. Most of his work is religious, with a distinctive imagery of judges, prostitutes and tragic clowns expressing the fallen condition of humanity.

Rousseau, Henri Julien ("Le Douanier") 1844–1910
French painter, the most famous of all naive artists. Before devoting himself to art in 1885 he worked as a toll inspector – hence his nickname.

Rousseau, Théodore 1812–67
French landscape painter, a leading figure in the Barbizon school. He caused controversy with his intense and boldly executed landscapes, and from 1836–43 his work was consistently excluded from the Salon, earning him the sobriquet "le grand refusé".

Rubens, Sir Peter Paul 1577–1640
The greatest Flemish painter of the 17thC and the dominant figure of Baroque art in northern Europe. He exerted a major influence on French artists, particularly through his huge cycle of paintings on the life of Marie de Médici (now in the Louvre, but originally commissioned for the Palais du Luxembourg).

Rubens: *Self-portrait, c.1630, Florence, Uffizi (Alinari)*

Rude, François 1784–1855
French sculptor. He was one of the finest sculptors of the Romantic movement, his ability to capture movement and emotion embodying the dynamic heroism of the Napoleonic era. His allegiance to Napoleon led him to leave Paris on the Emperor's abdication, and from 1814–27 he worked in Brussels.

Ruisdael, Jacob van 1628/9–82
The greatest Dutch landscape painter of the 17thC. His work is characterized by its power and emotional intensity. He is one of the most revered figures in the history of landscape painting, and the artists of the Barbizon school are among those who were influenced by him.

Sarrazin, Jacques 1588–1660
French sculptor. From 1610 to about 1627 he was in Rome, where he formed a dignified classical style, and on his return to France he became the leading sculptor of the day.

Schalken, Godfried 1643–1706
Dutch painter. He worked on a small scale, painting with exquisite detail, and had a penchant for candlelit scenes, often showing coquettish women.

Scheffer, Ary 1795–1858
Dutch painter, active mainly in France, the favourite painter of King Louis-Philippe. Much of his work is sentimental in flavour, and by the 1840s he was the leading painter of devotional art, his style being a rather vapid version of Ingres' classicism.

Schongauer, Martin d. 1491
German artist, the greatest northern engraver of the 15thC and also an accomplished painter. His work shows the influence of Netherlandish art, particularly Rogier van der Weyden, but he had a highly original imagination.
Sérusier, Paul 1863–1927
French painter, a founder of the Nabis, and the chief spokesman of the group.
Seurat, Georges 1859–91
French painter, the instigator and most important practitioner of Neo-Impressionism. Rather than conveying the sense of brevity of a particular moment, which had been a hallmark of Impressionism, Seurat sought to make that movement into something enduring. He devoted himself to the development of a few large canvases which in their concious monumentality reflected his study of the Old Masters. His work and ideas had wide influence.
Sickert, Walter Richard 1860–1942
British painter. He was a pupil of Whistler and knew Degas well, and his work was important in bringing French ideas to English art.
Signac, Paul 1863–1935
French Neo-Impressionist painter. He was important as the theoretician of the movement, and in 1899 he published *From Delacroix to Neo-Impressionism*, in which he advocated painting with scientific precision.

Signac: *Drawing by Seurat, 1889–90, Paris, G. Cachin-Signac coll.*

Simone Martini c. 1285–1344
One of the greatest of the Sienese artists.
Sisley, Alfred 1839–99
French-born Impressionist painter, of English parentage.
Sluter, Claus d. 1405/6
Netherlandish sculptor, the pioneer of a realistic trend in northern European sculpture that superseded Gothic. His powerful, solemn style was a major influence not only on sculptors but on painters such as Campin.
Snyders, Frans 1579–1657
Flemish painter of animals.
Solimena, Francesco 1657–1747
Influential Neapolitan painter.
Soutine, Chaim 1893–1943
Russian Expressionist painter, active in France from 1913.
Stael, Nicolas de 1914–55
French/Russian painter, one of the most influential artists in France after World War II. He settled in France in 1937 and in 1955 committed suicide.
Steen, Jan 1626–79
One of the more prolific Dutch genre painters of the 17thC.
Stella, Jacques 1596–1657
French history painter and engraver. He was one of Poussin's most faithful followers.
Stosskopf, Sébastien 1597–1657
French still-life painter.
Subleyras, Pierre-Hubert 1699–1749
French painter, most of whose career was spent in Rome. He was a fine portraitist, but his fame rests on his religious works.

Terborch, Gerard 1617–81
Dutch genre and portrait painter. He specialized in genteel interior scenes.
Tiepolo, Giambattista 1696–1770
The greatest Italian (and arguably European) painter of the 18thC and the last of the great line of fresco decorators. He worked mainly in his native Venice, but also in Germany and Spain. His output was enormous, and he was a superb etcher and draughtsman.
Tinguely, Jean b. 1925
Swiss artist whose work comments ironically on technology and mechanization. He was attracted to the work of Klee and Miró, but above all to Duchamp's anarchistic attitude to art. His most famous creation before the ***Fontaine Beaubourg***, 1980 (in collaboration with Nikki de St-Phalle) was the self-destroying ***Homage to New York***, 1960.
Tintoretto, Jacopo (Jacopo Robusti) 1518–94
Venetian painter, with Veronese the leading artist in the city after Titian's death. He produced a prodigious amount of work in a bold and dramatic style that often makes use of strange and vivid light effects.
Tissot, James Jacques Joseph 1836–1902
French painter and engraver. He is best known for his highly-finished society scenes, which cleverly capture nuances of social behaviour. His early works,

however, were mainly portraits, and his last 20 years, partly spent in Palestine, were devoted to religious works.

Titian (Tiziano Vecellio) d. 1576
The greatest Venetian painter and one of the most celebrated names in the history of art. He was famed throughout Europe, the Emperor Charles V and Philip II of Spain being among his most important patrons. In every department of painting he reigned supreme, and he revolutionized the oil technique, giving his paint an expressive life of its own independent of any representative function. His reputation as one of the supreme artists has never wavered.

Toulouse-Lautrec, Henri Marie Raymond de 1864–1901
French painter and graphic artist, an aristocrat by birth and one of the most colourful figures in 19thC art. Poor health and an accident in childhood left him stunted, and the misery of this deformity may have influenced his preference for the low life of Montmartre, his acid wit and alcoholism. His posters of dance halls and cabarets are considered among the finest in the history of the art.

Toulouse-Lautrec: *Self-portrait caricature, Rotterdam, Museum Boymans*

Tournier, Nicolas 1590–1638/9
French Caravaggesque painter. He was in Rome from 1619–27, and various genre scenes of eating, drinking and music-making have been attributed to him from this period. On his return to France, he worked mainly in Toulouse and turned to religious subjects. He is distinguished from most Caravaggesque artists by his elegance and refined physical types.

Troy, François de 1645–1730
French portrait painter. He worked in a somewhat subdued version of Flemish Baroque. His son and pupil **Jean-François Detroy** (1679–1752) was a history and genre painter.

Troyon, Constant 1810–65
French landscapist of the Barbizon school. He was an excellent animal painter, and in his last years painted some remarkable seascapes.

Turner, Joseph Mallard William 1775–1851
British painter, one of the greatest and most original of landscape artists. He first visited France and Switzerland in 1802, and the Alps became one of his favourite subjects.

Uccello, Paolo 1396/7–1475
Florentine painter. His virtuoso skill with perspective places him in the scientific current of the Renaissance, but his love of decorative display is typical of International Gothic.

Utrillo, Maurice 1883–1955
French painter. He was the son of Suzanne Valadon, who in 1903 encouraged him to take up painting to distract him from drinking and give him a reason to live. His finest works belong to his "White" period (c. 1909–15), in which he depicted deserted Montmartre streets in subtle, milky tones, his paint sometimes thickened with plaster.

Valadon, Suzanne 1867–1938
French painter, the mother of Utrillo and a friend of many of the Impressionists. She was an artist's model and became Renoir's mistress and a life-long friend of Degas.

Valenciennes, Pierre-Henri de 1750–1819
French landscape painter and art theorist. His formal, classical style was evolved in Italy and inspired by Poussin

Vallotton, Félix 1865–1925
Swiss painter and graphic artist, working mainly in France. His work is Realist in its monumentality and straightforward representation, but is distinguished by a strong sense of abstract design and simplification of form.

Van Loo family
Family of French painters of Flemish origin. **Jacob** (1614–70) the founder of the line, was a portrait painter who settled in Paris in 1662. His grandson **Jean-Baptiste** (1684–1745) produced portraits and history paintings. Jean-Baptiste's brother Charles André, known as **Carle** (1705–65), was by far the most important and successful member of the family. He was one of the leading Rococo decorators, and had a varied output of easel paintings, including many altarpieces for churches in Paris. Jean-Baptiste's son **Louis-Michel** (1707–71) painted portraits.

Vasarély, Victor b. 1908
French painter and graphic artist born in Hungary, the major pioneer of Op art. He began as a graphic designer, and turned to completely abstract painting in 1947.

Vasari, Giorgio 1511–74
Italian painter, architect and writer. He is best remembered for his *Lives of the Most Eminent Painters, Sculptors and Architects* (1550, revised 1568), the first great work of art history. His paintings are in a rather exaggerated and precious Mannerist style.

Velazquez (Velásquez) Diego Rodriguez de Silva y 1599–1660
The greatest of Spanish painters. Almost all his career was spent in Madrid as court painter to Philip II, and his paintings were largely unknown outside his native country until the Napoleonic Wars. In the 19thC, however, his work – particularly the freedom of his brushwork – came as a revelation to progressive artists, notably Manet.

Vermeer, Jan 1632–75
Dutch genre painter. Among Dutch artists he is now ranked second only to Rembrandt, but he was almost totally forgotten for two centuries after his death until he was rediscovered by the French critic Théophile Thoré. His paintings – quiet, small-scale interior scenes – are images of perfect serenity, clarity and balance, with wonderfully fresh colour harmonies.

Vernet family
Family of French painters working in the 18thC and 19thC. **Claude-Joseph** (1714–89) was one of the best French landscape painters of the day, and his dramatic scenes of shipwrecks anticipated the Romantics. His son **Carle** (1758–1836) specialized in horse racing pictures and Napoleonic battle pieces. Carle's grandson, **Horace** (1789–1863) also painted battle scenes, as well as Oriental subjects (then highly fashionable) and mawkishly sentimental animal studies.

Veronese, Paolo (Paolo Caliari) 1528–88
Italian painter, named after his birthplace Verona, but active mainly in Venice, where with Tintoretto he was the leading painter after Titian's death. He was essentially a great decorator, happiest working on a huge scale with scenes of extravagant pomp.

Vien, Joseph-Marie 1716–1809
French painter of history and genre. He was in Rome in the 1740s when the discoveries of antique paintings at Pompeii and Herculaneum were causing great excitement, but his importance as a precursor of Neoclassicism has been exaggerated, not least by himself.

Vigée-Lebrun, Elisabeth 1755–1842
French portrait painter. Her portraits are elegant, flattering, delicate in touch and charmingly sentimental. During the Revolution she sought refuge in Italy, and later made a successful career at many European courts before returning to France under Louis XVIII. She was renowned for her wit and charm, and her memoirs provide a fascinating account of the artistic and political events of the age.

Vigée-Lebrun: *Self-portrait, 1790, Florence, Uffizi (Alinari)*

Villon, Jacques (Gaston Duchamp) 1875–1963
French painter, the brother of Marcel Duchamp and of Raymond Duchamp-Villon. He worked in both abstract and representational styles.

Viollet-le-Duc, Eugène-Emmanuel 1814–79
French architect, archaeologist and writer, famous as a restorer of medieval buildings. He initially gained his commissions through his friendship with the writer Prosper Mérimée, who was Inspector of Ancient Monuments. Viollet-le-Duc became a profound and prolific scholar on medieval art and his restoration saved some buildings from destruction, but his work has often been condemned as insensitive. His original buildings are unmemorable compared to his restorations.

Vlaminck, Maurice de 1876–1958
French painter, principally of landscapes, a leading exponent of Fauvism. Eccentric and rebellious, he was a racing cyclist and violinist before taking up painting. His most characteristic paintings are vividly coloured, using pigments straight from the tube, but his work gradually became less brilliant and more mannered with the passing of time.

Vlaminck: *Portrait by Derain, 1905, Paris, Private coll. (Giraudon)*

Vouet, Simon 1590–1649
The most important French painter of the early 17thC. From 1613–27 he worked in Italy (mainly Rome) and the accomplished eclectic style he took back to France with him was highly successful, suiting French taste better than the full drama of Caravaggism or the rhetoric of Baroque would have done. His influence was enormous, and many of the leading painters of the next generation trained in his studio, among them Lebrun.

Vuillard, Edouard 1868–1940
French painter and printmaker. As with his friend Bonnard, his preferred subject was domestic interiors. His emphasis on flat pattern was much influenced by Japanese prints.

Watteau, Jean-Antoine 1684–1721
French painter, one of the greatest of Rococo artists. He is best known for his *fêtes galantes*, a type of painting he invented, in which elegant figures move in an aristocratic dreamworld where music, conversation and amorous dalliance hold sway. Their haunting sense of melancholy, born of the knowledge that all sensuous pleasure is transient, may be partly explained by the fact that for much of his life Watteau suffered from the consumption that was to cause his early death.

Weyden, Rogier van der
1399/1400–1464
Netherlandish painter, one of the greatest and most influential artists of the mid 15thC. A pupil of Campin at Tournai, his style is noble and elevated with a sense of refined spirituality. He is best known for religious works, but he also painted superb portraits. He worked for members of the Burgundian court.

Whistler, James Abbot McNeill
1834–1903
American painter and graphic artist, working principally in England after a period in Paris (1855–59). He was one of the leading figures of Aestheticism, whose adherents believed that painting, like music, should exist for its own sake, not for any social or moral purpose, and he often gave his pictures titles such as *Symphony* or *Nocturne* that stressed the musical parallel.

Wilkie, Sir David 1785–1841
Scottish genre, history and portrait painter.

Willumsen, Jens Ferdinand 1863–1958
Danish painter, sculptor, engraver, architect and ceramicist. His early work was influenced by Gauguin and Symbolism.

Winterhalter, Franz Xaver 1805–73
German painter and lithographer, based in Paris for most of his career. He was the most successful court painter of his day, portraying most of Europe's royalty and leading members of the aristocracy.

Witz, Konrad d.c.1444/6
German-born painter, active in Basel from 1434 and regarded as a member of the Swiss school.

Wolgemut, Michael 1434–1519
German woodcut designer and painter, the teacher of Dürer.

Wouwermans, Philips 1619–68
Dutch painter, specializing in scenes involving horses in landscapes – hunting parties, cavalry skirmishes and so on. He was immensely prolific and died very wealthy. His work is perhaps now underrated, for however many times he repeated his subjects he kept a sense of freshness – his lively touch probably owes something to his master Frans Hals.

Ziem, Félix 1821–1911
French painter. His high-keyed seascapes in watercolour and oils are in a style akin to late Turner, and he was especially skilled at sunsets and the effect of light on stonework. Venice was his favourite subject.

Zuloaga y Zabaleta, Ignacio 1870–1945
Spanish genre, landscape and portrait painter. He trained in Paris, where he knew Degas, Gauguin and Rodin, but he mainly painted Spanish life and customs and his style derived from the great masters of Spanish painting.

Zurbarán, Francisco 1598–1665
Spanish painter, mainly of religious works. His style combined severe and sombre realism with spiritual intensity, making him an ideal painter for the austere religious orders of Spain and South America.

GLOSSARY

A

Abstract art
Art that does not attempt to represent the appearance of objects, real or imaginary, though it may conjure up images for the viewer.

Académie Royale de Peinture et de Sculpture
French art academy founded in 1648 with the support of Louis XIV. It assumed great importance in the 1660s when the King's minister Colbert and its Director Lebrun reorganized it so as to control the teaching and commissioning of art throughout France.

Aisle
Lateral division of a church, flanking the nave or chancel on one or both sides.

Altarpiece
Picture, screen or decorated wall standing on or behind an altar.

Ambulatory
A continuous aisle around a circular building; an aisle around the apse of a church, originally used for processional purposes.

Apse
A semi-circular or polygonal termination of a building, particularly of a church.

Aquatint
Engraving process producing finely granulated tonal areas rather than lines.

Art Deco
The most fashionable style in interior decoration and design in the period between the two World Wars (1918–39). It was characterized by the use of geometrical shapes and stylized natural forms, paying more heed to the demands of mechanized production than Art Nouveau, with less interest in craftsmanship.

Art Nouveau
Decorative style that influenced all areas of design in the 1890s and was popular until World War I. It was characterized by the use of asymmetrical sinuous lines based on plant forms.

Avantgarde
French word meaning "vanguard", used to describe art or artists departing from accepted tradition or the academic norm to explore techniques or concepts of art in an original way.

B

Baldacchino
A canopy over an altar, throne or tomb, rising on columns or hanging down from the ceiling.

Baptistry
Part of a church containing the font for the baptismal rite. It is sometimes a separate building.

Barbizon school
Group of French landscape painters who worked in Barbizon, a village on the outskirts of the forest of Fontainebleau, in the 1840s. The basis of Barbizon art was direct study from nature, and this prepared the way for the Impressionists.

Baroque
Term broadly characterizing Western art produced from the beginning of the 17thC to the mid 18thC, or more precisely, applied to the most dominant stylistic trend within that period. Its salient qualities are dynamic movement, overt emotion and self-confident rhetoric. The Baroque originated in Italy, and in France is generally not found in its extreme forms, as French taste has usually leaned towards the classical. Louis XIV's palace at Versailles, however, is an archetypal example of the Baroque union of painting, sculpture and architecture (and here gardening) to create an overpowering effect.

Basilica
Originally, a Roman civic hall: later, an early Christian church with the rectangular construction typical of such halls. The term is also used in a completely different sense to refer to certain churches granted special rights by the Pope; they rank next in importance to cathedrals.

Boiserie
French term for wainscot (wooden panelling lining a wall), used particularly of the elaborately carved panelling found in 17thC and 18thC French interiors.

Byzantine art
Art associated with the Eastern Roman Empire, which was founded by the Emperor Constantine in 330 and ended when his capital Constantinople (formerly called Byzantium) was captured by the Turks in 1453. Byzantine art is characteristically flat and frontal in composition and serious and otherworldly in feeling.

C

Capital
The topmost part of a column or pilaster, often elaborately carved.

Carolingian art
European art of the late 8thC to early 10thC, taking its name from Charlemagne (crowned first Holy Roman Emperor in 800) and his descendants – the Carolingian dynasty.

Cassone
A large chest, either given as a wedding present or used to contain a bride's dowry. Cassoni were usually richly decorated, and painted panels from them are now often found as separate pictures.
Chancel
Part of a church reserved for clergy and containing the altar and choir; or, more generally, the whole of the church E of the nave, from which it is often separated by a screen.
Chiaroscuro
Term, from the Italian for "bright-dark", used to describe light and shade effects in painting. It is generally applied to a dramatic use of contrasting light and shade, pioneered by Leonardo but particularly associated with Caravaggio and his followers.
Chinoiserie
Style of interior decoration and design using Chinese (or pseudo-Chinese) motifs, particularly popular in the Rococo period.
Ciborium
An altar canopy; also a liturgical casket for holding the consecrated Host.
Classicism
Term used to describe the qualities or order, clarity and harmony associated with the art of ancient Greece and Rome. In its broadest sense, the term is used as the antithesis of Romanticism, denoting art that places adherence to accepted canons of beauty above personal inspiration.
Clerestorey
A row of windows in the upper part of the main walls of a church, above the level of the aisle roofs. The term refers also to the wall in which the windows are set.
Cloissonisme
Style of painting originated by Bernard in the late 1880s. Dark outlines surround flat bright forms, as in cloissoné enamelwork, in which thin strips of metal outline the enamel areas. In French, "cloissoner" means to divide up or compartmentalize.
Cope
An ecclesiastical cloak, worn particularly on ceremonial occasions.
Crypt
A room beneath the main floor of a church (but not necessarily underground), often used as a repository for relics.
Cubism
Movement in painting and sculpture originated jointly by Picasso and Braque from 1907 onwards. In the first stage of Cubism ("Analytical Cubism"), objects were depicted as if various parts of them were seen simultaneously from different angles, creating a multi-faceted appearance; in the second stage ("Synthetic Cubism"), objects were represented through simplified flat geometric forms, often with the addition of stencilled lettering or fragments of newspaper. Cubism was one of the most momentous turning-points in the history of art, breaking decisively from traditional methods of representation and emphasizing the flatness of the picture surface through a denial of illusionistic depth. It was immensely influential and one of the sources of abstraction.

D

Dada
Movement of revolt by European and American artists and writers, first appearing in 1915 and losing impetus by 1923. The title (French for "hobby-horse") was selected at random from a dictionary and symbolized the movement's deliberate anti-rational stance, in part a reaction to World War I. Dadaists aimed to destroy art as an aesthetic cult and to replace it with anti-art and non-art. They therefore rejected the art object, substituting the nonsense poem, the ready-made object and the collage. In Paris, the tendency to whimsical absurdity led, by about 1923, to Surrealism.
Diptych
A painting or other work of art consisting of two panels or sections, often hinged together.
Directory (Directoire) **style**
Style of interior decoration and design at its peak during the Directoire (1795–99), the period when France was governed by a body of five Directors. The style was simpler and more classical than the preceding Louis XVI style, its comparative austerity being in part caused by the country's bankruptcy.
Donjon
French term for a keep, the main tower of a castle, serving as the principal living quarters or as the final refuge in times of siege.

E

Empire style
Late Neoclassical style in France, associated closely with the personal tastes of Napoleon, Emperor from 1804–15.
Enamel
Smooth, glossy material made by fusing glass to a metal or similar base; also any

object made with, or decorated by, this material. Enamels were particularly popular during the Middle Ages, when Limoges was the most important center of production.

Engraving
Term referring both to the process of cutting a design into metal or wood and to the print taken from a plate or block so cut.

Etching
Term describing the process of biting out a design in a metal plate with acid, and also the print that results. The plate is coated with acid-resistant wax, in which the design is drawn with a needle. When the plate is immersed in acid, only the parts exposed by the needle are attacked by the acid, so the design is transferred to the plate. Etching allows greater spontaneity than other engraving processes, as the needle can be handled almost as freely as a pen.

Expressionism
Term describing, in its most general sense, a quality of expressive emphasis and distortion that may be found in the works of art of any place or period. In a narrower sense, the term is often used to characterize certain aspects of 20thC North European art, in which subjective stress is laid on heightened emotions and the artist's inner vision.

F

Faience
A kind of earthenware named after the city of Faenza in Italy, still an important center for pottery manufacture.

Fauvism
Style practised by a group of artists loosely associated with Matisse around 1905–7. The term "Fauve" (wild beast) was first used to describe paintings by Matisse, Rouault, Vlaminck and others exhibited together in 1905. The wildness that was objected to lay in their brilliant, luminous colour and their bold spontaneous handling of paint. Of the artists involved, only Matisse continued to explore the potential of pure colour.

Fête galante
Term invented by the Académie Royale de Peinture et de Sculpture to describe a type of painting introduced by Watteau that did not fit into any of the conventional genres. Such paintings feature figures in ball-dress or masquerade costume engaged in music, conversation and amorous dalliance.

Figurative art
Art that represents recognizable subjects – the opposite of abstract art.

Flamboyant
The last phase of Gothic architecture in France, at its peak in the 15thC. It is so called because the characteristic flowing lines of the tracery resemble flames.

Fontainebleau school
Term applied to artists associated with the court of Fontainebleau during the 16thC. A first and second school of Fontainebleau are recognized; the first, and more important, associated with François I, a great patron of Italian artists, the second – after the interruption of the Wars of Religion – with Henry III and Henry IV. The artists involved worked in an elegant Mannerist style.

Foreshortening
The application of the rules of perspective to a single figure or object; the term is generally used of extreme effects, as when a figure is seen steeply from below or a hand points directly out of a picture.

Found object
Object selected and displayed as art, without alteration to the form in which it was found. The idea originated with the Dadaists and Surrealists. The object may be a natural form, such as a shell or stone, or a manufactured one, usually called a **ready-made**.

Fresco
Method of wall painting using water-based paint applied to wet plaster. Paint and plaster fuse as they dry, forming a matt, stable surface, which in dry climates does not flake or rub off.

G

Gallo-Roman
Term applied to art produced under Roman rule in France (or more strictly, the ancient province of Gaul, which included parts of what are now neighbouring countries).

Genre
Term used to describe paintings of everyday life. In a more general sense, the term can be used to describe any distinctive type of painting, such as portraiture or landscape.

Gobelins factory
The most celebrated of all tapestry manufactories, on the outskirts of Paris. It was in existence by the early 17thC, but its great fame dates from 1662, when it was taken over by Louis XIV, with Lebrun as first Director. Until 1694, the factory produced not only tapestries, but everything needed for the furnishing of royal palaces – its official title was the Manufacture royale des meubles de la Couronne. In that year, however, the

factory closed because of Louis's financial difficulties, and after it re-opened in 1699 it produced only tapestries. It continues to produce them today. Apart from Lebrun, Boucher and Oudry are among the well-known artists who have been Directors of the Gobelins factory.

Gothic
Style of art and architecture prevailing in Europe from the mid 12thC to the 16thC. It is characterized chiefly in terms of architecture, above all by the use of pointed arches. Gothic was born in France and the great French cathedrals of the late 12thC and early 13thC, with their sculpture and stained glass, are the most sublime expressions of the style.

Gouache
Watercolour paint made opaque by the admixture of white pigment. In France it has often been preferred to the transparent watercolour so beloved of English artists.

Grisaille
Painting executed entirely in tones of grey or neutral greyish colours.

I

Illumination
Decoration of manuscripts (and some early printed books) with ornamental letters, borders and miniature paintings. Gouache and tempera were the usual media used for illumination.

Illusionism
The use of pictorial techniques to create a convincing or even deceptive sensation of real space and form on a two-dimensional surface.

Impasto
Thickly applied paint that creates a textured surface.

Impressionism
Movement in painting, originating in France in the 1860s, which sought to produce a spontaneous impression of a scene or object rather than a calculated, detailed portrayal. The artists involved were not a formal body, but to varying degrees they shared related outlooks and techniques and they grouped together for the purpose of exhibiting – there were eight exhibitions between 1874–86. After the final exhibition, the group dissolved, but the influence of the movement was enormous, causing painters everywhere to lighten their palettes. Reactions against it were also momentous; its lack of intellectual content was seen by many as a major failing, and the Post-Impressionists were concerned to bring back "meaning" – emotional or symbolic – to painting.

International Gothic
Style of painting and sculpture that flourished in the late 14thC/early 15thC in most of Europe. Essentially a courtly style, it was characterized by elegance, refinement and a development of interest in secular subjects.

L

Lady chapel
A chapel dedicated to the Virgin Mary; usually at the E end of a church, it forms an extension of the chancel or an aisle.

Lithograph
Print produced from a design drawn or painted onto a limestone block or metal plate.

Louis XIV style
Style of interior decoration and design associated with the reign of Louis XIV, effective ruler from 1661–1775. The style is massively rich, reflecting the formality and grandeur of Louis's court.

Louis XV style
Style of interior decoration and design named after Louis XV (reigned 1715–74) but in fact coinciding only very roughly with his period of rule. It is in effect synonymous with the Rococo style, which emerged around 1700, reached its peak from 1720–50, and was long outmoded by the time of Louis's death.

Louis XVI style
Style of interior decoration and design named after Louis XVI (reigned 1774–92), but in fact already fully developed before his accession. A reaction against the preceding Louis XV (Rococo) style, it was characterized by greater sobriety of form and a rich solidity of decoration.

M

Majolica
Type of pottery, said to have originated from Majorca (Latin *Majorica*), particularly popular in the Italian Renaissance.

Mannerism
The dominant style in European art from about 1520 to the end of the 16thC. It was characterized by hypersophistication and self-consciousness and often has disturbing emotional overtones, marking a reaction from the serene harmony of the High Renaissance.

Maquette
French term for a small model, usually in clay or wax, made by a sculptor as a rough sketch for a larger work.

Memento mori
Latin expression meaning "remember you must die" applied to works of art (or details of them) that symbolize the brevity of human life and the transience of earthly pleasures and achievements. A skull, a watch, a broken lute, smoking candles and flowers losing their petals are among the symbols of inevitable decay.

Menhir
A large prehistoric single standing stone, often carved.

Merovingian art
Art produced under the Merovingian dynasty, which ruled parts of France and Germany from the 6thC to the mid 8thC.

Mosaic
Picture or design made by setting small places of stone, glass or ceramic materials into cement or plaster. The pieces are called tesserae.

N

Nabis
Group of French painters, active in the 1890s, who rejected the naturalism of Impressionism and painted in flat areas of pure colour, stressing subjective, sometimes mystical perceptions. The name derives from the Hebrew for "prophet".

Naive art
Painting in a childlike or untrained fashion, characterized by a careful, descriptive style, non-scientific perspective, simple bright colours and often a literal depiction of imaginary scenes.

Narthex
A porch or vestibule at the W end of a church.

Nave
The western limb of a church, or more specifically, the central space of that area, usually bounded on either side by an aisle.

Neoclassicism
Movement dominating European art and architecture in the late 18thC and early 19thC. It was marked by an heroic severity of tone – a reaction against Rococo frivolity – and by the use of archaeologically correct detail. In France it is particularly associated with the Revolution and a desire to instil ancient Roman virtues into civic life.

Neo-Impressionism
Movement in French painting, both a development out of Impressionism and a reaction against it. The Neo-Impressionists tried to make Impressionism more scientific and rational by applying small touches of pure colour to the canvas in such a way that they would mix not on the picture surface but in the eyes of the spectator. The idea was to create an effect of great luminosity, but with a few exceptions (particularly the works of Seurat) posterity has often found Neo-Impressionist paintings dull and rigid.

O

Op art
Type of abstract art that exploits the optical effects of pattern. It uses hard-edged black-and-white or coloured patterns that appear to vibrate and change their shape as the viewer looks at them.

Orientalism
The production of or taste for paintings of exotic subject matter, at its peak in France in the mid 19thC. Orientalist paintings usually represented or evoked North Africa, the Holy Land or the Middle East rather than eastern Asia, which is now the part of the world that the term "Orient" usually refers to. Many leading artists, including Delacroix, visited these areas. In 1893 a Societé des Peintres Orientalistes was formed, with Gérôme as honorary president, but by then the genre was nearing exhaustion.

P

Paris, school of
Term applied to the large community of artists who made Paris the major center of avantgarde artistic activity during the first half of the 20thC. A lively and competitive atmosphere and the presence of writers, critics and dealers willing to support innovation and experiment attracted to Paris not only French artists, but also many major figures from abroad. No single style unified the school of Paris, but artists grouped themselves into a succession of movements, such as Fauvism, Cubism and Surrealism. The supremacy of Paris was unchallenged until the comparatively rapid emergence of New York as a major artistic center after World War II.

Pastel
Stick of colour made from powdered pigment bound with gum.

Perspective
The means by which a sensation of three-dimensional space is created on a flat picture surface, relying on the optical impressions that parallel lines converge as they recede and that subjects become

smaller and closer together in the distance.

Photorealism
Style of painting or sculpture, popular from the 1960s, in which the subject matter, usually banal, static and contemporary, is reproduced with minute exactitude, a high finish and a smooth and bland surface. Superrealism is an alternative name for the same style.

Pietà
Representation of the Virgin supporting the dead Christ on her lap; the word is Italian for "pity".

Plein-air
Term (French for "open-air") used to describe paintings that have been executed out of doors rather than in a studio.

Pleurant
French term meaning "weeper", used to describe the subsidiary figures in attitudes of grief or mourning often found on medieval tombs.

Pointillism
The technique of using small dots (in French "points") of pure colour employed by the Neo-Impressionists.

Polychrome
Term applied to a work or object (usually a piece of sculpture) that is made or decorated with various colours.

Polyptych
A painting or other work of art consisting of four or more panels or sections, often hinged together.

Pont-Aven school
Group of painters drawn to and inspired by Gauguin during his stay at Pont-Aven in 1886–91. The artists involved reacted against Impressionism in favour of a non-naturalistic style based on ideas and emotions.

Post-Impressionism
General term describing the various movements in painting, particularly in France, that developed out of Impressionism or reacted against it in the period from about 1880 to about 1905 (the later date marks the beginning of Expressionism and Fauvism). Post-Impressionist artists rejected naturalism in different ways: by a more scientific analysis of colour; by an emphasis on purely formal considerations; and by a renewed interest in religious and symbolic themes and in the power of colour and line to express emotion. Cézanne, Gauguin and van Gogh were the most influential of the Post-Impressionist artists.

Predella
One or more small panels fixed to the bottom of an altarpiece. The scenes shown generally relate to the main scene depicted above.

R

Ready-made see FOUND OBJECT

Realism
Term used in a general sense to describe unidealized and objective representation, and more specifically (usually with a capital R) applied to a movement in mid 19thC art, particularly in France. Realist painters rebelled against the idealized subjects of mythological and historical painting and turned to contemporary ones. The greatest Realist artist was Courbet, who proclaimed that "painting is essentially a concrete art and must be applied to real and existing things".

Regency (Régence) **style**
Term applied to early Rococo art in France c.1700–c.1730. It is named after the regency of Philippe d'Orleans.

Renaissance
Intellectual and artistic movement inspired by a rediscovery and reinterpretation of classical culture; it originated in 14thC Italy and eventually became the driving force behind the arts throughout much of Europe. The period from c.1500 to c.1520 in Italy is known as the High Renaissance, when the works of the three great giants – Leonardo, Michelangelo and Raphael – reached a peak of harmony and balance that has ever since been regarded as a touchstone in world art. In France, Renaissance influence was only sporadic before 1500, but thereafter quickly became dominant, partially as a result of the Italian campaigns of Louis XII and François I.

Repoussé
A technique of metalwork in which a malleable metal such as silver or copper is hammered over a block of wood carved to the requisite design.

Reredos
An altarpiece that rises from ground level behind the altar.

Retable
An altarpiece that stands on the back of the altar or on a pedestal behind it.

Rococo
The style, characterized by intimacy of scale, asymmetry, lightheartedness and grace, which in the early 18thC superseded the more formal grandeur of the Baroque. The Rococo was born in France and some of the finest expressions of the style are French. Boucher and Fragonard are archetypal Rococo artists.

Romanesque
Style of art and architecture prevailing in Europe in the 11thC and 12thC. Romanesque is characterized chiefly in terms of its architecture, which is massive and round-arched.

Romanticism
Artistic and literary movement flourishing in Europe from the late 18thC to the mid 19thC. Romantic art is characterized by the importance attached to the expression of the artist's personal feeling, an attitude summed up in Géricault's remark: "Genius is the fire of a volcano which must and will break forth."

S

Salon
Name given to the annual exhibition of the Académie Royale de Peinture et de Sculpture in Paris. By the early 19thC the Salon had assumed paramount importance in the artistic life of France, as acceptance of a work for exhibition there generally secured an artist's sales and reputation, while further prestige attached to the various medals it awarded. By 1870 the Salon had become synonymous with conventional art and had declined in importance.
Sinopia
The preliminary underdrawing of a fresco, sometimes exposed if a fresco is damaged or carefully removed from the wall for conservation.
Stela
An upright stone slab carved with inscriptions or figures, commonly used for commemorative purposes in the ancient world.
Stucco
Light, malleable plaster reinforced with powdered marble, used for architectural decoration and for sculpture.
Surrealism
Movement in art and literature, at its peak in the 1920s and 1930s that used incongruous juxtapositions of images in an effort to explore the subconscious. Its sources of inspiration were the nihilistic ideas of the Dadaists and a tradition in French poetry that acknowledged the supremacy of irrational inspiration and imaginative insight.
Symbolism
Movement in art providing an intellectual alternative to the purely visual painting of the Impressionists. It flourished principally in France during the 1880s and 1890s, but its currents spread throughout Europe. Symbolist paintings were not intended as concrete equivalents of ideas or emotions, but rather as evocations of them, and the subject matter of a picture was to be suggested rather than understood. Moreau was perhaps the archetypal Symbolist painter.

T

Tabernacle
A canopied niche to contain a sculptured figure or other image.
Tempera
Pigment mixed with egg white or yolk, the usual medium with which easel pictures were painted until the 15thC, when it began to be superseded by oil.
Tondo
A circular painting or sculpture; the word is Italian for "round".
Tracery
Intersecting ornament used in architecture or decorative work, particularly in Gothic windows.
Transept
Either of the two projecting arms of a cross-shaped church.
Transi
In medieval and Renaissance tomb sculpture, a representation of the effigy as a naked corpse. The word is the past participle of the verb "transir", meaning to freeze, paralyze or transfix.
Triptych
A painting or other work of art consisting of three panels or sections, often hinged together.
Trompe l'oeil
Term (French for "deceive the eye") used to describe the application of illusionistic skill to persuade the spectator that a painted object is a real one. *Trompe l'oeil* paintings often have a humorous intention, as when a fly is painted in a part of the picture where a real one might have alighted.
Tympanum
The space between the flat top of a doorway and the arch above it.

U

Ukiyo-e
Japanese term meaning "pictures of the floating world", which portrayed everyday life, with an emphasis on leisure pursuits; theaters, tea-houses and brothels are popular subjects. The flattened forms and unbroken colours of Ukiyo-e prints influenced some of the leading painters of the late 19thC, among them Gauguin and van Gogh.

V

Vault
An arched roof or ceiling.

INDEX

Page numbers in *italic* refer to the illustrations.

A

B

S

ACKNOWLEDGMENTS

31: Photo Michael Jacobs. 33: Photo Michael Jacobs. 43: Fouquet, *Heures d'Étienne Chevalier*/Lauros-Giraudon. 77: Grünewald, Isenheim altar (det.) Colmar, Unterlinden/Visual Arts Library. 99: Paris, Louvre/Photo Coll. Paul Stirton. 133: London, National Gallery/ Visual Arts Library. 145.1: Musées de St-Omer/Publications filmées d'Art et d'Histoire. 145.2: Autun, Musée Rolin/Visual Arts Library. 145.3: Bayeux, Musée/Photo Michael Holford. 146.1: Reims, Musée de l'Oeuvre de Notre-Dame/Edimedia. 146.2: Angers, Musée des Beaux-Arts/Edimedia. 146.3: Villeneuve-lez-Avignon, Musée/Photo Giraudon. 147.1: Beaune, Hotel-Dieu/La Goelette. 147.2: Dijon, Musée des Beaux-Arts/Giraudon. 148.1: Autun, Musée Rolin/Visual Arts Library. 148.2: Chantilly, Musée Condé/Giraudon. 149.1: Perpignan, Musée H. Rigaud. 149.2: Dijon, Musée des Beaux-Arts/Réunion des Musées Nationaux. 149.3: Colmar, Musée Unterlinden/Visual Arts Library. 150.1: Paris, Louvre/Réunion des Musées Nationaux. 150.2: Toulouse, Musée des Augustins/Giraudon. 151.1: Rouen, Musée des Beaux-Arts/Giraudon. 151.2: Rennes, Musée des Beaux-Arts/Photo Madec. 151.3: Paris, Louvre/Réunion des Musées Nationaux. 152.1: Perpignan, Musée H. Rigaud/Photo Parce. 152.2: St-Quentin, Musée Lecuyer/Visual Arts Library. 152.3: Valenciennes, Musée des Beaux-Arts/Giraudon. 153.1: Rennes, Musée des Beaux-Arts/Edimedia. 153.2: Douai, Musée des Beaux-Arts. 153.3: Paris, Louvre/Réunion des Musées Nationaux. 154.1: Rouen, Musée des Beaux-Arts/Giraudon. 154.2: Avignon, Musée Calvet. 154.3: Aix-en-Provence, Musée Granet/Bulloz. 155.1 Lyon, Palais Saint-Pierre. 155.2: Agen, Musée des Beaux-Arts/Lauros-Giraudon. 156.1: Pau, Musée des Beaux-Arts/Giraudon. 156.2: Nantes, Musée des Beaux-Arts/Photo Madec. 157.1: Paris, Musée d'Orsay/Visual Arts Library. 157.2: Montpellier, Musée Fabre/Bulloz. 157.3: Paris, Musée G. Moreau/Edimedia. 158.1: Orléans, Musée des Beaux-Arts/Photo Delatouche. 158.2: Rouen, Musée des Beaux-Arts/Lauros-Giraudon. 159.1: Troyes, Musée d'Art Moderne/Hamlyn. 159.2: Photo Lauros-Giraudon. 159.3: Saint-Tropez, Musée del'Annonciade/Visual Arts Library. 160.1: Grenoble, Musée des Beaux-Arts/Visual Arts Library. 160.2: Biot, Musée Léger/Giraudon. 160.3: Photo Pozorski. 185: Artists of the Fontainebleau School/Photo Coll. Michael Jacobs. 211: Photo Coll. Paul Stirton. 255: Visual Arts Library. 299: Photo I. Pozorski. 265: Photo Brassai/Victoria & Albert Museum. 265.2 Visual Arts Library. 267: John Topham Library. 269: Coll. Niarchos. 270: Paris, Louvre. 271: Florence, Uffizi (Alinari). 272: Paris, Louvre. 273: Florence, Uffizi (Alinari). 274: Sao Paolo (Alinari). 275: London, Courtauld Institute. 276: Paris, Louvre. 277: Paris, Louvre (Alinari). 279: Copenhagen, Statens Museum for Kunst. 280: Tours, M. des Beaux-Arts. 281: Philadelphia Museum of Art, A. E. Gallatin Coll. 282: Ari Redon Coll. 283: Florence, Uffizi (Alinari). 284: *Drawing* by Seurat, G. Cachin-Signac Coll. 285: Rotterdam, M. Boymans-Van Beuningen. 286: Florence, Uffizi (Alinari). 287: Private Coll. (Giraudon).